THE INCOHERENCE

OF THE PHILOSOPHERS

◆

Al-Ghazālī

The Incoherence
of the Philosophers

تهافت الفلاسفة

A parallel English–Arabic text
translated, introduced, and annotated by
Michael E. Marmura

Brigham Young University Press ✦ *Provo, Utah* ✦ *2000*

LIBRARY OF CONGRESS CATALOGING-IN-PUBLICATION DATA

Ghazzali, 1058–1111.
[Tahafut al-falasifah. English]
The incoherence of the philosophers = Tahafut al-falasifah:
a parallel English-Arabic text / translated, introduced, and annotated
by Michael E. Marmura. — 2nd ed.
p.   cm.— (Islamic translation series)
1. Philosophy—Early works to 1800. 2. Methodology—Early works to 1800.
3. Faith and reason—Islam—Early works to 1800. 4. Islam—Doctrines.
I. Marmura, Michael E., 1929– . II. Title. III. Series.
B753.G33T3313   2000
297.2'61—dc21   97-21195
                                              CIP

ISBN 978-0-8425-2466-5

PRINTED IN THE UNITED STATES OF AMERICA.

20 19 18 17 16   3 4 5 6 7

Second Edition

الى أخي عزيز

To my brother Aziz

—*M. Marmura*

Contents

Foreword to the Series

The Islamic Translation Series: Philosophy, Theology, and Mysticism (hereafter ITS) is designed not only to further scholarship in Islamic studies but, by encouraging the translation of Islamic texts into the technical language of contemporary Western scholarship, to assist in the integration of Islamic studies into Western academia and to promote global perspectives in the disciplines to which it is devoted. If this goal is achieved, it will not be for the first time: Historians well know that, during the so-called Middle Ages, a portion of the philosophical, scientific, and mathematical wealth of the Islamic tradition entered into and greatly enriched the West. Even Christian theology was affected, as is brilliantly evidenced in the works of St. Thomas Aquinas and other scholastics.

Manuscripts submitted to ITS for consideration are, of course, evaluated without regard to the religious, methodological, or political preferences of the translators or to their gender or national origins. The translator of each text, not the editors of the series nor the members of the advisory board, is solely responsible for the volume in question.

On behalf of Daniel C. Peterson, the executive editor, and members of the advisory board, I wish to express deep appreciation to the cosponsoring institutions—the Institute for the Study and Preservation of Ancient Religious Texts at Brigham Young University and the Foundation for Interreligious Diplomacy (and its director, Charles Randall Paul)—for their gracious support of this project.

—PARVIZ MOREWEDGE
Editor in Chief
Rutgers, The State University of New Jersey

❖ ❖ ❖

Brigham Young University and its Institute for the Study and Preservation of Ancient Religious Texts are pleased to sponsor and publish the Islamic Translation Series: Philosophy, Theology, and Mysticism (ITS). We wish to express our appreciation to the editor in chief of ITS, Parviz Morewedge, for joining us in this important project. We are especially grateful to James L. and Beverley Sorenson of Salt Lake City for their generous support, which made ITS possible, and to the Ashton Family Foundation of Orem, Utah, which kindly provided additional funding so that we might continue.

Islamic civilization represents nearly fourteen centuries of intense intellectual activity, and believers in Islam number in the hundreds of millions. The texts that will appear in ITS are among the treasures of this great culture. But they are more than that. They are properly the inheritance of all the peoples of the world. As an institution of The Church of Jesus Christ of Latter-day Saints, Brigham Young University is honored to assist in making these texts available to many for the first time. In doing so, we hope to serve our fellow human beings, of all creeds and cultures. We also follow the admonition of our own tradition, to "seek . . . out of the best books words of wisdom," believing, indeed, that "the glory of God is intelligence."

—DANIEL C. PETERSON
Executive Editor
Brigham Young University

❖ ❖ ❖

A NOTE ON SPELLING

In this work, terms of Arabic derivation found in *Webster's Third New International Dictionary* generally follow the first spelling given therein and are treated as regular English words. Otherwise, Arabic or Persian words and proper names have been transliterated following, with few exceptions, the standard recommended by the *International Journal of Middle East Studies.*

Acknowledgments

I owe a debt of thanks to Professors Parviz Morewedge and Daniel C. Peterson for their efforts expended in scrutinizing the present work and for their helpful comments; to Professor Fred C. Pinnegar for his careful reading of the English portion of this work and for pointing out ambiguities in the translation; to Mr. Steven Whiting, Mr. Kyle Hettinger, and Mr. Steven Dyches for their labors in preparing both the Arabic text and the translation for the printers, for help in preparing the index, and for many judicious suggestions; to my student, Mr. Timothy Gianotti, for reading and commenting on an early draft of the translation; and to my wife, Elizabeth, for her encouragement and for reading and commenting on sections of the translation.

I owe a special debt of thanks to Professor Paul Spade of Indiana University for making a careful comparative reading of the two texts, correcting grammatical errors, and making invaluable suggestions (editorial and linguistic) for the improvement of this second edition. Last but not least, I offer my thanks to Mr. Morgan Davis, Mr. Glen Cooper, Mr. Nathan Toronto, and Mrs. Elizabeth Watkins of the Islamic Translation staff of the Middle Eastern Texts Initiative at Brigham Young University for examining the text and offering suggestions for its improvement.

I also take this opportunity to pay tribute to my older brother Aziz who, very many years ago, was the first to instill in me a love of philosophy and whose sacrifices made my university education possible. It is to him that this work is dedicated.

—MICHAEL E. MARMURA
Toronto, February 2000

Translator's Introduction

I

Al-Ghazālī's *Tahāfut al-falāsifa* (The incoherence of the philosophers) marks a turning point in the intellectual and religious history of medieval Islam. It brought to a head a conflict between Islamic speculative theology *(kalām)* and philosophy *(falsafa)* as it undertook to refute twenty philosophical doctrines. Seventeen are condemned as heretical innovations, three as totally opposed to Islamic belief, and those upholding them as outright infidels. Not that the philosophers it condemned were atheists—far from it. Their entire philosophical system rested on affirming the existence of God, from whom all other existents emanated. But, according to the Islamic philosophers, these existents emanated as the necessary consequence of the divine essence. As al-Ghazālī saw it, this meant that God produces the world by necessity in the same way that an inanimate object like the sun was said to produce its light by its very nature—by its essence, necessarily. It meant for him the denial of the divine attributes of life, will, power, and knowledge. Denuded of these attributes, he maintained, the God of the philosophers was not the God of the Qurʾān. At issue was not the question of God's existence, but the nature of the godhead.

The *Tahāfut* certainly put Islamic philosophy on the defensive in a way that it had never been before. Paradoxically, however, it also served to make it better known in the Islamic world. It brought to the fore the conflict between philosophy and more traditional Islamic belief. But perhaps more to the point, in order to refute the Islamic philosophers, al-Ghazālī had to explain them. He explained them so clearly and so well that he rendered philosophical ideas accessible to nonphilosophers. Inadvertently, so to speak, the *Tahāfut* helped spread philosophical ideas, as it also set a new tradition in *kalām*. After al-Ghazālī, no Islamic theologian worth his salt avoided detailed discussion of the philosophical theories al-Ghazālī had criticized. *Kalām* thereafter became, as it had never been before, thoroughly involved with the theories of the *falāsifa*.

The *Tahāfut* also marks a high point in the history of medieval Arabic thought because of its intellectual caliber. Although its motivation is religious and theological, it makes its case through closely argued criticisms that are ultimately philosophical. A logical critique, largely of the emanative metaphysics, causal theory, and psychology of Avicenna (Ibn Sīnā, d. 1037), it is incisive and thorough. It is true that theological criticism of philosophy was not entirely new in medieval Islam: one does encounter prior to al-Ghazālī *kalām* criticisms of philosophical ideas. But one does not encounter anything like the comprehensive, sustained critique of the *Tahāfut*—a work entirely devoted to refuting the philosophers. Whatever its failings—some of these shown by the answer Averroës (Ibn Rushd, d. 1198) gave to it in his *Tahāfut al-Tahāfut* (The incoherence of the Incoherence)—it remains a brilliant, incisive critique.

II

Abū Ḥāmid Muḥammad ibn Muḥammad al-Ṭusī al-Ghazālī, perhaps the best known of medieval Islam's religious intellectuals, was trained as an Islamic lawyer *(faqīh)* and theologian *(mutakallim)* and became a noted Islamic mystic *(ṣūfī)*. He was born in 1058 in the city or district of Ṭūs, in northeast Persia. He studied in *madāris,* religious colleges that focused on the teaching of Islamic law, first in Ṭūs, then for a short period in Jurjān on the Caspian Sea, and then in 1077 at a major *madrasa* in Nishapur. There he was taught by Imām al-Ḥaramayn al-Juwaynī (d. 1085), a noted lawyer of the school of al-Shāfiᶜī (d. 820) and the then leading theologian of the school of al-Ashᶜarī (d. 935). In law, al-Ghazālī was a Shāfiᶜite; in *kalām,* he was an Ashᶜarite.

Ashᶜarism, by the eleventh century, was becoming the dominant school of *kalām.* It subscribed to a metaphysics of transient atoms and accidents, from which material bodies are composed. It regarded all temporal existents as the direct creation of God, decreed by His eternal attribute of will and enacted by His attribute of power. What humans habitually regard as sequences of natural causes and effects are in reality concomitant events whose constant association is arbitrarily decreed by the divine will. Between created things, there is no necessary causal connection— indeed, no causal interaction at all. God is the sole cause: all events are His direct creation. There is no inherent necessity in the uniformity of nature. Hence, when at certain times in history God interrupts this uniformity by creating a miracle on behalf of a prophet or holy man, no contradiction ensues. In his works of *kalām*, al-Ghazālī ardently defended this atomist-occasionalist doctrine on logical and epistemological grounds.

For some six years after the death of al-Juwaynī, al-Ghazālī spent much of his time at the court-camp of Niẓām al-Mulk (d. 1092), the vizier of the Seljuk sultans, but seems to have also taught in Nīshāpūr. He became known as a distinguished scholar and author of works on Islamic law. In 1091, at the invitation of Niẓām al-Mulk, he became the professor of law at the *Niẓāmiyya* in Baghdad. This was the most prestigious of a number of *madāris* instituted by Niẓām al-Mulk (hence their name *Niẓāmiyyas*) in various eastern Islamic cities for the teaching of Islamic law according to the school of al-Shāfiʿī. These colleges were intended in part to train scholars to counter the religious propaganda of the rulers of Egypt, the Fāṭimid caliphs. For in the eleventh century the Islamic world was divided, with two opposing caliphates—the "orthodox" Sunnī Abbasid caliphate in Baghdad, and the Shīʿite Fāṭimid caliphate in Cairo. The caliph in Baghdad, who wielded moral and religious authority rather than actual political power, stood as a symbol of Sunnī Islam. Real power rested with the Seljuk Turks, nomadic warriors who had occupied Baghdad in 1055. But the Seljuks had converted to Islam in its Sunnī form, and their power was legitimized by the Sunnī Abbasid caliph. There was hence an Abbasid-Seljuk establishment, and al-Ghazālī's appointment at the *Niẓāmiyya* of Baghdad made him part of it. Significantly, one of works he wrote during this period was *Faḍāʾiḥ al-bāṭiniyya* (Scandals of the esoterics), a critique of the esoteric *(bāṭini)* doctrine of the Ismāʿīlī Fāṭimids. This work was also entitled *Al-Mustaẓhirī*, after the Abbasid caliph, al-Mustaẓhir, who had asked al-Ghazālī to write a refutation of Ismāʿīlī doctrine.

It was during this period, which extended from 1091 to 1095, that al-Ghazālī wrote his *Tahāfut* and three other works closely related to it. The first of these was *Maqāṣid al-falāsifa* (The aims of the philosophers), an exposition in Arabic that closely follows Avicenna's Persian work, *Dānesh nāmeh ʿAlāī* (The book of science dedicated to ʿAlāʾ al Dawla). In the introduction of this work and at its conclusion, al-Ghazālī states that he wrote this work of exposition to explain the philosophers' theories as a prelude to his refuting them in the *Tahāfut*. (Strangely enough, in the *Tahāfut* there is never any mention of the *Maqāṣid al-falāsifa*, nor any allusion to it.) The second work, *Miʿyār al-ʿilm* (The standard for knowledge), is an exposition of Avicennan logic, the most comprehensive of such expositions that al-Ghazālī wrote. This logic, for al-Ghazālī, was philosophically neutral, no more than a tool for knowledge, differing from the logic used by the theologians only in its vocabulary and greater elaboration and refinement. He urged his fellow theologians and lawyers to adopt it. The *Miʿyār* was written expressly as an appendix to the *Tahāfut.* For, as al-Ghazālī proclaimed in introducing his *Tahāfut,* he would be using the very logic of the philosophers in refuting them. The third work, a sequel to the *Tahāfut,* is his *Al-iqtiṣād fī al-iʿtiqād* (Moderation in belief), an exposition of Ashʿarite theology. In the *Tahāfut* al-Ghazālī intended to refute and negate; in the *Iqtiṣād,* to build and affirm what he declared to be true doctrine, a point to which I will shortly return.

Probably around the time of his move to Baghdad, al-Ghazālī underwent a period of skepticism. As he recorded in his autobiography, written a few years before his death, he examined the various sciences he had studied but found that they did not yield certainty. Nor could he trust the senses, which, he maintained, deceive us. The faculty of sight, he wrote, "would look at the star and would see it small, the size of a dinar, but then astronomical proofs would show that it is greater in magnitude than the earth." Distrust of the senses, he then relates, extended itself to reason. He began to doubt the basis of all reason, the self-evident truths of logic. For two months, he states, he remained in this "illness," until in His mercy God restored to him his faith in reason.

In 1095, al-Ghazālī underwent another spiritual crisis that changed the course of his life. This came to a head in July when, for a period of time, he lost his ability to speak. Part of the reason, he stated in his autobiography, was that he came to realize that his motivation in pursuing his career was worldly glory, rather than genuine religious impulse. But he also hinted at a dissatisfaction with the purely doctrinal and intellectual approaches to religion. These, he maintained, bypassed the heart of the matter, that which is directly experiential in religion: the *dhawq,* a Sufi term that literally means "taste." He had read the works of the Islamic mystics and become convinced that their path was the one that led to true knowledge. He made the decision to forsake his career and follow their path.

After making arrangements for his family, he left Baghdad and went first to Damascus, where he secluded himself in the minaret of its great mosque. Next he went to Jerusalem, where again he secluded himself in the Dome of the Rock. He then traveled to Hebron, to Madina, and to Mecca. For some eleven years he lived the life of asceticism, pursuing the mystic's way. It was also during this period that he composed his magnum opus: his *Iḥyāʾ ʿulūm al-dīn* (The revivification of the sciences of religion). In this work, as well as other shorter treatises he wrote, he strove to reconcile traditional Islamic beliefs with Sufi teaching. This involved his reinterpretation of what Sufis declared to be the ultimate mystical experience: "annihilation" *(al-fanāʾ)* in the divine essence, a declaration that for the more traditional Muslim violated the fundamental Islamic concept of divine transcendence. For al-Ghazālī, the end of the mystical experience is proximity *(qurb)* to the divine attributes, which in Ashᶜarite dogma are "additional" to the divine essence. The divine essence, at least in this world, remains for al-Ghazālī beyond any human experience, although he adheres to the Ashᶜarite doctrine that God can be "seen" in the hereafter. He further suggests that the mystical experience of "annihilation" consists in seeing nothing in existence except the unity of all things and hence losing experience of oneself. In the *Ihyāʾ* he also sought a synthesis between Islamic theological principles, the Aristotelian doctrine of the mean, and the virtues expounded by the Sufis, the highest of which is the love of God.

In 1106 al-Ghazālī returned to teaching, first in Nīshāpūr and then in Ṭūs, until his death in 1111. His writings during this period included theological and mystical works, his autobiography, and a major book in Islamic law, *Al-mustasfā min uṣūl al-dīn* (The choice essentials of the principles of religion). Needless to say, all the works he wrote after he left Baghdad, which include the voluminous *Ihyāʾ*, are basic for understanding the religious views of this remarkable thinker and are certainly not without intrinsic philosophical interest and value. But speaking strictly from the point of view of the history of philosophy, the pivotal work remains his detailed critique of the Islamic philosophers, his *Tahāfut*.

III

In the *Tahāfut*, al-Ghazālī singles out for his criticism al-Fārābī (d. 950) and Avicenna (d. 1037) as the two most reliable Islamic exponents of Aristotle's philosophy. It should be stressed, however, that while these two philosophers were Aristotelian, they were also Neoplatonists who had formulated two closely related but quite distinct emanative schemes. There are, moreover, differences between these two thinkers, not only in their emanative schemes, but also in their theories of the soul, epistemologies, and eschatologies. At the same time, however, there is overlap in their ideas, so that many of al-Ghazālī's criticisms apply to both.

The main criticisms of al-Ghazālī, however, have Avicenna's philosophy as their direct target. Thus, to give only a few concrete examples, the third discussion includes a detailed critique of Avicenna's triadic emanative scheme, not the dyadic scheme of al-Fārābī. The doctrine that God knows only universals, or, rather, particulars "in a universal way," criticized and rejected in the thirteenth discussion, is a distinctly Avicennan theory. Again, al-Ghazālī devotes the last three discussions of the *Tahāfut* to a detailed critique of Avicenna's theory of an immaterial soul that denies bodily resurrection, not the theory of al-Fārābī. There are differences between the psychological theories of these two philosophers that include a marked difference between their eschatologies. Both maintain that it is only the immaterial soul that is immortal. But while Avicenna maintains that all human souls are immortal (living a life of bliss or misery in the hereafter, depending on their performance in this life), al-Fārābī in his extant writings confines immortality to the few.

The *Tahāfut* divides into two parts. The first, consisting of the first through sixteenth discussions, is devoted to metaphysical questions; the second, containing the seventeenth through twentieth discussions, covers the natural sciences. Two of the philosophical theories that al-Ghazālī condemns as utterly irreligious (not merely heretical innovations) are discussed in the metaphysical part. These are the theory of a pre-eternal world and the theory that God knows only the universal characteristics of particulars. The third doctrine condemned as irreligious—namely, the Avicennan doctrine of the human soul that denies bodily resurrection—belongs to the second part. It is debated in the eighteenth through twentieth discussions but more specifically in the twentieth discussion. This second part on natural science begins (in the seventeenth discussion) with al-Ghazālī's famous critique of causality and concludes with the lengthy discussion of Avicenna's psychology. In including psychology as part of natural science, al-Ghazālī follows the practice of the Islamic philosophers, who in turn follow Aristotle.

The theory of the world's pre-eternity debated in the first discussion is the longest in the *Tahāfut*. At the heart of this debate is the question of the nature of divine causality. As al-Ghazālī explains it, the philosophers maintain that the world is the necessitated effect of an eternally necessitating cause and hence must be eternal. At issue here is the question of whether God acts by the necessity of His nature or voluntarily. For al-Ghazālī, the doctrine of an eternal world means the denial of the divine attribute of will. The philosophers must demonstrate the impossibility of a world created in time by an eternal will, but he tries to show that they fail. At most, their theory of a pre-eternal world has not been demonstrated. It also leads to absurd consequences, he argues. Al-Ghazālī affirms that the world and time were created together at a finite moment in the past through the choice of the eternal divine will.

The second "irreligious doctrine" debated in the thirteenth discussion is Avicenna's theory that God knows particulars only "in a universal way." It should perhaps be said here that Avicenna makes a distinction between celestial and terrestrial particulars. (The distinction is implicit but is not explicitly discussed in al-Ghazālī's otherwise masterly exposition of Avicenna's theory). For Avicenna, a celestial particular like the sun, unlike a terrestrial particular, represents the only member of its species. As such, God knows that one sun exists and knows its universal qualities. In this sense, one might be able to argue that God knows the particular sun. But the concern is with the terrestrial world, where the particular is not the only member of its species. More specifically, the concern is with the individual human and the individual human act. These, as al-Ghazālī pointedly shows, cannot in Avicenna's system be known by God individually. This theory, he argues, has not been demonstrated and plainly contradicts Qurʾānic assertions about divine omniscience.

The case is similar with Avicenna's doctrine of the soul that denies bodily resurrection. Al-Ghazālī argues in detail that the theory of the soul's immateriality, on which Avicenna's denial is based, has not been demonstrated. He then argues that even if one were to concede that the soul is immaterial, bodily resurrection would still be possible. The language of the Qurʾān affirming bodily resurrection, he points out, is explicit and must be accepted literally, not metaphorically. The interpretation of scriptural language as merely metaphor is incumbent if and only if scriptural assertions are demonstrated—in the strictest sense of demonstration—to be impossible. Otherwise they must be accepted in their literal sense. (Elsewhere in his mystical writings al-Ghazālī insists that these statements have a deeper metaphorical and symbolic sense, beyond the literal. But this deeper sense must be based on their literal acceptance.) This criterion of demonstrability underlies the whole argument of the *Tahāfut*.

IV

Al-Ghazālī explains the purpose for his writing the *Tahāfut* in a religious preface and four short introductions. These relatively brief statements are extremely important for understanding the intention of this work. The religious preface reveals a "proximate cause" for his writing the book, as he inveighs in it against certain pseudo-intellectuals of his time. These, he says in effect, have been so impressed by such "high-sounding names such as 'Socrates,' 'Hippocrates,' 'Plato,' 'Aristotle,' and their likes" that they have become mere imitators of such philosophers and their followers, without having any real knowledge of their thought. Moreover, they have used the example of philosophers to rationalize their own disregard for the rituals and obligations imposed by the religious law, opting, in effect, for unbelief *(kufr)*. He thus has undertaken to write this book, he states, to show "the incoherence of [the philosophers'] beliefs and the contradiction of their metaphysical statements, relating at the same time their doctrine as it actually is, so as to make it clear to those who embrace unbelief in God through imitation that all the significant thinkers, past and present, agree in believing in God and the last day." In a tone of accommodation, adopted perhaps to stress the point that the "imitators" of the philosophers have totally misunderstood them, he states that his differences with the philosophers "reduce to matters of detail extraneous to those two pivotal points." These "matters of detail," however, turn out to be quite fundamental: they include the three philosophical doctrines he condemns as utterly irreligious, whose supporters, as he declares, should be punishable by death.

In the introductions that follow, he makes a number of basic points. His quarrel, he states, is not with the philosophers' mathematics, astronomical sciences, or logic, but only with those of their theories that contravene the principles of religion. His task, he further states, is not to defend any specific theological doctrine. On the contrary, in refuting the philosophers he will use against them arguments of various Islamic theological schools. His task, he explains, is simply to refute the philosophers, to show that, contrary to their claims, their theories contradicting religious principles have not been demonstrated; they have failed to fulfill the conditions for demonstration which they themselves had set down in their logical works. His assertion that the *Tahāfut* is intended only to refute is repeated at the conclusion of his critique of the philosophers' four proofs for the world's pre-eternity. He writes:

> We have not endeavored to defend a particular doctrine, and as such we have not departed from the objective of this book. We will not argue exhaustively for the doctrine of the temporal origination [of the world], since our purpose is to refute their claim of knowing [its] pre-eternity.

> As regards the true doctrine, we will write a book concerning it after completing this one—if success, God willing, comes to our aid—and will name it *The Principles of Belief.* We will engage in it in affirmation, just as we have devoted ourselves in this book to destruction.

Al-Ghazālī thus makes it quite clear that the *Tahāfut* is intended only to refute, not to defend any specific theological doctrine. He also tells us that he will write a sequel to the *Tahāfut* in which he will affirm true doctrine. These two points call for comment.

V

In his famous response to al-Ghazālī, his *Tahāfut al-Tahāfut*, Averroës repeatedly refers to al-Ghazālī's arguments as Ashʿarite. And it is true that more often than not al-Ghazālī argues from an Ashʿarite theological base and affirms Ashʿarite theological positions. But this is his preroga-tive. When he does this, he does it as part of his endeavor to refute. He does not develop a theological system in the *Tahāfut*. In one of his later works, *Jawāhir al-Qurʾān* (The gems of the Qurʾān) he mentions the *Tahāfut* with two Ashʿarite works as books intended to defend the faith. But while intended to defend the faith, the *Tahāfut*, strictly speaking, is not an Ashʿarite "manual," a systematically argued presentation of Ashʿarite doctrine. Moreover, al-Ghazālī sometimes defends non-Ashʿarite positions in this work. He defends them, to be sure, as I will shortly indicate, for the sake of argument, as a means for refuting the philosophers. Still, he defends them. Before turning to this point, however, a word is necessary about the title of the work he wrote intended as a sequel to the *Tahāfut*, the work mentioned in the quotation above. The title he gives is *Qawāʿid al-ʿaqāʾid* (The principles of belief). An Ashʿarite work bearing this title constitutes one of the books of al-Ghazālī's *Ihyāʾ*. But the work that best fulfills the purpose stated in his *Tahāfut* is another Ashʿarite work—namely, *Al-iqtisād fī al-iʿtiqād*. It is not that the two works do not com-plement each other; but the *Iqtisād*, written in Baghdād shortly after the writing of the *Tahāfut* and before the *Ihyāʾ*, refers directly to the *Tahāfut* and is closer to it in spirit and in terms of the issues with which it deals. Significantly, in the *Iqtisād*, al-Ghazālī states that its concern is with *qawāʿid al-ʿaqāʾid*, "the principles of belief." Perhaps more to the point, his statement that he will write a book in which he will engage "in affirma-tion" rather than "destruction" occurs, as already noted, at the end of the critique of the philosophers' first proof for the pre-eternity of the world. This statement comes after his assertion: "We will not argue exhaus-tively for the temporal origination [of the world] since our purpose is to refute their claim of knowing [its] pre-eternity." Such exhaustive argu-ment will be included in the book of affirmation he intends to write. The question of the world's origin, however, is not discussed exhaustively in the *Qawāᶜid,* although one of the *Tahāfut*'s arguments against infinite events in the past is repeated. The discussion in the *Iqtiṣād* is by far the more detailed. In it al-Ghazālī repeats his arguments in the *Tahāfut* for the temporal creation of the world much more fully, although admittedly he does not add much to them. It is the *Iqtiṣād,* not the *Qawāᶜid,* that is the sequel to the *Tahāfut.*

This returns the discussion to the question of al-Ghazālī's defense of non-Ashᶜarite positions. The two most important instances occur in his discussions of causality and of the doctrine of the soul's immateriality. I will begin with the causal question.

There are abundant statements in the *Tahāfut* indicating that its author subscribes to the Ashᶜarite occasionalist doctrine that confines all causal action to God. Nonetheless, in the seventeenth discussion, in which al-Ghazālī argues for the possibility of certain types of miracles whose possibility is rejected by the Islamic philosophers, he defends two different causal theories. He begins with his famous declaration and defense of the Ashᶜarite causal theory: "The connection between what is habitually believed to be a cause and what is habitually believed to be an effect is not necessary, according to us." The connection between such events, he then states, "is due to God's prior decree, who creates them side by side, not to its being necessary in itself, incapable of separation." Observation, he then argues, shows only concomitance—never any necessary causal connection. In the course of debating this question, however, al-Ghazālī puts into the mouth of his opponents an objection to this denial of necessary causal connection. According to this objection, such a denial leads inevitably to absurdities, to a confused, haphazard, irregular course of events. Al-Ghazālī answers quite emphatically that such a consequence does not follow. For God in His goodness has ordained a regular natural pattern (which in itself is not necessary but is inevitable because it is decreed by God) and has created in humanity knowledge that this uniformity will continue and will only be interrupted when a miracle takes place—an event also decreed and created by God. The opponent's contention that absurd consequences would result from the denial of causal necessity in things, al-Ghazālī declares, is hence an exercise in "sheer vilification" *(tashnīᶜ maḥḍ).* To avoid being subjected to such vilification, however, al-Ghazālī proposes another possible causal theory that would still allow the possibility of those miracles the philosophers deem impossible.

This second causal theory proposed by al-Ghazālī is perhaps best described as a modified Aristotelian theory. Created things would have causal efficacy, provided one maintains that the divine act remains voluntary, not necessitated by the divine essence. Moreover, according to this second theory, divine power is such that it can intervene in the natural order, creating new causal conditions that produce the miracle. Now al-Ghazālī elaborates this theory and insists that it is also possible. Hence he holds that there are two possible causal theories that allow the possibility of miracles. But while he holds both to be possible, he does not state that they are compossible. For they are mutually exclusive.

To which, then, of the two theories does al-Ghazālī actually subscribe? It is here that the *Iqtiṣād* provides the answer. For in it al-Ghazālī affirms without any equivocation the Ashʿarite causal theory. Divine power is pervasive and is the direct cause of each and every created existent and each and every temporal event. Inanimate things have no causal power (a point he also asserts more than once in the *Tahāfut*). Power belongs only to the animate. But this is a power which God "creates" in humanity. Created power, however, has no causal efficacy. It is created simultaneously with the event human beings ordinarily, but erroneously, regard as the effect of their created power. This effect is also the direct creation of divine power. (This is an expression of the Ashʿarite doctrine of acquisition *[kasb]* and finds corroboration in the *Qawāʿid*). Human power and the effect associated with it are both the simultaneous creations of God. Causal action belongs exclusively to divine power. This necessarily negates the second causal theory, the modified Aristotelian theory, introduced in the *Tahāfut*. Whatever other reason there might be for introducing it in the *Tahāfut*, it is clearly introduced there for the sake of argument, to demonstrate that even if one allows a measure of causal efficacy in things, one can still allow the possibility (denied by the philosophers) of certain kinds of miracles.

Turning to the question of the immateriality of the human soul, al-Ghazālī, as mentioned earlier, devotes an entire section (the eighteenth discussion) to it. He offers a detailed refutation of the proofs Avicenna had given for its immateriality, arguing that none of these proofs (ten in number) has demonstrated such an immateriality. The doctrine of an immaterial soul is the basis for Avicenna's insistence that there is no bodily resurrection. In the twentieth discussion, devoted to the question of bodily resurrection, however, al-Ghazālī does not choose to defend the Ashʿarite doctrine of the human soul that denies its immateriality. Instead, he strives to show that even if one accepts a doctrine of an immaterial soul, one can maintain the possibility of bodily resurrection. Moreover, he states that a doctrine of an immaterial soul need not be inconsistent with Islamic teaching, that it has support in the Qurʾān. His presentation of the possibility of an immaterial soul is so persuasive in the *Tahāfut* that one is prone to believe that this is the doctrine to which al-Ghazālī subscribes. In the *Iqtiṣād,* however, he defends an Ashʿarite doctrine of a material human soul and states quite explicitly that in the *Tahāfut* he defended a doctrine of an immaterial soul only for the sake of argument, in order to refute the philosophers.

These are the two notable instances where he defends a doctrine to which he does not actually subscribe. It is also clear that he defends them for the sake of argument, as a means to refute the philosophers. In this he is not inconsistent with his declarations that the *Tahāfut*'s primary aim is to refute.

VI

The term *tahāfut* has been variously translated—for example, as *destructio* by the Latins, "inconsistency," "disintegration," "collapse," as well as "incoherence," by modern scholars. A common meaning is "collapse," or "collapsing," sometimes with the nuance of rushing headlong and crowding to fall into disaster, into hellfire. It also is used to convey the idea of rushing and swarming into combat. The term also relates to *haft,* discourse that is not well thought out, that is unintelligible, incoherent. M. Bouyges, in the introduction to his edition of the text, gives a succinct discussion of the ways this term has been translated in English and other languages. He chose "incoherence" as perhaps conveying best what al-Ghazālī meant by the term *tahāfut.* His reasons for this choice are quite convincing and hence I have followed him in the translation of the term.

There have been two English translations of al-Ghazālī's *Tahāfut.* The first, published in 1954, is that of S. Van Den Bergh in his translation of Averroës's answer to al-Ghazālī—namely, the *Tahāfut al-Tahāfut*—which embodies most of al-Ghazālī's text. This translation (2 vols., London: Luzac, 1954), with its copious notes, is a veritable tour de force and is certainly a major contribution to the study of both al-Ghazālī and Averroës. At the same time, however, it is not free from serious errors. The second translation, by S. Kamali (Lahore: Pakistan Philosophical Congress, 1958), has for years served as a main introduction of this work to the English reader. Kamali's English version has the merit of conveying much of the argumentative flavor of the original—this in itself being a considerable achievement. This version, however, also has its share of inaccuracies and at times is more of a paraphrase than a translation.

A text sometimes poses difficulties for the translator, not because its author is a bad writer, but because its author is a good one. Al-Ghazālī is a master of Arabic prose. His style, however, is very personal and highly idiomatic; it carries with it nuances that are difficult to recapture in a translation. As such, the difficulties it often poses are not so much due to lack of clarity. For the most part, his presentation of complex and subtle arguments is remarkable for its clarity. But there are also lapses. Ambiguities do occur. And there are times when what is stated is so condensed that its intention is not immediately clear. There is also an ambiguity, frequently encountered in Arabic, relating to the use of pronouns, where the referents of these pronouns are not always immediately obvious. Hence, in translating the text, there is an ever-pressing need for clarification. In places where lengthy explanations are needed, I have placed these in notes. But there are numerous places where lengthy explanations are not needed. To place these in notes imposes unnecessary interruptions to the flow of the argument. For this reason, to clarify issues, I have made extensive use of square brackets. These include words or sentences which are not explicitly stated in the text but are implicit therein.

The Arabic text of the *Tahāfut* is based on the edition of Maurice Bouyges (Beirut: Imprimerie Catholique, 1927). I have, however, introduced new paragraphing, dictated by sense and flow of argument and determined also by the manner in which I thought it was best to paragraph the translation. To help the reader, I have also added considerably to the sparse punctuation of the original edition, and also to the sparse gemination marks, the *shaddas,* over the letters. On the whole, I have followed the readings of Bouyges adopted in the body of the texts, but there are departures. I have chosen other manuscript readings given in Bouyges's apparatus criticus, the choice dictated by grammar and sense. These departures from Bouyges's edition have been placed between square brackets, with a note indicating the reading in the body of Bouyges's text. Some changes—and these are few—dictated by language and sense, are my own. These are placed in angular brackets, with notes indicating the reading in Bouyges's text.

مقدّمة المترجم

كتاب «تهافت الفلاسفة» للإمام، «حجّة الاسلام»، أبي حامد الغزالي، كتاب ردّ على الفيلسوفين الاسلاميّين، «المعلّم الثاني»، أبي نصر الفارابي، وخاصّة «الشيخ الرئيس»، أبي عليّ ابن سينا. والغزالي لا يجد أيّ ضرر على الدين في علوم هذين الفيلسوفين الرياضيّة والمنطقيّة. فهذه من العلوم «التي لا يصدم مذهبهم فيه أصلا من أصول الدين.» وهو لا يجد أيضا أيّ ضرر في معظم علومهم الطبيعيّة. ولكنّه يرى الضرر كلّ الضرر في علومهم الالهيّة، وفي بعض علومهم الطبيعيّة، كنظريتهم في السببيّة، ونظريتهم في النفس البشريّة.

ينتقد الغزالي في كتابه عشرين نظريّة فلسفيّة، يفرد منها ثلاث مسائل على أنّها «لا تلائم الاسلام بوجه»، وهي نظريّة فلاسفة في قدم العالم، «وقولهم انّ لله تعالى لا يحيط علما بالجزئيّات الحادثة من الأشخاص... وانكارهم بعث الأجساد وحشرها». وأمّا باقي النظريّات التي ينتقدها فهو يعتبرها بدعا، قد نطق بها فريق من فرق الاسلام.

فالباعث لكتاب أبي حامد باعث دينيّ، غرضه الدفاع عن العقيدة. فالكتاب ― وهذا ما يصرّح به الغزالي في «جواهر القرآن» ― يجانس كتبه الكلاميّة التي مقصودها «حراسة» العقيدة. ولكنّ كتاب «تهافت

الفلاسفة)) يختلف عن كتب الغزالي الكلاميّة في انّه لا يروم فيه بناء مذهب، بل يقتصر فيه على الإبطال. وطريقة الغزالي في الابطال طريقة منطقيّة محضة. فهو يستعمل المنطق ليظهر ما في نطريّات الفلاسفة من تناقض. وهو يروم ابطال دعواهم انّ هذه النظريّات مبنيّة على حجج برهانيّة. فغرضه، كما يعبّر عنه في المقدّمة الرابعة لكتابه، هو ايضاح ((انّ ما شرّطوه في صحّة مادّة القياس في قسم البرهان من المنطق، وما شرّطوه في صورته في كتاب القياس... لم يتمكّنوا من الوفاء بشيء منه في علومهم الالهيّة)).

فالمنهج الذي يتّبعه الغزالي في ردّه على الفلاسفة منهج منطقيّ، على فهم تامّ للنظريّات الفلسفيّة التي يعارضها. فالكتاب كتاب نقد منطقيّ تحليليّ. وهو من أدقّ الكتب النقديّة المنطقيّة التحليليّة التي عرفها تاريخ الفكر البسريّ، ومن أهمّ الكتب الفكريّة التي أنتجته الحضارة الإسلاميّة. وكان له الأثر الكبير على الفكر الاسلاميّ، وتعدّى تأثيره الى أوروبا في القرون الوسطى وما بعد.

وإن كان باعث كتاب الغزالي دينيّ كلاميّ، فمنهجه منطقيّ فلسفيّ. فهو نقد فلسفيّ لآراء فلسفيّة، يناظر فيها مسائل فلسفيّة اساسيّة لا تزال تشغل الفكر البشريّ. فهو يتناول البحث مثلا في مسألة حدوث العالم، ومسألة التناهي واللاتناهي، ومسألة علاقة الصفات الالهيّة بالذات الالهيّة، ومسألة العلاقة بين ماهيّة الشيء ووجوده، ومسألة وجه الاقتران بين المسبّبات وأسبابها، ومسألة مصير الانسان بعد مفارقته الحياة، ومسائل أخرى تتعلّق بالتي ذكرناها، لا تقلّ عنها خطرا. فإدراج الترجمه الانكليزيّة مع النصّ العربي لكتاب ((تهافت الفلاسفة)) في ((سلسلة ترجمة الفلسفة الاسلاميّة)) لا ينبو عن غرض هذه السلسلة، بل يفي به كلّ الوفاء.

والنصّ العربيّ الذي أعددناه للترجمة الأنكليزيّة هو في جوهره نصّ
طبعة بيروت سنة ١٩٢٧ التي حقّقها العالم موريس بْويج. ولكنّا قد
أحدثنا بعض التغييرات. فقد قسّمنا النصّ الى فقرات جديدة كثيرة
مرقمة، يوازي ترقيمها ترقيم فقرات الترجمة. ثمّ انّا أضفنا الفواصل
والنقاط وعلامات الاستفهام، وأيضا الكثير من علامات التشديد فوق
الأحرف، تسهيلا للقراءه. ولقد استبدلنا عددا من العبارات في متن طبعة
بيروت بقراءات وردت في الجهاز النقديّ لهذه الطبعة. واساس اختيارنا
لهذه القراءات اللغة وسياق الفكر. وقد وضعنا لهذه القراءات التي
اخترناها من الجهاز النقدي ضمن معقّفين على هذه الصوره: [ ].
واشرنا في الحاشية في آخر الكتاب الى القراءات كما اوردها بويج في
متن طبعة بيروت. وهناك أيضا بعض القراءات، وهي قليلة جدّا، من
عندنا وضعناها امّا استبدالا لقراءات بويج، او اضافة اليها. وقد حصرنا
قراءاتنا هذه ضمن شكل ذى زوايا على هذه الصورة: < >، مشيرين في
الحاشية الى طبعة بيروت.

In the Name of God, the Compassionate, the Merciful

[The Religious Preface]

(1) We ask God in His majesty that transcends all bounds and His munificence that goes beyond all ends to shed upon us the lights of His guidance and to snatch away from us the darkness of waywardness and error; to make us among those who saw the truth as truth, preferring to
5   pursue and follow its paths, and who saw the false as false, choosing to avoid and shun it; to bring us to the felicity He promised His prophets and saints; to make us attain that rapture and gladness, favored bliss and joy (once we depart from this abode of delusion) from whose heights the greatest ascents of the understanding stand low and from whose dis-
10   tanced stretches the utmost reaches of the arrows of the imagination waste away; to grant us, after arriving at the bliss of paradise and emerging from the terror of the judgment day, "that which neither eye has seen, nor ear heard, nor occurred to the heart of men," and that He may bestow His prayers and His assured peace upon our prophet, the chosen,
15   Muḥammad, the best of men, and upon his virtuous family and his companions pure, keys of guidance and lanterns in the dark.

(2) I have seen a group who, believing themselves in possession of a distinctiveness from companion and peer by virtue of a superior quick wit and intelligence, have rejected the Islamic duties regarding acts
20   of worship, disdained religious rites pertaining to the offices of prayer and the avoidance of prohibited things, belittled the devotions and ordinances prescribed by the divine law, not halting in the face of its

بِسْمِ اللهِ الرَّحْمَنِ الرَّحِيمِ

(١) نسأل الله بجلاله الموفى على كل نهاية، وَجودِه المجاوز كلَّ غاية، ان يفيض علينا أنوار الهداية، ويقبض عنّا ظلمات الضلال والغواية، وان يجعلنا ممّن رأى الحقّ حقًّا فآثر اتّباعه واقتفاءه، ورأى الباطل باطلاً فاختار اجتنابه واجتواءه، وان يلقينا السعادة التى وعد بها انبياءه وأولياءه، وأن يبلغنا من الغبطة والسرور والنعمة والحبور، اذا ارتحلنا عن دار الغرور، ما ينخفض دون اعاليها مراقى الافهام، ويتضاءَل دون اقاصيها مرامى سهام الاوهام، وان يُنيلنا بعد الورود على نعيم الفردوس والصدور من هول المحشر، ما لا عين رأت ولا اذن سمعت ولا خطر على قلب بشر؛ وأن يصلى على نبينا المصطفى محمد خير البشر، وعلى آله الطيِّبين وأصحابِه الطاهرين، مفاتيح الهدى ومصابيح الدجى، ويسلّم تسليماً.

(٢) اما بعد فانى رأيت طائفة يعتقدون فى انفسهم التميّز عن الاتراب والنظراء بمزيد الفطنة والذكاء، قد رفضوا وظائف الاسلام من العبادات، واستحقروا شعائر الدين من وظائف الصلوات والتوقّى عن المحظورات، واستهانوا بتعبّدات الشرع وحدوده، و لم يقفوا عند توقيفاته وقيوده،

١

prohibitions and restrictions. On the contrary, they have entirely cast off the reins of religion through multifarious beliefs, following therein a troop "who repel away from God's way, intending to make it crooked, who are indeed disbelievers in the hereafter" [Qur'ān 11:19].

(3) There is no basis for their unbelief other than traditional, conventional imitation, like the imitation of Jews and Christians, since their[1] upbringing and that of their offspring has followed a course other than the religion of Islam, their fathers and forefathers having [also] followed [conventional imitation], and no [basis] other than speculative investigation, an outcome of their stumbling over the tails of sophistical doubts that divert from the direction of truth, and their being deceived by embellished imaginings akin to the glitter of the mirage, as has happened to groups of speculative thinkers, followers of heretical innovation and whim, in [their] investigation of beliefs and opinions.

(4) The source of their unbelief is in their hearing high-sounding names such as "Socrates," "Hippocrates," "Plato," "Aristotle," and their likes and the exaggeration and misguidedness of groups of their followers in describing their minds; the excellence of their principles; the exactitude of their geometrical, logical, natural, and metaphysical sciences—and in [describing these as] being alone (by reason of excessive intelligence and acumen) [capable] of extracting these hidden things. [It is also in hearing] what [these followers] say about [their masters—namely,] that concurrent with the sobriety of their intellect and the abundance of their merit is their denial of revealed laws and religious confessions and their rejection of the details of religious and sectarian [teaching], believing them to be man-made laws and embellished tricks.

(5) When this struck their hearing, that which was reported of [the philosophers'] beliefs finding agreement with their nature, they adorned themselves with the embracing of unbelief—siding with the throng of the virtuous, as they claim; affiliating with them; exalting themselves above aiding the masses and the commonality; and disdaining to be content with the religious beliefs of their forebears. [They have done this,] thinking that the show of cleverness in abandoning the [traditional] imitation of what is true by embarking on the imitation of the false is a beauteous thing, being unaware that moving from one [mode of] imitation to another is folly and confusedness.

(6) What rank in God's world is there that is lower than the rank of one who adorns himself with the abandonment of the truth that is traditionally believed by the hasty embracing of the false as true, accepting it without [reliable] report and verification? The imbeciles among the

بل خلعوا بالكلّية ربقة الدين بفنون من الظنون، يتبعون فيها رهطاً
«يصدّون عن سبيل الله ويبغونها عوجا وهم بالآخرة هم كافرون.»

(٣) ولا مستند لكفرهم غير تقليد سماعى الفى كتقليد اليهود
والنصارى، اذ جرى على غير دين الاسلام نشوؤهم وولادهم، وعليه درج
آباؤهم وأجدادهم؛ ولا غير بحث نظرى صادر عن التعثّر باذيال الشُّبه
الصارفة عن صوب الصواب، والانخداع بالخيالات المزخرفة كلامع
السراب، كما اتفق لطوائف من النظّار فى البحث عن العقائد والآراء من
أهل البدع والاهواء.

(٤) وانما مصدر كفرهم سماعهم اسامى هائلة كسقراط وبقراط
وافلاطن وأرسطاطاليس وأمثالهم، وإطناب طوائف من متبعيهم
وضلالهم فى وصف عقولهم وحسن أصولهم ودقة علومهم الهندسية
والمنطقية والطبيعية والالهية، واستبدادهم لفرط الذكاء والفطنة
باستخراج تلك الامور الخفيّة، وحكايتهم عنهم انهم مع رزانة عقلهم
وغزارة فضلهم منكرون للشرائع والنحل وجاحدون لتفاصيل الاديان
والملل، ومعتقدون انها نواميس مؤلّفة وحيل مزخرفة.

(٥) فلما قرع ذلك سمعهم ووافق ما حكى من عقائدهم طبعهم،
تجملوا باعتقاد الكفر تحيّزاً الى غمار الفضلاء بزعمهم، وانخراطاً فى
سلكهم، وترفّعاً عن مساعدة الجماهير والدهماء، واستنكافاً من القناعة
باديان الآباء، ظنًّا بأن إظهار التكايس فى النزوع عن تقليد الحق بالشروع
فى تقليد الباطل جمال، وغفلةً منهم عن ان الانتقال الى تقليد عن تقليد
خرق وخبال.

(٦) فايّة رتبة فى عالم الله أخس من رتبة من يتجمل بترك الحق المعتقد
تقليداً بالتسارع الى قبول الباطل تصديقاً دون أن يقبله خبراً وتحقيقاً؟

masses stand detached from the infamy of this abyss; for there is no crav-
ing in their nature to become clever by emulating those who follow the ways
of error. Imbecility is thus nearer salvation than acumen severed [from
religious belief]; blindness is closer to wholeness than cross-eyed sight.

(7) When I perceived this vein of folly throbbing within these dim-
wits, I took it upon myself to write this book in refutation of the ancient
philosophers, to show the incoherence of their belief and the contradiction of their word in matters relating to metaphysics; to uncover the dan-
gers of their doctrine and its shortcomings, which in truth ascertainable
are objects of laughter for the rational and a lesson for the intelligent—I
mean the kinds of diverse beliefs and opinions they particularly hold that
set them aside from the populace and the common run of men. [I will do
this,] relating at the same time their doctrine as it actually is, so as to
make it clear to those who embrace unbelief through imitation that all
significant thinkers, past and present, agree in believing in God and the
last day; that their differences reduce to matters of detail extraneous
to those two pivotal points (for the sake of which the prophets, supported
by miracles, have been sent); that no one has denied these two [beliefs]
other than a remnant of perverse minds who hold lopsided opinions, who
are neither noticed nor taken into account in the deliberations of the
speculative thinkers, [but who are instead] counted only among the com-
pany of evil devils and in the throng of the dim-witted and inexperienced.
[I will do this] so that whoever believes that adorning oneself with
imitated unbelief shows good judgment and induces awareness of one's
quick wit and intelligence would desist from his extravagance, as it will
become verified for him that those prominent and leading philosophers
he emulates are innocent of the imputation that they deny the religious
laws; that [on the contrary] they believe in God and His messengers; but
that they have fallen into confusion in certain details beyond these principles, erring in this, straying from the correct path, and leading others
astray. We will reveal the kinds of imaginings and vanities in which they
have been deceived, showing all this to be unproductive extravagance.
God, may He be exalted, is the patron of success in the endeavor to show
what we intend to verify.

والبله من العوامّ بمعزل عن فضيحة هذه المهواة؛ فليس فى سجيتهم حبّ التكايس بالتشبّه بذوى الضلالات. فالبلاهة أدنى الى الخلاص من فطانة بتراء، والعمى اقرب الى السلامة من بصيرة حولاء.

(٧) فلما رأيت هذا العرق من الحماقة نابضاً على هؤلاء الاغبياء، انتدبت لتحرير هذا الكتاب ردًّا على الفلاسفة القدماء، مبيناً تهافت عقيدتهم وتناقض كلمتهم فيما يتعلّق بالالهيات، وكاشفاً عن غوائل مذهبهم وعوراته التى هى على التحقيق مضاحك العقلاء وعبرة عند الاذكياء، أعنى ما اختصّوا بهِ عن الجماهير والدهماء من فنون العقائد والآراء. هذا مع حكاية مذهبهم على وجهه ليتبيّن [لهؤلاء]¹ الملحدة تقليداً اتفاق كل مرموق من الاوائل والاواخر على الايمان بالله واليوم الآخر، وان الاختلافات راجعة الى تفاصيل خارجة عن هذين القطبين الذين لاجلهما بعث الانبياء المؤيّدون بالمعجزات، وانه لم يذهب الى انكارهما الا شرذمة يسيرة من ذوى العقول المنكوسة والآراء المعكوسة الذين لا <يؤبه>² لهم، ولا يعبأ بهم فيما بين النظار، ولا يعدّون الا فى زمرة الشياطين الاشرار وغمار الاغبياء والاغمار، ليكفّ عن غلوائِه من يظن ان التجمل بالكفر تقليدا يدل على حسن رأيه ويشعر بفطنته وذكائه اذ يتحقق انّ هؤلاء الذين يتشبه بهم من زعماء الفلاسفة ورؤسائهم براء عمّا قرفوا به من جحد الشرائع، وانّهم مؤمنون بالله ومصدّقون، برسله، وانّهم اختبطوا فى تفاصيل بعد هذه الاصول، قد زلّو افيها فضلّوا واضلّوا عن سواء السبيل. ونحن نكشف عن فنون ما انخدعوا بهِ من التخاييل والاباطيل ونبيّن انّ كلّ ذلك تهويل ما وراءَه تحصيل والله تعالى ولىّ التوفيق لاظهار ما قصدناه من التحقيق.

(8) Let us now begin the book with introductions that express the pattern of discourse followed [therein].

[A first] introduction

(9) Let it be known that to plunge into narrating the differences among the philosophers would involve too long a tale. For their floundering about is lengthy, their disputes many, their views spread far apart, their ways divergent and convergent. Let us, then, restrict ourselves to showing the contradictions in the views of their leader, who is the philosopher par excellence and "the first teacher." For he has, as they claim, organized and refined their sciences, removed the redundant in their views, and selected what is closest to the principles of their capricious beliefs—namely, Aristotle. He has answered all his predecessors—even his teacher, known among them as "the divine Plato," apologizing for disagreeing with his teacher by saying: "Plato is a friend and truth is a friend, but truth is a truer friend."

(10) We have transmitted this story to let it be known that there is neither firm foundation nor perfection in the doctrine they hold; that they judge in terms of supposition and surmise, without verification or certainty; that they use the appearance of their mathematical and logical sciences as evidential proof for the truth of their metaphysical sciences, using [this] as a gradual enticement for the weak in mind. Had their metaphysical sciences been as perfect in demonstration, free from conjecture, as their mathematical, they would not have disagreed among themselves regarding [the former], just as they have not disagreed in their mathematical sciences.

(11) Moreover, the words of the translators of the words of Aristotle are not free from corruption and change, requiring exegesis and interpretation, so that this also has aroused conflict among them. The most reliable transmitters and verifiers among the philosophers in Islam are al-Fārābī Abū Naṣr and Ibn Sīnā. Let us, then, confine ourselves to refuting what these two have selected and deemed true of the doctrines

(٨) ولنصَدِّر الآن الكتاب بمقدّمات تُعرب عن مساق الكلام فى الكتاب.

مقدّمة

(٩) ليعلم ان الخوض فى حكاية اختلاف الفلاسفة تطويل، فانّ خبطهم طويل، ونزاعهم كثير، وآراءهم منتشرة، وطرقهم متباعدة متدابرة. فلنقتصر على اظهار التناقض فى رأى مقدّمهم الذى هو الفيلسوف المطلق والمعلم الاول. فانه رتّب علومهم وهذبها بزعمهم. وحذف الحشو من آرائهم وانتقى ما هو الاقرب الى اصول اهوائهم، وهو رسطاليس. وقد ردّ على كلّ من قبله حتى على استاذه الملقّب عندهم بافلاطن الالهى، ثم اعتذر عن مخالفته استاذه بان قال: افلاطن صديق والحقّ صديق ولكن الحقّ أصدق منه.

(١٠) وانّما نقلنا هذه الحكاية ليعلم انّه لا تثبّت ولا اتقان لمذهبهم عندهم، وانّهم يحكمون بظنّ وتخمين من غير تحقيق ويقين، ويستدلّون على صدق علومهم الالهية بظهور العلوم الحسابيّة والمنطقيّة، ويستدرجون به ضعفاء العقول. ولو كانت علومهم الالهيّة متقنة البراهين، نقيّة عن التخمين، كعلومهم الحسابيّة، لما اختلفوا فيها كما لم يختلفوا فى الحسابيّة.

(١١) ثم المترجمون لكلام رسطاليس، لم ينفكّ كلامهم عن تحريف وتبديل، محوج الى تفسير وتأويل، حتى أثار ذلك أيضا نزاعاً بينهم. وأقومهم بالنقل والتحقيق من المتفلسفة فى الاسلام الفارابى أبو نصر وابن سينا. فنقتصر على ابطال ما اختاروه ورأوه الصحيح من

of their leaders in error. For that which they have abandoned and scorned to pursue no one contests is error and needs no lengthy examination to refute. Let it, then, be known that we are confining ourselves to the [philosophers'] doctrines according to the transmission of these two
5   men so that the discussion would not spread [far and wide] with the spread of doctrines.

[A second] introduction

(12) Let it be known, then, that the dispute between [the philosophers] and others of the sects has three parts.

(13) There is a part in which the dispute reduces to the purely verbal,
10   as, for example, their naming the world's Creator—exalted be He above what they say—a substance, with their explanation of substance as that which does not exist in a subject—that is, [as] the self-subsisting that does not need that which substantiates it. They did not intend by substance, as their opponents intend, that which occupies space.

15   (14) We will not plunge into a refutation of this because, once the meaning of self-subsistence becomes agreed upon, then the discussion regarding the use of the term "substance" to express this meaning becomes a lexical investigation. If language sanctions its use, then the permissibility of its use in religion reverts to investigations within the
20   religious law. For the prohibiting and permitting of terms derives from what the outer meaning of the religious texts indicates. Now, you may say that this [type of] naming has been mentioned by the theologians in relation to the [divine] attributes but was not introduced by the lawyers in the discipline of the religious law. You must not, however, allow the
25   true nature of things to become confused for you because of customs and formalities. For you now know that it is an investigation about the permissibility of uttering an expression whose meaning is true of the thing named. It is thus similar to investigating the permissibility of a certain act[—hence, within the province of the religious law].

30   (15) The second part is one where their doctrine does not clash with any religious principle and where it is not a necessity of the belief in the prophets and [God's] messengers, God's prayers be upon them, to dispute with them about it. An example of this is their statement:

مذهب رؤسائهم فى الضلال؛ فانّ ما هجروه واستنكفوه من المتابعة فيه لا يتمارى فى اختلاله، ولا يفتقر الى نظر طويل فى ابطاله. فليعلم أنّا مقتصرون على رد مذاهبهم بحسب نقل هذين الرجلين كيلا ينتشر الكلام بحسب انتشار المذاهب.

مقدّمة ثانية

(١٢) ليعلم ان الخلاف بينهم وبين غيرهم من الفرق ثلاثة أقسام:

(١٣) قسم يرجع النزاع فيه الى لفظ مجرّد كتسميتهم صانع العالم تعالى عن قولهم جوهرا، مع تفسيرهم الجوهر بانه الموجود لا فى موضوع، أى القائم بنفسه الذى لا يحتاج الى مقوّم يقوّمه، ولم يريدوا بالجوهر المتحيّز على ما أراده خصومهم.

(١٤) ولسنا نخوض فى إبطال هذا، لانّ معنى القيام بالنفس اذا صار متّفقاً عليه، رجع الكلام فى التعبير باسم الجوهر عن هذا المعنى الى البحث عن اللغة وان [سوّغت]٣ اللغة إطلاقه، رجع جواز اطلاقه فى الشرع الى المباحث الفقهيّة. فان تحريم اطلاق الاسامى وإباحتها يؤخذ ممّا يدل عليه ظواهر الشرع. ولعلّك تقول، هذا انّما ذكره المتكلمون فى الصفات ولم يورده الفقهاء فى فن الفقه، فلا ينبغى ان يلتبس عليك حقائق الامور بالعادات والمراسم. فقد عرفت انه بحث عن جواز التلفظ بلفظ صدق معناه على المسمى به، فهو كالبحث عن جواز فعل من الأفعال.

(١٥) القسم الثانى ما لا يصدم مذهبهم فيه أصلاً من اصول الدين، وليس من ضرورة تصديق الانبياء والرسل صلوات الله عليهم منازعتهم

"The lunar eclipse consists in the obliteration of the moon's light due to the interposition of the earth between it and the sun, the earth being a sphere surrounded by the sky on all sides. Thus, when the moon falls in the earth's shadow, the sun's light is severed from it." Another example is their statement: "The solar eclipse means the presence of the lunar orb between the observer and the sun. This occurs when the sun and the moon are both at the two nodes at one degree."

(16) This topic is also one into the refutation of which we shall not plunge, since this serves no purpose. Whoever thinks that to engage in a disputation for refuting such a theory is a religious duty harms religion and weakens it. For these matters rest on demonstrations—geometrical and arithmetical—that leave no room for doubt. Thus, when one who studies these demonstrations and ascertains their proofs, deriving thereby information about the time of the two eclipses [and] their extent and duration, is told that this is contrary to religion, [such an individual] will not suspect this [science, but] only religion. The harm inflicted on religion by those who defend it in a way not proper to it is greater than [the harm caused by] those who attack it in the way proper to it. As it has been said: "A rational foe is better than an ignorant friend."

(17) If it is said that God's messenger—God's prayers and peace be upon him—said, "The sun and moon are two of God's signs that are eclipsed neither for the death nor the life of anyone; should you witness such [events], then hasten to the remembrance of God and prayer," how, then, does this agree with what [the philosophers] state? We say:

(18) There is nothing in this that contradicts what they have stated, since there is nothing in it except the denial of the occurrence of the eclipse for the death or life of anyone and the command to pray when it occurs. Why should it be so remote for the religious law that commands prayer at noon and sunset to command as recommendable prayer at the occurrence of an eclipse? If it is said that at the end of [this] tradition [the prophet] said, "But, if God reveals Himself to a thing, it submits itself to Him," thereby proving that the eclipse is submission by reason of revelation, we answer:

فيه، كقولهم: ان الكسوف القمرى عبارة عن امحاء ضوء القمر بتوسط الارض بينه وبين الشمس من حيث انه يقتبس نوره من الشمس، والارض كرة والسماء محيط بها من الجوانب؛ فاذا وقع القمر فى ظلّ الارض انقطع عنه نور الشمس. وكقولهم: ان كسوف الشمس معناه وقوف جرم القمر بين الناظر وبين الشمس، وذلك عند اجتماعهما فى العقدتين على دقيقة واحدة.

(١٦) وهذا الفن أيضاً لسنا نخوض فى ابطاله اذ لا يتعلق به غرض. ومن ظن ان المناظرة فى ابطال هذا من الدين، فقد جنى على الدين وضَعَّف أمره. فانّ هذه الامور تقوم عليها براهين هندسيّة حسابيّة لا يبقى معها ريبة؛ فمن تطلَّع عليها وتحقَّق ادلَّتها حتى يُخبر بسببها عن وقت الكسوفين وقدرهما ومدة بقائهما الى الانجلاء، اذا قيل لهُ ان هذا على خلاف الشرع، لم يسترب فيه، وانّما يستريب فى الشرع. وضرر الشرع ممَّن ينصره لا بطريقه اكثر من ضرره ممَّن يطعن فيه بطريقه. وهو كما قيل: عدوٌّ عاقل خير من صديق جاهل.

(١٧) فان قيل، فقد قال رسول الله صلى الله عليه وسلَّم: انّ الشمس والقمر لآيتان من آيات الله لا يخسفان لموت أحد ولا لحياته، فاذا رأيتم ذلك فافزعوا الى ذكر الله والصلاة، فكيف يلائم هذا ما قالوه. قلنا:

(١٨) وليس فى هذا ما يناقض ما قالوه، اذ ليس فيه الا نفى وقوع الكسوف لموت احد او لحياته والامر بالصلوة عنده؛ والشرع الذى يأمر بالصلوة عند الزوال والغروب والطلوع، من أين يبعد منه ان يأمر عند الكسوف بها استحباباً؟ فان قيل، فقد رُوى انه قال فى آخر الحديث: ولكنّ الله اذا تجلَّى لشىء خضع له، فيدلّ على انّ الكسوف خضوع بسبب التجلى، قلنا:

(19) This addition is not soundly transmitted and, hence, the one who transmits it must be judged as conveying what is false. The [correctly] related [tradition] is the one we have mentioned. How is this not so? For if the transmission [of the addition] were sound, then it would be easier to interpret it metaphorically rather than to reject matters that are conclusively true. For how many an apparent [scriptural] meaning has been interpreted metaphorically [on the basis of] rational proofs [rejecting their literal sense] that do not attain the degree of clarity [of the astronomical demonstrations regarding the eclipse]! The greatest thing in which the atheists rejoice is for the defender of religion to declare that these [astronomical demonstrations] and their like are contrary to religion. Thus, the [atheist's] path for refuting religion becomes easy if the likes [of the above argument for defending religion] are rendered a condition [for its truth].

(20) This is because the inquiry [at issue] about the world is whether it originated in time or is eternal. Moreover, once its temporal origination is established, it makes no difference whether it is a sphere, a simple body, an octagon, or a hexagon; [it makes] no difference whether the [highest] heavens and what is beneath are thirteen layers, as they say, or lesser or greater. For the relation of the inquiry into [these matters] to the inquiry into divine [matters] is similar to the relation of looking at the number of layers of an onion [or] the number of seeds in a pomegranate. What is intended here is only [the world's] being God's act, whatever mode it has.

(21) The third part is one where the dispute pertains to one of the principles of religion, such as upholding the doctrine of the world's origination and of the [positive] attributes of the Creator, [or] demonstrating the resurrection of bodies, all of which [the philosophers] have denied. It is in this topic and its likes, not any other, that one must show the falsity of their doctrine.

[A third] introduction

(22) Let it be known that [our] objective is to alert those who think well of the philosophers and believe that their ways are free from contradiction by showing the [various] aspects of their incoherence. For this reason, I do not enter into [argument] objecting to them, except as one who demands and denies, not as one who claims [and] affirms. I will render murky what they believe in [by showing] conclusively that they must hold to various consequences [of their theories]. Thus, I will force on them at one time necessary adherence to Muʿtazilite doctrine, at

(١٩) هذه الزيادة لم يصحّ نقلها، فيجب تكذيب ناقلها؛ وانّما المروى ما ذكرناه. كيف؟ ولو كان صحيحاً، لكان تأويله أهون من مكابرة أمور قطعيّة. فكم من ظواهر أُوّلت بالادلة العقليّة التى لا تنتهى فى الوضوح الى هذا الحد. وأعظم ما يفرح به الملحدة ان يصرّح ناصر الشرع بان هذا وأمثاله على خلاف الشرع فيسهل عليه طريق إبطال الشرع ان كان شرطه أمثال ذلك.

(٢٠) وهذا لانّ البحث فى العالم عن كونه حادثاً أو قديماً؛ ثم اذا ثبت حدوثه، فسواء كان كرة أو بسيطاً أو مثمّناً أو مسدّساً، وسواء كانت السموات وما تحتها ثلثة عشر طبقة كما قالوه أو أقلّ أو أكثر، فنسبة النظر فيه الى البحث الالهىّ كنسبة النظر الى طبقات البصل وعددها وعدد حبّ الرمان؛ فالمقصود كونه من فعل الله فقط كيف ما كانت.

(٢١) القسم الثالث ما يتعلق النزاع فيه بأصلٍ من اصول الدين، كالقول فى حدث العالم وصفات الصانع وبيان حشر الاجساد والابدان، وقد أنكروا جميع ذلك. فهذا الفن ونظائره هو الذى ينبغى أن يظهر فساد مذهبهم فيه دون ما عداه.

مقدّمة ثالثة

(٢٢) ليعلم ان المقصود تنبيه من حسنِ اعتقاده فى الفلاسفة وظنّ أن مسالكهم نقيّة عن التناقض ببيان وجوه تهافتهم. فلذلك أنا لا أدخل فى الاعتراض عليهم الا دخول مطالب منكر، لا دخول مدّعٍ مثبت؛ فاكدّر عليهم ما اعتقدوه مقطوعاً بالزامات مختلفة. فالزمهم تارة مذهب المعتزلة

another to that of the Karrāmiyya, at yet another to that of the Wāqifiyya.²
I, however, will not rise to the defense of any one doctrine but will make
all the sects as one group against them. For the rest of the sects may
differ from us in matters of detail, whereas these [philosophers] challenge
5   the [very] principles of religion. Let us [all], then, strive against them.
For in the face of hardships rancors depart.

[A fourth] introduction

(23) One of the tricks these [philosophers] use in enticing [people]
when confronted with a difficulty in the course of an argument is to say:
"These metaphysical sciences are obscure and hidden, being the most
10   difficult of the sciences for intelligent minds. One can only arrive at
knowing the answer to these difficulties through the introduction of
mathematics and logic." Thus, whoever imitates them in their unbelief
when confronted with a difficulty in their doctrine would think well of
them and say: "No doubt their sciences include a resolution of [this
15   difficulty]; but it is difficult for me to apprehend it, since I have neither
mastered logic nor attained mathematics."

(24) We say: "As regards [the branch of] mathematics which
consists of the examination of discrete quantity—namely, arithmetic—
metaphysics has no relation to it. The statement that the understanding
20   of metaphysics is in need of it is nonsense." It is as if one were to say that
medicine, grammar, and philology require it, or that arithmetic is in
need of medicine. As regards the geometrical sciences that consist in the
investigation of continuous quantity, [the investigation] in sum amounts
to showing that the [highest] heavens and what is below them to the
25   center are spherical in shape, to showing the number of their layers,
to showing the number of the spheres that move in the heavens, and to
showing the quantity of their [various] motions. Let us concede all this
to them, either dialectically or out of conviction.³ They do not need to
set up demonstrations for it. This has no bearing whatever on metaphys-
30   ical investigation. For this is as if someone were to say that the knowledge that this house came to be through the work of a knowing, willing,

واخرى مذهب الكرّاميّة وطوراً مذهب الواقفيّة. ولا أنتهض ذاباً عن مذهب مخصوص، بل اجعل جميع الفرق البأ واحداً عليهم. فانّ سائر الفرق ربما خالفونا فى التفصيل، وهؤلاء يتعرّضون لاصول الدين. فلنتظاهر عليهم؛ فعند الشدائد تذهب الاحقاد.

مقدّمة رابعة

(٢٣) من عظائم حيل هؤلاء فى الاستدراج اذا أورد عليهم اشكال فى معرض الحجاج قولهم: انّ هذه العلوم الالهيّة غامضة خفيّة، وهى أعصى العلوم على الافهام الذكيّة؛ ولا يتوصل الى معرفة الجواب عن هذه الاشكالات الا بتقديم الرياضيّات والمنطقيّات. فمن يقلدهم فى كفرهم، ان خطر له اشكال على مذهبهم، يُحسن الظنّ بهم ويقول: لا شكّ فى أن علومهم مشتملة على حلّه، وانما يعسر علىّ دركه لانّى لم أحكم المنطقيّات، ولم أحصل الرياضيّات.

(٢٤) فنقول: أمّا الرياضيّات التى هى نظر فى الكم المنفصل وهو الحساب فلا تعلق للالهيّات به؛ وقول القائل ان فهم الالهيّات يحتاج اليها خُرْق كقول القائل ان الطب والنحو واللغة يحتاج اليها، أو الحساب يحتاج الى الطب. واما الهندسيّات التى هى نظر فى الكم المتصل يرجع حاصله الى بيان ان السموات وما تحتها الى المركز كريّ الشكل، وبيان عدد طبقاتها، وبيان عدد الاكر المتحرّكة فى الافلاك، وبيان مقدار حركاتها. فلنسلم لهم جميع ذلك جدلاً أو اعتقاداً. فلا يحتاجون الى اقامة البراهين عليه؛ ولا يقدح ذلك فى شىء من النظر الالهىّ. وهو كقول القائل العلم بان هذا البيت حصل بصنع بنّاء عالم مريد قادر

living builder, endowed with power, requires that one knows that the
house is either a hexagon or an octagon and that one knows the number
of its supporting frames and the number of its bricks, which is raving, its
falsity obvious; or that one does not know that this onion is temporally
5   originated unless he knows the number of its layers and does not know
that this pomegranate is temporally originated unless one knows the
number of its seeds—[all] of which is abandonment of [rational] discourse, discredited by every rational person.

(25) Yes, when they say that the logical sciences must be mastered,
10   this is true. But logic is not confined to them. This is the principle which
in the discipline of theology we name "The Book of Reflection." They
changed its expression to "logic" to magnify it. We can [also] call it "The
Book of Argumentation," and we may call it "The Cognitions of the
Intellects." But when the one seeking to be clever, who is weak, hears the
15   name "logic," he thinks it an unfamiliar art, unknown to the theologians,
known only to the philosophers.

(26) In order to drive away this nonsense and uproot this ruse for
leading astray, we see [it fit] to set aside discussing "The Cognitions of
the Intellects" in this book, forsaking in it the terminology of the theolo-
20   gians and lawyers, but will express it in the idiom of the logicians, casting it in their molds, following their paths expression by expression, and
will dispute with them in this book in their language—I mean, their
expressions in logic. We will make it plain that what they set down as a
condition for the truth of the matter of the syllogism in the part on
25   demonstrating [their] logic, and what they set forth as a condition for
its form in the book of the syllogism, and the various things they posited
in the *Isagoge* and the *Categories* which are parts of logic and its prelimi-
naries, [are things] none of which have they been able to fulfill in their
metaphysical sciences.

30   (27) We judge it best, however, to introduce "The Cognitions of the
Intellects" at the end of the book. For it is like an instrument for apprehending the intention of the book. But perhaps some who engage in
theoretical reflection may not need it for comprehending [the book].
Hence, we will postpone it to the end so that those who do not need it
35   can set it aside. Whoever is unable to understand our expressions in
the individual questions in refuting [the philosophers] should begin by

حى يفتقر الى أن يعرف ان البيت مسدّس أو مثمّن وان يعرف عدد جذوعه وعدد لبناته. وهو هذيان لا يخفى فساده، وكقول القائل لا يعرف كون هذه البصلة حادثة ما لم يعرف عدد طبقاتها، ولا يعرف كون هذه الرمانة حادثة ما لم يعرف عدد حبّاتها؛ وهو هُجر من الكلام

٥ مستغثّ عند كل عاقل.

(٢٥) نعم قولهم ان المنطقيَّات لا بدّ من إحكامها، فهو صحيح. ولكن المنطق ليس مخصوصاً بهم، وانما هو الاصل الذى نسمّيه فى فن الكلام كتاب النظر. فغيّروا عبارته الى المنطق تهويلاً، وقد نسمّيه كتاب الجدل، وقد نسمّيه مدارك العقول. فاذا سمع المتكايس المستضعف اسم

١٠ المنطق ظنّ أنه فنّ غريب لا يعرفه المتكلّمون ولا يطّلع عليه الا الفلاسفة.

(٢٦) ونحن لدفع هذا الخبال واستئصال هذه الحيلة فى الاضلال، نرى ان نفرد القول فى مدارك العقول فى هذا الكتاب ونهجر فيه ألفاظ المتكلّمين والاصوليّين، بل نوردها بعبارات المنطقيِّين، ونصبّها فى قوالبهم ونقتفى آثارهم لفظا لفظا. ونناظرهم فى هذا الكتاب بلغتهم،

١٥ أعنى بعباراتهم فى المنطق، ونوضح ان ما شرّطوه فى صحّة مادة القياس فى قسم البرهان من المنطق وما شرّطوه فى صورته فى كتاب القياس وما وضعوه من الاوضاع فى ايساغوجى وقاطيغورياس التى هى من اجزاء المنطق ومقدّماته، لم يتمكّنوا من الوفاء بشىء منه فى علومهم الالهية.

(٢٧) ولكناً نرى ان نورد مدارك العقول فى آخر الكتاب، فانه

٢٠ كالآله لدرك مقصود الكتاب. ولكن ربّ ناظر يستغنى عنه فى الفهم، فنؤخّره حتى يعرض عنه من لا يحتاج اليه. ومن لا يفهم ألفاظنا فى آحاد

mastering the book, *The Standard for Knowledge*,[4] which is designated "logic" by them.

(28) Let us now, after [these] introductions, mention the table of contents of the problems wherein we show the inconsistency of their doctrine in this book. They are twenty problems.

[Author's table of contents]

المسائل فى الردّ عليهم فينبغى أن يبتدئ أوّلاً بحفظ كتاب معيار [العلم]؛ الذى هو الملقّب بالمنطق عندهم.

[فهرست المسائل]

٥ (٢٨) ولنذكر الان بعد المقدّمات فهرست المسائل التى أظهرنا تناقض مذهبهم فيها فى هذا الكتاب، وهى عشرون مسئلة:

١٠

١٥

٢٠

The fourteenth:	On [refuting their doctrine] that heaven is an animal that moves through volition.
The fifteenth:	On refuting what they mention regarding the purpose that moves heaven.
The sixteenth:	On refuting their doctrine that the souls of the heavens know all particulars.
The seventeenth:	On refuting their doctrine that the disruption of the habitual [course of nature] is impossible.
The eighteenth:	On [refuting] their statement that the human soul is a self-subsistent substance that is neither body nor accident.
The nineteenth:	On [refuting] their assertion that annihilation is impossible for the human soul.
The twentieth:	On refuting their denial of bodily resurrection [and] the accompanying bodily pleasures and pains in paradise and hell.

(29) These, then, among their metaphysical and physical sciences, are the things in which we wish to mention their contradictions. Regarding mathematical sciences, there is no sense in denying them or disagreeing with them. For these reduce in the final analysis to arithmetic and geometry. As regards the logical [sciences], these are concerned with examining the instrument of thought in intelligible things. There is no significant disagreement encountered in these. We will bring about in the book *The Standard for Knowledge* of its kind[5] what is needed for understanding the content of this book, God willing.

الرابعة عشرة،   فى قولهم انّ السماء حيوان متحرك بالارادة؛

الخامسة عشرة،   فى ابطال ما ذكروه من الغرض المحرّك للسماء؛

السادسة عشرة،   فى ابطال قولهم انّ نفوس السموات تعلم جميع الجزئيات؛

السابعة عشرة،   فى ابطال قولهم باستحالة خرق العادات؛

الثامنة عشرة،   فى قولهم انّ نفس الانسان جوهر قائم بنفسه ليس بجسم ولا عرض؛

التاسعة عشرة،   فى قولهم باستحالة الفناء على النفوس البشرية؛

العشرون،   فى ابطال انكارهم لبعث الاجساد مع التلذّذ والتألم فى الجنّة والنار باللذّات والآلام الجسمانيّة.

(٢٩) فهذا ما أردنا ان نذكر تناقضهم فيه من جملة علومهم الالهيّة والطبيعيّة. وأمّا الرياضيَّات فلا معنى لإنكارها ولا للمخالفة فيها؛ فانّها ترجع الى الحساب والهندسة. وأمّا المنطقيَّات فهى نظر فى آلة الفكر فى المعقولات ولا يتفق فيه خلاف به مبالاة. وسنورد فى كتاب معيار [العلم]° من جملته ما يحتاج اليه لفهم مضمون هذا الكتاب ان شاء الله.

[First] Discussion

On refuting their doctrine of the world's past eternity

(1) *Explicating [their] doctrine:* Philosophers have disagreed among themselves regarding the world's past eternity. However, the view of their multitudes, both ancient and modern, has settled on upholding its past eternity: that it has never ceased to exist with God, exalted be He, to
5   be an effect of His, to exist along with Him, not being posterior to Him in time, in the way the effect coexists along with the cause and light along with the sun; that the Creator's priority to [the world] is like the priority of the cause to the effect, which is a priority in essence and rank, not in time.

(2) It is related that Plato said: "The world is generated and origi-
10   nated in time." But, then, some among [the philosophers] have interpreted his language as metaphor, refusing [to maintain] that the world's temporal origination is a belief of his.

(3) Toward the end of his life, in the book entitled *What Galen Believes as Sound Judgment,* Galen adopted a noncommitted position on this ques-
15   tion, [stating] that he does not know whether the world is pre-eternal or temporally originated, that perhaps he can prove that [the answer] is unknowable to him, not because of any shortcoming on his part, but because of the inherent difficulty of this to [human] minds. This, however, appears to be most unusual in their doctrine. Rather, the doctrine
20   of all of them is that [the world] is pre-eternal and that altogether it is basically inconceivable for a temporal being to proceed from the eternal without mediation.

[قسم الاول]

مسئلة
فى إبطال قولهم بقدم العالم

(١) تفصيل المذهب. اختلفت الفلاسفة فى قدم العالم؛ فالذى استقر عليه رأى جماهيرهم، المتقدّمين والمتأخّرين، القول بقدمه وانّه لم يزلْ موجودا مع الله تعالى، ومعلولا له ومساوقا له، غير متأخّر عنه بالزمان، مساوقة المعلول للعلة، ومساوقة النور للشمس، وانّ تقدّم البارى عليه كتقدّم العلة على المعلول، وهو تقدّم بالذات والرتبة لا بالزمان.

(٢) وحكى عن أفلاطن انّه قال: العالم مكوّن ومحدث. ثم منهم من أوّل كلامه وأبى ان يكون [حدوث][1] العالم معتقدا له.

(٣) وذهب جالينوس فى آخر عمره فى الكتاب الذى سمّاه ما يعتقده جالينوس رأيا الى التوقّف فى هذه المسئلة، وانّه لا يدرى العالم قديم أو محدث، وربّما دلّ على انّه لا يمكن ان يعرف وان ذلك ليس لقصور فيه بل لاستعصاء هذه المسئلة فى نفسها على العقول. ولكن هذا كالشاذّ فى مذهبهم، وانّما مذهب جميعهم انه قديم وانّه بالجملة لا يتصوّر ان يصدر حادث من قديم بغير واسطة أصلا.

(4) *Presenting their proofs:* If I were to go into a description of what has been transmitted of [the philosophers' arguments] in the display of proofs and what has been said in objection to them, I would have to ink very many pages. But there is no virtue in lengthening matters. Let us,
5 then, delete from their proofs whatever belongs to the category of the arbitrary or of that which is feeble imagining, easily resolved by any reflective examiner. Let us [instead] confine ourselves to bringing forth those [proofs] that leave an impact on the soul and that are able to arouse doubt in the best speculative thinkers. For arousing doubt in the
10 weak is possible with the most feeble [of arguments].

(5) There are three[1] proofs of this sort.

The first [proof]
[First discussion: The first proof]

(6) They say, "It is absolutely impossible for a temporal to proceed from an eternal." For, if we suppose the Eternal without, for example, the world proceeding from Him, then it would not have proceeded
15 because existence would not have had that which gives [it] preponderance; rather, the world's existence would have been a pure possibility. If thereafter it were to come into existence, then a giver of preponderance either would have come into existence anew or would not have come into existence anew. If no giver of preponderance had come into existence
20 anew, the world would have then remained in a state of pure possibility as it had been before. If [on the other hand] a giver of preponderance did come into existence anew, then [the question arises]: "Who originated this giver of preponderance and why did it originate now and not earlier?" The question regarding the giver of preponderance persists.

25 (7) In brief, if the states of the Eternal are similar, then either nothing at all comes into existence through Him or else it comes into existence perpetually. As for [an existing divine] state of refraining [to act] standing differentiated from [another existing divine] state of commencing [to act, this] is impossible.

30 (8) The verifying [of this] consists in saying, "Why was the world not created before its creation?" This cannot be ascribed to His inability to originate [it earlier], nor to the impossibility of [an earlier] creation. For this would lead the Eternal to change from impotence to power and the world from impossibility to possibility, both of which are impossible.

(٤) ايراد ادلّتهم: لو ذهبت أصف ما نقل عنهم فى معرض الادلّة، وذكر فى الاعتراض عليه، لسوّدت فى هذه المسئلة أوراقا. ولكن لا خير فى التطويل، فلنحذف من أدلّتهم ما يجرى بجرى التحكّم أو التخيّل الضعيف الذى يهون على كلّ ناظر حلّه. ولنقتصر على ايراد ما له وقع فى النفس، ممّا يجوز أن ينهض مشككا لفحول النظّار؛ فان تشكيك الضعفاء بأدنى خبال ممكن.

(٥) وهذا الفنّ من الادلّة ثلاثة.

الاوّل

(٦) قولهم يستحيل صدور حادث من قديم مطلقاً؛ لانّا اذا فرضنا القديم و لم يصدر منه العالم مثلا، فانما لم يصدر لانه لم يكن للوجود مرجّح بل كان وجود العالم ممكنا إمكانا صرفا. فاذا حدث بعد ذلك لم يخلُ، اما ان تجدّد مرجّح او لم يتجدّد. فان لم يتجدّد مرجّح، بقى العالم على الامكان الصرف كما قبل ذلك؛ وان تجدّد مرجّح، فمن محدث ذلك المرجّح، ولِمَ حدث الآن ولَمْ يحدث من قبل؟ والسؤال فى حدوث المرجّح قائم.

(٧) وبالجملة، فأحوال القديم اذا كانت متشابهة، فإمّا أن لا يوجد عنه شىء قط، وإمّا أن يوجد على الدوام. فأمّا ان يتميّز حال الترك عن حال الشروع فهو محال.

(٨) وتحقيقه أن يقال، لِمَ لَمْ يحدث العالم قبل حدوثه؟ لا يمكن ان يحال على عجزه عن الاحداث، ولا على استحالة الحدوث. فان ذلك يؤدّى الى ان ينقلب القديم من العجز الى القدرة والعالم من الاستحالة الى

And it cannot be said that earlier there was no purpose, a purpose thereafter coming into existence anew. Nor can this be attributed to the loss of
an instrument which was thereafter found. Rather, the closest imaginative thing is to say: "He did not will its existence before this," from which
it follows that one must say: "Its existence occurred because He became
a willer of its existence after not having been a willer," in which case the
will would have been created. But its creation in Himself is impossible,
since He is not the receptacle of created things, and its creation not in
Himself would not make Him a willer.

(9) But let us leave speculation about the place [of the will's creation].
Does not the difficulty persist regarding the source of its[2] creation—
whence did [the source] originate, and why did it come into existence
now and not earlier? Did it come into existence now [but] not from the
direction of God? If a temporal event without an originator is allowed,
then let the world be an originated thing, having no maker. Otherwise,
what difference is there between one originated thing and another? If
[the world] is originated through God's origination of it, then why was it
originated now and not earlier? Is this because of a lack of an instrument,
power, purpose, or nature, such that, once these are replaced by existence,
[the world] came to be originated [now]? But then the same difficulty
recurs. Or is [its not being created earlier] due to the lack of a will? But
then the will would require another will to create it and likewise the first
will [and so on], regressing infinitely.[3]

(10) Thus, it is now ascertained through incontrovertible argument
that the proceeding of the temporal from the Eternal without a change
of state of affairs in the Eternal by way of power, instrument, time, purpose, or nature is impossible. To project a change of state [in the Eternal]
is impossible because the argument regarding that change that comes
about is similar to the argument regarding any other [change]. All this is
impossible. [Hence,] as long as the world exists and its origination in
time is impossible, its past eternity stands necessarily established.

(11) This, then, is the most imaginative of their proofs. In general,
their discussion in the rest of the metaphysical questions is weaker than
their discussion in this, since here they are able to [indulge in] various
types of imaginings they are unable to pursue in other [questions]. For
this reason we have given priority to this question, presenting first the
strongest of their proofs.

(12) The objection [to their proof] is in two respects.

الامكان، وكلاهما محالان. ولا امكن ان يقال لم يكن قبله غرض ثم تجدّد غرض ولا امكن ان يحال على فقد آلة ثم قد على وجودها؛ بل اقرب ما يتخيل ان يقال، لم يُرد وجوده قبل ذلك فيلزم ان يقال فيلزم حصل وجوده لانّه صار مريداً لوجوده بعد أن لم يكن مريدا، [فتكون]¹ قد حدثت الارادة.

٥ [وحدوثها]³ فى ذاته محال لانّه ليس محل الحوادث [وحدوثها]⁴ لا فى ذاته لا يجعله مريدا.

(٩) ولنترك النظر فى محلّ [حدوثها]⁵، أليس الاشكال قائما فى أصل [حدوثها]⁶، وانّه من أين حدث، ولِمَ حدث الآن ولَمْ يحدث قبله؟ أحدث الآن لا من جهة الله؟ فان جاز حادث من غير محدث، فليكن

١٠ العالم حادثا لا صانع له، والا فايّ فرق بين حادث وحادث؟ وان حدث باحداث الله، فلِمَ حدث الآن ولَمْ يحدث قبل؟ ألِعدم آلة أو قدرة أو غرض أو طبيعة، فلمّا ان تبدّل ذلك بالوجود حدث؟ عاد الاشكال بعينهِ. أو لعدم الارادة؟ فتفتقر الارادة الى ارادة وكذى الارادة الاولى ويتسلسل الى غير نهاية.

١٥ (١٠) فاذن قد تحقّق بالقول المطلق ان صدور الحادث من القديم من غير تغيّر أمر من القديم فى قدرة أو آلة أو وقت أو غرض أو طبع محال، وتقدير تغيّر حال محال، لانّ الكلام فى ذلك التغيّر الحادث كالكلام فى غيره والكل محال ومهما كان العالم موجودا واستحال حدوثه ثبت قدمه لا محالة.

(١١) فهذا [أخيل]⁷ ادلّتهم وبالجملة كلامهم فى سائر مسائل ٢٠ الالهيّات أركّ من كلامهم فى هذه المسألة، اذ يقدرون هاهنا على فنون من التخييل لا يتمكّنون منه فى غيرها. فلذلك قدّمنا هذه المسئلة وقدّمنا أقوى أدلّتهم.

(١٢) الاعتراض من وجهين:

[(1) The first objection]

(13) One of these is to say: With what [argument] would you deny one who says, "The world was temporally created by an eternal will that decreed its existence at the time in which it came to be; that [the preceding] nonexistence continued to the point at which [the world] began; that existence prior to this was not willed and for this reason did not occur; that at the time in which [the world] was created it was willed by the eternal will to be created at that time and for this reason it was created then"? What is there to disallow such a belief and what would render it impossible?

(14) To this [the opponent may] say:[4]

(15) This is impossible; its impossibility is very clear. For the temporal occurrence is necessitated and caused. And just as it is impossible for an event to exist without a cause and that which necessitates [it], it is impossible for that which necessitates [a thing] to exist with all the conditions of its being necessitating, [all the conditions] of its principles and causes fulfilled, such that nothing at all remains awaited, and then for the necessitated [effect] to be delayed. On the contrary, the existence of the necessitated [effect], when the conditions of the necessitating [cause] are fulfilled, is necessary and its delay impossible in accordance with the impossibility of the existence of the necessitated effect without the necessitating cause.

(16) Before the world's existence, the willer existed, the will existed, and its relation to what is willed existed. No willer came into existence anew, no will came into existence anew, and no relation that did not exist came to exist for the will anew. For all this is change. How, then, did the object of will come into existence anew, and what prevented its coming into existence anew earlier? [All this, moreover, would have taken place] when the state of renewal did not differ from the previous state in anything whatsoever—in any state of affairs, [in] any condition, or [in] any relation. Indeed, the state of affairs would have remained identical to what it was [before], the object of the will not having come into existence, and would remain thereafter as it was before when [lo and behold] the object of the will would come into existence! This is nothing but the ultimate in impossibility.

(17) Nor is the impossibility of this [restricted] to what necessitates and is necessitated in [the realm of] the necessary [and] the essential, but [it] is found in the customary and conventional. For if a man utters the [legal pronouncement] divorcing his wife and the separation does not occur immediately, it is inconceivable for it to occur thereafter. For he

(١٣) احدهما ان يقال: بِم تنكرون على من يقول انّ العالم حدث بارادة قديمة اقتضت وجوده فى الوقت الذى وجد فيه، وان يستمرّ العدم الى الغاية التى استمر اليها، وان يبتدئ الوجود من حيث ابتدأ، وانّ الوجود قبله لم يكن مرادًا فلم يحدث لذلك، وانّه فى وقته الذى حدث فيه مراد بالارادة القديمة، فحدث لذلك؟ فما المانع لهذا الاعتقاد، وما المحيل له؟

(١٤) فان قيل:

(١٥) هذا محال بيّن الاحالة، لانّ الحادث موجَب ومسبّب. وكما يستحيل حادث بغير سبب وموجب، يستحيل وجود موجِب قد تم بشرائط ايجابه وأركانه واسبابه، حتى لم يبق شىء منتظر البتّة، ثم يتأخّر الموجَب. بل وجود الموجَب عند تحقّق الموجب بتمام شروطه ضرورى وتأخّره محال حسب استحالة وجود الحادث الموجَب بلا موجب.

(١٦) فقبل وجود العالم كان المريد موجودا والارادة موجودة ونسبتها الى المراد موجودة، و لم يتجدّد مريد و لم [تتجدّد][8] ارادة، ولا تجدّد للارادة نسبة لم تكن، فانّ كل ذلك تغيّر، فكيف تجدّد المراد، وما المانع من التجدّد قبل ذلك؟ وحال التجدّد لم يتميّز عن الحال السابق فى شىء من الاشياء وأمر من الامور وحال من الاحوال ونسبة من النسب؛ بل الامور كما كانت بعينها ثم لم يكن يوجد المراد و بقيت بعينها كما كانت، فوجد المراد، ما هذا الا غاية الاحالة.

(١٧) وليس استحالة هذا الجنس فى الموجب والموجب الضرورىّ الذاتىّ، بل وفى العرفىّ والوضعىّ؛ فان الرجل لو تلفّظ بطلاق زوجته و لم تحصل البينونة فى الحال، لم يتصوّر ان تحصل بعده، لانّه جعل اللفظ علة

has made the utterance a cause of the judgment in terms of convention
and [legal] idiom. Thus, the delay of the effect is inconceivable unless he
ties the divorce with the coming of the next day or with the entry to the
house, in which case [the divorce] does not take place immediately but
5   will take place when the morrow comes about or with the entry into the
house. For he has made [the utterance] a cause [for the divorce] by relating it to an expected thing; and since this expected thing—namely, the
coming of the morrow and the entry [to the house]—is not now present,
the realization of the necessitated thing remains pending the occurrence
10 of what is not now at hand. Once the necessitated occurs, then something
would have necessarily come anew—namely, the entry into the house and
the coming of the morrow—so that if the man wants to delay the necessitated [divorce] beyond [the legal] pronouncement that is not made conditional on an occurrence [still] unrealized, this would be inconceivable,
15 even though he is the one who sets down the convention and has the
choice in explicating its details. If, then, we are unable by our own desire
to posit [such a delay] and cannot conceive it, how are we to conceive it in
what is necessitated [in the realm] of essential, rational, necessary things?

(18) As regards habitual things, what is brought about through our
20 intentional act is not delayed after the intent when the intent exists
except by an impediment. Once the intent and ability are realized, [all]
obstacles being removed, the delay of what is intended is not rationally
intelligible. This is only conceivable in the case of resolve, because
resolve is not sufficient for the existence of the act. Indeed, the resolve to
25 write does not produce writing unless an intent is renewed, this being a
renewed upsurge of motive within the human at the time of the act.

(19) If the eternal will belongs to the same category as that of our
intention to act, then, unless there is an impediment, neither the delay
of what is intended nor the [temporal] priority of the intent are conceiv-
30 able. Hence, an intent today that leads to an arising on the morrow is
incomprehensible except [if one thinks that this takes place] by way of
resolve. And if the eternal will is of the same category as our resolve, this
would not be sufficient for the object of the resolution to occur. Rather,
there would be the inescapable need for a renewed intentional upsurge
35 at the time of the [act of] bringing [something] into existence. But this
entails upholding change in the Eternal. Moreover, the very same difficulty persists in [that the question still] arises concerning this upsurge,
intention, will, or whatever you wish to call it: why did it occur now and
not earlier? [The consequence is that] there would be either a temporal
40 occurrence without a cause or an infinite regress [of causes].

للحكم بالوضع والاصطلاح، فلم يعقل تأخّر المعلول الا ان يعلّق الطلاق بمجىء الغد او بدخول الدار فلا يقع فى الحال ولكن يقع عند مجىء الغد وعند دخول الدار؛ فانه جعله علة بالاضافة الى شىء منتظر، فلمّا لم يكن حاضرا فى الوقت، وهو الغد والدخول، توقّف حصول الموجَب على

٥ حضور ما ليس بحاضر؛ فما حصل الموجب الا وقد تجدّد أمر وهو الدخول وحضور الغد، حتى لو اراد ان يؤخّر الموجب عن اللفظ غير منوط بحصول ما ليس بحاصل، لم يعقل، مع انّه الواضع وانّه المختار فى تفصيل الوضع. فاذا لم يمكننا وضع هذا بشهوتنا و لم نعقله، فكيف نعقله فى الايجابات الذاتية العقليّة الضروريّة؟

١٠ (١٨) وأما فى العادات فما يحصل بقصدنا لا يتأخر عن القصد مع وجود القصد اليه الا بمانع. فان تحقق القصد والقدرة وارتفعت الموانع لم يعقل تأخّر المقصود. وانّما يتصوّر ذلك فى العزم، لان العزم غير كاف فى وجود الفعل، بل العزم على الكتابة لا يوقع الكتابة ما لم يتجدّد قصد هو انبعاث فى الانسان متجدّد حال الفعل.

١٥ (١٩) فان كانت الارادة القديمة فى حكم قصدنا الى الفعل، فلا يتصوّر تأخر المقصود الا بمانع ولا يتصوّر تقدّم القصد فلا يعقل قصد فى اليوم الى قيام فى الغد الا بطريق العزم. وان كانت الارادة القديمة فى حكم عزمنا، فليس ذلك كافيا فى وقوع المعزوم عليه؛ بل لا بدّ من تجدّد انبعاث قصدىّ عند الايجاد، وفيه قول بتغيّر القديم. ثم يبقى عين الاشكال فى ان ذلك الانبعاث أو القصد أو الارادة أو ما شئت سمِّه، لِمَ

٢٠ حدث الآن ولَمْ يحدث قبل ذلك؟ فإمّا ان يبقى حادث بلا سبب أو يتسلسل الى غير نهاية.

(20) The sum total of this is that the necessitating [cause would] exist with all its conditions fulfilled, there remaining no expected thing; and yet, with [all] this, the necessitated [effect] would have been delayed and would not have existed in a period whose beginning the imagination cannot reach—indeed, [a period where] thousands of years [taken away from it] would not diminish it by a thing—and then suddenly the necessitated [effect] would turn [into an existent] without anything having come anew or any [new] condition having been realized. And this is in itself impossible.

(21) The answer is to say:

(22) Do you know the impossibility of an eternal will related to the temporal creation of something, whatever that thing is, through the necessity of reason or its theoretical reflection?[5] According to your language in logic, is the connection between the two terms [namely, "the eternal will" and "temporal creation"] known to you with or without a middle term? If you claim a middle term, which is the reflective theoretical method, then you must show it. [But this you have not shown.] If [on the other hand] you claim to know this [impossibility] through the necessity of reason, how is it, then, that those who oppose you do not share this knowledge, when the party believing in the world's temporal creation by an eternal will is [such] that no one land [can] contain it and [that its] number is beyond enumeration? And these certainly do not stubbornly defy reason while possessing the knowledge [which you claim is attainable through the necessity of reason]. Hence, it is incumbent on you to set up a demonstrative proof according to the condition of logic that would show the impossibility of this. For, in all of what you have stated, there is nothing but [an expression of] unlikelihood and the drawing of an analogy with our resolve and will, this being false, since the eternal will does not resemble temporal [human] intentions. As regards the sheer deeming of something as unlikely, without demonstrative proof, [this] is not sufficient.

(23) If it is said, "We know through the necessity of reason that a necessitating [cause] with all its conditions fulfilled is inconceivable without a necessitated [effect] and that the one who allows this is stubbornly defying the necessity of reason," we say:

(24) What difference is there between you and your opponents when they say to you, "We know by necessity the impossibility of someone's statement that one essence knows all the universals without this necessitating multiplicity [in the essence], without [this] knowledge's being [an attribute] additional to the essence,[6] and without knowledge's becoming

(٢٠) ورجع حاصل الكلام الى انّهُ وجد الموجِب بتمام شروطه و لم ييقَ أمر منتظر، ومع ذلك تأخر الموجَب و لم يوجد فى مدّة لا يرتقى الوهم الى أوّلها، بل الآف سنين لا تنقص شيئا منها، ثم انقلب الموجب بغتة من غير أمر تجدّد وشرط تحقّق؛ وهو محال فى نفسه.

(٢١) والجواب ان يقال:

(٢٢) استحالة ارادة قديمة متعلّقة باحداث شىء أىّ شىء كان، تعرفونه بضرورة العقل أو نظره؟ وعلى لغتكم فى المنطق، تعرفون الالتقاء بين هذين الحدّين بحدّ أوسط أو من غير حدّ أوسط؟ فان ادّعيتم حدًّا أوسط، وهو الطريق النظرىّ، فلا بد من اظهاره؛ وان ادّعيتم معرفة ذلك ضرورةً، فكيف لم يشاركم فى معرفته مخالفوكم، والفرقة المعتقدة [بحدوث]٩ العالَم بارادة قديمة لا يحصرها بلد ولا يحصيها عدد؟ ولا شك فى انهم لا يكابرون العقول عناداً مع المعرفة. فلا بدّ من اقامة برهان على شرط المنطق يدلّ على استحالة ذلك، اذ ليس فى جميع ما ذكرتموه الا الاستبعاد والتمثيل بعزمنا وارادتنا؛ وهو فاسد، فلا تضاهى الارادة القديمة القصود الحادثة. وأما الاستبعاد المجرّد، فلا يكفى من غير برهان.

(٢٣) فان قيل: نحن بضرورة العقل نعلم انّه لا يتصور موجِب بتمام شروطه من غير موجَب وجوّز ذلك مكابر لضرورة العقل، قلنا:

(٢٤) وما الفصل بينكم وبين خصومكم اذا قالوا لكم، انّا بالضرورة نعلم احالة قول من يقول ان ذاتا واحدا عالم بجميع الكليات من غير ان يوجب ذلك كثرة ومن غير ان يكون العلم زيادة على الذات ومن غير ان

multiple with the multiplicity of the object of knowledge?"—this being
your doctrine regarding God, which, in relation to us and our own sciences, is the ultimate in impossibility. But then you say, "Eternal knowledge is not to be compared with created [knowledge]." A group among
you, however, becoming aware of the impossibility [we indicated], said,
"God knows only Himself, so that He is the intellectual apprehender, the
intellect and the intelligible, all these being one and the same." Now, if
one were to say [to this], "The union of the intellect, the intellectual
apprehender, and the intelligible is known necessarily to be impossible,
since the supposition of a Maker of the world who does not know His
handiwork is necessarily impossible; and, if the Eternal—may He be
greatly exalted over what they and all the deviants [from the truth]
say—knows only Himself, He would not know His handiwork at all,"
[what would you say?]

(25) Indeed, we would not be going beyond the necessary implica-
tions of this question when we say:

(26) With what [argument] would you deny your opponents inasmuch as they have said [the following]? "The world's past eternity is
impossible because it leads to affirming circular movements of the
heavenly sphere whose number is infinite and whose individual units
are innumerable, even though they [divide into] a sixth, a fourth, a half
[and so on]. For the sphere of the sun rotates in one year, whereas
Saturn's rotates in thirty, so that the rotations of Saturn are a third of
a tenth of those of the sun. [Again,] the rotations of Jupiter are a half
of a sixth of the rotations of the sun; for it rotates once in every
twelve years. [Now,] just as the number of the rotations of Saturn is
infinite, the number of the solar rotations, although a third of a tenth
[of the latter], is [also] infinite. Indeed, the rotations of the sphere of
the fixed stars, which rotates [once in] every thirty-six thousand years,
are infinite, just as the sun's movement from east to west, taking place
in a day and a night, is [likewise] infinite." If one then were to say,
"This is one of the things whose impossibility is known by the necessity
[of reason]," how would your [position] differ from his statement?
Indeed, [how are you to answer] if one were to say, "Is the number of the
rotations even or odd, both even and odd, or neither even nor odd?"
Should you answer either that the number is both even and odd or that
it is neither even nor odd, then [again] this would be something whose
falsity is known through [rational] necessity. If you were to say that
the number is even, and the even becomes odd by [the addition of] one,
then how can the infinite be in need of one? If, on the other hand, you

يتعدّد العلم مع تعدّد المعلوم؟ وهذا مذهبكم فى حق الله، وهو بالنسبة الينا
والى علومنا فى غاية الإحالة؟ ولكن تقولون: لا يقاس العلم القديم
بالحادث. وطائفة منكُم استشعروا احالة هذا، فقالوا: ان الله لا يعلم الا
نفسه، فهو العاقل وهو العقل وهو المعقول، والكلّ واحد. فلو قال قائل
٥ اتّحاد العقل والعاقل والمعقول معلوم الاستحالة بالضرورة، اذ تقدير
صانع للعالم لا يعلم صُنعَه محال بالضّرورة، والقديم اذا لم يعلم الا نفسه،
تعالى عن قولكم وعن قول جميع الزائغين علوًّا كبيرا لم يكن يعلم صنعه
البتّة.

(٢٥) بل لا نتجاوز إلزامات هذه المسئلة فنقول:

١٠ (٢٦) بمَ تنكرون على خصومكم اذ قالوا قدم العالم محال لانّه يؤدّى
الى اثبات دورات للفلك لا نهاية لاعدادها ولا حصر لآحادها مع ان لها
سدساً وربعاً ونصفاً؟ فانّ فلك الشمس يدور فى سنة، وفلك زحل فى
ثلاثين سنة، فتكون ادوار زحل ثُلْث عشر ادوار الشمس، وادوار
المشترى نصف سدس ادوار الشمس، فانّه يدور فى اثنى عشر سنة؛ ثم
١٥ كما أنّه لا نهاية لاعداد دورات زحل، لا نهاية لاعداد دورات الشمس،
مع انّه ثُلْث عشره؛ بل لا نهاية لادوار فلك الكواكب الذى يدور فى ستة
وثلاثين ألف سنة مرة واحدة، كما لا نهاية للحركة المشرقيّة التى للشمس
فى اليوم والليلة مرة. فلو قال قائل، هذا ممّا يعلم استحالته ضرورةً، فبماذا
تنفصلون عن قوله؟ بل لو قال قائل: اعداد هذه الدورات شفع أو وتر، أو
٢٠ شفع ووتر جميعاً، أو لا شفع ولا وتر؟ فان قلتم شفع ووتر جميعا أو لا
شفع ولا وتر، فيعلم بطلانه ضرورةً، وان قلتم شفع، فالشفع يصير وترا
بواحد، فكيف أعوز ما لا نهاية له واحد؟ وان قلتم وتر، فالوتر يصير

answer that it is odd, then how would the infinite be in need of that one which would render it even? You are then necessarily forced to uphold the statement that it is neither even nor odd.

(27) If it is said, "It is only the finite that is described as either even or odd, but the infinite is not so described," we say:

(28) An aggregate composed of units having, as has been mentioned, a sixth and tenth, which is yet not described as either even or odd, is something whose falsity is known by necessity without theoretical reflection. With what [argument] can you disentangle yourselves from this? If it is then said, "The place of error lies in your statement that the heavenly movements consist of an aggregate composed of units; for these rotations are nonexistent, the past having ceased to exist, the future not yet existing; the 'aggregate' refers to existents that are present, but here there is no [such] existent," we say:

(29) Number divides into the even and the odd, and it is impossible for it to lie outside this [division], regardless of whether or not what is enumerated exists and endures or ceases to exist. For, if we suppose a number of horses, a necessary consequence of this is that [their number] is either even or odd, regardless of whether or not we reckon them existing or nonexisting. Should they cease to exist after existing, the proposition does not change. But we [furthermore] say to them:

(30) According to your own principles, it is not impossible that there should be existents, present here and now, which are individual entities varying in descriptions and which are infinite. These are the souls of humans that are separated from bodies after death. These, then, are existents that are not characterized as even and odd. With what [argument] would you deny [the statement] of someone who says: "The falsity of this is known through the necessity [of reason] in the same way you claim that the falsity of the connectedness of the eternal will with the act of temporal creation is known through the necessity [of reason]"? This view of souls is the one chosen by Avicenna, and perhaps it is Aristotle's doctrine.

(31) If it is said, "The truth is Plato's view—namely, that the soul is pre-eternal and one, that it is divided only in bodies, and that once it separates from them it returns to its origin and unites," we say:

بواحد شفعا، فكيف أعوز ذلك الواحدُ الذى به يصير شفعا؟ فيلزمكم القول بانّه ليس بشفع ولا وتر.

(٢٧) فان قيل: انما يوصف بالشفع والوتر المتناهى وما لا يتناهى لا يوصف به، قلنا:

(٢٨) فجملة مركبة من آحاد لها سُدْس وعُشر كما سبق، ثم لا توصف بشفع ولا وتر، يعلم بطلانه ضرورة من غير نظر. فبماذا تنفصلون عن هذا؟ فان قيل، محلّ الغلط فى قولكم انه جملة مركبة من آحاد، فان هذه الدورات معدومة، أما الماضى فقد انقرض وأما المستقبل فلم يوجد، والجملة إشارة الى موجودات حاضرة ولا موجود هاهنا، قلنا:

(٢٩) العدد ينقسم الى الشفع والوتر ويستحيل أن يخرج عنه، سواء كان المعدود موجودا باقيا أو فانيا؛ فاذا فرضنا عددا من الافراس لزمنا ان نعتقد انّه لا يخلوا من كونه شفعا أو وترا، سواء قدّرناها موجودة أو معدومة؛ فان انعدمت بعد الوجود لم تتغير هذه القضية.

على انّا نقول لهـم:

(٣٠) لا يستحيل على اصلكم موجودات حاضرة هى آحاد متغايرة بالوصف ولا نهاية لها، وهى نفوس الآدميين المفارقة للابدان بالموت، فهى موجودات لا توصف بالشفع والوتر. فبمَ تنكرون على من يقول: بطلان هذا يعرف ضرورة كما ادعيتم بطلان تعلّق الارادة القديمة بالاحداث ضرورة؟ وهذا الرأى فى النفوس هو الذى اختاره ابن سينا، ولعلّه مذهب رسطاليس.

(٣١) فان قيل: فالصحيح رأى أفلاطن وهو ان النفس قديمة وهى واحدة وانما تنقسم فى الابدان فاذا فارقتها عادت الى اصلها واتّحدت، قلنا:

(32) This is worse, more repugnant, and more worthy to uphold as contrary to rational necessity. For we say: "Is the soul of Zayd identical with the soul of ᶜAmr, or is it another?" If [it is stated that] it is identical, this would be necessarily false. For each individual is aware of his self and knows that he is not the self of another. [Moreover,] if identical, then both would be equal [in having the same] cognitions which are essential attributes of souls and which are included with the soul in every relation. If [on the other hand] you say that it is another, being individuated through attachments to bodies, we say: "The individuation of the one that has no magnitude in terms of size and quantitative measure is [known] by the necessity of reason to be impossible. How, then, will the one become two—nay, a thousand—then revert to becoming one? This is only intelligible in things that have magnitude and quantity, like the water of the sea that divides through streams and rivers and then returns to the sea. But how can that which is not quantitative be divided?"

(33) What is intended by all this is to show that they have not rendered their opponents unable to uphold belief in the connectedness of the eternal will with the act of temporal creation except by invoking [rational] necessity and that they are unable to disengage from those who [in turn] invoke [rational] necessity against them in those matters opposed to their own belief. From this [they have] no escape.

(34) To this it may be said: "This turns against you, in that before the world's creation God was able to create by a year or by years, there being no limit to His power. It is as though He waited, not creating, then created. What, then, of the duration of His refraining from creating; is it finite or infinite? If you say that it is finite, then the existence of God would be of a finite beginning. If you say that it is infinite, then a period wherein there are infinite possibilities would have elapsed."

(35) [To this] we say:

(36) According to us, duration and time are both created. We will be clarifying the true answer to this when we dissociate ourselves from their second proof.

(٣٢) فهذا أقبح وأشنع واولى بأن يُعتقد مخالفا لضرورة العقل. فانّا نقول: نفس زيد عين نفس عمرو أو غيره؟ فان كان عينه، فهو باطل بالضرورة. فان كل واحد يشعر بنفسه ويعلم انه ليس هو نفس غيره. ولو كان هو عينه لتساويا فى العلوم التى هى صفات ذاتيّة للنفوس داخلة مع النفوس فى كل اضافة. وان قلتم: انّه غيره، وانّما انقسم بالتعلّق بالابدان، قلنا: وانقسام الواحد الذى ليس له عظم فى الحجم وكميّة مقداريّة محال بضرورة العقل، فكيف يصير الواحد اثنين بل الفاً ثم يعود ويصير واحدا؟ بل هذا يعقل فيما له عظم وكميّة كماء البحر ينقسم بالجداول والانهار ثم يعود الى البحر فامّا ما لا كميّة له فكيف ينقسم؟

(٣٣) والمقصود من هذا كلّه ان نبين انّهم لم يعجزوا خصومهم عن معتقدهم فى تعلّق الارادة القديمة بالاحداث الا بدعوى الضرورة، وانّهم لا ينفصلون عمّن يدّعى الضرورة عليهم فى هذه الامور على خلاف معتقدهم، وهذا لا مخرج عنه.

(٣٤) فان قيل: هذا ينقلب عليكم فى أن الله قبل خلق العالم كان قادرا على الخلق بقدر سنة أو سنين، ولا نهاية لقدرته. فكأنّه صبر ولم يخلق ثم خلق، ومدّة الترك متناه أو غير متناه؟ فان قلتم متناه، صار وجود البارى متناهى الاول. وان قلتم غير متناه، فقد انقضى مدّة فيها امكانات لا نهاية لاعدادها.

(٣٥) قلنا:

(٣٦) المدّة والزمان مخلوق عندنا وسنبيّن حقيقة الجواب عن هذا فى الانفصال عن دليلهم الثانى.

(37) [The philosophers, however, may] say:

(38) With what [argument] would you deny one who relinquishes the appeal to the necessity [of reason] and proves [the impossibility of the connectedness of the eternal will with the act of temporal creation] in another way—namely, that the times are equal with respect to the possibility of the will's attachment to any of them? What, then, would have differentiated a specific time from what precedes and succeeds it when it is not impossible for [any of] the prior and posterior [times] to have been willed [as the beginning of creation]?[7] Indeed, in the case of whiteness and blackness, motion and rest, you [theologians] say: "Whiteness is created by the eternal will when the receptacle is as receptive of blackness as it is of whiteness." Why, then, did the eternal will attach itself to whiteness [and] not blackness, and what differentiated one of the two possibles from the other with respect to the will's attachment to it? We know by [rational] necessity that a thing is not distinguished from what is similar to it except through that which specifies. If this were allowed, then it would be permissible for the world, whose existence and nonexistence are equally possible, to originate in time; and the side of existence, similar in terms of possibility to the side of nonexistence, would thus be specified with existence without there being that which would specify [it]. If you say that the will specifies [it], then the question arises about the will's act of specifying and why it specified [one possible rather than another]. If you say that the "why" is not said of the eternal, then let the world be eternal and let there be no demand for its maker and cause— for "why" is not said of the eternal.

(39) For, if the eternal's specific relation to one of the two [equally] possible [existents] through [sheer] coincidence is allowed, then the uttermost unlikely thing would be to say that the world is specified with specific shapes when it is [equally] possible for it to have other shapes instead; whereupon one would then [also] say that this occurred in a manner coincidentally, in the same way that you [theologians] have said that the will has specifically related to one time rather than another and one shape rather than another by coincidence. If you then say that this question is superfluous because it can refer to anything the Creator wills and reverts to anything He decrees, we say, "No! On the contrary, this question is necessary because it recurs at all times and attaches to those who oppose us with every supposition [they make]."

(40) [To this] we say:

(٣٧) فان قيل:

(٣٨) فبمَ تنكرون على من يترك دعوى الضرورة ويدلّ عليه من وجه آخر، وهو انّ الاوقات متساوية فى جواز تعلّق الاراة بها؟ فما الذى ميّز وقتا معيّنا عمّا قبله وعمّا بعده وليس محالا ان يكون التقدّم والتأخّر مرادًا؟ بل فى البياض والسواد والحركة والسكون، فانّكم تقولون: يحدث البياض بالارادة القديمة، والمحلّ قابل للسواد قبوله للبياض. فلِمَ تعلقت الارادة القديمة بالبياض دون السواد، وما الذى ميّز أحد الممكنين عن الآخر فى تعلّق الارادة به؟ ونحن بالضرورة نعلم ان الشىء لا يتميّز عن مثله الا بمخصّص؛ ولو جاز ذاك لجاز أن يحدث العالم، وهو ممكن الوجود كما انه ممكن العدم، ويتخصّص جانب الوجود المماثل لجانب العدم فى الامكان بغير مخصّص. وان قلتم ان الارادة خصّصت، فالسؤال عن اختصاص الارادة وانها لِمَ اختصّت. فان قلتم القديم لا يقال له لِمَ، فليكن العالم قديماً ولا يطلب صانعه وسببه لانّ القديم لا يقال فيهِ لِمَ.

(٣٩) فإن جاز تخصّص القديم بالاتفاق بأحد الممكنين فغاية المستبعد ان يقال العالم مخصوص بهيئات مخصوصة كان يجوز أن يكون على هيئات أخرى بدلاً منها، فيقال وقع كذلك اتفاقاً، كما قلتم اختصّت الارادة بوقت دون وقت وهيئة دون هيئة اتفاقاً. وان قلتم ان هذا السؤال غير لازم لأنّه وارد على كل ما يريده، وعائد على كلّ ما يقدّره،، فنقول لا بل هذا السؤال لازم لأنّه عائد فى كل وقت وملازم لمن خالفنا على كلّ تقدير.

(٤٠) قلنا:

(41) The world came to existence whence it did, having the description with which it came to exist, and in the place in which it came to exist, through will, will being an attribute whose function is to differentiate a thing from its similar. If this were not its function, then power would be sufficient.[8] But since the relation of power to two contraries is the same and there was an inescapable need for a specifying [agent] that would specify one thing from its similar, it was said: "The Eternal has, beyond power, an attribute that has as its function the specifying of one thing from its similar." Hence, someone's statement, "Why did the will specifically relate to one of the two similars?" is akin to the statement, "Why does knowledge entail as a requirement the encompassing of the object of knowledge as it is?" For [to the latter] one would reply, "This is because 'knowledge' stands as an expression for an attribute that has this as a function." Similarly, "Will stands as an expression for an attribute whose function—nay, its essence—is to differentiate a thing from its similar."

(42) [To this the philosophers might then] say:

(43) Affirming an attribute whose function is to differentiate a thing from its similar is incomprehensible—indeed, contradictory. For to be similar means to be indiscernible, and to be discernible means that it is dissimilar. One should not think that two [instances of] blackness in two places are similar in every respect. For one is in one place, the other in another. And this necessitates a differentiation. Nor are two [instances] of blackness in the same place at two different times absolutely similar. For one differed from the other in terms of time— how could it be similar to it in every respect? If we say that the two [instances] of blackness are [two] things similar to each other, we mean by it [similar] in blackness related [to the two instances] in a special, not in an unrestricted, sense. Otherwise, if place and time are unified and no otherness remains, then neither the two [instances] of blackness nor duality itself is conceivable. This is shown to be true by [the fact] that the expression "will" [as applied to God] is a borrowing from our "will." It is inconceivable of us that we would differentiate through will one thing from its similar. Indeed, if in front of a thirsty person there are two glasses of water that are similar in every respect in relation to his purpose [of wanting to drink], it would be impossible for him to take either. Rather, he would take that which he would deem better, lighter,

(٤١) انّما وجد العالم حيث وجد وعلى الوصف الذى وجد، وفى المكان الذى وجد، بالارادة؛ والارادة صفة من شأنها تمييز الشىء عن مثله. ولَوْلا ان هذا شأنها، لوقع الاكتفاء بالقدرة. ولكن لما [تساوت]¹⁰ نسبة القدرة الى الضدّين، و لم يكن بدّ من مخصِّص يخصِّص الشىء عن مثله، فقيل: للقديم وراء القدرة صفة من شأنها تخصيص الشىء عن مثله. فقول القائل، لِمَ اختصّت الارادة بأحد المثلين، كقول القائل، لِمَ اقتضى العلم الاحاطة بالمعلوم على ما هو به؟ فيقال: لانّ العلم عبارة عن صفة هذا شأنها؛ فكذى الارادة عبارة عن صفة هذا شأنها، بل ذاتها تمييز الشىء عن مثله.

(٤٢) فان قيل:

(٤٣) اثبات صفة شأنها تمييز الشىء عن مثله غير معقول، بل هو متناقض. فانّ كونه مثلا معناه انه لا تميّز له وكونه مميّزا معناه أنه ليس مثلا. ولا ينبغى ان يظنّ ان السوادين فى محلّين متماثلان من كل وجه. لان هذا فى محلّ وذاك فى محلّ آخر، وهذا يوجب التميّز؛ ولا السوادان فى وقتين فى محلّ واحد متماثلان مطلقاً؛ لان هذا فارق ذلك فى الوقت، فكيف يساويه من كل وجه؟ واذا قلنا السوادان مثلان، عنينا به فى السواديّة مضافاً [اليهما]¹¹ على الخصوص لا على الاطلاق، والا فلو اتحد المحلّ والزمان و لم يبقَ تغاير، لم يعقل سوادان، ولا عقلت الاثنينية اصِلا. يحقق هذا ان لفظ الارادة مستعار من ارادتنا، ولا يتصوّر منّا ان نميّز بالارادة الشىء عن مثله. بل لو كان بين يدى العطشان قدحان من الماء يتساويان من كل وجه بالاضافة الى غرضه، لم يمكن ان يأخذ أحدهما. بل انما يأخذ

closer to his right side—if his habit was to move the right hand—or some such cause, whether hidden or manifest. Otherwise, differentiating something from its like is in no circumstance conceivable.

(44) The objection [to this argument of the philosophers] is in two ways:

[a]

5   (45) The first is regarding your statement that this is inconceivable: do you know this through [rational] necessity or through theoretical reflection? It is impossible [for you] to appeal to either of these. Moreover, your using our will as an example constitutes a false analogy that parallels the analogy [between human and divine] knowledge. God's knowledge
10   differs from human knowledge in matters we have [already] established. Why, then, should the difference between [the divine and the human] in the case of the will be unlikely? Rather, this is akin to someone's statement, "An essence existing neither outside nor inside the world, being neither connected nor disconnected with it, is inconceivable because we cannot
15   conceive it on our own terms," to which it would then be said, "This is the work of your estimative faculty[9]—rational proof has led rational people to believe this." With what [argument] would you then deny one who says that rational proof has led to the establishing of an attribute belonging to God, exalted be He, whose function is to differentiate a thing from its
20   similar? If the term "will" does not correspond [to this attribute], then let it be given another name; for there need be no dispute about names, and we ourselves have only used it because the religious law permits [its use]. Otherwise, "will" is conventionally used in language to designate that which has an objective [fulfilling a need], and there is never [such] an objective in
25   the case of God. What is intended is the meaning, not the utterance.

(46) Even so, in our [own human] case, we do not concede that [the choice between similar things] is inconceivable. For we will suppose that there are two equal dates in front of someone gazing longingly at them, unable, however, to take both together. He will inevitably take one of
30   them through an attribute whose function is to render a thing specific, [differentiating it] from its like. All the specifying things you have mentioned by way of goodness, proximity, and ease of taking we can suppose to be absent, the possibility of taking [one of the two] yet remaining. You are, hence, left between two alternatives. You could either say that
35   equality in relation to the individual's purpose is utterly inconceivable, which is sheer foolishness, the supposition [of this equality] being possible;[10] or else, that if the equality is supposed, the man yearning [for the dates] would ever remain undecided, looking at them but taking

ما يراه أحسن أو أخفّ أو أقرب الى جانب يمينه، ان كان عادته تحريك اليمين، أو سبب من هذه الاسباب، امّا خفى وامّا جلىّ. والا فلا يتصوّر تمييز الشىء عن مثله بحال.

(٤٤) والاعتراض من وجهين:

(٤٥) الاوّل، ان قولكم ان هذا لا يتصوّر، عرفتموه ضرورةً أو نظراً؟ ولا يمكن دعوى واحد منهما. وتمثيلكم بارادتنا مقايسة فاسدة تضاهى المقايسة فى العلم. وعلم الله يفارق علمنا فى امور قررناها. فلم تبعد المفارقة فى الارادة؟ بل هو كقول القائل: ذات موجودة لا خارج العالم ولا داخله ولا متّصلاً ولا منفصلاً، لا يعقل لانّا لا نعقله فى حقّنا، قيل: هذا عمل توهمك؛ وامّا دليل العقل فقد ساق العقلاء الى التصديق بذلك. فبمَ تنكرون على من يقول دليل العقل ساق الى اثبات صفة لله تعالى من شأنها تمييز الشىء عن مثله؟ فان لم يطابقها اسم الارادة، فلتسمَّ باسم آخر؛ فلا مشاحّة فى الاسماء، وانما أطلقناها نحن باذن الشرع. والا فالارادة موضوعة فى اللغة لتعيين ما فيه غرض، ولا غرض فى حق الله. وانما المقصود المعنى دون اللفظ.

(٤٦) على أنّه فى حقّنا لا نسلّم انّ ذلك غير متصوّر. فانّا نفرض تمرتين متساويتين بين يدى المتشوّف اليهما العاجز عن تناولهما جميعاً، فإنّه يأخذ احداهما لا محالة بصفة شأنها تخصيص الشىء عن مثله. وكلّ ما ذكرتموه من المخصّصات من الحسن أو القرب أو تيسّر الاخذ، فانّا نقدر على فرض انتفائه، ويبقى امكان الاخذ، فانتم بين أمرين: إمّا ان قلتم انّه لا يتصوّر التساوى بالاضافة الى اغراضه فقط، وهو حماقة وفرضه ممكن؛ وإمّا ان قلتم التساوى اذا فرض بقى الرجل المتشوّف أبدا متحيّرا

neither through pure will and choice that [according to you] are dissoci-
ated from the objective [of taking a specific one]. This also is impossible,
its falsity known by [rational] necessity. It is, hence, inescapable for anyone engaged in theoretical reflection on the true nature of the voluntary
act, whether in the realm of the observable or the unseen, but to affirm
the existence of an attribute whose function is to render one thing specifically distinct from its similar.

(47) The second way of objecting is for us to say:

[b]

(48) You in your own doctrine have not been able to dispense with
the rendering one of two similars specifically [distinct], for [you hold]
the world to have come into being through its necessitating cause, having specific configurations similar to their opposites. Why has it been
specified with [certain] aspects [and not others], when the impossibility
of differentiating one thing from its similar [as you uphold] does not
differ, [whether] in the [voluntary] act or in that which follows by nature
or by necessity?

(49) [To this you may] say:

(50) The universal order of the world can only be in the way it has
come to be. If the world were smaller or larger than it is at present, then
this order would not be complete. The same holds when speaking of the
number of these spheres and stars. You claim that the large differs from
the small and the numerous from the few in terms of what is required of
them. These, then, are not similar, but different, except that the human
faculty falls short of apprehending the modes of wisdom pertaining to
their quantities and details. It apprehends the wisdom only in some of
them—as, for example, the wisdom in the inclination of the sphere of the
zodiac away from the celestial equator, and the wisdom in [assigning]
the apogee and the spherical elliptical orbit. In most, the secret is not
apprehended, although their differences are known. It is not unlikely
that a thing is differentiated from its opposite by reason of its relation to
the established order. In the case of times, however, they are absolutely
similar in relation to possibility and the [established] order. It is impossible to claim that, if [the world] had been created later or earlier by one
moment, the order would be inconceivable. For the similarity of [temporal]
states is known by [rational] necessity.

(51) [To this we] say:

ينظر اليهما فلا يأخذ احداهما بمجرّد الارادة والاختيار المنفكّ عن الغرض وهو ايضا محال، يعلم بطلانه ضرورةً. فاذن لا بدّ لكلّ ناظر شاهدا أو غائبا فى تحقيق الفعل الاختيارى من اثبات صفة شأنها تخصيص الشىء عن مثله.

(٤٧) الوجه الثانى فى الاعتراض هو انّا نقول:

(٤٨) أنتم فى مذهبكم ما استغنيتم عن تخصيص الشىء عن مثله. فانّ العالم وجد من سببه الموجب له على هيئات مخصوصة تماثل نقائضها. فلمَ اختصّ ببعض الوجوه، واستحالة [تمييز]¹² الشىء عن مثله فى الفعل او فى اللزوم بالطبع أو بالضرورة لا تختلف؟

(٤٩) فان قلتم:

(٥٠) ان النظام الكلىّ للعالم لا يمكن الا على الوجه الذى وجد، وانّ العالم لو كان أصغر او اكبر مما هو الآن عليه، لكان لا يتمّ هذا النظام؛ وكذا القول فى عدد الافلاك وعدد الكواكب، وزعمتم انّ الكبير يخالف الصغير والكثير يفارق القليل فى ما يراد منه. فليست متماثلة، بل هى مختلفة الا انّ القوّة البشريّة تضعف عن درك وجوه الحكمة فى مقاديرها وتفاصيلها. وانما تدرك الحكمة فى بعضها كالحكمة فى ميل فلك البروج عن معدّل النهار، والحكمة فى الاوج والفلك الخارج <عن>¹³ المركز، والاكثر لا يدرك السرّ فيها ولكن يعرف اختلافها. ولا بعد فى أن يتميّز الشىء عن خلافه لتعلّق نظام الامر به. وامّا الاوقات فمتشابهة قطعاً بالنسبة الى الامكان والى النظام، ولا يمكن ان يدعى انّه لو خلق بعد ما خلق أو قبله بلحظة لما تصوّر النظام. فانّ تماثل الاحوال يعلم بالضرورة.

(٥١) فنقول:

(52) Even though we are able to use a similar argument against you in terms of [temporal] states, since there are those who say that God created the world at the time which was best for its creation, we will not restrict ourselves to this comparable [argument]. Rather, we will force [on you], in terms of your own principles, [the admission of] rendering specific [one similar as distinct from another] in two instances where it is not possible to suppose a difference [between their similars]. One is the difference of direction of [the world's] motion; the other is the assignment of the position of the pole in the ecliptic movement.

(53) Regarding the pole, its explanation is [as follows]: Heaven is a sphere rotating around two poles as though both are stationary. [Now,] the heavenly sphere is of similar parts. For it is simple—particularly the highest heaven, the ninth, for it has no stars at all. These two spheres [the ninth and the rest] rotate around two poles, northern and southern. Thus, we say, "There are no two opposite points among the points that, according [to the philosophers], are infinite but could be conceived as being the pole. Why is it, then, that the northern and southern points have been assigned to be the poles and to be stationary? And why does not the ecliptic line [shift], moving with [it] the two points so that the poles would revert to the two opposite points of the ecliptic? If, then, there is wisdom in the extent of the largeness of heaven and its shape, what differentiated the place of the pole from another [place], singling it out to be the pole from the rest of the parts and points, when all the points are similar and all parts of the sphere are equal?" There is no way out of this [for them].

(54) [To this the philosophers may] say:

(55) Perhaps the position where the point of the pole lies differs from other [positions] by a peculiarity that renders it suitable to be a place for the pole so as to be rendered stationary. It is, thus, as though it would not leave its "place," "space," "position," or whatever name is given it, while the rest of the positions on the [surface] of the [outermost] heaven in relation to the earth and [the rest of the] spheres change through rotation, the pole remaining stationary in its position. Perhaps, then, that position [for the pole] has precedence over others for being stationary.

(٥٢) نحن وان كنّا نقدر على معارضتكم بمثله فى الاحوال اذ قال قائلون، خلقه فى الوقت الذى كان الاصلح الخلق فيه؛ لكنّا لا نقتصر على هذه المقابلة، بل نفرض على أصلكم تخصّصا فى موضعين لا يمكن ان يقدر فيه اختلاف. احدهما اختلاف جهة الحركة؛ والآخر تعيّن موضع القطب فى الحركة عن المنطقة.

(٥٣) اما القطب، فبيانه انّ السماء كرة متحرّكة على قطبين كأنّهما ثابتان. وكرة السماء متشابهة الاجزاء. فانّها بسيطة، لا سيّما الفلك الأعلى الذى هو التاسع، فانّه غير مكوكب اصلا، وهما متحرّكان على قطبين شمالىّ وجنوبىّ. فنقول: ما من نقطتين متقابلتين من النقط التى لا نهاية لها عندهم الا ويتصوّر ان يكون هو القطب. فلم تعيّنت نقطتا الشمال والجنوب للقطبيّة والثبات؟ ولِمَ لَمْ يكن خط المنطقة مارًّا بالنقطتين حتّى يعود القطب الى نقطتين متقابلتين على المنطقة؟ فان كان فى مقدار كبر السماء وشكله حكمة، فما الذى ميّز محل القطب عن غيره حتى تعيّن لكونه قطبا دون سائر الاجزاء والنقط، وجميع النقط متماثلة وجميع اجزاء الكرة متساوية؟ وهذا لا مخرج عنه.

(٥٤) فان قيل:

(٥٥) لعلّ الموضع الذى عليه نقطة القطب يفارق غيره بخاصيَّة تناسب كونه محلا للقطب حتى يثبت، فكأنّه لا يفارق مكانه وحيّزه ووضعه أو ما يفرض اطلاقه عليه من الاسامى، وسائر مواضع الفلك يتبدّل بالدور وضعها من الارض ومن الافلاك، والقطب ثابت الوضع. فلعلّ ذلك الموضع كان أولى بان يكون ثابت الوضع من غيره.

(56) [To this] we say:

(57) In this there is a declared admission of a natural inequality
of the parts of the first sphere—that it is not of similar parts. This
is contrary to your principle, since one [of the principles] on which you
5   base your proof for the necessity for the heavens to be spherical in shape
is that it is a simple nature, similar [in its parts], having no inequality.
The simplest of the figures is the sphere. For being quadrangular and
hexagonal and so on entails the protrusion of angles and their inequality,
which can only be due to something additional to the simple nature.
10   Moreover, even though this [answer you have given] is contrary to your
doctrine, [the original] consequence forced on you is not removed by it.
For the question regarding that peculiarity remains: are the rest of the
parts receptive of this peculiarity or not? If they say, "Yes," then why
did [this] peculiarity attach specifically to one of the similars and not
15   the rest? If they say, "This [peculiarity] does not belong to any but that
position, the rest of the parts not being receptive of it," we say: "The rest
of the parts, inasmuch as they constitute a body receptive of forms, are
necessarily similar. The place is not deserving of that peculiarity by simply being a body or by simply being a heaven. For this intended meaning
20   is shared by all parts of heaven. It is thus the inescapable conclusion
that assigning [a particular place] with a specific characteristic is either
arbitrary or else [realized] through an attribute whose very function is to
render one thing [more] specific than its exact similar. For, just as it is
legitimate for them to say that the [temporal] states are equal in their
25   receptivity of the world's occurrence, it is legitimate for their opponents
to say that the parts of heaven are equal in terms of the receptivity of
the idea due to which precedence is given to the fixity of [one] position
[for the pole] as against its replacement." From this there is no escape.

(58) The second consequence forced on them is [this question]:
30   "What is the cause for assigning the direction of the motions of the
spheres—some from east to west, some in the opposite direction—[this]
despite the equivalence in direction when the equivalence in direction is
similar to the equivalence in times, there being no difference?"

(59) [To this they] may say:

(٥٦) قلنا:

(٥٧) ففى هذا تصريح بتفاوت اجزاء الكرة الاولى فى الطبيعة وانها ليست متشابهة الاجزاء. وهو على خلاف أصلكم، اذ أحد ما استدللتم بهِ على لزوم كون السماء كريّ الشكل أنه بسيط الطبيعة متشابه لا يتفاوت. وابسط الاشكال الكرة. فان التربيع والتسديس وغيرهما يقتضى خروج زوايا وتفاوتها، وذلك لا يكون الا بأمر زائد على الطبع البسيط. ولكنه وان خالف مذهبكم، فليس يندفع الالزام به. فان السؤال فى تلك الخاصيّة قائم اذ سائر الاجزاء هل كان قابلاً تلك الخاصيّة أم لا؟ فان قالوا: نعم، فلِمَ اختصت الخاصيّة من بين المتشابهات ببعضها؟ وان قالوا: لم يكن ذلك الا فى ذلك الموضع وسائر الاجزاء لا تقبلها، فنقول: سائر الاجزاء من حيث انها جسم قابل للصّور متشابه بالضّرورة؛ وتلك الخاصيّة لا يستحقها ذلك الموضع بمجرد كونه جسما ولا بمجرد كونه سماء. فان هذا المعنى يشاركه فيه سائر اجزاء السماء. فلا بدّ وأن يكون تخصيصه به بتحكّم أو بصفة من شأنها تخصيص الشىء عن مثله. والا فكما يستقيم لهم قولهم انّ الاحوال فى قبول وقوع العالم فيها متساوية، يستقيم لخصومهم انّ اجزاء السماء فى قبول المعنى الذى لاجلهِ صار ثبوت الوضع أولى به من تبدّل الوضع متساوية. وهذا لا مخرج منه.

(٥٨) الالزام الثانى تعيّن جهة حركة الافلاك بعضها من المشرق الى المغرب وبعضها بالعكس مع تساوى الجهات، ما سببها وتساوى الجهات كتساوى الأوقات من غير فرق؟

(٥٩) فان قيل:

(60) If all the whole [of the spheres] were to rotate in one direction, then their positions would not differ and the relationships between the stars in terms of being trine or sextine, having conjunction, and the like would not come about. The whole would then be in one state, without any differentiation at all, when [in fact] these [diverse] relationships are the principles of temporal events in the world.

(61) We say:

(62) We are not forced [into the position of affirming] the nonexistence of difference in the direction of the movement, but, on the contrary, say: "The highest sphere moves from east to west and what is beneath it in the opposite direction. Everything that can be achieved through this is achievable through its opposite—namely, in that the higher would move from west to east and that which is beneath it in the opposite direction, thereby differences taking place. [Now,] the directions of the motion after being circular and opposite are equivalent. Why, then, did one direction differ from another similar direction?"

(63) Should they say, "The directions are opposite and contrary; how, then, are they similar?" we would say:

(64) This is similar to someone's saying that priority and posteriority in terms of the world's [coming into] existence are contraries; how can one then claim their similarity? They claim, however, that one knows the similarity of times in relation to the possibility of existence and every beneficial end in existence whose conception is supposed. [But, then,] one can similarly [claim] that one knows the equivalence in space, position, and direction with respect to the receptivity of motion and every beneficial end related to it. If, then, they are allowed the claim of difference despite this similarity, their opponents are also allowed the claim of difference in times and configurations.

[(2) The second objection]

(65) The second objection against the basis of their proof is to say:

(66) You deem the occurrence of a temporal event through an eternal improbable when it is incumbent on you to acknowledge it. For in the world there are temporal events which have causes. If temporal events were to depend on [other] temporal events ad infinitum, this would be impossible—this is not the belief of a rational person. If this were

(٦٠) لو كان الكلّ يدور من جهة واحدة، لما تباينت أوضاعها، و لم تحدث مناسبات الكواكب بالتثليث والتسديس والمقارنة وغيرها؛ ولكان الكل على وضع واحد لا يختلف قطّ، وهذه المناسبات مبدأ الحوادث فى العالم.

(٦١) قلنا:

(٦٢) لسنا نلزم [عدم]¹¹ اختلاف جهة الحركة، بل نقول: الفلك الاعلى يتحرّك من المشرق الى المغرب والذى تحتهُ بالعكس؛ وكلّ ما يمكن تحصيله بهذا، يمكن تحصيله بعكسه، وهو ان يتحرّك الاعلى من المغرب الى المشرق وما تحته فى مقابلته فيحصل التفاوت؛ وجهات الحركة بعد كونها دورية وبعد كونها متقابلة متساوية، فلم تميّزت جهة عن جهة تماثلها؟

(٦٣) فان قالوا: الجهتان متقابلتان متضادّتان فكيف يتساويان؟ قلنا:

(٦٤) هذا كقول القائل التقدّم والتأخّر فى وجود العالم يتضادّا فكيف يدعى تشابههما؟ ولكن زعموا انّه يعلم تشابه الاوقات بالنسبة الى امكان الوجود والى كل مصلحة يتصوّر [فرضها]¹⁴ فى الوجود. فكذلك يعلم تساوى الاحياز والاوضاع والاماكن والجهات بالنسبة الى قبول الحركة وكل مصلحة تتعلّق بها. فان ساغ لهم دعوى الاختلاف مع هذا التشابه، كان لخصومهم دعوى الاختلاف فى الاحوال والهيئات أيضاً.

(٦٥) الاعتراض الثانى على أصل دليلهم ان يقال:

(٦٦) استبعدتم حدوث حادث من قديم، ولا بدّ لكم من الاعتراف به. فان فى العالم حوادث ولها أسباب. فان استندت الحوادث الى الحوادث الى غير نهاية، فهو محال، وليس ذلك معتقد عاقل. ولو كان ذلك ممكنا، لاستغنيتم عن الاعتراف بالصانع واثبات واجب وجود هو

possible, you would then have had no need to acknowledge [the existence of] the Maker and affirm a Necessary Existent who is the ground of [all] the possible [existents]. If, then, events have a limit with which their chain terminates, this limit would be the Eternal. It is, hence, inescapable
5   in terms of their [own] principle to allow the proceeding of a temporal from an eternal.

(67) [It may be] said:

(68) We do not deem improbable the proceeding of a temporal event, whichever event this is, from an eternal; rather, we deem improb-
10 able the proceeding from an eternal of an event which is a first event. For the state of coming into existence does not differ from what precedes it with respect to the preponderance of the direction of existence, whether in terms of the presence of a temporal moment, an organ, a condition, a nature, a purpose, or any cause. But if the event is not the first
15 event, then it is possible [for the temporal event] to proceed from [an eternal] with the temporal occurrence of some other thing, such as a preparedness in the receptacle, the presence of a suitable time, or something of this sort.

(69) [To this] we say:

20 (70) The question regarding the occurrence of the preparedness, the presence of the [suitable] time, and whatever comes into being anew, remains. Either [these occurrences] regress ad infinitum or terminate with an eternal from which a first temporal event comes about.

(71) [To this, however, it may be] said:

25 (72) None of the materials receptive of forms, accidents, and qualities are temporally created. The qualities that come into being in time are the movements of the spheres—I mean, the circular motion—and whatever descriptions relating to it by way of triadic, hexagonal, and quadratic configurations that come into existence anew. These consist of the
30 relation of some parts of heaven and the stars to each other and some to the earth—as with [the occurrences] that take place by way of astral ascent, appearance [in the firmament], the decline from the highest point and greatest distance from the earth by the star's being at its apogee, and its proximity by being at its perigee and inclining away from some

مستند الممكنات. واذا كانت الحوادث لها طرف ينتهى اليه تسلسلها، فيكون ذلك الطرف هو القديم؛ فلا بدّ اذن على أصلهم من تجويز صدور حادث من قديم.

(٦٧) فان قيل:

(٦٨) نحن لا نُبعد صدور حادث من قديم، أىّ حادث كان، بل نبعد صدور حادث هو أوّل الحوادث من القديم؛ اذ لا يفارق حال الحدوث ما قبله فى ترجّح جهة الوجود، لا من حيث حضور وقت ولا آلة ولا شرط ولا طبيعة ولا غرض ولا سبب من الاسباب. فأما اذا لم يكن هو الحادث الاول، جاز ان يصدر منه عند حدوث شىء آخر من استعداد المحل القابل وحضور الوقت الموافق أو ما يجرى هذا المجرى.

(٦٩) قلنا:

(٧٠) فالسؤال فى حصول الاستعداد وحضور الوقت وكل ما يتجدّد قائم. فإمّا ان يتسلسل الى غير نهاية، أو ينتهى الى قديم يكون أوّل حادث منه.

(٧١) فان قيل:

(٧٢) الموادّ القابلة للصور والاعراض والكيفيّات ليس شىء منها حادثا. والكيفيّات الحادثة هى حركة الافلاك، اعنى الحركة الدوريّة وما يتجدّد من الاوصاف الاضافية لها من التثليث والتسدبس والتربيع، وهى نسبة بعض أجزاء الفلك والكواكب الى بعض، وبعضها نسبة الى الارض، كما يحصل من الطلوع والشروق والزوال عن منتهى الارتفاع والبعد عن الارض بكون الكوكب فى الاوج، والقرب بكونه فى الحضيض،

climes by being in the north or in the south. This relation is by necessity
a concomitant to the circular motion; it is, hence, necessitated by the circular motion. As regards the events contained in the sublunar sphere—
namely, the elements with respect to what occurs in them by way of
generation and corruption, combination and separation, and transformation from one description to another—all these are events dependent
on each other in a lengthy, detailed [way]. In the end, the principles of
their causes terminate with the circular heavenly movement, the relations of the stars to each other, and their relation to the earth.

(73) The outcome of all this is that the perpetual, eternal circular
motion is the basis of all temporal events. That which imparts the circular motion of the heavens is the souls of the heavens. For these are alive,
having the same relation to the spheres as our souls to our bodies. The
[heavens'] souls are eternal. No wonder, then, that the heavenly motion
necessitated by the souls is also eternal. And, since the states of the souls
are similar, due to their being eternal, the states of the movements
become similar; that is, they circulate eternally.

(74) It is, hence, inconceivable for a temporal event to proceed from
an eternal except through the mediation of an eternal circular movement that in one respect resembles the Eternal, for He is everlasting;
and that in another respect resembles the temporal: for each of its parts
that are supposed comes into existence after not being. Hence, inasmuch as [the circular movement] is temporal in terms of its parts and
relationships, it is the principle of temporal events; and, inasmuch as it
is eternal [in terms] of similar states, it proceeds from an eternal soul.
Thus, if there are events in the world, there must then be a circular
motion. But in the world there are events. Hence, the eternal circular
motion is established.[11]

(75) [To this we] say:

(76) This lengthy elaboration does you no good. For is the circular
motion, which is the foundation [of all temporal events], temporally originated or eternal? If eternal, how does [this foundation] become a principle for the first temporal event? If temporal, it would require another

والميل عن بعض الاقطار بكونه فى الشمال والجنوب. وهذه الاضافة لازمة للحركة الدوريّة بالضرورة؛ فموجبها الحركة الدوريّة. وأما الحوادث فيما يحويه مقعّر فلك القمر [وهي]¹⁵ العناصر بما يعرض فيها من كون وفساد وامتزاج وافتراق واستحالة من صفة الى صفة، فكلّ ذلك حوادث مستند بعضها الى بعض فى تفصيل طويل. وبالآخرة تنتهى مبادىء اسبابها الى الحركة السماوية الدوريّة ونسب الكواكب بعضها الى بعض أو نسبتها الى الارض.

(٧٣) فيخرج من مجموع ذلك ان الحركة الدوريّة الدائمة الأبديّة مستند الحوادث كلها. ومحرّك السماء حركتها الدورية، نفوس السموات. فانّها حية، نازلة منزلة نفوسنا بالنسبة الى أبداننا. ونفوسها قديمة؛ فلا جرم [انّ]¹⁶ الحركة الدوريّة التى هى موجبها أيضا قديمة. ولما [تشابهت]¹⁷ احوال النفس لكونها قديمة، [تشابهت]¹⁸ أحوال الحركات، أى كانت دائرة ابدا.

(٧٤) فاذن لا يتصوّر ان يصدر الحادث من قديم الا بواسطة حركة دوريّة أبديّة تشبه القديم من وجه، فانّه دائم ابدا، وتشبه الحادث من وجه؛ فانّ كل جزء يفرض منه كان حادثا بعد ان لم يكن. فهو من حيث انه حادث بأجزائهِ وإضافاته مبدأ الحوادث، ومن حيث انه أبديّ متشابه الاحوال، صادر عن نفس أزليّة. فان كان فى العالم حوادث، فلا بدّ من حركة دوريّة؛ وفى العالم حوادث، فالحركة الدوريّة الابديّة ثابتة.

(٧٥) قلنا:

(٧٦) هذا التطويل لا يغنيكم. فان الحركة الدوريّة التى هى المستند [حادثة ام قديمة]¹⁹ فان [كانت قديمة]²⁰، فكيف صار مبدأ لاول

temporal event, [and so on,] regressing [ad infinitum]. [Regarding] your statement that in one respect it resembles the eternal and in one respect the temporal, being constant and renewed—that is, it is constant in being renewed, its constancy ever renewed—we say: "Is it the principle
5   of temporal events inasmuch as it is permanent or inasmuch as it is being renewed? If inasmuch as it is permanent, how is it, then, that there would proceed from something permanent whose states are similar something that occurs at [certain] times but not others? If inasmuch as it is renewed, what is the cause of [the] renewal in itself? It would then
10   require another cause, and [this] would regress [infinitely]." This, then, is the final [word] in confirming the necessary [absurd] consequences [of their position].

(77) They have, however, in the [endeavor to] escape this necessary consequence, [forced on them] a kind of ruse which we will bring forth
15   [not here, but] in some of the [forthcoming] discussions, lest the discourse in this discussion become prolonged through the branching of the diverse, diverting ways of speech. We shall, however, show that the circular motion is not suitable to be the principle of temporal events and that all events are inventions of God by [a first] initiation,[12] refuting what
20   they say regarding heaven being an animal that by choice undergoes a motion [caused] by the soul similar to our movements.

A second proof they have on this question
[First discussion: Second proof]

(78) They claim that whoever asserts that the world is posterior to God and God prior to it can mean by it [only one of two things]:[13]

(79) [He can mean] that He is prior in essence, not in time, in the way
25   that one is prior to two (which is [a priority] by nature, although it can temporally coexist with it); and like the priority of cause to effect, as with the priority of a person's movement to the movement of [his] shadow that follows him, the hand's movement and the movement of the ring, and the hand's movement in the water and the movement of the water—
30   for all these are simultaneous, some being a cause, some an effect. For

الحوادث؟ وان كان حادثا، افتقر الى حادث آخر وتسلسل. وقولكم انّه من وجه يشبه القديم ومن وجه يشبه الحادث، فانه ثابت متجدّد، أى هو ثابت التجدّد، متجدّد الثبوت، فنقول: أهو مبدأ الحوادث من حيث انه ثابت، أو من حيث انه متجدّد؟ ان كان من حيث انه ثابت، فكيف صدر من ثابت متشابه الاحوال شىء فى بعض الاوقات دون بعض؟ وان كان من حيث انه متجدّد، فما سبب تجدّده فى نفسه؟ فيحتاج الى سبب آخر ويتسلسل. فهذا غاية تقرير الالزام.

(٧٧) ولهم فى الخروج عن هذا الالزام نوع احتيال سنورده فى بعض المسائل بعد هذه كيلا يطول كلام هذه المسئلة بانشعاب شجون الكلام وفنونه. على انا سنبيّن انّ الحركة الدوريّة لا تصلح ان تكون مبدأ الحوادث وأن جميع الحوادث مخترعة لله ابتداءً، ونبطل ما قالوه من كون السماء حيوانا متحركا بالاختيار حركة نفسيّة كحركتنا.

دليل ثان لهم فى المسئلة

(٧٨) زعموا ان القائل بانّ العالم متأخّر عن الله والله متقدّم عليه ليس يخلوا:

(٧٩) امّا ان يريد به انه متقدّم بالذات لا بالزمان، كتقدّم الواحد على الاثنين، فانه بالطبع، مع انّه يجوز ان يكون ••• فى الوجود الزمانى، وكتقدّم العلّة على المعلول، مثل تقدّم حركة الشخص على حركة الظلّ التابع له وحركة اليد مع حركة الخاتم وحركة اليد فى الماء مع حركة الماء، فانّها متساوية فى الزمان وبعضها علّة وبعضها معلول، اذ يقال تحرّك

it is said, "The shadow moved because of the person's movement, and the water moved because of the hand's movement in the water," and it is not said, "The person moved because of the movement of his shadow, and the hand moved because of the water's movement," even though [each of the pair of movements is] simultaneous. If this, then, is meant by the Creator's priority to the world, it follows necessarily that both are either temporally finite or eternal, it being impossible for one to be eternal and the other temporally finite.

(80) If [on the other hand] it is meant that the Creator is prior to the world and time—not essentially, but in time—then, before the existence of the world and time, a time would have existed in which the world did not exist, since nonexistence precedes existence; and God would have preceded the world by a very lengthy duration, limited in the direction of its ending but having no limit in the direction of its beginning. Thus, before the existence of time, infinite time would have existed, and this is contradictory; for this reason the affirmation of the finitude of time is impossible. If, then, time, which is the expression of the measure of motion, is necessarily pre-eternal, motion is necessarily pre-eternal, and that which is in motion and through whose duration time endures is necessarily pre-eternal.

(81) The objection [to this] is to say:

(82) Time is originated and created, and before it there was no time at all. We mean by our statement that God is prior to the world and time: that He was and there was no world, and that then He was and with Him was the world. The meaning of our statement, "He was and there was no world," is only [the affirmation of] the existence of the Creator's essence and nonexistence of the world's essence. And the meaning of our statement, "He was and with Him was the world," is only [the affirmation of] the existence of two essences. Thus, by priority we mean only the appropriation of existence to Himself alone, the world being like an individual. If, for example, we said, "God was and there was no Jesus, and then He was and Jesus with Him," the utterance would not entail anything other than the existence of an essence and the nonexistence of an essence, then the existence of two essences. From this, the supposition of a third thing is not necessary, even though the estimative faculty does not refrain from supposing a third thing. But one must not heed the errors of estimative thoughts.

الظلّ لحركة الشخص وتحرّك الماء لحركة اليد فى الماء، ولا يقال تحرّك الشخص لحركة الظلّ وتحرك اليد لحركة الماء وان كانت متساوية؛ فان أُريد بتقدّم البارى على العالم هذا، لزم أن يكونا حادثين أو قديمين، واستحال أن يكون أحدهما قديما والآخر حادثا.

(٨٠) وان أُريد به أن البارى متقدّم على العالم والزمان، لا بالذات بل بالزمان فاذن قبل وجود العالم والزمان زمان كان العالم فيه معدوما، اذ كان العدم سابقا على الوجود، وكان الله سابقا بمدّة مديدة لها طرف من جهة الآخر ولا طرف لها من جهة الاوّل؛ فاذن قبل الزمان زمان لا نهاية له، وهو متناقض، ولأجله يستحيل القول بحدوث الزمان. واذا وجب قدم الزمان، وهو عبارة عن قدر الحركة، وجب قدم الحركة، ووجب قدم المتحرك الذى يدوم الزمان بدوام حركته.

(٨١) الاعتراض هو ان يقال:

(٨٢) الزمان حادث ومخلوق وليس قبله زمان أصلا، ونعنى بقولنا ان الله متقدّم على العالم والزمان انه كان ولا عالم ثم كان ومعه عالم. ومفهوم قولنا كان ولا عالم، وجود ذات البارى وعدم ذات العالم فقط؛ ومفهوم قولنا كان ومعه عالم، وجود الذاتين فقط. فنعنى بالتقدّم انفراده بالوجود فقط، والعالم كشخص واحد. ولو قلنا، كان الله ولا عيسى مثلا ثم كان وعيسى معهُ، لم يتضمّن اللفظ الا وجود ذات، وعدم ذات ثم وجود ذاتين. وليس من ضرورة ذلك تقدير شىء ثالث، وان كان الوهم لا يسكن عن تقدير ثالث. فلا التفات الى أغاليط الاوهام.

(83) [In response to this the philosophers may] say:

(84) There is to our saying, "God was and there was no world," a third meaning other than the existence of an essence and the non-existence of an essence, proved [by the fact that,] if we suppose the nonexistence of the world in the future, then the existence of an essence and the nonexistence of [another] essence would have been realized—where, however, it would then be incorrect to say, "God was and the world was not." On the contrary, the correct thing would then be to say, "God will be and the world will not be"; whereas we would say about the past, "God was and there was no world." Between our saying "was" and "will be" there is a difference, since neither [expression] is a substitute for the other. Let us, then, examine wherein the difference lies. There is no doubt that they do not differ in terms of the existence of the essence and the nonexistence of the world, but in a third thing. For if we say regarding the future nonexistence of the world, "God was and there was no world," it would be said to us, "This is an error." For "was" is only said about what has passed. This indicates that underlying the expression "was" is a third meaning—namely, the past. But the past in itself is time and through another is motion; for [the latter] passes with the passing of time. It follows by necessity, then, that before the world there would have been time that had passed, ending up with the world's existence.

(85) [To this we] say:

(86) The basic thing understood by the two expressions is the existence of an essence and the nonexistence of an essence. The third thing, by virtue of which there is a difference between the two expressions, is a relation necessary with respect to us [only]. The proof of this is that if we suppose the nonexistence of the world in the future and suppose for us a later existence, then we would say, "God was and the world was not," this statement being true regardless of whether we intend by it the first nonexistence or the second nonexistence, which is after existence. The sign that this is relative is that the future itself can become a past and is expressed in the past tense. All this is due to the inability of the estimative [faculty] to comprehend an existence that has a beginning except by supposing a "before" for it. This "before," from which the estimation does not detach itself, is believed to be a thing realized, existing—namely, time. This is similar to the inability of the estimation to suppose the finitude of body overhead, for example,

(٨٣) فان قيل:

(٨٤) لقولنا كان الله ولا عالم مفهوم ثالث سوى وجود الذات وعدم العالم، بدليل انا لو قدّرنا عدم العالم فى المستقبل، كان وجود ذات وعدم ذات حاصلا، و لم يصحّ ان نقول كان الله ولا عالم، بل الصحيح ان نقول يكون الله ولا عالم ونقول للماضى كان الله ولا عالم. فبين قولنا كان ويكون فرق اذ ليس ينوب أحدهما مناب الآخر، فلنبحث عن ما يرجع اليه الفرق. ولا شك فى انّهما لا يفترقان فى وجود الذات ولا فى عدم العالم، بل فى معنى ثالث. فانّا اذا قلنا لعدم العالم فى المستقبل، كان الله ولا عالم، قيل لنا، هذا خطأ فانّ كان انّما يقال على ماضٍ، فدلّ انّ تحت لفظ كان مفهوماً ثالثا وهو الماضى. والماضى بذاته هو الزمان والماضى بغيره هو الحركة، فانّها تمضى بمضىّ الزمان؛ فبالضّرورة يلزم أن يكون قبل العالم زمان قد انقضى حتى انتهى الى وجود العالم.

(٨٥) قلنا:

(٨٦) المفهوم الاصلىّ من اللفطين وجود ذات وعدم ذات. والامر الثالث الذى فيه افتراق اللفظين نسبة لازمة بالاضافة الينا بدليل انّا لو قدّرنا عدم العالم فى المستقبل ثم قدّرنا لنا بعد ذلك وجودا ثانيا لكُنّا عند ذلك نقول، كان الله ولا عالم، ويصحّ قولنا سواء أردنا به العدم الاول أو العدم الثانى الذى هو بعد الوجود. واية ان هذه نسبة، ان المستقبل بعينه يجوز أن يصير ماضيا فيعبّر عنه بلفظ الماضى. وهذا كلّه لعجز الوهم عن فهم وجود مبتدأ إلا مع تقدير قبل لهُ، وذلك القبل الذى لا ينفكّ الوهم عنه، يظنّ أنّه شىء محقّق موجود هو الزمان. وهو كعجز الوهم عن أن يقدّر تناهى الجسم فى جانب الرأس مثلاً الا على سطح له فوق، فيتوهّم

except in terms of a surface that has an "above," thereby imagining that beyond the world there is a place, either filled or void. Thus, if it is said that there is no "above" above the surface of the world and no distance more distant than it, the estimation holds back from acquiescing to it, just as if it is said that before the world's existence there is no "before" which is realized in existence, [and the estimation] shies away from accepting it.

(87) [Now,]¹⁴ one may hold estimation to be false in its supposition that above the world there is a void—namely, an infinite extension—by saying to it: "The void is in itself incomprehensible." As regards extension, it is a concomitant of body whose dimensions are extended. If body is finite, the extension which is its concomitant is finite and filled space terminates [with the surface of the world], whereas the void is incomprehensible. It is thus established that beyond the world there is neither void nor filled space, even though the estimation does not acquiesce to accepting [this]. Similarly, it will be said that, just as spatial extension is a concomitant of body, temporal extension is a concomitant of motion. For the latter is the spreading out of motion, just as the former is the spreading out of spatial dimensions. And, just as the proof for the finitude of the dimensions of the body prohibits affirming a spatial dimension beyond it, the proof for the finitude of motion at both ends prohibits affirming a temporal extension before it, even though the estimation clings to its imagining it and its supposing it, not desisting from [this]. There is no difference between temporal extension that, in relation [to us], divides verbally into "before" and "after" and spatial extension that, in relation [to us], divides into "above" and "below." If, then, it is legitimate to affirm an "above" that has no above, it is legitimate to affirm a "before" that has no real before, except an estimative imaginary [one], as with the "above." This is a necessary consequence. Let it then be contemplated. For they agreed that beyond the world there is neither void nor filled space.

(88) To this [the philosophers] may say:

(89) This comparison is contorted because the world has neither an "above" nor a "below," being, rather, spherical; and the sphere has neither an "above" nor a "below." Rather, if a direction is called "above"

انّ وراء العالم مكانا، امّا ملاء وامّا خلاء. واذا قيل، ليس فوق سطح العالم فوق ولا بعد ابعد منه، كاع الوهم عن الاذعان لقبوله، كما اذا قيل، ليس قبل وجود العالم قبل هو وجود محقّق، نفر عن قبوله.

(٨٧) وكما جاز أن يُكذّب الوهم فى تقديره فوق العالم خلاء هو بعد لا نهاية له بان يقال له، الخلاء ليس مفهوما فى نفسه، وأمّا البعد فهو تابع للجسم الذى تتباعد أقطاره، فاذا كان الجسم متناهيا كان البعد الذى هو تابع له متناهيا وانقطع الملاء، والخلاء غير مفهوم، فثبت انّه ليس وراء العالم لا خلاء ولا ملاء، وإن كان الوهم لا يذعن لقبوله، فكذلك يقال، كما ان البعد المكانىّ تابع للجسم، فالبعد الزمانىّ تابع للحركة؛ فانّه امتداد الحركة كما انّ ذلك امتداد اقطار الجسم. وكما انّ قيام الدليل على تناهى اقطار الجسم منع من اثبات بعد مكانىّ وراءَه، فقيام الدليل على تناهى الحركة من طرفيه يمنع من تقدير بعد زمانىّ وراءه، وإن كان الوهم متشبّثا بخياله وتقديره ولا يرعوى عنه. ولا فرق بين البعد الزمانى الذى تنقسم العبارة عنه عند الاضافة الى قبل وبَعْد وبين البعد المكانى الذى تنقسم العبارة عنه عند الاضافة الى فوق وتحت. فان جاز اثبات فوق لا فوق فوقه، جاز اثبات قبل ليس قبله قبل محقّق الا خيال وهمىّ كما فى الفوق. وهذا لازم. فليتأمل. فانهم اتفقوا على أنّه ليس وراء العالم لا خلاء ولا ملاء.

(٨٨) فان قيل:

(٨٩) هذه الموازنة معوجّة لان العالم ليس له فوق ولا تحت بل هو كرىّ، وليس للكرة فوق وتحت؛ بل إن سميت جهة فوقاً من حيث انّه

٥

١٠

١٥

٢٠

this is inasmuch as it is beyond your head; the other [direction is called] "below" insofar as it extends beyond your foot. [These are] innovated [names] given [them] in relation to you. The direction which is "below" in relation to you is "above" in relation to another if you suppose him to

5   be on the opposite side of the globe, standing in such a way that the arch of his foot is opposite the arch of your foot. Indeed, the direction of parts of the heavens which in the daytime you suppose to be "above" you is the very same one that at night is "below" the globe. What is "below" reverts to being "above" the earth through the heavenly rotation. As for the first

10   [point in time] for the world's existence, it cannot be conceived to change so as to become the last. An example of this is when we suppose a piece of wood, one end of which is thick [and] the other thin, agreeing to name the direction close to the narrow end "above," as far as it goes, [and] the other side "below"—through this, no essential difference in

15   the parts of the world manifests itself. Rather, these are different names dependent on the shape of this piece of wood, so that if its position is reversed, the name is reversed, the world remaining unchanged. "Above" and "below" [constitute] a relation purely to you in terms of which no change in the parts and surfaces of the world is effected.

20   (90) But the nonexistence that precedes the world [terminating with] the first limit of [the world's] existence is essential; [it is] inconceivable for it to interchange and become last. Nor is it conceivable for the supposed nonexistence when the world is extinguished, which is a subsequent nonexistence, to become antecedent. Thus, the two limits of the world's

25   nonexistence, one being the first, the other the second, are essential, established limits whose interchange through the change of relations is utterly inconceivable. This is different from the "above" and the "below." Hence, it is possible for us to say, "The world has neither an 'above' nor a 'below,'" whereas you cannot say, "There is neither a 'before' nor an

30   'after' for the world's existence." If, then, the "before" and "after" have been established, there is no meaning for time except in terms of what is expressed by "before" and "after."

         (91) [To this] we say:

يلى رأسك، والآخر تحتا من حيث انه يلى رجلك، فهو اسم تجدّد له
بالاضافة اليك، والجهة التى هى تحت بالاضافة اليك فوق بالاضافة الى
غيرك، اذا قدّرت على الجانب الآخر من كرة الارض واقفا يحاذى
أخمص قدمه أخمص قدمك. بل الجهة التى تقدّرها فوقك من أجزاء
السماء نهارا هو بعينه تحت الارض ليلا. وما هو تحت الارض يعود الى   ٥
فوق الارض فى الدور. وأما الاول لوجود العالم، لا يتصور ان ينقلب
آخرا. وهو كما لو قدّرنا خشبة أحد طرفيها غليظ والآخر دقيق
واصطلحنا على أن نسمى الجهة التى تلى الدقيق فوقا الى حيث ينتهى،
والجانب الآخر تحتاً، لم يظهر بهذا اختلاف ذاتى فى اجزاء العالم. بل هى
أسامى مختلفة قيامها بهيئة هذه الخشبة، حتى لو عكس وضعها انعكس   ١٠
الاسم، والعالم لم يتبدل. فالفوق والتحت نسبة محضة اليك لا تختلف
أجزاء العالم وسطوحه فيه.

(٩٠) وأمّا العدم المتقدّم على العالم والنهاية الاولى لوجوده ذاتىّ لا
يتصوّر أن يتبدل فيصير آخراً. ولا العدم المقدّر عند افناء العالم الذى هو
عدم لاحق يتصوّر ان يصير سابقاً. فطرفا نهاية وجود العالم الذى   ١٥
أحدهما أول والثانى آخر طرفان ذاتيّان ثابتان لا يتصوّر التبدّل فيه
بتبدّل الاضافات البتّة، بخلاف الفوق والتحت. فاذن امكننا ان نقول
ليس للعالم فوق ولا تحت، ولا يمكنكم أن تقولوا ليس اوجود العالم قبل
ولا بعد. واذا ثبت القبل والبعد فلا معنى للزمان سوى ما يعبّر عنه
بالقبل والبعد.   ٢٠

(٩١) قلنا:

(92) This makes no difference. There is no [particular] purpose in assigning the utterance "above" and "below," but we will shift to the expressions "beyond" and "outside" and say, "The world has an inside and an outside: is there, then, outside the world something which is either filled or empty space?" [The philosophers] will then say, "Beyond the world there is neither a void nor filled space. If by 'outside' you mean its outermost surface, then it would have an outside; but if you mean something else, then it has no outside." Similarly, if we are asked, "Does the world have a 'before'?" we answer, "If by this is meant, 'Does the world's existence have a beginning—that is, a limit in which it began?' then the world has a 'before' in this sense, just as the world has an 'outside' on the interpretation that this is its exposed limit and bounding surface. If you mean by it anything else, then the world has no 'before'— just as, when one means by 'outside the world' [something] other than its surface, then one would say, 'There is no exterior to the world.' Should you say that a beginning of an existence that has no 'before' is incomprehensible, it would then be said, 'A finite bodily existence that has no outside is incomprehensible.' If you say that its 'outside' is its surface with which it terminates, [and] nothing more, we will say that its 'before' is the beginning of its existence which is its limit, [and] nothing more."

(93) There remains for us to say:

(94) God has an existence without the world. [Saying] this much also does not necessarily entail affirming another thing. What proves that [affirming another thing] is the work of the estimation is that [this faculty] is specifically related to time and space. For, even though the opponent believes in the eternity of the [world's] body, his estimative faculty acquiesces to the supposition of its temporal origin. Although we believe in its temporal origination, our estimative faculty may yet acquiesce to the supposition of its eternity—this with respect to body. But when we return to time, the opponent is unable to suppose the coming into being of a time which has no "before." [Now, normally,] what is contrary to belief can be posited in the estimative faculty as a supposition and a hypothesis. But this, as with space, is one of the things that cannot be placed within the estimative faculty. For neither the believer in the body's finitude nor the one who disbelieves it is able to suppose a body beyond which there is neither a void nor a filled space, their estimative faculties not acquiescing to the acceptance of this. But it is said, "If clear reason, through proof, does not disallow the existence of

(٩٢) لا فرق؛ فانّه لا غرض فى تعيين لفظ الفوق والتحت، بل نعدل الى لفظ الوراء والخارج ونقول: للعالم داخل وخارج، فهل خارج العالم شىء من ملاء او خلاء؟ فسيقولون: ليس وراء العالم لا خلاء ولا ملاء؛ وان عنيتم بالخارج سطحه الاعلى، فله خارج، وان عنيتم غيره، فلا خارج له. فكذلك اذا قيل لنا، هل لوجود العالم قبل؟ قلنا: إن عنى بهٖ، هل لوجود العالم بداية أى طرف منه ابتدأ، فله قبل على هذا، كما للعالم خارج على تأويل انّه الطرف المكشوف والمنقطع السطحىّ، وان عنيتم بقبل شيئاً آخر، فلا قبل للعالم، كما انّه اذا عنى بخارج العالم شىء سوى السطح، قيل لا خارج للعالم. فان قلتم لا يعقل مبتدأ وجود لا قبل له، فيقال، ولا يعقل متناهى وجود من الجسم لا خارج له. فان [قلتم]٢١، خارجه [سطحه]٢٢ الذى هو منقطعه لا غير، قلنا: قبله بداية وجوده الذى هو طرفهُ لا غير.

(٩٣) بقى انّا نقول:

(٩٤) لله وجود ولا عالم معه، وهذا القدر ايضاً لا يوجب اثبات شىء آخر. والذى يدلّ على انّ هذا عمل الوهم انّهُ مخصوص بالزمان والمكان، فانّ الخصم وان اعتقد قدم الجسم، يذعن وهمه لتقدير حدوثه؛ ونحن، وان اعتقدنا حدوثه، ربما اذعن وهمنا لتقدير قدمه، هذا فى الجسم. فاذا رجعنا الى الزمان، لم يقدر الخصم على تقدير حدوث زمان لا قبل له. وخلاف المعتقد يمكن وضعه فى الوهم تقديرا وفرضا، وهذا ممّا لا يمكن وضعه فى الوهم كما فى المكان فانّ من يعتقد تناهى الجسم ومن لا يعتقد، كل واحد يعجز عن تقدير جسم ليس وراءَه لا خلاء ولا ملاء، بل لا يذعن وهمه لقبول ذلك. ولكن قيل، صريح العقل اذا لم يمنع وجود

a finite body, then one must not heed the estimation." Similarly, clear reason does not disallow a first beginning that is preceded by nothing; and if the estimation falls short of grasping this, one must not heed it. For the estimative faculty, never being acquainted with a finite body that
5   does not have beside it [either] another body or air, which it imagines to be a void, is unable to grasp [its contrary] in the unseen. Similarly, the estimative faculty has never had acquaintance with an event that does not occur after something else. It is thus incapable of supposing a temporal event that has no "before," this being [for it] an existing thing
10   that has passed.

(95) This, then, is the cause of the error. With this objection, resistance [to the philosophers] achieves [its end].

Another pattern [of argument the philosophers] have
for rendering the pre-eternity of time necessary

(96) They say:

(97) No doubt, according to you, God was able to create the world
15   before He created it by a year, a hundred years, a thousand years, [and so on,] and these hypothesized [magnitudes] surpass each other in measure and quantity. There is, hence, no escape from affirming [the existence] of something prior to the world's existence—[something] that is extended and measured, parts of which are more extended and
20   longer than others. If you say, "One cannot apply the expression 'years' except after the heavens' creation and its rotation," we will abandon the expression "years" and put the matter in a different mold, saying: "If we suppose that since the world's first existence its sphere up to the present has made, for example, a thousand revolutions, would God [praised
25   be He] have been able to create before it a second world, similar to it, such that it would have made up to the present time eleven hundred rotations?" If you say, "No," it would be as though the Eternal has changed from impotence to capability or the world from impossibility to possibility[—which is absurd]. If you say, "Yes"—and this [you] must—
30   [it would then be asked,] "Would He have been able to create a third world that would have rotated up to the present twelve hundred times?" A "Yes" here is inevitable. We would then say: "Could this world, which, according to the order of our hypothesizing, we have named 'third,' even

جسم متناهٍ بحكم الدليل لا يلتفت الى الوهم، فكذلك صريح العقل لا يمنع وجودا مفتتحا ليس قبله شىء وان قصر الوهم عنه فلا يلتفت اليه؛ لانّ الوهم لمّا لم يألف جسما متناهيا الا وبجنبه جسم آخر أو هواء تخيّله خلاء، لم يتمكّن من ذلك فى الغائب. فكذلك لم يألف الوهم حادثا الا بعد شىء آخر، فكاع عن تقدير حادث ليس له قبل هو شىء موجود قد انقضى.

(٩٥) فهذا هو سبب الغلط والمقاومة حاصلة بهذه المعارضة.

صيغة ثانية لهم فى الزام قدم الزمان

(٩٦) قالوا:

(٩٧) لا شك فى ان الله عندكم كان قادرا على ان يخلق العالم قبل أن خلقه بقدر سنة ومائة سنة وألف سنة وان هذه التقديرات متفاوتة فى المقدار والكميّة، فلا بد من اثبات شىء قبل وجود العالم ممتدّ مقدّر، بعضه أمدّ وأطول من البعض. وان قلتم، لا يمكن اطلاق لفظ سنين الا بعد حدوث الفلك ودوره، فلنترك لفظ سنين ولنورد صيغة أُخرى فنقول: اذا قدّرنا ان العالم من اول وجوده قد دار فلكه الى الآن بالف دورة مثلاً، فهل كان الله قادرا على أن يخلق قبله عالًما ثانياً مثله بحيث ينتهى الى زماننا هذا بالف ومائة دورة؟ فان قلتم، لا، فكأنه انقلب القديم من العجز الى القدرة او العالم من الاستحالة الى الامكان، وان قلتم، نعم، ولا بدَ منه، فهل كان يقدر على أن يخلق عالما ثالثا بحيث ينتهى الى زماننا بالف ومائتى دورة؟ ولا بد من نعم. فنقول: هذا العالم الذى سمّيناه بحسب ترتيبنا فى التقدير ثالثا، وان كان هو الأسبق، فهل امكن خلقه مع العالم

though it is the earlier, have been created with the world which has been called 'second,' the former making up to the present twelve hundred rotations, the latter eleven hundred, yet both equivalent as regards the distance covered by their motions and velocities?" If you say, "Yes," this would be impossible. For it is impossible for two motions to be equal in rapidity and slowness and then reach the same point in time when the number [of their rotations] is unequal. If [on the other hand] you say [as you must]: [(a)] that the third world, which up to now has made twelve hundred revolutions, cannot be created simultaneously with the second world, which up to the present has made eleven hundred revolutions; [(b)] that, indeed, God must have created [the former] earlier by a measure equal to the one by which the second world precedes the first— we call [this latter] the first because it is closer to our estimative faculty, since it is to it, in making our hypothetical measure, [that] we date back from the present; [(c)] that [consequently] the measure of one possible would be double that of the other and that [hence] there would have to be another possible that is double the whole—[if you must admit all this,] then the possibility measured by quantity, parts of which are lengthier than others by a known amount, has no other reality except time.

(98) For these hypothetical measures do not constitute an attribute of the Creator's essence—exalted be He above hypothesized measures. Nor are they an attribute of the world's nonexistence, since nonexistence is not a thing so as to be measured by different magnitudes. [Now,] quantity is an attribute. Hence, it calls for something that has quantity. This [something] is none other than motion; and quantity is none other than time, which is the measure of motion. Hence, there is, for you, prior to the world something that had different quantities—namely, time. Hence, for you, before the world there was time.

(99) [Our] objection [to this is to say]:

(100) All this is the work of the estimation. The quickest way to rebut it is to put space in the place of time. For we would then say: "Did it lie within God's power to create the highest heaven greater in thickness by one cubit than the one He had created?" If they say, "No," this would be [the attribution to Him of] impotence. If they say, "Yes," then [it follows that God could have created it] greater by two cubits, three cubits, and so on, ascending ad infinitum. We would then say: "In this there is

الذى سمّيناه ثانيا وكان ينتهى الينا بالف ومائتّى دورة والآخر بالف
ومائة دورة وهما متساويان فى مسافة الحركة وسرعتها؟ فان قلتم، نعم،
فهو محال، اذ يستحيل أن يتساوى حركتان فى السرعة والبطء ثم تنتهيان
الى وقت واحد والاعداد متفاوتة. وان قلتم انّ العالم الثالث الذى ينتهى

٥ الينا بألف ومائتّى دورة لا يمكن ان يخلق مع العالم الثانى الذى ينتهى الينا
بالف ومائة دورة بل، لا بدّ وان يخلقه قبله بمقدار يساوى المقدار الذى
تقدّم العالم الثانى على العالم الاول، وسمّيّنا الاوّل ما هو أقرب الى وهمنا
[اذ]٢٣ ارتقينا من وقتنا اليه بالتقدير، فيكون قدر امكان هو ضعف امكان
آخر ولا بدّ من امكان آخر هو ضعف الكلّ؛ فهذا الامكان المقدّر المكمّم

١٠ الذى بعضه أطول من البعض بمقدار معلوم، لا حقيقة له الا الزمان.

(٩٨) فليست هذه الكمّيّات المقدّرة صفة ذات البارى، تعالى عن
التقدير، ولا صفة عدم العالم، اذ العدم ليس شيئا حتى يتقدّر بمقادير
مختلفة. والكمّيّة صفة، فتستدعى ذا كمّيّة. وليس ذلك الا الحركة،
والكمّيّة الا الزمان الذى هو قدر الحركة. فاذن قبل العالم عندكم شىء ذو

١٥ كمّيّة متفاوتة وهو الزمان. فقبل العالم عندكم زمان.

(٩٩) الاعتراض:

(١٠٠) انّ كلّ هذا من عمل الوهم، وأقرب طريق فى دفعه المقابلة
للزمان بالمكان. فانا نقول: هل كان فى قدرة الله أن يخلق الفلك الاعلى
فى سمكه أكبر مما خلقه بذراع؟ فان قالوا، لا، فهو تعجيز، وان قالوا،

٢٠ نعم، فبذراعين وثلاثة أذرع وكذلك يرتقى الى غير نهاية. ونقول، فى

the affirmation of a dimension beyond the world that has measure and quantity, since that which is greater by two cubits does not occupy [the equivalent space] which the [one] greater by one cubit occupies. According to this, then, beyond the world there is quantity, requiring thus that
5   which is quantified—namely, either body or the void. Hence, beyond the world there is either void or filled space. What, then, is the answer to this?" Similarly [we can ask]: "Was God able to create the world's sphere smaller by one cubit, then by two, and is there not between the two hypothetical possibilities a difference in terms of what is eliminated by way
10 of filled space and the occupation of space?" For the abolished filled space with the lessening by two cubits is greater than what is abolished with the lessening of one cubit. As such, the void would be measured.[15] But the void is nothing: how could it be measured? Our answer regarding the estimative faculty's act of making one imagine the supposition
15 of temporal possibilities before the world's existence is similar to your answer regarding the estimative faculty's act of inducing one to imagine the supposition of spatial possibilities beyond the world's existence. There is no difference [here].

(101) [The philosophers, however,] may say:

20 (102) We do not say that that which is not possible is within [divine] power. The world's being greater or smaller than it is, is impossible. Hence, it is not within [divine] power.

(103) [We answer:] This excuse is false in three respects.

(104) The first is that this is an affront to reason. For, in supposing
25 the world larger or smaller than it is by a cubit, the mind is not supposing what is akin to conjoining blackness and whiteness [in one and the same place: namely, existence and nonexistence. The impossible consists of conjoining negation and affirmation. All impossibilities reduce to this. [Your argument,] hence, is arbitrary, silly, false.

30 (105) The second is that, if the world as it is cannot be greater or smaller, then its existence as it is would be necessary, not possible. But the necessary has no need for a cause. Uphold, then, what the materialists uphold by way of denying the Maker and denying the cause that is the Cause of [all] Causes. But this is not your doctrine.

هذا اثبات بعد وراء العالم له مقدار وكمّية، اذ الاكبر بذراعين ما كان يشغل ما يشغله الاكبر بذراع. فوراء العالم بحكم هذا كمّية، فتستدعى ذا كم. وهو الجسم أو الخلاء، فوراء العالم خلاء أو ملاء. فما الجواب عنه؟ وكذلك هل كان الله قادرا على أن يخلق كرة العالم

٥ أصغر مما خلقه بذراع ثم بذراعين وهل بين التقديرين تفاوت فيما ينتفى من الملاء والشغل للاحياز؟ اذ الملاء المنتفى عند نقصان ذراعين أكثر مما ينتفى عند نقصان ذراع، فيكون الخلاء مقدّرا، والخلاء ليس بشىء، فكيف يكون مقدّرا؟ وجوابنا فى تخييل الوهم تقدير الامكانات الزمانيّة قبل وجود العالم كجوابكم فى تخييل الوهم تقدير

١٠ الامكانات المكانيّة وراء وجود العالم، ولا فرق.

(١٠١) فان قيل:

(١٠٢) نحن لا نقول ان ما ليس بممكن فهو مقدور، وكون العالم أكبر مما هو عليهِ ولا أصغر منهُ ليس بممكن، فلا يكون مقدورا.

(١٠٣) وهذا العذر باطل من ثلاثة أوجه:

١٥ (١٠٤) احدها، ان هذا مكابرة العقل، فان العقل فى تقدير العالم أكبر أو أصغر ممّا هو عليه بذراع ليس هو كتقديره الجمع بين السواد والبياض والوجود والعدم. والممتنع هو الجمع بين النفى والاثبات، واليه ترجع المحالات كلها. فهو تحكّم بارد فاسد.

(١٠٥) الثانى: انّه اذا كان العالم على ما هو عليهِ لا يمكن أن يكون

٢٠ أكبر منه ولا اصغر، فوجوده على ما هو عليه واجب لا ممكن. والواجب مستغن عن علّة. فقولوا بما قاله الدهريون من نفى الصانع ونفى سبب هو مسبب الاسباب. وليس هذا مذهبكم.

(106) The third is that the opponent is not unable to oppose this false [argument] with its like. Thus, we would say, "The world's existence prior to its existence was not possible, but existence coincided with possibility—nothing more, nothing less." Should you say that [in this case] the Eternal would have changed from power to impotence, we answer: "No, because existence then was not possible and, hence, not [enactable by] power; and the impossibility of realizing what is not possible does not indicate impotence." Should you say, "How was it impossible and how did it then become possible?" we answer, "Why should it not be impossible at one [temporal] state [and] possible at another?" Should you say, "But the [temporal] states are equal," it would be said to you, "[Spatial] magnitudes are equal; how, then, can one magnitude be possible, while one larger or smaller by the measure of a fingernail is impossible? If this, then, is not impossible, the [former] is not impossible." This, then, is the way of opposition.

(107) The verification in answering [them] is [to say that] what they have mentioned regarding the hypothesized possibilities is meaningless. What one [must] admit is that God, exalted be He, is eternal and powerful. Action is never impossible for Him, if He wills it. In all this there is nothing that necessitates affirming [a limitless] extended time, unless the estimative faculty, in its confusion, adds [to time] some other thing.

A third proof they have for the world's pre-eternity
[First discussion: Third proof]

(108) They held fast [to their view] by saying:

(109) The existence of the world is possible before its existence, since it is impossible for it to be impossible and then to become possible. This possibility has no beginning; that is, it is ever established, the world's possibility never ceasing, since there is no temporal state whatsoever in which the world's existence can be described as impossible. If, then, [this] possibility never ceases, the possible in conformity with possibility also never ceases. For the meaning of our saying that its existence is possible is that its existence is not impossible. Hence, if its existence is eternally possible,

(١٠٦) الثالث هو انّ هذا الفاسد لا يعجز الخصم عن مقابلته بمثله، فنقول: انّه لم يكن وجود العالم قبل وجوده ممكنا بل وافق الوجود الامكان من غير زيادة ولا نقصان. فان قلتم فقد انتقل القديم من القدرة الى العجز، قلنا، لا، لان الوجود لم يكن ممكنا فلم يكن مقدورا، وامتناع حصول ما ليس بممكن لا يدل على العجز. وان قلتم انّه كيف كان ممتنعا فصار ممكنا؟ قلنا: ولَم يستحيل ان يكون ممتنعا فى حال ممكنا فى حال؟ فان قلتم، الاحوال متساوية، قيل لكم، والمقادير متساوية، فكيف يكون مقدار ممكنا وأكبر منه أو أصغر بمقدار ظفر ممتنعا؟ فان لم يستحل ذلك، لم يستحل هذا. [فهذه]²⁴ طريقة المقاومة.

(١٠٧) فالتحقيق فى الجواب ان ما ذكروه من [تقدير]²⁵ الامكانات لا معنى [له]²⁶ وانما المسلّم ان الله تعالى²⁷ قديم قادر، لا يمتنع عليهِ الفعل أبدًا لو أراد؛ وليس فى هذا القدر ما يوجب اثبات زمان ممتد، الا أن يضيف الوهم بتلبيسه اليه شيئا آخر.

دليل ثالث لهم على قدم العالم

(١٠٨) تمسّكوا بان قالوا:

(١٠٩) وجود العالم ممكن قبل وجوده، اذ يستحيل أن يكون ممتنعا ثم يصير ممكنا؛ وهذا الامكان لا أوّل له، أى لم يزل ثابتا، ولم يزل العالم ممكنا وجوده، اذ لا حال من الاحوال يمكن أن يوصف العالم فيه بانّه ممتنع الوجود؛ فاذا كان الامكان لم يزل، فالممكن على وفق الامكان أيضاً لم يزل، فانّ معنى قولنا انّه ممكن وجوده، أنه ليس محالا وجوده؛ فاذا كان

its existence is eternally not impossible. Otherwise, if the impossibility of its existence is eternal, our saying that its existence is eternally possible is false. And if our statement that its existence is eternally possible is false, then our statement that the possibility never ceases is false. And, if our statement that the possibility never ceases is false, then our statement that possibility has a beginning becomes true. But, if it is true that it has a beginning, then before that it was impossible. This leads to affirming a time in which the world was impossible and over which God had no power.

(110) The objection [to this] is to say:

(111) The world [is such] that it is eternally possible for it to be temporally originated. No doubt, then, that there is no [single] moment of time but wherein its creation could not but be conceived; but, if it is supposed to exist eternally, then it would not be temporally originated. The factual, then, would not be in conformity with possibility, but contrary to it. This is similar to what you [philosophers] say about place—namely, that supposing it [to be] larger than it is or [that] creating a body above the world is possible, and likewise another on top of the latter, and so on ad infinitum. Thus, there is no limit to the possibility of increase. Despite this, the existence of filled space which is absolute, having no limit, is impossible. Similarly, an existence whose [temporal] end [in the past] is not finite is not possible. Rather, just as it is said that the possible is a body whose surface is finite, but whose measures in terms of largeness and smallness are not specified, so, too, [it is] for that whose creation in time is possible. The beginnings of existence are not specified with respect to priority and posteriority, but [it is only] the principle of being temporally created that is specified. For [the temporally created world alone] is the possible—no other.

A fourth proof
[First discussion: Fourth proof]

(112) They say:

(113) [In the case of] every temporal existent, the matter in it precedes it, since no temporal existent dispenses with matter. Matter, then, is not a temporally created [existent], the temporally created [existents] being the forms, accidents, and qualities [that occur] to materials. The

ممكنا وجوده أبدا، لم يكن محالا وجوده أبدا؛ والا فان كان محالا وجوده
أبدا، بطل قولنا انه ممكن وجوده ابدا؛ وان بطل قولنا انه ممكن وجوده
ابدا، بطل قولنا ان الامكان لم يزل؛ وان بطل قولنا ان الامكان لم يزل،
صح قولنا ان الامكان لهُ أوّل؛ واذا صحّ ان له أوّلا، كان قبل ذلك غير
ممكن؛ فيؤدى الى اثبات حال لم يكن العالم ممكنا ولا كان الله عليه قادرا. ٥

(١١٠) الاعتراض ان يقال:

(١١١) العالم لم يزل ممكن الحدوث. فلا جرم ما من وقت الا
ويتصوّر احداثه فيه. واذا قدّر موجودا ابدا، لم يكن حادثا، فلم يكن
الواقع على وفق الامكان بل خلافه. وهذا كقولهم فى المكان، وهو ان
تقدير العالم أكبر مما هو أو خلق جسم فوق العالم ممكن، وكذى آخر فوق ١٠
ذلك الآخر وهكذى الى غير نهاية. فلا نهاية لامكان الزيادة؛ ومع ذلك
فوجود ملاء مطلق لا نهاية له غير ممكن. فكذلك وجود لا ينتهى طرفه
غير ممكن بل كما يقال، الممكن جسم متناهى السطح، ولكن لا تتعيّن
مقاديره فى الكبر والصغر. فكذلك الممكن الحدوث؛ ومبادى الوجود لا
تتعيّن فى التقدّم والتأخّر، وأصل كونه حادثا متعيّن. فانّه الممكن لا غير. ١٥

دليل رابع

(١١٢) وهو انّهم قالوا:

(١١٣) كلّ حادث فالمادة التى فيه تسبقه، اذ لا يستغنى الحادث عن
مادّة؛ فلا تكون المادّة حادثة، وانما الحادث الصور والاعراض والكيفيّات

proof for this is that, prior to existence, every temporal being is either
possible in existence, impossible in existence, or necessary in existence.
It cannot be impossible, because that which in itself is impossible never
exists at all. It is impossible for it to be a necessary existent in itself, for
5   that which is necessary in itself never ceases to exist at all. This proves
that it is possible in existence in itself. Hence, the possibility of existence
obtains for it before its existence. But the possibility of existence is a
relative characterization that is not self-subsistent. It must, hence, need a
receptacle to which to relate, and there is no receptacle except matter.[16]
10 [This is just] as when we say, "This matter is receptive of heat and cold,
blackness and whiteness, or motion and rest," meaning that it is possible
for it to have these qualities originate in it and these changes occur to it.
Possibility thus becomes a description of matter. But matter does not
have matter [receptive of it], and it is, hence, impossible for it to origi-
15 nate in time. For, if it were to originate in time, then the possibility of its
existence would precede its existence and the possibility would then
be self-subsistent, not related to anything, when it is [in fact] a relative
description [and is] incomprehensible as self-subsisting.

(114) It is not possible to say that the meaning of possibility reduces
20 to its being [something] within the power [of enactment] and to the
Eternal's having the power [to enact it]. For we do not know that a thing
is within the power [of being enacted] except by its being possible. Thus,
we say, "It is within the power [of being enacted] because it is possible
and not within the power [of being enacted] because it is not possible."
25 If our statement, "It is possible," reduces to its being within the power
[of being enacted], then it is as if we have said, "It is within the power [of
being enacted] because it is within the power [of enactment] and it is
not within the power [of being enacted] because it is not within the
power [of enactment]," which is defining a thing in terms of itself. This
30 indicates that its being possible is another proposition in the mind that
is clear, in terms of which the second proposition—namely, that it is
within the power [of being enacted]—is known. It is [further] impossible
for this to reduce to the knowledge of the Eternal of its being possible.
For knowledge requires a knowable. Hence, the possibility that is known
35 is necessarily other than the knowledge. Moreover, [possibility] is a relative description. It inevitably requires an entity to which it is related.
And this is nothing other than matter. Hence, every temporally originated thing is preceded by matter. Primary matter is thus in no circumstance originated.

على المواد. وبيانه انّ كل حادث فهو قبل حدوثه لا يخلوا امّا أن يكون
ممكن الوجود، أو ممتنع الوجود، أو واجب الوجود. ومحال ان يكون
ممتنعا، لان الممتنع فى ذاته لا يوجد قطّ، ومحال ان يكون واجب الوجود
لذاته، فان الواجب لذاته لا يعدم قطّ، فدلّ انّه ممكن الوجود بذاته. فاذن

٥ امكان الوجود حاصل له قبل وجوده، وامكان الوجود وصف اضافىّ لا
قوام له بنفسه، فلا بدّ له من محلّ يضاف اليه، ولا محلّ الا المادّة، فيضاف
اليها، كما نقول: هذه المادّة قابلة للحرارة والبرودة أو السواد والبياض أو
الحركة والسكون، أى ممكن لها حدوث هذه الكيفيّات وطريان هذه
التغيّرات، فيكون الامكان وصفا للمادة. والمادة لا يكون لها مادة. فلا

١٠ يمكن أن تحدث، اذ لو حدثت لكان امكان وجودها سابقا على وجودها،
وكان الامكان قائما بنفسه غير مضاف الى شىء، مع انه وصف اضافىّ لا
يعقل قائما بنفسه.

(١١٤) ولا يمكن أن يقال ان معنى الامكان يرجع الى كونه مقدورا
وكون القديم قادرا عليهِ؛ لانا لا نعرف كون الشىء مقدورا الا بكونه
١٥ ممكنا، فنقول: هو مقدور لانّه ممكن، وليس بممكن لانّه ليس بممكن. فان
كان قولنا، هو ممكن، يرجع الى انّه مقدور، فكأنّا قلنا هو مقدور لانّه
مقدور، وليس بمقدور لانّه ليس بمقدور وهو تعريف الشىء بنفسه. فدلّ
انّ كونه ممكنا قضيّة أُخرى فى العقل ظاهرة، بها تعرف القضيّة الثانية،
وهو كونه مقدورا. ويستحيل ان يرجع ذلك الى علم القديم بكونه ممكنا.
٢٠ فانّ العلم يستدعى معلوما. فالامكان المعلوم غير العلم، لا محالة. ثم هو
وصف اضافىّ، فلا بدّ من ذات يضاف اليه، وليس الا المادّة فكلّ حادث
فقد سبقه مادّة. فلم تكن المادّة الاولى حادثة بحال.

(115) The objection [to this] is to say:

(116) The possibility which they have mentioned reverts to a judgment of the mind. Anything whose existence the mind supposes, [nothing] preventing its supposing it, we call "possible"; and, if [it is] prevented, we call [it] "impossible"; and, if it is unable to suppose its nonexistence, we name it "necessary." For these are rational propositions that do not require an existent so as to be rendered a description thereof, as proven by three things.

(117) One of them is that, if possibility requires something existing to which to relate and of which it is said that it is its possibility, then impossibility would require something existing of which one would say that it is its impossibility. But the impossible in itself has no existence, and there is no matter to which impossibility occurs such that impossibility would be [rendered] related to matter.

(118) The second is that the mind judges blackness and whiteness to be possible before their existence. If this possibility is related to the body to which they occur, so as to say, "This means that it is possible for the body to become black or white," then whiteness in itself is not possible and does not have the description of possibility. The possible would then be only the body, possibility being related to it [alone]. [To this,] then, we would say, "What is the judgment [pertaining] to blackness in itself—is it possible, necessary, or impossible?" But there is no way out of saying that it is possible. This shows that the mind, in judging possibility, does not need to posit [something] having existence to which it would relate possibility.

(119) The third is that the souls of humans, according to [the philosophers], are substances that subsist in themselves, neither in a body nor in matter, and are not imprinted in matter. [Moreover,] they are created in time, according to what Avicenna and the rigorous among [the philosophers] have chosen [to believe]. These [souls, according to them,] have [their] possibility before their creation, but they have neither entity nor matter. Their possibility, hence, is a relative description. It does not reduce to the power [to create them] of the One endowed with power and to the Agent. To what, then, does it revert? This difficulty is thus turned against them.

(١١٥) الاعتراض ان يقال:

(١١٦) الامكان الذى ذكروه يرجع الى قضاء العقل. فكل ما قدّر العقل وجوده، فلم يمتنع عليهِ تقديرُه، سمّيناه ممكناً، وان امتنع سمّيناه مستحيلا، وان لم يقدر على تقدير عدمه سميناه واجبا. فهذه قضايا عقليّة لا تحتاج الى موجود حتّى تجعل وصفاً له، بدليل ثلاثة امور:

(١١٧) أحدها ان الامكان لو استدعى شيئا موجودا يضاف اليه ويقال انّه امكانه لاستدعى الامتناعُ شيئا موجودا يقال انّه امتناعه. وليس للممتنع وجود فى ذاته، ولا مادّة يطرى عليها المحال حتّى يضاف الامتناع الى المادّة.

(١١٨) والثانى أن السواد والبياض يقضى العقل فيهما قبل وجودهما بكونهما ممكنين؛ فان كان هذا الامكان مضافا الى الجسم الذى يطريان عليه حتى يقال معناه ان هذا الجسم يمكن أن يسوّد وان يبيضّ، فاذن ليس البياض فى نفسه ممكنا ولا له نعت الامكان، وانّما الممكن الجسم، والامكان مضاف اليه. فنقول: ما حكم نفس السواد فى ذاته، أهو ممكن او واجب أو ممتنع؟ ولا بدّ من القول بانّه ممكن؛ فدلّ انّ العقل فى القضية بالامكان لا يفتقر الى وضع ذات موجود يضيف اليه الامكان.

(١١٩) والثالث انّ نفوس الآدميين عندهم جواهر قائمة بانفسها ليس بجسم ومادّة ولا [منطبعة]٢٨ فى مادّة؛ وهى حادثة على ما اختاره ابن سينا والمحقّقون منهم. ولها امكان قبل حدوثها، وليس لها ذات ولا مادّة. فامكانها وصف اضافىّ، ولا يرجع الى قدرة القادر والى الفاعل. فإلى ماذا يرجع؟ فينقلب عليهم هذا الاشكال.

(120) [The philosophers, however,] may say:

(121) Reducing possibility to the judgment of the mind is impossible, since there is no meaning to the judgment of the mind except knowledge of possibility. Possibility is, hence, known, and it is other than knowledge. Rather, knowledge encompasses it, follows it, and relates to it as it is.[17] If knowledge is supposed to cease, the object of knowledge does not cease; whereas if the object of knowledge ceases to exist, knowledge [of it] ceases. Hence, knowledge and its object are two [distinct] things; one follows, [and] the other is followed. If we [were to] suppose rational people [to] desist from supposing possibility and [to] be unaware of it, we would say, "Possibility is not removed, the possibles being, rather, [possible] in themselves; but the minds are oblivious of them." Or, [if we suppose] minds and rational people to cease to exist, possibility would inevitably remain.

(122) As regards the three things, these do not entail a [valid] argument. For impossibility is also a relative description that requires an existent to which it would relate. The meaning of the impossible is the [simultaneous] combining of two opposites [in one place]. Thus, if the receptacle is white, it would be impossible for it to become black with the [continued] existence of white. Hence, there must be a subject to which one refers, qualified with a description, and [it is] then that it is said: "Its opposite is impossible for it to have." Impossibility would thus be a relative description subsisting in the subject to which it is related. As for necessity, it is no hidden matter that it relates to necessary existence.

(123) As for the second—namely, blackness being in itself possible— this is an error. For, if it is taken in abstraction without a receptacle in which it inheres, it would be impossible, not possible. It only becomes possible when it is reckoned as an appearance[18] in a body. The body is disposed for the interchange of appearance, interchange [of appearances] over the body being possible. Otherwise, blackness has no identity unto itself so as to have possibility ascribed to it.

(124) With regards to the third—namely, the soul—for some it is eternal but has the possibility of attaching to bodies. Thus, with respect to this [doctrine, what you say] does not necessarily follow. Among those who admit its temporal origination, one group has believed that it is

(١٢٠) فان قيل:

(١٢١) ردّ الامكان الى قضاء العقل محال، اذ لا معنى لقضاء العقل الا العلم بالامكان. فالامكان معلوم وهو غير العلم بل العلم يحيط به ويتبعه ويتعلق به على ما هو. والعلم لو قدّر عدمه، لم ينعدم المعلوم، والمعلوم اذا قدّر انتفاؤه، انتفى العلم. فالعلم والمعلوم أمران اثنان أحدهما تابع والآخر متبوع. ولو قدّرنا إعراض العقلاء عن تقدير الامكان وغفلتهم عنه، لكنّا نقول: لا يرتفع الامكان، بل الممكنات فى أنفسها، ولكن العقول غفلت عنها؛ أو عدمت العقول والعقلاء فيبقى الامكان لا محالة.

(١٢٢) وأمّا الامور الثلاثة، فلا حجّة فيها. فان الامتناع أيضاً وصف اضافىّ يستدعى موجودا يضاف اليه. ومعنى الممتنع الجمع بين الضدّين، فاذا كان المحلّ أبيض، كان ممتنعا عليه أن يسوّد مع وجود البياض، فلا بدّ من موضوع يشار اليه، موصوف بصفة، فعند ذلك يقال: ضدّه ممتنع عليه. فيكون الامتناع وصفا اضافيّا قائما بموضوع مضافا اليه. واما الوجوب فلا يخفى انه مضاف الى الوجود الواجب.

(١٢٣) وأمّا الثانى، وهو كون السواد فى نفسه ممكنا، فغلط. فانّه ان أخذ مجرّدا دون محلّ يحلّه، كان ممتنعا لا ممكنا، وانّما يصير ممكنا اذا قدّر هيئة فى جسم. فالجسم مهيّأً لتبدّل هيئة، والتبدّل ممكن على الجسم، والا فليس للسواد نفس مفردة حتى يوصف بامكان.

(١٢٤) وأمّا الثالث، وهو النفس، فهى قديمة عند فريق ولكن ممكن لها التعلّق بالابدان، فلا يلزم على هذا. ومن سلّم حدوثه، فقد اعتقد فريق

imprinted in matter, consequent upon [the bodily] humors, as Galen has indicated in certain places. As such, [the soul] would be in matter and its possibility related to its matter.

(125) With respect to the doctrine of those who admit that it is temporally originated but is not imprinted [in matter], this means that matter has the possibility of being managed by a rational soul. The possibility that precedes origination would thus be related to matter. For, although not imprinted in [matter, the soul] has a relation to it, since it is that which governs and uses it. Possibility would thus refer back to [matter] in this way.

(126) The answer [to all this is to say]:

(127) To refer possibility, necessity, and impossibility back to rational judgments is correct. [In reference] to what has been mentioned—namely, that the meaning of the mind's judgment is [its] knowledge and that knowledge requires an object of knowledge—we say: "[Modality as a judgment of the mind] has an object of knowledge in the same way that being a color, animality, and the rest of the universal propositions are, according to them, fixed in the mind, these being cognitions that are not said to have no objects of knowledge." Yet the objects of their knowledge have no existence in the concrete—so [much so] that the philosophers have declared that universals exist in the mind, not in the concrete: what exist in the concrete are only individual particulars that are perceived by the senses, not conceived, but are the cause for the mind's snatching from them an intellectual proposition, abstracted from matter. Hence, being a color is a single proposition in the mind, other than blackness and whiteness. One cannot conceive in existence a color which is neither white nor black nor some other color. The form of being a color, however, is established in the mind without detailing [different species of color], and one says of it that it is a form whose existence is in minds, not in concrete things. If this is not impossible, then what we have mentioned is not impossible.

(128) As for their saying that, if one supposes the nonexistence of rational beings or their unawareness [of possibility], possibility would not cease, we say: "If their nonexistence is supposed, would the universal propositions—namely, genera and species—cease to exist?" If they say, "Yes, since they have no meaning except as propositions in the mind,"

منهم انّه منطبع فى المادّة تابع للمزاج على ما دلّ عليه كلام جالينوس فى بعض المواضع فتكون فى مادّة وامكانها مضاف الى مادّتها.

(١٢٥) وعلى مذهب من سلّم انها حادثة وليست منطبعة، فمعناه ان المادّة ممكن لها ان يدبّرها نفس ناطقة، فيكون الامكان السابق على الحدوث مضافا الى المادّة. فانّها وان لم تنطبع فيها فلها علاقة معها اذ هى المدبّرة المستعملة لها. فيكون الامكان راجعا اليها بهذا الطريق.

(١٢٦) والجواب:

(١٢٧) انّ ردّ الامكان والوجوب والامتناع الى قضايا عقلية صحيح؛ وما ذكر بانّ معنى قضاء العقل علم والعلم يستدعى معلوما فنقول: له معلوم، كما انّ اللونيّة والحيوانيّة وسائر القضايا الكلّيّة ثابتة فى العقل عندهم وهى علوم لا يقال لا معلوم لها، ولكن لا وجود لمعلوماتها فى الاعيان، حتى صرّح الفلاسفة بان الكلّيّات موجودة فى الاذهان، لا فى الاعيان، وانّما الموجود فى الاعيان جزئيّات شخصيّة، وهى محسوسة غير معقولة، ولكنّها سبب لأن ينتزع العقل منها قضيّة مجرّدة عن المادّة عقليّة. فاذن اللونيّة قضيّة مفردة فى العقل سوى السواديّة والبياضيّة. ولا يتصوّر فى الوجود لون ليس بسواد ولا بياض ولا غيره من الالوان، ويثبت فى العقل صورة اللونيّة من غير تفصيل، ويقال هى صورة وجودها فى الاذهان لا فى الاعيان. فان لم يمتنع هذا لم يمتنع ما ذكرناه.

(١٢٨) أمّا قولهم لو قدّر عدم العقلاء أو غفلتهم ما كان الامكان ينعدم فنقول: ولو قدّر عدمهم، هل كانت القضايا الكلّيّة، وهى الاجناس والانواع، تنعدم؟ فاذا قالوا، نعم، اذ لا معنى لها الا قضيّة فى العقول،

then this is what we would say about possibility, there being no difference
between the two cases. If, however, they claim that they remain in the
knowledge of God, the same would be said of possibility. The necessary
consequence [forced on them] hence obtains. What is intended [here] is
to show the contradiction of their words.

(129) As for [their] excuse regarding impossibility—namely, that it is
[always] related to matter qualified by something, the opposite of which is
prevented from [being with] it—this is not the case with everything that
is impossible. For the existence of a partner to God is impossible when
there is no matter to which [this] impossibility would be related. Should
they claim that the meaning of the impossibility of a partner is [simply]
that the singularity of God, exalted be He, in His essence and His being
alone, are necessary, singularity being related to Him, we would say:

(130) [This singularity] is not necessary, according to their principles.
For the world [they maintain] coexists with Him. He is, thus, not solitary.
If they claim that His being singularly set aside from a similar [being] is
necessary, the opposite of the necessary being the impossible, which is a
relation to Him, we say: "We mean that God's being set aside from [the
world] is not akin to His being set aside from the similar. For His being
set aside from the similar is necessary, whereas His being set aside from
the created contingent things is not necessary." We thus undertake relating possibility to Him by this device,[19] as they have undertaken it in
returning impossibility to His essence by changing the expression
"impossibility" to "necessity," then relating singularity to Him using the
qualification "necessary."

(131) As for the excuse regarding blackness and whiteness—namely,
that they have neither a singular self nor essence—the answer is, "Yes,"
if by this is meant in [extramental] existence. If, however, they mean by
this in the mind, then [the answer is], "No." For the mind apprehends
universal blackness and judges it to be in itself possible.

(132) Furthermore, the excuse regarding the created souls is false.
For they have singular entities and a possibility preceding [their] origination. But there is nothing [material] to which this [possibility] relates.
[Regarding] their statement that matter [is such] that it is possible for
it to be governed by the soul, this is a far-fetched relation. If you find
this sufficient, then it would not be far-fetched to say that the meaning
of the possibility of the created [souls] is that it is possible within the
realm of the One capable of creating them to create them. [Possibility]
would thus be a relation [belonging] to the Agent without its being
imprinted in Him, in the same way as it would be [for the philosophers]

فكذلك قولنا فى الامكان، ولا فرق بين البابين. وان زعموا انّها تكون باقية فى علم الله، فكذى القول فى الامكان. فالالزام واقع، والمقصود اظهار تناقض كلامهم.

(١٢٩) وأمّا العذر عن الامتناع بانّه مضاف الى المادّة الموصوفة بالشىء اذ يمتنع عليه ضدّه، فليس كلّ محال كذلك؛ فانّ وجود شريك لله محال، وليس ثم مادّة يضاف اليها الامتناع. فان زعموا انّ معنى استحالة الشريك انّ انفراد الله تعالى بذاته وتوحّده واجب، والانفراد مضاف اليه، فنقول:

(١٣٠) ليس بواجب [على اصلهم؛][٢٩] فانّ العالم موجود معه، فليس منفردا. فان زعموا ان انفراده عن النظير واجب ونقيض الواجب ممتنع وهو اضافة اليه، قلنا: نعنى انّ انفراد الله عنها ليس كانفراده عن النظير؛ فانّ انفراده عن النظير واجب، وانفراده عن المخلوقات الممكنة غير واجب. فنتكلّف اضافة الامكان اليه بهذه الحيلة، كما تكلّفوه فى ردّ الامتناع الى ذاته بقلب عبارة الامتناع الى الوجوب، ثم باضافة الانفراد اليه بنعت الوجوب.

(١٣١) وأمّا العذر عن السواد والبياض بانه لا نفس له ولا ذات منفردا، ان عنى بذلك فى الوجود، فنعم، وان عنى بذلك فى العقل، فلا؛ فانّ العقل يعقل السواد الكلّىّ وبحكم عليه بالامكان فى ذاته.

(١٣٢) ثم العذر باطل بالنفوس الحادثة. فانّ لها ذواتا مفردة وامكانا سابقا على الحدوث، وليس ثمّ ما يضاف اليه. وقولهم ان المادّة ممكن لها ان يدبّرها النفس، فهذه اضافة بعيدة. فان اكتفيتم بهذا، فلا يبعد ان يقال معنى امكان الحادث ان القادر عليها يمكن فى حقّه ان يحدثها؛ فيكون اضافة الى الفاعل مع انّه ليس منطبعا فيه، كما انّه اضافة الى البدن المنفعل

a relation to the body receptive of action, even though it is not imprinted
in it. There is no difference between the relation to the agent and the
relation to the patient if there is no imprinting in either case.

(133) If it is said, "In all the objections, you have relied on counter-
acting difficulties by [raising other] difficulties, without solving any
of the problematic [the philosophers] have brought with them," we say:

(134) The objection necessarily shows the falsity of the argumentation.
The problematic facet is resolved in evaluating the objection and what is
being demanded [of the opponent]. In this book we have undertaken
only to muddy their doctrine and throw dust in the face of their proofs
with that which would reveal their incoherence. We have not undertaken
to defend a specific doctrine and thus have not departed from the purpose of this book. We will not go exhaustively into the proofs for the
[world's] temporal creation, since our purpose is to refute their claim
that they have knowledge of [its] pre-eternity. As regards affirming the
true doctrine, we will write another book concerning it after completing
this one, if success comes to our aid, God willing, and we will name it *The
Principles of Belief*.[20] In it we will devote ourselves to affirming, just as in
this work we have devoted ourselves to destroying; and God knows best.

مع انّه لا ينطبع فيه. ولا فرق بين النسبة الى الفاعل والنسبة الى المنفعل اذا لم يكن انطباع فى الموضعين.

(١٣٣) فان قيل: فقد عوّلتم فى جميع الاعتراضات على مقابلة الإشكالات بالاشكالات، و لم تحلّوا ما أوردوه من الاشكال، قلنا:

(١٣٤) المعارضة تبيّن فساد الكلام لا محالة وينحلّ وجه الاشكال فى تقدير المعارضة والمطالبة. ونحن لم نلتزم فى هذا الكتاب الا تكدير مذهبهم والتغيير فى وجوه أدلّتهم بما نبيّن تهافتهم. و لم نتطرق للذبّ عن مذهب معيّن، فلم نخرج لذلك عن مقصود الكتاب. ولانستقصى القول فى الادلّة الدالّة على الحدث اذ غرضنا ابطال دعواهم معرفة القدم. واما اثبات المذهب الحق، فسنصنّف فيهِ كتاباً بعد الفراغ من هذا، ان ساعد التوفيق، ان شاءَ الله، ونسميه قواعد العقائد، ونعتنى فيه بالاثبات كما اعتنينا فى هذا الكتاب بالهدم، والله أعلم.

[Second] Discussion

On refuting their statement on the
post-eternity of the world, time, and motion

(1) Let it be known that this question is a branch of the first. For, according to them, just as the world is pre-eternal, having no beginning for its existence, it is [also] post-eternal, having no end, its corruption and annihilation being inconceivable. Rather, it has always continued [to be] in this way, and in this way it will also continue [to be].

(2) Their four proofs for the [world's] pre-eternity which we have mentioned are applicable to its post-eternity, and the objection [to them] is the same, without difference. For they say that the world is caused, its cause being eternal in the past and the future, the effect thus [coexisting] with the cause. They [also] say that, if the cause does not change, the effect does not change; and on this [premise] they built [the proof] for the impossibility of the world's temporal origination. This very [argument] is applicable to [the argument for] the [world's not] coming to an end. This is their first approach.

(3) Their second approach is to argue that, if the world is annihilated, its annihilation would take place after its existence. It would thus have an "after," and this entails the affirmation of time.

(4) Their third approach is that the possibility of existence never ceases. Similarly, possible existence can be[1] [eternal] in conformity with [ceaseless] possibility. This proof, however, has no strength. For we maintain that it is impossible for it to be pre-eternal but do not hold it impossible for it to be post-eternal if God, exalted be He, makes it endure everlastingly. For it is not a necessary requirement for that which is temporally originated that it should have an end, whereas it is a necessary requirement of the act to be temporally originated and have a beginning. No one maintains that the world should necessarily have an

مسئلة

فى ابطال قولهم فى ابديّة العالم والزمان والحركة

(١) ليعلم ان هذه المسئلة فرع الاولى؛ فانّ العالم عندهم كما انّه أزلىّ لا بداية لوجوده، فهو أبدىّ لا نهاية لآخره، ولا يتصوّر فساده وفناؤه، بل لم يزل كذلك ولا يزال أيضاً كذلك.

(٢) وادلّتهم الاربعة التى ذكرناها فى الازليّة جارية فى الابديّة، والاعتراض كالاعتراض من غير فرق. فانّهم يقولون انّ العالم معلول، علّته أزليّة ابديّة، فكان المعلول مع العلّة. ويقولون: اذا لم تتغير العلّة لم يتغير المعلول. وعليهِ بنوا منع الحدوث؛ وهو بعينه جار فى الانقطاع. وهذا مسلكهم الاول.

(٣) ومسلكهم الثانى انّ العالم اذا عدم، فيكون عدمه بعد وجوده، فيكون له بعد؛ ففيه اثبات الزمان.

(٤) ومسلكهم الثالث انّ امكان الوجود لا ينقطع، فكذلك الوجود الممكن يجوز ان يكون على وفق الامكان. الا ان هذا الدليل لا يقوى. فانّا نحيل ان يكون أزليّا ولا نحيل أن يكون أبديّا لو أبقاه الله تعالى أبدا، اذ ليس من ضرورة الحادث ان يكون له آخر، ومن ضرورة الفعل ان يكون حادثا وان يكون له أول. ولم يوجب ان يكون للعالم لا محالة آخر

٤٧

end except Abū al-Hudhayl al-ʿAllaf.[2] For he said: "Just as an infinite
number of past [heavenly] rotations is impossible, the same is true of the
future." But this is false, because the future does not enter at all into
existence, either successively or concomitantly, whereas all of the past
5   has entered into existence successively, even though not concomitantly.
And, if it has become evident that we do not deem it rationally remote
for the world's duration to be everlasting, but regard either its rendering
it eternal in the future or annihilating it as [both] possible, then which of
the two possibilities becomes fact is only known through the revealed
10   law. Hence, the examination of this [question] is not connected with
what is rationally apprehended.

(5) As for their fourth approach, it runs [a course parallel to their
fourth proof of the world's pre-eternity]. For they say that, if the world is
annihilated, the possibility of its existence remains, since the possible
15   does not change into the impossible. But [possibility] is a relational
description. Hence, every temporal existent, as they claim, needs a previous matter, and every annihilated thing needs matter from which it is
annihilated. For materials and principles are not annihilated. It is only
the forms and accidents inherent in them that are annihilated.

20   (6) The answer to all this is identical with what has been previously
stated [in refuting their doctrine of a pre-eternal world]. We have only
singled out this problem [for additional discussion] because they have
two other proofs regarding it.

(7) The first is that to which Galen has held fast inasmuch as he said:
25   (8) If the sun, for example, were receptive of annihilation, then in
[the course of] a long period of time some withering would have appeared
in it. But the astronomical observations indicating its size, [carried out]
in the course of thousands of years, indicate only this [same] size. Hence,
inasmuch as it has not withered throughout these lengthy ages, [this]
30   shows that it will not be corrupted.

(9) The objection to this [is raised] from several perspectives.

(10) The first is that the form of the proof is expressed by saying:
"If the sun will be corrupted, then it must undergo withering." But the
consequent is impossible; hence, the antecedent is impossible. This is a
35   syllogism termed by them "the [hypothetical] conjunctive conditional."
This conclusion, however, does not follow necessarily because the antecedent is not true unless another condition is added—namely, his [hav-
ing] to say that, if [something] is corrupted, then it must wither. This
latter does not follow from the first premise except with the addition of

الا أبو الهذيل العلّاف. فانّه قال: كما يستحيل فى الماضى دورات لا نهاية لها، فكذلك فى المستقبل. وهو فاسد، لانّ كلّ المستقبل قطّ لا يدخل فى الوجود، لا متلاحقا ولا متساوقا، والماضى قد دخل كله فى الوجود متلاحقا، وان لم يكن متساوقا. واذا تبين انّا لا نبعد بقاء العالم أبدا من حيث العقل بل نجوّز ابقاءه وافناءه، فانّما يعرف الواقع من قسمَى الممكن بالشرع. فلا يتعلّق النظر فيه بالمعقول.

(٥) وامّا مسلكهم الرابع فهو جار. لأنّهم يقولون اذا عدم العالم، بقى امكان وجوده، اذ الممكن لا ينقلب مستحيلا، وهو وصف اضافىّ، فيفتقر كل حادث بزعمهم الى مادّة سابقة وكل منعدم فيفتقر الى مادّة ينعدم عنها. فالموادّ والاصول لا تنعدم، وانما تنعدم الصور والاعراض الحالَّة فيها.

(٦) والجواب عن الكل ما سبق. وانّما أفردنا هذه المسئلة لانّ لهم فيها دليلين آخرين.

(٧) والاوّل ما تمسّك به جالينوس اذ قال:

(٨) لو كان الشمس مثلا تقبل الانعدام، لظهر فيها ذبول فى مدة مديدة، والارصاد الدالّة على مقدارها منذ آلاف سنين لا تدلّ الا على هذا المقدار. فلمّا لم تذبل فى هذه الآماد الطولة، دلّ انّها لا تفسد.

(٩) الاعتراض عليه من وجوه:

(١٠) الاوّل، انّ شكل هذا الدليل ان يقال: ان [كانت][1] الشمس تفسد، فلا بدّ وان يلحقها ذبول؛ لكن التالى محال؛ فالمقدّم محال. وهو قياس يسمى عندهم الشرطى المتصل. وهذه النتيجة غير لازمة، لان المقدّم غير صحيح ما لم يُضَفْ اليه شرط آخر وهو قوله، ان [كانت][2] تفسد، فلا بدّ وان تذبل. فهذا التالى لا يلزم هذا المقدّم الا بزيادة شرط وهو ان نقول:

a condition—namely, that we say, "If it is to be corrupted by way of withering, then it must wither in the long period of time," or if it is shown
that there is no corruption except by way of withering so [as to have] the
consequent necessarily follow [from] the antecedent. But we do not concede that a thing is corrupted only by way of withering. Rather, withering
is but one way of [a thing's] corruption. It is not improbable for a thing,
when in its state of perfection, to be corrupted suddenly [all at once].

(11) The second is that, even if this is conceded—namely, that there
can be no corruption except through withering—how would [Galen]
know that no withering afflicted [the sun]? As to his turning to astronomical observations, it is impossible [for these to yield such information],
since they only give knowledge of the size [of the sun] by approximation.
Should the sun—which is said to be a hundred and seventy times larger
than the earth, or close to this—be diminished by the size of mountains,
for example, this would not be apparent to the senses. Thus, it may well
be undergoing a process of withering and [may] have been, up till now,
diminished by the amount of [several] mountains and more. The senses,
however, would have been unable to apprehend this because estimating
[such an amount] is known in the science of optics only by approximation.
This is similar to the case of rubies and gold, which, according to [the
philosophers], are composed of elements and are subject to corruption.
If, then, a ruby is placed [somewhere] for a hundred years, what diminished of it would be imperceptible. Perhaps the ratio of what diminishes
from the sun during the period of the history of astronomical observations
is the same as what diminishes of the ruby in a hundred years, this being
something imperceptible. This shows that his proof is exceedingly bad.

(12) We have refrained from introducing many a proof of this kind,
which rational people find feeble, bringing forth this one [only] to pro-
vide a lesson and [as] an example of what we have left out. We have confined ourselves to the four proofs that require exertion in resolving their
sophistical difficulties, as we have seen.

(13) The second proof they have for the impossibility of the world's
annihilation consists in their saying:

(14) The substances of the world never cease to exist because a cause
for their annihilation is not rationally comprehensible. That which had
not been nonexistent and then becomes nonexistent would inevitably
have become [nonexistent] due to a cause. This cause would have had to

ان [كانت]٣ تفسد فسادا ذبوليًّا فلا بدّ وان تذبل فى طول المدة، أو يبيّن انّه لا فساد الا بطريق الذبول، حتّى يلزم التالى للمقدّم. ولا نسلّم انّه لا يفسد الشىء الا بالذبول؛ بل الذبول احد وجوه الفساد. ولا يبعد ان يفسد الشىء بغتة وهو على حال كماله.

(١١) الثانى، انّه لو سلّم له هذا وانّه لا فساد الا بالذبول، فمن أين عرف انّه ليس يعتريها الذبول؟ وامّا التفاته الى الارصاد، فمحال، لانّها لا تعرّف مقاديرها الا بالتقريب. والشمس التى يقال انها كالارض مائة وسبعين مرّة أو ما يقرب منه، لو نقص منها مقدار جبال مثلا، لكان لا يتبين للحس. فلعلّها فى الذبول والى الآن قد نقص مقدار جبال وأكثر، والحس لا يقدر على ان يدرك ذلك لانّ تقديره فى علم المناظر لم يعرف الا بالتقريب. وهذا كما انّ الياقوت والذهب مركّبان من العناصر عندهم وهى قابلة للفساد، ثم لو وضع ياقوت مائة سنة، لم يكن نقصانه محسوسا. فلعلّ نسبة ما ينقص من الشمس فى مدّة تاريخ الارصاد كنسبة ما ينقص من الياقوت فى مائة سنة، وذلك لا يظهر للحس. فدلّ انّ دليله فى غاية الفساد.

(١٢) وقد أعرضنا عن إيراد أدلّة كثيرة من هذا الجنس يستركّها العقلاء، وأوردنا هذا الواحد ليكون عبرة ومثالا لما تركناه، واقتصرنا على الادلّة الاربعة التى يحتاج الى تكلّف فى حلّ شبهها كما سبق.

(١٣) الدليل الثانى لهم فى استحالة عدم العالم ان قالوا:

(١٤) العالم لا تنعدم جواهره لانّه لا يعقل سبب معدم [لها]٤، وما لم يكن منعدما ثم انعدم فلا بدّ وان يكون بسبب. وذلك السبب لا يخلوا

be either the will of the Eternal (an impossibility, since, if He were not a willer of [the world's] annihilation and then became a willer of it, He would have changed); or this may lead to the consequence that the Eternal and His will are of the same description in all states, but that the object of the will would change from nonexistence to existence, then from existence to nonexistence. But what we have stated of the impossibility of the existence of a temporal event through an eternal will proves the impossibility of the [world's future] annihilation.

(15) There is here, moreover, an additional difficulty, stronger than this—namely, that the thing willed is necessarily the act of the willer. [In the case of] anyone who was not acting and then becomes an actor, even if he were not to change in himself, his act would [still] necessarily have come into existence after being nonexistent. For if [the agent] remains as he had been, having not acted and now also not acting, he would then not have enacted a thing. Nonexistence is not a thing. How could it then be an act? If, then, He annihilates the world and an act which did not previously exist comes anew for Him, what, then, is this act? Is it the world's existence? But this is impossible, since [its] existence would have ceased. Or is His act the nonexistence of the world? But the nonexistence of the world is not a thing so as to be an act. For the least degree of an act is for it to be existing. But the nonexistence of the world is not a thing that exists so as to say that it is the thing which the agent enacted and which was brought into existence by the One who brings about existence.

(16) Due to the difficulty posed by this, [the philosophers] claimed, the theologians, in striving to disengage from it, have divided into four groups, each group committing an impossible [absurdity].

(17) As for the Muᶜtazila, they said: "His act that proceeds from Him exists, [this] being annihilation, which He creates in no place. The whole world then ceases to exist all at once, and the created annihilation ceases to exist by itself so as not to require another annihilation [to annihilate it, and so on,] leading to an infinite regress."

(18) This [argument, the philosophers continue,] is false in several respects. One of them is that "annihilation" is not an existent that is rationally comprehensible such that one [can] hypothesize its creation. Moreover, if it were an existent, how is it, then, that it would cease to exist by itself without an annihilator? Again, by what would the world be annihilated? For, if [annihilation] were to be created in the world itself and indwell therein, this would be impossible. This is because what inheres

امّا ان يكون ارادة القديم، وهو محال لانّه اذا لم يكن مريدا لعدمه ثم صار مريدا فقد تغيّر، أو يؤدّى الى ان يكون القديم وارادته على نعت واحد فى جميع الاحوال، والمراد يتغير من العدم الى الوجود ثم من الوجود الى العدم. وما ذكرناه من استحالة وجود حادث بارادة قديمة يدلّ على

٥ استحالة العدم.

(١٥) ويزيد هاهنا اشكال آخر اقوى من ذلك، وهو انّ المراد فعل المريد لا محالة، وكلّ من لم يكن فاعلا ثم صار فاعلا، فان لم يتغيّر هو فى نفسه، فلا بدّ وان يصير فعله موجودا بعد ان لم يكن موجودا. فانّه لو بقى كما كان، اذ لم يكن له فعل، والآن أيضا لا فعل له، فاذن لم يفعل شيئا.

١٠ والعدم ليس بشىء، فكيف يكون فعلا؟ واذا أعدم العالم وتجدّد له فعل لم يكن، فما ذلك الفعل؟ أهو وجود العالم؟ وهو محال اذ انقطع الوجود. أو فعله عدم العالم؟ وعدم العالم ليس بشىء حتى يكون فعلا؛ فانّ أقلّ درجات الفعل ان يكون موجودا، وعدم العالم ليس شيئا موجودا حتّى يقال هو الذى فعله الفاعل وأوجده الموجد.

١٥ (١٦) ولاشكال هذا، زعموا افترق المتكلّمون فى التفصّى عن هذا أربع فرق وكل فرقة اقتحمت محالا.

(١٧) اما المعتزلة فانهم قالوا: فعله الصادر منه موجود، وهو الفناء، يخلقه لا فى محلّ. فينعدم كلٍ العالم دفعة واحدة وينعدم الفناء المخلوق بنفسه، حتّى لا يحتاج الى فناء آخر، فيتسلسل الى غير نهاية.

٢٠ (١٨) وهو فاسد من وجوه. أحدها ان الفناء ليس موجودا معقولا حتّى يقدّر خلقه؛ ثم ان كان موجودا، فلم ينعدم بنفسه من غير معدم؟ ثم [بما]ه يعدم العالم، فانّه ان خلق فى ذات العالم وحلّ فيه فهو مُحالٌ، لان

meets the receptacle, so that they combine, even if for but one moment. But, if their combining is possible, they would not be two contraries, and [the created annihilation] would not annihilate [the world]. If [on the other hand] He were to create [annihilation] neither in the world nor in a receptacle, then how would its existence oppose the world's existence? Then there is an additional repugnancy in this doctrine—namely, that God is incapable of annihilating some of the world's substances but not others. Indeed, He would be capable only of bringing about an annihilation that annihilates the whole world. For, if [annihilation] is not in any place, then its relation to [each of] the totality [of things] is of one pattern.[3]

(19) The second party is the Karrāmiyya, inasmuch as they have said that His act is [the act of] annihilation, annihilation being, in effect, an existent which He creates in His own essence—may He be exalted above what they say—through which the world becomes annihilated. Similarly, existence, according to them, [takes place] through an act of bringing existence into being which He creates in Himself, whereby that which [would] exist through [such an act] becomes an existent. This is also false, since it entails the Eternal's being a receptacle of temporal happenings. Moreover, it is a departure from what is intelligible, since the only thing comprehensible about an act that brings about existence is that the existent [it produces] is related to Will and Power. Hence, to affirm anything other than Will and Power and the existence of the enactable by Power— namely, the world—is unintelligible. The same applies to annihilation.

(20) The third group are the Ash^carites, who said: "Regarding the accidents, these cease to exist by themselves, their enduring being inconceivable. For, if their enduring is conceivable, then their annihilation becomes inconceivable for this [very] meaning.[4] As for substances, they do not endure by themselves but endure by virtue of an endurance which is additional to their existence. If God does not create endurance, [the substance] is annihilated due to the nonexistence of that which renders it enduring."

(21) This is also false, for it entails a contradiction of what is perceived by the senses [when it maintains that] blackness does not endure—likewise whiteness—and that [their] existence is constantly renewed. The mind is repelled by this as it is repelled by someone's statement that the existence of the body at every moment is [continually] renewed. The mind that judges the hair on the head of a human at one day to be identical [with the hair] that was there the previous day, [and] not its replica, makes the same judgment regarding the blackness of the hair. To this there is another difficulty—namely, that, if the enduring endures by virtue of an endurance, it follows necessarily that the divine

الحالّ يلاقى المحلول فيجتمعان، ولو فى لحظة. فاذا جاز اجتماعهما لم [يكونا ضدّين]، فلم يفنِه. وان خلقه لا فى العالم ولا فى محلّ، فمن أين يضادّ وجوده وجود العالم؟ ثم فى هذا المذهب شناعة اخرى، وهو انّ الله لا يقدر على اعدام بعض جواهر العالم دون بعض؛ بل لا يقدر الا على احداث فناء يعدم العالم كلّه. لانّها اذا لم تكن فى محلّ، كان نسبتها الى الكلّ على وتيرة.

(١٩) الفرقة الثانية الكرّاميّة حيث قالوا انّ فعله الاعدام، والاعدام عبارة عن موجود يحدثه فى ذاته، تعالى عن قولهم، فيصير العالم به معدوما. وكذلك الوجود عندهم بايجاد يحدثه فى ذاته، فيصير الموجود به موجودا. وهذا أيضا فاسد، اذ فيه كون القديم محلّ الحوادث؛ ثم خروج عن المعقول، اذ لا يعقل من الايجاد الا وجود منسوب الى ارادة وقدرة. فاثبات شىء آخر سوى الارادة والقدرة ووجود المقدور، وهو العالم، لا يعقل وكذى الإعدام.

(٢٠) الفرقة الثالثة الاشعريّة اذ قالوا: امّا الأعراض فانّها تفنى بانفسها ولا يتصوّر بقاؤها؛ لانّه لو تصوّر بقاؤها، لما تصوّر فناؤها لهذا المعنى. وأمّا الجواهر فليست باقية بانفسها ولكنّها باقية ببقاء زائد على وجودها؛ فاذا لم يخلق الله البقاء انعدم لعدم المبقى.

(٢١) وهو أيضا فاسد لما فيه من مناكرة المحسـوس فى انّ السواد لا يبقى، والبياض كذلك، وانّه متجدد الوجود. والعقل ينبو عن هذا كما ينبو عن قول القائل انّ الجسم متجدّد الوجود فى كل حالة. والعقل القاضى بانّ الشعر الذى على رأس الانسان فى يوم هو الشعر الذى كان بالامس، لا مثله، يقضى أيضا بهِ فى سواد الشعر. ثم فيه إشكال آخر وهو

attributes would have to endure through an endurance, this [latter] endurance being [something] enduring and, hence, requiring [yet] another endurance, this regressing infinitely.

(22) The fourth party is another group of Ashᶜarites, inasmuch as they said that the accidents cease to exist by themselves, while the substances are annihilated in that God does not create in them motion and rest, combination and separation. It is impossible for a body which is neither in motion nor at rest to endure, and, hence, it becomes annihilated.⁵ It is as though both Ashᶜarite groups, inasmuch as they did not conceive nonexistence to be an act, inclined [to the view] that annihilation is not an act, but only the refraining from action.

(23) If these methods [for explaining the world's annihilation] are false, [the philosophers argue,] then there remains no way for upholding the possibility of annihilating the world.

(24) [They maintain] this even if it is held that the world is created. For, with their admission of the creation of the human soul, they claim the impossibility of its annihilation in a manner similar to what we have mentioned.⁶ In brief, according to them, the nonexistence after existence of anything that subsists by itself, not in a substratum, is inconceivable, regardless of whether it is pre-eternal or temporally originated. And if it is said to them that, whenever one ignites fire under water, the water ceases to exist, they answer that it does not cease to exist but turns into vapor and then into water. For matter—namely, hyle—remains in the air, it being the matter for the form, water. It is only that the hyle has shed off the form of water and put on the form of air. If cold meets the air, it condenses and changes into water. It is not the case that a new water has come into being; rather, the materials are shared by the elements. It is only the [successive] turnover of their forms that changes.

(25) [Our] answer [is as follows]:

(26) Although we can defend each of the divisions you have mentioned, showing that their refutation on the basis of your principles is not sound, since your own principles include the same kind [of difficulty you attribute to them], we will not go into this at any length. We will confine ourselves to one part and say: With what [argument] would you deny someone who says: "The bringing about of existence and annihilation obtains through the will of the one endowed with power. Thus, if God wills, He brings about existence; and, if He wills, He annihilates. This is the meaning of His being powerful in the [most] perfect [sense].

انّ الباقى اذا بقى ببقاء، فيلزم ان تبقى صفات الله ببقاء، وذلك البقاء يكون باقيا فيحتاج الى بقاء آخر، ويتسلسل الى غير نهاية.

(٢٢) والفرقة الرابعة طائفة اخرى من الاشعريّة اذ قالوا انّ الاعراض تفنى بأنفسها، وأمّا الجواهر فانّها تفنى بان لا يخلق الله فيها حركة ولا سكونا ولا اجتماعا ولا افتراقا؛ فيستحيل ان يبقى جسم ليس بساكن ولا متحرّك فينعدم. وكأنّ فرقَى الاشعريّة مالوا الى انّ الإعدام ليس بفعل انّما هو كفّ عن الفعل لمّا لم يعقلوا كون العدم فعلا.

(٢٣) واذا بطلت هذه الطرق لم يبق وجه للقول بجواز اعدام العالم.

(٢٤) هذا لو قيل بانّ العالم حادث. فانّهم مع تسليمهم حدوث النفس الانسانيّة يدّعون استحالة انعدامها بطريق يقرب ممّا ذكرناه. وبالجملة عندهم كلّ قائم بنفسه لا فى محلّ، لا يتصوّر انعدامه بعد وجوده، سواء كان قديما أو حادثا. واذا قيل لهم، مهما [أوقدت][٧] النار تحت الماء، انعدم الماء، قالوا، لم ينعدم، ولكن انقلب بخارا ثم ماء. فالمادّة، وهى الهيولى، باقية فى الهواء، وهى المادّة التى كانت لصورة الماء، وانما خلعت الهيولى صورة المائيّة ولبست صورة الهوائيّة. واذا اصاب الهواء برد، كثف وانقلب ماء، لا انّ مادّة تجددت، بل الموادّ مشتركة بين العناصر؛ وانما يتبدّل عليها صورها.

(٢٥) الجواب:

(٢٦) ان ما ذكرتموه من الاقسام، وان أمكن ان نذبّ عن كلّ واحد، ونبيّن ان إبطاله على اصلكم لا يستقيم، لاشتمال اصولكم على ما هو من جنسه، ولكنّا لا نطول بهِ، ونقتصر على قسم واحد ونقول، بمَ تنكرون على من يقول: الايجاد والاعدام بارادة القادر؟ فاذا أراد الله أوجد، واذا أراد اعدم، وهذا معنى كونه قادرا على الكمال، وهو فى جملة ذلك لا

In all, this He in Himself does not change, what changes being only the act"? As to your statement that the agent [is such] that an act inevitably proceeds from Him, [asking] what then proceeds from Him, we say: "What proceeds from Him is that which occurs anew—namely, nonexis-
5   tence—since hitherto there was no nonexistence and then nonexistence came about anew. This, then, is what proceeds from Him."

(27) Should you then say, "Nonexistence is not a thing; how did it proceed from Him?" we answer:

(28) It is not a thing. How, then, did it come about? The only mean-
10   ing of its proceeding from Him is that what occurs relates to His power. Hence, if its occurrence is apprehended by the mind, why should its rela-tion to [His] power not be apprehended by the mind? And what is the difference between you and the one who utterly denies the occurrence of nonexistence to accidents and forms, saying, "Nonexistence is not a thing;
15   how would it then occur and be described as occurring and coming about anew?" We do not doubt that the occurrence of nonexistence to accidents is conceivable. Hence, the coming about of what is described as occurring [to something] is apprehensible by the mind, regardless of whether or not it is called a thing. Thus, the relating of that comprehensible occurrence
20   to the power of the one endowed with power is also comprehensible.

(29) [To this it may be] said:

(30) This is a necessary consequence only for the doctrine of one who allows the possibility of the nonexistence of a thing after its exis-tence, where it would then be said to him, "What is it that occurred?"
25   According to us, however, the existing thing is not annihilated. The meaning of the annihilation of accidents is the occurrence of their oppo-sites, which are existents, not the occurrence of pure nonexistence, which is not anything. For how can one describe that which is not any-thing as occurring? Thus, when hair turns white, the occurring thing is
30   whiteness only, which is an existent. We do not say that what has occurred is the privation of blackness.

(31) [Our answer is that] this is false in two respects:

(32) The first [is embodied in the question]: "Does the occurrence of whiteness entail the privation of blackness, or does it not?" If they say,
35   "No," they would affront what is intelligible, and if they say, "Yes," [then the question would be asked:] "Is what is entailed other than the thing

يتغيّر فى نفسه وانما يتغيّر الفعل. وأمّا قولكم، انّ الفاعل لا بدّ وان يصدر منه فعل فما الصادر منه، قلنا: الصادر منه ما تجدّد، وهو العدم، اذ لم يكن عدم ثم تجدّد العدم. فهو الصادر عنه.

(٢٧) فان قلتم انّه ليس بشىء، فكيف صدر منه؟ قلنا:

(٢٨) وهو ليس بشىء، فكيف وقع؟ وليس معنى صدوره منه الا أنّ ما وقع مضاف الى قدرته. فاذا عقل وقوعه، لَم لا تعقل اضافته الى القدرة؟ وما الفرق [بينكم]٨ وبين من ينكر طريان العدم أصلا على الاعراض والصور ويقول، العدم ليس بشىء فكيف يطرى، وكيف يوصف بالطريان والتجدّد؟ ولا نشك فى انّ العدم يتصوّر طريانه على الاعراض؛ فالموصوف بالطريان معقول وقوعه، سمّى شيئا أو لم يسمّ. فاضافة ذلك الواقع المعقول الى قدرة القادر أيضا معقول.

(٢٩) فان قيل:

(٣٠) هذا انما يلزم على مذهب من يجوّز عدم الشىء بعد وجوده، فيقال له، ما الذى طرى؟ وعندنا لا ينعدم الشىء الموجود، وانّما معنى انعدام الاعراض طريان اضدادها التى هى موجودات، لا طريان العدم المجرّد الذى ليس بشىء. فانّ ما ليس بشىء، كيف يوصف بالطريان؟ فاذا ابيضّ الشعر، فالطارى هو البياض فقط، وهو موجود. ولا نقول الطارى عدم السواد.

(٣١) وهذا فاسد من وجهين.

(٣٢) أحدهما: ان طريان البياض، هل تضمّن عدم السواد أم لا؟ فان قالوا، لا، فقد كابروا المعقول، وان قالوا، نعم، فالمتضمّن غير

that entails, or identical with it?" If they say that it is identical, this would be contradictory, since a thing does not entail itself; and, if they say that it is another, then one would ask: "Is this other intelligible or not?" If they say, "No," then we would say: "How did you know that it is entailed, when judging it to be entailed is a recognition that it is intelligible?" If they say, "Yes," then [it would be asked whether] that which is entailed and intelligible—namely, the privation of blackness—is eternal or temporally originated. If they say, "Eternal," this would be impossible; and if they say, "Temporally originated," then how can that which is described as temporal not be intellectually apprehensible? If they say that it is neither eternal nor temporally originated, then this would be impossible. For, if it is said of blackness, prior to the occurrence of whiteness, that it did not exist, this would be false; and, if after [the occurrence of whiteness] it is said that [blackness] is nonexistent, this would be true. It is, hence, inescapably an occurrence. Such an occurrence is thus intellectually apprehensible, and, hence, it is permissible for it to be related to the power of one endowed with power.

(33) The second respect [in which their argument is false] is that there are accidents that, according to them, cease to exist, not through [the occurrence of] their opposite. For motion has no opposite, the opposition between it and rest, according to them, being that of the opposition between [what is] a positive disposition and privation—that is, the opposition between existence and nonexistence. The meaning of rest is the absence of motion, so that, if motion ceases, there is no occurrence of a rest which is its opposite, [rest] being pure nonexistence. The same is true of those qualities that pertain to the class of the realization of perfections, as, for example, the imprinting of images of sensible things in the moist humor of the eye—nay, the impression of the forms of the intelligibles in the soul. For these amount to the commencement of an existence without the ceasing to exist of its opposite. If these are annihilated, this means the ceasing of existence without its being followed by its opposite. Their ceasing to exist then represents a pure privation that has occurred. Hence, the coming about of the occurring privation is apprehended intellectually. And, [in the case of] that whose occurrence as such (even though not a thing) is apprehended intellectually, its relation to the power of the one endowed with power becomes [likewise] apprehended intellectually.

(34) Through [all] this it becomes clear that, so long as the occurrence of an event by an eternal will is conceivable, there is no difference in the state of affairs whether what occurs is a privation or an existence.

المتضمّن أم عينه؟ فان قالوا، هو عينه، كان متناقضا، اذ الشيء لا يتضمّن نفسه؛ وان قالوا، غيره، فذلك الغير معقول أم لا؟ فإن قالوا، لا، قلنا، فبم عرفتم انهُ متضمّن، والحكم عليه بكونه متضمّنا اعتراف بكونه معقولا؟ وان قالوا، نعم، فذلك المتضمّن المعقول وهو عدم السواد قديم او حادث؟ فان قالوا، قديم، فهو محال، وان قالوا، حادث، فالموصوف بالحدوث كيف لا يكون معقولا؟ وان قالوا لا قديم ولا حادث، فهو محال، لانّه قبل طريان البياض، لو قيل السواد معدوم، كان كذبا، وبعده، اذا قيل انه معدوم، كان صدقا. فهو طار لا محالة، فهذا الطارى معقول؛ فيجوز ان يكون منسوبا الى قدرة قادر.

(٣٣) الوجه الثانى: انّ من الاعراض ما ينعدم عندهم لا بضدّه. فانّ الحركة لا ضدّ لها، وانّما التقابل بينها وبين السكون عندهم تقابل الملكة والعدم، أى تقابل الوجود والعدم. ومعنى السكون عدم الحركة، فاذا عدمت الحركة لم يطر سكون هو ضدّه، بل هو عدم محض. وكذلك الصفات التى هى من قبيل الاستكمال، كانطباع أشباح المحسوسات فى الرطوبة الجليديّة من العين، بل النطباع صور المعقولات فى النفس. فانّها ترجع الى استفتاح وجود من غير زوال ضدّه. واذا [عدمت][٩]، كان معناها زوال الوجود من غير استعقاب ضدّه. فزوالها عبارة عن عدم محض قد طرى. فعقل وقوع العدم الطارى، وما عقل وقوعه بنفسه، وان لم يكن شيئا، عقل ان ينسب الى قدرة القادر.

(٣٤) فتبيّن بهذا أنّه مهما تصوّر وقوع حادث بارادة قديمة، لم يفترق الحال بين أن يكون الواقع عدما أو وجودا.

[Third] Discussion

On showing their obfuscation in saying that
God is the world's enactor and maker,
that the world is His handiwork and act; showing
that with them this is metaphor, not reality

(1) The philosophers, with the exception of the materialists, have agreed that the world has a maker, that God is the maker and enactor of the world, that the world is His act and handiwork. This, however, is obfuscation in terms of their principle. Indeed, it is inconceivable, in accordance with their principle, for the world to be the work of God, in three respects: with respect to the agent, with respect to the act, and with respect to a relationship common to act and agent.

(2) Regarding [the aspect pertaining to] the agent, it is incumbent that He should be a willer, a chooser, and a knower of what He wills, so as to be the agent of what He wills. But, according to [the philosophers], God, exalted be He, is not one who wills, but has no attribute at all. Whatever proceeds from Him proceeds by compulsory necessity. [As for] the second [aspect, which pertains to the act], the world [for the philosophers] is eternal, whereas the act is the temporally originated. [Regarding] the third [aspect], God for them is one in every respect; and from the One, according to them, nothing but that which is one in all respects proceeds. But the world is composed of various [things]; how does it then proceed from Him?

(3) Let us, then, ascertain each one of these three aspects, together with [showing] their insanity in defending it.

مسئلة

في بيان تلبيسهم بقولهم انّ الله فاعل العالم
وصانعه وانّ العالم صنعه وفعله وبيان انّ ذلك
مجاز عندهم وليس بحقيقة

(١) وقد اتفقت الفلاسفة، سوى الدهريّة، على ان للعالم صانعا وان الله هو صانع العالم وفاعله وان العالم فعله وصنعه. وهذا تلبيس على أصلهم؛ بل لا يتصوّر على مساق أصلهم ان يكون العالم من صنع الله من ثلاثة أوجه، وجه في الفاعل، ووجه في الفعل، ووجه في نسبة مشتركة بين الفعل والفاعل.

(٢) امّا الذي في الفاعل، فهو انّه لا بدّ وان يكون مريدا مختارا عالما بما يريده حتّى يكون فاعلا لما يريده. والله تعالى عندهم ليس مريدا بل لا صفة له أصلا، وما يصدر عنه فيلزم منه لزوما ضروريّا. والثاني ان العالم قديم، والفعل هو الحادث. والثالث ان الله واحد عندهم من كلّ وجه، والواحد لا يصدر منه عندهم الا واحد من كلّ وجه؛ والعالم مركب من مختلفات، فكيف يصدر عنه؟

(٣) ولنحقّق وجه كل واحد من هذه الوجوه الثلاثة، مع خبالهم في دفعه.

Regarding the first [aspect]

(4) We say: "'Agent' is an expression [referring] to one from whom the act proceeds, together with the will to act by way of choice and the knowledge of what is willed." But, according to you [philosophers], the world [proceeds] from God [exalted be He] as the effect from the cause, as a necessary consequence, inconceivable for God to prevent, in the way the shadow is the necessary consequence of the individual and light [the necessary consequence] of the sun. And this does not pertain to action in anything. Indeed, whoever says that the lamp enacts the light and the individual enacts the shadow has ventured excessively into metaphor and stretched it beyond [its] bound, being satisfied with the occurrence of one common description between the expression borrowed for one thing and that from which it is borrowed, [as in this instance, where] the agent is cause in a general sense, whereas the lamp is the cause of illumination and the sun the cause of light. The agent, however, is not called an agent and a maker by simply being a cause, but by being a cause in a special respect—namely, by way of will and choice—so that if one were to say, "The wall is not an agent; the stone is not an agent; the inanimate is not an agent, action being confined to animals," this would not be denied and the statement would not be false. But [according to the philosophers] the stone has an action—namely, falling due to heaviness and an inclination toward [the earth's] center—just as fire has an action, which is heating, and the wall has an action—namely, the inclination toward the center and the occurrence of the shadow—for all [these latter things] proceed from [the wall]. But this is impossible.

(5) [The philosophers, however, may] say:

(6) [In the case of] every existent whose existence is not in itself necessary, but which exists through another, we call that thing an enacted thing and its cause an agent. We do not care whether the cause acts by nature or voluntarily, just as you do not care whether it acts by an instrument or without an instrument. Rather, [for you] action is a genus that divides into that which occurs through an instrument and that which occurs without an instrument. Similarly, it is a genus and divides into that which occurs naturally and that which occurs by choice. Proof of this is

امّا الاول

(٤) فنقول: الفاعل عبارة عمّن يصدر منه الفعل مع الارادة للفعل على سبيل الاختيار ومع العلم بالمراد. وعندكم انّ العالم من الله كالمعلول من العلة، يلزم لزوما ضروريّا، لا يتصوّر من الله دفعه، لزوم الظلّ من الشخص والنور من الشمس. وليس هذا من الفعل فى شىء. بل من قال ان السراج يفعل الضوء والشخص يفعل الظلّ، فقد جازف وتوسّع فى التجوّز توسعا خارجا من الحدّ، واستعار اللفظ اكتفاء بوقوع المشاركة بين المستعار له والمستعار منه فى وصف واحد، وهو انّ الفاعل سبب على الجملة والسراج سبب الضوء والشمس سبب النور. ولكنّ الفاعل لم يسمّ فاعلا صانعا بمجرّد كونه سببا، بل بكونه سببا على وجه مخصوص، وهو على وجه الارادة والاختيار، حتى لو قال القائل، الجدار ليس بفاعل والحجر ليس بفاعل والجماد ليس بفاعل، وانّما الفعل للحيوان، لم ينكر ذلك ولم يكن قوله كاذبا. وللحجر فعل عندهم وهو الهوى [بالثقل][1] والميل الى المركز، كما ان للنار فعلا وهو التسخين، وللحائط [فعلا][2] وهو الميل الى المركز، ووقوع الظلّ. فان كلّ ذلك صادر منه، وهذا محال.

(٥) فان قيل:

(٦) كل موجود ليس واجب الوجود بذاته بل هو موجود بغيره، فانّا نسمّى ذلك الشىء مفعولا، ونسمّى سببه فاعلا. ولا نبالى كان السبب فاعلا بالطبع أو بالارادة، كما انّكم لا تبالون أنّه كان فاعلا بآلة أو بغير آلة؛ بل الفعل جنس وينقسم الى ما يقع بآلة والى ما يقع بغير آلة، فكذلك هو جنس وينقسم الى ما يقع بالطبع والى ما يقع بالاختيار، بدليل انّا اذا

that, if we say, "He acted by nature," our saying "by nature" would not
be contrary to our saying "he acted," neither repelling nor contradicting
it. Rather, it would be a clarification of the kind of action, just as, when
we say, "He acted directly, without an instrument," this would not be a
contradiction, but an indication of [the] kind [of action] and a clarification. If we say, "He acted by choice," this would not be repetition as
[when we repeat ourselves] in our statement, "animal, human," but an
explication of the kind of action, as [in] our statement, "He acted
[using] an instrument." Had our statement, "He acted," entailed will,
will being essential to the action inasmuch as it is action, then our statement, "He acted by nature," would be [as] contradictory as our statement,
"He acted and he has not acted."

(7) We say:

(8) This naming is false. It is not permissible to call any cause, in
whatever aspect, an agent, nor any effect an enacted thing. Had this
been the case, it would not then be correct to say that the inanimate has
no action, action belonging only to animals, when these are among the
well-known, true universals. If the inanimate is called an agent, then this
is as metaphor, just as it is called a seeker and willer by way of figurative
speech. For it is said that the stone falls because it wills [to move to] the
center and seeks it, when seeking and willing in reality are only conceivable in conjunction with the knowledge of what is willed and sought after
and are [thus] conceivable only of animals.

(9) As for your statement that our saying, "He acts," is a general statement and divides into what is by nature and what is by will, this is not
admitted. It is akin to someone saying that our statement, "He willed," is a
general expression and divides [in its reference] into one who wills and
knows what he wills and one who wills and does not know what he wills.
And this is false, since will necessarily entails knowledge. Similarly, action
necessarily entails will. Regarding your statement that [the second part
of] our saying, "He acted by nature," does not contradict the first, this is
not the case. For it contradicts it in terms of what is real. But the contradiction does not impress itself immediately on the understanding, and
[our] nature's repulsion to it does not become intense because it remains
a metaphor. For, since it is in some respect a cause, the agent also being a
cause, ["the action by nature"] is called an action metaphorically. If one

قلنا، فعل بالطبع، لم يكن قولنا بالطبع ضدًّا لقولنا فعل ولا دفعا ونقضا له، بل كان بيانا لنوع الفعل، كما اذا قلنا: فعل مباشرة بغير آلة، لم يكن نقضا، بل كان تنويعا وبيانا؛ واذا قلنا فعل بالاختيار، لم يكن تكرارا مثل قولنا، حيوان انسان، بل كان بيانا لنوع الفعل، كقولنا فعل بآلة. ولو كان

٥ قولنا فعل يتضمّن الارادة، وكانت الارادة ذاتيّة للفعل من حيث انه فعل، لكان قولنا فعل بالطبع متناقضا، كقولنا فعل وما فعل.

(٧) قلنا:

(٨) هذه التسمية فاسدة، ولا يجوز أن يسمّى كل سبب بايّ وجه كان فاعلا ولا كل مسبّب مفعولا؛ ولو كان كذلك، لما صحّ ان يقال

١٠ الجماد لا فعل له، انما الفعل للحيوان، وهذه من [الكلّيّات]٣ المشهورة الصادقة. فان سمّى الجماد فاعلا، فبالاستعارة كما قد يسمّى طالبا مريدا على سبيل المجاز، اذ يقال الحجر يهوى لانه يريد المركز ويطلبه؛ والطلب والارادة حقيقة لا يتصوّر الا مع العلم بالمراد المطلوب ولا يتصوّر الا من الحيوان.

١٥ (٩) وأمّا قولكم انّ قولنا، فعل، عامّ وينقسم الى ما هو بالطبع والى ما هو بالارادة، غير مسلّم؛ وهو كقول القائل قولنا، أراد، عامّ وينقسم الى من يريد مع العلم بالمراد والى من يريد ولا يعلم ما يريد. وهو فاسد اذ الارادة تتضمّن العلم بالضرورة، فكذلك الفعل يتضمّن الارادة بالضرورة. وأمّا قولكم ان قولنا، فعل بالطبع، ليس بنقض للأوّل،

٢٠ فليس كذلك. فانه نقض له من حيث الحقيقة، ولكن لا يسبق الى الفهم التناقض، ولا يشتدّ نفور الطبع عنه، لانّه يبقى مجازا. فانّه لما أن كان سببا بوجه ما، والفاعل أيضا سبب، سمّى فعلا مجازا. واذا [قيل]٤؛

says, "He acted by choice," this is ascertainable as repetition, as when one says, "He willed, knowing what he willed." But, since it is conceivable to say "he acted" when this is metaphor and "he acted" when this is real, the soul is not repelled by the statement, "He acted by choice," the
5   meaning being that he performed a real action not [in the] metaphorical [sense], as when one says [in the real sense], "He spoke with his tongue," or, "He saw with his eye." For, since it is [linguistically] permissible to use [the expression] "seeing with the heart" metaphorically and "speak-ing" with reference to one's moving the head and the hand, such that one
10   would say, "He spoke with his head," meaning [that he said], "Yes," it is not deemed repugnant to say, "He spoke with his tongue" and "saw with his eye," where the intention is to remove the possibility of [taking these expressions as] metaphor. This, then, is where the foot will slip. Let one then be alerted to [the place] where these naïve people are deceived.
15   (10) [The philosophers may] say:

(11) Naming the agent "agent" is known from linguistic usage. Other-wise, it is evident to the mind that what is a cause for a thing divides into that which is voluntary and that which is not. The dispute, hence, pertains to whether or not the term "action" is truly applicable to both
20   divisions. There is no way to deny [its applicability to both], since the Arabs say, "Fire burns," "The sword cuts," "Snow cools," "Scammony moves the bowels," "Bread satiates," and "Water quenches." Our saying, "He strikes," means, "He enacts the striking"; our saying, "It burns," means, "It enacts the burning"; and our saying, "It cuts," means, "It
25   enacts the cutting." If you say, "All of this is metaphor," you would be arbitrary about it, without support.

(12) [To this we] answer:

(13) All this is by way of metaphor. Real action is that which comes about only through will. Proof of this is that, if we suppose that a temporal
30   event depends for its occurrence on two things, one voluntary and the other not, reason relates the act to the voluntary. [It is] the same with language. For, if someone throws another into the fire and [the latter] dies, it is said that [the former], not the fire, is the killer, so that if it is said, "None

فعل بالاختيار، فهو تكرير على التحقيق، كقوله، أراد وهو عالم بما أراده؛ الا انه لما تصوّر ان يقال فعل وهو مجاز، ويقال فعل، وهو حقيقة، لم تنفر النفس عن قوله فعل بالاختيار، وكان معناه فعَل فعلا حقيقيّا لا مجازيّا، كقول القائل، تكلم بلسانهٖ، ونظر بعينهٖ؛ فانّه لما جاز ان يستعمل النظر فى القلب مجازا والكلام فى تحريك الرأس واليد حتى يقال قال برأسه، أى نعم، لم يستقبح ان يقال قال بلسانه ونظر بعينه، ويكون معناه نفى احتمال المجاز. فهذا مزلّة القدم، فليتنبّه لمحل انخداع هؤلاء الاغبياء.

(١٠) فان قيل:

(١١) تسمية الفاعل فاعلا انما يعرف من اللغة، والا فقد ظهر فى العقل أن ما يكون سببا للشىء ينقسم الى ما يكون مريدا والى ما لا يكون، ووقع النزاع فى ان اسم الفعل على كلى القسمين حقيقة أم لا؛ ولا سبيل الى انكاره اذ العرب تقول، النار تحرق، والسيف يقطع، والثلج يبرد، والسقمونيا تسهل، والخبز يشبع، والماء يروى؛ وقولنا، يضرب، معناه يفعل الضرب، وقولنا تحرق، معناه تفعل الاحتراق، وقولنا يقطع معناه يفعل القطع. فان قلتم إنّ ذلك كلّ مجاز، كنتم متحكّمين فيه من غير مستند.

(١٢) والجواب:

(١٣) ان كلّ ذلك بطريقٖ المجاز؛ وانّما الفعل الحقيقىّ ما يكون بالارادة. والدليل عليه انّا لو فرضنا حادثا توقف فى حصوله على أمرين أحدهما ارادىّ والآخر غير ارادىّ، أضاف العقل الفعل الى الارادىّ. وكذى اللغة، فانّ من ألقى انسانا فى نار فمات، يقال هو القاتل دون النار،

other than So-and-so killed him," the speaker of this would have said the truth. For if the term "agent" is [applicable to both] willer and nonwiller in the same way, not by way of one of them being the basis [and] the other derived as a metaphor from it, why is it, then, that, on the basis of language, custom, and reason, killing is related to the willer, even though fire is the proximate cause of the killing? [Here the opponent is speaking] as though the one who throws [the victim] would have only undertaken bringing [the victim] and the fire together. But, since the joining [of victim and fire] came about through will, whereas the efficacy of fire is without will, [the willer] is called the killer and the fire is not called a killer except through some kind of metaphor. This shows that the agent is the one from whom the act proceeds through his will. Hence, if God, according to [the philosophers], has neither will nor choice, He would be neither an agent nor a maker except in a metaphorical [sense].

(14) [The philosophers may] say:

(15) We mean by God's being an agent that He is the cause of every other existent; and that the world's subsistence is through Him; and that, had it not been for the existence of the Creator, the existence of the world would be inconceivable. And, should the nonexistence of God be supposed, then [in terms of such a supposition] the world would cease to exist—just as, if the nonexistence of the sun is supposed, light [in terms of such a supposition] would cease to exist. This is what we mean by His being an agent. If the opponent refuses to call this meaning "action," there is no need to squabble about names, once the meaning is clear.

(16) We say:

(17) Our [whole] purpose is to show that this meaning is not [properly] termed "action" and "handiwork." Rather, that which is meant by "action" and "handiwork" is that which truly proceeds from the will. You [philosophers] have denied the true meaning of "action" and have uttered its expression to endear yourselves to Muslims. Religion is not fulfilled by uttering expressions devoid of [their real] meaning. Declare openly, then, that God has no action, so that it becomes clear that your belief is contrary to the religion of Muslims. Do not confuse matters by [stating] that God is the maker of the world and that the world is His doing. For this is

حتى اذا قيل ما قتله الا فلان صدق قائله. فان كان اسم الفاعل على المريد
وغير المريد على وجه واحد، لا بطريق كون أحدهما أصلا وكون الآخر
مستعارا منه، فلِمَ يضاف القتل الى المريد لغة وعرفا وعقلا، مع انّ النار
هى العلة القريبة فى القتل؟ وكان الملقى لم يتعاط الا الجمع بينه وبين النار،
ولكن لما ان كان الجمع بالارادة وتأثير النار بغير ارادة، سمّى قاتلا، و لم
تسمّ النار قاتلا الابنوع من الاستعارة. فدلّ انّ الفاعل من صدر الفعل عن
ارادته. [فإذا]° لم يكن الله مريدا عندهم ولا مختارا لفعل، لم يكن صانعا
ولا فاعلا الا بجازا.

(١٤) فان قيل:

(١٥) نحن نعنى بكون الله فاعلا انّه سبب لوجود كل موجود سواه،
وانّ العالم قوامه به، ولولا وجود البارى لما تصوّر وجود العالم. ولو قدّر
عدم البارى، لانعدم العالم، كما لو قدّر عدم الشمس، لانعدم الضوء.
فهذا ما نعنيه بكونه فاعلا. فان كان الخصم يأبى ان يسمّى هذا المعنى
فعلا، فلا مشاحة فى الاسامى بعد ظهور المعنى.

(١٦) قلنا:

(١٧) غرضنا ان نبيّن انّ هذا المعنى لا يسمّى فعلا وصنعا. وانّما
المعنى بالفعل والصنع ما يصدر عن الارادة حقيقة، وقد نفيتم حقيقة معنى
الفعل ونطقتم بلفظه تجمّلا بالاسلاميين. ولا يتمّ الدبن باطلاق الالفاظ
الفارغة عن المعانى؛ فصرّحوا بانّ الله لا فعل له، حتى يتّضح انّ معتقدكم
مخالف لدين المسلمين. ولا تلبسوا بانّ الله صانع العالم وانّ العالم صنعه.

an expression which you have uttered, but [you have] denied its reality.
The purpose of this discussion is only to clear this deceptive beclouding.

The second aspect

(18) [This is] concerned with refuting [the idea] that the world,
according to their principle, is the act of God. [The refutation] pertains
to a condition regarding the act—namely, that the act means temporal
creation, whereas the world, according to them, is pre-eternal and not
temporally created. The meaning of "action" is the bringing forth of the
thing from nonexistence to existence by creating it. But this is inconceivable of the pre-eternal, since what [already] exists cannot be brought
into existence. Hence, the condition of the act [to be something enacted]
is for it to be temporally created. But the world, according to [the philoso-
phers], is pre-eternal. How could it, then, be the act of God?

(19) [The philosophers] may say:[1]

(20) The meaning of "the created" is "an existent after nonexistence."
Let us, then, investigate the case when the agent creates: is that which
proceeds from Him, that relates to Him, pure existence, pure nonexistence, or both? It is false to say that what relates to Him is the prior
nonexistence, since the agent has no influence on nonexistence. And it is
false to say that both [relate to Him], since it has become clear that nonexistence basically does not relate to Him and that nonexistence, in being
nonexistence, does not require an agent at all. It remains, then, that it
relates to Him inasmuch as it exists and that what proceeds from Him is
pure existence and that there is no relation to Him except existence. If
existence is supposed to be permanent, the relation would be supposed
permanent. And if the relation is permanent, then the one to whom it
relates would be the more efficacious and more permanent in influence
because nonexistence did not attach to the agent in any state. It [then]
remains to say that [the world] relates to [the agent] inasmuch as it is
created. There is no meaning for its being created except that it exists
after nonexistence but that nonexistence is not related to it. If, then, the

فانّ هذه لفظة اطلقتموها ونفيتم حقيقتها. ومقصود هذه المسئلة الكشف عن هذا التلبيس فقط.

الوجه الثانى

(١٨) فى ابطال كون العالم فعلا لله على اصلهم، بشرط فى الفعل، وهو انّ الفعل عبارة عن الاحداث، والعالم عندهم قديم وليس بحادث. ومعنى الفعل اخراج الشىء من العدم الى الوجود باحداثه. وذلك لا يتصوّر فى القديم، اذ الموجود لا يمكن ايجاده. فاذن شرط الفعل ان يكون حادثا، والعالم قديم عندهم، فكيف يكون فعلا لله؟

(١٩) فان قيل:

(٢٠) معنى الحادث موجود بعد عدم. فلنبحث انّ الفاعل اذا أحدث، كان الصادر منه المتعلّق به الوجود المجرّد، أو العدم المجرّد، أو كلاهما؟ وباطل ان يقال ان المتعلّق به العدم السابق، اذ لا تأثير للفاعل فى العدم. وباطل ان يقال كلاهما، اذ بان أنّ العدم لا يتعلق به أصلا وانّ العدم فى كونه عدما لا يحتاج الى فاعل البتّة. فبقى انّه متعلق به من حيث انه موجود وان الصادر منه مجرّد الوجود وانّه لا نسبة اليه الا الوجود. فان فرض الوجود دائما، فرضت النسبة دائمة؛ واذا دامت هذه النسبة، كان المنسوب اليه أفعل وأدوم تأثيرا لانّه لم يتعلّق العدم بالفاعل بحال. فبقى ان يقال انّه متعلّق به من حيث انّه حادث. ولا معنى لكونه حادثا الا انّه وجود بعد عدم، والعدم لم يتعلّق به. فان

precedence of nonexistence is made a description of existence and it is said that what relates [to the agent] is a special [kind of] existence, not all existence—namely, existence preceded by nonexistence—it would be said:

(21) Its being preceded by nonexistence is not an act of an agent and
5   the work of a maker. For the proceeding of this existence from its agent is only conceivable with nonexistence preceding it. But the precedence of nonexistence is not the enactment of the agent—thus, its being preceded by nonexistence is not through the act of the agent. It thus has no connection with it. Hence, having [the previous nonexistence] as a con-
10   dition for [the act] to be an act is to set as a condition that over which the agent in no circumstance has any influence. As for your statement that the existent cannot be brought into existence, if you mean by this that an existence does not commence for it after nonexistence, this would be correct. If [on the other hand] you mean by this that in the
15   state of its being existent it would not be [something] brought into existence, we have shown that it is [something] brought into existence in the state of its being existent, not in the state of its being nonexistent. For a thing is only brought into existence if the agent brings about existence; and the agent is not an enactor of existence in a state of [a thing's]
20   nonexistence, but in the state of a thing's [being in] existence [due to it]. Bringing into existence is concomitant with the agent's being that which brings about existence and the thing enacted being that which is brought into existence. [This is] because it is an expression of the relation of the thing that brings about existence to the thing whose exis-
25   tence is brought about. All [this obtains] with existence, not before it. Hence, there is no bringing about of existence except for an existent, if by "bringing into existence" is meant the relation through which the agent is that which brings about existence and the thing enacted that which is brought into existence.

30   (22) [The philosophers] say [further]:

(23) For this reason we have ruled that the world is the act of God from eternity and everlastingly and that there is no time wherein He is not the Enactor of it. For what is connected with the agent is existence. Hence, if the connection continues, existence continues; and if it is
35   severed, [existence] is severed. It is not what you [theologians] imagine— namely, that, if one supposes the Creator's existence to cease, the world would [still] endure, since you have thought Him to be akin to the builder [in relation to] the building. For [the builder] would cease to exist, whereas the building would remain. The continued endurance of the building is

جعل سبق العدم وصف الوجود، وقيل المتعلّق به وجود مخصوص، لا كلّ وجود، وهو وجود مسبوق بالعدم، فيقال:

(٢١) كونه مسبوقا بالعدم ليس من فعل فاعل وصنع صانع؛ فانّ هذا الوجود لا يتصوّر صدوره من فاعله الا والعدم سابق عليه، وسبق العدم ليس بفعل الفاعل؛ فكونه مسبوق العدم ليس بفعل الفاعل، فلا تعلّق له به، فاشتراطه فى كونه فعلا اشتراط ما لا تأثير للفاعل فيه بحال. وأمّا قولكم ان الموجود لا يمكن ايجاده، ان عنيتم به انّه لا يستأنف له وجود بعد عدم، فصحيح؛ وان عنيتم بهِ انّه فى حال كونه موجودا، لا يكون موجدا، فقد بيّنّا انه يكون موجدا فى حال كونه موجدا، لا فى حال كونه معدوما. فانّه انّما يكون الشىء موجدا اذا كان الفاعل موجدا، ولا يكون الفاعل موجدا فى حال العدم بل فى حال وجود الشىء منه. والايجاد مقارن لكون الفاعل موجدا وكون المفعول موجدا، لانّه عبارة عن نسبة الموجد الى الموجد. وكل ذلك مع الوجود لا قبله. فاذن لا ايجاد الا للموجود، ان كان المراد بالايجاد النسبة التى بها يكون الفاعل موجدا والمفعول موجدا.

(٢٢) قالوا:

(٢٣) ولهذا قضينا بانّ العالم فعل الله أزلا وأبدا وما من حال الا وهو فاعل له، لانّ المرتبط بالفاعل الوجود. فان دام الارتباط، دام الوجود، وان انقطع انقطع، لا كما تخيّلتموه من ان البارئ لو قدر عدمه لبقى العالم، اذ ظننتم انه كالبنّاء مع البناء، فانه ينعدم ويبقى البناء، فانّ بقاء البنّاء

not due to the builder, but to the dryness that holds its structure together, since, if it did not have the sustaining power—like water, for example, does not—the endurance of the original shape brought about by the act of the agent would be inconceivable.[2]

(24) [To this we] answer:

(25) The act attaches to the agent in terms of its temporal origination, not in terms of its previous nonexistence, nor in terms of its being an existent only. For, according to us, it does not attach to it in the subsequent state after origination when it [already] exists, but attaches to it at the moment of its temporal origination, inasmuch as [this] is temporal origination and an exodus from nonexistence to existence. If the meaning of temporal existence is denied it, then neither its being an act nor its being attached to an agent would be intelligible. Your statement that its being temporally originated reduces to its being preceded by nonexistence and [that] its being preceded by nonexistence is not the act of the agent and the deed of the maker [expresses what, in fact,] is the case. But its being preceded by nonexistence is a condition for existence to be the act of the agent. Thus, existence which is not preceded by nonexistence, but is perpetual, is not fit to be the act of the agent. Not everything that is made a condition for the act to be an act should [come about] through the act of the agent. Thus, the agent's essence, his power, his will, and his knowledge are a condition for his being [an agent]. But this is not the effect of the agent. But one cannot comprehend an act unless [it proceeds] from an existent. Hence, the agent's existence, his will, his power, and his knowledge [constitute] a condition for his being an agent, although these are not the effects of the agent.

(26) [To this the philosophers may] say:

(27) If you have acknowledged the possibility of the act's coexistence with the agent [rather than] its being posterior to him, then it follows necessarily from this that the act would be temporally originated if the agent is temporally originated, and [the act would be] pre-eternal if [the agent] is pre-eternal. If you make it a condition that the act should be temporally posterior to the agent, this would be impossible, since, if someone moves his hand in a glass of water, the water moves with the movement of the hand, neither before nor after it. For if it moved after it,

ليس بالبانى بل هو باليبوسة الممسكة لتركيبه، اذ لو لم يكن فيه قوة ماسكة كالماء مثلا، لم يتصوّر بقاء الشكل الحادث بفعل الفاعل فيه.

(٢٤) والجواب:

(٢٥) ان الفعل يتعلّق بالفاعل من حيث حدوثه لا من حيث عدمه السابق ولا من حيث كونه موجودا فقط، فانه لا يتعلّق به فى ثانى حال الحدوث عندنا، وهو موجود، بل يتعلّق به فى حال حدوثه من حيث انّه حدوث وخروج من العدم الى الوجود. فان نفى منه معنى الحدوث لم يعقل كونه فعلا ولا تعلقه بالفاعل. وقولكم انّ كونه حادثا يرجع الى كونه مسبوقا بالعدم وكونه مسبوقا بالعدم ليس من فعل الفاعل وجعل الجاعل فهو كذلك، لكنّه شرط فى كون الوجود فعل الفاعل، أعنى كونه مسبوقا بالعدم. فالوجود الذى ليس مسبوقا بعدم، بل هو دائم، لا يصلح لان يكون فعل الفاعل؛ وليس كل ما يشترط فى كون الفعل فعلا، ينبغى ان يكون بفعل الفاعل. فانّ ذات الفاعل وقدرته وإرادته وعلمه شرط فى كونه، وليس ذلك من اثر [الفاعل]؛ ولكن لا يعقل فعل الا من موجود. فكان وجود الفاعل شرطا، وارادته وقدرته وعلمه، ليكون فاعلا، وان لم يكن من اثر الفاعل.

(٢٦) فان قيل:

(٢٧) ان اعترفتم بجواز كون الفعل مع الفاعل غير متأخر عنه، فيلزم منه ان يكون الفعل حادثا ان كان الفاعل حادثا، وقديما ان كان قديما. وان شرّطتم ان يتأخر الفعل عن الفاعل بالزمان فهذا محال، اذ من حرّك اليد فى قدح ماء، تحرّك الماء مع حركة اليد، لا قبله ولا بعده، اذ لو تحرّك بعده

then, before [the water] gives way, the hand would be with the water in
one and the same space; and if it moved before it, then the water would be
separated from the hand—this with its being [simultaneous] with it [as]
its effect and an act proceeding from its direction. If, then, we suppose
5   the hand to be pre-eternal in the water, [ever] moving, then the movement of the water would also be perpetual, being, despite its perpetuity,
an effect and an enacted thing. This [latter] is not prevented by supposing perpetuity. The case is similar with the relation of the world to God.
        (28) [To this] we say:
10   (29) We do not deem it impossible that the act [should coexist] with
the agent, [provided that] the act is created, as with the movement of
the water. For it is created out of nonexistence. It is, hence, possible [for
something] to be an act, regardless of whether it is posterior to the essence
of the agent or concomitant with it. We only deem impossible the eternal
15   act. For naming that which is not created out of nothing an "act" is pure
metaphor, having no reality. As regards the effect with the cause, it is
possible for both to be created or to be eternal, as [when] it is said that
eternal knowledge is a cause for the Eternal to be a knower. This is not
what is being discussed. The discussion is only concerned with what is
20   termed an "act." The effect of the cause is not called an act of the cause
except metaphorically. Rather, what is called an act has as a condition its
being created out of nothing. If someone allows himself to call the Eternal,
the Permanently Existent, an[3] act of another, he would be indulging in
metaphor. Your statement, "If we suppose the movement of the finger
25   and the finger to be eternal, this would not remove the movement of the
water from being an act," is obfuscation. This is because the finger has no
act; rather, the agent is only the one who has the finger, and he is the one
who wills [the act]. If we suppose him to be eternal, the movement of the
finger would [still] be an act of his, inasmuch as each part of the move-
30   ment is a temporal creation out of nothing. Considered in this way, it
would be an act. As for the movement of the water, we might not say that
it is a result of his action, but of the action of God. But in whatever way
we take [the water's movement in the supposition to be caused], it is an
act inasmuch as it is created, except that it is eternally being created—
35   it being an act inasmuch as it is created.
        (30) [The philosophers] may say:

لكان اليد مع الماء قبل تنحِّيه فى حيّز واحد، ولو تحرّك قبله، لانفصل الماء عن اليد. وهو مع كونه معه معلوله، وفعل من جهته. فان فرضنا اليد قديمة فى الماء متحرّكة، كانت حركة الماء أيضاً دائمة. وهى مع دوامها معلولة ومفعولة. ولا يمتنع ذلك بفرض الدوام. فكذلك نسبة العالم الى الله.

(٢٨) قلنا: ٥

(٢٩) لا نحيل ان يكون الفعل مع الفاعل بعد كون الفعل حادثا، كحركة الماء. فانّها حادثة عن عدم، فجاز ان يكون فعلا ثم، سواء كان متأخرا عن ذات الفاعل أو مقارنا له. وانّما نحيل الفعل القديم. فانّ ما ليس حادثا عن عدم فتسميته فعلا مجاز مجرّد لا حقيقة له. وأما المعلول مع العلّة فيجوز ان يكونا حادثين وان يكونا قديمين، كما يقال ان العلم القديم ١٠ علّة لكون القديم عالما، ولا كلام فيه. وانّما الكلام فيما يسمّى فعلا. ومعلول العلّة لا يسمى فعل العلّة الا مجازا؛ بل ما يسمّى فعلا، فشرطه ان يكون حادثا عن عدم. فان تَجوّز متجوّز بتسمية القديم الدائم الوجود فعلا لغيره، كان متجوّزا فى الاستعارة. وقولكم لو قدّرنا حركة الاصبع مع الاصبع قديما دائما، لم يخرج حركة الماء عن كونه فعْلا، تلبيس، لأنّ ١٥ الاصبع لا فعْل له، وانّما الفاعل ذو الاصبع، وهو المريد. ولو قدّر قديما لكانت حركة الاصبع فعلا له من حيث انّ كلّ جزء من الحركة فحادث عن عدم. فبهذا الاعتبار كان فعلا. وأمّا حركة الماء فقد لا نقول انّه من فعله، بل هو من فعل الله. وعلى أى وجه كان، فكونه فعلا من حيث انّه حادث، إلا انّه دائم الحدوث، وهو فعل من حيث انه حادث. ٢٠

(٣٠) فان قيل:

(31) You have, hence, acknowledged that the relation of the act to the agent, inasmuch as it exists, is akin to the relation of the effect to the cause, and then admitted that the permanence of the relation between cause [and effect] is conceivable. We do not mean by the world's being an "act" anything other than its being an effect whose relation to God, exalted be He, is permanent. If you do not call this an "act," there is no need for conflict over naming once the meanings are clear.

(32) We say:

(33) Our sole purpose in this question is to show that you have used these terms as an affectation, without [the proper] ascertaining of their real meaning; that God, according to you, is not an agent in the real sense nor the world His act in a real sense; and that the application of such a term on your part is metaphorical, having no basis in reality. And this has become manifest.

The third aspect

(34) [This is concerned with showing] the impossibility of the world's being an act of God according to their principle, due to a condition common to agent and act—namely, in that they said, "From the one only one thing proceeds." But the First Principle [they hold] is one in every respect. The world, however, is composed of varied things. Hence, as necessarily demanded by their own principle, it is inconceivable for it to be an act of God.

(35) [The philosophers] may say:

(36) The world as a whole does not proceed from God without an intermediary. Rather, what proceeds from Him is one existent which is the first of the created things. It is a pure intellect—that is, it is a substance that is self-subsisting; that has no position in space; that knows itself and knows its principle; and, in the language of the revealed law, is referred to as an "angel." A third existent proceeds from it and from the third a fourth, the existents becoming multiple through mediation. For the variance in the act and its multiplicity are due either: [(a)] to the differences in the acting powers—just as we enact with the appetitive

(٣١) فاذا اعترفتم بانّ نسبة الفعل الى الفاعل من حيث انّه موجود كنسبة المعلول الى العلة، ثم سلّمتم تصوّر الدوام فى نسبة العلة، فنحن لا نعنى بكون العالم فعلا الا كونه معلولا دائم النسبة الى الله تعالى. فان لم تسمّوا هذا فعلا، فلا مضايقة فى التسميات بعد ظهور المعانى.

(٣٢) قلنا:

(٣٣) ولا غرض من هذه المسئلة الا بيان انكم تتجمّلون بهذه الاسماء من غير تحقيق، وانّ الله عندكم ليس فاعلا تحقيقا، ولا العالم فعله تحقيقا، وانّ اطلاق هذا الاسم مجاز منكم، لا تحقيق له. وقد ظهر هذا.

الوجه الثالث

(٣٤) فى استحالة كون العالم فعلا لله على اصلهم بشرط مشترك بين الفاعل والفعل، وهو انّهم قالوا: لا يصدر من الواحد الا شىء واحد. والمبدأ واحد من كل وجه، والعالم مركّب من مختلفات. فلا يتصوّر ان يكون فعلا لله بموجب أصلهم.

(٣٥) فان قيل:

(٣٦) العالم بجملته ليس صادرا من الله بغير واسطة؛ بل الصادر منه موجود واحد هو أوّل المخلوقات، وهو عقل مجرد، اى هو جوهر قائم بنفسه غير متحيّز، يعرف نفسه، ويعرف مبدأه، ويعبّر عنه فى لسان الشرع بالملك. ثم يصدر منه ثالث، ومن الثالث رابع، وتكثر الموجودات بالتوسّط. فانّ اختلاف الفعل وكثرته، امّا ان يكون لاختلاف القوى الفاعلة، كما انّا نفعل بقوة الشهوة خلاف ما نفعل

power that which is different from what we enact with irascible power;
[(b)] to the different materials—just as the sun whitens the washed garments, darkens the face of man, melts some substances, and solidifies
some; [(c)] to differences in the instruments [used]—as with the one
5   carpenter who saws with the saw, chisels with the adz, and bores holes
with the drill; or [(d)] the multiplicity in the act comes about through
mediation where one act is performed, then that act enacts another, the
act thereby becoming multiple.

(37) All these divisions are impossible with respect to the First Prin-
10   ciple, since there is neither difference, nor duality, nor multiplicity in His
essence, as will be shown in the proofs of divine unity. Moreover, there is no
difference in materials. For the discussion would [then] pertain to the first
effect and that which is first matter, for example.[4] And, moreover, there
is no difference in instrument, since there is no existent having the same
15   rank as God. The discussion would then pertain [only] to the origination
of the first instrument. Thus, there only remains for the multiplicity in the
world to proceed from God by way of mediation, as mentioned earlier.

(38) We say:

(39) It follows necessarily from this that there will be no one thing in
20   the world that is composed of individuals. Rather, all the existents would
be ones, each one the effect of another one above it and the cause of
another below it, until an effect without an effect is reached, just as [this
chain] terminates in the direction of ascent with a cause that has no
cause. But this is not the case. For body, according to them, is composed
25   of form and matter, becoming by their combination one thing. [Again,]
man is composed of body and soul, the existence of neither being from
the other, the existence of both being through another cause. The heavenly sphere, according to them, is likewise. For it is a body with a soul
where neither is the soul caused by the body nor the body by the soul,
30   both proceeding from a cause other than both. How, then, did these com-
posites come into existence? [Did they come about] from one [simple]
cause—in which case their statement that from the one only one proceeds becomes false—or from a composite cause? [If the latter,] then the

بقوة الغضب، وإمّا ان يكون لاختلاف الموادّ، كما انّ الشمس تبيّض الثوب المغسول وتسوّد وجه الانسان وتذيب بعض الجواهر وتصلّب بعضها، وإما لاختلاف الآلات، كالنجار الواحد ينشر [بالمنشار][٧] وينحت بالقدّوم ويثقب بالمثقب، وإمّا ان تكون كثرة الفعل بالتوسّط،

٥ بان يفعل فعلا واحدا، ثم ذلك الفعل يفعل غيره، فيكثر الفعل.

(٣٧) وهذه الاقسام كلّها محال فى المبدأ الاول، اذ ليس فى ذاته اختلاف واثنينيّة وكثرة، كما سيأتى فى أدلّة التوحيد، ولا ثمّ اختلاف موادّ. فانّ الكلام فى المعلول الاول والذى هى المادّة الاولى مثلا. ولا ثمّ اختلاف آلة، اذ لا موجود مع الله فى رتبته. فالكلام فى حدوث الآلة

١٠ الاولى. فلم يبق الا ان تكون الكثرة فى العالم صادرة من الله بطريق التوسّط كما سبق.

(٣٨) قلنا:

(٣٩) فيلزم من هذا ان لا يكون فى العالم شىء واحد مركب من افراد، بل تكون الموجودات كلها آحادا، وكل واحد معلول لواحد

١٥ آخر فوقه وعلة لآخر تحته الى أن ينتهى الى معلول لا معلول له، كما انتهى فى جهة التصاعد الى علّة لا علّة له. وليس كذلك. فانّ الجسم عندهم مركّب من صورة وهيولى، وقد صار باجتماعهما شيئا واحدا؛ والانسان مركّب من جسم ونفس، ليس وجود أحدهما من الآخر، بل وجودهما جميعا بعلّة اخرى؛ والفلك عندهم كذلك، فانّه جرم ذو

٢٠ نفس، لم تحدث النفس بالجرم، ولا الجرم بالنفس، بل كلاهما صدرا من علة سواهما. فكيف وجدت هذه المركبات؟ أمن علّة واحدة، فيبطل قولهم لا يصدر من الواحد الا واحد، أو من علّة مركّبة؟ فيتوجّه

question becomes directed to the composition of the cause [and is pursued] until one arrives at [the conclusion that] a composite necessarily meets a simple. For the principle is simple, whereas in [all] other [things] there is composition. This is inconceivable unless [the simple and the complex] meet; and, inasmuch as a meeting takes place, [the philosophers'] statement that from the one only one proceeds becomes false.

(40) [The philosophers may] say:

(41) Once our doctrine is [properly] known, the difficulty is resolved. Existents divide into those that are in receptacles, such as accidents and forms, and those that are not in receptacles. These [latter] divide into those, like bodies, that are receptacles for others and those that are not receptacles, such as the existents that are self-subsisting substances. These [in turn] divide into those that exert influence on bodies—and these we call souls—and those that do not exert influence on bodies, but only on souls, which we call pure intellects. As for the existents, such as accidents, that indwell in receptacles, these are temporal and have temporal causes that terminate in a principle that is in one respect temporal and in one respect permanent—namely, the circular [celestial] motion, which, however, is not the object of the discussion. The discussion is only concerned with the principles that are self-subsistent that do not [inhere] in receptacles. These are three: [(1)] bodies, which are the lowliest; [(2)] pure intellects that do not relate to bodies, either through the relation of action or by being impressed [in them], these being the noblest; [(3)] souls, which hold the middle ground. For these [souls] attach to bodies in some manner of attachment—namely, the exertion of influence and action on them. They are, hence, medial in the rank of value. For they are influenced by the intellects and exert influence on bodies.

(42) Moreover, the bodies are ten: nine heavens and a tenth which [consists of] the matter which is the filling of the concavity of the sphere of the moon. The nine heavens are animals that have bodies and souls and have an order in existence, which we will [now] mention.

السؤال فى تركيب العلّة الى ان يلتقى بالضرورة مركّب ببسيط. فانّ المبدأ بسيط، وفى الاواخر تركيب. ولا يتصوّر ذلك الا بالتقاء، وحيث يقع التقاء، يبطل قولهم ان الواحد لا يصدر منه الا واحد.

(٤٠) فان قيل:

(٤١) اذا عرف مذهبنا، اندفع الاشكال. فان الموجودات تنقسم الى ما هى فى محالّ كالاعراض والصور، والى ما ليست فى محالّ. وهذا ينقسم الى ما هى محالّ لغيرها كالاجسام والى ما ليست بمحالّ، كالموجودات التى هى جواهر قائمة بانفسها. وهى تنقسم الى ما يؤثر فى الاجسام ونسمّيها نفوسا والى ما لا يؤثر فى الاجسام بل فى النفوس ونسمّيها عقولا مجرّدة. أمّا الموجودات التى تحلّ فى المحالّ، كالاعراض، فهى حادثة ولها علل حادثة وتنتهى الى مبدأ هو حادث من وجه دائم من وجه، وهى الحركة الدورية وليس الكلام فيها. وانّما الكلام فى الاصول القائمة بانفسها لا فى محالّ، وهى ثلاثة: اجسام، وهى اخسّها، وعقول مجرّدة وهى التى لا تتعلّق بالاجسام، لا بالعلاقة الفعليّة ولا بالانطباع فيها، وهى أشرفها، ونفوس، وهى أوسطها. فانّها تتعلّق بالاجسام نوعا من التعلّق، وهو التأثير والفعل فيها. فهى متوسّطة فى الشرف. فانّها تتأثّر من العقول وتؤثّر فى الاجسام.

(٤٢) ثم الاجسام عشرة: تسع سموات، والعاشر المادّة التى هى حشو مقعّر فلك القمر. والسموات التسع حيوانات لها اجرام ونفوس ولها ترتيب فى الوجود كما نذكره.

(43) From the existence of the First Principle the first intellect emanated, it being a self-subsisting existent, neither body nor imprinted in body, that knows itself and knows its principle. (We have named it "the first intellect," but there is no need for dispute about names— whether it is called "angel," "intellect," or whatever one wishes). From its existence three things are rendered necessary: an intellect; the soul of the most distant [that is, the outermost] sphere, which is the ninth heaven; and the body of the most distant sphere. Then, from the second intellect, there necessarily [comes into existence] a third intellect: the soul of the sphere of the [fixed] stars, and its body. Then, from the third intellect there necessarily [proceeds] a fourth intellect: the soul of Saturn and its body. From the fourth intellect there necessarily [comes into existence] a fifth intellect: the soul of the sphere of Jupiter and its body. [The process continues] in this manner until it reaches the intellect from which proceeds [the existence] of the [last] intellect: the soul of the sphere of the moon and its body. The last intellect is the one termed "the active intellect." That which fills the sphere of the moon—namely, matter subject to generation and corruption—[proceeds] necessarily from the active intellect and the natures of the spheres. The matters intermix due to the motion of the stars in various combinations from which the minerals, plants, and animals come about. It does not follow necessarily that from each intellect another intellect would ensue without end. For these intellects are of different species,[5] so that what holds for one does not necessarily hold for the other.

(44) From [all] this, it comes out that the intellects, after the First Principle, are ten in number, and the spheres nine. The sum of these noble principles, after the First [Principle], is nineteen. From this it [also] comes out that under each of the first intellects there are three things: an intellect, the soul of a sphere, and its body. Hence, there must necessarily be a trinity in the principle [of each of these intellects]. No multiplicity is conceivable in the first effect except in one respect—namely, in that it intellectually apprehends its principle and intellectually apprehends itself. [Now,] with respect to itself, it is [only] possible of existence because the necessity of its existence is through another, not itself. These, then, are three different meanings, and the noblest of the three effects

(٤٣) وهو انّ المبدأ الاوّل فاض من وجوده العقل الاوّل، وهو موجود قائم بنفسه، ليس بجسم ولا منطبع فى جسم، يعرف نفسه ويعرف مبدأه، وقد سمّيناه العقل الاول ولا مشاحة فى الاسامى، سمّى ملكا أو عقلا أو ما أُريد. ويلزم عن وجوده ثلاثة أُمور، عقل ونفس الفلك الاقصى، وهى السماء التاسعة، وجرم الفلك الاقصى. ثم لزم من العقل الثانى عقل ثالث، ونفس فلك الكواكب، وجرمه. ثم لزم من العقل الثالث عقل رابع، ونفس فلك زحل، وجرمه. ولزم من العقل الرابع عقل خامس، ونفس فلك المشترى، وجرمه، وهكذى حتى انتهى الى العقل الذى لزم منه عقل، ونفْس فلك القمر، وجرمه. والعقل الاخير هو الذى يسمّى العقل الفَعَّال. ولزم حشو فلك القمر وهى المادة القابلة للكون والفساد من العقل الفعّال وطبائع الافلاك. ثم انّ الموادّ تمتزج بسبب حركات الكواكب امتزاجات مختلفة يحصل منها المعادن والنبات والحيوان. ولا يلزم ان يلزم من كلّ عقل عقل الى غير نهاية لانّ هذه العقول مختلفة الانواع فما ثبت لواحد، لا يلزم للآخر.

(٤٤) فخرج منه انّ العقول بعد المبدأ الاول عشرة، والافلاك تسعة، ومجموع هذه المبادى الشريفة بعد الاول تسعة عشر؛ وحصل منه أن تحت كلّ عقل من العقول الاول ثلاثة أشياء، عقل، ونفس فلك، وجرمه. فلا بدّ وان يكون فى مبدئه تثليث لا محالة، ولا يتصور كثرة فى المعلول الاول الا من وجه واحد. وهو انّه يعقل مبدأه، ويعقل نفسه؛ وهو باعتبار ذاته ممكن الوجود، لانّ وجوب وجوده بغيره، لا بنفْسه؛ وهذه معان ثلاثة مختلفة، والاشرف من المعلولات الثلاثة ينبغى أن ينسب الى الاشرف من هذه المعانى، فيصدر منه العقل من حيث انّه

ought to be related to the noblest of these meanings. Thus, an intellect proceeds from it inasmuch as it intellectually apprehends its principle. The soul of the sphere proceeds from it inasmuch as it intellectually apprehends itself, whereas the body of the sphere proceeds from it inasmuch as it in itself is [only] possible of existence.

(45) It remains [for the opponent] to say, "Whence did this trinity in the first effect come about when its principle is one?" We say:

(46) Nothing proceeded from the First Principle except one [thing]: namely, the essence of this intellect by which it apprehends itself intellectually. It has as a necessary consequence—not, however, from the direction of the Principle—that it apprehends the Principle intellectually.[6] In itself it is possible of existence; but it does not derive [this] possibility from the First Principle, but [has it] due to itself. We do not deem it improbable that, from the one, one comes into existence, where the [latter] effect would have as a necessary concomitant—[but] not from the direction of the First Principle—necessary matters, relative or non-relative, because of which multiplicity comes about, [this effect] becoming thereby the principle for the existence of plurality. In this manner, then, it becomes possible for the composite to meet the simple, since such a meeting is inevitable; and it can only happen in this way. This, then, is the way the [matter] must be adjudged. This, then, is the discourse explaining their doctrine.

(47) [To this] we say:

(48) What you have mentioned are arbitrary assertions which, when truly ascertained, constitute [nothing but] darkness atop darkness. If a human were to relate this as something seen in sleep, one would infer from it the illness of his temperament; or, if its kind were brought about in legal matters, where the most one can hope for is conjecture, it would be said that these are trifles that bestow no likely suppositions. The [possible] openings in objecting to such [statements] are limitless. We will, however, bring forth aspects that are limited in number.

(49) The first is to say: "You have claimed that one of the meanings of plurality in the first effect is that it is possible of existence." [To this we] say: "Is its being possible of existence identical with its existence or other than it? If identical, then no plurality would arise from it; and, if other than it, then why would you not say that there is plurality in the First Principle because He exists and, in addition to this, He is necessary of existence?" For the necessity of existence is other than existence itself. Let one then

يعقل مبدأه، ويصدر نفس الفلك من حيث انّه يعقل نفسه، ويصدر جرم الفلك من حيث انّه ممكّن الوجود بذاته.

(٤٥) فيبقى ان يقال: هذا التثليث، من أين حصل فى المعلول الاول، ومبدؤه واحد؟ فنقول:

٥ (٤٦) لم يصدر من المبدأ الاوّل الا واحد، وهو ذات هذا العقل الذى به يعقل نفسه. ولزمه ضرورة، لا من جهة المبدأ، ان عقل المبدأ. وهو فى ذاته ممكن الوجود، وليس له الامكان من المبدأ الاول، بل هو لذاته. ونحن لا نبعد ان يوجد من الواحد واحد يلزم ذلك المعلول، لا من جهة المبدأ، أمور ضروريّة اضافيّة أو غير اضافيّة، فيحصل بسببه كثرة ويصير

١٠ بذلك مبدأ لوجود الكثرة. فعلى هذا الوجه يمكن ان يلتقى المركب بالبسيط، اذ لا بد من الالتقاء، ولا يمكن الا كذلك. فهو الذى يجب الحكم به. فهذا هو القول فى تفهيم مذهبهم.

(٤٧) قلنا:

(٤٨) ما ذكرتموه تحكّمات وهى على التحقيق ظلمات فوق
١٥ ظلمات، لو حكاه الانسان عن منام رآه لاستدل به على سوء مزاجه، أو اورد جنسه فى الفقهيّات التى قصارى المطلب فيها تخمينات، لقيل انها ترهات لا تفيد غلبات الظنون. ومداخل الاعتراض على مثلها لا تنحصر. ولكنّا نورد وجوها معدودة.

(٤٩) الاوّل، هو انّا نقول: ادعيتم ان أحد معانى الكثرة فى المعلول الاول انّه ممكن الوجود، فنقول: كونه ممكن الوجود، عين وجوده أو غيره؟
٢٠ فان كان عينه، فلا ينشأ منه كثرة، وان كان غيره، فهلا قلتم فى المبدا الاول كثرة لانّه موجود وهو مع ذلك واجب الوجود؟ فوجوب الوجود غير نفس

allow the proceeding of various things from Him due to this plurality. If it is said, "There is no meaning to the necessary of existence except existence," then [we would say that] there is no meaning to the possibility of existence except existence. If you then say, "It is possible to know its being an existent without knowing its being possible; hence, [being possible] is other than it," [we would say that,] similarly with the Necessary Existent, it is possible to know His existence without knowing its necessity except after another proof; hence, let [the necessity] be other than Him.

(50) In sum, existence is a general thing that divides into the necessary and the contingent. If, then, the differentia in one of the two divisions is additional to the general [meaning], the same applies to the second differentia. There is no difference [between the two].

(51) If it is then said, "The possibility of existence belongs to it from itself, whereas its existence derives from another; then how would that which belongs to it from itself and that which it has from another be the same?" we say:

(52) How can the necessity of existence be identical with existence, when the necessity of existence can be denied and existence affirmed?[7] The true one[8] in every respect is the one not subject to [simultaneous] affirmation and negation, since it cannot be said of it that it exists and does not exist and that it is necessary of existence and not necessary of existence. But it is possible to say that [something] exists but is not necessary of existence, just as it can be said that it exists and is not possible of existence. It is through this that unity is known. Hence, it would be incorrect to suppose this [identity of the necessity of existence and existence] in the case of the First, if what they say—namely, that the possibility of existence is other than existence that is possible—is true.

(53) The second objection is to say: "Is [the first intellect's] intellectual apprehension of its Principle identical with its existence and identical with its apprehension of itself, or is it another?" If identical, then there is no plurality in its essence—only in the verbal expression about its essence. If another, then this plurality exists in the First. For He intellectually apprehends His essence and intellectually apprehends [what is] other. If they claim [(a)] that His intellectual apprehension of Himself is His very self, [(b)] that He only apprehends Himself if He apprehends that He is a principle for another, [and (c)] that [this is] because the act of intellectual apprehension[9] coincides with the apprehended intelligible, whereby [His apprehending another] reverts to [being] His [very] essence, we say:

الوجود. فليجز صدور المختلفات منه لهذه الكثرة. وان قيل، لا معنى لوجوب الوجود الا الوجود، فلا معنى لامكان الوجود الا الوجود. فان قلتم يمكن ان يعرف كونه موجودا ولا يعرف كونه ممكنا، فهو غيره، فكذا واجب الوجود، يمكن ان يعرف وجوده ولا يعرف وجوبه الا بعد دليل آخر، فليكن غيره. ٥

(٥٠) وبالجملة الوجود أمر عام ينقسم الى واجب والى ممكن، فان كان فصل احد القسمين زائدا على العام، فكذى الفصل الثانى ولا فرق.

(٥١) فان قيل: امكان الوجود له من ذاته ووجوده من غيره، فكيف يكون ما له من ذاته وما له من غيره واحدا؟ قلنا:

(٥٢) وكيف يكون وجوب الوجود عين الوجود ويمكن أن ينفى ١٠ وجوب الوجود ويثبت الوجود؟ والواحد الحقّ من كل وجه هو الذى لا يتّسع للنفى والاثبات اذ لا يمكن أن يقال موجود وليس بموجود او واجب الوجود وليس بواجب الوجود، ويمكن ان يقال موجود وليس بواجب الوجود، كما يمكن ان يقال موجود وليس بممكن الوجود. وانّما [تعرف]٨ الوحدة بهذا. فلا يستقيم تقدير ذلك فى الاوّل ان صحّ ما ١٥ ذكروه من أنّ امكان الوجود غير الوجود الممكن.

(٥٣) الاعتراض الثانى هو ان نقول: عقله مبدأه، عين وجوده وعين عقله نفسه أم غيره؟ فان كان عينه، فلا كثرة فى ذاته الا فى العبارة عن ذاته، وان كان غيره، فهذه الكثرة موجودة فى الاوّل. فانّه يعقل ذاته ويعقل غيره. فان زعموا ان عقله ذاته عين ذاته، ولا يعقل ذاته ما لم يعقل ٢٠ انه مبدأ لغيره، فانّ العقل يطابق المعقول، فيكون راجعا الى ذاته، فنقول:

(54) The [first] effect's intellectual apprehension of itself is identical with itself. For it is intellect in its substance, and thus it intellectually apprehends itself. Intellect, that which intellectually apprehends, and that of it which is intellectually apprehended are also one. Moreover, if
5   its intellectual apprehension of itself is identical with itself, then let it apprehend itself as an effect of a cause. For this is the case. Intellect and intelligible coincide, all thus reverting to the essence [of the first effect]. Hence, there is no multiplicity. If this were to constitute plurality, then it would exist in the First. Let, then, the varied things proceed from Him.
10 And let us then forsake the claim of His unity in every respect, if unity ceases with this kind of plurality.

(55) If it is then said, "The First does not apprehend intellectually [that which is] other than Himself. His intellectual apprehension of Himself is identical with Himself, intellect, intellectual apprehension,
15 and what is apprehended being one [and the same]; and [thus] He does not intellectually apprehend another," we answer in two ways:

(56) One is that because of the repugnancy of this doctrine Avicenna and the rest of the exacting [philosophers] abandoned it. They claimed that the First knows Himself as the source for what emanates from Him
20 and intellectually apprehends all the existents in their [various] kinds by a universal, not particular, intellectual apprehension, since they deemed it reprehensible for one to say that from the First Principle only an intellect proceeds and then that He does not intellectually apprehend what proceeds from Him. And His effect [those who hold that the First knows
25 only Himself then maintain][10] is an intellect from which another intellect, the soul of a sphere, and a body of a sphere emanate. [This other intellect] apprehends itself, its three effects, its [own] cause, and its principle.

(57) The effect [it should be pointed out] would thus be nobler than the cause, inasmuch as from the cause only one [existent] emanated,
30 whereas from this one three emanated. Moreover, the First apprehends intellectually only Himself, whereas this [effect] apprehends itself, the Principle itself, and the effects themselves. Whoever is content [with holding] that what he says about God reduces to this level would have rendered Him lower than every existent that apprehends itself and Him.
35 For that which apprehends Him and apprehends itself is nobler than He, since He apprehends only Himself.

(58) Hence, their endeavor to go deep into magnifying [God] has ended up in their negating everything that is understood by greatness. They have rendered His state approximating that of the dead person who

(٥٤) والمعلول عقله ذاته عين ذاته. فانّه عقل بجوهره، فيعقل نفسه. والعقل والعاقل والمعقول منه أيضا واحد. ثم اذا كان عقله ذاته عين ذاته، فليعقل ذاته معلولا لعلّة، فانّه كذلك. والعقل يطابق المعقول فيرجع الكلّ الى ذاته؛ فلا كثرة اذن. وان كانت هذه كثرة، فهى موجودة فى الاول.

فليصدر منه المختلفات. ولنترك دعوى وحدانيّته من كلّ وجه، ان كانت الوحدانيّة تزول بهذا النوع من الكثرة.

(٥٥) فان قيل الاول لا يعقل الا ذاته وعقله ذاته هو عين ذاته فالعقل والعاقل والمعقول واحد ولا يعقل غيره، [فالجواب]٩ من وجهين.

(٥٦) احدهما، انّ هذا المذهب لشناعته هجره ابن سينا وسائر المحقّقين، وزعموا انّ الاول يعلم نفسه مبدأ لفيضان ما يفيض منه ويعقل الموجودات كلّها بانواعها عقلا كلّيًّا لا جزئيًّا، اذ استقبحوا قول القائل المبدأ الاوّل لا يصدر منه الا عقل واحد ثم لا يعقل ما يصدر منه. ومعلوله عقل ويفيض منه عقل ونفس فلك وجرم فلك ويعقل نفسه ومعلولاته الثلاث وعلّته ومبدأه.

(٥٧) فيكون المعلول أشرف من العلّة من حيث انّ العلة ما فاض منها الا واحد، وقد فاض من هذا ثلاثة أمور، والاوّل ما عقل الا نفسه وهذا عقل نفسه ونفس المبدأ ونفس المعلولات. ومن قنع ان يكون قوله فى الله راجعا الى هذه الرتبة، فقد جعله احقر من كلّ موجود يعقل نفسه ويعقله. فانّ ما يعقله ويعقل نفسه أشرف منه اذا كان هو لا يعقل الا نفسه.

(٥٨) فقد انتهى منهم التعمق فى التعظيم الى ان أبطلوا كلّ ما يفهم من العظمة، وقرّبوا حاله من حال الميت الذى لا خبر له [بما]١٠ يجرى

has no information of what takes place in the world, differing from the dead, however, only in His self-awareness. This is what God does with those who are deviators from His path and destroyers of the way of guidance; who deny His saying, "I did not make them witness the creation of the heavens and the earth, nor the creation of themselves" [Qurʾān 18:51]; who think of God in evil terms; who believe that the depth of the "lordly" things is grasped by the human faculties; who are full of conceit about their minds, claiming that they have in them a [better] alternative to the tradition of imitating the apostles and following them. No wonder, then, that they are forced to acknowledge that the substance of their intellectual apprehensions reduces to that which would be astonishing [even] if it were uttered in a slumber.

(59) The second answer is that whoever upholds that the First intellectually apprehends only Himself [has done so] to avoid plurality as a necessary consequence. For, if he were to uphold [the doctrine that He knows other than Himself], then it would follow necessarily that one must say that His apprehending another is other than His apprehending Himself. But this is [also] necessary with the first effect, and, hence, it ought to apprehend [nothing] but itself. For, if it apprehends the First or another, then this act of intellectual apprehension would be other than itself; and it would require a cause other than the cause of itself when there is no cause other than the cause of itself—namely, the First Principle. Hence, it ought to know only itself, and the plurality that ensues in [the] way [the philosophers hold] ceases.

(60) If it is said, "When it came into existence and apprehended itself, it became necessary for it to apprehend the Principle," we say:

(61) Did this become necessary for it by a cause or without a cause? If by a cause, there is no cause except the First Principle. He is one, and it is inconceivable that anything but one should proceed from Him. And this [one thing] has [already] proceeded—namely, the effect. How, then, did the second [thing, the necessity of the first effect to apprehend Him,] proceed from Him? If [on the other hand] it became necessary without a cause, let, then, the existence of the First [Principle] be followed necessarily by numerous existents without a cause, and let plurality be their resultant consequence. If this is incomprehensible—inasmuch as necessary existence cannot be but one, that which is more than one being [only] possible, the possible requiring a cause—then this thing which is necessary in terms of the [first] effect [—namely, that it must apprehend the First Principle— would have to be either necessary in itself or possible]. But if [it is] necessary in itself, then [the philosophers'] statement that the Necessary Existent is one becomes false. If possible, then it must require a cause. But it has no

فى العالم، الا انّه فارق الميت فى شعوره بنفسه فقط. وهكذى يفعل الله بالزائغين عن سبيله والناكبين لطريق الهدى، المنكرين لقوله ‹‹ما اشهدتهم خلق السموات والارض ولا خلق أنفسهم،›› الظانّين بالله ظنّ السوء، المعتقدين انّ الامور الربوبيّة يستولى على كنهها القوى البشريّة، المغرورين بعقولهم، زاعمين انّ فيها مندوحة عن تقليد الرسل واتباعهم. فلا جرم اضطروا الى الاعتراف بانّ لباب معقولاتهم رجعت الى ما لو حكى فى منام لتعجب منه.

(٥٩) الجواب الثانى هو انّ من ذهب الى انّ الاوّل لا يعقل الا نفسه انّما حاذر من لزوم الكثرة، اذ لو قال به، للزم ان يقال عقله غيره غير عقله نفسه. وهذا لازم فى المعلول الاوّل، فينبغى ان لا يعقل الا نفسه؛ لانّه لو عقل الاوّل أو غيره، لكان ذلك غير ذاته، ولافتقر الى علّة غير علّة ذاته، ولا علّة الا علّة ذاته وهو المبدأ الاوّل. فينبغى ان لا يعلم الا ذاته، وتبطل الكثرة التى نشأت من هذا الوجه.

(٦٠) فان قيل لمّا وجد وعقل ذاته، لزمه ان يعقل المبدأ، قلنا:

(٦١) لزمه ذلك بعلّة أو بغير علّة؟ فان كان بعلّة، فلا علّة الا المبدأ الاول، وهو واحد، ولا يتصوّر ان يصدر منه الا واحد، وقد صدر، وهو ذات المعلول. فالثانى كيف يصدر منه؟ وان لزم بغير علّة، فليلزم وجود الاوّل موجودات بلا علّة كثيرة وليلزم منها الكثرة. فان لم يُعقل هذا من حيث انّ واجب الوجود لا يكون الا واحدا، والزائد على الواحد ممكن، والممكن يفتقر الى علّة، فهذا اللازم فى حق المعلول. وان كان واجب الوجود بذاته، فقد بطل قولهم واجب الوجود واحد. وان كان ممكنا فلا بدّ له من علّة. ولا علّة له. فلا يعقل وجوده. وليس هو من ضرورة

cause. Its existence is, hence, incomprehensible. Nor is [this necessity of apprehending the First] a necessity [required] by the first effect by reason of its being possible of existence. For the possibility of existence is necessary in every effect. As for an effect's having knowledge of its cause, this is not necessary for its existence, just as the cause's being cognizant of its effect is not necessary for its existence. Rather, the concomitance [of a cause] and the knowledge of [its] effect is more evident than the concomitance [of an effect] and the knowledge of [its] cause. It becomes clear, then, that the plurality resulting from [the first effect's] knowledge of its principle is impossible. For there is no initiating principle for this [knowledge], and it is not a necessary consequence of the existence of the effect itself. This also is inescapable.

(62) The third objection is [to ask]: "Is the first effect's intellectual apprehension of its own essence identical with its essence or other than it?" If it is identical, this would be impossible, because knowledge is other than the object known. If it is other, then let this be the same with the First Principle: plurality would then necessarily ensue from Him. Moreover, there would necessarily proceed from [the first effect] a quadruplication and not, as they claim, a trinity [of existents]. For this would consist of [the first effect] itself, its apprehension of itself, its apprehension of its Principle, and its being in itself possible of existence. One could also add that it is necessary of existence through another, wherewith a quintuplicating would appear. By this one gets to know the deep delving of these [philosophers] into lunacy.

(63) The fourth objection is for us to say: "Trinity in the first effect does not suffice." For the body of the first heaven, according to them, proceeds necessarily from one idea in the essence of [its] principle. [But] in it there is composition in three respects.

(64) One of them is that it is composed of form and matter—this, according to them, being applicable to every body. It is incumbent, then, that each of the two should have a [different] principle, since form differs from matter. Neither one of them, according to their doctrine, is an independent cause of the other, whereby one of them would come about through the mediation of the other without another additional cause.

(65) The second is that the outermost body is of a specific extent in size. Its having this specific quantity from among the rest of quantities is something additional to the existence of itself, since it can be smaller

المعلول الاوّل لكونه ممكن الوجود. فانّ امكان الوجود ضروريّ فى كل معلول. أمّا كون المعلول عالما بالعلة ليس ضروريّا فى وجود ذاته، كما انّ كون العلّة عالما بالمعلول ليس ضروريّا فى وجود ذاته، بل لزوم العلم بالمعلول اظهر من لزوم العلم بالعلّة. فبان انّ الكثرة الحاصلة من علمه بالمبدأ محال. فانّه لا مبدأ له وليس هو من ضرورة وجود ذات المعلول. وهذا ايضا لا مخرج منه.

(٦٢) الاعتراض الثالث هو انّ عقل المعلول الاوّل ذات نفسه عين ذاته أو غيره؟ فان كان عينه، فهو محال، لانّ العلم غير المعلوم. وان كان غيره، فليكن كذلك فى المبدأ الاول، فيلزم منه كثرة ويلزم فيه تربيع لا تثليث بزعمهم. فانّه ذاته، وعقله نفسه، وعقله مبدأه، وانّه ممكن الوجود بذاته. ويمكن ان يزاد انّه واجب الوجود بغيره، فيظهر تخميس. وبهذا يتعرف تعمّق هؤلاء فى الهوس.

(٦٣) الاعتراض الرابع ان نقول التثليث لا يكفى فى المعلول الاول. فانّ جرم السماء الاوّل لزم عندهم من معنى واحد من ذات المبدأ وفيه تركيب من ثلاثة أوجه.

(٦٤) احدها انه مركّب من صورة وهيولى، وهكذا كل جسم عندهم. فلا بدّ لكلّ واحد من مبدأ، اذ الصورة تخالف الهيولى، وليست كل واحدة على مذبهم علّة مستقلة للاخرى بكون أحدها بوساطة الآخر من غير علّة أُخرى زائدة عليه.

(٦٥) الثانى انّ الجرم الاقصى على حدّ مخصوص فى الكبر. فاختصاصه بذلك القدر من بين سائر المقادير زائد على وجود ذاته اذ كان

or larger than it is. It must have, then, something that specifies that quantity—[something] which is additional to the simple idea that necessitates its existence and which is unlike the existence of the intellect. For [the latter] is pure existence, unspecified with a quantity contrary to all other quantities, so that one can say that [the intellect] needs only a simple cause. If it is said, "The reason for this is that, if it were larger than it is, it would not be needed for realizing the universal order; and, if smaller, it would not be suitable for the intended order," we say:

(66) Is the assigning of the mode of the order sufficient for the existence of that through which the order comes to be, or does it need a cause that brings about [the latter's] existence? If sufficient, then you would not need to posit causes. Rule, then, that the existence of order in these existents decreed these existents without an additional cause. If not sufficient, but requiring a cause, then this also would not be sufficient to specify quantities, but would also require a cause for composition.

(67) The third is that the outermost heaven divides along two points, these being the two poles. These two are of fixed positions, never departing from their positions, while the parts of the zone differ in position. For then it follows either [(a)] that all parts of the outermost heaven are similar, [and hence it can be asked,] "Why was the assigning of two points from among the rest of the points to be the two poles rendered necessary?" or [(b)] their parts are different. In some, then, there would be special characteristics not [found] in others. What, then, is the principle of these differences, when the outermost body proceeded only from one simple idea, and when the simple necessitates only what is simple in shape (namely, the spherical) and what is similar in idea (namely, one devoid of differentiated characteristics)? From this, also, there is no escape [for them].

(68) It may be said: "Perhaps there are in the principle [of these differences] kinds of multiplicity that are necessary, [but] not from the direction of the [First] Principle, of which only three or four have become apparent to us and of the rest [of which] we have no knowledge. Our not coming across [the rest] in the concrete does not make us doubt that the principle of multiplicity is multiple and that from the one many do not proceed." [To this] we say:

ذاته ممكنا أصغر منه وأكبر. فلا بدّ له من مخصّص بذلك المقدار، زائد على المعنى البسيط الموجب لوجوده لا كوجود العقل. فانّه وجود محض لا يختصّ بمقدار مقابل لسائر المقادير، فيجوز ان يقال: لا يحتاج إلا الى علّة بسيطة. فان قيل، سببه انّهُ لو كان منه اكبر لكان مستغنى عنه فى تحصيل،

٥   النظام الكلّيّ لو كان أصغر منه لم يصلح للنظام المقصود، فنقول:

(٦٦) وتعيّن جهة النظام، هل هو كاف فى وجود ما به النظام أم يفتقر الى علّة موجدة؟ فان كان كافيا، فقد استغنيتم عن وضع العلل. فاحكموا بانّ كون النظام فى هذه الموجودات اقتضى هذه الموجودات بلا علّة زائدة. وان كان ذلك لا يكفى، بل افتقر الى علّة، فذلك أيضاً لا

١٠   يكفى للاختصاص بالمقادير، بل يحتاج أيضاً الى علّة التركيب.

(٦٧) الثالث انّ الفلك الاقصى انقسم الى نقطتين، هما القطبان، وهما ثابتا الوضع، لا يفارقان وضعهما، واجزاء المنطقة يختلف وضعها. فلا يخلوا امّا ان كان جميع أجزاء الفلك الاقصى متشابها، فلم لزم تعيّن نقطتين من بيّن سائر النقط لكونهما قطبين؟ أو أجزاؤها مختلفة. ففى

١٥   بعضها خواصّ ليست فى البعض. فما مبدأ تلك الاختلافات، والجرم الاقصى لم يصدر الا من معنى واحد بسيط، والبسيط لا يوجب الا بسيطا فى الشكل، وهو الكرى، ومتشابها فى المعنى، وهو الخلو عن الخواصّ المميّزة؟ وهذا أيضا لا مخرج منه.

(٦٨) فان قيل: لعلّ فى المبدأ أنواعا من الكثرة لازمة لا من جهة المبدأ وانما ظهر لنا ثلاثة أو أربعة والباقي لم نطلع عليه. وعدم عثورنا على عينه

٢٠   لا يشكّكنا فى انّ مبدأ الكثرة كثرة وانّ الواحد لا يصدر منه كثير، قلنا:

(69) If you allow this, then say that all the existents, with all their great number—and they are in the thousands—have proceeded from the first effect, and there is no need to restrict [what proceeds from it] to the body of the outermost heaven and its soul. Rather, it is possible that all celestial and human souls, all terrestrial and celestial bodies, have proceeded from it with many kinds of multiplicity necessary in them [that] they have not known. Hence, there would be no need for the first effect. Furthermore, from this there follows the absence of [any] need for the First Cause. For, if the generation of plurality that is said to be necessary without a cause, even though not necessary for the existence of the first effect, is permitted, it becomes allowed to suppose this with the First Cause and [to suppose] that their existence would be without a cause. It would then be said that these are necessary, but their number is not known. Whenever their existence without a cause with the First [Cause] is imagined, this [existence] without a cause is imagined with the second [cause]. Indeed, there is no meaning to our saying "[their being] with the First [Cause]" and "[with] the second," since there is no difference between them in either time or space. For that which does not differ from the two in space and time and can exist without a cause will not have one of the two [rather than the other] specifically related to it.

(70) If it is said, "Things have become numerous so as to exceed a thousand, and it is unlikely that multiplicity in the first effect should reach this extent, and for this reason we have increased the [number of] intermediaries," we say:

(71) Someone's saying, "This is unlikely," is sheer supposition in terms of which no judgment is made in rational [arguments], unless he says, "It would be impossible," in which case we would then say:

(72) Why would it be impossible? What prevents it, and what [operative] deciding criterion is there, once we go beyond the one and believe that it is possible [that there may] follow necessarily from the first effect—not by way of the [First] Cause—one, two, or three concomitants? What would render four, five, and so on up to a thousand impossible? Otherwise, [when] anyone arbitrarily decides on one quantity rather than another, then, after going beyond the one, there is nothing to prevent [greater numbers]. This [answer] is also conclusive.

(٦٩) فاذا جوَّزتم هذا، فقولوا ان الموجودات كلّها على كثرتها وقد بلغت آلافا صدرت من المعلول الاوّل، فلا يحتاج ان يقتصر على جرم الفلك الاقصى ونفسه، بل يجوز ان يكون قد صدر منه جميع النفوس الفلكيّة والانسانيّة وجميع الاجسام الارضيّة والسماويّة بانواع كثرة لازمة فيها لم يطلعوا عليها، فيقع الاستغناء بالمعلول الأول. ثم يلزم منه الاستغناء بالعلّة الاولى. فانّه اذا جاز تولّد كثرة يقال انّها لازمة لا بعلّة، مع انّها ليست ضرورية فى وجود المعلول الاوّل، جاز ان يقدر ذلك مع العلّة الاولى ويكون وجودها لا بعلّة، ويقال انّها لزمت ولا يدرى عددها. وكلّما تخيّل وجودها بلا علة مع الاول، تخيّل ذلك بلا علّة مع الثانى. بل لا معنى لقولنا مع الاوّل والثانى، اذ ليس بينهما مفارقة فى زمان ولا مكان. فما لا يفارقهما فى مكان وزمان ويجوز ان يكون موجودا بلا علّة لم يختصّ أحدهما بالاضافة اليه.

(٧٠) فان قيل لقد كثرت الاشياء حتّى زادت على ألف وييعد ان تبلغ الكثرة فى المعلول الاول الى هذا الحدّ فلذلك أكثرنا الوسائط، قلنا:

(٧١) قول القائل ييعد، هذا رجم ظنّ، لا يحكم به فى المعقولات، الا ان يقول، انه يستحيل، فنقول:

(٧٢) لم يستحيل؟ وما المرّد والفيصل مهما جاوزنا الواحد واعتقدنا انّه يجوز ان يلزم المعلول الاول لا من جهة العلّة لازم واثنان وثلث؟ فما المحيل لأربع وخمس وهكذى الى الالف؟ والا فمن يتحكم بمقدار دون مقدار فليس بعد مجاوزة الواحد مرّد. وهذا أيضا قاطع.

(73) We further say: "This is false with respect to the second effect. For from it proceeded the sphere of the fixed stars, which includes over twelve hundred stars. These vary in size, shape, position, color, influence—in being bad omens and in being omens of bliss. Some have the figure of the ram, [some] of the bull, [some] of the lion, [some] the figure of a human. Their influence in one place in the lower world differs in terms of cooling [or] heating [or] bringing about good and bad luck. Moreover, their sizes differ in themselves. Thus, with all these differences, it cannot be said that the whole constitutes one species. If this were possible, it would be possible to say that all the bodies of the world are one in corporeality, and, hence, it would be sufficient for them to have one cause. If, then, the differences in the qualities [of the bodies of the world], their substances, and [their] natures indicate their differences, then likewise the fixed stars are necessarily different, each requiring a cause for its form; a cause for its matter; a cause for its having a particular nature that either heats [or] cools, brings about a good omen or a bad omen; [a cause] for its belonging specifically to its place; and [a cause] for [the resemblance of] their groups to specific figures of different beasts. And, if the intellectual apprehension of this multiplicity is conceivable in the second effect, it is conceivable in the first effect, wherewith there comes about the dispensing [with the second effect]."

(74) The fifth objection is that we say:

(75) We will concede these insipid postulates and false arbitrary [assertions]. But how is it that you are not embarrassed by your statement that the first effect, being possible of existence, required the existence from it of the outermost sphere, [that] its intellectual apprehension of itself required the existence from it of the soul of the sphere, and [that] its apprehension of the First requires the existence from it of an intellect? What is the difference between this and someone who—knowing the existence of a man who is absent, [knowing] that [such a man] is possible of existence, [knowing] that he apprehends himself and his Maker—then [goes on to] say: "The existence of a celestial sphere follows necessarily from [this man's] being possible of existence"? To this it would then be said: "What relationship is there between his being possible of existence and the existence from him of a celestial sphere?" Similarly, from his intellectual apprehension of himself and of his Maker, two things would have to follow necessarily. This, when spoken of in

(٧٣) ثم نقول: هذا باطل بالمعلول الثانى. فانّه صدر منه فلك الكواكب وفيه ألف ونيف ومئتا كوكب، وهى مختلفة العظم والشكل والوضع واللون والتأثير والنحوسة والسعادة؛ فبعضها على صورة الحمل والثور الاسد، وبعضها على صورة الانسان؛ ويختلف تأثيرها فى محل واحد من العالم السفلى فى التبريد والتسخين والسعادة والنحوس؛ وتختلف مقاديرها فى ذاتها. فلا يمكن ان يقال الكلّ نوع واحد مع هذا الاختلاف. ولو جاز هذا لجاز ان يقال كلّ اجسام العالم نوع واحد فى الجسميّة فيكفيها علّة واحدة. فان كان اختلاف صفاتها وجواهرها وطبائعها دلّ على اختلافها، فكذى الكواكب مختلفة لا محالة ويفتقر كلّ واحد الى علّة لصورته وعلّة لهيولاه وعلّة لاختصاصه بطبيعته المسخّنة أو المبرّدة أو المسعدة أو المنحسة ولاختصاصه. بموضعه ثم لاختصاص جملها باشكال البهائم المختلفة. وهذه الكثرة ان تصوّر ان تعقل فى المعلول الثانى تصوّر فى الاول ووقع الاستغناء.

(٧٤) الاعتراض الخامس هو انا نقول:

(٧٥) سلّمنا هذه الاوضاع الباردة والتحكّمات الفاسدة، ولكن كيف لا تستحيون من قولكم ان كون المعلول الاول ممكن الوجود اقتضى وجود جرم الفلك الاقصى منه، وعقله نفسه اقتضى وجود نفس الفلك منه، وعقله الاول يقتضى وجود عقل منه؟ وما الفصل بين هذا وبين قائل، عرف وجود انسان غائب وانه ممكن الوجود وانه يعقل نفسه وصانعه، فقال يلزم من كونه ممكن الوجود وجود فلك؟ فيقال، وأىّ مناسبة بين كونة ممكن الوجود وبين وجود فلك منه؟ وكذلك يلزم من كونه عاقلا لنفسه ولصانعه شيئان آخران. وهذا اذا قيل فى انسان

terms of a human, evokes [nothing but] laughter, and it would [evoke] the same [when said of any] other existent. For the possibility of existence is a proposition that does not differ with the difference of that which is possible, be this a human, an angel, or a celestial sphere. I do not know how [even] a madman would in himself be satisfied by the likes of such postulates, to say nothing of [those] rational people who split hairs in what they claim in matters intellectual.

(76) It may be said:

(77) If you have refuted their doctrine, what do you yourselves say? Do you claim that, from the thing that is one in every respect, two different things proceed, thereby affronting what is intelligible; would you say that the First Principle possesses multiplicity, thereby abandoning divine unity; would you say that there is no plurality in the world, denying thereby [the evidence of] the senses; or, would you say that [plurality] is necessitated through intermediaries, being compelled thereby to acknowledge what [the philosophers] say?

(78) We say:

(79) We have not plunged into this book in the manner of one who is introducing [doctrine], our purpose being to disrupt their claims—and this has been effected. Nonetheless, we say: "Whoever claims that whatever leads to the proceeding of two things from one is an affront to reason, or that describing the First Principle as having eternal, everlasting attributes contradicts [the doctrine of] divine unity, [should note] that these two claims are false and [that the philosophers] have no demonstration to prove them." For the impossibility of the proceeding of two things from one is not known in the way the impossibility of an individual's being in two places is known. In brief, this is known neither through [rational] necessity nor through theoretical reflection. What is there to prevent one from saying that the First Principle is knowing, powerful, willing; that He enacts as He wishes, governs what He wills, creates things that are varied and things that are homogeneous as He wills and in the way He wills? The impossibility of this is known neither through rational necessity nor through theoretical reflection. [That this is the case] has been conveyed by the prophets, [and the veracity of their prophethood has been] supported by miracles. Hence, it must be accepted. Investigating the manner of the act's proceeding from God through will is presumption and a coveting of what is unattainable. The end product of the reflection of those who have coveted seeking [this]

ضحك منه فكذى فى موجود آخر، اذ إمكان الوجود قضيّة لا تختلف باختلاف ذات الممكن، انسانا كان أو ملكا أو فلكا. فلست ادرى كيف يقنع الجنون فى نفسه.بمثل هذه الاوضاع، فضلاً من العقلاء الذين يشقّون الشعر بزعمهم فى المعقولات.

(٧٦) فان قال قائل:

(٧٧) فاذا أبطلتم مذهبهم فماذى تقولون أنتم؟ أتزعمون أنّه يصدر من الشىء الواحد من كل وجه شيئان مختلفان، فتكابرون المعقول، أو تقولون المبدأ الاول فيه كثرة، فتتركون التوحيد، أو تقولون لا كثرة فى العالم فتنكرون الحس، أو تقولون لزمت بالوسائط فتضطرون الى الاعتراف.بما قالوه؟

(٧٨) قلنا:

(٧٩) نحن لم نخض فى هذا الكتاب خوض ممهّد، وانّما غرضنا ان نشوّش دعاويهم وقد حصل. على أنّا نقول ومن زعم انّ المصير الى صدور اثنين من واحد مكابرة المعقول أو اتصاف المبدأ بصفات قديمة أزلية مناقض للتوحيد، فهاتان دعوتان باطلتان لا برهان لهم عليهما. فانّه ليس يعرف استحالة صدور الاثنين من واحد كما يعرف استحالة كون الشخص الواحد فى مكانين، وعلى الجملة لا يعرف بالضرورة ولا بالنظر. وما المانع من أن يقال: المبدأ الاول، عالم قادر مريد، يفعل ما يشاء ويحكم ما يريد، يخلق المختلفات والمتجانسات كما يريد وعلى ما يريد. فاستحالة هذا لا يعرف بضرورة ولا نظر، وقد ورد به الانبياء المؤيّدون بالمعجزات فيجب قبوله. وأما البحث عن كيفيّة صدور الفعل من الله بالارادة ففضول وطمع فى غير مطمع. والذين طمعوا فى طلب المناسبة

relationship and knowing it reduces to [the notion] that the first effect, inasmuch as it is possible of existence, [results in the] procession from it of a celestial sphere; and, inasmuch as it intellectually apprehends itself, the soul of the sphere proceeds from it. This is stupidity, not the showing

5   of a relationship.

(80) Let, then, the principles of these things be accepted from the prophets, and let [the philosophers] believe in them, since reason does not render [these principles] impossible. Let investigating quality, quantity, and quiddity be abandoned. For this is not something which the human

10   faculties can encompass. And, for this reason, the one who conveyed the religious law has said: "Think on the creation of God and do not think on the essence of God."

[ومعرفتها]^{١١} رجع حاصل نظرهم الى ان المعلول الاول من حيث انّه ممكن الوجود صدر منه فلك ومن حيث انّه يعقل نفسه صدر منه نفس الفلك. وهذه حماقة لا اظهار مناسبة.

(٨٠) فلتتقبل مبادى هذه الامور من الانبياء وليصدّقوا فيها، اذ العقل لا يحيلها. وليترك البحث عن الكيفيّة والكميّة والماهيّة. فليس ذلك مما يتسع له القوى البشرية. ولذلك قال صاحب الشرع تفكّروا فى خلق الله ولا تتفكّروا فى ذات الله.

[Fourth] Discussion

*On showing their inability to prove the
existence of the Maker of the world*

(1) We say:

(2) People divide into two groups: [(1)] The group of people that follow the truth and have perceived that the world is created and have known
necessarily that the created does not exist by itself and, hence, needs a
maker, their doctrine upholding [belief in] the Maker being therefore
comprehensible; [(2)] another group—namely, the materialists—who
perceive the world to have existed pre-eternally in the way that it exists
[now] and have not affirmed [the existence of] the Maker. The belief [of
the latter] is understandable, even though proof shows its falsity. As for
the philosophers, they perceived the world to be pre-eternal, then,
despite this, have affirmed for it a maker. This doctrine is, as it stands,
contradictory, there being no need in [its postulation] for a refutation.

(3) [It may, however,] be said:

(4) When we say that the world has a maker, we do not intend by it
an agent who chooses, who acts after not having acted, as we observe in
the different kinds of agents such as the tailor, the weaver, and the
builder. Rather, we mean by it the cause of the world, naming it the First
Principle, in the sense that His existence has no cause, whereas He
is the cause of the existence of [all] other [existents]. If we name Him
"Maker," it is in this figurative sense. The affirmation of an existent that
has no cause rests on conclusive demonstration which is nigh, for we
[philosophers] say:

مسئلة

فى بيان عجزهم عن الاستدلال
على وجود الصانع للعالم

(١) فنقول:

(٢) الناس فرقتان: فرقة أهل الحقّ، وقد رأوا ان العالم حادث وعلموا ضرورة ان الحادث لا يوجد بنفسه، فافتقر الى صانع، فيعقل مذهبهم فى القول بالصانع؛ وفرقة أُخرى، هم الدهريّة، وقد رأوا العالم قديما كما هو عليه ولم يثبتوا له صانعا، ومعتقدهم مفهوم، وان كان الدليل يدلّ على بطلانه. وأمّا الفلاسفة فقد رأوا أن العالم قديم ثم أثبتوا له مع ذلك صانعا. وهذا المذهب بوضعه متناقض لا يحتاج فيه الى ابطال.

(٣) فان قيل:

(٤) نحن اذا قلنا للعالم صانع، لم نرد به فاعلا مختارا يفعل بعد ان لم يفعل، كما نشاهد فى اصناف الفاعلين من الخيّاط والنسّاج والبنّاء، بل نعنى به علّة العالم، ونسمّيه المبدأ الاوّل على معنى انّه لا علّة لوجوده وهو علّة لوجود غيره. فان سمّيناه صانعا فبهذا التأويل. وثبوت موجود لا علّة لوجوده يقوم عليه البرهان القطعىّ على قرب، فانّا نقول:

٧٨

(5) The world (with its existents) either has a cause or does not have a cause. If it has a cause, then [the question arises]: "Does this cause have a cause or is it without a cause?" [If it has a cause,] the same [question] applies to the cause of the cause. This would either regress infinitely, which would be impossible, or terminate with a limit. The latter, then, is a first cause that has no cause for its existence. We call this the First Principle. If [on the other hand it is maintained that] the world exists by itself, having no cause, the First Principle would become evident. For we did not mean by it anything other than an uncaused existent.[1] This is established necessarily.

(6) Yes, it is not permissible for the First Principle to be the heavens, because they constitute a number [of things], and the proof of divine oneness prohibits this. Its falsity is thus known by examining the attribute of the [First] Principle. Nor can it be said that it is one heaven, one body, one sun, or some other thing. For [such a thing] would be a body, and body is composed of form and matter, whereas the First Principle cannot be composite. This is known through another theoretical investigation. What is intended is that an existent that has no cause for its existence is affirmed necessarily and by agreement. The disagreement, however, pertains only to the attributes [of the Principle].

(7) This [the philosophers conclude] is what we mean by the First Principle.

(8) [Our] answer [to this] is in two ways:

(9) The first is that it follows necessarily, according to the pattern of your doctrine, that the bodies of the world are also pre-eternal, having no cause. Your statement that the falsity of this is known through another theoretical investigation will be refuted in the discussion on [divine] unity and [your] denial of the [divine] attributes, following this discussion.

(10) The second [way], which pertains specifically to this discussion, is to say: "It [becomes] established, by way of supposition,[2] that these existents have a cause, but that their cause has a cause, and the cause of the cause a cause, and so on ad infinitum. Your statement that it is impossible to affirm causes that are infinite [cannot] be in line with [what you hold]. For we say: 'Do you know this through the necessity of rational thought, without a middle term; or do you know it through a middle term?' There is no recourse [for you] to invoke rational necessity.

(٥) العالم وموجوداته امّا ان يكون له علّة أو لا علّة له. فان كان له علّة، فتلك العلّة لها علّة أم لا علّة لها؟ وكذى القول فى علّة العلّة. فامّا ان يتسلسل الى غير نهاية، وهو محال، وامّا ان ينتهى الى طرف. فالاخير علّة أولى لا علّة لوجودها فنسمّيه المبدأ الاوّل. وان كان العالم موجودا بنفسه لا علّة له فقد ظهر المبدأ الاوّل. فانّا لم نعن به الا موجودا لا علّة له، وهو ثابت بالضرورة.

(٦) نعم، لا يجوز ان يكون المبدأ الاوّل هى السموات لانّها عدد ودليل التوحيد يمنعه فيعرف بطلانه بنظر فى صفة المبدأ؛ ولا يجوز ان يقال انّه سماء واحد أو جسم واحد أو شمس <واحدة>[1] أو غيره، لانّه جسم والجسم مركّب من الصورة والهيولى، والمبدأ الاوّل لا يجوز ان يكون مركّبا. وذلك يعرف بنظر ثان. والمقصود ان موجودا لا علّة لوجوده ثابت بالضرورة والاتفاق، وانما الخلاف فى الصفات.

(٧) وهو الذى نعنيه بالمبدأ الاول.

(٨) والجواب من وجهين:

(٩) احدهما، انّه يلزم على مساق مذهبكم ان تكون اجسام العالم قديمة كذلك لا علّة لها. وقولكم ان بطلان ذلك يعلم بنظر ثان، فسيبطل ذلك عليكم فى مسئلة التوحيد وفى نفى الصفات بعد هذه المسئلة.

(١٠) الثانى، وهو الخاصّ بهذه المسئلة، هو ان يقال: ثبت تقديرا، انّ هذه الموجودات لها علّة، ولكن لعلّتها علّة ولعلّة العلّة علّة كذلك وهكذى الى غير نهاية. وقولكم انّه يستحيل اثبات علل لا نهاية لها لا يستقيم منكم. فانّا نقول: عرفتم ذلك ضرورة بغير وسط، او عرفتموه

And [in the case of argument involving a middle term] every path you mentioned in theoretical investigation has proved false for you by [your] allowing the existence of events that have no beginning. If, then, it is possible that that which is infinite should enter existence, then it is not unlikely that some [existents] are causes for others, terminating in the final end with an effect that has no effect, but not terminating in the other direction with a cause that has no cause—just as past time [according to you] has an end, being the existing 'now,' but [having] no beginning. If you claim that past events do not coexist at one time nor at some times and that what has ceased to exist is not characterized with either finitude or the privation of finitude, then there is necessarily forced on you [the case of] the human souls that separate from bodies. For, according to you, these do not perish; and the existing souls that separate from the body are infinite in their number, since there continues to come about endlessly a sperm from a human and a human from a sperm. Moreover, the soul of each human that dies continues to exist, being numerically other than the soul of the one who died before him, [who dies] with him, and [who will die] after him, even though all are one in species. Hence, according to you, within existence, at every [moment of] time, there are souls whose number is infinite."

(11) [The philosophers may] say:

(12) Souls have no connection one with another and have no order either by nature or position. We only deem impossible an infinity of existents if they have order in position, as with bodies—for these are arranged one atop the other—or by nature, as with causes and effects. But this is not the case with souls.

(13) We say:

(14) The consequence of this judgment regarding position has no greater claim [to truth] than its opposite. Why did you deem impossible one of the two alternatives and not the other? What is the decisive demonstrative proof here? And with what would you deny one who says that these souls [which, according to you] are infinite, are not without order, since the existence of some precedes others? For the past days and nights

بوسط؟ ولا سبيل الى دعوى الضرورة، وكلّ مسلك ذكرتموه فى النظر بطل عليكم بتجويز حوادث لا أوّل لها. واذا جاز ان يدخل فى الوجود ما لا نهاية له، فلم يبعد ان يكون بعضها علّة للبعض، وينتهى من الطرف الاخير الى معلول لا معلول له، ولا ينتهى من الجانب الآخر الى علّة لا علّة لها، كما انّ الزمان السابق له آخر وهو الآن الراهن ولا اوّل له. فان زعمتم ان الحوادث الماضية ليست موجودة معاً فى الحال ولا فى بعض الاحوال، والمعدوم لا يوصف بالتناهى وعدم التناهى، فيلزمكم النفوس البشريّة المفارقة للأبدان، فانّها لا تفنى عندكم، والموجود المفارق للبدن من النفوس لا نهاية لاعدادها، اذ لم تزل نطفة من انسان وانسان من نطفة الى غير نهاية. ثم كل انسان مات فقد [بقيت]² نفسه [وهي]³ بالعدد غير نفس من مات من قبله ومعه وبعده وان كان الكلّ بالنوع واحدا. فعندكم فى الوجود فى كلّ حال نفوس لا نهاية لاعدادها.

(١١) فان قيل:

(١٢) النفوس ليس لبعضها ارتباط بالبعض، ولا ترتيب لها لا بالطبع ولا بالوضع، وانّما نحيل نحن موجودات لا نهاية لها اذا كان لها ترتيب بالوضع، كالاجسام فانّها مرتّبة بعضها فوق البعض، أو كان لها ترتيب بالطبع كالعلل والمعلولات، وأمّا النفوس فليست كذلك.

(١٣) قلنا:

(١٤) وهذا الحكم فى الوضع ليس طرده بأولى من عكسه. فلم أحلتم أحد القسمين دون الآخر؟ وما البرهان المفرق؟ وبم تنكرون على من يقول ان هذه النفوس التى لا نهاية لها لا يخلوا عن ترتيب اذ وجود

are infinite. If we suppose the existence of one soul in each day and night, the sum of existence up to the present would be infinite, occurring in an order of existence—that is, one after another. With reference to the cause, the most that can be said about it is that it is by nature prior to the effect,
just as it is said that it is above the effect in essence, not in place. If, then, [the infinite] is not impossible in the real temporal "before," it ought not to be impossible in the essential, natural "before." And why is it that they do not allow bodies on top of each other infinitely in space, but allow existents temporally preceding each other ad infinitum? Is this not an
arbitrary, insipid judgment that is groundless?

(15) [The philosophers may] say:

(16) The conclusive demonstration for the impossibility of infinite causes is to say: "Each one of the individual causes is either in itself possible or necessary. If [it is] necessary, then it would not need a cause.[3]
If [it is] possible, then the whole is characterized with possibility. Every possible needs a cause additional to itself. The whole, then, needs an extraneous cause."

(17) We say:

(18) The expressions "the possible" and "the necessary" are vague
expressions, unless by "the necessary" is intended that whose existence has no cause and by "the possible" that whose existence has a cause. If this, then, is what is intended, let us, then, turn again to this expression. We will thus say: "Each one [of the causes] is possible in the sense that it has a cause additional to itself, and the whole is not possible [but nec-
essary] in the sense that it does not have a cause additional to itself, extraneous to it."[4] If the expression "the possible" is intended to mean other than what we intended, this would be incomprehensible.

(19) If it is said, "This leads to [the consequence] that the necessary existent would have [its] subsistence through [things] possible of existence, which is impossible," we say:

بعضها قبل البعض؟ فان الايّام والليالى الماضية لا نهاية لها. واذا قدّرنا وجود نفس واحد فى كل يوم وليلة، كان الحاصل فى الوجود الآن خارجا عن النهاية واقعا على ترتيب فى الوجود أى بعضها بعد البعض. والعلّة غايتها ان يقال انّها قبل المعلول بالطبع، كما يقال انّها فوق المعلول بالذات، لا بالمكان. فاذا لم يستحل ذلك فى القبل الحقيقى الزمانىّ، فينبغى ٥ ان لا يستحيل فى القبل الذاتىّ الطبعىّ. وما بالهم لم يجوّزوا أجساما بعضها فوق البعض بالمكان الى غير نهاية، وجوّزوا موجودات بعضها قبل البعض بالزمان الى غير نهاية؟ وهل هذا الا تحكّم بارد لا أصل له؟

(١٥) فان قيل:

(١٦) البرهان القاطع على استحالة علل الى غير نهاية ان يقال: كلّ ١٠ واحد من آحاد العلل ممكنة فى نفسها او واجبة. فان كانت واجبة، فلم تفتقر الى علّة، وان كانت ممكنة، فالكل، موصوف بالامكان. وكل ممكن فيفتقر الى علّة زائدة على ذاته؛ فيفتقر الكلّ الى علة خارجة عنها.

(١٧) قلنا:

(١٨) لفظ الممكن والواجب لفظ مبهم، الا ان يراد بالواجب ما لا ١٥ علّة لوجوده ويراد بالممكن ما لوجوده علّة. وان كان المراد هذا، فلنرجع الى هذه اللفظة فنقول كلّ واحد ممكن على معنى انّ له علّة زائدة على ذاته، والكلّ ليس بممكن، على معنى انه ليس له علّة زائدة على ذاته خارجة عنه منه. وان أُريد بلفظ الممكن غير ما اردناه فهو ليس بمفهوم.

(١٩) فان قيل فهذا يؤدّى الى أن يتقوّم واجب الوجود بممكنات ٢٠ الوجود وهو محال، قلنا:

(20) If you intended by "the necessary" and "the possible" that which we have mentioned, then this is the very thing we are after. We do not admit that it is impossible. It is similar to one's saying, "It is impossible for the pre-eternal to have its subsistence in temporal events," when time, according to them, is eternal and the individual celestial movements are temporal events, having beginnings, whereas [their] totality has no beginning. Hence, that which has no beginning has been rendered subsistent by those things that have beginnings, and what is true of those that have beginnings is applicable to the individual units but not true of the totality. Similarly, it can be said about each individual unit that it has a cause, but it is not said that the totality has a cause. Not everything that is true of the individual units is true of the totality. For it would be true of each individual that it is one, that it is a part, and that it has a part, but it would not be true of the totality. Every place on earth that we specify is lit by the sun during the day becomes dark at night, and each [of these events] comes into temporal existence after not being—that is, it has a beginning. But the totality, for [the philosophers], is that which has no beginning. Hence, it has become evident that whoever allows the possibility of events that have no beginning—namely, the forms of the four elements and of [all] the things that undergo change— is unable to deny causes that are infinite. From this it comes about that they have no way of reaching [the point] of affirming the First Principle, for this [very] difficulty. Their distinguishing [between the two cases], hence, reduces to that which is sheer arbitrariness.

(21) [The philosophers may] say:

(22) The [celestial] circular motions do not exist at the present, nor [do] the forms of the elements. The existent among these is only [the] one form that is in actuality. What does not exist is not characterized by being either finite or infinite, unless their existence is supposed in the estimative faculty. What is supposed in the estimation is not improbable [when viewed within this faculty], even though the things that are supposed are causes of each other. For man may hypothesize this in his estimation. But what is being discussed is the existent in the concrete, not in the mind.

(23) The only [problematic] thing that remains is [the question of] the souls of dead humans. Some philosophers have held that they are eternal [and were] one before joining the bodies, and that with their separation [after death] from the bodies they reunite. Thus, they will have no

(٢٠) ان اردتم بالواجب والممكن ما ذكرناه، فهو نفس المطلوب. فلا نسلّم انّه محال. وهو كقول القائل: يستحيل ان يتقوّم القديم بالحوادث. والزمان عندهم قديم، وآحاد الدورات حادثة، وهى ذوات أوائل، والمجموع لا أوّل له. فقد تقوّم ما لا أوّل له بذوات أوائل وصدق ذوات الاوائل على الآحاد ولم يصدق على المجموع. فكذلك يقال على كلّ واحد انّ له علّة ولا يقال للمجموع علّة. وليس كل ما صدق على الآحاد يلزم ان يصدق على المجموع، اذ يصدق على كلّ واحد انّه واحد، وانّه بعض، وانّه جزء، ولا يصدق على المجموع. وكلّ موضع عيّناه من الارض فانّه قد استضاءَ بالشمس فى النهار وأظلم بالليل، وكلّ واحد حادث بعد ان لم يكن، أى له أوّل. والمجموع عندهم ما له أوّل. فتبين انّ من يجوّز حوادث لا أوّل لها، وهى صور العناصر الاربعة والمتغيّرات، فلا يتمكن من انكار علل لا نهاية لها. ويخرج من هذا انّه لا سبيل لهم الى الوصول الى اثبات المبدأ الاول لهذا الاشكال. ويرجع فرقهم الى التحكّم المحض.

(٢١) فان قيل:

(٢٢) الدورات ليست موجودة فى الحال، ولا صور العناصر؛ وانّما الموجود منها صورة واحدة بالفعل. وما لا وجود له، لا يوصف بالتناهى وعدم التناهى، الا اذا قدّر فى الوهم وجردها. ولا يبعد ما يقدّر فى الوهم، وان كانت المقدّرات أيضا بعضها عللا لبعض. فالانسان قد يفرض ذلك فى وهمه. وانّما الكلام فى الموجود فى الاعيان لا فى الاذهان.

(٢٣) لا يبقى الا نفوس الاموات. وقد ذهب بعض الفلاسفة الى انّها كانت واحدة أزليّة قبل التعلق بالابدان وعند مفارقة الابدان تتّحد. فلا

number, to say nothing about their being described as infinite. Others
have said that the soul is dependent on the composition of the body and
that the meaning of death is its annihilation, [as] it has no subsistence
in terms of its [own] substance without the body. Thus, there is no existence for souls except with respect to the living. But the living that exist
are restricted [in number], and finitude is not removed from them. The
nonexistents are fundamentally not described in terms of the existence
of finitude or its nonexistence, except in the estimation if hypothesized
as existing.

(24) The answer [is as follows]:

(25) We brought the difficulty regarding the souls against Avicenna,
Al-Fārābī, and the exacting among [the philosophers], inasmuch as they
have judged that the soul is a self-subsistent substance, this being the
choice of Aristotle and the commentators among the early [thinkers].
With respect to those who have swerved away from this course, we say:

(26) Is it or is it not conceivable that something should originate [at
a moment in time] and endure? If they say, "No," [they would be stating
what is] impossible; and, if they answer, "Yes," we would then say:

(27) If we suppose the temporal occurrence and endurance of one
thing in each day, there would necessarily accrue for us, up to the present, existents that are infinite. For, even though the [past celestial] circular motion ceases to exist, the occurrence in it of an existent that
endures and does not cease to exist is not impossible. With this possibility considered [in the mind], the difficulty becomes firmly established. It
makes no difference whether that which endures is the soul of a human,
of a genie, of a devil, of an angel, or of whatever existent you wish. It is a
necessary consequence of every doctrine they have, inasmuch as they
have affirmed [celestial] motions that are infinite.

يكون [فيها]؛ عدد، فضلا من ان توصف [انّها]ؕ لا نهاية لها. وقال آخرون: النفس [تابعة]ؖ للمزاج، وانما معنى الموت عدمها ولا قوام لها بجوهرها دون الجسم. فاذن لا وجود فى النفوس الا فى حقّ الاحياء. والاحياء الموجودون محصورون ولا تنتفى النهاية عنهم.

والمعدومون لا يوصفون أصلا لا بوجود النهاية ولا بعدمها، الا فى الوهم اذا فرضوا موجودين.

(٢٤) والجواب:

(٢٥) انّ هذا الاشكال فى النفوس أوردناه على ابن سينا والفارابى والمحققين منهم، اذ حكموا بان النفس جوهر قائم بنفسه، وهو اختيار ارسطاليس [والمفسرين]ؗ من الاوائل. ومن عدل عن هذا المسلك فنقول له:

(٢٦) هل يتصوّر ان يحدث شىء يبقى أم لا؟ فان قالوا لا، فهو محال، وان قالوا نعم، قلنا:

(٢٧) فاذا قدّرنا كل يوم حدوث شىء وبقاءه اجتمع الى الآن لا محالة موجودات لا نهاية لها. فالدورة وان كانت منقضية، فحصول موجود فيها يبقى ولا ينقضى غير مستحيل. وبهذا التقدير يتقرر الاشكال. ولا غرض فى ان يكون ذلك الباقى نفس آدمىّ أو جنىّ أو شيطان أو ملك أو ما شئت من الموجودات. وهو لازم على كلّ مذهب لهم اذ اثبتوا دورات لا نهاية لها.

[Fifth] Discussion

*On showing their inability to prove that
God is one and that it is impossible to suppose
two necessary existents, each having no cause*

(1) Their proof for this is in two ways.

(2) The first is their statement that, if there were two [necessary existents], then the species, being necessary of existence, would be predicable of each one of them. That of which being "necessary of existence"
is predicated must either be [such] that it is necessary of existence in itself [and] its existence through another thus inconceivable, or [such] that the necessity of existence belongs to it through a cause, whereby the essence of the necessary existent would be caused, and some cause it has had required [for it] the necessity of existence.[1] We do not intend by the "necessary of existence" anything other than that whose existence is not linked in any way to a cause.

(3) [The philosophers, moreover,] claim that the human species is predicated of [both] Zayd and ʿAmr and that Zayd is not [rendered] human by reason of his [very] self, since, if he were [rendered] human by reason of his [very] self,[2] then ʿAmr would not be human; rather, [Zayd is rendered human] through a cause which rendered him human and which rendered ʿAmr also human.[3] Thus, humanity has become multiple through the multiplicity of the matter that is its substratum. Its attachment to matter is an effect and is not due to humanity itself. In the same way, if the establishing of the necessity of existence for the Necessary Existent is through Himself, [the necessity of existence] would belong only to Him; [but,] if [it is] through a cause, He then becomes an effect and not necessary of existence. From this it has become evident that the Necessary Existent must be one.

– 84 –

مسئلة

فى بيان عجزهم عن اقامة الدليل على انّ الله
واحد وانه لا يجوز فرض اثنين واجبى الوجود
كلّ واحد منهما لا علّة له

(١) واستدلالهم على هذا بمسلكين.

(٢) المسلك الاول قولهم انّهما لو كانا اثنين، لكان نوع وجوب
الوجود مقولا على كلّ واحد منهما. وما قيل عليه انّه واجب الوجود فلا
يخلوا امّا ان يكون وجوب وجوده لذاته، فلا يتصور ان يكون لغيره، أو
وجوب الوجود له لعلّة، فيكون ذات واجب الوجود معلولا وقد اقتضت
علّة له وجوب الوجود. ونحن لا نريد بواجب الوجود الا ما لا ارتباط
لوجوده بعلّة بجهة من الجهات.

(٣) وزعموا انّ نوع الانسان مقول على زيد وعلى عمرو وليس زيد إنسانا
لذاته، اذ لو كان انسانا لذاته، لما كان عمرو وانسانا، بل لعلّة [جعلته]¹ انسانا وقد
[جعلت]² أيضا عمرا انسانا. فتكثّرت الانسانيّة بتكثّر المادّة الحاملة لها. وتعلّقها
بالمادّة معلول ليس لذات الانسانية. فكذلك ثبوت وجوب الوجود لواجب
الوجود، ان كان لذاته، فلا يكون الا له، وان كان لعلّة اذن فهو معلول، وليس
بواجب الوجود. وقد ظهر بهذا انّ واجب الوجود لا بدّ وان يكون واحدا.

٨٤

(4) [To this first way] we reply:

(5) Your statement, "The species 'necessity of existence' belonging to the Necessary Existent is either by reason of Himself or due to a cause," is a division that is faulty in its formulation. For we have shown that in the utterance "necessary of existence" there is imprecision, unless one intends by it the denial of [having] a cause. Let, then, this expression be used [in this sense]. We say:

(6) Why is it impossible for two existents having no cause, neither being the cause of the other, to stand firmly? For your statement that that which has no cause has no cause either by reason of itself or due to a cause is a faulty division. For the denial of a cause and the absence of the need of a cause for existence do not need a cause. What sense is there to one's saying, "That which has no cause has no cause either by reason of itself or due to a cause"? For our statement, "It has no cause," is pure negation; and pure negation has no cause, and one does not speak of it as being either by reason of itself or not by reason of itself. And, if you intend by the necessity of existence a permanent description of the Necessary Existent other than His being an existent whose existence has no cause, this in itself would be incomprehensible. What is forged from uttering [the expression "necessary existent"] is the denial of a cause for His existence, which is pure negation about which it is said, "It is neither by reason of itself nor due to a cause," so as to build on the formulation of this disjunction a [meaningful] purpose. This shows that this is a demonstration of one who has waxed senile and is baseless. Rather, we say:

(7) The meaning that He is necessary of existence is that there is no cause for His existence and no cause for His being without a cause. Nor, moreover, is His being without a cause causally explicable in terms of Himself. Rather, there is fundamentally neither a cause for His existence nor a cause for His being without a cause. How is this not so, when this division does not apply to some of the positive attributes, to say nothing of those that reduce to negation? Someone, however, may say:

(8) Blackness is either a color in virtue of itself or due to a cause. If by virtue of itself, then it follows necessarily that redness is not a color and that this species—I mean, being a color—would belong only to the essence of blackness. If blackness were a color due to a cause that rendered it a color, then one ought to [be able to] conceive of a blackness which is not

(٤) قلنا:

(٥) قولكم نوع وجوب الوجود لواجب الوجود لذاته أو لعلّة تقسيم خطأ فى وضعه. فانّا قد بينا انّ لفظ وجوب الوجود فيه اجمال، الا ان يراد به نفى العلّة. فنستعمل هذه العبارة، فنقول:

(٦) لم يستحيل ثبوت موجودين لا علّة لهما وليس أحدهما علّة للآخر؟ فقولكم انّ الذى لا علّة له لا علّة له لذاته او لسبب تقسيم خطأ، لانّ نفى العلّة واستغناء الوجود عن العلّة لا يطلب له علة. فاىّ معنى لقول القائل، انّ ما لا علّة له لا علّة له لذاته أو لعلّة؟ اذ قولنا لا علّة له سلب محض، والسلب المحض لا يكون له سبب، ولا يقال فيه انّه لذاته أو لا لذاته. وان عنيتم بوجوب الوجود وصفا ثابتا لواجب الوجود سوى انّه موجود لا علّة لوجوده، فهو غير مفهوم فى نفسه. والذى ينسبك من لفظه، نفى العلة لوجوده، وهو سلب محض، لا يقال فيه انّه لذاته أو لعلّة، حتّى يبنى على وضع هذا التقسيم غرض. فدلّ ان هذا برهان من خرف لا اصل له. بل نقول:

(٧) معنى انّه واجب الوجود انّه لا علّة لوجوده ولا علّة لكونه بلا علّة. وليس كونه بلا علّة معلّلا أيضا بذاته؛ بل لا علّة لوجوده ولا لكونه بلا علّة أصلا. كيف، وهذا التقسيم لا يتطرّق الى بعض صفات الاثبات، فضلا عمّا يرجع الى السلب؟ اذ لو قال قائل:

(٨) السواد لون لذاته أو لعلّة، فان كان لذاته فينبغى ان لا تكون الحمرة لونا وان لا يكون هذا النوع، أعنى اللونية، الا لذات السواد. وان كان السواد لونا لعلّة جعلته لونا، فينبغى ان يعقل سواد ليس بلون، أى لم

a color—that is, [one] that the cause did not render as a color. For whatever is affirmed for the essence as something additional to the essence through a cause, the supposition of [that thing's] nonexistence in the estimative faculty is possible, even if this is not realized in [extramental] existence.

5   (9) But [to this] one says: "This division is faulty in [its] postulation." For one does not say of blackness that it is a color in itself in such a way that this prevents [color] from belonging to another essence. Similarly, one does not say that this existent is necessary in itself—that is, that it has no cause for its essence, in such a way that this prevents this ["necessity of 10   existence"] from belonging, under any circumstance, to another entity.

(10) The second way consists in their saying:

(11) If we suppose two necessary existents, these would either be similar in every way or be different. If similar in every way, then multiplicity and duality would be unintelligible. For two instances of black are 15   two when they are in two places or in one place but at two [different] times, since blackness and motion in one place at one time are two because their essences differ. But, if the two essences, such as the two instances of black, do not differ, time and place coinciding, [their] multiplicity becomes unintelligible. If it were permissible to say that in the same time 20   and in the same place there are two instances of black, it would become permissible to say with respect to each individual that it is two individuals but that no difference between them is evident. If, then, similarity in every respect is impossible and difference is inevitable—the difference, however, being neither in time nor in space—there only remains the 25   difference in essence.

(12) So long, then, as the two [hypothesized necessary existents] differ in something, then they must either share in something or not share in anything. If they do not share in something, this would be impossible, since it would follow necessarily that they neither share in existence, nor 30   in the necessity of existence, nor in their being individually self-subsistent, nor [inhering] in a subject. Alternatively, if they share in something and differ in another, then that which constitutes the sharing would be other than that which constitutes the difference. There would then be composition and lexical division. But the necessary of existence has no compo- 35   sition and is not qualitatively divisible; hence, it is not divided in [terms of] the lexical explanatory statement.[4] For its essence is not composed of

تجعله العلّة لونا. فان ما يثبت للذات زائدا على الذات بعلّة يمكن تقدير عدمه فى الوهم، وان لم يتحقّق فى الوجود.

(٩) ولكن يقال: هذا التقسيم خطأ فى الوضع. فلا يقال للسواد انّه لون لذاته قولا يمنع ان يكون ذلك لغير ذاته. وكذلك لا يقال انّ هذا الموجود واجب لذاته أو لا علّة له لذاته قولا يمنع ان يكون ذلك لغير ذاته بحال.

(١٠) مسلكهم الثانى ان قالوا:

(١١) لو فرضنا واجبى الوجود لكانا متماثلين من كلّ وجه أو مختلفين. فان كانا متماثلين من كلّ وجه، فلا يعقل التعدّد والاثنينيّة، اذ السوادان هما اثنان اذا كانا فى محلّين أو فى محلّ واحد ولكن فى وقتين، اذ السواد والحركة فى محلّ واحد فى وقت واحد هما اثنان لاختلاف ذاتيهما. أمّا اذا لم يختلف الذاتان كالسوادين، ثم اتحد الزمان والمكان، لم يعقل التعدّد. ولو جاز ان يقال فى وقت واحد فى محلّ واحد سوادان، لجاز ان يقال فى حقّ كل شخص انّه شخصان، ولكن ليس [يتبيّن]٣ بينهما مغايرة. واذا استحال التماثل من كلّ وجه، ولا بدّ من الاختلاف، ولم يمكن بالزمان ولا بالمكان، فلا يبقى الا الاختلاف فى الذات.

(١٢) ومهما اختلفا فى شىء، فلا يخلوا امّا ان يشتركا فى شىء أو لم يشتركا فى شىء. فان لم يشتركا فى شىء، فهو محال، اذ يلزم ان لا يشتركا فى الوجود ولا فى وجوب الوجود ولا فى كون كلّ واحد قائما بنفسه لا فى موضوع. واذا اشتركا فى شىء واختلفا فى شىء، كان ما فيه الاشتراك غير ما فيه الاختلاف. فيكون ثم تركيب وانقسام بالقول. وواجب الوجود لا تركيب فيه وكما لا ينقسم بالكمّية فلا ينقسم أيضا

things [whereby] the explanatory statement would indicate its being multiple, as with the indication "animal" and "rational," [which points] to that through which the quiddity of man subsists. For [man] is [both] animal and rational; but the indication of the expression "animal," with respect to man, is other than the indication of the expression "rational." Man, hence, is composed of parts that are ordered in the definition through utterances that point to these parts, whereby the term "man" indicates [their] composite. This is inconceivable [in the Necessary Existent], and without [this composition] duality is inconceivable.

(13) [Our] answer [is as follows]:

(14) It is admitted that duality is only conceivable through difference in something and that the difference between two things that are similar in every respect is inconceivable. Your statement, however, that this kind of composition is impossible in the First Principle is sheer arbitrariness. What demonstration is there for this?

(15) Let us describe this problem [as it stands] independently.[5] Among their well-known statements is that the First Principle is not divisible in terms of verbal definition, just as It is not divisible quantitatively. For them, the proof of God's unity is built on this. Indeed, they claim that the doctrine of divine unity is only completed by establishing unity for the essence of the Creator in every respect and that proving unity obtains through the denial of plurality in all respects. Plurality [they continue] finds access to essences in five ways.

(16) The first is through the reception of division either in actuality or in the estimation. For this reason, the one body is not absolutely one. For it is one through the continuity that stands [existing for it], which is subject to cessation. It is, thus, quantitatively divisible in the estimation. And this is impossible in [the case of] the First Principle.

(17) The second is that a thing is divisible in the mind into two different meanings, not by way of quantity. An example of this would be the division of the body into matter and form. For, although it is inconceivable for each one of matter and form to subsist by itself without the other, these are two things different in definition and reality through whose

بالقول الشارح، اذ لا تتركّب ذاته من أمور يدلّ القول الشارح على [تعدّدها]، كدلالة الحيوان والناطق على ما تقوم به ماهيّة الانسان. فانّه حيوان وناطق، ومدلول لفظ الحيوان من الانسان غير مدلول لفظ الناطق. فيكون الانسان متركّبا من اجزاء تنتظم فى الحدّ بالفاظ تدلّ على تلك الاجزاء، ويكون اسم الانسان بمجموعه. وهذا لا يتصوّر ودون هذا لا تتصوّر التثنية.

(١٣) والجواب:

(١٤) انّه مسلّم انه لا تتصوّر الأثنيّة الا بالمغايرة فى شىء ما، وأن المتماثلين من كلّ وجه لا يتصوّر تغايرهما. ولكن قولكم انّ هذا النوع من التركيب محال فى المبدأ الاول تحكّم محض. فما البرهان عليه؟

(١٥) ولنرسم هذه المسئلة على حيالها. فانّ من كلامهم المشهور انّ المبدأ الاوّل لا ينقسم بالقول الشارح كما لا ينقسم بالكميّة وعليه ينبنى اثبات وحدانيّة الله عندهم. بل زعموا ان التوحيد لا يتمّ الا باثبات الوحدة لذات البارى من كلّ وجه، واثبات الوحدة بنفى الكثرة من كلّ وجه. والكثرة تتطرّق الى الذوات من خمسة اوجه.

(١٦) الاوّل، بقبول الانقسام فعلا أو وهما. فلذلك لم يكن الجسم الواحد واحدا مطلقا. فانّه واحد بالاتصال القائم القابل للزوال. فهو منقسم فى الوهم بالكميّة. وهذا محال فى المبدأ الاوّل.

(١٧) الثانى ان ينقسم الشىء فى العقل الى معنيين مختلفين لا بطريق الكميّة، كانقسام الجسم الى الهيولى والصورة. فانّ كل واحد من الهيولى والصورة، وان كان لا يتصوّر ان يقوم بنفسه دون الآخر، فهما شيئان

combination one thing is realized—namely, body. This also is denied of God. For the Creator can be neither form in a body, nor matter in a hyle for a body, nor a combination of both. As regards the combination of the two, this is due to two causes. One of them is that [when division takes place] it is quantitatively divisible either in actuality or in the estimation. The second is that it is divisible in terms of meaning into form and matter. [God] cannot be matter, since [matter] needs form; and the Necessary Existent is not in any respect in need [of anything], so that His existence cannot be linked to any condition besides itself. And He cannot be form, because [form] needs matter.

(18) The third way [in which plurality finds access to essences] is through the [positive] attributes, by supposing the attributes of knowledge, power, and will. Now, if these attributes are necessary of existence, then the necessity of existence would become common to the essence and these attributes. Plurality in the Necessary Existent becomes a necessary consequence, and unity ceases to be.

(19) The fourth is an intellectual plurality that comes about through the composition of genus and species. For black is [both] black and color. But blackness to the mind is other than being a color. Rather, being a color is a genus, and blackness is a differentia. Hence, [black] is composed of a genus and differentia. [Again] in the mind, animality is other than humanity. For man is [both] animal and rational. Animal is a genus, rational a differentia, [man] being composed of genus and differentia. This is a kind of plurality. [The philosophers] thus claimed that this also is denied of the First Principle.

(20) The fifth is a plurality that becomes necessary by way of supposing a quiddity and hypothesizing an existence for this quiddity. For there belongs to man a quiddity before existence.[6] Existence occurs to [this quiddity] and is related to it. This, for example, is the case with the triangle; it has a quiddity—namely, its being a figure surrounded by three sides. Existence, however, is not part of the constitutive being of this quiddity, giving it subsistence. For this reason, the rational individual can apprehend the quiddity of man and the quiddity of the triangle without knowing whether or not they have an existence in concrete reality.[7] If existence were to give subsistence to [the] quiddity [of a thing], one would not [be able to] conceive its standing firm in the mind prior to its

مختلفان بالحدّ والحقيقة يحصل بمجموعهما شيء واحد هو الجسم. وهذا ايضا منفى عن الله. فلا يجوز ان يكون البارى صورة فى جسم، ولا مادّة فى هيولى لجسم، ولا مجموعهما. أما مجموعهما فلعلّتين: احديهما انّه منقسم بالكمّية عند التجزئة فعلا أو وهما، والثانية انه منقسم بالمعنى الى الصورة والهيولى. ولا يكون مادّة، لأنّها تحتاج الى الصورة، وواجب الوجود مستغنٍ من كلّ وجه، فلا يجوز ان يرتبط وجوده بشرط آخر سواه. ولا يكون صورة لأنّها تحتاج الى مادّة.

(١٨) الثالث، الكثرة بالصفات، بتقدير العلم والقدرة والارادة، فانّ هذه الصفات ان كانت واجبة الوجود، كان وجوب الوجود مشتركا بين الذات وبين هذه الصفات، ولزمت كثرة فى واجب الوجود، وانتفت الوحدة.

(١٩) الرابع، كثرة عقليّة تحصل بتركيب الجنس والنوع. فانّ السواد سواد ولون، والسواديّة غير اللونيّة فى حقّ العقل. بل اللونيّة جنس، والسواديّة فصل. فهو مركّب من جنس وفصل. والحيوانيّة غير الانسانيّة فى العقل. فانّ الانسان حيوان وناطق والحيوان جنس والناطق فصل وهو مركّب من الجنس والفصل. وهذا نوع كثرة. فزعموا انّ هذا أيضاً منفيّ عن المبدأ الاول.

(٢٠) الخامس، كثرة تلزم من جهة تقدير ماهيّة وتقدير وجود لتلك الماهيّة. فانّ للانسان ماهيّة قبل الوجود والوجود يرد عليها ويضاف اليها وكذى المثلث مثلا له ماهيّة وهى أنّه شكل يحيط به ثلاثة اضلاع. وليس الوجود جزءا من ذات هذه الماهيّة مقوّما لها، ولذلك يجوز ان يدرك العاقل ماهيّة الانسان وماهيّة المثلّث وليس يدرى ان لهما وجودا فى الاعيان أم لا. ولو كان الوجود مقوّماً لماهيّته، لما تصوّر ثبوت ماهيّته فى

existence. Existence is, hence, [something] related to the quiddity—whether as a necessary concomitant such that that quiddity would [always] exist, as with the heavens, or as an occurrence after not being, as with the quiddity of humanity with respect to Zayd and ʿAmr and the quiddities of accidents and temporal forms.

(21) [The philosophers] thus claim that this plurality must also be removed from the First [Principle]. It is thus said [that] He does not have a quiddity to which existence is related. Rather, necessary existence belongs to Him as quiddity belongs to others. Thus, necessary existence is a quiddity, a universal reality, and a true nature in the way that humanity, "tree-ness," and "heaven-ness" are quiddities. Now, if a quiddity [other than the necessity of existence] were to be affirmed [as belonging] to Him, then the necessity of existence would be a necessary concomitant of this quiddity, not [something] that renders it subsistent. But the necessary concomitant is consequent [on something] and is caused. Necessary existence would then be caused, which contradicts its being necessary.

(22) Despite this, they say of the Creator that He is a principle, a first, an existent, a substance, one, pre-eternal, everlasting, knowing, an intellect, one who apprehends intellectually, intelligible, an agent, a creator, a willer, powerful, living, a lover, a beloved, enjoyable, one who enjoys, generous, and pure good. They claim that all this is an expression of one meaning that has no plurality. This [truly] is a wonder. Hence, we must first ascertain their doctrine for the purpose of explaining [it], then engage in objection. For the objection to doctrines before complete explanation is blind shooting.

(23) The basic point for understanding their doctrine consists in their saying [that] the essence of the First Principle is one, the names becoming many by relating something to it, relating it to something, or negating something of it. Negation does not necessitate plurality in the essence of Him of whom [things] are negated, nor does relation necessitate plurality. Hence, they do not deny a multiplicity of negations and a multiplicity of relations, but the task [they maintain] is to reduce all these matters to negation and relation. They thus said:

العقل قبل وجوده. فالوجود مضاف الى الماهيّة، سواء كان لازما بحيث لا تكون تلك الماهيّة الا موجودة، كالسماء، أو عارضا بعد ما لم يكن كماهيّة الانسانيّة من زيد وعمرو وماهيّة الاعراض والصوّر الحادثة.

(٢١) فزعموا انّ هذه الكثرة أيضاً يجب ان تنفى عن الاوّل. فيقال ليس له ماهيّةٌ، الوجود مضاف اليها؛ بل الوجود الواجب له كالماهيّة لغيره. فالوجود الواجب ماهيّة وحقيقة كليّة وطبيعة حقيقيّة، كما ان الانسانيّة والشجريّة والسمائيّة ماهيّة. اذ لو ثبت [له]° ماهيّة، لكان الوجود الواجب لازما لتلك الماهيّة غير مقوّم لها. واللازم تابع ومعلول. فيكون الوجود الواجب معلولا، وهو مناقض لكونه واجبا.

(٢٢) ومع هذا، فانّهم يقولون للباري انّه مبدأ، وأوّل، وموجود، وجوهر وواحد، وقديم، وباق، وعالم، وعقل، وعاقل، ومعقول، وفاعل، وخالق، ومريد، وقادر، وحيّ، وعاشق، ومعشوق، ولذيذ، وملتذّ، وجواد، وخير محض. وزعموا ان كلّ ذلك عبارة عن معنى واحد لا كثرة فيه. وهذا من العجائب. فينبغى ان نحقّق مذهبهم للتّفهيم أوّلا ثم نشتغل بالاعتراض. فانّ الاعتراض على المذهب قبل تمام التّفهيم رمى فى عماية.

(٢٣) والعمدة فى فهم مذهبهم انّهم يقولون: ذات المبدأ واحد وانّما تكثر الاسامى باضافة شىء اليه، أو اضافته الى شىء، أو سلب شىء عنه؛ والسلب لا يوجب كثرة فى ذات المسلوب عنه، ولا الاضافة توجب كثرة. فلا ينكرون اذن كثرة السلوب وكثرة الاضافات، ولكنّ الشأن فى ردّ هذه الامور كلّها الى السلب والاضافة. فقالوا:

(24) If it is said of Him, "First," this is in relation to the existents after Him; and, if it said, "Principle," this is an indication that the existence of [what is] other than Him is from Him, He being the cause of it. This, then, is a relation to His effects. If it is said, "Existent," it means, "He is known."[8] If it is said, "Substance," it means that inherence in a subject is negated of [His] existence. This, then, is a negation. If it is said, "Pre-eternal," this means the negation of nonexistence of Him in terms of a first [beginning]; and if it is said, "Everlasting," this means the negation of nonexistence of Him in terms of a last [ending]. Thus, in the final analysis, the pre-eternal and the everlasting amount to an existence neither preceded by nonexistence nor succeeded by nonexistence. If it is said, "The Necessary Existent," this means that He is an existent that has no cause, while He is the cause of what is other than Him. This would thus be a combination of negation and relation, since the denial of a cause is a negation, while rendering Him a cause of another is a relation. If it is said, "Intellect," [this] means that He is an existent free of matter. Every existence having this description is an intellect; that is, it apprehends itself, is aware of it, and apprehends intellectually another. The essence of God has this as its characterization, and, hence, He is intellect, the two expressions ["being free from matter" and "intellect"] expressing one thing. If it is said, "Intellectual Apprehender," [this] means that His essence, which is an intellect, has an intelligible, which is His essence. For He is aware of Himself and apprehends Himself. Hence, His essence is an intelligible, His essence is an intellectual apprehender, and His essence is Intellect, all being one. For He is an intelligible, inasmuch as He is a quiddity free from matter, not concealed from His essence—which is intellect in the sense of being a quiddity devoid of matter—where nothing is concealed from Him. Inasmuch as He intellectually apprehends Himself, He is an intellectual apprehender; inasmuch as He Himself is an intelligible for Himself, He is an intelligible; and inasmuch as His intellectual apprehension is by His essence, not by [something] additional to His essence, He is an intellect. It is not [an] unlikely [thing] for the intellectual apprehender and the intelligible to become one. For, if the intellectual apprehender apprehends his being an apprehender, he apprehends it by being an apprehender. Hence, the intellectual apprehender and the intelligible become in some respect one. And if, in this, our intellect differs from the mind of the First, this is because what belongs to the First is ever in actuality, while what belongs to us is at one time in potentiality and at another in act.

(٢٤) اذا قيل له اوّل، فهو اضافة الى الموجودات بعده، واذا قيل مبدا
فهو اشارة الى ان وجود غيره منه وهو سبب له. فهو اضافة الى معلولاته.
واذا قيل موجود، فمعناه معلوم. واذا قيل جوهر، فمعناه الوجود مسلوبا
عنه الحلول فى موضوع، وهذا سلب. واذا قيل قديم، فمعناه سلب العدم
عنه أوّلا، واذا قيل باق، فمعناه سلب العدم عنه آخرا. فيرجع حاصل
القديم والباقى الى وجود ليس مسبوقا بعدم ولا ملحوقا بعدم. واذا قيل
واجب الوجود، فمعناه انّه موجود لا علّة له، وهو علّة لغيره؛ فيكون
جمعا بين السلب والاضافة، اذ نفى علّة له سلب، وجعله علّة لغيره
اضافة. واذا قيل عقل، فمعناه انّه موجود برىء عن المادة، وكلّ موجود
هذا صفته فهو عقل، أى يعقل ذاته ويشعر به، ويعقل غيره. وذات الله
هذا صفته أى هو برىء عن المادة، فاذن هو عقل وهما عبارتان عن معبّر
واحد. واذا قيل عاقل، فمعناه انّ ذاته الذى هو عقل فله معقول هو ذاته.
فانّه يشعر بنفسه ويعقل نفسه. فذاته معقول، وذاته عاقل، وذاته عقل،
والكلّ واحد؛ اذ هو معقول من حيث انّه ماهيّة مجرّدة عن المادّة، غير
مستورة عن ذاته الذى هو عقل، بمعنى انّه ماهيّة مجرّدة عن المادّة لا يكون
شىء مستورا عنه. ولمّا عقل نفسه، كان عاقلا، ولمّا كان نفسه معقولا
لنفسه، كان معقولا، ولمّا كان عقله بذاته، لا بزائد على ذاته، كان عقلا.
ولا يبعد ان يتّحد العاقل والمعقول. فانّ العاقل اذا عقل كونه عاقلا، عقله
بكونه عاقلا. فيكون العاقل والمعقول واحدا بوجه ما. وان كان [عقلنا
فى]* ذلك يفارق عقل الاوّل، فانّ ما للاوّل بالفعل أبدا، وما لنا يكون
بالقوّة تارة وبالفعل أخرى.

(25) If it is said [of Him], "Creator, Agent, and Maker [of the world]" and the rest of the attributes of action, [all these] mean that His existence is a noble existence from which the existence of everything emanates in a necessary manner, and that the existence of other [things] comes about through Him and is consequent on His existence in the same way as light follows the sun and heat [follows] fire. The relation of the world to Him is similar to the relation of light to the sun only in [the world's] being an effect. And, if [they are similar only in this],[9] then He is not akin [to the sun]. For the sun is not aware of the emanation of light from it, nor fire of the emanation of heat [from it]. For this is pure nature. Rather, the First knows His essence and that His essence is the principle of the existence of others. Hence, the emanation of whatever emanates from Him is known to Him. There is, therefore, no unawareness on His part of what proceeds from Him. Nor is [God], moreover, akin to one of us who stands between a sick person and the sun, whereby the heat of the sun is deflected from the sick person because of him, [though the deflection is] not [caused] by his choice. The individual [intervening between sun and patient], however, is cognizant [of the deflection], without, moreover, being averse to it. For that which casts the shade, that which enacts the shadow, is his person and body, whereas the one who is cognizant of the falling of the shadow and is satisfied with it is his soul, not his body. This is not the case with respect to the First. For the enactor in Him is the knower and the one satisfied—that is, the one not averse [to the act]. For He knows that His perfection lies in having another emanate from Him. Indeed, if it were possible to suppose the body itself casting the shade, to be itself the knower of the falling of the shadow and to be the one satisfied [with this], this would also not be equal to the First. For the First is the knower and the doer, and His knowledge is the principle of His act. For His knowledge of Himself in being the principle of everything is the cause of the emanation of all things.

(26) The existing order is a consequent of the intelligible order in the sense that [the former] comes about through [the latter]. Hence, His being an agent is not additional to His being a knower of the whole, since His knowledge of the whole is the cause of the emanation of the whole from Him. His being a knower of the whole is not [something] additional to His knowledge of Himself. For He would not know Himself without His knowing that He is the Principle for the whole. Thus, what is known by the first intention is Himself, and the whole would be known to Him by the second intention. This, then, is the meaning of His being an agent.

(٢٥) واذا قيل خالق، وفاعل، وبارئ، وسائر صفات الفعل، فمعناه
انّ وجوده وجود شريف يفيض عنه وجود الكلّ فيضانا لازما، وانّ
وجود غيره حاصل منه وتابع لوجوده كما يتبع النور الشمس والاسخان
النار. ولا تشبه نسبة العالم اليه نسبة النور الى الشمس الا فى كونه معلولا
فقط؛ والا فليس هو كذلك. فانّ الشمس لا تشعر بفيضان النور عنها ولا
النار بفيضان الاسخان، فهو طبع محض. بل الاوّل عالم بذاته، وانّ ذاته
مبدأ لوجود غيره. ففيضان ما يفيض عنه معلوم له، فليس به غفلة عما
يصدر منه. ولا هو ايضاً كالواحد منا اذا وقف بين مريض وبين الشمس
فاندفع حر الشمس عن المريض بسببه، لا باختياره؛ ولكنّه عالم به، وهو
غير كاره أيضا له. فانّ المظلّ الفاعل للظلّ شخصه وجسمه والعالم
الراضى بوقوع الظلّ نفسه لا جسمه. وفى حق الاوّل ليس كذلك. فانّ
الفاعل منه هو العالم وهو الراضى أى انّه غير كاره. [فانّه]٧ عالم بانّ
كماله فى ان يفيض منه غيره. بل لو أمكن ان يفرض كون الجسم المظلّ
بعينه هو العالم بعينه بوقوع الظل وهو الراضى، لم يكن أيضا مساويا
للاول. فانّ الاول هو العالم وهو الفاعل، وعلمه هو مبدأ فعله. فان علمه
بنفسه فى كونه مبدأ للكلّ علّة فيضان الكلّ.

(٢٦) فانّ النظام الموجود تبع للنظام المعقول. بمعنى انّه واقع به. فكونه
فاعلا غير زائد على كونه عالما بالكلّ، اذ علمه بالكلّ علّة فيضان الكلّ
عنه. وكونه عالما بالكلّ لا يزيد على علمه بذاته. فانّه لا يعلم ذاته، ما لم
يعلم انّه مبدأ للكلّ. فيكون المعلوم بالقصد الاوّل ذاته، ويكون الكلّ
معلوما عنده بالقصد الثانى. فهذا معنى كونه فاعلا.

(27) If it is said [of Him], "Powerful," we do not mean by it [anything] other than His being an agent in the manner we have established— namely, that His existence is an existence from which [all] things under His power emanate and through whose emanation the arrangement of the whole is ordered according to the highest reaching of the modes of possibility in terms of perfection and beauty. If it is said, "Willer," we do not mean by it [anything] other than that He is not oblivious of what emanates from Him and is not averse to it, but, rather, that He knows His perfection consists in having the whole emanate from Him. It is thus permissible to say in this sense that He is satisfied, and it is permissible to say of the One Satisfied that He is a Willer. Thus, Will would be nothing other than Power itself, Power nothing other than Knowledge itself, Knowledge nothing other than the Essence itself. All, then, reduces to the Essence itself. This is because His knowledge of things does not derive from things. Otherwise, He would be acquiring an attribute or a perfection from another, which is impossible in the Necessary Existent.

(28) Our [own] knowledge, however, is of two divisions: [(a)] knowledge of a thing that occurs as a result of the form of that thing, as with our knowledge of the form of heaven and the earth; and [(b)] knowledge which we invent, as with something whose form we did not perceive but which we formed in our souls, then brought into existence, in which case the existence of the form would be derived from knowledge, not knowledge from [the] existence [of the form]. Knowledge [that belongs to] the First is in accordance with the second division. For the representation of the order in His essence is a cause for the emanation of the order from His essence.

(29) Yes, if the sheer presence of an etching or of the writing of a line in our souls is sufficient for the occurrence of such a form, then knowledge itself with respect to us is [one and the same as] power itself and will itself. But, because of our shortcomings, our conception is not sufficient to bring about the existence of the form but requires, in addition to that, a renewed will that springs forth from an appetitive power so that, through both, the power that moves the muscles and nerves in the organic parts [is able to] move [them]. Thus, through the movement of the muscles and nerves the hand or some other [organ] moves, and

(٢٧) واذا قيل قادر، لم نعن بهِ الا كونه فاعلا على الوجه الذى قرّرناه، وهو انّ وجوده وجود يفيض عنه المقدورات التى بفيضانها ينتظم الترتيب فى الكلّ على أبلغ وجوه الامكان فى الكمال والحسن. واذا قيل، مريد لم نعن به الا انّ ما يفيض عنه ليس هو غافلا عنه وليس كارها له، بل هو عالم بانّ كماله فى فيضان الكلّ عنه. فيجوز بهذا المعنى ان يقال هو راض وجاز ان يقال للراضى انّه مريد. فلا تكون الارادة الا عين القدرة ولا القدرة الا عين العلم ولا العلم الا عين الذات. فالكلّ اذن يرجع الى عين الذات. وهذا لانّ علمه بالأشياء ليس مأخوذا من الاشياء؛ والا لكان مستفيدا وصفا أو كمالا من غيره، وهو محال فى واجب الوجود.

(٢٨) ولكنّ علمنا على قسمين علم شىء حصل من صورة ذلك الشىء، كعلمنا بصورة السماء والارض، وعلم اخترعناه كشىء لم نشاهد صورته، ولكن صوّرناه فى أنفسنا ثم أحدثناه، فيكون وجود الصورة مستفادا من العلم لا العلم من الوجود. وعلم الاول بحسب القسم الثانى. فانّ تمثّل النظام فى ذاته سبب لفيضان النظام عن ذاته.

(٢٩) نعم، لو كان مجرّد حضور صورة نقش أو كتابة خطّ فى نفوسنا كافيا فى حدوث تلك الصورة، لكان العلم بعينه منا هو القدرة بعينها والارادة بعينها. ولكنّا لقصورنا، فليس يكفى تصوّرنا لايجاد الصورة، بل نحتاج مع ذلك الى ارادة متجدّدة تنبعث من قوّة شوقيّة ليتحرّك منهما معا القوّة المحرّكة للعضل والاعصاب فى الاعضاء الآليّة. فيتحرّك بحركة العضل والاعصاب اليد أو [غيرها]٨ ويتحرّك [بحركتها]٩ القلم او آلة

with its movement the pen or some other external instrument moves. Then, by the movement of the pen, matter such as ink or some other thing is moved, after which the form conceived in our souls is realized. For this reason, the very existence of this form in our souls is neither power nor will. Rather, power in us exists with the principle that moves the muscle, while this form [we conceive in ourselves] is the mover of that mover which is the principle of power. This is not the case with the Necessary Existent. For He is not composed of bodies in whose limbs power is infused. Hence, Power, Will, Knowledge, and Essence are, with respect to Him, one [and the same].

(30) If it is said of Him, "Living," by this is only intended that He knows by a knowledge through which the existent that is termed an act of His emanates. For the Living is the doer and the knower. Thus, what is intended [by "Living"] is His essence, together with a relation to actions in the way we have mentioned. [This] is not like our life. For it is not completed except through two diverse faculties from which apprehension and action spring forth. Hence, His Life is also identical with His essence.

(31) If it is said of Him, "Generous," by this is intended that the whole emanates from Him, not for any purpose [fulfilling a need] that reverts to Him. Generosity is fulfilled by two things. The first is that there should be for the one on whom the act of generosity is bestowed a benefit in what has been granted. For one may not ascribe generosity to whoever grants a person something for which [the person] has no need. The second is that the generous person is in no need of generosity when his undertaking [the act of] generosity would be for fulfilling a personal need. Whoever is generous in order to be praised and lauded or to escape from being blamed is someone seeking compensation and is not being generous. True generosity belongs to God. For He does not seek by it escape from blame, nor any perfection acquired through praise. "The Generous," hence, becomes a name indicating His existence in conjunction with a relation to [His] act and a negation of a purpose. Therefore, it does not lead to plurality in His essence.

(32) If it is said [of Him], "Pure Good," by this is intended either [one of two things. The first is] the existence of a creator free from deficiency and from the possibility of nonexistence. For evil has no entity unto itself, but reduces to the privation of a substance or a privation of the soundness of state of the substance. Otherwise, existence inasmuch

أُخرى خارجة، وتتحرك المادة بحركة القلم، كالمداد أو غيره، ثم تحصل الصورة المتصوّرة فى نفوسنا. فلذلك لم يكن نفس وجود هذه الصورة فى نفوسنا قدرة ولا ارادة. بل كانت القدرة فينا عند المبدأ المحرّك للعضل، وهذه الصورة محرّكة لذلك المحرّك الذى هو مبدأ القدرة. وليس كذلك فى واجب الوجود. فانّه ليس مركّبا من اجسام تنبث القوى فى اطرافه. فكانت القدرة والارادة والعلم والذات منه واحدا.

(٣٠) واذا قيل له حىّ، لم يرد به الا انّه عالم يفيض عنه الموجود الذى يسمى فعلا له. فانّ الحىّ هو الفعّال الدرّاك. فيكون المراد به ذاته مع اضافة الى الافعال على الوجه الذى ذكرناه، لا كحياتنا. فانّها لا تتمّ الا بقوّتين مختلفتين ينبعث عنهما الادراك والفعل. فحياته عين ذاته أيضا.

(٣١) واذا قيل له، جواد اريد به انّه يفيض عنه الكلّ، لا لغرض يرجع اليه. والجود يتمّ بشيئين: احدهما ان يكون للمنعم عليه فائدة فيما وهب منه، فلعلّ من يهب شيئا ممّن هو مستغن عنه لا يوصف بالجود؛ والثانى ان لا يحتاج الجواد الى الجود فيكون اقدامه على الجود لحاجة نفسه. وكلّ من يجود ليمدح أو يثنى عليه أو يتخلّص من مذمّة، فهو مستعيض، وليس بجواد. وانما الجود الحقيقىّ لله. فانّه ليس يبغى به خلاصا عن ذم ولا كمالا مستفادا بمدح. فيكون الجواد اسما منبئا عن وجوده مع اضافة الى الفعل وسلب للغرض. فلا يؤدّى الى الكثرة فى ذاته.

(٣٢) واذا قيل خير محض، فامّا ان يراد به وجوده بريئا عن النقص وإمكان العدم، فانّ الشر لا ذات لهُ، بل يرجع الى عدم جوهر او عدم صلاح حال الجوهر، والا فالوجود من حيث انّه وجود خير، فيرجع هذا

as it is existence is good. The term consequently reduces to the negation
of the possibility of imperfection and evil. [The second is when] it is also
said, "Good," to that which is the cause of the order of things. [Now,] the
First is the Principle of the order of all things. He is thus "Good," the
name indicating existence together with a kind of relation.

(33) If it is said [of Him], "Necessary Existent," [this] means this
existence [of His] with the negation of a cause for His existence and the
impossibility for a cause for His nonexistence, whether at a beginning
[of His existence] or at an end.

(34) If it is said [of Him], "Lover, Beloved, Enjoyer, and Enjoyed,"
[this] means that all beauty, splendor, and perfection are the object of
love and ardor in the One who has perfection. There is no meaning
for "enjoyment" other than apprehending the appropriate perfection.
Whoever knows his own perfection in knowing [all] the knowable things
(supposing he were to know them)—the beauty of his form, the perfection of his power, the strength of his organs, and, in general, his apprehension of the presence of every perfection possible for him—if this
were conceivable in one human, he would be a lover of his own perfection
and one who enjoys it. His enjoyment, however, decreases by supposing
privation and deficiency. For joy is rendered incomplete by what ceases
to exist or by that whose ceasing to exist is feared. The First, however, has
the most perfect splendor and the most complete beauty, since every perfection that is possible for Him is present to Him. He apprehends this
perfection with the assurance against the possibility of [its] decrease and
ceasing to be. The perfection that is realized for Him is above every perfection. Hence, His love and ardor for this perfection is above every love,
and His enjoyment of it is above every enjoyment. Indeed, our enjoyment
has no comparison to it at all. Rather, it is more exalted than to be
expressed [in terms of] enjoyment, joy, and gladness, except that we
have no expressions for these ideas [as they pertain to the divine]; one
cannot escape from using remote metaphor. [This is] just as when we
borrow as metaphor for Him from the expressions "Willer," "Chooser,"
and "Enactor," [used to refer to] ourselves, while at the same time giving
conclusive argument for the remoteness of His will from our will and the
remoteness of His power and knowledge from our power and knowledge.
It is not unlikely that one would deem the [use of the term] "enjoyment"
[with reference to God] repugnant and would use another. What is
intended, however, is that His state is nobler than the states of the
angels and [is] more worthy to be the object of exultation—and the state
of the angels is nobler than our states.

الاسم الى السلب لامكان النقص والشرّ؛ وقد يقال خير لما هو السبب لنظام الاشياء. والاوّل مبدأ لنظام كل شىء. فهو خير، ويكون الاسم دالا على الوجود مع نوع اضافة.

(٣٣) واذا قيل واجب الوجود، فمعناه هذا الوجود مع سلب علّة لوجوده واحالة علّة لعدمه اوّلا وآخرا.

(٣٤) واذا قيل عاشق ومعشوق ولذيذ وملتذّ، فمعناه هو انّ كلّ جمال وبهاء وكمال فهو محبوب ومعشوق لذى الكمال. ولا معنى للذّة الا ادراك الكمال الملائم. ومن عرف كمال نفسه فى احاطته بالمعلومات، لو أحاط بها، وفى جمال صورته وفى كمال قدرته وقوّة أعضائه، وبالجملة ادراكه لحضور كلّ كمال هو ممكن له، لو امكن ان يتصوّر ذلك فى انسان واحد، لكان محبّا لكماله وملتذّا به. وانما تنتقص لذّته بتقدير العدم والنقصان. فان السرور لا يتمّ بما يزول أو يخشى زواله. والأوّل له البهاء الاكمل والجمال الاتمّ اذ كل كمال هو ممكن له فهو حاضر له. وهو مدرك لذلك الكمال مع الامن من امكان النقصان والزوال. والكمال الحاصل له فوق كلّ كمال؛ فاحبابه وعشقه لذلك الكمال فوق كل احباب، والتذاذه به فوق كل التذاذ، بل لا نسبة للذّاتنا اليها البتّة، بل هى أجلّ من ان يعبّر عنها باللذّة والسرور والطيبة. الا أنّ تلك المعانى ليس لها عبارات عندنا، فلا بدّ من الابعاد فى الاستعارة، كما نستعير له لفظ المريد والمختار والفاعل منّا، مع القطع ببعد ارادته عن ارادتنا وبعد قدرته وعلمه عن قدرتنا وعلمنا. ولا بعد فى ان [يستبشع]¹⁰ عبارة اللذّة فيستعمل [غيرها]¹¹. والمقصود انّ حالته أشرف من أحوال الملائكة وأحرى بان يكون مغبوطا، وحالة الملائكة أشرف من أحوالنا.

(35) If there is no enjoyment other than the pleasure of eating and copulation, then the state of the donkey and the pig would be nobler than the state of the angels. These—that is [to say], the principles [in the realm] of the angels that are devoid of matter—have no enjoyment other than joy in the awareness of that with which they have been specifically endowed by way of perfection and beauty, whose cessation is never feared. But that which belongs to the First is above that which belongs to the angels. For the existence of the angels that are intelligences separate [from matter] is an existence that is possible in itself and necessary of existence through another. The possibility of nonexistence is a kind of evil and an imperfection. Hence, nothing is absolutely free from every evil except the First. For He is the Pure Good. To Him belong the most perfect splendor and beauty. Moreover, He is beloved, regardless of whether others love Him or not, just as He is [both] intellectual apprehender and intelligible, regardless of whether or not others apprehend Him. All these meanings reduce to His essence and His apprehension of His essence. His intellectual apprehension [of all this] and His intellectual apprehension of His essence are identical with His essence. For He is pure intellect. All, then, reduce to one meaning.

(36) This, then, is the way to explain their doctrine. These matters divide into those [things] in which belief is permissible—where, however, we will show that it cannot be correctly held in terms of [the philosophers' own] principles—and those in which belief is not correct, where we will show its falsity. Let us, then, return to the five levels in the divisions of plurality and their claim of negating them, showing their impotence in establishing a proof. And let us describe each problem independently.

(٣٥) ولو لم تكن لذّة إلا فى شهوة البطن والفرج، لكان حال الحمار والخنزير أشرف من حال الملائكة، وليس لها لذّة، أى للمبادى من الملائكة المجرّدة عن المادّة، الا السرور بالشعور بما خص بها من الكمال والجمال الذى لا يخشى زواله. ولكن الذى للاوّل فوق الذى للملائكة.

فانّ وجود الملائكة التّى هى العقول المجرّدة وجود ممكن فى ذاته واجب الوجود بغيره؛ وامكان العدم نوع شرّ ونقص. فليس شىء بريئا عن كل شرّ مطلقا سوى الاول. فهو الخير المحض، وله البهاء والجمال الاكمل. ثم هو معشوق، عشقه غيره أو لم يعشقه، كما انّه عاقل ومعقول، عقله غيره أو لم يعقله. وكلّ هذه المعانى راجعة الى ذاته، والى ادراكه لذاته. وعقله له وعقله لذاته هو عين ذاته. فانّه عقل مجرّد. فيرجع الكلّ الى معنى واحد.

(٣٦) فهذا طريق تفهيم مذهبهم. وهذه الامور منقسمة الى ما يجوز اعتقاده، فنبيّن انّه لا يصح على أصلهم، والى ما لا يصح اعتقاده، فنبيّن فساده. ولنعد الى المراتب الخمسة فى اقسام الكثرة ودعواهم نفيها، ولنبيّن عجزهم عن اقامة الدليل. ولنرسم كلّ واحد مسئلة على حيالها.

[Sixth] Discussion

[On the divine attributes]

(1) The philosophers have agreed, just as the Muᶜtazila have agreed, on the impossibility of affirming knowledge, power, and will for the First Principle. They claimed that all these names have come about through the religious law and that it is permissible to use them verbally, but that, as has been previously explained, they reduce [referentially] to one essence. Moreover, [they claim that] it is not permissible to affirm attributes that are additional to His essence in the way it is allowable in our case for our knowledge and power to constitute a description of ourselves that is additional to our essence. They claim that this necessitates plurality because, if these attributes were to occur for us, we would know that they are additional to the essence, since they would have come about anew. If one supposes them to be attached to our existence without [temporal] delay, [their constant] attachment would not render them outside their being additional to the essence. For [in the case of any] two things, if one of them occurs to the other, and it is known that "this" is not "that" and "that" is not "this," should they also be [constantly] connected, their being two things would [still] be rationally apprehended. Hence, these attributes in being [always] connected with the essence of the First are not removed from being things other than the essence. This would, then, necessitate plurality in the Necessary Existent, which is impossible. For this reason they all agreed on the denial of the attributes.

(2) [To this] one would say to them:

(3) In terms of what have you known the impossibility of this mode of plurality? You are opposed [in this] by all the Muslims, with the exception of the Muᶜtazila. What is the demonstration for this? For one's saying

مسئلة

(١) اتفقت الفلاسفة على استحالة اثبات العلم والقدرة والارادة للمبدأ الاوّل كما اتفقت المعتزلة عليه، وزعموا ان هذه الاسامى وردت شرعاً ويجوز اطلاقها لغة، ولكن ترجع الى ذات واحدة، كما سبق، ولا يجوز اثبات صفات زائدة على ذاته كما يجوز فى حقّنا ان يكون علمنا وقدرتنا وصفاً لنا زائدا على ذاتنا. وزعموا ان ذلك يوجب كثرة، لانّ هذه الصفات لو [طرأت]١ علينا، لكنّا نعلم انها زائدة على الذات اذ تجدّدت. ولو [قدّرت مقارنة]٢ لوجودنا من غير تأخّر، لما خرج عن كونه زائدا على الذات بالمقارنة. فكلّ شيئين، اذا [طرأ]٣ احدهما على الآخر، وعلم انّ هذا ليس ذاك وذاك ليس هذا، فلو اقترنا أيضا، عقل كونهما شيئين. فاذن لا تخرج هذه الصفات بان تكون مقارنة لذات الاوّل عن ان تكون أشياء سوى الذات. فيوجب ذلك كثرة فى واجب الوجود، وهو محال. فلهذا اجمعوا على نفى الصفات.

(٢) فيقال لهم:

(٣) وبم عرفتم استحالة الكثرة من هذا الوجه، وأنتم مخالفون من كافّة المسلمين سوى المعتزلة. فما البرهان عليه؟ فان قول القائل الكثرة محال فى

that plurality is impossible in the Necessary Existent when the essence is described as one reduces to maintaining that a plurality of attributes is impossible, which is the point at issue. Its impossibility is not known through rational necessity, so one inescapably needs a demonstration.

(4) [In answering this, the philosophers] adopt two ways.

[(1)]

(5) The first is their statement that the demonstration of this [is as follows: in the case of] both the attribute and the thing to which it is ascribed, if "this" is not "that" and "that" is not "this," then either [(a)] neither one will need the other for its existence, [(b)] each one will need the other, or [(c)] one will not need the other, the other needing [the former]. If each is supposed not to need the other, then both would be necessary of existence, which is the absolute rendering of duality and is impossible. But [if it is supposed] that each of the two is in need of the other, then neither would be necessary of existence, since the meaning of the necessary of existence is that which is self-subsistent and which has no need for another in any respect. For whatever is in need of another, that other would be its cause, since, if that other is removed [from existence], the existence [of the former] would become impossible. Hence, its existence would not be of itself, but through another. If it is said that only one of them needs [the other], that which has the need is an effect, the Necessary Existent being the other. And as long as it is an effect, it needs a cause. This leads to having the essence of the Necessary Existent be connected with a cause [other than it].[1]

(6) [Our] objection to this [first way] is to say:

(7) Of these divisions, the one to be chosen is the last. But your refuting the first division—namely, [that this leads to] absolute duality—is [something] we have shown in the previous question for which you have no demonstration; moreover, it is only complete by basing it on the denial of plurality [to be discussed] in this question and the one that follows. But how can that which is a branch of this question be the foundation on which the question is based? But the chosen [division consists] in saying that the essence in its subsistence does not need the attributes, but that the attribute, as with our case, is in need of that to which it is ascribed. There then remains their statement that that which needs another is not necessary of existence.

واجب الوجود مع كون الذات الموصوفة واحدة يرجع الى انّه يستحيل كثرة الصفات، وفيه النزاع. وليس استحالته معلومة بالضرورة. فلا بدّ من البرهان.

(٤) ولهم مسلكان.

(٥) الاوّل قولهم: البرهان عليه انّ كلّ واحد من الصفة والموصوف، اذا لم يكن هذا ذاك ولا ذاك هذا، فامّا ان يستغنى كل واحد عن الآخر فى وجوده، أو يفتقر كلّ واحد الى الآخر، أو يستغنى واحد عن الآخر، ويحتاج الآخر. فان فرض كلّ واحد مستغنيا، فهما واجبا وجود وهو التثنية المطلقة وهو محال. وامّا ان يحتاج كل واحد منهما الى الآخر، فلا يكون واحد منهما واجب الوجود، اذ معنى واجب الوجود ما قوامه بذاته وهو مستغن من كلّ وجه عن غيره. فما احتاج الى غيره، فذلك الغير علّته، اذ لو رفع ذلك الغير لامتنع وجوده، فلا يكون وجوده من ذاته بل من غيره. وان قيل احدهما يحتاج، دون الآخر، فالذى يحتاج معلول والواجب الوجود هو الآخر. ومهما كان معلولا افتقر الى سبب. فيؤدّى الى ان ترتبط ذات واجب الوجود بسبب.

(٦) والاعتراض على هذا ان يقال:

(٧) المختار من هذه الاقسام هو القسم الاخير. ولكن ابطالكم القسم الاوّل، وهو التثنية المطلقة، قد بيّنا انّه لا برهان لكم عليها فى المسئلة التى قبل هذه، وانّها لا تتمّ الا بالبناء على نفى الكثرة فى هذه المسئلة وما بعدها. فما هو فرع هذه المسئلة، كيف تبنى هذه المسئلة عليه؟ ولكن المختار ان يقال الذات فى قوامه غير محتاج الى الصفات والصفة محتاجة الى الموصوف كما فى حقّنا. فيبقى قولهم ان المحتاج الى غيره لا يكون واجب الوجود.

(8) To this it is said, "If by the necessary of existence you mean that which has no efficient cause, why do you say this? Why is it impossible to say that, just as the essence of the Necessary Existent is pre-eternal, having no agent, His attribute is co-eternal with Him, having no agent? And, if by the necessary of existence you mean that which has no receptive cause, then, according to this interpretation, [the attribute] is not necessary of existence, but despite this it is pre-eternal, having no agent. What renders this impossible?"

(9) If it is said, "The absolutely necessary existent is the one that has a cause that is neither efficient nor receptive; if it is admitted that it has a receptive cause, then it is admitted that it is an effect," we say:

(10) Naming the receptive essence a receptive cause is an idiom of yours. The proof [you offer] does not prove the existence of a necessary existent in terms of the idiom you adopt, proving only a limit with which the chain of causes and effects terminates. It proves only this much. The termination of the regress is possible with one [existent] that has eternal attributes that have no agent in the same way that there is no agent for His essence. These, however, are established in His essence. Let, then, the term "necessary existent" be cast aside, for one can be misled by it. Demonstration only shows the termination of regress, proving nothing else at all. To claim for it other than this is [sheer] arbitrariness.

(11) If it is said, "Just as one must terminate regression with respect to the efficient cause, one must then terminate it with the receptive, since, if every existent needs a receptacle to subsist therein, the receptacle also requiring a receptacle, regress would necessarily ensue, just as when every existent requires an [efficient] cause and that cause also a cause," we say:

(12) You have said what is true. No doubt this regress must also be terminated. We have said that the attribute is in His essence, while His essence does not subsist in another. [This is] just as our knowledge is in our essence, our essence being a receptacle for it, while our essence is not in a receptacle. Hence, a regress of efficient causes for the [eternal] attribute is eliminated, along with [any efficient cause for] the essence, since it has no agent, just as the essence has no agent.[2] Rather, the essence continues to exist [eternally] with this attribute without a cause for itself or for its

(٨) فيقال: ان اردت بواجب الوجود انه ليس له علّة فاعليّة، فلِمَ قلت ذلك؟ و لِم استحال ان يقال، كما انّ ذات واجب الوجود قديم، لا فاعل له، فكذلك صفته قديمة معه، ولا فاعل لها؟ وان أردت بواجب الوجود ان لا يكون له علّة قابليّة، فهو ليس بواجب الوجود على هذا التأويل، ولكنّه مع هذا قديم لا فاعل له. فما المحيل لذلك؟

(٩) فان قيل: واجب الوجود المطلق هو الذى ليس له علّة فاعليّة ولا قابليّة، فاذا سلّم ان له علّة قابليّة فقد سلّم كونه معلولا، قلنا:

(١٠) تسمية الذات القابلة علّة قابليّة من اصطلاحكم. والدليل لم يدلّ على ثبوت واجب وجود بحكم اصطلاحكم، وانّما دلّ على اثبات طرف ينقطع به تسلسل العلل والمعلولات. و لم يدلّ الا على هذا القدر. وقطع التسلسل ممكن بواحد له صفات قديمة لا فاعل لها كما لا فاعل لذاته، ولكنّها تكون متقرّرة فى ذاته. فليطرح لفظ واجب الوجود، فانه ممكن التلبّس فيه. فانّ البرهان لم يدل الا على قطع التسلسل و لم يدلّ على غيره البتّة. فدعوى غيره تحكّم.

(١١) فان قيل: كما يجب قطع التسلسل فى العلّة الفاعليّة، يجب قطعها فى القابليّة، اذ لو افتقر كل موجود الى محلّ يقوم فيه، وافتقر المحلّ أيضا، للزم التسلسل، كما لو افتقر كل موجود الى علّة وافتقرت العلّة أيضا الى علّة، قلنا:

(١٢) صدقتم. فلا جرم قطعنا هذا التسلسل أيضاً. وقلنا ان الصفة فى ذاته وليس ذاته قائما بغيره، كما انّ علمنا فى ذاتنا وذاتنا محلّ له، وليس ذاتنا فى محلّ. فالصفة انقطع تسلسل علتها الفاعليّة مع الذات، اذ لا فاعل لها كما لا فاعل للذات. بل لم تزل الذات بهذه الصفة موجودة

attribute. As for the receptive cause, its regress terminates only with the essence. Whence is it necessary that the receptacle should cease [to exist] so that [its having an efficient] cause should terminate? Demonstration only compels the termination of the regress. Any method through which the termination of the regress becomes possible constitutes a fulfillment of the dictate of the demonstration that requires [as its conclusion] the Necessary Existent. If by "necessary existent" is meant something other than an existent that does not have an efficient cause, wherewith regress terminates, we would basically not concede this as necessary. And as long as the mind encompasses the acceptance of an eternal existent whose existence has no cause, it encompasses the acceptance of an eternal characterized by attributes[—an existent] that has no cause for its existence either in its essence or in its attributes.

[(2)]

(13) The second way is their statement:

(14) Knowledge and power in us are not included in the quiddity of ourselves, but are accidental. If these attributes are established for the First, they also would not be included in the quiddity of Himself[3] but would be accidental in relation to Himself, even though they are permanent for Him. Many an accidental [thing] does not separate from the quiddity or is a concomitant of a quiddity without becoming for this reason [something that] substantiates its essence. If accidental, it is a dependent ancillary of the essence, and the essence becomes a cause for it. It thus becomes an effect. How, then, would it be necessary of existence?

(15) This [we say] is the same as the first [way], but with a change in expression. We thus say:

(16) If you mean by its being ancillary to the essence and the essence being a cause for it that the essence is an efficient cause of it and that it is enacted by the essence, this is not the case. For this does not follow necessarily in the case of our knowledge in relation to our essence, since our essences do not constitute an efficient cause for our knowledge. If you mean that the essence is a receptacle and that the attribute does not subsist by itself without a receptacle, this is conceded. But why should this be impossible? For it to be referred to as "ancillary," as "accidental," as an "effect," or whatever the person expressing it intends does not change the

بلا علّة [لها]؛ ولا [لصفتها]°. وامّا العلّة القابليّة، لم ينقطع تسلسلها الا على الذات. ومن أين يلزم ان ينتفى المحلّ حتى تنتفى العلّة؟ والبرهان ليس يضطرّ الا الى قطع التسلسل. فكلّ طريق امكن قطع التسلسل به، فهو وفاء بقضية البرهان الداعى الى واجب الوجود. وان أريد بواجب الوجود شىء سوى موجود ليس له علّة فاعليّة حتّى ينقطع به التسلسل، فلا نسلّم ان ذلك واجب أصلا. ومهما اتسع العقل لقبول موجود قديم لا علّة لوجوده، اتسع لقبول قديم موصوف لا علّة لوجوده فى ذاته وفى صفاته جميعا.

(١٣) المسلك الثاني قولهم:

(١٤) انّ العلم والقدرة فينا ليس داخلا فى ماهيّة ذاتنا بل هو عارض. واذا [اثبتت]٦ هذه الصفات للأوّل٧، لم [تكن]٨ أيضا [داخلة]٩ فى ماهيّة ذاته بل [كانت عارضة]١٠ بالاضافة اليه وان <كانت>١١ دائما له. وربّ عارض لا يفارق أو يكون لازما لماهيّة ولا يصير بذلك مقوما لذاته. واذا كان عارضا، كان تابعا للذات <وكانت>١٢ الذات سببا فيه، فكان معلولا. فكيف يكون واجب الوجود؟

(١٥) وهذا هو الاوّل مع تغيير عبارة. فنقول:

(١٦) ان عنيتم بكونه تابعا للذات وكون الذات سببا له، انّ الذات علّة فاعليّة له وانه مفعول للذات، فليس كذلك. فان ذلك ليس يلزم فى علمنا بالاضافة الى ذاتنا، اذ ذواتنا ليست بعلّة فاعلة لعلمنا. وان عنيتم ان الذات محلّ وانّ الصفة لا تقوم بنفسها فى غير محلّ، فهذا مسلّم فلم يمتنع هذا؟ فبأن يعبّر عنه بالتابع أو العارض او المعلول أو ما اراده المعبّر لم يتغيّر

meaning, if the meaning is nothing other than its being subsistent in the essence in the way attributes subsist in the things that have attributes. It is not impossible for [the attribute] to be in an essence, being at the same time pre-eternal, having no agent. All their proofs [are in reality] horrifying, saddling an expression with bad connotations by calling [the attribute] "possible," "permissible," "ancillary," "concomitant," and "effect," [maintaining that] this is reprehensible.

(17) [To this] it is said, "If by this is intended that [the attribute] has an agent, this is not the case. If by this is only intended that it has no agent but has a receptacle in which it subsists, then let this be given whatever expression one wants. For there is no impossibility in this."

(18) They may, however, [attempt to] frighten by linking the expression with bad connotations in another way, saying: "This leads to [the conclusion] that the First needs these attributes. Hence, He would not be absolutely self-sufficient. For the absolutely self-sufficient is the one who does not need anything other than His self." This, however, is a language of [rhetorical] preaching that is feeble in the extreme. For the attributes of perfection do not separate from the essence of the Perfect, so as to say that He is in need of another. If He never ceased and never ceases [throughout eternity] to be perfect in terms of knowledge, power, and life, how could He be in need, and how can one express adherence to perfection as a need? This is similar to someone's statement: "The perfect is the one who does not need perfection. Hence, the one who needs the attributes of perfection for himself is deficient"—to which one [replies]: "There is no meaning to his being perfect other than the existence of perfection for himself. Similarly, there is no meaning to his being self-sufficient other than the existence in himself of the attributes that negate needs. How, then, are the attributes of perfection through which divinity is perfected denied through such verbal [acts] that arouse [sheer] imaginings?"

(19) If it is said, "If you affirm an essence, and an attribute, and an inherence of the attribute in the essence, then this would constitute composition, and every composition requires a composer; and for this reason the First cannot be a body, because [the body] is composite," we say:

المعنى، اذا لم يكن المعنى سوى انّه قائم بالذات قيام الصفات بالموصوفات. ولم [يستحل]¹٢ ان يكون قائما فى ذات، وهو مع ذلك قديم ولا فاعل له. فكلّ ادلّتهم تهويل بتقبيح العبارة بتسميته ممكنا وجائزا وتابعا ولازما ومعلولا وانّ ذلك مستنكر.

(١٧) فيقال: ان أُريد بذلك ان له فاعلا، فليس كذلك. وان لم يرد به الا انّهُ لا فاعل لهُ ولكن هو محلّ لهُ قائم فيهِ، فليعبّر عن هذا المعنى باىّ عبارة أُريد. فلا استحالة فيه.

(١٨) وربما هوّلوا بتقبيح العبارة من وجه آخر فقالوا: هذا يؤدّى الى ان يكون الاوّل محتاجا الى هذه الصفات فلا يكون غنيّا مطلقا اذ الغنىّ المطلق من لا يحتاج الى غير ذاته. وهذا كلام وعظى فى غاية الركاكة. فانّ صفات الكمال لا تباين ذات الكامل، حتّى يقال انّه محتاج الى غيره. فاذا لم يزل ولا يزال كاملا بالعلم والقدرة والحياة، فكيف يكون محتاجا، [و]¹⁴ كيف يجوز ان يعبّر عن ملازمة الكمال بالحاجة؟ وهو كقول القائل: الكامل من لا يحتاج الى كمال، فالمحتاج الى وجود صفات الكمال لذاته، ناقص. فيقال: لا معنى لكونه كاملا، الا وجود الكمال لذاته؛ فكذلك لا معنى لكونه غنيّا، الا وجود الصفات المنافية للحاجات لذاته. فكيف تنكر صفات الكمال التى بها تتم الالهيّة بمثل هذه التخييلات اللفظية؟

(١٩) فان قيل، اذا أُثبتم ذاتا وصفة وحلولا للصفة بالذات، فهو تركيب؛ وكل تركيب يحتاج الى مركّب، ولذلك لم يجز ان يكون الاوّل جسما لانه مركّب، قلنا:

(20) One's statement, "Every composition requires a composer," is similar to his saying, "Every existent requires that which brings into existence." It is then further said to him:

(21) "The First is an eternal existent that has neither a cause nor
5   that which brings about [His] existence." Similarly, it is said: "He is an eternal [being] having attributes. There is neither a cause for His essence, [nor] for His attributes, nor for the subsistence of His attributes in His essence. Rather, all are eternal without a cause. As regards body, it is impossible for it to be the First because it is temporally created inasmuch
10 as it is not devoid of temporal events. Anyone for whom the creation of the body is not established must—as we shall force as a necessary consequence on you later on—allow that the first cause is a body." All their approaches in this problem are [things] that induce [mere] imaginings.

(22) Moreover, they are unable to reduce all [the attributes] they
15 affirm to the essence itself. For they affirm His being a knower, and this necessarily forces upon them [the admission] that this is [something] additional to pure existence. Thus, it would be said to them: "Do you admit that the First knows [anything] other than Himself?" Some admit this, while some maintain that He knows only Himself.

20 (23) The first [of these two positions] is the one Avicenna chose. For he claimed that [God] knows all things in a universal kind [of knowing] that does not fall under time and that He does not know [those] particulars the renewal of whose knowledge necessitates change in the essence of the knower. [To this] we say:

25 (24) Is the First's knowledge of the existence of all the species and genera that are infinite identical with His knowledge of Himself, or is it [some] other [thing]? If you say that it is other, you would have affirmed plurality and contradicted the principle [of divine unity]. And if you say it is identical, then you are no different from one who claims that man's
30 knowledge of another is identical with his knowledge of himself and identical with himself. Whoever says this [is afflicted with] folly in his mind. [For] it is said: "The definition of one thing is that it is impossible to combine [its] negation and affirmation in the estimation." Hence, knowledge of one thing, since it is one thing, renders it impossible to sup-
35 pose in the estimation its existing and not existing at the same time. And since it is not impossible to suppose in the estimation man's knowledge of

(٢٠) قول القائل، كل تركيب يحتاج الى مركّب، كقوله كل موجود يحتاج الى موجد. فيقال له:

(٢١) الاوّل موجود قديم لا علّة له، ولا موجد. فكذلك يقال هو موصوف قديم، ولا علّة لذاته، ولا لصفته، ولا لقيام صفته بذاته. بل الكلّ قديم بلا علّة. وامّا الجسم، فانّما لم يجز ان يكون هو الاوّل لانّه حادث من حيث انّه لا يخلوا عن الحوادث. ومن لم يثبت له حدوث الجسم يلزمه ان يجوز ان تكون العلّة الاولى جسما كما سنلزمه عليكم من بعد. وكل مسالكهم فى هذه المسألة تخييلات.

(٢٢) ثم انّهم لا يقدرون على ردّ جميع ما يثبتونه الى نفس الذات. فانّهم اثبتوا كونه عالما ويلزمهم ان يكون ذلك زائدا على مجرّد الوجود. فيقال لهم: أتسلّمون انّ الاوّل يعلم غير ذاته؟ ومنهم من يسلّم ذلك ومنهم من قال لا يعلم الا ذاته.

(٢٣) فامّا الاول، فهو الذى اختاره ابن سينا. فانه زعم انّه يعلم الاشياء كلّها بنوع كلّىّ لا يدخل تحت الزمان ولا يعلم الجزئيات التى يوجب تجدّد الاحاطة بها تغيّرا فى ذات العالم. فنقول:

(٢٤) علم الاوّل بوجود كلّ الانواع والاجناس التى لا نهاية لها، عين علمه بنفسه، أو غيره؟ فان قلتم انه غيره، فقد أثبتّم كثرة، ونقضتم القاعدة. وان قلتم انه عينه، لم تتميّزوا عن من يدّعى انّ علم الانسان بغيره عين علمه بنفسه وعين ذاته. ومن قال ذلك سفه فى عقله. وقيل حدّ الشىء الواحد ان يستحيل فى الوهم الجمع فيه بين النفى والاثبات. فالعلم بالشىء الواحد، لمّا كان شيئا واحدا، استحال ان يتوهّم فى حالة واحدة موجودا ومعدوما. ولمّا لم يستحل فى الوهم ان يقدّر علم الانسان

himself without knowledge of another, it is said that his knowledge of another is other than his knowledge of himself, since, if it were identical, then denying [self-knowledge] would be a denial [of knowledge of the other] and affirming [the former] would be an affirmation [of the latter].
⁵ For it is impossible for Zayd to be existing and not existing—I mean, he, himself—at the same time, whereas this is not impossible with respect to knowledge of another and knowledge of oneself.

(25) The same applies to the First's knowledge of Himself with respect to His knowledge of another, since it is possible to [suppose in the]
¹⁰ estimation the existence of one without the other. Consequently, they are two things; whereas it is not possible to suppose in the estimation the existence of His essence without the existence of His essence. If all [knowledge of self and knowledge of another] were thus [identical], then this estimative supposition would be impossible. Hence, all those
¹⁵ among the philosophers who confess that the First knows what is other than Himself inevitably affirm plurality.

(26) [The philosophers] may say:

(27) He does not know the other by first intention. Rather, He knows Himself as the principle of all things, knowledge of the whole becoming
²⁰ necessary for Him by the second intention, since He can only know Himself as a principle. For this, in reality, is His essence. And He cannot know Himself as the principle for another without the other's becoming included in His knowledge by way of entailment and necessary consequence. It is not improbable that His essence should have necessary consequences,
²⁵ but this does not necessitate plurality in the quiddity of the self. What is impossible is only that there should be plurality in the very essence.

(28) The answer to this is in [a number of] ways:

(29) The first is that your statement that He knows Himself as a principle is arbitrary. Rather, He must know only the existence of
³⁰ Himself. As regards the knowledge of His being a principle, this is additional to knowledge of existence, because being a principle is a relation to the essence and it is possible [for Him] to know the essence without knowing its relation. If being a principle were not a relation, then His essence would be multiple and He would have existence and the [property of] being a principle, and these are two things. And just as it is
³⁵ possible for a human to know himself without knowing himself to be an effect until he is taught [this], because being an effect is a relation he has

بنفسه دون علمه بغيره، قيل انّ علمه بغيره غير علمه بنفسه، اذ لو كان هو
هو، لكان نفيه نفيا له واثباته اثباتا له؛ اذ يستحيل ان يكون زيد موجودا
وزيد معدوما، اعنى هو بعينه فى حالة واحدة، ولا يستحيل مثل ذلك فى
العلم بالغير مع العلم بنفسه.

(٢٥) وكذى فى علم الاوّل بذاته مع علمه بغيره، اذ يمكن ان يتوهّم
وجود احدهم دون الآخر. فهما اذن شيئان، ولا يمكن ان يتوهّم وجود
ذاته دون وجود ذاته. فلو كان الكلّ كذلك، لكان هذا التوهّم محالا. فكلّ
من اعترف من الفلاسفة بانّ الاوّل يعرف غير ذاته فقد اثبت كثرة لا محالة.

(٢٦) فان قيل:

(٢٧) هو لا يعلم الغير بالقصد الاوّل، بل يعلم ذاته مبدأ للكلّ
فيلزمه، العلم بالكلّ بالقصد الثانى، اذ لا يمكن ان يعلم ذاته الا مبدأ. فانّه
حقيقة ذاته. ولا يمكن ان يعلم ذاته مبدأ لغيره الا ويدخل الغير فى علمه
بطريق التضمن واللزوم. ولا يبعد ان يكون لذاته لوازم وذلك لا يوجب
كثرة فى ماهيّة الذات. وانما يمتنع ان يكون فى نفس الذات كثرة.

(٢٨) والجواب من وجوه.

(٢٩) الاول، انّ قولكم انّه يعلم ذاته مبدأ تحكّم. بل ينبغى ان يعلم
وجود ذاته فقط. فامّا العلم بكونه مبدأ يزيد على العلم بالوجود، لانّ
المبدئيّة اضافة للذات. ويجوز ان يعلم الذات ولا يعلم اضافته. ولو لم
تكن المبدئيّة اضافة [لتكثرت]¹⁵ ذاته وكان له وجود ومبدئيّة وهما
شيئان. وكما يجوز ان يعرف الانسان ذاته ولا يعلم كونه معلولا الى ان

to his cause, similarly, [God's] being a cause is a relation He has to His effect. Thus, the necessary consequence [against them] remains standing in their mere saying that He knows Himself to be a principle, since it includes knowledge of the self and of being a principle, which is a relation. The relation is other than the self. Knowledge of the relation is other than knowledge of the self, [as shown] by the proof we have [just] mentioned—namely, that knowledge of the self without knowledge of being a principle can be supposed in the estimation—whereas one cannot suppose in the estimation knowledge of the self without knowledge of the self, because the self is one.

(30) The second way [of answering them] is that their statement that the whole is known to Him by the second intention is nonsensical speech. For as long as His knowledge encompasses another, just as it encompasses Himself, He would have two different objects of knowledge and He would have knowledge of both. The multiplicity and variance of what is known necessitates the multiplicity of knowledge, since one of the two objects of knowledge is amenable to separation from the other in one's estimation. Hence, knowledge of one of them would not be identical with knowledge of the other. For if this were the case, then it would not be possible to suppose the existence of the one without the other. Moreover, there would be no "other" as long as the whole [as they maintain] is one. Expressing [this] as "[knowledge] by the second intention" does not change anything.

(31) Upon my word, how can one who says that "not even the weight of an atom in the heavens or the earth escapes His knowledge" [Qur'ān 10:61], except that He knows the whole by a universal kind [of knowing], have the audacity to deny plurality, when the universals known [to God] are infinite, [and to maintain that] the knowledge relating to them with their multiplicity and variety remains one in all respects? In this Avicenna has differed with other philosophers who, in order to safeguard against the consequence of plurality, have held that God knows only Himself. How, then, does he share with them their denial of plurality but disagree with them in affirming [God's] knowledge of other [things]? When he was ashamed that it should be said that God does not know anything at all in this world and the next, but knows only Himself, whereas another knows Him and also knows himself and others, thereby becoming nobler than Him in knowledge, [Avicenna] forsook this [position], being embarrassed and repelled by this doctrine. But he was not ashamed in insisting on the denial of plurality in all respects, claiming

يعلّم لان كونه معلولا اضافة له الى علّته، فكذلك كونه علة اضافة له الى معلوله. فالالزام قائم فى مجرّد قولهم انّه يعلم كونه مبدأ، اذ فيه علم بالذات وبالمبدئيّة، وهو الاضافة والاضافة غير الذات. فالعلم بالاضافة غير العلم بالذات بالدليل الذى ذكرناه، وهو انّه يمكن ان يتوهّم العلم بالذات دون العلم بالمبدئيّة، ولا يمكن ان يتوهّم العلم بالذات دون العلم بالذات، لان الذات واحدة.

(٣٠) الوجه الثانى، هو انّ قولهم انّ الكلّ معلوم له بالقصد الثانى كلام غير معقول. فانّه مهما كان علمه محيطا بغيره كما يحيط بذاته، كان له معلومان متغايران وكان له علم بهما. وتعدّد المعلوم وتغايره يوجب تعدّد العلم اذ يقبل أحد المعلومين الفصل عن الآخر فى الوهم، فلا يكون العلم باحدهما عين العلم بالآخر، اذ لو كان، لتعذّر تقدير وجود احدهما دون الآخر. وليس ثمّ آخر مهما كان الكلّ واحدا. فهذا لا يختلف بان يعبّر عنه بالقصد الثانى.

(٣١) تم ليت شعرى، كيف يقدم على نفى الكثرة من يقول انّه لا يعزب عن علمه مثقال ذرّة فى السموات ولا فى الارض الا انّه يعرف الكلّ بنوع كلىّ، والكلّيّات المعلومة له لا تتناهى، فيكون العلم المتعلق بها مع كثرتها وتغايرها واحدا من كلّ وجه؟ وقد خالف ابن سينا فى هذا غيره من الفلاسفة الذين ذهبوا الى انّه لا يعلم الا نفسه احترازا من لزوم الكثرة. فكيف شاركهم فى نفى الكثرة ثم باينهم فى اثبات العلم بالغير؟ ولمّا استحيا ان يقال انّ الله لا يعلم شيئا أصلا فى الدنيا والآخرة، وانّما يعلم نفسه فقط، وأمّا غيره فيعرفه ويعرف ايضاً نفسه وغيره، فيكون غيره أشرف منه فى العلم، فترك هذا حياء من هذا المذهب واستنكافا منه. ثم لم يستحى من الاصرار على نفى الكثرة من كلّ وجه وزعم انّ علمه بنفسه

that [God's] knowledge of Himself and of others—indeed, of all things—constitutes His essence without any addition. This is the very contradiction of which the rest of the philosophers were ashamed because of the manifest contradiction [in Avicenna's doctrine] at first reflection. Hence, no party among them is free from shame as regards his doctrine. This is what God does with those who stray from His path, thinking that the inner nature of divine matters is grasped by their reflection and imagination.

(32) [The philosophers may] say:

(33) If it is established that He knows Himself as a principle by way of relation, then the knowledge of what is related is one. For whoever knows the son knows him by one knowledge; and [this knowledge of what is related] includes by entailment knowledge of the father, of fatherhood, and [of] sonship. Thus, what is known becomes multiple, but knowledge remains one. Similarly, [God] knows Himself as the principle for others, knowledge remaining one even though what is known becomes multiple. If, then, this is rationally comprehended in the case of one effect and its relation to Him, this not necessitating plurality, then the increase in that whose genus does not necessitate plurality [in turn] does not necessitate plurality. Similarly, whoever knows a thing and knows his knowledge of the thing knows it with that [same] knowledge. Thus, every knowledge is knowledge of itself and of its object. The object of knowledge becomes multiple, while knowledge remains one. What also shows this is that you [theologians] perceive that the objects of God's knowledge are infinite, while His knowledge is one, and [you] attribute to Him cognitions that are infinite in number. If the multiplicity of what is known necessitates the multiplicity of the essence of knowledge, then let there be in the divine essence cognitions that are numerically infinite, which would be impossible.

(34) [To this] we say:

(35) As long as knowledge is one in every respect, then its attachment to two objects of knowledge is inconceivable. Rather, this exacts some multiplicity according to what the philosophers posit and [express in] their idiom when considering [the notion of] multiplicity—so [much so] that they exaggerate, saying: "If the First were to have a quiddity characterized by existence,[4] this would constitute multiplicity." They did not

وبغيره بل وبجميع الاشياء هو ذاته من غير مزيد؛ وهو عين التناقض الذى استحيا منه سائر الفلاسفة لظهور التناقض فيه فى أوّل النظر. فاذن ليس ينفكّ فريق منهم عن خزى فى [مذهبه][١٦]. وهكذى يفعل الله بمن ضلّ عن سبيله وظنّ انّ الامور الالهيّة يستولى على كنهها بنظره [وتخيّله][١٧].

(٣٢) فان قيل:

(٣٣) اذا ثبت انّه يعرف نفسه مبدأ على سبيل الاضافة فالعلم بالمضاف واحد، اذ من عرف الابن عرفه بمعرفة واحدة، وفيه العلم بالاب وبالابوّة والبنوّة ضمنا، فيكثر المعلوم ويتّحد العلم، فكذلك هو يعلم ذاته مبدأ لغيره فيتّحد العلم وان تعدّد المعلوم. ثمّ اذا عقل هذا فى معلول واحد واضافته اليه ولم يوجب ذلك كثرة، فالزيادة فيما لا يوجب جنسه كثرة لا توجب كثرة. وكذلك من يعلم الشىء ويعلم علمه بالشىء فانّه يعلمهُ بذلك العلم. فكلّ علم هو علم بنفسه وبمعلومهِ، فيتعدّد المعلوم ويتّحد العلم. ويدلّ عليهِ أيضا انكم ترون انّ معلومات الله لا نهاية لها وعلمهُ واحد، ولا تصفونهُ بعلوم لا نهاية لاعدادها. فان كان تعدّد المعلوم يوجب تعدد ذات العلم، فليكن فى ذات الله علوم لا نهاية لاعدادها وهذا محال.

(٣٤) قلنا:

(٣٥) مهما كان العلم واحدا من كل وجه لم يتصوّر تعلّقهُ بمعلومين، بل يقتضى ذلك كثرة ما على ما هو وضع الفلاسفة واصطلاحهم فى تقدير الكثرة، حتّى بالغوا فقالوا، لو كان للاول ماهيّة موصوفة بالوجود

deem it intelligible for one thing to have a reality to which thereafter existence is attributed but claimed that existence related to reality, being other than it, exacts multiplicity as its consequence. It is, then, in this way [we maintain] that one cannot suppose knowledge to be attached to many objects of knowledge without this necessitating in it a kind of multiplicity clearer and greater than what is necessitated by supposing an existence related to a quiddity.

(36) As for knowledge of the son, and likewise the rest of the relations, this includes multiplicity. For there is no escape from knowing the essence of the son and the essence of the father, [this knowledge consisting of] two cognitions, and [having] a third knowledge—namely, [knowledge of] the relation. Yes, this third is entailed in the two previous cognitions, since these two are a condition and a necessary requirement for it. For, unless the related thing is first known, the relation is not known. These, then, are manifold cognitions, some conditioned by others. Similarly, if the First knows Himself as related to the rest of the genera and species by being a principle for them, He needs to know Himself and the individual genera and to know His relation [to the latter] in terms of being a principle to them. Otherwise, the relation's being known to Him becomes unintelligible.

(37) Regarding their statement that whoever knows a thing knows that he is a knower by virtue of that very knowledge, so that, while the object of his knowledge constitutes a plurality, knowledge remains one, this is not the case. Rather, he knows his being a knower by another knowledge [and so on] until this terminates in a knowledge of which he is oblivious and does not know. We do not say that this regresses ad infinitum but that it stops [at a point] with a knowledge relating to its object, where [the individual] is oblivious to the existence of the knowledge but not [to that] of the object known. This is similar to a person who knows blackness, being, in his state of knowing, psychologically absorbed with the object of his knowledge—namely, blackness—but unaware of his [act of] knowing blackness, paying no heed to it. If he pays heed to it, he will require another knowledge [and so on] until his heeding ceases.

(38) As regards their saying, "This is turned against you regarding the objects of God's knowledge, for these are infinite, whereas knowledge, according to you, is one," we say:

لكان ذلك كثرة. فلم يعقلوا شيئا واحدا لهُ حقيقة ثم يوصف بالوجود، بل زعموا ان الوجود مضاف الى الحقيقة وهو غيره، فيقتضى كثرة. فعلى هذا الوجهِ لا يمكن تقدير علم يتعلّق بمعلومات كثيرة الا ويلزم فيه نوع كثرة اجلى وأبلغ من اللازم فى تقدير وجود مضاف الى ماهيّة.

(٣٦) وامّا العلم بالابن وكذى سائر المضافات، ففيه كثرة، اذ لا بدّ من العلم بذات الابن وذات الاب وهما علمان وعلم ثالث وهو الاضافة. نعم، هذا الثالث مضمن بالعلمين السابقين، اذ هما من شرطه وضرورته، والا فما لم يعلم المضاف أولاً لا تعلم الاضافة. فهى علوم متعددة، بعضها مشروطة فى البعض؛ فكذلك، اذا علم الاوّل ذاته مضافا الى سائر الاجناس والانواع بكونه مبدأ لها، افتقر الى ان يعلم ذاته وآحاد الاجناس، وأن يعلم اضافة نفسه بالمبدئيّة اليها، والا لم يعقل كون الاضافة معلومة له.

(٣٧) وامّا قولهم ان من علم شيئا علم كونه عالما بذلك العلم بعينه فيكون المعلوم متعدّدا والعلم واحدا، فليس كذلك. بل يعلم كونه عالما بعلم آخر وينتهى الى علم يغفل عنه ولا يعلمه. ولا نقول يتسلسل الى غير نهاية بل ينقطع على علم متعلّق بمعلومه وهو غافل عن وجود العلم، لا عن وجود المعلوم، كالذى يعلم السواد وهو فى حال علمه مستغرق النفس بمعلومه الذى هو سواد، وغافل عن علمه بالسواد وليس ملتفتا اليه. فان التفت اليه افتقر الى علم آخر الى ان ينقطع التفاته.

(٣٨) وامّا قولهم، انّ هذا ينقلب عليكم فى معلومات الله فانّها غير متناهية والعلم عندكم واحد، فنقول:

(39) We did not plunge into this book in the manner of those who introduce [what is constructive], but in the manner of those who are destroyers and objectors. For this reason we have named the book *The Incoherence of the Philosophers*, not *The Introduction to Truth*. Hence, it is not incumbent on us to answer this.

(40) [The philosophers may] say:

(41) We do not force upon you adherence to the doctrine of one specific sect. But that which turns against the rest of mankind, where all are equal in facing its difficulty, is not [something] you should be allowed to bring [against us]. This difficulty turns against you, and no sect can escape it.

(42) We say:

(43) No. What is intended is to show your impotence in your claim of knowing the true nature of things through conclusive demonstrations, and to shed doubt on your claims. Once your impotence becomes manifest, then [one must point out that]there are among people those who hold that the realities of divine matters are not attained through rational reflection—indeed, that it is not within human power to know them. For this reason, the giver of the law has said: "Think on God's creation and do not think on God's essence."

(44) What, then, is your disavowal of this group that believes the truth of the apostle through the proof of the miracle, that confines itself in intellectual judgment to prove the existence of the apostle, that avoids reflecting on the attributes by intellectual reflection, that follows the law-giver in what he has revealed of God's attributes, that follows [the prophet's] example in using the terms "knower," "willer," "powerful," and "living," that refrains from using those terms that have been prohibited, and that acknowledges the inability of the mind to apprehend [divine things]? You only disapprove of them by attributing to them ignorance of the methods of demonstration and the manner of arranging the premises according to syllogistic figures, and by your claims that we have known [all] this through rational ways. But your impotence, the incoherence of

(٣٩) نحن لم نخض فى هذا الكتاب خوض الممهدين بل خوض الهادمين المعترضين. ولذلك سمّينا الكتاب تهافت الفلاسفة لا تمهيد الحق فليس يلزمنا هذا الجواب.

(٤٠) فان قيل:

(٤١) انّا لا نلزمكم مذهب فرقة معيّنة من الفرق. فامّا ما ينقلب على كافّة الخلق وتستوى الاقدام فى اشكاله فلا يجوز لكم ايراده. وهذا الاشكال منقلب عليكم ولا محيص لأحد من الفرق عنه.

(٤٢) قلنا:

(٤٣) لا. بل المقصود تعجيزكم عن دعواكم معرفة حقائق الامور بالبراهين القطعيّة وتشكيككم فى دعاويكم. واذا ظهر عجزكم، ففى الناس من يذهب الى انّ حقائق الامور الالهيّة لا تنال بنظر العقل، بل ليس فى قوّة البشر الاطلاع عليه. ولذلك قال صاحب الشرع، تفكّروا فى خلق الله ولا تتفكّروا فى ذات الله.

(٤٤) فما انكاركم على هذه الفرقة المعتقدة صدق الرسول بدليل المعجزة، المقتصرة من قضيّة العقل على اثبات ذات المرسل، المحترزة عن النظر فى الصفات بنظر العقل، المتّبعة صاحب الشرع فيما أتى به من صفات الله، المقتفية اثره فى اطلاق العالم والمريد والقادر والحى، المنتهية عن اطلاق ما لم يؤذن فيه، المعترفة بالعجز عن درك العقل؟ وانّما انكاركم عليهم بنسبتهم الى الجهل .بمسالك البراهين ووجه ترتيب المقدمات على اشكال المقاييس، ودعواكم أنّا قد عرفنا ذلك .بمسالك عقلية، وقد بان عجزكم وتهافت مسالككم وافتضاحكم فى

your ways, and the exposure [of your ignorance] in what you [claim to] know have become manifest. And [showing] this is what is intended in this explanatory discussion. Where, then, are those who claim that metaphysical demonstrations are as conclusive as geometrical demonstrations?

(45) [The philosophers may] say:

(46) This difficulty is forced as a necessary consequence on Avicenna, inasmuch as he claimed that the First knows other [than Himself]. The exacting philosophers, however, have agreed that He knows only Himself. [With this] the difficulty is thus removed.

(47) We say:

(48) Sufficient is the shame on you with this doctrine. Had it not reached the limit in feebleness, the later [philosophers] would not have refrained from supporting it. We will [now] draw attention to the shameful aspect in it. For it entails the rendering of [God's] effects better than He. For angel, man, and every one among the rational beings knows himself and his principle, and knows others, whereas the First knows only Himself. He is thus deficient in relation to individual people, to say nothing of the angels. Indeed, the beasts, in addition to their awareness of themselves, know things other than themselves. There is no doubt that knowledge is nobility and its absence deficiency. Where, then, is their statement, "He is the Lover and the Beloved, because to Him belongs majesty most perfect and beauty most complete?" What beauty is there for an existence that is simple, having neither quiddity nor reality, that has no knowledge of what takes place in the world and no knowledge of what is necessitated by itself? And what deficiency in God's world is greater than this?

(49) A rational person would indeed be astonished by a party that claims to delve deeply into [the world of] the intelligibles but whose reflection in the end leads to [the conclusion] that the Lord of Lords and the Cause of Causes has basically no knowledge of what occurs in the world. What difference is there between Him and the dead, except for His knowledge of Himself? And what perfection is there in His knowledge of Himself, with His ignorance of what is other than Himself? This is a

دعوى معرفتكم، وهو المقصود من هذا البيان. فاين من يدّعى انّ براهين الالهيّات قاطعة كبراهين الهندسيّات؟

(٤٥) فان قيل:

(٤٦) هذا الاشكال انما لزم على ابن سينا حيث زعم انّ الاوّل يعلم غيره. فامّا المحققون من الفلاسفة قد اتفقوا على انّه لا يعلم الا نفسه. فيندفع هذا الاشكال.

(٤٧) فنقول:

(٤٨) ناهيكم خزيا بهذا المذهب. ولولا انّه فى غاية الركاكة، لما استنكف المتأخرون عن نصرته. ونحن ننبّه على وجه الخزى، فيه، فانّ فيه تفضيل معلولاته عليه، اذ الملك والانسان وكلّ واحد من العقلاء يعرف نفسه ومبدأه ويعرف غيره، والاوّل لا يعرف الا نفسه. فهو ناقص بالاضافة الى آحاد الناس، فضلا عن الملائكة. بل البهيمة مع شعورها بنفسها تعرف امورا أُخر سواها. ولا شكّ فى ان العلم شرف وان عدمه نقصان. فاين قولهم انه عاشق ومعشوق لانّ له البهاء الاكمل والجمال الاتمّ؟ وأيّ جمال لوجود بسيط لا ماهيّة له ولا حقيقة ولا خبر له بما يجرى فى العالم ولا ممّا يلزم ذاته ويصدر منه؟ وأيّ نقصان فى عالم الله يزيد على هذا؟

(٤٩) وليتعجب العاقل من طائفة يتعمّقون فى المعقولات بزعمهم ثم ينتهى آخر نظرهم الى انّ ربّ الارباب ومسبّب الاسباب لا علم له أصلا بما يجرى فى العالم. وأى فرق بينه وبين الميت الا فى علمه بنفسه؟ وأيّ كمال فى علمه بنفسه مع جهله بغيره؟ وهذا مذهب تغنى صورته فى

doctrine whose scandalous visage renders elaboration and clarification needless. Further, it is said to those, "You have also not escaped multiplicity, in addition to your plunging into these shameful things." For we say:

(50) Is His knowledge of Himself identical with Himself or other than Himself? If you say that it is other than Himself, then multiplicity comes about. If [on the other hand] you say that it is identical with Himself, then what difference is there between you and one who says that a human's knowledge of himself is identical with himself? This is foolishness. For the existence of himself in a state where he is unaware of himself is conceivable. His unawareness thereafter ceases, and he becomes awakened to himself. Hence, his awareness of himself becomes necessarily other than himself. If, however, you say, "A human may be devoid of the knowledge of himself, and then [self-knowledge] would occur to him so that his awareness of himself would necessarily be other than himself," we say:

(51) Otherness is known neither through occurrence nor [through] connection. For the identical thing cannot occur to the [identical] thing. When that which is other than the thing connects with the thing, it does not become identical with it and does not cease to be another. That the First should be eternally knowing Himself does not prove that His knowledge of Himself is identical with Himself. The estimative [power] is wide enough [to allow] postulating [the existence of] the [divine] essence [by itself] and then the occurrence of [God's] awareness [of Himself]. If [this awareness] were identical with the [divine] essence itself, then this estimative act [of hypothesizing essence and awareness of essence separately] would have been inconceivable.

(52) If it is said, "His essence is intellect and knowledge; hence, He does not possess an essence [and] then a knowledge subsisting in it," we say:

(53) The folly is obvious in this speech. For knowledge is an attribute and an accident that requires that to which the attribute is ascribed. The statement of someone that [God] in His essence is intellect and knowledge is the same as his saying that He is power and will; [the latter] would then be self-subsisting. If this is upheld, then it is akin to someone's statement concerning blackness and whiteness, that [they] are self-subsistent; and, with respect to quantity, squareness, and three-foldness, that [they] are self-subsistent. The same holds with all the accidents. [Now,] in the way that it is impossible for the attributes of bodies to be self-subsistent without a body which is other than the attributes, in [this very] same way it is known that the attributes of the living by way of knowledge, life,

الافتضاح عن الاطناب والايضاح. ثم يقال لهؤلاء: لم تتخلصوا عن الكثرة، مع اقتحام هذه المجازى، أيضاً فانّا نقول:

(٥٠) علمه بذاته عين ذاته أو غير ذاته؟ فان قلتم انّه غيره، فقد جاءَت الكثرة، وان قلتم انّه عينه، فما الفصل بينكم وبين قائل، انّ علم الانسان بذاته عين ذاته؟ وهو حماقة، اذ يعقل وجود ذاته فى حالة هو فيها غافل عن ذاته ثم تزول غفلته ويتنبّه لذاته فيكون شعوره بذاته غير ذاته لا محالة. فان قلتم، انّ الانسان قد يخلوا عن العلم بذاته فيطرى عليه فيكون غيره لا محالة، فنقول:

(٥١) الغيّرية لا تعرف بالطريان والمقارنة؛ فانّ عين الشىء لا يجوز ان يطرى على الشىء. وغير الشىء اذا قارن الشىء لم يصر هو هو، و لم يخرج عن كونه غيرا. فبأن كان الاوّل لم يزل عالما بذاته، لا يدلّ على انّ علمه بذاته عين ذاته. ويتّسع الوهم لتقدير الذات ثم طريان الشعور. ولو كان هو الذات بعينه لما تصور هذا التوهّم.

(٥٢) فان قيل ذاته عقل وعلم، فليس له ذات ثم علم قائم به، قلنا:

(٥٣) الحماقة ظاهرة فى هذا الكلام، فانّ العلم صفة وعرض يستدعى موصوفا. وقول القائل هو فى ذاته عقل وعلم، كقوله هو قدرة وارادة، وهو قائم بنفسه. ولو قيل به، فهو كقول القائل فى سواد وبياض انّه قائم بنفسه، وفى كمّية وتربيع وتثليث انّه قائم بنفسه، وكذى فى كل الاعراض. وبالطريق الذى يستحيل ان تقوم صفات الاجسام بنفسها دون جسم هو غير الصفات، بعين ذلك الطريق يعلم أنّ صفات الاحياء

power, and will are also not self-subsistent but subsist in an essence. Life then subsists in an essence. [God's] life would, hence, be through [the attribute of life]. The same applies to the rest of [the divine] attributes.

(54) Consequently, [the philosophers] are not content with denying the First the rest of the attributes, nor with denying Him reality and quiddity, but have reached the point of denying Him self-subsistence, reducing Him to the realities of accidents and attributes that have no self-subsistence. Nonetheless, we will, after this, in a separate discussion, show their inability to prove His being a knower of Himself and of others.

من العلم والحياء والقدرة والارادة أيضا لا تقوم بنفسها، وانما تقوم بذات. فالحياة تقوم بالذات، فيكون حياته بها، وكذلك سائر الصفات.

(٥٤) فاذن لم يقنعوا بسلب الاوّل سائر الصفات، ولا بسلبه الحقيقة والماهيّة، حتّى سلبوه أيضاً القيام بنفسه وردّوه الى حقائق الاعرض والصفات التى لا قوام لها بنفسها. على انا سنبيّن بعد هذا عجزهم عن اقامة الدليل على كونه عالما بنفسه وبغيره فى مسئلة مفردة.

[Seventh] Discussion

*On refuting their statement that the First cannot
share with another in terms of genus and differ from
it in differentia—that an intellectual division in
terms of genus and differentia never frequents to Him*

(1) They have agreed on this, building on it [the argument] that, if [the First] does not share a generic meaning with another, He also does not differ from it in terms of a differential meaning. Hence, He has no definition, since definition is formed in terms of genus and differentia. And that which has no composition has no definition and [according to them] this [namely, having genus and difference] is a kind of composition.

(2) They [further] claimed that the statement of someone that He equals the first effect in being an existent, a substance, and a cause of another and necessarily differs from it in another thing does not constitute generic participation but participation in [what is] a necessary common concomitant. There is a difference between genus and the necessary concomitant in reality, even if they did not differ in commonness, as is known in logic. For the essential genus is the common predicate in the answer [to the question], "What is it?" and is included in the quiddity of the defined thing and is a giver of substance to its essence. Thus, a human's being animate is included in the quiddity of the human—I mean animality—and is therefore a genus. His being born and created is a concomitant of his, never separating from him, but is not included in the quiddity, even though it is a common concomitant. This is known in logic in a manner that is indisputable.

مسئلة

فى ابطال قولهم: إنّ الاوّل لا يجوز ان يشارك
غيره فى جنس ويفارقه بفصل وانّه لا يتطرق
اليه انفسام فى حق العقل، بالجنس والفصل

(١) وقد اتفقوا على هذا وبنوا عليهِ انّهُ اذا لم يشارك غيره بمعنى
جنسى لم ينفصل عنهُ بمعنى فصلى، فلم يكن له حدّ، اذ الحدّ ينتظم من
الجنس والفصل؛ وما لا تركيب فيه فلا حدّ لهُ. وهذا نوع من التركيب.

(٢) وزعموا أنّ قول القائل انّهُ يساوى المعلول الاوّل فى كونه
موجودا وجوهرا وعلّة لغيره، ويباينه بشىء آخر لا محالة، فليس هذا
مشاركة فى الجنس بل هو مشاركة فى لازم عامّ. وفرق بين الجنس
واللازم فى الحقيقة وان لم يفترقا فى العموم، على ما عرف فى المنطق. فانّ
الجنس الذاتىّ هو العامّ المقول فى جواب ما هو ويدخل فى ماهيّة الشىء
المحدود ويكون مقوما لذاتهِ. فكون الانسان حيّا داخل فى ماهيّة الانسان،
أعنى الحيوانيّة، فكان جنسا؛ وكونهُ مولودا ومخلوقا لازم لهُ لا يفارقهُ قطّ،
ولكنّهُ ليس داخلا فى الماهيّة، وان كان لازما عامّا. ويعرف ذلك فى
المنطق معرفة لا يتمارى فيها.

١١٠

(3) Moreover, they claimed that existence is never included in the quiddity of things but is related to the quiddity either as a concomitant that never separates, as with heaven, or as occurring after not being, as with temporal things. Hence, participation in existence is not participation in a genus. As regards [God's] participation in being a cause of another, as with the rest of the causes, this is participation in a necessary relation that is also not included in the quiddity. For neither being a principle nor [being in] existence substantiates the essence, but [both become] necessary concomitants of the essence after the substantiation of the essence by the parts of its quiddity. Hence, participation in it is nothing but the participation in a common concomitant whose necessity is consequent on the essence, its necessary concomitance not being in [terms of] genus. For this reason, things are not defined except in terms of matters that substantiate [them]. If defined through [their] necessary concomitants, this would constitute a description[1] for the purpose of differentiation, not for the purpose of giving a conception of the reality of the thing. Thus, it is not said regarding the definition of the triangle that it is that whose angles are equal to two right angles, even though this is a necessary concomitant of every triangle; but it is said that it is a figure encompassed by three straight lines.

(4) It is the same with participation in His being a substance. For the meaning of His being a substance is that He does not exist in a subject. Existence is not a genus. That something negative is related to it—namely, that it is not in a subject—does not make [existence] become a substantiating genus. Indeed, if [something positive][2] were related to it and it is said that it exists in a subject, it would not become a genus in terms of being an accident. This is because whoever knows a substance by its definition, which is like a description to it—namely, that it does not exist in a subject—does not know that it exists, to say nothing of its either being in a subject or not [being] in a subject. Rather, the meaning of our statement in describing the substance is that it is the existent not in a subject—that is, that it is some reality which, if it comes into existence, comes to exist not in a subject. We do not mean by it that it actually exists at the time in which it is being defined. Hence, the participation in it is not the participation in a genus.

(5) Rather, participation in the things substantiating the quiddity is participation in the genus, requiring thereafter differentiation through

(٣) وزعموا انّ الوجود لا يدخل قطّ فى ماهيّة الاشياء، بل هو مضاف الى الماهيّة، امّا لازما لا يفارق، كالسماء أو واردا بعد ان لم يكن، كالاشياء الحادثة. فالمشاركة فى الوجود ليس مشاركة فى الجنس. وأمّا مشاركته فى كونهِ علّةً لغيره كسائر العلل، فهو مشاركة فى اضافة لازمة لا تدخل أيضاً فى الماهيّة. فانّ المبدئيّة والوجود لا يقوّم واحد منهما الذات، بل يلزمان الذات بعد تقوّم الذات باجزاء ماهيّته. [فليست]¹ المشاركة فيه الا مشاركة فى لازم عامّ يتبع الذات، لزومه لا فى جنس. ولذلك لا تحدّ الاشياء الا بالمقوّمات. فان حدّت باللوازم، كان ذلك رسما للتمييز، لا لتصوير حقيقة الشىء. فلا يقال فى حدّ المثلّث انّه الذى تساوى زواياه القائمتين، وان كان ذلك لازمًا لكلّ مثلّث، بل يقال انّه شكل يحيط به ثلاثة اضلاع.

(٤) كذلك المشاركة فى كونه جوهرا. فانّ معنى كونه جوهرا انّه موجود لا فى موضوع. والموجود ليس يجنس فبأن يضاف اليه أمر سلبى، وهو انّه لا فى موضوع، [لا]² يصير جنسا مقوّما. بل لو أُضيف اليه ايجابه وقيل موجود فى موضوع، لم يصر جنسا فى العرض. وهذا لانّ من عرف الجوهر بحدّه الذى هو كالرسم له، وهو انّه موجود لا فى موضوع، فليس يعرف كونه موجودا، فضلاً من ان يعرف انّه فى موضوع أو لا فى موضوع. بل معنى قولنا فى رسم الجوهر انّه الموجود لا فى موضوع، أى انّه حقيقة ما، اذا وجد، وجد لا فى موضوع. ولسنا نعنى به انه موجود بالفعل حالة التحديد؛ فليس المشاركة فيه مشاركة فى جنس.

(٥) بل المشاركة فى مقوّمات الماهيّة هى المشاركة فى الجنس المحوج الى المباينة بعده بالفصل. وليس للاول ماهيّة سوى الوجود الواجب.

a differentia. There is no quiddity for the First other than necessary existence. Necessary existence is in itself a true nature and a quiddity; it belongs to Him, not to another. If, then, necessary existence belongs only to Him, then He does not share [it] with another; hence, He is not differentiated from [the other] by a specific differentia. Consequently, He has no definition.

(6) This, then, is the explanation of their doctrine. The reply to it is in two respects: a demand and a refutation.

(7) Regarding the demand, it consists of saying: "This is [merely] the relating of the doctrine. But how[3] do you know the impossibility of this with respect to the First so as to have built on it the denial of duality, when you said that [the] second [existent—namely, His first effect—]would have to share one thing with Him and differ in another, and that whatever contains that by means of which sharing and differentiating takes place is composite, and the composite [with the First] is impossible?"

(8) We [further] say:

(9) Whence do you know the impossibility of this kind of composition? There is no proof for it other than your statement, reported of you, in your denial of the attributes—namely, that [whatever] is composed of genus and differentia is an aggregate of parts, so that, if it is true for one of the parts or for the whole to exist without the other, then [what is independent] is the necessary existent and not anything else; and, if it is not true for either the parts to exist without the aggregate or the aggregate without the parts, then the whole is caused and is in need [of a cause]. We have spoken of this in [discussing] the attributes and have shown that this [namely, the existence of uncaused attributes] is not rendered impossible by terminating the regress of causes, and that demonstration only proved the termination of regress.

(10) As for the great things which they invented concerning the necessity of attributing [composition] to the Necessary Existent, there is no proof to demonstrate it. If, then, the Necessary Existent is [the being] they described—namely, that there is no multiplicity in Him, so that He does not need another for His subsistence—there is no proof for establishing the Necessary Existent. Proof shows only the termination of [the causal] regress. This is [something] we have finished with in [discussing] the attributes. In this kind [of argument] it is more obvious. For the division of a thing into genus and difference is not the same as the division of that which has an attribute into an essence and an attribute.

فالوجود الواجب طبيعة حقيقيّة وماهيّة فى نفسه، هو له لا لغيره. واذا لم يكن وجود الوجود الا له، لم يشارك غيره، فلم ينفصل عنه بفصل نوعى؛ فلم يكن له حدّ.

(٦) فهذا تفهيم مذهبهم. والكلام عليه من وجهين: مطالبة وابطال.

(٧) اما المطالبة، فهو ان يقال: هذا حكاية المذهب. فبم عرفتم استحالة ذلك فى حقّ الاوّل، حتّى بنيتم عليه نفى التثنية، اذ قلتم انّ الثانى ينبغى ان يشاركه فى شىء ويباينه فى شىء، والذى فيه ما يشارك به وما يباين به فهو مركب، والمركب محال؟

(٨) فنقول:

(٩) هذا النوع من التركيب من أين عرفتم استحالته؟ ولا دليل عليه الا قولكم المحكىّ عنكم فى نفى الصفات، وهو انّ المركب من الجنس والفصل مجتمع من اجزاء، فان كان يصح لواحد من الاجزاء أو الجملة وجود دون الآخر، فهو واجب الوجود دون ما عداه، وان كان لا يصح للاجزاء وجود دون المجتمع ولا للمجتمع وجود دون الاجزاء، فالكلّ معلول محتاج. وقد تكلّمنا عليه فى الصفات، وبيّنا انّ ذلك ليس بمحال فى قطع تسلسل العلل والبرهان لم يدلّ الا على قطع التسلسل.

(١٠) فامّا العظائم التى اخترعوها فى لزوم اتصاف واجب الوجود به، فلم يدلّ عليه دليل. فان كان واجب الوجود ما وصفوه به، وهو أنّه لا يكون فيه كثرة فلا يحتاج فى قوامه الى غيره، فلا دليل اذن على اثبات واجب الوجود، وانّما الدليل دل على قطع التسلسل فقط. وهذا قد فرغنا منه فى الصفات. وهو فى هذا النوع اظهر. فانّ انقسام الشىء الى

The attribute is other than the essence, and the essence is other than the attribute, whereas the species is not other than the genus in all respects. Thus, whenever we mention the species, we mention the genus and an addition. When we mention man, we are not mentioning anything but animal with the additional rationality. Hence, someone's question, "Does humanity dispense with animality?" is similar to someone's asking, "Does humanity dispense with itself when something else is added to it?" This is more removed from multiplicity than the attribute and the thing to which it is attributed.

(11) In what respect is it impossible for the chain of effects to terminate with two causes—one of the two being the cause of the heavens [and] the other the cause of the elements, or one of the two being the cause of intellects [and] the other being the cause of all bodies—and that there should be between them a difference and a separation in meaning, as there is between redness and heat in the same place? For [the latter] differ in meaning, without our supposing that there is in redness a generic and differential composition such that it[4] is receptive of separation. Rather, should there be multiplicity in it, it would be a kind of multiplicity that does not violate the unity of the essence. In what respect, then, is this impossible [in the case of] causes? With this, their inability to deny two creating gods becomes clear.

(12) [It may be] said:

(13) This is impossible, inasmuch as, if that through which there is a difference between the two essences constitutes a condition for necessary existence, then it must exist for every necessary existent; hence, the two will not differ. But if neither this nor the other [namely, a difference that is not a condition] constitutes a condition, then the existence of that which is not a condition for necessary existence becomes dispensable, and the necessity of existence is fulfilled by [what is] other than [it].[5]

(14) [To this] we say:

(15) This is the very thing you mentioned with respect to the attributes, and we have [already] discussed it. The source of the obfuscation in all this lies in the expression "the necessary existent." Let [the expression] be cast aside. For we do not admit that proof proves the "necessary existent," unless what is meant by it is an existent that has no agent [and

الجنس والفصل ليس كانقسام الموصوف الى ذات وصفة. فان الصفة غير الذات والذات غير الصفة، والنوع ليس غير الجنس من كلّ وجه. فمهما ذكرنا النوع، فقد ذكرنا الجنس وزيادة. واذا ذكرنا الانسان، فلم نذكر الا الحيوان مع زيادة نطق. فقول القائل: انّ الانسانيّة هل تستغنى عن الحيوانيّة؟ كقوله: ان الانسانيّة، هل تستغنى عن نفسها اذا انضم اليها شىء آخر؟ فهذا ابعد عن الكثرة من الصفة والموصوف.

(١١) ومن اىّ وجه يستحيل أن تنقطع سلسلة المعلولات على علّتين، احديهما علّة السموات والآخرى علّة العناصر، أو أحدهما علّة العقول والآخر علّة الاجسام كلّها، ويكون بينهما مباينة ومفارقة فى المعنى كما بين الحمرة والحرارة فى محلّ واحد؟ فانّهما يتباينان بالمعنى من غير أن نفرض فى الحمرة تركيبا جنسيّا وفصليّا بحيث يقبل الانفصال. بل ان كان فيه كثرة فهو نوع كثرة لا يقدح فى وحدة الذات. فمن أىّ وجه يستحيل هذا فى العلل؟ وبهذا يتبيّن عجزهم عن نفى الهين صانعين.

(١٢) فان قيل:

(١٣) انّما يستحيل هذا من حيث انّ ما به المباينة بين الذاتين، ان كان شرطا فى وجوب الوجود، فينبغى أن يوجد لكلّ واجب وجود، فلا يتباينان. وان لم يكن هذا شرطا ولا الآخر شرطا، فكلّ ما لا يشترط فى وجوب الوجود، فوجوده مستغنًى عنه ويتمّ وجوب الوجود بغيره.

(١٤) قلنا:

(١٥) هذا عين ما ذكرتموه فى الصفات وقد تكلّمنا عليه. ومنشأ التلبيس فى جميع ذلك فى لفظ واجب الوجود. فليطّرح. فانّا لا نسلّم انّ الدليل يدلّ على واجب الوجود، ان لم يكن المراد به موجود لا فاعل له

is] eternal. If this is what is intended, then let the expression "necessary existent" be abandoned and let it be shown that it is impossible for an existent that has no cause or agent to have in it multiplicity and [attributional] differentiation. But there is no proof for this. There thus remains
5   their question: "Is this [difference between the supposed uncaused causes] not a condition for its not having a cause?" But this is madness. For we have shown [that, in the case of] that which has no cause, its being without a cause is not causally explained so as to have its condition sought after. This is akin to saying: "Is blackness a condition for color
10   to be color and, if a condition, then why would redness be a color?" To this it would be answered that, as regards the reality [of color], neither [blackness nor redness] is made a condition—that is, [for] establishing the reality of being a color in the mind. In [external] existence, however, the condition would be one of the two [or any other color], but not specifi-
15   cally [one and not the other]. In other words, there can be no genus in [external] existence but that which must have a differentia. The same applies to whoever affirms two causes and terminates the regress with the two. He would thus say: "They are separated through a differentia, and one of the differentiae is necessarily a condition for [external] existence;
20   but [this must] not [be confined] to [one] specific [differentia]."

(16) It may be said:

(17) This is possible in the case of color. For it has an existence related to the quiddity [and] additional to the quiddity. This, however, is not pos-sible with the Necessary Existent, since nothing belongs to Him other
25   than the necessity of existence, there being no quiddity to which existence is added. And just as the differentia blackness and the differentia redness are not conditions for color in being color, but only for its existence that comes about through a cause, similarly, no condition must be made for necessary existence. For the necessity of existence is for the First as
30   being a color[6] is to a color, not as existence that is related to being color.

(18) We say:

(19) We do not admit [this]. Rather, He has a reality which is char-acterized by existence, as we shall show in the discussion following this one. Their statement that He is existence without quiddity is beyond
35   [what is] intelligible. The sum of the discussion is that they have based the denial of duality on the denial of generic and differential composition and then built this on the denial of quiddity behind [God's] existence.

قديم. وان كان المراد هذا، فليترك لفظ واجب الوجود وليبيّن انّ موجودا لا علّة له ولا فاعل يستحيل فيه التعدّد والتباين. ولا يقوم عليه دليل. فيبقى قولهم: انّ ذلك، هل هو شرط فى أن لا يكون له علّة؟ فهو هوس. فانّ ما لا علّة له قد بيّنا انّه لا يعلّل كونه لا علّة له حتّى يطلب شرطه. [و]

٥ هو كقول القائل: انّ السواديّة هل هى شرط فى كون اللون لونا، فان كان شرطا، فلم [كانت] الحمرة لونا؟ فيقال: أمّا فى حقيقته، فلا يشترط واحد منهما، أعنى ثبوت حقيقة اللونيّة، فى العقل. وأمّا فى وجوده، فالشرط أحدهما، لا بعينه؛ أى لا يمكن جنس فى الوجود الا وله فصل. فكذلك من يثبت علّتين ويقطع التسلسل بهما. فيقول: يتباينان بفصل

١٠ وأحد الفصول شرط الوجود لا محالة، ولكن لا على التعيّن.

(١٦) فان قيل:

(١٧) هذا يجوز فى اللون. فان له وجودا مضافا الى الماهيّة زائدا على الماهيّة. ولا يجوز فى واجب الوجود، اذ ليس له الا وجوب الوجود، وليس ثم ماهيّة يضاف الوجود اليها. وكما ان فصل السواد

١٥ وفصل الحمرة لا يشترط للونيّة فى كونها لونيّة، انّما يشترط فى وجودها الحاصل بعلّة، فكذلك ينبغى ان لا يشترط فى الوجود الواجب. فانّ الوجود الواجب للاول كاللونيّة للون، لا كالوجود المضاف الى اللونيّة.

(١٨) قلنا:

(١٩) لا نسلّم. بل له حقيقة موصوفة بالوجود على ما سنبيّنهُ فى المسئلة التى [بعد هذه]. وقولهم انّه وجود بلا ماهيّة خارج عن المعقول.

٢٠ ورجع حاصل الكلام الى انّهم بنوا نفى التثنية على نفى التركيب الجنسىّ والفصلىّ ثم بنوا ذاك على نفى الماهيّة وراء الوجود. فمهما ابطلنا الاخير

Thus, once we refute the last, which is the foundation of the foundation, the whole becomes refuted. This is a structure that is weak in its standing, similar to a spider's web.

(20) The second way [of answering the philosophers] is forcing on them necessarily [an absurd consequence]. This consists of our saying: "If existence, substantiality, and being a principle is not a genus because it is not [that of which something is] said in the answer to 'What is it?', the First [nonetheless] is, according to you, an intellect denuded [of matter], just as the rest of the intellects that are principles for existence—named 'angels,' according to them—and that are the effects of the First are [also] intellects denuded of matter. This reality pervades the First and His first effect. For the first effect is also simple, having no composition in itself, except with respect to its necessary concomitants. Both share, in that each is of them is an intellect denuded of matter. But this is a generic reality. For being an intellect denuded [of matter] is not, with respect to the essence, one of the necessary concomitants but is the quiddity. This quiddity is a common thing shared between the First and the rest of the [celestial] intellects. If He does not differ from them through some other thing, then you [philosophers] would have conceived duality without there being a difference. If He differs, then that through which the difference obtains is other than that which constitutes sharing and being intellect. The sharing in [this] is in reality a sharing. For the First apprehended Himself intellectually and apprehended another (for those who hold this) inasmuch as He is, in Himself, mind denuded of matter. Similarly, the first effect, which is the first intellect, which God creates without mediation, shares [with God] in this meaning. The proof of this is that the [celestial] intellects that are effects constitute different species, sharing in being intellect and differing through differences other than this. Similarly, the First shares with all [these intellects] in being intellect." [The philosophers] are thus [caught] between [two things:] either contradicting the principle [of divine uniqueness], or else coming to [uphold the view] that being intellect does not substantiate the essence. Both of these, according to them, are impossible.

الذى هو أساس الاساس، بطل عليهم الكلّ. وهو بنيان ضعيف الثبوت، قريب من بيوت العنكبوت.

(٢٠) المسلك الثانى، الالزام، وهو انّا نقول: ان لم يكن الوجود والجوهريّة والمبدئيّة جنسا لانّه ليس مقولا فى جواب ما هو، فالاوّل عندكم عقل مجرّد كما ان سائر العقول التى هى المبادى للوجود المسّمى بالملائكة عندهم التّى هى معلولات الاوّل عقول مجرّدة عن المواد. فهذه الحقيقة تشمل الاوّل ومعلوله الاول. فانّ المعلول الاوّل أيضا بسيط لا تركيب فى ذاته، الا من حيث لوازمه. وهما مشتركان فى ان كلّ واحد عقل مجرّد عن المادة. وهذه حقيقة جنسيّة. [فليست]٦ العقليّة المجرّدة للذات من اللوازم بل هى الماهيّة. وهذه الماهيّة مشتركة بين الاول وسائر العقول. فان لم يباينها بشىء آخر، فقد عقلتم اثنينية من غير مباينة. وان باينها فما به المباينة غير ما به المشاركة والعقليّة. والمشاركة فيها مشاركة فى الحقيقة. فانّ الاوّل عقل نفسه وعقل غيره، عند من يرى ذلك، من حيث انّه فى ذاته عقل مجرّد عن المادة. وكذى المعلول الاوّل، وهو العقل الاول الذى ابدعه الله من غير واسطة، مشارك فى هذا المعنى. والدليل عليه انّ العقول التّى هى معلولات أنواع مختلفة. وانّما اشتراكها فى العقليّة وافتراقها بفصول سوى ذلك. وكذلك الاول شارك جميعها فى العقليّة. فهم فيه بين نقض القاعدة أو المصير الى انّ العقليّة ليست مقوّمة للذات. وكلاهما محالان عندهم.

[Eighth] Discussion

*On refuting their statement that the existence of
the First is simple—that is, that He is pure existence,
and that there is no quiddity or reality to which
existence is related, but that necessary existence is
for Him akin to a quiddity for another*

The discourse against this is in two respects.

(1) The first is to demand a proof. It is thus asked, "How do you know this? By [rational] necessity or through reflection?" This, however, is not [known by rational] necessity; hence, the method of reflection would
5   have to be mentioned.

(2) If [then] it is said, "This is because, if [God] has a quiddity, then existence would be related to it, consequent on it, and a necessary concomitant of it; but the consequence is an effect, and necessary existence would thus be an effect—but this is contradictory," we say:

10   (3) This is a return to the source of the confusion in using the expression "necessary existence." For we say [that] He has a reality and a quiddity. This reality exists—that is, it is not nonexistent [or] negated, and its existence is related to it. If [the philosophers] want to call [this existence] consequent and necessary concomitant, then there is no quarrel in names
15   once it is known that there is no agent for [His] existence, but that this existence continues to be pre-eternal without [having] an efficient cause. If, however, they mean by "the consequent" and "the effect" that it has an efficient cause, this is not the case. If they mean something else, this is conceded; and there is nothing impossible in it, since proof has only
20   shown the termination of the regress of causes. Its termination in an

مسئلة

فى ابطال قولهم: انّ وجود الاول بسيط اى
هو وجود محض ولا ماهيّة ولا حقيقة يضاف
الوجود اليها بل الوجود الواجب له كالماهيّة لغيره

والكلام عليه من وجهين:

(١) الاوّل المطالبة بالدليل فيقال: بم عرفتم ذلك؟ أبضرورة أو نظر؟
وليس بضروريّ؛ فلا بد من ذكر طريق النظر.

(٢) فان قيل: لانّه لو كان له ماهيّة لكان الوجود مضافا اليها وتابعا
لها ولازما لها، والتابع معلول، فيكون الوجود الواجب معلولا، وهو
متناقض، فنقول:

(٣) هذا رجوع الى منبع التلبيس فى اطلاق لفظ الوجود الواجب.
فانّا نقول له حقيقة وماهيّة وتلك الحقيقة موجودة اى ليست معدومة
منفيّة ووجودها مضاف اليها. وان أحبّوا أن يسمّوه تابعا ولازما، فلا
مشاحة فى الاسامى بعد ان يعرف انّه لا فاعل للوجود، بل لم يزل هذا
الوجود قديما من غير علّة فاعلية. فان عنوا بالتابع والمعلول انّ له علة
فاعلية، فليس كذلك. وان عنوا غيره، فهو مسلّم ولا استحالة فيه، اذ

١١٦

existing reality and a fixed quiddity is possible. Hence, there is no need in this for the negation of quiddity.

(4) If it is said, "The quiddity then becomes a cause of the existence which is consequent on Him,[1] existence becoming caused and enacted," we say:

(5) The quiddity in created things is not a cause of existence; how, then, [can this be] in the case of [what is] pre-eternal, if they mean by "cause" that which enacts it? If they mean by ["cause"] some other facet—namely, that [existence] does not dispense with it[2]—let this be the case, since there is no impossibility in [this]. The impossibility is only in the [infinite] regress of causes. If the regress is terminated, then the impossibility is prevented. The impossibility of other than this is not known. Hence, there is a necessary need for a demonstration [to show] its impossibility. But all their "demonstrations" are arbitrary [matters] built on taking the expression "necessary existent" in a sense that has necessary consequences [following from it] and on the acceptance that proof has demonstrated a necessary existent having the quality they attributed to it. But this is not the case, as previously [shown].

(6) In brief, their proof in this goes back to their proof denying [the divine] attributes and their denial of generic and specific division [in the divine], except that it is more obscure and weaker. [This] is because this multiplicity reduces only to sheer verbal utterance. Otherwise, the mind accommodates the supposition of one [divine] existing quiddity, whereas [the philosophers] say that every existing quiddity is a plurality, since it includes quiddity and existence.

(7) But this is the ultimate in waywardness. For the existent which is one is intelligible, whatever [the] state [one attributes to it]. There is never an existent without a real [nature], and the existence of a real [nature] does not negate unity.

(8) The second way is for us to say:

(9) Existence without quiddity and a real [nature] is unintelligible. And just as we do not comprehend an unattached nonexistence, but only [one] in relation to an existent whose nonexistence is supposed, we do not

الدليل لم يدلّ الا على قطع تسلسل العلل. وقطعه بحقيقة موجودة وماهيّة ثابتة ممكن. فليس يحتاج فيه الى سلب الماهيّة.

(٤) فان قيل: فتكون الماهيّة سببا للوجود الذى هو تابع له فيكون الوجود معلولا ومفعولا، قلنا:

(٥) الماهيّة فى الاشياء الحادثة لا تكون سببا للوجود، فكيف فى القديم ان عنوا بالسبب الفاعل له؟ وان عنوا به وجها آخر، وهو انّه لا يستغنى عنه، فليكن كذلك، فلا استحالة فيه. انّما الاستحالة فى تسلسل العلل. فاذا انقطع فقد اندفعت الاستحالة، وما عدى ذلك لم تعرف استحالته، فلا بد من برهان على استحالته. وكلّ براهينهم تحكمّات مبناها على أخذ لفظ واجب الوجود.بمعنى له لوازم وتسلّم ان الدليل قد دلّ على واجب وجود بالنعت الذى وصفوه. وليس كذلك كما سبق.

(٦) وعلى الجملة، دليلهم فى هذا يرجع الى دليل نفى الصفات ونفى الانقسام الجنسىّ والفصلىّ، الا انه اغمض واضعف، لانّ هذه الكثرة لا ترجع الا الى مجرّد اللفظ، والا فالعقل يتسع لتقدير ماهيّة واحدة موجودة، وهم يقولون: كلّ ماهيّة موجودة فمتكثّرة، اذ فيه ماهيّة ووجود.

(٧) وهذا غاية الضلال. فانّ الموجود الواحد معقول بكلّ حال، ولا موجود الا وله حقيقة، ووجود الحقيقة لا ينفى الوحدة.

(٨) المسلك الثانى هو ان نقول:

(٩) وجود بلا ماهيّة ولا حقيقة غير معقول. وكما لا نعقل عدما مرسلا الا بالاضافة الى موجود يقدّر عدمه، فلا نعقل وجودا مرسلا الا

comprehend an unattached existence, but only in relation to a determinate real [nature], particularly if it is determined as one entity. How, then, is one thing that differs from another in meaning determined, when no real [nature] belongs to it? For the negation of quiddity is a negation of a real [nature]; and if the real [nature] of an existent is negated, existence becomes incomprehensible. It is as though [the philosophers] have said, "[There is] existence without [there being] an existent," which is contradictory.

(10) What proves this is that if this were intelligible, then there could be among caused things an existent that shares with the First in being [an existent] that has neither a real [nature] nor a quiddity, differing from [the First] in that it has a cause, whereas the First has no cause. Why is this inconceivable in effects? Does it have a cause other than its being in itself unintelligible? And that which in itself is unintelligible does not become intelligible through the denial of its cause. And what is intelligible does not cease to be intelligible by supposing for it a cause.

(11) Their going to such an extreme is the ultimate in [their wallowing in] their darkness. For they thought that they are elevating [God above all similitudes to His creation] in what they say, but the end result of their discourse is pure negation. For the denial of the quiddity is the denial of reality. Nothing remains with the denial of reality save the verbal utterance "existence," having basically no referent when not related to a quiddity.

(12) If it is said, "His reality consists in His being necessary, and [this] is [His] quiddity," we say:

(13) There is no meaning for [His being] necessary other than the denial of [a] cause [for His existence]. This [denial] is [pure] negation, through which the reality of an essence is not established. Denying the cause for [God's] reality is a necessary concomitant of [this] reality. Let, then, reality be [something] intelligible so as to be described as having no cause and [as something] whose nonexistence is inconceivable, since there is no other meaning for "necessity" except this. However, if necessity is [something] additional to existence, then multiplicity [in the divine] would ensue; and, if not additional, [which must be the case,] how can it be the quiddity when existence is not a quiddity? Such is the case with whatever is not additional to existence.[3]

بالاضافة الى حقيقة معيّنة، لا سيّما اذا تعيّن ذاتا واحدة. فكيف يتعيّن واحدا متميّزا عن غيره بالمعنى، ولا حقيقة له؟ فانّ نفى الماهيّة نفى للحقيقة، واذا [نفيت]١، حقيقة الموجود، لم يعقل الوجود. فكأنّهم قالوا: وجود ولا موجود، وهو متناقض.

(١٠) ويدلّ عليه انّه لو كان هذا معقولا، لجاز ان يكون فى المعلولات وجود حقيقة له يشارك الاول فى كونه لا حقيقة ولا ماهيّة له ويباينه فى انّ له علّة، والاوّل لا علّة له. فلمَ لا يتصوّر هذا فى المعلولات؟ وهل له سبب الا انّه غير معقول فى نفسه؟ وما لا يعقل فى نفسه فبأن <تنفى>٢ علّته لا يصير معقولا. وما يعقل فبأن يقدّر له علّة لا يخرج عن كونه معقولا.

(١١) والتناهى الى هذا الحدّ غاية ظلماتهم. فقد ظنّوا انهم ينزّهون فيما يقولون، فانتهى كلامهم الى النفى المجرّد. فانّ نفى الماهيّة نفى للحقيقة. ولا يبقى مع نفى الحقيقة الا لفظ الوجود، ولا مسمّى له أصلاً اذا لم يضف الى ماهيّة.

(١٢) فان قيل: حقيقته انّه واجب وهو الماهيّة، قلنا:

(١٣) ولا معنى للواجب الا نفى العلّة، وهو سلب، لا يتقوّم به حقيقة ذات. ونفي العلّة عن الحقيقة لازم [للحقيقة]٣. فلتكن الحقيقة معقولة حتّى توصف [بأنّا]؛ لا علّة لها ولا يتصوّر عدمها، اذ لا معنى للوجوب الا هذا. على انّ الوجوب ان زاد على الوجود، فقد جاءت الكثرة، وان لم يزد، فكيف يكون هو الماهيّة والوجود ليس بماهيّة؟ فكذى ما لا يزيد عليه.

[Ninth] Discussion

On showing their inability to sustain
a proof that the First is not a body

(1) We say: "[The proof that God is not a body] would only proceed correctly for someone who perceives [(a)] that the body is temporally originated, inasmuch as it is not devoid of temporal events, and
[(b)] that every temporal event requires an originator." But if you
[philosophers are able to] apprehend intellectually an eternal body
whose existence has no beginning, even though it is not devoid of
temporal events, why would it then be impossible for the First to be a
body—either the sun, the outermost sphere, or some other thing?

(2) [To this it may be] said:

(3) [This is] because body [can] only be composite, divisible into two
parts quantitatively: into matter and form in terms of conceptual division, and into descriptions necessarily proper to it, so as to differ from
other bodies—for [all] bodies, in being bodies, are otherwise similar. But
the Necessary Existent is one and is not receptive of divisions in [any of]
these respects.

(4) We say:

(5) We have refuted this against you and have shown that you have
no proof for it except [to argue] that if parts of the composite are in need
of the [other] parts, then it is caused. We have discussed this, showing
that if the supposition of an existent that does not have that which brings

مسئلة
فى تعجيزهم عن اقامة الدليل
على انّ الاوّل ليس بجسم

(١) فنقول: هذا انّما يستقيم لمن يرى انّ الجسم حادث من حيث انّه لا يخلو عن الحوادث، وكلّ حادث فيفتقر الى محدث. فامّا أنتم اذا عقلتم جسما قديما لا أوّل لوجوده، مع انّه لا يخلو عن الحوادث، فلمَ يمتنع ان يكون الاوّل جسما، امّا الشمس واما الفلك الاقصى وامّا غيره؟

(٢) فان قيل:

(٣) لانّ الجسم لا يكون الا مركّبا منقسما الي جزئين بالكمّيّة، والى الهيولى والصورة بالقسمة المعنويّة، والى أوصاف يختص بها لا محالة، حتّى يباين سائر الاجسام، والا فالاجسام متساوية فى انّها أجسام. وواجب الوجود واحد لا يقبل القسمة بهذه الوجوه.

(٤) قلنا:

(٥) وقد أبطلنا هذا عليكم وبيّنا انّه لا دليل لكم عليه سوى انّ المجتمع اذا افتقر بعض اجزائهِ الى البعض، كان معلولا. وقد تكلّمنا عليه، وبيّنا انّه اذا لم يبعد تقدير موجد لا موجود له، لم يبعد تقدير مركّب لا مركّب له.

١١٩

about its existence is not improbable, then the supposition of a composite that has no composer and the supposition of [many] existents without a cause of their existence[1] are [likewise] not improbable—[this] since you have built the denial of number and duality on the denial of composition,

5   and the denial of composition on the denial of a quiddity [that is other] than existence. And [the latter], which is the final foundation [of your argument, is something] we had uprooted, showing your arbitrariness in [affirming it].

(6) If it is said, "If body has no soul, it would not be an active agent;
10   and if it has a soul, then the soul would be a cause of it and it would not be 'a first,' " we say:

(7) Our soul is not a cause for the existence of our bodies, nor is the soul of the celestial [sphere] by itself a cause for the existence of its body, according to you; rather, both exist through a cause that is other than
15   both. If the eternal existence of both is allowed, then the nonexistence of a cause for either becomes allowed.

(8) If it is then asked, "How did the joining of soul and body happen [to come about]?" we say:

(9) This is like someone saying, "How did the existence of the First
20   happen?" to which it would be said, "This is a question [applicable to] an originated thing. But as regards [the Being] who has never ceased to exist, one does not say, 'How did [His existence] happen?' The same applies to the body and its soul: if each continues to exist [from eternity], then why is it unlikely that [each] is a creator?"

25   (10) If it is said, "This is because body qua body does not create another; and the soul that is attached to the body only acts through the mediation of the body, the body [never] being an intermediary for the soul in the creating of bodies or the originating of souls and things not appropriate to bodies," we say:

30   (11) Why is it not allowable that there exists among souls a soul characterized with a property through which it becomes predisposed to have bodies and nonbodies come into being from it? The impossibility of this is not known as a [rational] necessity, and there is no demonstration to prove it. The only thing is that it has not been observed among these
35   observable [bodies]. Nonobservation does not prove impossibility. For [the philosophers] have related to the First Existent that which is not related to an existent at all and [that which] we have not observed in [existents]

وتقدير موجودات لا موجد لها، اذ نفى العدد والتثنية بنيتموه على نفى التركيب، ونفى التركيب على نفى الماهيّة، سوى الوجود. وما هو الاساس الاخير فقد استأصلناه وبيّنا تحكّمكم فيه.

(٦) فان قيل: الجسم، ان لم يكن له نفس لا يكون فاعلا، وان كان له نفس فنفسه علّة له فلا يكون الجسم أوّلا، قلنا:

(٧) نفسنا [ليست]¹ علّة لوجود جسمنا، ولا نفس الفلك بمجرّدها علّة لوجود جسمه عندكم بل هما يوجدان بعلّة سواهما. فاذا جاز وجودهما قديما جاز ان لا يكون لهما علّة.

(٨) فان قيل: كيف اتفق اجتماع النفس والجسم؟ قلنا:

(٩) هو كقول القائل كيف اتفق وجود الاوّل؟ فيقال هذا سؤال عن حادث فاما ما لم يزل موجودا فلا يقال كيف اتفق. فكذلك الجسم ونفسه اذا لم يزل كل واحد موجودا، لِمَ يبعد ان يكون صانعا؟

(١٠) فان قيل: لانّ الجسم من حيث انّه جسم لا يخلق غيره والنفس المتعلّقة بالجسم، لا تفعل الا بواسطة الجسم، ولا يكون الجسم واسطة للنفس فى خلق الاجسام، ولا فى ابداع النفوس، واشياء لا تناسب الاجسام، قلنا:

(١١) ولِمَ لا يجوز ان يكون فى النفوس نفس تختصّ بخاصيّة تتهيّأ بها لان توجد الاجسام وغير الاجسام منها؟ فاستحالة ذلك لا يعرف ضرورة ولا برهان يدلّ عليه. الا انه لم [يشاهد]² من هذه المشاهدة. وعدم المشاهدة لا يدلّ على الاستحالة. فقد أضافوا الى الموجود الاوّل ما

other than Him. The absence of observing [this] in others does not prove that it is impossible in His case. The same [can be argued] in the case of the body's soul and the body.

(12) If it is said, "The furthermost sphere, the sun, or whatever body is supposed has been specified with a quantity that can be increased or decreased, so that its specification with that possible quantity is in need of something that specifies it with it, and [hence such a body] would not be 'a first,'" we say:

(13) With what [argument] would you deny one who says that that body would have a quantity which it must necessarily have [as required by] the order of the whole [world], and that, if it were smaller or larger, [this] would be impossible? This is similar to what you have said: [namely,] that the outermost sphere emanates from the first effect, being quantified by [a certain] quantity, when all other quantities relative to the essence of the first effect are equal, but that a certain quantity was specified because the [world] order is connected to it. Hence, the quantity that came about is necessary, its contrary not allowable. The same would be the case if [the celestial body] is supposed to be uncaused. Indeed, if [the philosophers] affirm for the first effect—which to them is the cause of the outermost sphere—a principle of specification such as the will, for example, the question does not cease. For then, in the same way that [the philosophers] forced on Muslims the question of the relation of things to the eternal will, it would be said: "Why did [the principle] will this quantity and not any other?" We have turned their argument against them with respect to specifying the direction of the movement of the heaven and the assigning [of] the two spherical nodes.[2]

(14) If, then, it has become clear that they are compelled to allow the differentiating of one thing from its [exact] similar when [the differentiation] is due to a cause, [it follows] that allowing [the differentiation] when not due to a cause is similar to allowing it when due to a cause. For there is no difference in directing the question to that very thing when it is asked, "Why is it specified with this quantity?" and in directing it to the cause when it is asked, "Why did it specify it with this quantity and not with a similar one?" For, if it is possible to answer the question regarding the cause by [arguing] that the [assigned] quantity is not like another, since the world order is connected with it and not with any other, it would [also] be possible to answer the question [in the same way] about the thing itself, where [the differentiation] needs no cause. There is no escape [for them] from this. For, if this specific quantity that

لا يضاف الى موجود أصلاً، ولم نشاهد من غيره. وعدم المشاهدة من غيره لا يدلّ على استحالته منه. فكذى فى نفس الجسم والجسم.

(١٢) فان قيل: الجسم الاقصى أو الشمس أو ما قدّر من الاجسام، فهو متقدّر بمقدار يجوز أن يزيد عليه وينقص منه، فيفتقر اختصاصه

٥ بذلك المقدار الجائز الى مخصص، فلا يكون أوّلا، قلنا:

(١٣) بم تنكرون على من يقول انّ ذلك الجسم يكون على مقدار يجب ان يكون عليه لنظام الكلّ، ولو كان أصغر منه أو أكبر لم يجز؟ كما انكم قلتم ان المعلول الاوّل يفيض الجرم الاقصى منه متقدّرا بمقدار، وسائر المقادير بالنسبة الى ذات المعلول الاول متساوية، ولكن تعيّن بعض

١٠ المقادير لكون النظام متعلّقا به؛ فوجب المقدار الذى وقع ولم يجز خلافه. فكذى اذا قدّر غير معلول. بل لو اثبتوا فى المعلول الاوّل الذى هو علّة الجرم الاقصى عندهم مبدأ للتّخصيص مثل ارادة مثلا، لم ينقطع السؤال؛ اذ يقال: ولم أراد هذا المقدار دون غيره؟ كما ألزموه على المسلمين فى اضافتهم الاشياء الى الارادة القديمة. وقد قلبنا عليهم ذلك فى تعيّن جهة

١٥ حركة السماء وفى تعيّن نقطتى القطبين.

(١٤) فاذا بان انّهم مضطرّون الى تجويز [تمييز]٣ الشىء عن مثله فى الوقوع بعلّة، فتجويزه بغير علّة كتجويزه بعلّة، اذ لا فرق بين ان يتوجّه السؤال فى نفس الشىء فيقال: لم اختصّ بهذا القدر؟ وبين ان يتوجّه فى العلّة فيقال: ولم خصّصه بهذا القدر عن مثله؟ فان أمكن دفع السؤال عن

٢٠ العلّة بانّ هذا المقدار ليس مثل غيره، اذ النظام مرتبط به دون غيره، أمكن دفع السؤال عن نفس الشىء، ولم يفتقر الى علّة. وهذا لا مخرج عنه. فانّ

occurs is similar to that which did not occur, the question [continues] to be posed, [namely:] "How is something distinguished from its similar?" particularly in terms of their [own] principle when they deny a will that differentiates [between similars]. If [on the other hand] it is not similar to it, the possibility [of an alternative quantity] does not hold. Rather, it would be said that [the quantity] came about in this way pre-eternally, in the same way that the cause, as they claim, came about pre-eternally. Let the person who reflects on this discussion draw on what we have brought against [the philosophers] in directing the question regarding the eternal will and our turning the matter against them in the case of the node and the direction of the movement of the sphere.

(15) From this it becomes clear that whoever does not believe in the temporal origination of bodies is fundamentally incapable of erecting a proof that the First is not a body.

هذا المقدار المعيّن الواقع ان كان مثل الذى لم يقع، فالسؤال متوجّه انه: كيف ميّز الشىء عن مثله؟ خصوصاً على أصلهم وهم ينكرون الارادة المميّزة. وان لم يكن مثلا له، فلا يثبت الجواز، بل يقال: وقع كذلك قديما كما وقعت العلّة القديمة بزعمهم. وليستمد الناظر فى هذا الكلام ممّا أوردناه لهم من توجيه السؤال فى الارادة القديمة وقلبنا ذلك عليهم فى نقطة القطب وجهة حركة الفلك.

(٥١) وتبيّن بهذا انّ من لا يصدّق بحدوث الاجسام فلا يقدر على اقامة دليل على انّ الاوّل ليس بجسم أصلاً.

[Tenth] Discussion

On their inability to show that
the world has a maker and a cause

(1) We say:

(2) [When] those who maintain that every body is temporally originated because it is never devoid of temporal events state that [the world]
needs a maker and a cause, their doctrine is intelligible. But as for you
[philosophers], what is there to prevent you from [upholding] the doctrine of the materialists—namely, that the world is eternal, that it likewise has no cause and no maker, that only temporal events have a cause,
that no body in the world is originated and no body annihilated, but
[that] what occurs temporally is forms and accidents? For [according to
this doctrine] the bodies consist of the heavens, which are eternal, [and]
the four elements constituting the stuff of the sublunar sphere. The bodies
and materials [of the latter] are [likewise] eternal. It is only that the
forms, through mixtures and transformations, undergo successive change
over [these bodies]; the human and the vegetative souls come into temporal existence. The causes of [all] these [temporal] events terminate in
the circular motion, the circular motion being eternal, its source an eternal soul of the heavens. Hence, [according to the materialists] there is no
cause for the world and no maker of its bodies, but it continues eternally
to be in the manner that it is, without a cause (I mean, [without a cause
of its] bodies). What, then, is the sense of their saying that these bodies
come into being through a cause, when [such bodies] are eternal?

(3) If it is said, "Whatever has no cause is necessary of existence, and
we have made a statement concerning those attributes of the Necessary

مسئلة

فى تعجيزهم عن إقامة الدليل
على انّ للعالم صانعا وعلّة

(١) فنقول:

(٢) من ذهب الى انّ كلّ جسم فهو حادث لأنّه لا يخلوا عن الحوادث، عقل مذهبهم فى قولهم انّه يفتقر الى صانع وعلّة. وأمّا انتم فما الذى يمنعكم من مذهب الدهريّة. وهو انّ العالم قديم كذلك ولا علّة له ولا صانع، وانّما العلّة للحوادث، وليس يحدث فى العالم جسم ولا ينعدم جسم وانّما تحدث الصور والاعراض؟ فانّ الاجسام هى السموات وهى قديمة، والعناصر الاربعة التّى هى حشو فلك القمر، واجسامها وموادّها قديمة، وانّما تتبدّل عليها الصور بالامتزاجات والاستحالات، وتحدث النفوس الانسانيّة والنباتيّة. وهذه الحوادث تنتهى عللها الى الحركة الدوريّة، والحركة الدوريّة قديمة، ومصدرها نفس قديمة للفلك. فاذن لا علّة للعالم ولا صانع لاجسامه، بل هو كما هو عليهِ لم يزل قديما كذلك بلا علّة، اعنى الاجسام. فما معنى قولهم انّ هذه الاجسام وجودها بعلّة وهى قديمة؟

(٣) فان قيل: كلّ ما لا علّة له فهو واجب الوجود، وقد ذكرنا من صفات واجب الوجود ما تبيّن به انّ الجسم لا يكون واجب الوجود، قلنا:

١٢٣

Existent through which it was shown that body cannot be a necessary existent," we say:

(4) We have shown the falsity of what you have claimed concerning the attributes of the Necessary Existent [and have shown] that demonstration only proves the termination of the [causal] series. And this, for the materialist, has already terminated at the outset. For he states that bodies have no cause and that, as regards forms and accidents, [these] cause each other, until [such causes and effects] reach the circular motion [of the heavens], parts of which [in turn] are causes of [other] parts (as it is with the doctrine of the philosophers), the regress [of the series of the causes of forms and accidents] terminating [with the circular motion]. Whoever reflects on what we have said will know the inability of the one who believes in the eternity of bodies to claim for them a cause; and the necessary consequence for him is materialism and atheism, as openly declared by a group. For these [latter] are the ones who [in reality] have fulfilled the requirements of the speculation of [the philosophers].

(5) If it is said, "The proof of this is that these bodies are either necessary in existence, which is impossible, or [that they are] possible [in existence], and every possible is in need of a cause," we say:

(6) The expression "necessary existent" and the expression "possible existent" are incomprehensible. All their obfuscations are hidden in these two expressions. Let us, then, turn to what is comprehensible—namely, the negation or affirmation of the cause. It would then be as though they ask, "Do these bodies have a cause or do they not have a cause?" To this the materialist replies, "They have no cause." What is [so] disavowable in this? If, then, this is what is meant by possibility, we [disagree and] say, "[Body] is necessary and not contingent." Their statement that it is not possible for body to be necessary is arbitrary and groundless.

(7) If it is said, "It is undeniable that body has parts and that the aggregate is substantiated by the parts and that the parts essentially precede the aggregate,"[1] we say:

(8) Let this be the case. The aggregate, then, is substantiated by the parts and their combination—there being no cause, however, for the parts or their combination. Rather, these are likewise eternal, having no efficient cause. They are unable to refute this except with what they had mentioned of the necessity of denying multiplicity in the First Existent. But we have refuted this, and they have no other way [to argue for their position] except it.

(9) Hence, it has become clear that whoever does not believe in the creation of bodies has no basis whatsoever for his belief in the maker.

(٤) وقد بيّنا فساد ما ادعيتموه من صفات واجب الوجود وأنّ البرهان لا يدلّ الا على قطع السلسلة، وقد انقطع عند الدهرى فى أوّل الامر، اذ يقول لا علّة للاجسام، وامّا الصور والاعراض فبعضها علّة للبعض الى ان تنتهى الى الحركة الدورية، وهى بعضها سبب للبعض كما هو مذهب الفلاسفة، وينقطع تسلسلها بها. ومن تأمل ما ذكرناه، علم عجز كلّ من يعتقد قدم الاجسام عن دعوى علّة لها، ولزمه الدهر والالحاد، كما صرّح به فريق. فهم الذين وفوا.بمقتضى نظر هؤلاء.

(٥) فان قيل: الدليل عليه انّ هذه الاجسام امّا ان كانت واجبة الوجود، وهو محال، وامّا ان كانت ممكنة، وكلّ ممكن يفتقر الى علّة، قلنا:

(٦) لا يفهم لفظ واجب الوجود وممكن الوجود. فكلّ تلبيساتهم مغباة فى هاتين اللفظتين، فلنعدل الى المفهوم وهو نفى العلّة واثباته. فكأنّهم يقولون: هذه الاجسام لها علّة أم لا علّة لها؟ فيقول الدهرىّ: لا علّة لها. فما المستنكر؟ واذا عنى بالامكان هذا فنقول: انّه واجب وليس بممكن. وقولهم الجسم لا يمكن ان يكون واجبا تحكّم لا أصل له.

(٧) فان قيل: لا ينكر انّ الجسم له اجزاء وانّ الجملة انّما تتقوّم بالاجزاء وانّ الاجزاء تكون سابقة فى الذات على الجملة، قلنا:

(٨) ليكن كذلك. فالجملة تقوّمت بالاجزاء واجتماعها، ولا علّة للاجزاء ولا لاجتماعها. بل هى قديمة كذلك بلا علّة فاعليّة. فلا يمكنهم ردّ هذا الا بما ذكروه من لزوم نفى الكثرة عن الموجود الاوّل. وقد ابطلناه عليهم ولا سبيل لهم سواه.

(٩) فبان انّ من لا يعتقد حدوث الاجسام فلا أصل لاعتقاده فى الصانع أصلا.

[Eleventh] Discussion

On showing the impotence of those among them who believe that the First knows other[s] and knows the genera and species in a universal way

(1) We say:

(2) Inasmuch as existence for the Muslims[1] is confined to the temporally originated and the eternal, there being for them no eternal other than God and His attributes, [all things] other than Him being originated from His direction through His will, a necessary premise regarding His knowledge became realized for them. For that which is willed must necessarily be known to the willer. On this they built [the argument] that everything is known to Him because all [things] are willed by Him and originated by His will. Hence, there is no generated being that is not originated by His will, nothing remaining [uncreated] except Himself. And as long as it is established that He is a willer, knowing what He wills, He is necessarily a living being. And with any living being that knows another, knowing himself takes priority. Hence, for [Muslims] all existents are known to God, and they came to know this in this way after it became evident to them that He wills the temporal origination of the world. As for you [philosophers], if you claim the world to be pre-eternal, not originated through His will,[2] how, then, do you know that He knows [what is] other than Himself? A proof for this is necessary.

(3) The sum of what Avicenna mentioned in ascertaining this in the course of his discussion reduces to two sorts [of argument].

مسئلة

فى تعجيز من يرى منهم انّ الاوّل يعلم غيره ويعلم الانواع والاجناس بنوع كلّىّ

(١) فنقول:

(٢) امّا المسلمون، لما انحصر عندهم الوجود فى حادث وفى قديم، ولم يكن عندهم قديم الا الله وصفاته، وكان ما عداه حادثا من جهته بارادته، حصل عندهم مقدّمة ضروريّة فى علمه. فانّ المراد بالضرورة لا بدّ وان يكون معلوما للمريد. فبنوا عليه انّ الكلّ معلوم له، لانّ الكلّ مراد له وحادث بارادته. فلا كائن الا وهو حادث بارادته ولم يبق الا ذاته. ومهما ثبت انّه مريد عالم بما اراده، فهو حىّ بالضرورة. وكلّ حىّ يعرف غيره، فهو بأن يعرف ذاته أولى. فصار الكلّ عندهم معلوما لله وعرفوه بهذا الطريق بعد ان بان لهم انّه مريد لاحداث العالم. فامّا أنتم، فاذا زعمتم انّ العالم قديم، لم يحدث بارادته، فمن أين عرفتم انّه يعرف غير ذاته؟ فلا بدّ من الدليل عليه.

(٣) وحاصل ما ذكره ابن سينا فى تحقيق ذلك فى ادراج كلامه يرجع الى فنّين.

(4) The first sort [of argument consists in saying] that the First does not exist in matter: whatever does not exist in matter is a pure intellect, and whatever is pure intellect has all the intelligibles laid bare to it.[3] For the impediment to apprehending all things is attachment to matter and preoccupation with it. The soul of the human being is preoccupied with managing matter—that is, the body. Once [the human's] preoccupation [with the body] ceases with death, [the individual,] not having been tarnished by bodily appetites and base qualities that come to him from natural things, has the realities of all the intelligibles unveiled to him. For this reason, [Avicenna] adjudged it that all the angels know all the intelligibles, nothing escaping them, since they, too, are pure intellects, not existing in matter.

(5) [To this] we say:

(6) If, by your statement that the First does not exist in matter, it is meant that He is neither body nor imprinted in a body, but, rather, that He is self-subsistent without being spatial or specified with spatial position, this is admitted. There remains your statement that that which has this description is a pure intellect. What, then, do you mean by "intellect"? If you mean by it that which apprehends intellectually the rest of things, this would be the very thing sought after and the point at dispute. How, then, did you include it in the premises of the syllogism for [establishing] what is being sought after? If you mean by it something else—namely, that it apprehends itself intellectually—some of your philosopher brethren may concede this to you, but it amounts to saying that whatever conceives itself conceives another, in which case it would be asked, "Why do you claim this, when it is not necessary?" This is [something] which Avicenna held, setting himself apart from the rest of the philosophers. How, then, do you claim it to be necessary? If it is [attained through] reflection, what demonstration is there for it?[4]

(7) If it is then said, "This is because the impediment to the apprehension of things is matter, but [here] there is no matter," we say:

(8) We concede that it is an impediment, but we do not concede that it is the only impediment. Their syllogism is ordered according to the form of the conditional syllogism—namely, in saying: "If this is in matter, then it does not apprehend things intellectually. It is not in matter. Therefore,

(٤) الفنّ الاوّل: انّ الاوّل موجود لا فى مادّة، وكلّ موجود لا فى مادّة، فهو عقل محض، وكلّ ما هو عقل محض، فجميع المعقولات مكشوفة له. فانّ المانع عن درك الاشياء كلّها التعلّق بالمادّة والاشتغال بها. ونفس الآدمى مشغول بتدبير المادّة أىّ البدن. واذا انقطع شغله بالموت، ولم يكن قد تدنّس بالشهوات البدنيّة والصفات الرذيلة المتعدّية اليه من الامور الطبيعيّة، [انكشفت]¹ له حقائق المعقولات كلّها. ولذلك قضى بانّ الملائكة كلّهم يعرفون جميع المعقولات ولا يشذّ عنهم شىء لانّهم أيضاً عقول مجرّدة لا فى مادّة.

(٥) فنقول:

(٦) قولكم: الاوّل موجود لا فى مادّة، ان كان المعنى به انّه ليس يجسم ولا هو منطبع فى جسم بل هو قائم بنفسه من غير تحيّز واختصاص بجهة، فهو مسلّم. فيبقى قولكم: وما هذا صفته، فهو عقل مجرّد. فماذا تعنى بالعقل؟ ان عنيت ما يعقل سائر الاشياء، فهذا نفس المطلوب، وموضع النزاع، فكيف اخذته فى مقدّمات قياس المطلوب؟ وان عنيت به غيره، وهو انّه يعقل نفسه، فربما يسلّم لك اخوانك من الفلاسفة ذلك، ولكن يرجع حاصله الى انّ ما يعقل نفسه يعقل غيره. فيقال: ولم ادعيت هذا، وليس ذلك بضرورىّ؟ وقد انفرد به ابن سينا عن سائر الفلاسفة، فكيف تدّعيه ضروريّا؟ وان كان نظريا، فما البرهان عليه؟

(٧) فان قيل: لان المانع من درك الاشياء المادّة ولا مادّة، فنقول:

(٨) نسلّم انه مانع، ولا نسلم انّه المانع فقط. وينتظم قياسهم على شكل القياس الشرطىّ وهو ان يقال: ان كان هذا فى المادّة، فهو لا يعقل

it apprehends things intellectually." This [way of arguing] consists in adding the contradictory of the antecedent.[5] But, as all agree,[6] adding the contradictory of the antecedent does not yield a valid conclusion. This is similar to one's saying: "If this is a human, then it is an animal. It is not a human. Therefore, it is not an animal." But this does not follow. For it may not be a human, but a horse, whereby it would be an animal.

(9) Yes, [it is true that] repeating the antecedent negatively would yield the consequent as a valid conclusion, as mentioned in logic, [but] with a condition—namely, establishing the convertibility of the consequent and the antecedent through restriction. An example of this is their saying: "If the sun has risen, then it is daytime. But the sun has not risen. Therefore, it is not daytime." This is [valid] because the existence of daytime has no other cause than the rising of the sun. Hence, each [namely, antecedent and consequent] is convertible to the other. The showing of these modes and terms is explained in the book *The Standard for Knowledge*, which we have composed and appended to this book.

(10) If it is said, "We claim convertibility—namely, in that the impediment is restricted to matter, there being no impediment other than it," we say:

(11) This is arbitrary assertion. Where is the proof for it?

(12) The second sort [of argument] is [Avicenna's] statement: "Even though we did not say that the First wills origination nor that the whole [world] is temporally originated, we [nonetheless] say that [the world] is His act and has come to existence through Him, except that He continues to have the attribute of [those who are] agents and, hence, is ever enacting. We differ from others only to this extent. But as far as the basis of the act is concerned, [the answer is,] 'No.' And if the agent's having knowledge of His act is necessary, as all agree, then the whole, according to us, is due to His act."

(13) The answer [to this] is in two respects.

الاشياء، ولكنّه ليس فى المادة، فاذن يعقل الاشياء. فهذا استثناء نقيض المقدّم واستثناء نقيض المقدّم غير منتج بالاتفاق. وهو كقول القائل: ان كان هذا انسانا فهو حيوان؛ لكنّه ليس بانسان؛ فاذن ليس بحيوان. فهذا لا يلزم، اذ ربما لا يكون انسانا ويكون فرسا فيكون حيوانا.

(٩) نعم، استثناء نقيض المقدّم ينتج نقيض التالى، على ما ذكر فى المنطق بشرط، وهو ثبوت انعكاس التالى على المقدّم وذلك بالحصر. وهو كقولهم ان كانت الشمس طالعة، فالنهار موجود، لكنّ الشمس ليست طالعة، فالنهار غير موجود، لانّ وجود النهار لا سبب لهُ سوى طلوع الشمس. فكان أحدهما منعكسا على الآخر. وبيان هذه الاوضاع والالفاظ يفهم فى كتاب [معيار العلم][2] الذى صنّفناه مضموماً الى هذا الكتاب.

(١٠) فان قيل: فنحن ندّعى التعاكس، وهو انّ المانع محصور فى المادة، فلا مانع سواه، قلنا:

(١١) وهذا تحكّم فما الدليل عليه؟

(١٢) الفن الثانى قوله: انّا وان لم نقل انّ الاوّل مريد الاحداث، ولا ان الكلّ حادث حدوثا زمانيا، فانّا نقول: انّه فعله، وقد وجد منه، الا أنّه لم يزل بصفة الفاعلين، فلم يزل فاعلا. فلا نفارق غيرنا الا فى هذا القدر. وأمّا فى أصل الفعل، فلا. واذا وجب كون الفاعل عالما بالاتفاق بفعله، فالكل عندنا من فعله.

(١٣) والجواب من وجهين:

(14) The first is that action divides into two [kinds]: voluntary, like the action of animal[s] and human[s], and natural, like the action of the sun in shedding light, fire in heating, and water in cooling. Knowledge of the act is only necessary in the voluntary act, as in the human arts.
5   As regards natural action, [the answer is,] "No." [Now,] according to you [philosophers], God enacted the world by way of necessity from His essence, by nature and compulsion, not by way of will and choice. Indeed, the whole [of the world] follows necessarily from His essence in the way that light follows necessarily from the sun. And just as the sun has no
10   power to stop light and fire [has no power] to stop heating, the First has no power to stop His acts, may He be greatly exalted above what they say. This mode [of expression], [even] if metaphorically named an "act," does not at all entail knowledge for the agent.
       (15) [To this it may be] said:
15   (16) There is a difference between the two—namely, that the whole proceeded from His essence because of His knowledge of the whole. Thus, the representation of the whole order is the cause of the emanation of the whole. There is no principle for [the existence of the whole] other than [His] knowledge of the whole. [His] knowledge of the whole is identical
20   with His essence. Had He had no knowledge of the whole, the whole would not have come into existence. This is unlike [the case] of light and the sun.
       (17) [To this] we say:
       (18) In this your [philosopher] brethren disagreed with you. For they said, "His essence is an essence from which the existence of the whole
25   in its order follows necessarily, naturally, and by compulsion, not inasmuch as He has knowledge of [this essence]." As long as you [Avicenna] agree with them in denying [God's] will, what is there that would render their doctrine impossible? And since knowledge of the sun of light was not made a condition for the necessity of light, light rather proceeding
30   from it necessarily, let this be supposed with the First. There is nothing to prevent this [view].
       (19) The second way [of answering the philosophers] is to concede that the proceeding of something from the agent also requires knowledge of what proceeds. [Now,] according to them, the act of God is one—namely,

(١٤) احدهما: انّ الفعل قسمان: ارادىّ كفعل الحيوان والانسان، وطبيعىّ كفعل الشمس فى الاضاءَة، والنار فى التسخين، والماء فى التبريد. وانّما يلزم العلم بالفعل فى الفعل الارادىّ، كما فى الصناعات البشريّة. وامّا الفعل الطبيعىّ، فلا. وعندكم انّ الله فعل العالم بطريق اللزوم عن ذاته بالطبع والاضطرار، لا بطريق الارادة والاختيار. بل لزم الكلّ ذاته كما يلزم النور الشمس؛ وكما لا قدرة للشمس على كفّ النور، ولا للنار على كفّ التسخين، فلا قدرة للاوّل على الكفّ عن افعاله، تعالى عن قولهم علوّا كبيرا. وهذا النمط، وان تجوّز بتسميته فعلا، فلا يقتضى علما للفاعل أصلاً.

(١٥) فان قيل:

(١٦) بين الامرين فرق، وهو ان صدر الكلّ عن ذاته بسبب علمه بالكلّ. فتمثّل النظام الكلّىّ هو سبب فيضان الكلّ. ولا مبدأ له سوى العلم بالكلّ. والعلم بالكلّ عين ذاته. فلو لم يكن له علم بالكلّ، لما وجد منه الكلّ، بخلاف النور من الشمس.

(١٧) قلنا:

(١٨) وفى هذا خالفك اخوانك. فانّهم قالوا: ذاته ذات يلزم منه وجود الكلّ على ترتيبه بالطبع والاضطرار لا من حيث انّه عالم بها. فما المحيل لهذا المذهب، مهما وافقتهم على نفى الارادة؟ ولمّا لم يشترط علم الشمس بالنور للزوم النور، بل يتبعه النور ضرورة، فليقدّر ذلك فى الاول. ولا مانع منه.

(١٩) الوجه الثانى: هو انّه ان سلّم انّ صدور الشىء من الفاعل يقتضى العلم بالصادر أيضا، فعندهم فعل الله واحد، وهو المعلول الاول

the first effect, which is a simple intellect. [From this it follows] that He must know only it. The first effect would [also] know only what proceeds from it. For the whole did not come into existence from God all at once, but through mediation, generation, and necessity. [Regarding] that which
5   proceeds from what proceeds from Him, why should it be known to Him, when only one thing proceeds from Him? Indeed, [if] this [knowledge extending beyond the first effect] is not necessary with the voluntary act, how much more so [is it unnecessary] with the natural? For the [downward] motion of the stone from the top of a mountain may be due
10   to a voluntary [act] that sets [it] in motion that necessitates knowledge of the source of the motion but does not necessitate knowledge of what is generated by [the initial voluntary act] through the mediation [of the movement] by way of [the stone's] colliding and its breaking another. For this, also, [Avicenna] has no answer.
15   (20) [To this it may be] said:

(21) If we judge it that He knows only Himself, this would be the ultimate in repugnancy. For that which is other [than Him] knows itself, knows Him, and knows another. Hence, it would be above Him in nobility. How can the effect be nobler than the cause?
20   (22) [To this] we say:

(23) This repugnancy is a necessary consequence of [the doctrine] to which philosophy leads in terms of denying [the divine] will and denying the world's temporal origination; hence, [the repugnancy] must either be committed in the same way that the rest of the philosophers have
25   committed [it], or else one must forsake philosophy and confess that the world is temporally originated by the [divine] will.

(24) Moreover, one would say: "With what would you disavow those among the philosophers who say that [the effect's having more knowledge than the cause] does not constitute greater honor? For knowledge is
30   needed by [a being] other [than God] only in order to acquire perfection. For [such a being] in himself is deficient. Man is ennobled by the intelligibles, either in order to acquire knowledge of what benefits him in terms of consequences in this world or the next, or to perfect his dark, deficient self. The same is the case with all other creatures. As for God's

الذى هو عقل بسيط. فينبغى أن لا يكون عالما الا به. والمعلول الاوّل يكون عالما أيضا بما صدر منه فقط. فانّ الكلّ لم يوجد من الله دفعة، بل بالوساطة والتولّد واللزوم. فالذى يصدر ممّا يصدر منه، لم ينبغى ان يكون معلوما له، ولم يصدر منه الا شيء واحد؟ بل هذا لا يلزم فى الفعل الارادىّ، فكيف فى الطبيعىّ؟ فانّ حركة الحجر من فوق جبل قد [تكون]³ بتحريك ارادىّ يوجب العلم باصل الحركة ولا يوجب العلم بما يتولد [منه بوسطتها]⁴، من مصادمته وكسره غيره. فهذا أيضا لا جواب له عنه.

(٢٠) فان قيل:

(٢١) لو قضينا بانه لا يعرف الا نفسه، لكان ذلك فى غاية الشناعة. فان غيره يعرف نفسه ويعرفه ويعرف غيره، فيكون فى الشرف فوقه. وكيف يكون المعلول اشرف من العلّة؟

(٢٢) قلنا:

(٢٣) فهذه الشناعة لازمة من مقاد الفلسفة فى نفى الارادة ونفى حدث العالم. فيجب ارتكابها، كما ارتكب سائر الفلاسفة أو لا بدّ من ترك الفلسفة والاعتراف بانّ العالم حادث بالارادة.

(٢٤) ثم يقال: بم تنكر على من قال من الفلاسفة انّ ذلك ليس بزيادة شرف؟ فانّ العلم انّما احتاج اليه غيره ليستفيد به كمالا. فانّه فى ذاته قاصر. والانسان شرف بالمعقولات امّا ليطلع على مصلحته فى العواقب فى الدنيا والآخرة، وامّا لتكمل ذاته المظلمة الناقصة. وكذى

essence, it has no need for an act of perfecting [itself]. On the contrary, if one were to suppose for Him knowledge through which He is perfected, then His essence qua His essence would be deficient."

(25) This is similar to what you [Avicenna] have said regarding hearing, seeing, and knowledge of the particulars that fall under time. For you have agreed with the rest of the philosophers that God is above [such knowledge] and that the First does not know the things that undergo change in the realm of the temporal that divide into "what was" and "what will be," because that would necessitate change in His essence [and the reception of] influence. [Accordingly,] no deficiency [is involved] in denying Him [such knowledge]; rather, it is perfection, deficiency belonging to the senses and the need thereof. If it were not for the deficiency of the human, he would have no need of the senses to protect him against whatever subjects him to change. The same applies to knowledge of temporal particular events. You [philosophers] claim that it constitutes deficiency. If, then, we know all temporal events and apprehend all sensible things, but the First knows nothing of the particulars and apprehends nothing of the sensible things, this not being a deficiency [in Him], then knowledge of the intellectual universals can also be affirmed as belonging to another, but not affirmed of Him, this also not constituting deficiency [in Him]. From this [conclusion] there is no escape.

سائر المخلوقات. وامّا ذات الله فمستغنية عن التكميل. بل لو قدّر له علم يكمل به لكان ذاته من حيث ذاته ناقصا.

(٢٥) وهذا كما قلت فى السمع والبصر وفى العلم بالجزئيّات الداخلة تحت الزمان. فانّك وافقت سائر الفلاسفة بانّ الله منزّه عنه وان المتغيّرات الداخلة فى الزمان المنقسمة الى ما كان ويكون لا يعرفه الاوّل لانّ ذلك يوجب تغيّرا فى ذاته وتأثّرا. و لم يكن فى سلب ذلك عنه نقصان؛ بل هو كمال، وانّما النقصان فى الحواس والحاجة اليها ولولا نقصان الادمىّ، لما احتاج الى حواس لتحرسهُ عمّا يتعرّض للتغيّر به. وكذلك العلم بالحوادث الجزئيّة زعمتم انه نقصان. فاذا كنّا نعرف الحوادث كلّها وندرك المحسوسات كلّها والاوّل لا يعرف شيئا من الجزئيّات ولا يدرك شيئا من المحسوسات ولا يكون ذلك نقصانا، فالعلم بالكليّات العقلية أيضا يجوز ان يثبت لغيره ولا يثبت له، ولا يكون فيه نقصان أيضا. وهذا لا مخرج عنه.

[Twelfth] Discussion

On showing their inability to prove that He also knows Himself

(1) We say: "Inasmuch as the Muslims recognized the world to be temporally originated through His will, they inferred knowledge from the will and then inferred life from both will and knowledge. From life they then [inferred] that every living being is aware of himself. [But God] is alive; hence, He also knows Himself." This becomes a pattern of reasoning that is comprehensible and exceedingly strong. But in your case, [philosophers,] once you deny will and temporal origination, claiming that whatever proceeds from Him follows by way of necessity and nature, why [would you hold] it improbable that His essence is such that there would proceed from Him only the first effect, and then from the first effect a second effect, [and so on] to the completion of the order of existents, but that, despite all this, He is unaware of Himself—just as, with fire from which heat necessarily proceeds and with the sun from which light necessarily proceeds, neither one knows itself, just as it does not know another? On the contrary, that which knows itself knows what proceeds from it and, hence, knows another. We have shown that in terms of their doctrine [God] does not know another and [that we] have forced on those who oppose them on this the necessary consequence of [actually] agreeing with them by dint of the [very] position [these opponents] take. If, then, He does not know another, it is not unlikely that He does not know Himself.

(2) If it is said, "Whoever does not know himself is dead; how could the First be dead?" we say:

مسئلة
فى تعجيزهم عن اقامة الدليل
على انّه يعرف ذاته ايضا

(١) فنقول: المسلمون لمّا عرفوا حدوث العالم بارادته استدلّوا بالارادة على العلم، ثم بالارادة والعلم جميعا على الحياة، ثم بالحياة على انّ كلّ حىّ يشعر بنفسه. وهو حىّ، فيعرف أيضا ذاته. فكان هذا منهجا معقولا فى غاية المتانة. فامّا انتم، فاذا نفيتم الارادة والاحداث وزعمتم انّ ما يصدر منه يصدر بلزوم على سبيل الضرورة والطبع، فاىّ بعد فى ان تكون ذاتا ذاته من شأنها ان يوجد منه المعلول الاول فقط، ثم يلزم المعلول الاول المعلول الثانى الى تمام ترتيب الموجودات، ولكنّه مع ذلك لا يشعر بذاته، كالنار يلزم منها السخونة والشمس يلزم منها النور، ولا يعرف واحد منهما ذاته كما لا يعرف غيره؟ بل ما يعرف ذاته، يعرف ما يصدر منه فيعرف غيره، وقد بيّنا من مذهبهم انّه لا يعرف غيره وألزمنا من خالفهم فى ذلك موافقتهم بحكم وضعهم. واذا لم يعرف غيره لم يبعد ان لا يعرف نفسه.

(٢) فان قيل: كلّ من لا يعرف نفسه فهو ميت، فكيف يكون الاوّل ميتا؟ قلنا:

(3) This is a necessary consequence forced on you by the logic of your doctrine. For there is no difference between you and the one who says, "Whoever does not act through will, power, and choice, and who neither hears nor sees, is dead; and [moreover,] he who does not know another is dead." If, then, it is possible for the First to be devoid of all these attributes, what need is there for Him to know Himself? If they return to [the argument] that everything free from matter is in itself intellect and, hence, apprehends itself, we have shown that this is an arbitrary assertion, having no demonstration to prove it.

(4) [To this it may be] said:

(5) The demonstration for this is that the existent divides into the living and the dead, the living being prior to the dead and nobler. But the First is prior and nobler and is thus living—everything alive being aware of itself—since it is impossible that the living should be included among His effects while He Himself is not alive.

(6) We say:

(7) These are arbitrary [assertions]. For we say: "Why is it impossible that there should proceed from that which does not know itself that which knows itself, either through many intermediaries or without an intermediary? If that which renders this impossible is [the consequence] that the effect becomes nobler than the cause, why should it be impossible for the effect to be nobler than the cause? This is not [self-evident] to the natural intelligence. Moreover, with what [argument] would you deny [the assertion] that His nobility lies in [the fact] that the existence of the whole [universe] is a consequence of His essence [and yet is] not in His knowledge?" Proof for this is that some other [existent] may know things other than itself, [being one] who sees and hears, whereas He neither sees nor hears. For if one were to say, "The existent divides into the seeing and the blind, the knower and the ignorant," let, then, the seeing be prior and let, then, the First be a seer and a knower of things. But you [philosophers] deny this and say that nobility does not lie in the seeing and knowing of things, but, rather, in dispensing with seeing and knowing [particular things]; and [that it] lies in the essence, being such that from it the whole [universe], which includes knowers and those with sight, comes to exist.

(٣) فقد لزمكم ذلك على مساق مذهبكم، اذ لا فصل بينكم وبين من قال: كلّ من لا يفعل بارادة وقدرة واختيار ولا يسمع ولا يبصر فهو ميت ومن لا يعرف غيره فهو ميت. فان جاز ان يكون الاوّل خاليا عن هذه الصفات كلّها، فاىّ حاجة به الى ان يعرف ذاته؟ فان عادوا الى انّ كلّ برى عن المادة عقل بذاته فيعقل نفسه، فقد بيّنا انّ ذلك تحكّم لا برهان عليه.

(٤) فان قيل:

(٥) البرهان عليه ان الموجود ينقسم الى حىّ والى ميت، والحى اقدم واشرف من الميت. والاول أقدم وأشرف، فليكن حيّا، وكل حىّ يشعر بذاته، اذ يستحيل ان يكون فى معلولاته الحىّ، وهو لا يكون حيّا.

(٦) قلنا:

(٧) هذه تحكّمات. فانّا نقول: لم يستحيل ان يلزم ممّا لا يعرف نفسه ما يعرف نفسه بالوسائط الكثيرة أو بغير واسطة؟ فان كان المحيل لذلك كون المعلول أشرف من العلّة، فلم يستحيل ان يكون المعلول أشرف من العلّة؟ وليس هذا بديهيًّا. ثم بم تنكرون ان شرفه فى ان وجود الكلّ تابع لذاته لا فى علمه؟ الدليل عليه أنّ غيره ربما عرف اشياء سوى ذاته، ويرى ويسمع، وهو لا يرى ولا يسمع. ولو قال قائل: الموجود ينقسم الى البصير والاعمى والعالم والجاهل، فليكن البصير أقدم، وليكن الاول بصيرا وعالما بالاشياء. لكنّكم تنكرون ذلك وتقولون: ليس الشرف فى البصر والعلم بالاشياء بل فى الاستغناء عن البصر والعلم، وكون الذات بحيث يوجد منه

Similarly, there would be no nobility in [His] knowledge of [His] essence, but in His being the Principle of those possessing knowledge, this being a nobility peculiar to Him.

(8) Hence, it is by necessity that they are compelled to deny also His
5 knowledge of Himself, since nothing gives evidence for this except will, and nothing proves will except the world's temporal origination. With the rendering false [of their doctrine that He knows Himself], everything becomes false for those who approach these things in terms of rational reflection. They have no proof for all that they have mentioned
10 or denied regarding the attributes of the First, [but] only suppositions and opinions, disdained by the lawyers [even] in [their treatment of] the conjectural. There is neither wonder nor astonishment if the mind is perplexed as regards the divine attributes. One is only astonished at their conceit in themselves and in their proofs and at their belief that they
15 have come to know these things with certainty, despite the confusion and error [their arguments] contain.

الكلّ الذى فيه العلماء وذوو الابصار. فكذلك لا شرف فى معرفة الذات،
بل فى كونه مبدأ لذوات المعرفة، وهذا شرف مخصوص به.

(٨) فبالضرورة يضطرّون الى نفى علمه أيضا بذاته، اذ لا يدلّ على
شىء من ذلك سوى الارادة ولا يدلّ على الارادة سوى حدث العالم.
وبفساد ذلك يفسد هذا كلّه على من يأخذ هذه الامور من نظر العقل.
فجميع ما ذكروه من صفات الاوّل أو نفوه لا حجّة لهم عليها، الا
تخمينات وظنون تستنكف الفقهاء منها فى الظنيّات. ولا غرو لو حار
العقل فى الصفات الالهية ولا عجب. انما العجب من عجبهم بانفسهم
وبأدلّتهم ومن اعتقادهم انّهم عرفوا هذه الامور معرفة يقينيّة مع ما فيها
من الخبط والخبال.

[Thirteenth] Discussion

On refuting their statement that God, may
He be exalted above what they say, does not know
the particulars divisible in terms of temporal
division into what is, what was, and what will be

(1) They agreed on this. In the case of the one among them who maintained that He knows only Himself, this is evident from his doctrine. And those who maintain that He knows others, this being [the position] which Avicenna chose, claim that He knows things through a universal knowledge which does not enter time and which does not change in terms of the past, the future, and the present. Despite this, [Avicenna] claims that not even the weight of an atom, either in the heavens or on earth, escapes His knowledge, except that He knows the particulars by a universal kind [of knowing].

(2) One must begin by understanding their doctrine and then engage in objecting [to it].

(3) We will explain this with an example—namely, that the sun, for example, becomes eclipsed after not being eclipsed, then becomes bright again. Three things occur to it—I mean, to the eclipse:

(4) [(1)] A state in which it is nonexistent, but its existence is expected—that is, it will be; [(2)] a state in which it exists—that is, it is; [(3)] a third state in which it is nonexistent, having, however, been previously existent. Alongside these three states, we have three different

مسئلة

فى ابطال قولهم انّ الله تعالى عن قولهم لا يعلم الجزئيّات المنقسمة بانقسام الزمان الى الكائن وما كان وما يكون

(١) وقد اتفقوا على ذلك. فانّ من ذهب منهم الى انّه لا يعلم الا نفسه فلا يخفى هذا من مذهبه. ومن ذهب الى انه يعلم غيره، وهو الذى اختاره ابن سينا، فقد زعم انّه يعلم الاشياء علما كلّيّا لا يدخل تحت الزمان ولا يختلف بالماضى والمستقبل والآن. ومع ذلك، زعم انّه لا يعزب عن علمه مثقال ذرّة فى السموات ولا فى الارض، الا انّهُ يعلم الجزئيّات بنوع كلّىّ.

(٢) ولا بدّ أولا من فهم مذهبهم ثم الاشتغال بالاعتراض.

(٣) ونبيّن هذا بمثال، وهو انّ الشمس مثلا [تنكسف]¹ بعد ان لم [تكن]² [منكسفة]³ ثم [تتجلى]⁴، فيحصل له ثلثة أحوال أعنى [الكسوف]⁵:

(٤) [حال]⁶ هو فيها معدوم منتظر الوجود، اى سيكون، وحال هو فيها موجود، اى هو كائن، وحالة ثالثة هو فيها معدوم، ولكنّه كان من قبل. ولنا بازاء هذه الاحوال الثلثة، ثلثة علوم مختلفة. فانّا نعلم أوّلا انّ الكسوف معدوم وسيكون؛ وثانيا انّه كائن؛ وثالثا انّه كان وليس كائنا

cognitions. For we know, first of all, that the eclipse is nonexistent but will be; secondly, that it is; and, thirdly, that it was but is not presently existing. These three cognitions are numbered and different. Their succession over the [one] receptacle necessitates a change in the knowing essence. For, if, after the clearing [of the eclipse], one were to "know" that the eclipse presently exists, this would be ignorance, not knowledge; and if, when [the eclipse actually] exists, one were to "know" that it does not exist, this [also] would be ignorance [and not knowledge]. For none of [these states] can take the place of the other.

(5) [The philosophers] thus claim that God's state does not differ in these three states, for this leads to change. It is inconceivable [they maintain] for that whose state does not differ to know these three matters, for knowledge follows the object known. Thus, if the object known changes, knowledge changes; and if knowledge changes, the knower inescapably changes. But change in God is impossible. Despite this, [Avicenna] claims that [God] knows the eclipse and all its attributes and accidents, but by a knowledge eternally attributed to Him which does not change—as, for example, knowing that the sun exists and the moon exists. For these came to exist through Him by the mediation of the angels, which, according to their idiom, they termed "pure intellects." [God] knows that [these two orbs] undergo a circular motion and that their sphere's paths intersect at two points—namely, the head and the tail—and that at certain times they meet at the two nodes, whereby the sun becomes eclipsed—that is, the body of the moon intercedes between it and the eyes of the observers so that the sun is concealed from [sight]. Moreover, [He knows] that if [the sun] moves beyond the node by a certain period of time—a year, for example—it would suffer an eclipse once again, and that that eclipse would cover all of it, a third of it, or half of it, and that it would last an hour or two hours, and so on to include all the states of the eclipse and its accidental occurrences, such that nothing escapes His knowledge. But His knowledge of [all] this—before the eclipse, at the time of the eclipse, and when it clears—is of one unchanging pattern and does not necessitate change in His essence. The same applies to His knowledge of all temporal events. For these occur as a result of causes, and these causes through other causes, until they terminate with the circular heavenly motion. The cause of [this] movement is the soul of the heavens, and the cause of the soul's causing motion is the desire to imitate God and the angels close to

الآن. وهذه العلوم الثلثة متعدّدة ومختلفة وتعاقبها على المحلّ يوجب تغيّر الذات العالمة. فانّه لو علم بعد الانجلاء انّ الكسوف موجود الآن، كان جهلا لا علما؛ ولو علم عند وجوده انّه معدوم، كان جهلا. فبعض هذه لا يقوم مقام بعض.

(٥) فزعموا انّ الله لا يختلف حاله فى هذه الاحوال الثلثة، فانّه يؤدّى الى التغيّر، وما لم يختلف حاله، لم يتصوّر ان يعلم هذه الامور الثلثة. فانّ العلم يتبع المعلوم. فاذا تغيّر المعلوم، تغيّر العلم، واذا تغيّر العلم فقد تغيّر العالم، لا محالة، والتغيّر على الله محال. ومع هذا، زعم انّه يعلم الكسوف وجميع صفاته وعوارضه ولكن علما هو يتّصف به فى الازل ولا يختلف، مثل ان يعلم مثلا انّ الشمس موجود وانّ القمر موجود؛ فانّهما حصلا منه بواسطة الملائكة التى سمّوها باصطلاحهم عقولا مجرّدة. ويعلم انّها تتحرّك حركات دوريّة، ويعلم ان بين فلكيهما تقاطع على نقطتين، هما الرأس والذنب، وانّهما يجتمعان فى بعض الاحوال فى العقدتين [فتنكسف]⁷ الشمس أى يحول جرم القمر بينها وبين أعين الناظرين، [فتستتر]⁸ الشمس عن الاعين، وانّه اذا جاوز العقدة مثلا بمقدار كذى، وهو سنة مثلا، فانّه ينكسف مرّة أخرى، وان ذلك الانكساف يكون فى جميعه أو ثلثه أو نصفه، وانّه يمكث ساعة او ساعتين، وهكذى الى جميع أحوال الكسوف وعوارضه. فلا يعزب عن علمه شىء، ولكن علمه بهذا قبل الكسوف وحالة الكسوف وبعد الانجلاء على وتيرة واحدة، لا يختلف ولا يوجب تغيّرا فى ذاته. وكذى علمه بجميع الحوادث؛ فانّها انّما تحدث باسباب وتلك الاسباب لها اسباب أخر الى ان تنتهى الى الحركة الدوريّة السماويّة؛ وسبب الحركة نفس السموات، وسبب تحريك النفس الشوق الى التشبّه بالله والملائكة

Him.[1] The whole is thus known to Him—that is, unveiled to Him—in one homogeneous unveiling, unaffected by time. With all this, however, one does not say at the time of the eclipse that He knows that the eclipse presently exists; and thereafter He does not know at the time that it has
5   cleared. Now, it is inconceivable that [God] knows anything that necessarily requires in defining it a relation to time, because this necessitates a change in [Him]. This, then, [is what they hold] regarding what is divisible in terms of time.

(6) Their doctrine is similar regarding what is divisible in terms
10   of matter and space—as, for example, individual humans and animals. For they say that [God] does not know the accidents of Zayd, ᶜAmr, and Khālid, but only man [in the] absolute [sense] by a universal knowledge. He thus knows [absolute man's] accidents and properties: that his body must be composed of organs, some for attacking, some for walking, some
15   for apprehending; that some [of his organs] are pairs, some single; that his powers must be spread throughout his parts; and so on to the inclusion of every attribute external and internal to man, all that belongs to his appendages, attributes, and necessary concomitants, such that nothing escapes His knowledge, knowing [all that constitutes man] universally.
20   As for the individual Zayd, he becomes distinguished from the individual ᶜAmr to the senses, not the intellect. For the basis of the distinction is the pointing to him in a specific direction, whereas the intellect apprehends [only] absolute, universal direction and universal space. As regards our saying "this" and "this," this is a reference to a relation obtaining between
25   the sensible object and the perceiver by being close to him, far from him, or in a specific direction—[all of which] is impossible in the case of [God].

(7) This is a principle which they believed and through which they uprooted religious laws in their entirety, since it entails that if Zayd, for example, obeys or disobeys God, God would not know what of his states
30   has newly come about, because He does not know Zayd in his particularity. For [Zayd] is an individual, and his actions come temporally into existence after nonexistence. And if He does not know the individual, He does not know his states and acts. Indeed, He does not know Zayd's unbelief or [acceptance of] Islam but only knows man's unbelief or [accep-
35   tance of] Islam absolutely and universally, not as specified in [particular] individuals. Indeed, it follows necessarily that one would have to say that

المقرّبين. فالكلّ معلوم له أى هو منكشف له انكشافا واحدا متناسبا لا يؤثّر فيه الزمان. ومع هذا [فحال]⁹ الكسوف لا يقال انّه يعلم ان الكسوف موجود الآن، ولا يعلم بعده انّه انجلى الآن، وكل ما يجب فى تعريفه الاضافة الى الزمان فلا يتصوّر ان يعلمه، لانّه يوجب التغير. هذا ٥ فيما ينقسم بالزمان.

(٦) وكذى مذهبهم فيما ينقسم بالمادّة والمكان كاشخاص الناس والحيوانات فانهم يقولون: لا يعلم عوارض زيد وعمرو وخالد وانّما يعلم الانسان المطلق بعلم كلّيّ، ويعلم عوارضه وخواصه وانّه ينبغى ان يكون بدنه مركّبا من اعضاء بعضها للبطش، وبعضها للمشى وبعضها ١٠ للادراك، وبعضها زوج وبعضها فرد؛ وانّ قواه ينبغى أن تكون مبثوثة فى أجزائه، وهلمّ جرّا الى كل صفة فى [خارج]¹⁰ الادمى وباطنه، وكل ما هو من لواحقه وصفاته ولوازمه حتى لا يعزب عن علمه شىء ويعلمه كلّيّا. فامّا شخص زيد، فانّما يتميّز عن شخص عمرو للحس لا للعقل. فانّ عماد التمييز اليه الاشارة الى جهة معيّنة، والعقل يعقل الجهة المطلقة الكلّيّة والمكان الكلّى. فامّا قولنا هذا وهذا، فهو اشارة الى نسبة حاصلة ١٥ لذلك المحسوس الى الحاسّ بكونه منه على قرب أو بعد أو جهة معيّنة؛ وذلك يستحيل فى حقّه.

(٧) وهذه قاعدة اعتقدوها واستأصلوا بها الشرائع بالكلّيّة، اذ مضمونها انّ زيدا مثلا، لو أطاع الله أو عصاه، لم يكن الله عالما بما يتجدّد من أحواله، لانّه لا يعرف زيدا بعينه. فانّه شخص وافعاله حادثة بعد ان لم ٢٠ تكن. واذا لم يعرف الشخص، لم يعرف أحواله وافعاله؛ بل لا يعلم كفر زيد ولا اسلامه، وانّما يعلم كفر الانسان واسلامه مطلقا كلّيا، لا

when Muḥammad, God's prayers and peace be upon him, challenged [the heathen] with his prophethood, [God] did not know then that he made the challenge, the same being the case with every individual prophet, that [God] only knows that among people there would be those
5   who would make the prophetic challenge and that their description would be such and such. However, as regards the specific prophet individually, He does not know him. For that is [only] known to the senses. [Likewise,] He does not know the [individual] states proceeding from [the prophet] because these are states divisible through the division of
10   time pertaining to a specific individual. The apprehension of [these states] in their diversity necessitates change [in the knower].

(8) This, then, is what we wished to mention by way of, first, reporting their doctrine; second, explaining it; and third, [indicating] the repugnancies necessarily ensuing from it. Let us now mention their confusion
15   [in supporting this doctrine] and [then] the manner in which it is false.

(9) Their confusion [lies in saying] that these [the temporal sequence of events relating to the eclipse] are three different states and that different things, when succeeding each other over one receptacle, must necessitate a change [in the knower]. Thus, if at the time of the eclipse
20   [God] "knows" that [the one receptacle] would be [in the same state] as it had been prior [to the eclipse], He would be ignorant, not knowing. If, [on the other hand, at the time of the eclipse] He has knowledge that [the eclipse] exists, but prior to this [time knowledge] that it will be, then His knowledge would change and His state would change. Change is thus
25   the necessary consequence, since there is no other meaning for change except a difference in the knower. For whoever does not know a thing undergoes change when he comes to know it; and whoever has had no knowledge that [the eclipse] exists undergoes change when [this knowledge] is realized at the time of the existence [of the eclipse]. They ascer-
30   tained this by maintaining that the states are three:

(10) [The first is] a state which is a pure relation—as [for example] your being to the right or the left [of something]; for this does not refer to an essential attribute but is a pure relation. Thus, if the thing which was to your right changes to your left, your relation changes but your
35   essence does not change in any way. For this is a change of a relation to the essence but [does] not [come about] through a change in the essence.

(11) [The second] of this sort [is the case] when you are able to move bodies in front of you and these bodies, or some of them, cease to exist, where neither your innate capacity nor [other] power changes. This is

مخصوصا بالاشخاص. بل يلزم ان يقال: تحدّى محمد صلى الله عليه وسلّم
بالنبوّة، وهو لم يعرف فى تلك الحالة انّه تحدّى بها، وكذلك الحال مع كلّ
نبى معيّن، وانه انما يعلم أن من الناس من يتحدّى بالنبوّة وانّ صفة اولئك
كذى وكذى. فاما النبىّ المعيّن بشخصه، فلا يعرفه. فانّ ذلك يعرف
بالحسّ؛ والاحوال الصادرة منه لا يعرفها، لانّها أحوال تنقسم بانقسام
الزمان من شخص معيّن ويوجب ادراكها على اختلافها تغيّرا.

(٨) فهذا ما أردنا ان نذكره من نقل مذهبهم أوّلا، ثم تفهيمه ثانيا،
ثم من القبايح اللازمة عليه ثالثا. فلنذكر الآن خبالهم ووجه بطلانه.

(٩) وخبالهم انّ هذه أحوال ثلثة مختلفة والمختلفات اذا تعاقبت على
محلّ واحد أوجبت فيه تغيّرا لا محالة. فان كان حالة الكسوف عالما بانّه
سيكون كما كان قبله فهو جاهل لا عالم. وان كان عالما بانّه كائن وقبل
ذلك كان عالما بانه ليس بكائن وانّه سيكون، فقد اختلف علمه واختلف
حاله، فلزم التغير، اذ لا معنى للتغيّر الا اختلاف العالم. فانّ من لم يعلم
شيئا ثم علمه فقد تغيّر، ولم يكن له علم بانّه كائن ثم حصل حالة الوجود،
فقد تغيّر. وحقّقوا هذا بانّ الاحوال ثلثة:

(١٠) [حال]¹¹ هى اضافة محضة ككونك يميناً وشمالاً، فانّ هذا لا
يرجع الى وصف ذاتىّ بل هو اضافة محضة. فان تحوّل الشىء الذى كان
على يمينك الى شمالك تغيّرت اضافتك ولم تتغيّر ذاتك بحال. [فهذا]¹²
تبدّل اضافة على الذات وليس بتبدّل الذات.

(١١) ومن هذا القبيل اذا كنت قادرا على تحريك اجسام حاضرة بين
يديك فانعدمت الاجسام او انعدم بعضها لم تتغيّر قوتك الغريزيّة ولا قدرتك.

because power is the power over the moving of body; first of all in the
absolute [general sense], and secondly over a specific [body] inasmuch as
it is body. Thus, the relating of power to the specific body would not constitute an essential attribute, but [only] a pure relation. Therefore, the
5   ceasing [of the bodies] to exist necessitates [only] the ceasing of the relation, not a change in the state of the one endowed with power.

(12) The third [state is one which involves] change in essence—
namely, that He would not be knowing and then knows, or would not be
one endowed with power and then [becomes endowed with] power. This
10   constitutes change. The change in the object known necessitates change
in the knowledge. For the reality of the essence of knowledge includes
the relation to the specific object of knowledge, since the reality of the
specific knowledge consists in its attachment to the specific object of
knowledge as it [actually] is. Its attachment to it in a different manner
15   necessarily constitutes another knowledge. Its succession necessitates a
change in the state of the knower. It is impossible to say that the essence
has one knowledge which becomes knowledge of "what is" after having
been knowledge of "what will be" and then becomes knowledge of "what
was" after being knowledge of "what is." For knowledge is one, similar
20   in its states; but [here] the relation [to the object] has changed, since
the relation in knowledge is the reality of the essence of knowledge.
Hence, its change necessitates a change in the essence of knowledge. As
a consequence, change [in the knower] necessarily ensues; and this is
impossible in the case of God.

25   (13) The objection [to this] is in two respects:

(14) The first is to say, "With what [argument] do you deny one who
says that God, exalted be He, has one knowledge of the existence of the
eclipse, for example, at a specific time; and that this [same] knowledge
before [the existence of the eclipse] is knowledge that it will be, being
30   identical with the knowledge at the time of the eclipse and identical with
the knowledge after the clearing [of the eclipse]; and that these differences reduce to relations that do not necessitate change in the essence of
knowledge and, hence, do not necessitate change in the essence of the
knower; and that [these differences] have the status of a pure relation?"
35   For, [in moving past you, an] individual [is first] on your right, [then]
moves on to be in front of you, and then [moves] to your left. The relations thus succeed each other for you; but the one undergoing change is

لانّ القدرة قدرة على تحريك الجسم المطلق أوّلا، ثم على المعيّن ثانيا من حيث انه جسم. فلم تكن اضافة القدرة الى الجسم المعين وصفا ذاتيا، بل اضافة محضة. فعدمها يوجب زوال اضافة لا تغيّرا فى حال القادر.

(١٢) والثالث تغير فى الذات، وهو ان لا يكون عالما فيعلم، أو لا يكون قادرا فيقدر. فهذا تغيّر. وتغيّر المعلوم يوجب تغيّر العلم. فانّ حقيقة ذات العلم تدخل فيه الاضافة الى المعلوم الخاص، اذ حقيقة العلم المعيّن تعلّقه بذلك المعلوم المعيّن على ما هو عليه. فتعلّقه به على وجه آخر علم آخر بالضرورة. فتعاقبه يوجب اختلاف حال العالم. ولا يمكن ان يقال انّ للذات علم واحد فيصير علما بالكون بعد كونه علما بانّه سيكون، ثم هو يصير علما بانّه كان بعد ان كان علما بانّه كائن. فالعلم واحد متشابه الاحوال، وقد تبدّلت عليه الاضافة، لانّ الاضافة فى العلم حقيقة ذات العلم. فتبدّلها يوجب تبدّل ذات العلم. فيلزم منه التغيّر وهو محال على الله.

(١٣) والاعتراض من وجهين:

(١٤) احدهما ان يقال: بمَ تنكرون على من يقول انّ الله تعالى له علم واحد بوجود الكسوف مثلا فى وقت معيّن وذلك العلم قبل وجوده علم بانّه سيكون وهو بعينه عند الوجود علم بالكون وهو بعينه بعد الانجلاء علم بالانقضاء، وانّ هذه الاختلافات ترجع الى اضافات لا توجب تبدّلا فى ذات العلم، فلا توجب تغيّرا فى ذات العالم، وأنّ ذلك ينزل منزلة الاضافة المحضة؟ فانّ الشخص الواحد يكون على يمينك ثم يرجع الى قدامك ثم الى شمالك فتتعاقب عليك الاضافات، والمتغيّر ذلك الشخص

that moving individual, not yourself. This is how the state of affairs ought to be understood as regards God's knowledge. For we admit that He knows things by one knowledge in the eternal past and future, [His] state never changing. Their purpose is to deny change [in God], and on this there is agreement. Their statement, however, that change [in the knower] follows necessarily from affirming knowledge of a present existence and its termination thereafter is not admitted. How do they know this? For if God creates for us knowledge of the arrival of Zayd tomorrow at sunrise [and] perpetuates this knowledge, neither creating another knowledge nor inattention to this knowledge, we would then, at the time of the sunrise, know of his arriving now purely by the previous knowledge; and, [moreover, we would know] afterwards that he had arrived earlier. This one permanent knowledge would be sufficient to encompass these three states.

(15) There remains for them to say that the relation to the specific object of knowledge is included in its reality, so that whenever the relation changes, the thing for which the relation is essential changes; and as long as difference and succession [in the object of knowledge] occur, change [in the knower] takes place. [To this we] say:

(16) If this is true, then follow the path of [those of] your philosopher brethren who maintain that [God] knows only Himself and that His knowledge of Himself is identical with Himself, because if He knew absolute [universal] man and absolute [universal] animal and absolute [universal] inanimate [object], these being necessarily different, the relations to them are inevitably different. Thus, the one knowledge would not be suitable to be knowledge of different things because the thing related is different and the relation is different, the relation to the object known being essential for knowledge. This necessitates multiplicity and difference—and not multiplicity only with respect to similar things, since among similar things there are those that substitute for others. Knowledge of animal, however, is not a substitute for knowledge of the inanimate, and knowledge of whiteness is not a substitute for knowledge of blackness. For [each of] these [examples] constitute[s] two different [things].

(17) Moreover [we say]: "These species, genera, and universal accidents are infinite and are different. How can the different cognitions be subsumed under one knowledge—this knowledge, moreover, being the

المنتقل دونك. وهكذى ينبغى ان يفهم الحال فى علم الله. فانّا نسلّم انّه يعلم الاشياء بعلم واحد فى الازل والابد، والحال لا يتغيّر. وغرضهم نفى التغيّر وهو متّفق عليه. وقولهم من ضرورة اثبات العلم بالكون الان والانقضاء بعده تغيّر، فليس بمسلّم. فمن أين عرفوا ذلك؟ بل لو خلق الله لنا علما بقدوم زيد غدا عند طلوع الشمس وادام هذا العلم و لم يخلق لنا علما آخر ولا غفلة عن هذا العلم، لكُنّا عند طلوع الشمس عالمين بمجرّد العلم السابق بقدومه الآن، وبعده بانّه قدم من قبل. وكان ذلك العلم الواحد الباقى كافيا فى الاحاطة بهذه الاحوال الثلثة.

(١٥) فيبقى قولهم: انّ الاضافة الى المعلوم المعيّن داخلة فى حقيقته، ومهما اختلفت الاضافة اختلف الشىء الذى الاضافة ذاتيّة له، ومهما حصل الاختلاف والتعاقب، فقد حصل التغيّر. فنقول:

(١٦) ان صحّ هذا، فاسلكوا مسلك اخوانكم من الفلاسفة حيث قالوا انّه لا يعلم الا نفسه، وانّ علمه بذاته عين ذاته، لانّه لو علم الانسان المطلق والحيوان المطلق والجماد المطلق، وهذه مختلفات لا محالة، فالاضافات اليها تختلف لا محالة. فلا يصلح العلم الواحد لان يكون علما بالمختلفات، لانّ المضاف مختلف والاضافة مختلفة، والاضافة الى المعلوم ذاتيّة للعلم. فيوجب ذلك تعدّدا واختلافا، لا تعدّدا فقط مع التماثل، اذ المتماثلات ما يسدّ بعضها مسدّ البعض. والعلم بالحيوان لا يسدّ مسدّ العلم بالجماد، ولا العلم بالبياض يسدّ مسدّ العلم بالسواد؛ فهما مختلفان.

(١٧) ثمّ هذه الانواع والاجناس والعوارض الكلّيّة لا نهاية لها، وهى مختلفة. فالعلوم المختلفة كيف تنطوى تحت علم واحد، ثم ذلك العلم

essence of the Knower—without this constituting an addition to Him?"
By my word, how does the rational person allow himself to deem impossible the unifying of knowledge of one thing whose states divide into the
past, present, and future but not allow as impossible the unification of
knowledge connected with all the different genera and species, when the
differences and remoteness between the various remote genera and
species are far greater than the differences that occur between the states
of the one thing that divide in terms of time? And if [the former] did not
necessitate multiplicity and difference, why should this necessitate multiplicity and difference? Once it is established by demonstration that the
differences in times are less than the differences between genera and
species and that the [latter] did not necessitate multiplicity and difference, [the former], then, does not necessitate difference. And if it does
not necessitate difference, then the encompassing of all [things][2] by one
knowledge, permanent in the eternal past and future, becomes possible
without this necessitating change in the essence of the Knower.

(18)   The second objection is to say:

(19)   What is the preventive in terms of your own principle for Him to
know these particular matters, even though [this means] He would
undergo change? And why would you not hold that this kind of change
is not impossible for him, just as Jahm, among the Mu^ctazilites,[3] held, to
the effect that His cognitions of temporal events are [themselves] temporal and, just as some of the later Karrāmiyya believed, that He is the
receptacle of temporal events? The multitudes of the people following
true doctrine only denounced this against them inasmuch as that whatever undergoes change is not free of change, and what is not free of
change and temporal happenings is temporally originated and is not
eternal. But you hold the doctrine that the world is eternal and is not free
from change. If, then, you rationally comprehend an eternal that changes,
there is nothing to prevent you from upholding this belief [that God
undergoes change].

(20)   [To this, however,] it may be said:

هو ذات العالم، من غير مزيد عليه؟ وليت شعرى كيف يستجيز العاقل من
نفسه ان يحيل الاتحاد فى العلم بالشىء الواحد المنقسم أحواله الى الماضى
والمستقبل والآن، وهو لا يحيل الاتحاد فى العلم المتعلق بجميع الاجناس
والانواع المختلفة، والاختلاف والتباعد بين الاجناس والانواع المتباعدة
أشدّ من الاختلاف الواقع بين أحوال الشىء الواحد المنقسم بانقسام
الزمان؟ واذا لم يوجب ذلك تعدّدا واختلافا، كيف يوجب هذا تعدّدا
واختلافا؟ ومهما ثبت بالبرهان انّ اختلاف الازمان دون اختلاف
الاجناس والانواع، وانّ ذلك لم يوجب التعدّد والاختلاف، فهذا أيضا
لا يوجب الاختلاف. واذا لم يوجب الاختلاف، جاز الاحاطة بالكلّ
بعلم واحد دائم فى الازل والابد، والا يوجب ذلك تغيّرا فى ذات العالم.

(١٨) الاعتراض الثانى هو ان يقال:

(١٩) وما المانع على أصلكم من أن يعلم هذه الامور الجزئيّة وان
كان يتغيّر؟ وهلا اعتقدتم انّ هذا النوع من التغيّر لا يستحيل عليه كما
ذهب جهم من المعتزلة الى انّ علومه بالحوادث حادثة، وكما اعتقد
الكرّاميّة من عند آخرهم، انّه محلّ الحوادث؟ ولم ينكر جماهير اهل
الحق عليهم الا من حيث انّ المتغيّر لا يخلو عن التغيّر وما لا يخلو عن
التغيّر والحوادث فهو حادث وليس بقديم. وأمّا أنتم فمذهبكم انّ
العالم قديم وانّه لا يخلو عن التغيّر. فاذا عقلتم قديما متغيّرا، فلا مانع
لكم من هذا الاعتقاد.

(٢٠) فان قيل:

(21) We have only deemed this impossible because the [supposed] knowledge, temporally originating in His essence, must either originate from His direction or from the direction of another. It is false that it originates from Him. For we have shown that from the Eternal a temporal event does not proceed, and that He does not become engaged in action[4] after not being engaged in action. For this necessitates change. We have established this in the question of the world's temporal origination. If, then, this [temporal knowledge] occurs in His essence from the direction of another, how could another be effective in Him and cause Him to change, such that His states would change by way of force and compulsion from the direction of another?

(22) We say:

(23) Each of these two alternatives is not impossible in terms of your own principle. Regarding your saying that it is impossible for a temporal event to proceed from the eternal, [this] is a [statement] we have refuted in the question [of the world's temporal creation]. And how [is this not the case] when, according to you, it is impossible for a temporal event which is a first temporal event to proceed from an eternal, where the condition for its impossibility is its being first? Otherwise, these events do not have temporal causes that are infinite, but terminate through the mediation of this circular movement to an eternal thing—namely, the soul and life of the sphere. Thus, the celestial soul is eternal and the circular motion is originated by it. Each part of the motion comes into being in time and passes away, and what comes after it is inevitably renewed. Temporal events then proceed from the eternal, according to you; but since the states of the eternal are similar, the emanation of the events from it is perpetually similar, just as the parts of the movement are similar because it proceeds from an eternal whose states are similar. It thus becomes clear that each party among them confesses that it is possible for a temporal event to proceed from an eternal, if it proceeds uniformly and perpetually. Let, then, these temporal cognitions [in the divine] be of this sort.

(24) As to the second alternative—namely, the proceeding of this knowledge in Him from another—we say, "Why is this impossible for you?" For it entails only three things:

(٢١) انّما احلنا ذلك لانّ العلم الحادث فى ذاته لا يخلوا امّا ان يحدث من جهته أو من جهة غيره. وباطل ان يحدث منه. فانّا بيّنا انّ القديم لا يصدر منه حادث، ولا يصير فاعلا بعد ان لم يكن فاعلا. فانّه يوجب تغيّرا. وقد قرّرناه فى مسئلة حدث العالم. وان حصل ذلك فى ذاته من جهة غيره، فكيف يكون غيره مؤثّرا فيه ومغيّرا له حتّى تتغيّر أحواله على سبيل التسخّر والاضطرار من جهة غيره؟

(٢٢) فلنا:

(٢٣) كلّ واحد من القسمين غير محال على أصلكم. أمّا قولكم انه يستحيل أن يصدر من القديم حادث، فقد أبطلناه فى تلك المسئلة. كيف، وعندكم يستحيل أن يصدر من القديم حادث، هو أوّل الحوادث، فشرط استحالته كونه أوّلا؟ والا فهذه الحوادث ليست لها اسباب حادثة الى غير نهاية بل تنتهى بواسطة الحركة الدوريّة الى شىء قديم هو نفس الفلك وحياته. فالنفس الفلكيّة قديمة والحركة الدوريّة تحدث منها. وكل جزء من اجزاء الحركة يحدث وينقضى وما بعده متجدّد لا محالة. فاذن الحوادث صادرة من القديم عندكم. ولكن اذ [تشابهت]¹² احوال القديم تشابه فيضان الحوادث منه على الدوام كما [تتشابه]¹⁴ أحوال الحركة لما ان كانت تصدر من قديم متشابه الاحوال. فاستبان انّ كل فريق منهم معترف بانّه يجوز صدور حادث من قديم اذا كانت تصدر على التناسب والدوام. فلتكن العلوم الحادثة من هذا القبيل.

(٢٤) وأمّا القسم الثانى، وهو صدور هذا العلم فيه من غيره، فنقول: و لم يستحيل ذلك عندكم؟ وليس فيه الا ثلثة أمور:

(25) The first is change [in God], but we have shown its necessity in terms of your own principle.

(26) The second is the other's being a cause for the change of another, which, however, is not impossible according to you. Let, then, the temporal occurrence of something be a cause for the temporal occurrence of the knowledge of it. [This is] just as when you say: "The colored figure's presenting itself in front of the perceiving pupil is the cause of the imprinting of the image of the figure in the moist layer of the eye with the mediation of the transparent air between the pupil and the object seen." If, then, it is possible for an inanimate thing to be a cause for the imprinting of the form in the pupil, this being the meaning of seeing, why should it be impossible for the occurrence of temporal events to be a cause for the occurrence of the knowledge of them by the First? For, just as the seeing faculty is prepared for apprehension and [as] the occurrence of the colored figure, with the removal of [all] barriers, [is] a cause for the occurrence of the apprehension, let, then, the essence of the First Principle for you be prepared to receive knowledge, changing from potentiality to actuality with the existence of that temporal event. If this entails a change of the Eternal, the changing eternal, according to you, is not impossible. And if you claim that this is impossible with the Necessary Existent, you have no proof for the necessary existent other than the termination of the chain of causes and effects, as previously [shown]. And we have shown that terminating the regress is possible with an eternal that undergoes change. [To] the third thing entailed in this—namely, [that] the Eternal [is] being changed by another and that this is akin to subjugation [imposed on Him] and His being held in the power of another—it would be said:

(27) Why is this impossible according to you—namely, that He would be the cause for the occurrence of temporal events through intermediaries and that then the occurrence of temporal events would become the cause for the occurrence of their knowledge for Him? It would be as though He is the cause for realizing knowledge for Himself, but through intermediaries. [Regarding] your statement that this would be akin to enforcement— [well,] let it be so. For this is appropriate to your principle, since you

(٢٥) أحدها: التغيّر وقد بيّنا لزومه على أصلكم.

(٢٦) والثانى كون الغير سببا لتغيّر الغير. وهو غير محال عندكم. فليكن حدوث الشىء سببا لحدوث العلم به، كما انّكم تقولون: تمثّل الشخص المتلوّن بازاء الحدقة الباصرة سبب لانطباع مثال الشخص فى الطبقة الجليديّة من الحدقة عند توسّط الهواء المشفّ بين الحدقة والمبصر. فاذا جاز أن يكون جماد سببا لانطباع الصورة فى الحدقة، وهو معنى الابصار، فلم يستحيل أن يكون حدوث الحوادث سببا لحصول علم الاوّل بها؟ فانّ القوة الباصرة، كما انها مستعدّة للادراك، ويكون حصول الشخص المتلوّن مع ارتفاع الحواجز سببا لحصول الادراك، فليكن ذات المبدأ الاول عندكم مستعدا لقبول العلم ويخرج من القوّة الى الفعل بوجود ذلك الحادث. فان كان فيه تغيّر القديم، فالقديم المتغيّر عندكم غير مستحيل. وان زعمتم انّ ذلك يستحيل فى واجب الوجود، فليس لكم على اثبات واجب الوجود دليل، الا قطع سلسلة العلل والمعلولات، كما سبق. وقد بيّنا ان قطع التسلسل ممكن بقديم متغيّر. والامر الثالث الذى يتضمّنه هذا هو كون القديم متغيّرا بغيره وان ذلك يشبه التسخّر واستيلاء الغير عليه، فيقال:

(٢٧) ولم يستحيل عندكم هذا وهو أن يكون هو سببا لحدوث الحوادث بوسائط، ثم يكون حدوث الحوادث سببا لحصول، العلم له بها؟ فكأنّه هو السبب فى تحصيل العلم لنفسه، ولكن بالوسائط. وقولكم انّ ذلك يشبه [التسخير]١٥، فليكن كذلك. فانّه لائق باصلكم اذ زعمتم

claim that what proceeds from God proceeds by way of necessity and [by] nature and that He has no power not to act. This also is similar to a kind of enforcement [imposed on Him] and indicates that He is akin to one compelled with respect to what proceeds from Him.

5   (28) If it is said, "This is not compulsion because His perfection consists in His being a source of all things," [we say:]

          (29) This [namely, His being the cause of realizing knowledge for Himself] is [also] not an enforcement. For His perfection consists in His knowledge of all things. If there would occur to us knowledge corre-

10   sponding to every temporal event, this would be a perfection for us, [and] neither a deficiency nor an enforcement [on us]. So let this be the case with respect to Him.

انّ ما يصدر من الله يصدر على سبيل اللزوم والطبع، ولا قدرة له على ان لا يفعل. وهذا أيضاً يشبه نوعا من [التسخير]١٦ ويشير الى انّه كالمضطرّ فى ما يصدر منه.

(٢٨) فان قيل: انّ ذلك ليس باضطرار لانّ كماله فى ان يكون مصدرا لجميع الاشياء.

(٢٩) فهذا ليس [بتسخير]١٧. فانّ كماله فى ان يعلم جميع الاشياء. ولو حصل لنا علم مقارن لكلّ حادث، لكان ذلك كمالا لنا لا نقصانا [وتسخيرا]١٧. فليكن كذلك فى حقّه.

[Fourteenth] Discussion

On their inability to set a proof [to show]
that heaven is an animal that obeys God,
the Exalted, through its circular motion

(1) They had said:

(2) Heaven is an animal, and it has a soul whose relation to the body of heaven is similar to the relation of our souls to our bodies. Just as our bodies move voluntarily toward their goals through [their being] moved by the soul, the same [is the case] with the heavens; and the purpose of the heavens in their essential motion is to worship the Lord of the worlds, in a manner we will be mentioning.

(3) Their doctrine in this question is one of those [views] whose possibility is not to be denied, nor its impossibility claimed. For God is capable of creating life in every body. For neither does the largeness of the body prevent its being animate, nor does its being circular. For the special shape is not a condition for life, since the animals, despite the differences in their shapes, share in their reception of life.

(4) We claim, however, that they are unable to know this through rational proof and that, if [what they maintain] is true, it would only be known to prophets through an inspiration from God or [through] revelation. The rational syllogism,[1] however, does not prove it. Yes, it is not improbable that the likes of this may become known through a proof, if proof were to be found and is helpful. But we say: "What they have brought forth as a proof is suitable only for the bestowal of an opinion; as to [the claim] that it bestows a conclusive [argument, the answer is], 'No.'"

مسئلة

فى تعجيزهم عن إقامة الدليل على أن السماء حيوان مطيع لله تعالى بحركته الدورية

(١) وقد قالوا:

(٢) انّ السماء حيوان وانّ له نفسا نسبته الى بدن السماء كنسبة نفوسنا الى ابداننا؛ وكما انّ ابداننا تتحرّك بالارادة نحو اغراضها بتحريك النفس، فكذى السموات؛ وانّ غرض السموات بحركتها الذاتيّة عبادة رب العالمين على وجه سنذكره.

(٣) ومذهبهم فى هذه المسئلة ممّا لا ينكر امكانه ولا يدّعى استحالته. فانّ الله قادر على ان يخلق الحياة فى كلّ جسم. فلا كبر الجسم يمنع من كونه حيا، ولا كونه مستديرا. فانّ الشكل المخصوص ليس شرطا للحياة، اذ الحيوانات مع اختلاف أشكالها مشتركة فى قبول الحياة.

(٤) ولكنّا ندّعى عجزهم عن معرفة ذلك بدليل العقل، وانّ هذا ان كان صحيحاً، فلا يطّلع عليه الا الانبياء بالهام من الله أو وحى. وقياس العقل ليس يدلّ عليه. نعم، لا يبعد ان يتعرّف مثل ذلك بدليل ان وجد الدليل وساعد؛ ولكنّا نقول ما أوردوهُ دليلا لا يصلح الا لافادة ظنّ؛ فامّا ان يفيد قطعا، فلا.

١٤٤

(5) Their confusion in this [lies in] that they said:

(6) Heaven is in motion, this being a premise based on sensory perception. Every body in motion has a mover. This is a rational premise, since if [a] body were to move by virtue of being [a] body, then every body would be in motion. Either every mover comes forth out of the essence of the thing in motion, as with the nature [of a thing] in the downward motion of the stone and [with] the will, together with power, in the motion of the animal; or else the mover is external but moves by compulsion, as with propelling a stone upwards. And everything that moves due to a notion in itself [is such] that that thing is either unaware of the motion—and this we call a nature, as with the downward motion of the stone—or is aware of it, and we call it voluntary and endowed with soul. Thus, motion, through these exhaustive divisions that revolve between negation and affirmation, becomes either natural, compulsory, or voluntary; and if two of these divisions are false, the third becomes assigned [as true].

(7) [Now, the mover] cannot be compulsory, because the mover by compulsion would be another body that is either moved voluntarily or by compulsion. This [forms a regress that] terminates necessarily with a will [that moves a body]. And once one establishes [that] a body among the heavenly bodies is moved by will, the objective [of the argument] is achieved. What use is there for positing compulsory motions, when in the end there is no escape from returning to the will? Alternatively, it may be said that [the heavenly body] moves by compulsion, God being the mover without mediation. But this is impossible, because if [the heavenly body], inasmuch as it is body, were moved by [God], He being its creator, then it follows necessarily that every body is moved. It is inevitable, then, that the movement would have a specific quality that differentiates [the heavenly body] from other bodies. This quality would then have to be the proximate mover, either voluntarily or by nature. [But] it is impossible to say that God moves it by will. This is because His will has the same relation to all bodies. Why, then, would this body, and not another, become specifically disposed for its motion to be willed? Nor can this [take place] as an arbitrary venture. For this is impossible, as previously [shown] in the question of the world's origin.

(٥) وخبالهم فيه ان قالوا:

(٦) السماء متحرّك وهذه مقدمة حسيّة. وكل جسم متحرّك فله محرّك، وهذه مقدمة عقلية، اذ لو كان الجسم يتحرّك لكونه جسما لكان كلّ جسم متحركا. وكل محرّك فامّا ان يكون منبعثا عن ذات المتحرك كالطبيعة فى حركة الحجر الى أسفل، والارادة فى حركة الحيوان مع القدرة، وامّا ان يكون المحرك خارجا ولكن يحرّك على طريق القسر كدفع الحجر الى فوق. وكلّ ما يتحرّك بمعنى فى ذاته، فامّا أن لا يشعر ذلك الشىء بالحركة، ونحن نسمّيه طبيعة، كحركة الحجر الى اسفل، وامّا ان يشعر به، ونحن نسمّيه اراديّا ونفسانيّا. فصارت الحركة بهذه التقسيمات الحاصرة الدائرة بين النفى والاثبات، امّا قسريّة واما طبيعيّة وامّا اراديّة، واذا بطل قسمان تعيّن الثالث.

(٧) ولا يمكن ان يكون قسريّا، لانّ المحرك القاسر امّا جسم آخر يتحرك بالارادة أو بالقسر، وينتهى لا محالة الى ارادة. ومهما اثبت فى اجسام السموات متحرك بالارادة، فقد حصل الغرض. فاىّ فائدة فى وضع حركات قسريّة، وبالآخرة لا بدّ من الرجوع الى الارادة. وامّا ان يقال: انّه يتحرك بالقسر، والله هو المحرك بغير واسطة. وهو محال لانّهُ لو تحرّك بهٖ من حيث انّه جسم وانّه خالقه، للزم ان يتحرّك كلّ جسم. فلا بدّ وان تختصّ الحركة بصفة يتميّز به عن غيره من الاجسام. وتلك الصفة هى المحرّك القريب امّا بالارادة أو الطبع، ولا يمكن ان يقال انّ الله يحرّكه بالارادة، لانّ ارادته تناسب الاجسام نسبة واحدة. فلم استعد هذا الجسم على الخصوص لان يراد تحريكه دون غيره؟ ولا يمكن ان يكون ذلك جزافا. فانّ ذلك محال كما سبق فى مسئلة حدث العالم.

(8) If, then, it is established that this [heavenly] body must have within it a quality which is the principle of motion, then the first alternative—namely, the supposition of a compulsory motion—becomes false. It remains, then, to say that [this intrinsic characteristic] is natural. But this is impossible, because nature by itself is never a cause of movement. This is because the meaning of motion is escape from one place and a seeking of another place. If the place in which the body exists is suitable, it would not move away from it. For this reason, a leather flask full of air placed on the surface of the water will not move, but if submerged [it] will move to the surface. For it would have found the suitable place and come to rest, the nature continuing to be there. But if [a body] is moved to an unsuitable place, it escapes to the suitable place, as [with the air-filled flask that] escapes from the midst of water to the place of air. It is inconceivable that the circular motion [of the heavenly body] is natural, because each position and place one supposes for [the body] to escape from [is something] to which it returns. And that from which one naturally escapes cannot be that which is naturally sought after. For this reason, the air flask does not go to the interior of the water, nor would the [flung] stone, after settling on earth, return to the air. Thus, the only remaining alternative is the third—namely, the voluntary motion.

(9) The objection [to this] is to say: "We will hypothesize three possible [alternatives] to your doctrine for which there is no demonstration [showing them] to be false."

(10) The first is to suppose the movement of heaven to be made compulsory by another body that wills its motion, rotating it perpetually. This body that moves [it] is neither a sphere nor a circumference. Hence, it would not be a heaven. Thus, their statement that the heavenly motion is voluntary and that the heaven is an animal becomes false. This which we have mentioned is possible, and [the only argument] for rejecting it is the mere deeming of it as unlikely.

(11) The second is to say that the motion is compulsory, its source being God's will. For we say: "The movement of the stone downward is also compulsory, originating by God's creating motion in it. The same is to be

(٨) واذا ثبت ان هذا الجسم ينبغى ان يكون فيه صفة هو مبدأ الحركة، بطل القسم الاول وهو تقدير الحركة القسريّة. فيبقى ان يقال هى طبيعيّة، وهو غير ممكن لانّ الطبيعة بمجرّدها قطّ لا تكون سببا للحركة، لانّ معنى الحركة هرب من مكان وطلب لمكان آخر. فالمكان الذى فيه الجسم ان كان ملائما له فلا يتحرّك عنه. ولهذا لا يتحرّك زقّ مملوء من الهواء على وجه الماء، واذا غمس فى الماء تحرّك الى وجه الماء. فانّه وجد المكان الملائم فسكن، والطبيعة قائمة. ولكن ان نقل الى مكان لا يلائمه هرب منه الى الملائم، كما هرب من وسط الماء الى حيّز الهواء. والحركة الدوريّة لا يتصوّر ان تكون طبيعيّة لانّ كلّ وضع وأين يفرض الهرب منه فهو عائد اليه. والمهروب عنه بالطبع لا يكون مطلوبا بالطبع. ولذلك لا ينصرف زقّ الهواء الى باطن الماء ولا الحجر ينصرف بعد الاستقرار على الارض فيعود الى [الهواء]¹. فلم يبق الا القسم الثالث وهى الحركة الارادية.

(٩) الاعتراض هو انّا نقول: نحن [نقدّر]² ثلث احتمالات سوى مذهبكم لا برهان على بطلانها.

(١٠) الاوّل: ان يقدّر حركة السماء قهرا لجسم آخر مريد لحركتها يديرها على الدوام. وذلك الجسم المحرك لا يكون كرة ولا يكون محيطا؛ فلا يكون سماء. فيبطل قولهم انّ حركة السماء اراديّة وان السماء حيوان. وهذا الذى ذكرناه ممكن، وليس فى دفعه الا مجرّد استبعاد.

(١١) الثانى هو ان يقال: الحركة قسريّة ومبدؤها ارادة الله. فانّا نقول: حركة الحجر الى أسفل أيضا قسرىّ [تحدث]³ بخلق الله الحركة

said of the motion of all inanimate bodies." There remains their [asking a question] rendering the matter unlikely, [namely:] "Why did the will attach specifically to that [body] when the rest of the bodies share corporeality with it?" But we have shown that the eternal will is such that its function is to specify one thing from its similar and that [the philosophers] are forced to affirm an attribute with such a function in assigning the direction of the circular motion and in assigning the place of the pole and node—hence, we will not repeat it. To put it briefly, what they deem unlikely regarding the specifying of a body in terms of the will's connection with it without [the latter's] being differentiated by an attribute is turned against them in [their] having [the body, in fact,] being differentiated by such an attribute. For we say: "Why is it that the heavenly body [in undergoing circular motion] has been distinguished by this attribute that differentiated it from other bodies, when the rest of the bodies are also bodies?" Why did this occur in it and not in another? If this is causally explained in terms of [the positing of] another attribute, the question is then directed toward this other attribute and would thus regress infinitely. In the end, they are forced to judge that there is a [discerning] will and that there exists among the principles that which distinguishes one thing from its similar, specifying it with a quality [distinguishing it] from its similars.

(12) The third is to concede that heaven is specified with a quality, that quality being the principle of motion, as they believe in the case of the stone's downward fall, but that, as with the stone, it is unaware of it. Moreover, their statement that that which is naturally sought after is not that from which one flees is obfuscation. For, according to them, there are no numerically separate places, there being only one body and the circular motion being one. For neither body has in actuality a [determinate] part, nor does movement have in actuality a part, but [these are] divided in the estimation. Hence, this motion is neither for the sake of seeking a place, nor for the sake of fleeing from a place. It is, hence, possible to create a body that has in itself a notion that requires circular movement, the movement itself being the requirement of that notion—not that the requirement of the notion is to seek after a place whereby there would be a motion for the purpose of moving toward it. If your statement that every motion is for the sake of seeking a place or escaping from it

فيه. وكذى القول فى سائر حركات الاجسام التى ليست حيوانيّة. فيبقى استبعادهم ان الارادة، لمَ اختصت به وسائر الاجسام تشاركها فى الجسميّة؟ فقد بيّنا انّ الارادة القديمة من شأنها تخصيص الشىء عن مثله وانّهم مضطرّون الى اثبات صفة هذا شأنها فى تعيين جهة الحركة الدوريّة

٥ وفى تعيين موضع القطب والنقطة، فلا نعيده. والقول الوجيز انّ ما استبعدوه فى اختصاص الجسم بتعلّق الارادة به من غير تميّز بصفة، ينقلب عليهم فى تميّزه بتلك الصفة. فانّا نقول: ولم تميّز جسم السماء بتلك الصفة التى بها فارق غيره من الاجسام وسائر الاجسام أيضا أجسام؟ فلمَ حصل فيه ما لم يحصل فى غيره؟ فان علّل ذلك بصفة أُخرى، توجّه

١٠ السؤال فى الصفة الآخرى، وهكذى يتسلسل الى غير نهاية. فيضطرّون بالآخرة الى [الحكم]؛ فى الارادة وانّ فى المبادئ ما يميّز الشىء عن مثله ويخصّصه بصفة عن أمثاله.

(١٢) الثالث: هو ان يسلّم انّ السماء [اختصت]° بصفة تلك الصفة مبدأ الحركة، كما اعتقدوه فى هوى الحجر الى أسفل، الا أنّه لا يشعر به

١٥ كالحجر. وقولهم ان المطلوب بالطبع لا يكون مهروبا عنه بالطبع فتلبيس. لانّهُ ليس ثمّ أماكن متفاصلة بالعدد عندهم، بل الجسم واحد والحركة الدوريّة واحدة، فلا للجسم جزء بالفعل، ولا للحركة جزء بالفعل، وانما [يتجزأ]° بالوهم. فليست تلك الحركة لطلب المكان ولا للهرب من المكان؛ فيمكن ان يخلق جسم وفى ذاته معنى يقتضى حركة

٢٠ دوريّة وتكون الحركة نفسها مقتضى ذلك المعنى، لا أن مقتضى المعنى طلب المكان، ثم تكون حركة للوصول اليه. وقولكم انّ كل حركة فهو لطلب مكان أو هرب منه اذا كان ضروريّا، فكأنّكم جعلتم طلب المكان

were necessary, it would be as though you have made the seeking of a place the requirement of the nature and have rendered movement not intended in itself, but only a means to [reaching the place]. We, however, say that it is not unlikely that the motion is the very requirement [of the notion and is] not for the purpose of seeking a place. What makes this impossible?

(13) It has thus become clear that, even if one thinks that what they have mentioned is more probable than another supposition, it does not follow as a conclusive certainty that another [hypothesis] would have to be denied. Hence, [their] judgment that heaven is an animal is a purely arbitrary [assertion] that has no support.

مقتضى الطبع، وجعلتم الحركة غير مقصودة فى نفسها، بل وسيلة اليه. ونحن نقول: لا يبعد ان تكون الحركة نفس المقتضى، لا لطلب مكان. فما الذى يحيل ذلك؟

(١٣) فاستبان انّ ما ذكروه ان ظنّ انّه أغلب من احتمال آخر، فلا يتيقّن قطعا انتفاء غيره. فالحكم على السماء بانّه حيوان تحكّم محض، لا مستند له.

[Fifteenth] Discussion

*On refuting what they mentioned concerning
the purpose that moves heaven*

(1) They said: "Heaven, through its motion, obeys God and seeks to draw nigh to Him because every motion that is voluntary is for an end; for it is inconceivable that action and movement should proceed from an animal unless it is more suitable for [the animal] to act than to refrain [from the act]. Otherwise, if action and refraining from action were on a par, action would be inconceivable. Moreover, to seek closeness to God does not mean to solicit [His] satisfaction and to take precaution against [His] wrath. For God's sanctity is above wrath and satisfaction [with His creatures]. If these expressions are used, [they are used] by way of metaphor to express the intent to punish and the intent to reward. Nor is it permissible that endeavoring to draw near to God consists in seeking spatial closeness to Him, for this is impossible. Thus, there only remains the seeking of closeness to Him in terms of [His] attributes. For the most perfect existence is His, every existence being deficient in relation to His existence. Deficiency has degrees and disparities. The angel is closer to Him in terms of attributes, not of space. This is what is meant by 'the angels drawn close to Him'; that is, the intellectual substances that neither change, perish, nor undergo transformation and that know things as they [really] are. And as man becomes closer to the angels in terms of attributes, he becomes closer to God. The ultimate that the class of men can reach is [to become] similar to the angels."

(2) If it is established that this is the meaning of seeking closeness to God, [this] then reduces to seeking closeness to Him in terms of attributes. This, for the human, consists in his knowing the realities of things and

– 149 –

مسئلة

فى ابطال ما ذكروه من الغرض المحرّك للسماء

(١) وقد قالوا: انّ السماء [مطيعة]١ لله [بحركتها]٢ ومتقرّب اليه لانّ
كلّ حركة بالارادة [فهي]٣ لغرض، اذ لا يتصوّر ان يصدر الفعل والحركة
من حيوان الا اذا كان الفعل أولى به من الترك. والا فلو استوى الفعل
والترك، لما تصوّر الفعل. ثم التقرّب الى الله ليس معناه طلب [الرضى]٤
والحذر من السخط. فانّ الله يتقدس عن السخط [والرضى]٥، وان
[أطلقت]٦ هذه الالفاظ، فعلى سبيل المجاز، يكنى بها عن ارادة العقاب
وارادة الثواب. ولا يجوز ان يكون التقرّب بطلب القرب منه فى المكان؛
فانّه محال. فلا يبقى الا طلب القرب فى الصفات. فانّ الوجود الاكمل
وجوده، وكلّ وجود فبالاضافة الى وجوده ناقص. وللنقصان درجات
وتفاوت. فالملك أقرب اليه صفة، لا مكانا. وهو المراد بالملائكة المقرّبين،
أى الجواهر العقليّة الّتى لا تتغيّر ولا تفنى ولا تستحيل، وتعلم الاشياء على
ما هى عليه. والانسان كلّما ازداد قربا من الملك فى الصفات، ازداد قربا
من الله. ومنتهى طبقة الآدميين التشبّه بالملائكة.

(٢) واذا ثبت انّ هذا معنى التقرّب الى الله، [فانّه]٧ يرجع الى طلب
القرب منه فى الصفات. وذلك للآدمى بان يعلم حقائق الاشياء وبان يبقى

١٤٩

his remaining [after death] eternally in the most perfect state that is possible for him. For eternal existence in the most perfect state belongs to
God [alone]. All the perfection that is possible for the angels that are close
to God is [ever] present to them in existence, since nothing [of this per-
fection] is in potency so as to change into actuality. Hence, their perfection
is of the highest degree, [but only] in relation to what is other than God.

(3) The "celestial angels" is an expression denoting the souls that
move the heavens. They have within them what is potential. Their perfection divides into that which is actual, such as spherical shape and
configuration, which are [ever] present, and that which is in potency—
namely, [their] appearance in [terms of] position and place. No determinate position [in the circular movement] is possible [for the spherical
form]. It does not, however, cover the rest of the positions [other than
the one it occupies in actuality]. For encompassing all [positions at once]
is impossible. And since it cannot at one time completely [encompass]
the individual positions, it seeks to fulfill [or encompass] them [as] a
species. Hence, it continues to seek one position after another, and one
place after another, this possibility never ending; and, as such, these
motions never end. Its aim is to imitate the First Principle by attaining
the utmost perfection according to [what is] possible with respect to
Him. This is the meaning of the heavenly angels' obedience to God. This
is realized for them in two ways. One is the complete encompassing of
every possible position [as] a species, this being what is intended by the
first intention. The second is the order dependent on its movement
by way of the difference in relations in triangularity, squareness, conjunction, and opposition and the differences in the astral ascendants in
relation to the earth. Consequently, the good emanates from it onto the
sublunary sphere, and all these events come about through it. This, then,
is the way the heavenly soul is perfected. Every rational soul is in itself
desirous of perfection.

بقاءً مؤبّدًا على أكمل أحواله [الممكنة]^ له. فانّ البقاء على الكمال الاقصى هو لله. والملائكة المقرّبون كلّ ما يمكن لهم من الكمال، فهو حاضر معهم فى الوجود، اذ ليس فيهم شىء بالقوة حتى يخرج الى الفعل. فاذن كمالهم فى الغاية القصوى بالاضافة الى ما سوى الله.

٥ (٣) والملائكة السماويّة هى عبارة عن النفوس المحرّكة للسموات. وفيها ما بالقوّة. وكمالاتها منقسمة الى ما هو بالفعل كالشكل الكرىّ والهيئة، وذلك حاضر، والى ما هو بالقوة، وهو الهيئة فى الوضع والاين. وما من وضع معين الا وهو ممكن له. ولكن ليست له سائر الاوضاع بالفعل؛ فانّ الجمع بين جميعها غير ممكن. فلمّا لم يمكنها استيفاء آحاد

١٠ الاوضاع على الدوام قصد استيفاءها بالنوع. فلا يزال يطلب وضعاً بعد وضع وأيناً بعد أين ولا ينقطع قطّ هذا الامكان فلا تنقطع هذه الحركات. وانّما قصده التشبّه بالمبدا الاول فى نيل الكمال الاقصى على حسب الامكان فى حقّه وهو معنى طاعة الملائكة السماويّة لله. وقد حصل لها التشبّه من وجهين: أحدهما: استيفاء كلّ وضع ممكن له بالنوع وهو

١٥ المقصود بالقصد الاول؛ والثانى: ما يترتب على حركته من اختلاف النسب فى التثليث والتربيع والمقارنة والمقابلة واختلاف الطوالع بالنسبة الى الارض. فيفيض منه الخير على ما تحت فلك القمر ويحصل منه هذه الحوادث كلّها. فهذا وجه استكمال النفس السماويّة. وكلّ نفس عاقلة فمتشوقة الى الاستكمال بذاتها.

(4) The objection to this is that the premises of this discourse include that which one can dispute. We will not, however, prolong matters with this, returning [instead] to the purpose you specified at the end and refuting it in two ways.

(5) One of them is that seeking to perfect oneself by being in every place that is possible for one [to be] is folly, not obedience. This [resembles] nothing [so much as] a human who, having nothing to do and having satisfied the needs of his appetites and wants, arises and begins to move around in a town or a house and claims that he is drawing near to God. For [according to him] he attains perfection by realizing for himself presence in every possible place. He [further] claims that being in [different] places "is possible for me, but I cannot combine them numerically, so I will encompass them [as a] species; for in this there is a perfecting [of oneself] and a drawing close [to God]." As such, his reasoning in this would be adjudged folly, and he would be deemed foolish. It would be said, "Moving from one realm to another and from one place to another is not a perfection that is significant or desirable." There is no difference between what they have said and this.

(6) The second is that we say:

(7) What you have mentioned of the purpose is attainable by the [celestial] movement from the west to the east. Why, then, is the first movement from the east, and why are not the movements of everything in one direction? If there is a purpose in their variance, why would they not vary [when the movement is] reversed such that movements from the east become movements from the west and those from the west from the east? For all that they have stated regarding the occurrence of events through the differences of motions by way of being threefold and sixfold and so on are obtainable through their reverse. The same applies to what they have said regarding completing the encompassing of positions and places. And why [not], when motion in the opposite direction is possible for it? Why does it not move from one side at one time and from another at another time in fulfillment of what is possible for it, if there is perfection in the fulfillment of all possibilities? [All this] indicates that these

(٤) والاعتراض على هذا هو انّ فى مقدمات هذا الكلام ما يمكن النزاع فيه. ولكنّا لا نطوّل بهِ ونعود الى الغرض الذى عيّنتموه اخِراً ونبطله من وجهين:

(٥) احدهما: ان طلب الاستكمال بالكون فى كلّ أين يمكن ان يكون له حماقة لا طاعة. وما هذا الا كانسان لم يكن له شغل وقد كفى المؤونة فى شهواته وحاجاته فقام وهو يدور فى بلد أو بيت ويزعم انّه يتقرّب الى الله. فانّه يستكمل بان يحصّل لنفسه الكون فى كل مكان أمكن؛ وزعم ان الكون فى الاماكن ممكن لى، ولست أقدر على الجمع بينها بالعدد، فاستوفيه بالنوع، فانّ فيه استكمالا وتقرّبا. فيسفّه عقله فيه ويحمل على الحماقة، ويقال: الانتقال من حيّز الى حيّز ومن مكان الى مكان ليس كمالا يعتدّ به أو يتشوف اليه. ولا فرق بين ما ذكروه وبين هذا.

(٦) والثانى هو انّا نقول:

(٧) ما ذكرتموه من الغرض حاصل بالحركة المغربيّة. فلمَ كانت الحركة الاولى مشرقيّة، وهلا كانت حركات الكلّ الى جهة واحدة؟ فان كان فى اختلافها غرض، فهلا اختلفت بالعكس، فكانت التى هى مشرقيّة مغربيّة، والتى هى مغربيّة مشرقيّة؟ فانّ كل ما ذكروه من حصول الحوادث باختلاف الحركات من التثليثات والتسديسات وغيرها يحصل بعكسه. وكذى ما ذكروه من استيفاء الاوضاع والايون. كيف، ومن الممكن لها الحركة الى الجهة الآخرى. فما بالها لا تتحرّك مرّة من جانب ومرّة من جانب استيفاء لما يمكن لها ان كان فى استيفاء كلّ ممكن كمال؟ فدلّ انّ هذه خيالات لا حاصل لها وانّ اسرار ملكوت السموات لا

are imaginings that achieve nothing, and that the secrets of the heavenly
kingdom are not known with the likes of these imaginings. God makes
them known only to his prophets and saints by way of inspiration, not by
way of inferential proof. For this reason, the philosophers to their last
have been unable to show the reason for the direction of the [celestial]
motion and for its choice.

(8) Some of them, however, have said:

(9) Since their perfection is realized through motion, from whatever
direction it is, and the ordering of the terrestrial events calls for diversity
in movements and the determination of directions, the motive prompting
them toward the [very] principle of motion is the quest after proximity
to God, and the motive for the direction of the movement is the emanation of the good on the lower world.

(10) [We answer that] this is false in two respects. One is that if it
is possible to imagine this, then let it be judged that the requirement of
the nature [of the heaven] is rest in avoidance of motion and change,
which in true ascertainment would be imitating God. For He is sanctified
above change, motion being change. He, however, has chosen motion
for the purpose of emanating the good. For this is of benefit for others,
while motion neither burdens nor tires Him. What is there to prevent
such an imagining?

(11) The second is that events are based on the variations in the
relations generated by the differences in the directions of motions. Let,
then, the first motion be western and the rest eastern, through which
differences and hierarchies of relations come about. Why, then, has one
direction been determined? These differences require only the principle
of these changes. A determinate direction, however, has no priority over
its opposite in [the accomplishment of such an] end.

يطّلع عليه بامثال هذه الخيالات. وانّما يطلع الله عليه انبياءه وأولياءه على سبيل الالهام لا على سبيل الاستدلال. ولذلك عجز الفلاسفة من عند آخرهم عن بيان السبب فى جهة الحركة واختيارها.

(٨) وقال بعضهم:

(٩) لمّا كان استكمالها يحصل بالحركة من أىّ جهة كانت، وكان انتظام الحوادث الارضيّة يستدعى اختلاف حركات وتعيّن جهات، كان الداعى لها الى أصل الحركة التقرّب الى الله، والداعى الى جهة الحركة افاضة الخير على العالم السفلىّ.

(١٠) وهذا باطل من وجهين: أحدهما انّ ذلك ان أمكن ان يتخيّل فليقض بان مقتضى طبعه السكون احترازاً عن الحركة والتغيّر وهو التشبه بالله على التحقيق. فانّه مقدّس عن التغيّر، والحركة تغيّر. ولكنّه اختار الحركة لافاضة الخير، فانّه كان ينتفع به غيره وليس يثقل عليه الحركة وليس تتعبه، فما المانع من هذا الخيال؟

(١١) والثانى انّ الحوادث تنبنى على اختلاف النسب المتولّدة من اختلاف جهات الحركات، فلتكن الحركة الاولى مغربيّة وما عداها مشرقيّة وقد حصل به الاختلاف ويحصل به تفاوت النسب. فلمَ تعيّنت جهة واحدة؟ وهذه الاختلافات لا تستدعى الا أصل الاختلاف. فامّا جهة بعينها فليس باولى من نقيضها فى هذا الغرض.

[Sixteenth] Discussion

On refuting their statement that the souls of the heavens
know all the particulars that occur in this world;
that what is meant by "the preserved tablet" [Qur'ān 85:22]
is the souls of the heavens; that the impression of the
world's particulars in them is similar to the impressions of
the retained [images] in the retentive faculty entrusted in the
human brain, not that the [preserved tablet] is a solid
wide body on which things are inscribed in the way boys
write on a slate, since the abundance of this writing requires
a widening of the thing written on and, if the thing
written is infinite, the thing written on would have to
be infinite—but an infinite body is inconceivable, and it
is impossible to have infinite lines on a body, and it is
impossible to make known infinite things with limited lines

(1) They claim that the heavenly angels are the celestial souls and that the cherubim that are drawn close [to God] are the pure intelligences that are self-subsisting substances that do not occupy space and do not administer bodies; that these particular forms emanate from [the celestial intelligences] onto the celestial souls; that [pure intelligences] are nobler than heavenly angels because they are bestowers, whereas [the latter] are bestowed upon, the bestower being nobler than the bestowed upon. For

مسئلة

فى ابطال قولهم انّ نفوس السموات مطّلعة على جميع الجزئيّات الحادثة فى هذا العالم، وانّ المراد باللوح المحفوظ نفوس السموات، وانّ انتقاش جزئيّات العالم فيها يضاهى انتقاش المحفوظات فى القوّة الحافظة المودعة فى دماغ الانسان، لا انّه جسم صلب عريض مكتوب عليه الاشياء كما يكتبه الصبيان على اللوح، لانّ تلك الكتابة يستدعى كثرتها اتساع المكتوب عليه، واذا لم يكن للمكتوب نهاية، لم يكن للمكتوب عليه نهاية؛ ولا يتصوّر جسم لا نهاية له ولا يمكن خطوط لا نهاية لها على جسم، ولا يمكن تعريف أشياء لا نهاية لها بخطوط معدودة.

(١) وقد زعموا انّ الملائكة السماويّة هى نفوس السموات، وانّ الملائكة الكروبيّين المقرّبين هى العقول المجرّدة التى هى جواهر قائمة بانفسها لا تتحيّز ولا تتصرف فى الاجسام؛ وانّ هذه الصور الجزئيّة تفيض على النفوس السماويّة منها، وهى أشرف من الملائكة السماويّة

this reason the nobler has been expressed [by the term] "the pen," so that God has said, "He taught by the pen" [Qur'ān 96:44], because it is like the one who etches, who bestows [knowledge] as the teacher [bestows it], and He likened the bestowed upon to the tablet. This is their doctrine.

(2) The dispute in this question differs from the one which preceded it. For what they had stated earlier is not impossible, since at most [it says] that heaven is an animal that moves for a purpose—and this is possible. But this [question, in the final analysis,] ends up in affirming a creature's knowledge of particulars that are infinite. And this is [something] whose impossibility one may well believe. We thus ask them for proof of it. [As it stands,] it is in itself sheer arbitrary [assertion].

(3) For proof of this they say:

(4) It has been established that the circular motion is voluntary, the will following the thing willed.[1] To the thing willed that is a universal, only a universal will is directed. Nothing, however, proceeds from the universal will. For every existent that is actual is [something] determinate, a particular. The relation of the universal will to [each] one of the particulars is of one [uniform] pattern. Hence, nothing particular proceeds from it. Rather, there must be for the designated motion a particular will. For in the heavenly sphere, for every designated particular movement from one point to another, there is a particular will for that motion. It thus necessarily has a representation[2] of particular motions by a bodily faculty, since particulars are apprehended only by bodily faculties. For it is a necessity [inherent] in every will that it [undergo] a representational apprehension[3] of that thing which is willed; that is, [it has] knowledge of it, regardless of whether [the thing willed] is particular or universal. And as long as the celestial sphere has a representation of the particular motions and knowledge of them, it must comprehend what necessarily follows from them by way of differing relations to the earth, in having some parts [of the heavens] rising, some waning, some being at the center of the sky of some folk and [conversely] beneath the feet of [another] folk. Likewise, it knows what necessarily follows by way of the different relations that are renewed through motion, such as being threefold and

لأنّها مفيدة، وهى مستفيدة، والمفيد أشرف من المستفيد. ولذلك عبّر عن الاشرف بالقلم، فقال تعالى، «علّم بالقلم»، لانّه كالنقاش المفيد مثل المعلّم، وشبّه المستفيد باللوح. هذا مذهبهم.

(٢) والنزاع فى هذه المسئلة يخالف النزاع فيما قبلها. فانّ ما ذكروه من قبل ليس محالا، اذ منتهاه كون السماء حيوانا متحرّكا لغرض، وهو ممكن. أمّا هذه [فيرجع]١ الى اثبات علم لمخلوق بالجزئيّات التى لا نهاية لها. وهذا ربّما يعتقد استحالته. فنطالبهم بالدليل عليه. فانّه تحكّم فى نفسه.

(٣) استدلوا فيه بأن قالوا:

(٤) ثبت انّ الحركة الدوريّة إراديّة، والارادة تتبع المراد، والمراد الكلّىّ لا يتوجّه اليه الا ارادة كلّيّة، والارادة الكلّيّة لا يصدر منها شىء. فانّ كلّ موجود بالفعل معيّن جزئىّ. والارادة الكلّيّة نسبتها الى آحاد الجزئيّات على وتيرة واحدة، فلا يصدر عنها شىء جزئىّ. بل لا بدّ من ارادة جزئيّة للحركة المعيّنة. فللفلك بكلّ حركة جزئية معيّنة من نقطة الى نقطة معيّنة ارادة جزئيّة لتلك الحركة. فله لا محالة تصور لتلك الحركات الجزئيّة بقوّة جسمانيّة، اذ الجزئيّات لا تدرك الا بالقوى الجسمانية. فانّ كلّ ارادة فمن ضرورتها تصوّر لذلك المراد، أى علم به سواء كان جزئيّا او كلّيّا. ومهما كان للفلك تصوّر لجزئيّات الحركات واحاطة بها، احاط لا محالة بما يلزم منها من اختلاف النسب مع الارض من كون بعض اجزائه طالعة، وبعضها غاربة، وبعضها فى وسط سماء قوم، وتحت قدم قوم؛ وكذلك يعلم ما يلزم من اختلاف النسب التى تتجدّد بالحركة من التثليث والتسديس والمقابلة والمقارنة، الى غير ذلك من الحوادث

sixfold, [or being] in opposition, conjunction, and so on to the rest of the celestial events. All of the terrestrial events depend on the celestial events, either without an intermediary, through one intermediary, or through many intermediaries.

5   (5) In brief, every event has a temporal cause, until the chain of causes terminates with the eternal celestial motion, where each part is a cause for another. Hence, the causes and effects in their chain terminate with the particular celestial motions. Thus, that which has a representation of the movements has a representation of their consequences and 10 the consequences of their consequences, to the end of the chain. In this way, what will happen is known. For [in the case of] everything that will happen, its occurrence is a necessary consequence of its cause, once the cause is realized. We do not know what will happen in the future only because we do not know all the causes [of the future effects]. If we were 15 to know all the causes, we would know all the effects. For once we know, for example, that fire will contact cotton at a specific time, we would know the burning of the cotton. And once we know that an individual will eat, we would know that he will be satiated. And if we know that a person will step across such and such a place in which is a treasure covered by some 20 light thing such that if a pedestrian walks over it his foot would stumble over the treasure and would recognize it, we would then know that he will become rich by finding the treasure. But we do not know these causes. Sometimes we may know some of them, whereby we would have an intuition of the occurrence of the effect. If we know the more frequent 25 and the greater number of [the causes], we would acquire a clear, [well-founded] opinion [regarding the effects'] occurrence.[4] If knowledge of all the causes were to occur to us, knowledge of all the effects would occur to us. But the celestial [events] are numerous. Moreover, they have an admixture with terrestrial events. It is not within human power to know 30 them, whereas the celestial souls know them because they know the First Cause, the consequences [of their own occurrences], and the consequences of their consequences, to the end of the chain.

    (6) For this reason they claimed that the sleeper sees in his sleep what will happen in the future—this [taking place] through his contact 35 with "the preserved tablet" and viewing it. Whenever he sees something, that very thing may remain in his memory. Sometimes, however, the

السماويّة. وسائر الحوادث الارضيّة تستند الى الحوادث السماويّة، امّا بغير واسطة، وامّا بواسطة واحدة، وامّا بوسائط كثيرة.

(٥) وعلى الجملة، فكلّ حادث فله سبب حادث الى ان ينقطع التسلسل بالارتقاء الى الحركة السماويّة الابديّة التى بعضها سبب للبعض. فاذن الاسباب والمسبّبات فى سلسلتها تنتهى الى الحركات الجزئية السماويّة. فالمتصوّر للحركات متصوّر للوازمها ولوازم لوازمها الى آخر السلسلة. فبهذا يطّلع على ما يحدث. فانّ كلّ ما سيحدث، فحدوثه واجب عن علّته مهما تحقّقت العلّة. ونحن انّما لا نعلم ما يقع فى المستقبل لانّا لا نعلم جميع أسبابها. ولو علمنا جميع الاسباب، لعلمنا المسبّبات. فانّا مهما علمنا انّ النار [ستلتقى]٢ بالقطن مثلاً فى وقت معيّن، فنعلم احتراق القطن. ومهما علمنا انّ شخصاً سيأكل، فنعلم انّه سيشبع؛ واذا علمنا انّ شخصاً سيتخطّى الموضع الفلانىّ الذى فيه كنز مغطى بشىء خفيف، اذا مشى عليه الماشى تعثّر رجله بالكنز وعرفه، فنعلم انّه سيستغنى بوجود الكنز، ولكن هذه الاسباب لا نعلمها. وربّما نعلم بعضها، فيقع لنا حدس بوقوع المسبّب. فان عرفنا أغلبها وأكثرها، حصل لنا ظنّ ظاهر بالوقوع. فلو حصل لنا العلم بجميع الاسباب، لحصل بجميع المسبّبات. الا انّ السماويّات كثيرة. ثمّ لها اختلاط بالحوادث الارضيّة، وليس فى القوة البشريّة الاطلاع عليه، ونفوس السموات مطّلعة عليها لاطلاعها على السبب الاوّل، ولوازمها، ولوازم لوازمها، الى اخر السلسلة.

(٦) ولهذا زعموا يرى النائم فى نومه ما يكون فى المستقبل، وذلك باتصاله باللوح المحفوظ ومطالعته. ومهما اطلع على الشىء، ربّما بقى

imaginative faculty may hasten to imitate it. For by its innate nature, [its function is the] imitating of things through examples that have some correspondence to them or else the transferring of them to their opposite, whereby the truly apprehended thing is erased from the memory,
5   the imaged example [alone] remaining in the memory. Hence, there is a need for interpreting what the imagination symbolizes; for example, a man may be exemplified by trees, a wife by a shoe, a servant by some of the household utensils, the trustee of pious property and alms by the oil of seeds—for the seeds constitute a cause for the lamp, which is the
10   cause of illumination. The science of [dream] interpretation branches out from this principle. They [also] claimed that the contact with these [celestial] souls is openly given, since [at the time of sleep] there is no veil, but that in our waking hours we are preoccupied with what the senses and the appetites bring to us. Thus, our preoccupation with these
15   sensory matters diverts us from [this contact]. When, during sleep, some of the preoccupation with the senses falls off, then there comes about with it some disposition toward the contact.[5]

(7) [In addition,] they claimed that the prophet has knowledge of the unknown also in this way, except that the prophetic psychological
20   faculty can attain such strength that the external senses do not submerge it. No wonder, then, that he perceives while awake what others see in sleep. The imaginative faculty, moreover, makes for him representations of what he sees. Sometimes the very thing remains in his memory, sometimes [only] its symbol, whereby this inspiration requires [meta-
25   phorical] interpretation, just as that which resembles it in sleep requires [dream] interpretation. If it were not the case that all beings firmly exist in "the preserved tablet," the prophets would not know the unseen, either in wakefulness or in sleep. But the pen runs dry in recording all of what would be until the date of the resurrection. The meaning of this
30   is what we have stated.

(8) This, then, is what we wanted to convey in explaining [the philosophers'] doctrine.

(9) The answer is to say:

(10) With what [argument] would you deny someone who says that
35   the prophet knows the hidden through God's apprising him of it by way of [direct] initiation? The same applies to someone who has a vision in his

ذلك بعينه فى حفظه؛ وربما تسارعت القوّة المتخيّلة الى محاكاتها. فانّ من
غريزتها محاكاتها الاشياء بامثلة تناسبها بعض المناسبة، أو الانتقال منها الى
أضدادها، فينمحى المدرك الحقيقىّ عن الحفظ ويبقى مثال الخيال فى
الحفظ. فيحتاج الى تعبير ما يمثّل الخيال، [كما يمثّل]² الرجل بشجر،
والزوجة بخفّ، والخادم ببعض أوانى الدار، وحافظ مال البرّ والصدقات

٥

بزيت البذر؛ فانّ البذر سبب للسراج الذى هو سبب الضياء. وعلم التعبير
يتشعّب عن هذا الاصل. وزعموا ان الاتصال بتلك النفوس مبذول، اذ
ليس ثمّ حجاب، ولكنّا فى يقظتنا مشغولون بما تورده الحواس
والشهوات علينا. فاشتغالنا بهذه الامور الحسّيّة صرفنا عنه. واذا سقط
عنّا فى النوم بعض اشتغال الحواس، ظهر به استعداد ما للاتصال.

١٠

(٧) وزعموا انّ النبىّ مطّلع على الغيب بهذا الطريق أيضا، الا انّ القوّة
النفسيّة النبويّة قد تقوى قوّة لا تستغرقها الحواسّ الظاهرة. فلا جرم يرى
هو فى اليقظة ما يراه غيره فى المنام. ثم القوّة الخيالية تمثّل له أيضاً ما رآه.
وربّما يبقى الشىء بعينه فى ذكره وربّما يبقى مثاله، فيفتقر مثل هذا الوحى
الى التأويل، كما يفتقر مثل ذلك المنام الى التعبير. ولولا انّ جميع الكائنات

١٥

ثابتة فى اللوح المحفوظ، لما عرف الانبياء الغيب فى يقظة ولا منام. لكن
جفّ القلم بما هو كائن الى يوم القيامة. ومعناه هذا الذى ذكرناه.

(٨) فهذا ما أردنا ان نورده لتفهيم مذهبهم.

(٩) والجواب ان نقول:

(١٠) بم تنكرون على من يقول انّ النبىّ يعرف الغيب بتعريف الله
على سبيل الابتداء؟ وكذى من يرى فى المنام فانّما يعرفه بتعريف الله، أو

٢٠

sleep who only knows [the hidden] through his being apprised [of it] by God or one of the angels. There is no need for any of the things you [philosophers] have mentioned, for there is no proof in this. Nor do you have a proof [for your interpretation] of what the religious law conveyed

5   regarding "the tablet" and "the pen." For the people versed in the law do not understand by "the tablet" and "the pen" the meaning [you have given to these terms] at all. Consequently, there is nothing for you to cling to [for your interpretation] in the religious law. [The only thing that] remains [for you] to cling to is the ways of reason. But the existence of

10   what you have mentioned—even if one acknowledges its possibility (as long as this [acknowledgment] is not conditional on the denial of the finitude of these objects of knowledge)—is not known and its being is not ascertained. The only way [for this] to be known would be from the religious law, not through reason.

15   (11) Regarding what you have first mentioned by way of rational proof, this is built on many premises, for which [reason] we will not prolong matters [by] refuting [all of them]. We will confine ourselves to disputing three premises of these.

(12) The first premise is your statement that the heavenly move-
20   ment is voluntary. But we have [already] finished with this question and [with] refuting the claim you made for it.

(13) The second is that even if, for the sake of being tolerant, one concedes this [view of the voluntary movement of the heavens], your statement that [the heavens] need a particular representation of the
25   particular motions is [a premise that is] not conceded. Rather, according to you, [the spherical] body does not have a part, since it is one thing and is only rendered divisible within the faculty of estimation—nor does [the circular] motion, for it is one in being continuous. Hence, the desire [of the celestial soul]⁶ suffices to [make the celestial body] complete,
30   [traversing all] the places that are possible for it, as [the philosophers] have mentioned. Universal representation and a universal will are sufficient for [the continuous circular motion of the heavens].

(14) Let us, then, represent the universal and the particular will by an example to explain [the philosophers'] intention. If a human, for exam-
35   ple, has a universal purpose to make a pilgrimage to the house of God, from this universal will no motion will proceed. This is because motion occurs as [something] particular in a determined direction, having a determined quantity. Indeed, there continues to be renewed for man in his traveling to the house [of God] one [mental] representation after
40   another for the place he will pass and the direction he will take, each

بتعريف ملك من الملائكة، فلا يحتاج الى شىءٍ ممّا ذكرتموه. فلا دليل فى هذا، ولا دليل لكم فى ورود الشرع باللوح والقلم. فانّ أهل الشرع لم يفهموا من اللوح والقلم هذا المعنى قطعا. فلا متمسّك [لكم]ٔ فى الشرعيّات. [ويبقى]ٔ التمسّك بمسالك العقول. وما ذكرتموه، وان اعترف بامكانه، مهما لم يشترط نفى النهاية عن هذه المعلومات، فلا يعرف وجوده، ولا يتحقّق كونه. وانّما السبيل فيه ان يتعرّف من الشرع لا من العقل.

(١١) وأمّا ما ذكرتموه من الدليل العقلىّ أوّلاً، فمبنىّ على مقدّمات كثيرة لسنا نطول بابطالها. ولكنّا ننازع فى ثلث مقدّمات منها.

(١٢) المقدمة الاولى: قولكم انّ حركة السماء اراديّة؛ وقد فرغنا من هذه المسئلة وابطال دعواكم فيها.

(١٣) الثانية انّه ان سلّم ذلك مسامحة به، فقولكم انّه يفتقر الى تصوّر جزئى للحركات الجزئيّة، فغير مسلّم. بل ليس ثمّ جزء عندكم فى الجسم، فانّه شىء واحد، وانما يتجزّأ بالوهم. ولا فى الحركة؛ فانّها واحدة بالاتصال. فيكفى تشوقها الى استيفاء الايون الممكنة لها كما ذكروه، ويكفيها التصوّر الكلّىّ والارادة الكلّيّة.

(١٤) ولنمثّل للارادة الكلّيّة والجزئيّة مثالا لتفهيم غرضهم. فاذا كان للانسان غرض كلّىّ فى أن يحج بيت الله مثلاً، فهذه الارادة الكلّيّة لا يصدر منها الحركة، لان الحركة تقع جزئيّة فى جهة مخصوصة بمقدار مخصوص. بل لا يزال يتجدّد للانسان فى توجّه الى البيت تصوّر بعد تصوّر للمكان الذى يتخطّاه، والجهة التى يسلكها، ويتبع كل تصوّر جزئى ارادة جزئيّة للحركة عن المحلّ الموصول اليه بالحركة. فهذا ما أرادوه بالارادة الجزئيّة التابعة للتصوّر الجزئىّ.

particular representation being followed by a particular will to move from the place [already] reached through [a previous] motion. This is what they meant by the particular will that follows the particular representation.

(15) One concedes this because the directions in going to Mecca are many, the distance not determined. Thus, [each act of] determining one place after another and one direction after another requires another [renewed] particular will. But in the case of the heavenly movement, it has only one direction. For the sphere revolves around itself and in its space, not going beyond it, and the movement is willed. There is, moreover, nothing but one movement, one body, and one direction. This is similar to the fall of the stone downward. For it seeks the earth in the shortest way, the shortest way being the straight line. The straight line is determined, and it has no inherent need for the renewal of a temporal cause other than the universal nature that seeks the center, together with the renewal of proximity and remoteness, arriving at a limit and proceeding from it. Similarly, in this [heavenly] motion the universal will is sufficient for the motion and does not need anything more. Hence, this is a premise[7] which [the philosophers] posited arbitrarily.

(16) The third premise—which is arbitrary in the extreme—is their statement that, if [the celestial sphere] forms representations of the particular motions, it also forms representations of their attendants and necessary consequences. This is pure insanity, as when one says, "If a human moves and knows his movement, he must know what follows necessarily from his movement in terms of being parallel and not parallel, these being his relation to the bodies that are above him, below him, and to his sides; that if he walks in the sun he ought to know the places on which his shadow falls and those where it does not fall and what occurs as a result of his shadow by way of coolness through the obstructing of the sun's rays in these places; [that he must know] what occurs by way of pressure on the parts of the earth under his foot and what happens in terms of separation in them; [that he must know] what happens to his humors internally in terms of change toward heat due to [his] motion, and what of his parts changes into sweat, and so on to all the happenings in his body, and in other than it, for which [his] movement constitutes a cause, a condition, a preparation, a disposition." This is insanity which no rational being can imagine, [but] only the ignorant being deceived by it. It is to this that [their] arbitrary assertion reduces.

(١٥) وهو مسلّم لانّ الجهات متعدّدة فى التوجّه الى مكّة، والمسافة غير متعيّنة؛ فيفتقر تعيّن مكان عن مكان وجهة عن جهة الى ارادة أُخرى جزئيّة. وأمّا الحركة السماويّة فلها [جهة واحدة]. فانّ الكرة انّما تتحرّك على نفسها وفى حيّزها والحركة مرادة. وليس ثمّ الا [جهة واحدة] وجسم واحد وصوب واحد. فهو كهوى الحجر الى أسفل. فانّه يطلب الارض فى أقرب طريق، وأقرب الطرق الخطّ المستقيم. فتعيّن الخط المستقيم، فلم يفتقر فيه الى تجدد سبب حادث سوى الطبيعة الكلّيّة الطالبة للمركز، مع تجدّد القرب والبعد والوصول الى حدّ والصدور عنه. فكذلك يكفى فى تلك الحركة الارادة الكلّيّة للحركة. ولا يفتقر الى مزيد. فهذه مقدّمة تحكّموا بوضعها.

(١٦) المقدّمة الثالثة، وهى التحكّم البعيد جدّا قولهم: انّه اذا تصوّر الحركات الجزئيّة، تصوّر أيضاً توابعها ولوازمها. وهذا هوس محض كقول القائل: انّ الانسان اذا تحرّك وعرف حركته ينبغى ان يعرف ما يلزم من حركته من موازاة ومجاوزة، وهو نسبته الى الاجسام التى فوقه وتحته ومن جوانبه، وانّه اذا مشى فى شمس، ينبغى ان يعلم المواضع التى يقع عليها ظلّه، والمواضع التى لا يقع، وما يحصل من ظلّه من البرودة بقطع الشعاع فى تلك المواضع، وما يحصل من الانضغاط لاجزاء الارض تحت قدمه، وما يحصل من التفرّق فيها وما يحصل فى اخلاطه فى الباطن من الاستحالة بسبب الحركة الى الحرارة، وما يستحيل من أجزائه الى العرق، وهلمّ جرّا الى جميع الحوادث فى بدنه وفى غيره من بدنه ممّا الحركة علّة فيه أو شرط أو مهيىء ومعد. وهو هوس لا يتخيّله عاقل ولا يغترّ به الا جاهل. والى هذا يرجع هذا التحكّم.

(17) But we further say, "Do these discrete particulars known to the soul of the heavenly sphere exist at the present, or does one add to them that which one expects to be in the future?" If you restrict them to the present, then [the heavens'] knowledge of the hidden ceases, and its mediated knowledge of the future [possessed by] the prophets while awake and by the rest of men while asleep [would also cease]. Moreover, what the proof leads to no longer holds. For it is arbitrary [to maintain] that, when one knows a thing, one knows its consequences and attendants, so that if we knew the causes of all things we would know all future events. [Now,] the causes of all events exist now. For they consist of the heavenly movement—which, however, requires [as its consequence] the effect through either an intermediary or many intermediaries. But if this goes beyond to the future, it would have no ending. How, then, are the infinite details of the particulars in the future known, and how would there combine in the soul of one created being at one time, without succession, detailed particular cognitions whose number is infinite and whose units have no end?[8] Let anyone whose intellect does not testify to the impossibility of this despair of his intellect. Should they turn this against us as regards God's knowledge, [we would point out] that the attachment of God's knowledge to His objects of knowledge through correspondence is not in the same manner as the attachment of the cognitions belonging to creatures. But as long as the soul of the heavens plays the same role[9] as the human soul, it is of the same kind as the human soul. For it shares with it apprehending particulars through a mediator. For if it does not affiliate with it in a definitive way, it is probable that it is of its kind. But even if it is not probable, it is possible. And [this] possibility refutes their claim of conclusiveness in what [they argued] as being conclusive.

(18) [It may be said]:

(19) It rightly belongs to the human soul in its [very] essence also to apprehend all things.[10] But its preoccupation is with the consequences of appetite, anger, covetousness, rancor, envy, hunger, pain, and, in general, the things to which the body is prone and what the senses bring to it, so that when the soul attends to one thing, [this thing] diverts it from some

(١٧) على انّا نقول: هذه الجزئيّات المفصّلة المعلومة لنفس الفلك هى الموجودة فى الحال أو ينضاف اليها ما يتوقّع كونها فى الاستقبال؟ فان قصرتموه على الموجود فى الحال، بطل اطلاعه على الغيب واطلاع الانبياء فى اليقظة وسائر الخلق فى النوم على ما سيكون فى الاستقبال [بواسطته]٨. ثم بطل مقتضى الدليل. فانّه تحكّم بان من عرف الشىء عرف لوازمه وتوابعه حتّى لو عرفنا جميع أسباب الاشياء لعرفنا جميع الحوادث المستقبلة. وأسباب جميع الحوادث حاضرة فى الحال. فانّها هى الحركة السماويّة ولكن تقتضى المسبب اما بواسطة أو بوسائط كثيرة. واذا تعدّى الى المستقبل لم يكن له آخر فكيف يعرف تفصيل الجزئيّات فى الاستقبال الى غير نهاية وكيف يجتمع فى نفس مخلوق فى حالة واحدة من غير تعاقب علوم جزئيّة مفصّلة لا نهاية لأعدادها ولا غاية لآحادها؟ ومن لا يشهد له عقله باستحالة ذلك فلييأس من عقله. فان قلبوا هذا علينا فى علم الله، فليس تعلّق علم الله بالاتفاق بمعلوماته على نحو تعلق العلوم التى هى للمخلوقات. بل مهما دار نفس الفلك دورة نفس الانسان، كان من قبيل نفس الانسان. فانّه شاركه فى كونه مدركا للجزئيّات بواسطة. فان لم يلتحق به قطعا، كان للغالب على الظنّ انّه من قبيله. فان لم يكن غالبا على الظن فهو ممكن. والامكان يبطل دعواهم القطع بما قطعوا به.

(١٨) فان قيل:

(١٩) حقّ النفس الانسانيّة فى جوهرها ان تدرك أيضا جميع الاشياء ولكن اشتغالها بنتائج الشهوة والغضب والحرص والحقد والحسد والجوع والالم، وبالجملة عوارض البدن وما يورده الحواس عليه، حتّى

other. The celestial souls, on the other hand, are free from these attributes; no distraction afflicts them, and no worry, pain, or feeling preoccupies them. Hence, they know all things.

(20) We say:

5   (21) How do you know that they have nothing which preoccupies them? Are not their worship of the First and their longing [for Him things] that absorb them and distract them from apprehending discrete particulars? Or, what makes it impossible to suppose [the existence of] an impediment other than anger, appetite, and [such] sensory impediments?

10   How does one know that the impediments are restricted to the number we have witnessed in ourselves? [Now,] for rationally mature humans there are preoccupations such as high purpose and the quest for leadership which children cannot imagine and which [such adults] do not believe constitute preoccupation and impediment. How does one know

15   the impossibility of [the existence of] things that play a similar role among the celestial souls?

(22) This is what we have wanted to mention concerning the sciences to which [the philosophers] have given the name "metaphysical."

اذا أقبلت النفس الانسانيّة على شىء واحد شغلها عن غيره. وأمّا النفوس الفلكيّة [فبريئه] عن هذه الصفات، لا يعتريها شاغل، ولا يستغرقها هم وألم واحساس. فعرفت جميع الاشياء.

(٢٠) قلنا:

(٢١) وبم عرفتم انّه لا شاغل لها؟ وهلا كانت عبادتها واشتياقها الى الاوّل مستغرقا لها وشاغلا لها عن تصوّر الجزئيّات المفصّلة؟ أو ما الذى يحيل تقدير مانع آخر سوى الغضب والشهوة وهذه الموانع المحسوسة؟ ومن أين عرف انحصار المانع فى القدر الذى شاهدناه من أنفسنا؟ وفى العقلاء شواغل من علوّ الهمة وطلب الرئاسة ما يستحيل تصوّره عند الاطفال ولا يعتقدونها شاغلا ومانعا. فمن أين يعرف استحالة ما يقوم مقامها فى النفوس الفلكيّة؟

(٢٢) هذا ما أردنا ان نذكره فى العلوم الملقّبة عندهم بالالهيّة.

[The Natural Sciences]

[Introduction]

(1) Regarding what are called "the natural sciences," these consist of many sciences, whose divisions we will [now] mention so that it would be known that the religious law does not require disputing them nor denying them, except in places we will mention. [These sciences] divide into roots and branches. Their roots consist of eight divisions.

(2) In the first is mentioned what adheres to body inasmuch as it is body by way of divisibility, motion, and change, and what is concomitant with motion and [what is] a consequent to it by way of time, space, and the void. This is covered by the book *Physics*.

(3) The second makes known the states of the divisions of the elements of the world—namely, the heavens and what exists in the sublunary world by way of the four elements, their natures, and the cause for each of them deserving a specific place. This is covered by the book *On the Heavens and the World*.

(4) In the third, one [gets to] know the states of generation and corruption: of generation and procreation, of growth and withering, of transformations and the manner in which species are retained after the corruption of the particulars through the two heavenly movements, the eastern and the western. This is covered by the book *On Generation and Corruption*.

[القسم الثاني]

[الطبيعيّات]

(١) امّا الملقّب بالطبيعيّات [فهي]١ علوم كثيرة نذكر اقسامها ليعرف انّ الشرع ليس يقتضى المنازعة فيها ولا انكارها الا فى مواضع ذكرناها. وهى منقسمة الى أُصول وفروع. واصولها ثمانية أقسام.

(٢) الاوّل يذكر فيه ما يلحق الجسم من حيث انّه جسم من الانقسام والحركة والتغيّر، وما يلحق الحركة ويتبعه من الزمان والمكان والخلاء. ويشتمل عليه كتاب سمع الكيان.

(٣) الثانى يعرّف احوال اقسام اركان العالم التى هى السموات وما فى مقعّر فلك القمر من العناصر الاربعة وطبائعها وعلّة استحقاق كلّ واحد منها موضعا متعيّنا، ويشتمل عليه كتاب السماء والعالم.

(٤) الثالث يعرّف فيه أحوال الكون والفساد والتولّد والتوالد والنشوء والبلى والاستحالات وكيفيّة استبقاء الانواع على فساد الاشخاص بالحركتين السماويّتين الشرقيّة والغربيّة، ويشتمل عليه كتاب الكون والفساد.

(5) The fourth is on the states that occur to the four elements by way of mixtures through which meteorological effects such as clouds, rain, thunder, lightning, the halo, the rainbow, storms, winds, and earthquakes come about.

(6) The fifth is on the mineral substances.

(7) The sixth is the laws [governing] plants.

(8) The seventh is on animals and is covered by the book *The Natures of the Animals*.[1]

(9) The eighth is on the animal soul and the apprehending faculties, [showing] that the human soul does not perish with the death of the body and that it is a spiritual substance, corruption for it being impossible.

(10) As for their branches, they are seven.

(11) The first is medicine. Its objective is to become acquainted with the principles of the human body, its states in terms of health and illness, and their causes and symptoms, so as to remove illness and preserve health.

(12) The second is astral determinations, which consist of suppositional inferences [based on] the configurations and interrelationships of the stars, and of their mingling of what will happen concerning the conditions of the world—the [political] realm, births, and [what] the years [will bring about].

(13) The third is physiognomy, which is the inference of moral dispositions from appearance.

(14) The fourth is interpretation—namely, a detection from the imaginings in dreams of what the soul had witnessed in the world of the unseen [and] which the imaginative faculty has rendered as image, representing [what the soul had witnessed by] some other [thing].

(15) The fifth is the science of talismanic things—namely, the combining of celestial powers with the powers of some terrestrial bodies so as to have composed from this a power that enacts some strange acts in the terrestrial world.

(16) The sixth science is magic—namely, the mixing of the powers of earthly substances so as to produce strange things.

(٥) الرابع فى الاحوال التى تعرض للعناصر الاربعة من الامتزاجات التى منها تحدث الآثار العلويّة من الغيوم والامطار والرعد والبرق والهالة وقوس قزح والصواعق والرياح والزلازل.

(٦) الخامس فى الجواهر المعدنيّة.

(٧) السادس فى احكام النبات.

(٨) السابع فى الحيوانات وفيه كتاب طبائع الحيوانات.

(٩) الثامن فى النفس الحيوانيّة والقوى الدراكة وانّ نفس الانسان لا [تموت]¹ بموت البدن [وانها]² جوهر روحانيّ³ يستحيل [عليها]⁴ الفناء.

(١٠) اما فروعها فسبعة:

(١١) الاوّل الطب. ومقصوده معرفة مبادى بدن الانسان وأحواله من الصحّة والمرض وأسبابها ودلائلها ليدفع المرض ويحفظ الصحّة.

(١٢) الثانى فى احكام النجوم. وهو تخمين فى الاستدلال من اشكال الكواكب وامتزاجاتها على ما يكون من أحوال العالم والملك والمواليد والسنين.

(١٣) الثالث علم الفراسة، وهو استدلال من الخلق على الاخلاق.

(١٤) الرابع التعبير، وهو استدلال من المتخيّلات الحلميّة على ما شاهدته النفس من عالم الغيب فخيّلته القوّة المتخيّلة بمثال غيره.

(١٥) الخامس علم الطلسمات، وهو تأليف للقوى السماويّة بقوى بعض الاجرام الارضيّة ليأتلف من ذلك قوّة تفعل فعلا غريا فى العالم الارضيّ.

(١٦) السادس علم النيرنجات، وهو مزج قوى الجواهر الارضيّة ليحدث منه أُمور غريبة.

(17) The seventh is the science of alchemy, whose intent is to transform the properties of mineral substances so as to arrive at the attainment of gold and silver through [special] kinds of devices.

(18) There is no necessity to oppose them in terms of the revealed law in any of these sciences. We only oppose them in these sciences with respect to four questions.

(19) The first is their judgment that this connection between causes and effects that one observes in existence is a connection of necessary concomitance, so that it is within neither [the realm of] power nor within [that of] possibility to bring about the cause without the effect or the effect without the cause.[2]

(20) The second is their statement that human souls are self-subsisting substances, not imprinted in the body, and that the meaning of death is the severing of its relation with the body by severing its management [thereof]. Otherwise, [the body] would be self-subsistent in the state of death. They claimed that this is known through rational demonstration.

(21) The third is their statement that annihilation is impossible for these souls, but that once they are brought into existence they are eternal and perpetual and their annihilation inconceivable.

(22) The fourth is their statement that it is impossible to return these souls to bodies.

(23) The contention over the first [theory] is necessary, inasmuch as [on its refutation] rests the affirmation of miracles that disrupt [the] habitual [course of nature], such as the changing of the staff into a serpent, revival of the dead, and the splitting of the moon. Whoever renders the habitual courses [of nature] a necessary constant makes all these [miracles] impossible. [The philosophers] have thus interpreted what is said in the Qur'ān about the revivification of the dead metaphorically, saying that what is meant by it is the cessation of the death of ignorance through the life of knowledge. And they interpreted the staff devouring the magic of the magicians as[3] the refutation by the divine proof, manifest at the hand of Moses, of the doubts of those who deny [the one God]. As regards the splitting of the moon, they often deny the existence [of this occurrence] and claim that there has been no soundly transmitted, indubitable reporting of it.[4]

(24) It is only in three instances that the philosophers have affirmed miracles that disrupt the habitual courses of nature.

(١٧) السابع علم الكيمياء ومقصوده تبديل خواصّ الجواهر المعدنيّة ليتوصّل الى تحصيل الذهب والفضة بنوع من الحيل.

(١٨) وليس يلزم مخالفتهم شرعا فى شىء من هذه العلوم وانّما نخالفهم من جملة هذه العلوم فى أربعة مسائل.

(١٩) الاولى: حكمهم بانّ هذا الاقتران المشاهد فى الوجود بين الاسباب والمسبّبات اقتران تلازم بالضرورة، فليس فى المقدور ولا فى الامكان ايجاد السبب دون المسبّب ولا وجود المسبّب دون السبب.

(٢٠) الثانية: قولهم انّ النفوس الانسانيّة جواهر قائمة بانفسها ليست منطبعة فى الجسم وانّ معنى الموت انقطاع علاقتها عن البدن بانقطاع التدبير؛ والا فهو قائم بنفسه فى [حال الموت]°. وزعموا ان ذلك عرف بالبرهان العقلىّ.

(٢١) الثالثة: قولهم انّ هذه النفوس يستحيل عليها العدم، بل هى اذا وجدت، فهى أبديّة سرمديّة لا يتصوّر فناؤها.

(٢٢) والرابعة: قولهم يستحيل ردّ هذه النفوس الى الاجساد.

(٢٣) وانّما يلزم النزاع فى الاولى من حيث انّه ينبنى عليها اثبات المعجزات الخارقة للعادة، من قلب العصا ثعبانا واحياء الموتى وشقّ القمر. ومَن جعل مجارى العادات لازمة لزوما ضروريا أحال جميع ذلك؛ وأوّلوا ما فى القرآن من احياء الموتى، وقالوا: أراد به ازالة موت الجهل بحياة العلم؛ وأوّلوا تلقّف العصا سحر السحرة على ابطال الحجّة الالهيّة الظاهرة على يد موسى شبهات المنكرين. وأما شقّ القمر، فربّما انكروا وجوده وزعموا انّه لم يتواتر.

(٢٤) ولم يثبت الفلاسفة من المعجزات الخارقة للعادات الا فى ثلثة أُمور:

(25) One of these pertains to the imaginative faculty. For they maintain that once it becomes dominant and strong and does not become absorbed by the senses and preoccupation [with them], it sees the preserved tablet, the forms of future particular events becoming imprinted in it. This happens to prophets in their waking hours, to the rest of people in their sleep. This, then, is the prophetic property belonging to the imaginative faculty.[5]

(26) The second is a special property belonging to the theoretical rational faculty. This pertains to the power of intuition—namely, the quick transition from one object of knowledge to another. For with many a quick-witted person, when a thing proved is mentioned to him, he [immediately] awakens to the proof [that led to the conclusion]; and, when the proof is mentioned, he by himself [immediately] awakens to what is proved. In brief, once the middle term comes to his attention, he [immediately] notices the conclusion; and, if the conclusion's two terms present themselves to his mind, he [immediately] becomes aware of the middle term connecting the conclusion's two terms. In this, people are divided into classes. Some by themselves become [immediately] aware [of the middle term], some become aware with the slightest directing of attention, and some do not become aware [of it, even] with the directing of attention, except after much toil. If, then, the side of deficiency can terminate with someone who has no intuition at all so that he does not become disposed, even with direction, to comprehend the intelligibles, it becomes possible that the side of strength and increase would terminate [with one] who becomes aware of all the intelligibles—or most of them—in the shortest and quickest of times. This differs quantitatively in all things sought after—or some of them—and in such a manner that [the intuitive apprehension] varies in speed and [temporal] proximity [to what is apprehended]. Hence, it may well be the case[6] that the intuition of a holy and pure soul would proceed uninterruptedly [so as to grasp] all the intelligibles in the quickest of times. [The one endowed with such a soul] would thus be the prophet who [performs] a miracle relating to the theoretical faculty. He would thus have no need of instruction in [attaining] the intelligibles. It is as though he learns by himself. He is the one described as the person "whose oil almost gives light, even though no fire touches it; light upon light" [Qurʾān 24:35].

(27) The third is the practical faculty of the soul, which may reach a point [in strength] whereby [natural things] are influenced by it and do its bidding. An example of this is [that], when the soul of one of us imagines something, the limbs and the powers therein serve him and are

(٢٥) أحدها فى القوّة المتخيّلة. فانّهم زعموا انّها اذا استولت وقويت و لم يستغرقها الحواس والاشتغال، اطلعت على اللوح المحفوظ، [فانطبعت] فيها صور الجزئيّات الكائنة فى المستقبل. وذلك فى اليقظة للانبياء ولسائر الناس فى النوم. فهذه خاصيّة النبوّة للقوّة المتخيّلة.

(٢٦) الثانية: خاصيّة فى القوّة العقليّة النظريّة. وهو راجع الى قوّة الحدس، وهو سرعة الانتقال من معلوم الى معلوم؛ فربّ ذكىّ اذا ذكر له المدلول تنبّه للدليل واذا ذكر له الدليل تنبّه للمدلول من نفسه؛ وبالجملة اذا خطر له الحدّ الاوسط تنبّه للنتيجة، واذا حضر فى ذهنه حدّا النتيجة، خطر بباله الحدّ الاوسط الجامع بين طرفى النتيجة. والناس فى هذا منقسمون. فمنهم من يتنبّه بنفسه، ومنهم من يتنبّه بأدنى تنبيه، ومنهم من لا يدرك مع التنبيه الا بتعب كثير. واذا جاز ان ينتهى طرف النقصان الى من لا حدس له اصلا حتى لا يتهيّأ لفهم المعقولات مع التنبيه، جاز ان ينتهى طرف القوّة والزيادة الى ان يتنبّه لكلّ المعقولات أو لاكثرها، وفى أسرع الاوقات وأقربها. ويختلف ذلك بالكمّية فى جميع المطالب أو بعضها وفى الكيفيّة حتى يتفاوت فى السرعة والقرب. فربّ نفس مقدّسة صافية يستمر حدسها فى جميع المعقولات وفى اسرع الاوقات. فهو النبى الذى له معجزة من القوّة النظريّة. فلا يحتاج فى المعقولات الى تعلّم، بل كانه يتعلّم من نفسه، وهو الذى وصف بانّه ﴿يكاد زيتها يضىء ولو لم تمسسه نار نور على نور﴾.

(٢٧) الثالث: القوّة النفسيّة العمليّة، وقد تنتهى الى حدّ تتأثّر بها الطبيعيّات وتتسخّر. ومثاله انّ النفس منا، اذا [توهّمت] شيئا، خدمته

put into motion toward the imagined thing sought after so that, if he imagines some tasty thing, the sides of his mouth begin to water and the faculty producing saliva arises, flowing with the saliva from its elemental sources. [Again,] if he imagines copulation, the faculty [in question] is aroused and renders the organ erected. Indeed, if he walks on a branch stretched in space, whose ends [rest] on two walls, [the sensation of] his imagining himself falling would become quite intense, [with] the body reacting to his imagination, and he falls. Were this [branch] on the ground, he would walk on it without falling. This is because bodies and bodily powers were created to serve souls and do their bidding. This varies with the variance of the souls' purity and strength. It is not improbable that the power of the soul should reach a degree where the natural power outside his body would serve it. For the soul is not imprinted in his body, except that it has a kind of inclination and desire for managing it, created as part of its nature.

(28) If, then, it is possible for the parts of his body to obey it, it is not impossible for parts other [than his] to obey it. His soul then looks toward the blowing of a wind, the falling of rain, an attack of a storm, or a quaking of the earth for the annihilating of a people—all this being contingent on the occurrence of coldness, heat, or motion in the atmosphere—causing the cold or heat in his soul, from which these things are generated without the presence of a manifest natural cause. This, then, would be a miracle for the prophet; but it would only occur in an atmosphere disposed to receive [such action], and it would not extend to having wood change into an animal and to having the moon, [which is] not receptive of cleavage, be split.

(29) This, then, is their doctrine regarding miracles. We do not deny anything they have mentioned and [agree] that this belongs to prophets. We only deny their confining themselves to it and their denying the possibility of the changing of the staff into a serpent, the revivification of the dead, and other [miracles of the kind]. For this reason it becomes necessary to plunge into this question to affirm miracles and [to achieve] something else—namely, to support what all Muslims agree on, to the effect that God has power over all things. Let us, then, plunge into what is intended.

الاعضاء والقوى التى فيها، فحرّكت الى الجهة المتخيّلة المطلوبة، حتّى اذا توهّم شيئا طيّب المذاق، تحلّبت أشداقه وانتهضت القوّة الملعبة فياضّة باللعاب من معادنها؛ واذا تصوّر الوقاع انتهضت القوّة فنشرت الالة. بل اذا مشى على جذع ممدود على فضاء طرفاه على حائطين، اشتدّ توهّمه

٥ للسقوط، فانفعل الجسم بتوهّمه، وسقط. ولو كان ذلك على الارض لمشى عليه و لم يسقط. وذلك لانّ الاجسام والقوى الجسمانية خلقت خادمة مسخّرة للنفوس. ويختلف ذلك باختلاف صفاء النفوس وقوّتها. فلا يبعد ان تبلغ قوّة النفس الى حدّ تخدمه القوّة الطبيعيّة فى غير بدنه؛ لانّ نفسه ليست منطبعة فى بدنه، الا انّ [لها]^٨ نوع نزوع وشوق الى

١٠ تدبيره، خلق ذلك فى [جبلتها]^٩.

(٢٨) فاذا جاز ان [تطيعها]^١٠ اجسام بدنه، لم يمتنع أن [يطيعها غيرها، فتطّلع]^١١ نفسه الى هبوب ريح أو نزول مطر أو هجوم صاعقة أو تزلزل أرض لتخسف بقوم، وذلك موقوف حصوله على حدوث برودة أو سخونة أو حركة فى الهواء، فيحدث فى نفسه تلك السخونة

١٥ والبرودة، ويتولّد منه هذه الامور من غير حضور سبب طبيعىّ ظاهر. ويكون ذلك معجزة للنبى، ولكنّه انّما يحصل ذلك فى هواء مستعد للقبول. ولا ينتهى الى ان ينقلب الخشب حيوانا، وينفلق القمر الذى لا يقبل الانخراق.

(٢٩) فهذا مذهبهم فى المعجزات. ونحن لا ننكر شيئا ممّا ذكروه وانّ ذلك ممّا يكون للانبياء. وانّما ننكر اقتصارهم عليه، ومنعهم قلب

٢٠ العصا ثعبانا، واحياء الموتى وغيره. فلزم الخوض فى هذه المسئلة لاثبات المعجزات ولأمر آخر وهو نصرة ما اطبق عليه المسلمون من انّ الله قادر على كلّ شىء. فلنخض فى المقصود.

[Seventeenth] Discussion

[On causality and miracles]

(1) The connection between what is habitually believed to be a cause and what is habitually believed to be an effect is not necessary, according to us. But [with] any two things, where "this" is not "that" and "that" is not "this"[1] and where neither the affirmation of the one entails the affirmation of the other nor the negation of the one entails negation of the other,[2] it is not a necessity of the existence of the one that the other should exist, and it is not a necessity of the nonexistence of the one that the other should not exist—for example, the quenching of thirst and drinking, satiety and eating, burning and contact with fire, light and the appearance of the sun, death and decapitation, healing and the drinking of medicine, the purging of the bowels and the using of a purgative, and so on to [include] all [that is] observable among connected things in medicine, astronomy, arts, and crafts. Their connection is due to the prior decree of God, who creates them side by side,[3] not to its being necessary in itself, incapable of separation. On the contrary, it is within [divine] power to create satiety without eating, to create death without decapitation, to continue life after decapitation, and so on to all connected things. The philosophers denied the possibility of [this] and claimed it to be impossible.

(2) To examine these matters that are beyond enumeration will take a long time. Let us, then, take a specific example—namely, the burning of cotton, for instance, when in contact with fire. For we allow the possibility

مسئلة

[في السببيّة والمعجزات]

(١) الاقتران بين ما يعتقد فى العادة سببا وما يعتقد مسبّبا ليس ضروريّا عندنا. بل كل شيئين، ليس هذا ذاك ولا ذاك هذا، ولا اثبات أحدهما متضمّن لاثبات الآخر، ولا نفيه متضمّن لنفى الآخر، فليس من ضرورة وجود احدهما وجود الآخر، ولا من ضرورة عدم أحدهما عدم الآخر؛ مثل الرىّ والشرب، والشبع والاكل، والاحتراق ولقاء النار، والنور وطلوع الشمس، والموت وجزّ الرقبة، والشفاء وشرب الدواء، واسهال البطن واستعمال المسهل، وهلمّ جرّا الى كل المشاهدات من المقترنات فى الطبّ والنجوم والصناعات والحرف. وانّ اقترانها لما سبق من تقدير الله سبحانه يخلقها على التساوق، لا لكونه ضروريّا فى نفسه، غير قابل للفرق. بل فى المقدور خلق الشبع دون الاكل، وخلق الموت دون جزّ الرقبة، وادامة الحيوة مع جزّ الرقبة. وهلمّ جرّا الى جميع المقترنات. وأنكر الفلاسفة امكانه وادعوا استحالته.

(٢) والنظر فى هذه الامور الخارجة عن الحصر يطول. فلنعيّن مثالا واحدا، وهو الاحتراق فى القطن مثلا مع ملاقاة النار. فانّا نجوز وقوع

١٦٦

of the occurrence of the contact without the burning, and we allow as possible the occurrence of the cotton's transformation into burnt ashes without contact with the fire. [The philosophers], however, deny the possibility of this.

(3) The discussion of this question involves three positions.[4]

(4) The first position is for the opponent to claim that the agent of the burning is the fire alone, it being an agent by nature [and] not by choice—hence, incapable of refraining from [acting according to] what is in its nature after contacting a substratum receptive of it. And this is one of the things we deny. On the contrary, we say:

(5) The one who enacts the burning by creating blackness in the cotton, [causing] separation in its parts, and making it cinder or ashes is God, either through the mediation of His angels or without mediation. As for fire, which is inanimate, it has no action. For what proof is there that it is the agent? They have no proof other than observing the occurrence of the burning at the [juncture of] contact with the fire. Observation, however, [only] shows the occurrence [of burning] at [the time of the contact with the fire] but does not show the occurrence [of burning] by [the fire] and [the fact] that there is no other cause for it. For there is no disagreement [with the philosophers] that the infusion of spirit and of the apprehending and motive powers into the animal sperm is not engendered by the natures confined in heat, cold, moistness, and dryness; that the father does not produce his son by placing the sperm in the womb; and that he does not produce his life, sight, hearing, and the rest of the [powers][5] in him. It is known that these [come to] exist *with* [the placing of the sperm], but no one says that they [come to] exist *by* it. Rather, they exist from the direction of the First, either directly or through the mediation of the angels entrusted with temporal things. This is what the philosophers who uphold the existence of the creator uphold in a conclusive manner, [our] discourse being [at this point in agreement] with them.[6]

(6) It has thus become clear that [something's] existence *with* a thing does not prove that it exists *by* [that thing]. Indeed, we will show this by an example. If a person, blind from birth, who has a film on his eyes and who has never heard from people the difference between night and day, were to have the film cleared from his eyes in daytime, [then] open his

الملاقاة بينهما دون الاحتراق، ونجوّز حدوث انقلاب القطن رمادا محترقا دون ملاقاة النار. وهم ينكرون جوازه.

(٣) وللكلام فى المسئلة ثلثة مقامات

(٤) المقام الأوّل: ان يدّعى الخصم انّ فاعل الاحتراق هو النار فقط، وهو فاعل بالطبع لا بالاختيار، فلا يمكنه الكفّ عمّا هو طبعه بعد ملاقاته لمحلّ قابل له. وهذا مما ننكره بل نقول:

(٥) فاعل الاحتراق بخلق السواد فى القطن والتفرّق فى اجزائه وجعله حراقا أو رمادا هو الله، اما بواسطة الملائكة أو بغير واسطة. فأمّا النار، وهى جماد، فلا فعل لها. فما الدليل على انّها الفاعل؟ وليس [لهم]¹ دليل الا مشاهدة حصول الاحتراق عند ملاقاة النار. والمشاهدة تدلّ على الحصول عنده ولا تدلّ على الحصول به وانّه لا علّة سواه؛ اذ لا خلاف فى ان انسلاك الروح والقوى المدركة والمحرّكة فى نطفة الحيوانات ليس يتولّد عن الطبائع المحصورة فى الحرارة والبرودة والرطوبة واليبوسة، ولا انّ الاب فاعل ابنه بايداع النطفة فى الرحم، ولا هو فاعل حيوته وبصره وسمعه وسائر المعانى التى هى فيه. ومعلوم انّها موجودة عنده ولم [يقل أحد]² انها موجودة به، بل وجودها من جهة الاوّل امّا بغير واسطة، وامّا بواسطة الملائكة الموكّلين بهذه الامور الحادثة. وهذا ممّا يقطع به الفلاسفة القائلون بالصانع، والكلام معهم.

(٦) فقد تبيّن ان الوجود عند الشىء لا يدلّ على انّه موجود به. بل نبيّن هذا بمثال وهو انّ الاكمه لو كان فى [عينيه]³ غشاوة ولم يسمع من الناس الفرق بين الليل والنهار، لو انكشفت الغشاوة عن [عينيه]⁴ نهارا

eyelids and see colors, [such a person] would believe that the agent [causing] the apprehension of the forms of the colors in his eyes is the opening of his sight and that, as long as his sight is sound, [his eyes] opened, the film removed, and the individual in front of him having color,

5   it follows necessarily that he would see, it being incomprehensible that he would not see. When, however, the sun sets and the atmosphere becomes dark, he would then know that it is sunlight that is the cause for the imprinting of the colors in his sight.

(7) Whence can the opponent safeguard himself against there being

10   among the principles of existence grounds and causes from which these [observable] events emanate when a contact between them[7] takes place— [admitting] that [these principles], however, are permanent, never ceasing to exist; that they are not moving bodies that would set; that, were they either to cease to exist or to set, we would apprehend the dissocia-

15   tion [between the temporal events] and would understand that there is a cause beyond what we observe? This [conclusion] is inescapable in accordance with the reasoning based on [the philosophers' own] principle.

(8) It is because of this that the exacting among them have agreed that these accidents and events that occur when the contact between

20   bodies takes place—and, in general, when the relationships between them change—emanate from the bestower of forms, who is one of the angels, so that they have said: "The imprinting of the form of color in the eye comes from the bestower of forms,[8] the sun's appearance, the healthy pupil and the colored body being only 'readiers' and preparers

25   for the receptacle's acceptance of these forms." They have made this the case with all temporal events. With this, the claim of those who proclaim that it is fire that enacts the burning, that it is bread that enacts satiety, that it is medicine that produces health, and so on, becomes false.

(9) The second position belongs to those who admit that these tem-

30   poral events emanate from the principles of temporal events but that the preparation for the reception of the forms comes about through these present, observed causes—except that these principles are also [such that] things proceed from them necessarily and by nature, not by way of deliberation and choice, in the way [that] light proceeds from the

35   sun, receptacles differing in their reception because of the differences [of] disposition. For the shiny body receives the sun's ray and reflects it,

وفتح اجفانه فرأى الالوان، ظنّ انّ الادراك الحاصل فى [عينيه]ه لصور الالوان فاعله فتح البصر، وانّه مهما كان بصره سليما مفتوحا، والحجاب مرتفعا والشخص المقابل متلوّنا، فيلزم لا محالة أن يبصر، ولا يعقل ان لا يبصر؛ حتّى اذا غربت الشمس وأظلم الهواء علم ان نور الشمس هو السبب فى انطباع الالوان فى بصره.

(٧) فمن أين يأمن الخصم ان يكون فى المبادى للوجود علل واسباب يفيض منها هذه الحوادث عند حصول ملاقاة بينها، الا انّها ثابتة ليست تنعدم، ولا هى اجسام متحرّكة، فتغيب. ولو انعدمت او غابت لأدركنا التفرقة وفهمنا انّ ثمّ سببا وراء ما شاهدناه؟ وهذا لا مخرج منه، على قياس اصلهم.

(٨) ولهذا اتفق محقّقوهم على انّ هذه الاعراض والحوادث التى تحصل عند وقوع الملاقاة بين الاجسام وعلى الجملة عند اختلاف نسبها، انما تفيض من عند واهب الصور، وهو ملك [من الملائكة]٦ حتّى قالوا: انطباع صورة الالوان فى العين يحصل من جهة واهب الصور، وانّما طلوع الشمس والحدقة السليمة والجسم المتلوّن معدات ومهيئات لقبول المحلّ [لهذه الصور]٧، وطردوا هذا فى كلّ حادث. وبهذا يبطل دعوى من يدّعى انّ النار هى الفاعلة للاحتراق والخبز هو الفاعل للشبع والدواء هو الفاعل للصحّة الى غير ذلك من الاسباب.

(٩) المقام الثانى، مع من يسلّم انّ هذه الحوادث تفيض من مبادى الحوادث ولكن الاستعداد لقبول الصور يحصل بهذه الاسباب المشاهدة الحاضرة، الا انّ [تلك]٨ المبادى أيضا تصدر الاشياء عنها باللزوم والطبع لا على سبيل التروى والاختيار، صدور النور من الشمس، وانما افترقت المحالّ فى القبول لاختلاف استعدادها. فانّ الجسم الصقيل يقبل شعاع

whereby another place is illuminated by it, whereas mud does not; air does not prevent the penetration of light, whereas stone does; some things are softened by the sun, some hardened; some [are] whitened, as with the bleacher's garment, [and] some blackened, as with his face. [In all this, they maintain that] the principle is one but [that] the effects differ because of the differences of the dispositions in the receptacle. Similarly, the principles of existence are ever inundating with what proceeds from them, having neither restraint from granting nor stinginess: the short-coming is only due to the receptacles. This being the case [they argue] then as long as we suppose a fire having the quality [proper to it] and we suppose two similar pieces of cotton that come into contact with it in the same way, how would it be conceivable that one should burn and not the other, when there is no choice [on the part of the agent]? Based on this notion, they denied the falling of Abraham in the fire without the burning taking place, the fire remaining fire, and claimed that this is only possi-ble by taking the heat out of the fire—which makes it no longer fire—or by changing the essence and body of Abraham into a stone or something over which fire has no effect. But neither is this [latter] possible, nor is that [former] possible.

(10) The answer [to this] has two approaches.

(11) The first is to say: "We do not concede that the principles do not act by choice and that God does not act voluntarily." We have finished with refuting their claim concerning this in the question of the world's creation. If, then, it is established that the Agent creates the burning through His will when the piece of cotton comes into contact with the fire, it becomes rationally possible [for God] not to create [the burning] with the existence of the contact.

(12) [To this] it may be said:

(13) This leads to the commission of repugnant contradictions. For if one denies that the effects follow necessarily from their causes and relates them to the will of their Creator, the will having no specific designated course but [a course that] can vary and change in kind, then let each of us allow the possibility of there being in front of him ferocious beasts, raging fires, high mountains, or enemies ready with their weapons [to kill him],

الشمس ويردّه حتى يستضىء به موضع آخر، والمدر لا يقبل؛ والهواء لا يمنع نفوذ نوره، والحجر يمنع؛ وبعض الاشياء يلين بالشمس، وبعضها يتصلّب، وبعضها يبيّض كثوب القصّار، وبعضها يسوّد كوجهه؛ والمبدأ واحد، والآثار مختلفة لاختلاف الاستعدادت فى المحلّ. فكذى مبادى

٥ الوجود، فيّاضة بما هو صادر منها لا منع عندها ولا بخل، وانّما التقصير من القوابل. واذا كان كذلك، فمهما فرضنا النار بصفتها، وفرضنا قطنتين متماثلتين، لاقتا النار على وتيرة واحدة، فكيف يتصوّر ان تحترق احديهما دون الآخرى، وليس ثمّ اختيار؟ وعن هذا المعنى انكروا وقوع ابرهيم فى النار مع عدم الاحتراق، وبقاء النار نارا، وزعموا ان ذلك لا

١٠ يمكن الا بسلب الحرارة من النار، وذلك [يخرجها]٩ عن [كونها]١٠ نارا أو بقلب ذات ابرهيم وبدنه حجرا أو شيئا لا يؤثّر فيه النار. ولا هذا ممكن، ولا ذاك ممكن.

(١٠) والجواب له مسلكان:

(١١) الاوّل ان نقول: لا نسلّم انّ المبادى ليست تفعل بالاختيار وانّ

١٥ الله لا يفعل بالارادة. وقد فرغنا عن ابطال دعواهم فى ذلك فى مسئلة حدث العالم. واذا ثبت انّ الفاعل يخلق الاحتراق بارادته عند ملاقاة القطنة النار، أمكن فى العقل ان لا يخلق، مع وجود الملاقاة.

(١٢) فان قيل:

(١٣) فهذا يجر الى ارتكاب محالات شنيعة. فانه اذا [أنكر]١١ لزوم المسببات عن اسبابها [وأضيفت]١٢ الى ارادة مخترعها، ولم يكن للارادة

٢٠ أيضا منهج مخصوص متعيّن بل أمكن تفنّنه وتنوّعه، فليجوّز كلّ واحد منّا ان يكون بين يديه سباع ضارية، ونيران مشتعلة وجبال راسية، واعداء

but [also the possibility] that he does not see them because God does not create for him [vision of them]. And if someone leaves a book in the house, let him allow as possible its change on his returning home into a beardless slave boy—intelligent, busy with his tasks—or into an animal; or if he leaves a boy in his house, let him allow the possibility of his changing into a dog; or [again] if he leaves ashes, [let him allow] the possibility of its change into musk; and let him allow the possibility of stone changing into gold and gold into stone. If asked about any of this, he ought to say: "I do not know what is at the house at present. All I know is that I have left a book in the house, which is perhaps now a horse that has defiled the library with its urine and its dung, and that I have left in the house a jar of water, which may well have turned into an apple tree. For God is capable of everything, and it is not necessary for the horse to be created from the sperm nor the tree to be created from the seed—indeed, it is not necessary for either of the two to be created from anything. Perhaps [God] has created things that did not exist previously." Indeed, if [such a person] looks at a human being he has seen only now and is asked whether such a human is a creature that was born, let him hesitate and let him say that it is not impossible that some fruit in the marketplace has changed into a human—namely, this human—for God has power over every possible thing, and this thing is possible; hence, one must hesitate in [this matter]. This is a mode wide open in scope for [numerous] illustrations, but this much is sufficient.

(14) [Our] answer [to this] is to say:

(15) If it is established that the possible is such that there cannot be created for man knowledge of its nonbeing, these impossibilities would necessarily follow. We are not, however, rendered skeptical by the illustrations you have given because God created for us the knowledge that He did not enact these possibilities. We did not claim that these things are necessary. On the contrary, they are possibilities that may or may not occur. But the continuous habit of their occurrence repeatedly, one time after another, fixes unshakably in our minds the belief in their occurrence according to past habit.

مستعدّة بالاسلحة، وهو لا يراها، لانّ الله تعالى ليس يخلق الرؤية له. ومن وضع كتابا فى بيته، فليجوّز ان يكون قد انقلب عند رجوعه الى بيته غلاما أمرد عاقلا متصرّفا، أو انقلب حيوانا، أو لو ترك غلاما فى بيته فليجوّز انقلابه كلبا، أو ترك الرماد، فليجوّز انقلابه مسكا، وانقلاب الحجر ذهبا والذهب حجرا، واذا سئل عن شىء من هذا فينبغى ان يقول:

٥ لا ادرى ما فى البيت الآن، وانّما القدر الذى اعلمه انّى تركت فى البيت كتابا، ولعلّه الآن فرس وقد لطّخ بيت الكتب ببوله وروثه؛ وانّى تركت فى البيت جرة من الماء، ولعلها انقلبت شجرة تفاح. فانّ الله قادر على كلّ شىء، وليس من ضرورة الفرس أن يخلق من النطفة، ولا من ضرورة الشجرة ان [تخلق]١٣ من البذر، بل ليس من [ضرورتهما]١٤ ان

١٠ [تخلق]١٥ من شىء. فلعلّه خلق أشياء لم يكن لها وجود من قبل. بل اذا نظر الى انسان لم يره الا الآن، وقيل له هل هذا مولود، فليتردّد وليقل يحتمل ان يكون بعض الفواكه فى السوق قد انقلب انسانا وهو ذلك الانسان. فانّ الله قادر على كلّ شىء ممكن، وهذا ممكن، فلا بدّ من التردّد

١٥ فيه. وهذا فنّ يتّسع المجال فى تصويره وهذا القدر كاف فيه.

(١٤) والجواب ان نقول:

(١٥) ان ثبت أن الممكن كونه لا يجوز ان يخلق للانسان علم بعدم كونه، لزم هذه المحالات. ونحن لا نشكّ فى هذه الصور التى اوردتموها. فانّ الله خلق لنا علما بانّ هذه الممكنات لم يفعلها. و لم ندّع انّ هذه

٢٠ الامور واجبة، بل هى ممكنة يجوز ان تقع ويجوز ان لا تقع. واستمرار العادة بها مرّة بعد اخرى يرسخ فى اذهاننا جريانها على وفق العادة الماضية ترسّخا لا تنفكّ عنه.

(16) Indeed, it is possible for one of the prophets to know through the ways [the philosophers] have mentioned that a certain individual will not arrive from his journey tomorrow when his arrival is possible, the prophet [knowing, however,] the nonoccurrence of this possible thing. Nay, this is just as when one looks at a common man and knows that he neither knows the occult in any manner whatsoever nor apprehends the intelligibles without instruction; and yet, with all that, one does not deny that the soul and intuition [of this ordinary man] may become stronger so as to apprehend what the prophets apprehend, in accordance with what [the philosophers] acknowledge—although they know that such a possibility has not taken place.

(17) If, then, God disrupts the habitual [course of nature] by making [the miracle] occur at the time in which disruptions of habitual [events] take place, these cognitions [of the nonoccurrence of such unusual possibilities] slip away from [people's] hearts, and [God] does not create them. There is, therefore, nothing to prevent a thing being possible, within the capabilities of God, [but] that by His prior knowledge He knew that He would not do it at certain times, despite its possibility, and that He creates for us the knowledge that He will not create it at that time. Hence, in [all] this talk [of theirs], there is nothing but sheer vilification.[9]

(18) The second approach, with which there is deliverance from these vilifications,[10] is for us to admit[11] that fire is created in such a way that, if two similar pieces of cotton come into contact with it, it would burn both, making no distinction between them if they are similar in all respects. With all this, however, we allow as possible that a prophet may be cast into the fire without being burned, either by changing the quality of the fire or by changing the quality of the prophet. Thus, there would come about either from God or from the angels a quality in the fire which restricts its heat to its own body so as not to transcend it (its heat would thus remain with it, and it would [still] have the form and true nature of fire, its heat and influence, however, not going beyond it), or else there will occur in the body of the prophet a quality which will not change him from being flesh and bone [but] which will resist the influence of the fire. For we see [that] a person who covers himself with talc and sits in a fiery furnace is not affected by it. The one who has not witnessed this will deny it. Hence, the opponent's denial that [divine] power includes the ability to establish a

(١٦) بل يجوز ان يعلم نبيّ من الانبياء بالطرق التى ذكروها انّ فلانا لا يقدم من سفره غدا، وقدومه ممكن ولكن يعلم عدم وقوع ذلك الممكن. بل كما ينظر الى العاميّ فيعلم انّه ليس يعلم الغيب فى امر من الامور ولا يدرك المعقولات من غير تعلّم، ومع ذلك فلا ينكر ان تتقوّى نفسه وحدسه بحيث يدرك ما يدركه الانبياء، على ما اعترفوا بامكانه، ولكن يعلمون انّ ذلك الممكن لم يقع.

(١٧) فان خرق الله العادة بايقاعها فى زمان خرق العادات فيها، انسلت هذه العلوم عن القلوب، و لم يخلقها. فلا مانع اذن من ان يكون الشىء ممكنا فى مقدورات الله، ويكون قد جرى فى سابق علمه انّه لا يفعله مع امكانه فى بعض الاوقات، ويخلق لنا العلم بانّه ليس يفعله فى ذلك الوقت. فليس فى هذا الكلام الا تشنيع محض.

(١٨) المسلك الثانى، وفيه الخلاص من هذه التشنيعات، وهو ان نسلّم انّ النار خلقت خلقة اذا لاقاها قطنتان متماثلتان أحرقتهما و لم تفرّق بينهما اذا تماثلتا من كلّ وجه. ولكنّا مع هذا نجوّز ان يلقى نبيّ فى النار فلا يحترق، امّا بتغيير صفة النار، أو بتغيير صفة النبيّ. فيحدث من الله أو من الملائكة صفة فى النار يقصر سخونتها على جسمها بحيث لا تتعدّاه، [فتبقى]١٦ معها سخونتها وتكون على صورة النار وحقيقتها ولكن لا تتعدّى سخونتها واثرها، أو يحدث فى بدن الشخص صفة [لا تخرجه]١٧ عن كونه لحما وعظما [فتدفع]١٨ اثر النار. فانّا نرى من يطلى نفسه بالطلق ثم يقعد فى تنّور [موقد]١٩ ولا يتأثّر به. والذى لم يشاهد ذلك ينكره. فانكار الخصم اشتمال القدرة على اثبات صفة من الصفات

certain quality either in the fire or in the human body that would prevent burning is like the denial of one who has never seen talc and its influence. Among the objects lying within God's power there are strange and wondrous things, not all of which we have seen. Why, then, should we deny their possibility and judge them to be impossible?

(19) Similarly, the raising of the dead and the changing of the staff into a snake are possible in this way—namely, that matter is receptive of all things. Thus, earth and the rest of the elements change into plants, plants—when eaten by animals—into blood, blood then changing into sperm. Sperm is then poured into the womb and develops in stages as an animal; this, in accordance with habit, takes place in a lengthy period of time. Why, then, should the opponent deem it impossible that it lies within God's power to cycle matter through these stages in a time shorter than has been known? And if this is possible within a shorter time, there is no restriction to its being [yet] shorter. These powers would thus accelerate in their actions, and through [this] there would come about what is a miracle for the prophet.

(20) If it is said, "Does this proceed from the prophet's soul or from some other principle at the suggestion of the prophet?" we say:

(21) [In] what you have admitted regarding the possibility of the coming down of rain [and] of hurricanes and the occurrence of earthquakes through the power of the prophet's soul, do [such events] come about from him or from another principle? Our statement in [answering your question] is the same as your statement in [answering ours].[12] It is, however, more fitting for both you and us to relate this to God, either directly or through the mediation of the angels.[13] The time meriting its appearance, however, is when the prophet's attention is wholly directed to it and the order of the good[14] becomes specifically [dependent] on its appearance so that the order of the revealed law may endure. [All] this gives preponderance to[15] the side of [the] existence [of the miracle], the thing in itself being possible [and] the principle [endowing it being] benevolent and generous. But it does not emanate from Him except when the need for its existence becomes preponderant and the order of the good becomes specified therein. And the order of the good becomes specified therein only if a prophet needs it to prove his prophethood in order to spread the good.

فى النار أو فى البدن يمنع الاحتراق، كانكار من لم يشاهد الطلق واثره. وفى مقدورات الله غرائب وعجائب ونحن لم نشاهد جميعها. فلِم ينبغى ان ننكر امكانها ونحكم باستحالتها؟

(١٩) وكذلك احياء الميت وقلب العصا ثعبانا يمكن بهذا الطريق، وهو انّ المادّة قابلة لكلّ شىء. فالتراب وسائر العناصر يستحيل نباتا ثم النبات يستحيل عند أكل الحيوان دما، ثم الدم يستحيل منيا، ثم المنى ينصب فى الرحم فيتخلّق حيوانا، وهذا بحكم العادة واقع فى زمان متطاول. فلم يحيل الخصم ان يكون فى مقدور الله ان يدير المادّة فى هذه الاطوار فى وقت أقرب مما عهد فيه؟ واذا جاز فى وقت أقرب، فلا ضبط للاقلّ. فتستعجل هذه القوى فى عملها ويحصل به ما هو معجزة النبىّ.

(٢٠) فان قيل: وهذا يصدر من نفس النبىّ أو من مبدأ آخر من المبادىء عند اقتراح النبىّ؟ قلنا:

(٢١) وما سلّمتموه من جواز نزول الامطار والصواعق وتزلزل الارض بقوّة نفس النبىّ، يحصل منه أو من مبدأ آخر؟ فقولنا فى هذا، كقولكم فى ذاك. والاولى بنا وبكم اضافة ذلك الى الله، امّا بغير واسطة أو بواسطة الملائكة. ولكن وقت استحقاق حصولها انصراف همّة النبى [اليها]٢٠ وتعيّن نظام الخير فى [ظهورها]٢١ لاستمرار نظام الشرع، فيكون ذلك مرجّحا جهة الوجود، ويكون الشىء فى نفسه ممكنا، والمبدأ به سمحا جوادا، ولكن لا يفيض منه الا اذا ترجحت الحاجة الى وجوده وصار الخير متعيّنا فيه. ولا يصير الخير متعينا فيه الا اذا احتاج نبىّ فى اثبات نبوّته اليه لافاضة الخير.

(22) All this is consistent with the drift of what they say and a necessary consequence for them as long as they bring up the topic [of the doctrine to which they subscribe—namely,] of the prophet's special endowment with a characteristic contrary to what is customary with people. For the possible amounts of such special [prophetic qualities] are not encompassed by the mind. Why, then, with [all] this, must one disbelieve that whose transmission has been corroborated by innumerable reports, and belief in which is enjoined by the religious law?

(23) [To proceed] in general, since only the sperm is receptive of the animal form, the animal powers emanating to it from the angels who, according [to the philosophers], are principles of being, [it follows that]^{16} from the human sperm only a human is created and from the sperm of the horse only a horse, since [to take the latter case] its realization from the horse is the more necessitating of preponderance because of the greater appropriateness of the equine form over all other forms. In this way, it thus accepts only the preponderant form. For this reason, wheat has never sprouted from barley and apples never from the seed of pears.

(24) Moreover, we have seen genera of animals that are [spontaneously] generated from earth and are never procreated—as, for example, worms—and others like the mouse, the snake, and the scorpion that are both [spontaneously] generated and procreated, their generation being from the earth. Their dispositions to receive forms differ due to things unknown to us, it being beyond human power to know them, since, according to [the philosophers], forms do not emanate from the angels by whim or haphazardly. On the contrary, there emanates to each receptacle only that to which its reception is specified by being in itself disposed to receive [that thing]. [Now,] dispositions vary, their principles, according to them, being the configuration of the stars and the differing relations of the heavenly bodies in their movements.

(25) From this it has become clear that the principles of dispositions include strange and wondrous things—so much so that the masters of the talismanic art have arrived, through their knowledge of the special properties of mineral substances and knowledge of the stars, [at the ability] to combine the heavenly powers and the special properties of minerals. They have thus taken certain forms of the terrestrial [properties] and sought for them a specific horoscope, bringing about through them

(٢٢) فهذا كلّه لائق بمساق كلامهم ولازم لهم مهما فتحوا باب الاختصاص للنبيّ بخاصيّة تخالف عادة الناس. فانّ مقادير ذلك الاختصاص لا ينضبط فى العقل امكانه. فلم يجب معه التكذيب لما تواتر نقله وورد الشرع بتصديقه؟

٥

(٢٣) وعلى الجملة، لمّا كان لا يقبل صورة الحيوان الا النطفة وانّما تفيض القوى الحيوانية عليها من الملائكة التى هى مبادى الموجودات عندهم، و لم يتخلّق قطّ من نطفة الأنسان الا انسان، ومن نطفة الفرس الا فرس، من حيث ان حصوله من الفرس أوجب ترجيحا، لمناسبة صورة الفرس على سائر الصور، فلم يقبل الا الصورة المترجّحة بهذا الطريق. ولذلك لم ينبت قط من الشعير حنطة ولا من بذر الكمثرى تفاح.

١٠

(٢٤) ثم رأينا اجناسا من الحيوانات تتولّد من التراب ولا تتوالد قطّ، كالديدان ومنها ما يتولّد ويتوالد جميعاً كالفار والحيّة والعقرب، وكان تولّدها من التراب. ويختلف استعدادها لقبول الصور بامور غابت عنا، و لم يكن فى القوة البشرية الاطلاع عليها، اذ ليس تفيض الصور عندهم من الملائكة بالتشهّى ولا جزافا، بل لا يفيض على كلّ محلّ الا ما تعيّن قبوله له بكونه مستعدّا فى نفسه. والاستعدادات مختلفة، ومبادئها عندهم امتزاجات الكواكب واختلاف نسب الاجرام العلوية فى حركاتها.

١٥

(٢٥) فقد [اتّضح]²² من هذا ان مبادى الاستعدادات فيها غرائب وعجائب حتّى توصّل ارباب الطلسمات من علم خواصّ الجواهر المعدنيّة وعلم النجوم الى مزج القوى السماويّة بالخواصّ المعدنيّة، فاتخذوا اشكالاً من هذه الارضيّة وطلبوا لها طالعا مخصوصا من الطوالع، وأحدثوا بها أمورا غريبة فى العالم. فربّما دفعوا الحيّة والعقرب

٢٠

strange things in the world. Thus, they have at times repelled from [one] town the snake and the scorpion, from [another] town the bedbug, and so on to matters known in the talismanic art. If, then, the principles of dispositions are beyond enumeration, the depth of their nature beyond our ken, there being no way for us to ascertain them, how can we know that it is impossible for a disposition to occur in some bodies that allows their transformation in phase of development in the shortest time so that they become prepared for receiving a form they were never prepared for receiving previously, and that this should not come about as a miracle? The denial of this is only due to our lack of capacity to understand, [our lack of] familiarity with exalted beings, and our unawareness of the secrets of God, praised be He, in creation and nature. Whoever studies [inductively] the wonders of the sciences will not deem remote from the power of God, in any manner whatsoever, what has been related of the miracles of the prophets.

(26) [It may be] said:

(27) We help you by maintaining that every possible thing is within the power of God, while you help us by maintaining that whatever is impossible is not within [divine] power. There are things whose impossibility is known and there are things whose possibility is known, while there are things the mind confronts undecided, judging them neither to be impossible nor possible. Now, then, what, according to you, is the definition of the impossible? If it reduces to the combining of negation and affirmation in the one thing, then [go on and] say, "In the case of two things, where 'this' is not 'that' and 'that' is not 'this,' the existence of the one does not require the existence of the other," and say that God can create a will without knowledge of the object willed and can create knowledge without life; that He can move a dead man's hand, seating him and with the hand writing volumes and engaging in crafts, the man being all the while open-eyed, staring ahead of him, but not seeing and having no life and no power over [what is being done]—all these ordered acts being created by God together with the moving of [the man's] hand, the moving coming from the direction of God. By allowing the possibility of this, there ends the distinction between the voluntary movement and the tremor. The well-designed act would no longer prove either the knowledge or the

عن بلد، والبق عن بلد، الى غير ذلك من امور تعرف من علم الطلسمات. فاذا خرجت عن الضبط مبادى الاستعدادات، ولم نقف على كنهها، ولم يكن لنا سبيل الى حصرها، فمن أين نعلم استحالة حصول الاستعداد فى بعض الاجسام للاستحالة فى الاطوار فى أقرب زمان حتّى يستعدّ لقبول صورة ما كان يستعدّ لها من قبل وينتهض ذلك معجزة؟ ما انكار هذا الا لضيق الحوصلة والانس بالموجودات العالية والذهول عن اسرار الله سبحانه فى الخلقة والفطرة. ومن استقرأ عجائب العلوم لم يستبعد من قدرة الله ما يحكى من معجزات الانبياء بحال من الاحوال.

(٢٦) فان قيل:

(٢٧) فنحن نساعدكم على انّ كلّ ممكن مقدور لله، وأنتم تساعدون على انّ كلّ محال فليس.بمقدور. ومن الاشياء ما يعرف استحالتها ومنها ما يعرف امكانها ومنها ما يقف العقل فلا يقضى فيه باستحالة ولا امكان. فالآن ما حدّ المحال عندكم؟ فان رجع الى الجمع بين النفى والاثبات فى شىء واحد، فقولوا: انّ كل شيئين، ليس هذا ذاك ولا ذاك هذا، فلا يستدعى وجود أحدهما وجود الآخر؛ وقولوا: انّ الله يقدر على خلق ارادة من غير علم بالمراد، وخلق علم من غير حيوة، ويقدر على ان يحرّك يد ميت ويقعده ويكتب بيده مجلدات ويتعاطى صناعات، وهو مفتوح العين محدق بصره نحوه، ولكنّه لا يرى، ولا حيوة فيه ولا قدرة له عليه، وانّما هذه الافعال المنظومة يخلقها الله تعالى مع تحريك يده، والحركة من جهة الله. وبتجويز هذا يطل الفرق بين الحركة الاختيارية وبين الرعدة. فلا يدلّ الفعل المحكم على العلم ولا على قدرة الفاعل. وينبغى ان يقدر

power of the agent. [God] ought then to be able to change genera. He would thus change substance into accident, knowledge into power, blackness into whiteness, sound into smell, just as He had been able to change the inanimate into the animate and stone into gold, and there would follow as necessary consequences impossibilities beyond enumeration.

(28) [We] answer:

(29) The impossible is not within the power [of being enacted]. The impossible consists in affirming a thing conjointly with denying it, affirming the more specific while denying the more general, or affirming two things while negating one [of them]. What does not reduce to this is not impossible, and what is not impossible is within [divine] power.

(30) As for combining blackness and whiteness, this is impossible. For by the affirmation of the form of blackness in the receptacle we understand [(a)] the negation of the appearance of whiteness and [(b) the affirmation of] the existence of blackness. Once the negation of whiteness becomes understood from the affirmation of blackness, then the affirmation of whiteness, together with its negation, becomes impossible.

(31) It is [further] impossible for the individual to be in two places, because we understand by his being in the house [for example] his not being in [a place] other than the house. Hence, it is impossible to suppose him in [a place] other than the house together with his being in the house, [his being in the house] signifying the denial of [his being] elsewhere other than the house.

(32) Similarly, we understand by the will the seeking after something known [to the willer]. If, then, a quest is supposed without knowledge, there would be no will. This entails the denial of what we have understood [by will].

(33) It is impossible, moreover, to create knowledge in inanimate matter. For we understand by the inanimate that which does not apprehend. If apprehension is created in it, then to call it inanimate in the sense we have understood becomes impossible. And if it does not apprehend, then to call what has been created "knowledge" when its receptacle does not apprehend anything is [also] impossible. This, then, is the way in which this is impossible.

(34) As for the changing of genera, some of the Islamic dialectical theologians have said that it is within God's capacity [to enact]. We, however, say:

على قلب الاجناس. فيقلب الجوهر عرضا، ويقلب العلم قدرة، والسواد بياضا، والصوت رائحة، كما اقتدر على قلب الجماد حيوانا، والحجر ذهبا، ويلزم عليه أيضا من المحالات ما لا حصر له.

(٢٨) والجواب:

(٢٩) انّ المحال غير مقدور عليه؛ والمحال اثبات الشيء مع نفيه، أو اثبات الاخصّ مع نفى الاعمّ، أو اثبات الاثنين مع نفى الواحد. وما لا يرجع الى هذا فليس بمحال، وما ليس بمحال فهو مقدور.

(٣٠) أمّا الجمع بين السواد والبياض فمحال. لانّا نفهم من اثبات صورة السواد فى المحلّ، نفى هيئة البياض ووجود السواد. فاذا صار نفى البياض مفهوما من اثبات السواد، كان اثبات البياض مع نفيه محالا.

(٣١) وانّما لا يجوز كون الشخص فى مكانين لانّا نفهم من كونه فى البيت عدم كونه فى غير البيت، فلا يمكن تقديره فى غير البيت مع كونه فى البيت، المفهم لنفيه عن غير البيت.

(٣٢) وكذلك نفهم من الارادة طلب معلوم. فان فرض طلب ولا علم، لم تكن ارادة. فكان فيه نفى ما فهمناه.

(٣٣) والجماد يستحيل ان يخلق فيه العلم، لانّا نفهم من الجماد ما لا يدرك. فان خلق فيه ادراك، فتسميته جمادا بالمعنى الذى فهمناه محال. وان لم يدرك فتسمية الحادث علما ولا يدرك به محلّه شيئا محال. فهذا وجه استحالته.

(٣٤) وامّا قلب الاجناس، فقد قال بعض المتكلمين انّه مقدور لله. فنقول:

(35) A thing's becoming something else is unintelligible. For if blackness changes into a cooking pot,[17] does the blackness continue to exist or not? If it ceases to exist, it does not change [into something else]; rather, the thing ceases to exist and something else comes into existence. If it [continues to] exist with the cooking pot, then it did not change, but something was added to it. If [on the other hand] the blackness remains while the cooking pot is nonexistent, then the former did not change, but remained as it had been. [Again,] if we say that blood has changed into sperm, we mean by this that that matter itself took off one form and put on another. This, then, amounts to the fact that one form has ceased to exist and one has come into existence, there being a subsistent matter over which the two forms passed in succession. And when we say that water through heating has changed into air, we mean that the matter receptive of the form of water took off this form and received another form. Matter is thus common, while the quality changes. The same holds when we say that the staff has changed into a serpent and earth into animal.

(36) Between accident and substance, there is no common matter—nor between blackness and the cooking pot. And there is no common matter between the rest of the genera. It is in this respect, then, that [the transformation of different genera one into another] is impossible.

(37) As for God's moving the hand of the dead man, setting him up in the form of a living person who is seated and writes so that through the movement of his hand ordered writing ensues, [this] in itself is not impossible as long as we turn over [the enactment of] temporal events to the will of a choosing being. It is only disavowed because of the continuous habit of its opposite occurring. Your statement that, with this, the well-designed act ceases to indicate the [existence of] the knowledge of the agent is not true. For the agent now is God, who is the performer of the well-designed act and [the] knower of it.

(38) As for your statement that there would be no difference between the tremor and the voluntary movement, we say:

(39) We apprehend [this difference] in ourselves. For we have perceived in ourselves a necessary distinction between the two states and have given expression to this difference by the term "power." We thus know that what takes place in the two possible alternatives [is two things],

(٣٥) مصير الشيء شيئا آخر غير معقول، لانّ السواد اذا انقلب قدرة، مثلا فالسواد باق أم لا؟ فان كان معدوما فلم ينقلب، بل عدم ذاك ووجد غيره، وان كان موجودا مع القدرة، فلم ينقلب ولكن انضاف اليه غيره. وان بقى السواد، والقدرة معدومة، فلم ينقلب، بل بقى على ما هو عليه. واذا قلنا انقلب الدم منيا أردنا به انّ تلك المادة بعينها خلعت صورة ولبست صورة اخرى، فرجع الحاصل الى انّ صورة عدمت وصورة حدثت، وثمّ مادّة قائمة تعاقب عليها الصورتان. واذا قلنا انقلب الماء هواء بالتسخين أردنا به أن المادّة القابلة لصورة المائيّة خلعت هذه الصورة وقبلت صورة اخرى. فالمادة مشتركة والصفة متغيّرة. وكذلك اذا قلنا انقلب العصا ثعبانا، والتراب حيوانا.

(٣٦) وليس بين العرض والجوهر مادّة مشتركة، ولا بين السواد والقدرة، ولا بين سائر الاجناس مادّة مشتركة. فكان هذا محالا من هذا الوجه.

(٣٧) وأمّا تحريك الله يد ميت ونصبه على صورة حىّ يقعد ويكتب حتّى يحدث من حركة يده الكتابة المنظومة، فليس بمستحيل فى نفسه مهما احلنا الحوادث الى ارادةٍ مختارٍ. وانّما هو مستنكر لاطراد العادة بخلافه. وقولكم تبطل به دلالة احكام الفعل على علم الفاعل، فليس كذلك. فانّ الفاعل الان هو الله وهو المحكم وهو [عالم]²³ به.

(٣٨) وأمّا قولكم انّه لا يبقى فرق بين الرعشة والحركة المختارة فنقول:

(٣٩) انّما ادركنا ذلك من انفسنا، لانّا شاهدنا من أنفسنا تفرقة بين الحالتين، فعبّرنا عن ذلك الفارق بالقدرة، فعرفنا انّ الواقع من القسمين

one of them [occurring] in one state, the other in [another] state—
namely, the bringing to existence of a motion with the power over it[18]
in the one state, and the bringing of motion into existence without the
power in the other state. If, however, we look at another person and see
5   many ordered motions, there occurs to us knowledge of their being
within his power. For these are cognitions which God creates according to
the habitual course [of events], by which we know the existence of one of
the two possible alternatives [but] by which the impossibility of the other
alternative is not shown, as has been previously said.

الممكنين أحدهما فى حالة والآخر فى حالة وهو ايجاد الحركة مع القدرة عليها فى حالة، وايجاد الحركة دون القدرة فى حالة اخرى. وأمّا اذا نظرنا الى غيرنا ورأينا حركات كثيرة منظومة حصل لنا علم [بقدرته]٢٤، فهذه علوم يخلقها الله تعالى بمجارى العادات يعرف بها وجود أحد قسمىّ الامكان ولا يتبيّن به استحالة القسم الثانى، كما سبق.

٥

[Eighteenth] Discussion

On their inability to sustain a rational demonstration
[proving] that the human soul is a self-subsistent
spiritual substance that does not occupy space; that it is
neither body nor imprinted in the body; that it is neither
connected with nor disconnected from the body, just as
God is neither outside nor inside the world, the same
being the case with the angels, according to them

(1) To plunge into this requires explaining their doctrine of the animal and human [psychological] faculties.

(2) The animal faculties, according to [the philosophers], divide into two parts: motive and apprehending. The apprehending consists of two parts: external and internal. The external consists of the five senses, which are meanings imprinted in bodies—I mean these faculties. As for the internal, they are three. One of them is the imaginative faculty [located] in the front of the brain, behind the faculty of sight. In it, the forms of seen things are retained after closing the eye; indeed, there is imprinted in it what all the five senses bring in. These assemble therein, and for this reason it is [then] termed "the common sense." If it were not for [this common sense], then if someone who had seen white honey and [in the past] had not apprehended its sweetness except through taste were to see it again, he would not apprehend its sweetness unless he tasted [it] as he did the first time. But [the common sense] includes[1] a meaning that judges that this white thing is the sweet thing. Hence, it is

مسئلة

فى تعجيزهم عن اقامة البرهان العقلى على انّ
النفس الانسانى جوهر روحانىّ قائم بنفسه لا يتحيّز
وليس بجسم ولا منطبع فى الجسم ولا هو متّصل بالبدن
ولا هو منفصل عنه، كما أنّ الله ليس خارج العالم ولا
داخل العالم، وكذى الملائكة عندهم.

(١) والخوض فى هذا يستدعى شرح مذهبهم فى القوى الحيوانيّة
والانسانيّة.

(٢) والقوى الحيوانيّة تنقسم عندهم الى قسمين، محرّكة ومدركة.
والمدركة قسمان، ظاهرة وباطنة. والظاهرة هى الحواسّ الخمس وهى
معان منطبعة فى الاجسام اعنى هذه القوى. واما الباطنة فثلثة: احديها ٥
القوة الخياليّة فى مقدّم الدماغ وراء القوة الباصرة. [وفيها]¹ تبقى صور
الاشياء المرئيّة بعد تغميض العين، بل ينطبع فيها ما تورده الحواس الخمس.
فيجتمع فيه، ويسمّى الحسّ المشترك لذلك. ولولاه لكان من رأى العسل
الابيض ولم يدرك حلاوته الا بالذوق، فاذا رآه ثانيا لا يدرك حلاوته ما لم
يذق كالمرّة الاولى. ولكن فيه معنى يحكم بانّ هذا الابيض هو الحلو. ١٠

١٧٨

inevitable that he have with him a judge where the two things—I mean color and sweetness—have been assembled, such that with the existence of the one he judges that the other exists.

(3) The second is the estimative faculty,[2] which apprehends meanings, whereas the first faculty apprehends the forms. By "form" one intends that whose existence requires matter—that is, a body—and by "meanings" that whose existence does not require a body but which happens to be in a body—as, for example, enmity and harmony. Thus, the ewe apprehends of the wolf its color, shape, and appearance, which can only exist in a body, but she also apprehends its being disagreeable to her. [Again,] the kid apprehends the color and shape of the mother, then it apprehends her harmony and agreeableness. For this reason it flees from the wolf and runs after the mother. Unlike color and shape, it is not a necessity for disagreeableness and agreeableness to be in bodies; but it so happens that they also exist in bodies. Hence, this [imaginative] faculty differs from the second faculty [the estimative]. The place of this [latter] faculty is the hindmost concavity of the brain.

(4) As regards the third [inner sense], this is the faculty which in animals is called the imaginative and in humans the cogitative. Its task is to combine the sensible forms with each other and to construct meanings over forms. It is in the middle concavity of the brain, between that which retains the forms and that which retains the meanings. For this reason the human can imagine a horse that flies, [or] an individual whose head is the head of a man and whose body is the body of a horse, or other compositions [of this sort], even though the likes of these have never been seen. It is more appropriate that this faculty should be attached to the motive faculty, as will be discussed shortly, [and] not with the apprehending faculties. The place of these faculties is known through the medical art. For when a malady afflicts any of these concavities, these [apprehending] things become defective.

(5) They then claimed that the faculty in which the forms of the sensible things experienced by the five senses are impressed retains these forms so that they endure after [their] reception. A thing does not retain [another] thing by the [same] faculty by which it receives it. For water receives but does not retain, whereas wax receives through its moistness and retains through its dryness, unlike water. Thus, the retentive [faculty]

فلا بدّ وان يكون عنده حاكم قد اجتمع عنده الامران، اعنى اللون والحلاوة، حتّى قضى عند وجود احدهما بوجود الآخر.

(٣) والثانية القوّة الوهميّة وهى التى تدرك المعانى <وكانت>[٢] القوّة الاولى تدرك الصور. والمراد بالصور ما لا بدّ لوجوده من مادّة أى جسم، والمراد بالمعانى ما لا يستدعى وجوده جسما، ولكن قد يعرض له أن يكون فى جسم، كالعداوة والموافقة. فانّ الشاة تدرك من الذئب لونه وشكله وهيئته وذلك لا يكون الا فى جسم وتدرك أيضا كونه مخالفا لها؛ وتدرك السخلة شكل الام ولونه، ثم تدرك موافقته وملاءمته ولذلك تهرب من الذئب وتعدو خلف الام. والمخالفة والموافقة ليس من ضرورتها ان تكون فى الاجسام، لا كاللون والشكل، ولكن قد يعرض لها ان تكون فى الاجسام أيضا. فكانت هذه القوّة مباينة للقوة الثانية. وهذا محلّه التجويف الاخير من الدماغ.

(٤) اما الثالثة، فهى القوّة التى تسمّى فى الحيوانات متخيّلة، وفى الانسان مفكّرة. وشأنها أن تركّب الصور المحسوسة بعضها مع بعض وتركّب المعانى على الصور. وهى فى التجويف الاوسط بين حَافظ الصور وحافظ المعانى. ولذلك يقدر الانسان على أن يتخيّل فرسا يطير وشخصا رأسه رأس انسان وبدنه بدن فرس، الى غير ذلك من التركيبات، وان لم يشاهد مثل ذلك. والاولى أن تلحق هذه القوة بالقوى المحرّكة، كما سيأتى، لا بالقوى المدركة. وانما عرفت مواضع هذه القوى بصناعة الطبّ. فان الآفة اذا نزلت بهذه التجويفات اختلت هذه الامور.

(٥) ثم زعموا ان القوّة التى تنطبع فيها صور المحسوسات بالحواس الخمس تحفظ تلك الصور حتّى تبقى بعد القبول. والشىء يحفظ الشىء لا بالقوة التى بها يقبل. فانّ الماء يقبل ولا يحفظ، والشمع يقبل برطوبته

through this consideration becomes other than the receptive. Hence, this [latter faculty] is termed "the retentive." The same applies to meanings. [These] are impressed on the estimative [faculty], and a faculty termed "memory" retains them. Thus, the internal apprehensions through this
5 consideration, when the imaginative is added to them, become five, just as the external [senses] are five.

(6) Regarding the motive faculties, they divide into a motive [faculty] in the sense that it motivates toward movement and into a motive [faculty] in the sense that it initiates the movement, enacting [it].

10 (7) The motive in the sense that it motivates is the appetitive, desirous [faculty]. This is the one which, when the form of the object of either desire or aversion is imprinted in the imaginative faculty which we have mentioned, impels the active motive faculty into motion. It has two branches: a branch termed "the concupiscent," a faculty that impels
15 toward motion through which one is drawn near to the things imagined, whether necessary or useful, in the quest of pleasure; and a branch termed "irascible"—namely, a faculty that impels toward motion that repels the imagined thing, whether harmful or destructive, seeking to overcome [it]. With this faculty is fulfilled the complete resolution to
20 [perform] the act termed "voluntary."

(8) As regards the motive faculty, in the sense that it enacts [movement], it is a power that is imprinted in the nerves and muscles whose function is to contract the muscles, pulling thereby the sinews and tendons that are connected with the limbs to the direction wherein is the power,
25 or else to relax and stretch them lengthwise so that the sinews and tendons move in the opposite direction. These, then, are the faculties of the animal soul [described] by way of brevity and the abandoning of detail.

(9) Regarding the rational human soul, called by them "the discursive"—by "discursive" being meant "rational" (because discourse is exter-
30 nally the most particular of the fruits of reason and is hence attributed to it)—it has two faculties, a cognitive faculty and a practical faculty. Each of the two may be called an "intellect," but equivocally. The practical is a

ويحفظ بيبوسته، بخلاف الماء. فكانت الحافظة بهذا الاعتبار غير القابلة. فتسمّى هذه قوّة حافظة. وكذى المعانى، تنطبع فى الوهميّة وتحفظها قوّة تسمّى ذاكرة. فتصير الادراكات الباطنة بهذا الاعتبار اذا ضمّ اليها المتخيّلة خمسة، كما كانت الظاهرة خمسة.

(٦) وامّا [القوى]٢ المحرّكة، فتنقسم الى محرّكة على معنى انّها باعثة على الحركة، والى محرّكة على معنى انها مباشرة للحركة، فاعلة.

(٧) والمحرّكة على انّها باعثة هى القوة النزوعيّة الشوقيّة. وهى التى اذا ارتسم فى القوة الخياليّة التى ذكرناها صورة مطلوب أو مهروب عنه، بعثت القوة المحركة الفاعلة على التحريك. ولها شعبتان، شعبة تسمى قوّة شهوانيّة، وهى قوّة تبعث على تحريك يقرّب به من الاشياء المتخيّلة ضروريّة او نافعة طلبا للذة، وشعبة تسمّى قوّة غضبيّة، وهى قوّة تبعث على تحريك يدفع به الشىء المتخيّل ضارّا أو مفسدا طلبا للغلبة. وبهذه القوّة يتمّ الاجماع التام على الفعل المسمّى [اراديّا]٤.

(٨) واما القوّة المحرّكة على انّها فاعلة، هى قوة تنبعث فى الاعصاب والعضلات من شأنها أن تشنج العضلات، فتجذب الاوتار والرباطات المتّصلة بالاعضاء الى جهة الموضع الذى فيه القوّة أو ترخيها وتمدّدها طولا، فتصير الاوتار والرباطات الى خلاف الجهة. فهذه قوى النفس الحيوانيّة على طريق الاجمال وترك التفصيل.

(٩) فامّا النفس العاقلة الانسانيّة المسماة الناطقة عندهم، والمراد بالناطقة العاقلة، لانّ النطق اخصّ ثمرات العقل فى الظاهر، فنسبت اليه، فلها قوّتان قوّة عالمة وقوّة عاملة. وقد [تسمّى]٥ كلّ واحدة عقلا، ولكن

faculty which is a principle that moves the body of man toward the ordered human arts whose order is drawn out by deliberation, [the activity] proper to man. As for the cognitive, this is the one termed "theoretical." This is a faculty whose function is to apprehend the true natures of the intelligibles stripped from matter, place, and [spatial] direction. These are the universal propositions[3] which the speculative theologians call "states" at one time [and] "aspects" at another, and which the philosophers call "abstract universals."

(10) Hence, the soul has two faculties in relation to two sides: the theoretical faculty in relation to the side of the angels, since through it [the soul] takes from the angels the true sciences—and this faculty ought to be constantly [open to] reception from the side above; and the practical faculty, which belongs to [the soul] in relation to what is below—namely, the direction of the body to its management and the rectification of moral dispositions. This is a faculty that ought to take control over all the rest of the bodily faculties, whereby the rest of the faculties would be disciplined by its educative action [and be] vanquished by it, so that it is not influenced by [the bodily faculties], but, rather, that these faculties [themselves] are influenced by it—[this] lest there occur in the soul by way of bodily qualities submissive dispositions called vices. Rather, [this practical faculty ought] to be dominant so that because of it there would be realized for the soul dispositions called virtues.

(11) This, in brief, is what they have detailed regarding the animal and human faculties, going to great length in mentioning them, abandoning any discussion of the vegetative powers, since talking about them is not to our purpose. There is nothing in what they have mentioned that must be denied in terms of the religious law. For these are observed matters which God has ordained to flow according to habit.[4]

(12) We only want now to object to their claim of their knowing through rational demonstrations that the soul is a self-subsistent substance. We do not offer against [their claim] the objection of one who deems this remote from God's power or who perceives that the religious law has brought forth what is contrary to it. Indeed, we may well show in detailing the explanation of the resurrection and the afterlife that the law gives credence to it. We deny, however, their claim that reason alone

باشتراك الاسم. فالعاملة قوّة هى مبدأ محرّك لبدن الانسان الى الصناعات المرتّبة الانسانيّة المستنبط ترتيبها بالرويّة الخاصّة بالانسان. وأمّا العالمة فهى التى تسمّى النظريّة. وهى قوّة من شأنها أن تدرك حقائق المعقولات المجرّدة عن المادّة والمكان [والجهة]٦ وهى القضايا الكلّيّة التى يسمّيها المتكلمون احوالا مرة ووجوها أخرى، وتسميها ٥ الفلاسفة الكلّيّات المجرّدة.

(١٠) فاذن للنفس قوّتان بالقياس الى جنبتين، القوّة النظريّة بالقياس الى جنبة الملائكة، اذ بها تأخذ من الملائكة العلوم الحقيقيّة، وينبغى ان تكون هذه القوّة دائمة القبول من جهة فوق، والقوّة العمليّة لها بالنسبة الى أسفل، وهى جهة البدن وتدبيره واصلاح الاخلاق. ١٠ وهذه القوّة ينبغى أن تتسلّط على سائر القوى البدنيّة وأن تكون سائر القوى متأدّبة بتأديبها مقهورة دونها حتّى لا تنفعل ولا تتأثّر هى عنها، بل تنفعل تلك القوى عنها، لئلا يحدث فى النفس من الصفات البدنيّة هيآت انقياديّة تسمّى رذائل. بل تكون هى الغالبة، ليحصل للنفس بسببها هيآت تسمّى فضائل. ١٥

(١١) فهذا ايجاز ما فصّلوه من القوى الحيوانيّة والانسانيّة وطوّلوا بذكرها، مع الاعراض عن ذكر القوى النباتيّة، اذ لا حاجة الى ذكرها فى غرضنا. وليس شىء ممّا ذكروه ممّا يجب انكاره فى الشرع. فانّها امور مشاهدة اجرى الله العادة بها.

(١٢) وانّما نريد ان نعترض الآن على دعواهم معرفة كون النفس ٢٠ جوهرا قائما بنفسه ببراهين العقل. ولسنا نعترض اعتراض من يبعد ذلك من قدرة الله، أو يرى ان الشرع جاءَ بنقيضه. بل ربما نبيّن فى تفصيل

indicates this and that there is no need in it for the religious law. Let us, then, demand of them proofs. They have for this many demonstrations, as they claim.

The first [proof]⁵

(13) They say:

(14) Intellectual cognitions indwell in the human soul, being restricted [in number], and include units that are indivisible. It is inevitable, therefore, that their receptacle is also indivisible. [Now,] every body is divisible. [This] proves that their receptacle is something that is indivisible. One can formulate this according to the condition of logic in its [various] figures, but the easiest [to grasp] is to say: "If the receptacle of knowledge is a divisible body, knowledge that indwells therein is also divisible; but the knowledge indwelling therein is not divisible; the receptacle, hence, is not a body." This is a hypothetical syllogism in which the contradictory of the consequent is given as a second statement,⁶ deriving thereby as the conclusion the contradictory of the antecedent, by agreement.⁷ There is, hence, no need to examine the correctness of the figure of the syllogism, nor also [the truth] of the two premises. For the first [consists of] our statement that everything that indwells in what is divisible becomes necessarily divisible by the [very] supposition of divisibility in its receptacle. This is a primary [truth] that cannot be doubted. The second is our statement that the one knowledge indwells in the human and is indivisible. For if it were divisible infinitely, this would be impossible; and if it were to have a limit, then it would necessarily include unities that are indivisible. In brief, we know things but cannot suppose that some [of the things in our knowledge] cease while some remain, since there is no "some" in these [things].

(15) The objection is from two standpoints.

(16) The first standpoint is to say: "With what [argument] would you deny one who says, 'The receptacle for knowledge is single, indivisible, space-occupying substance'?" This is known from the doctrine of the speculative theologians. The only response that remains [for the philosophers]

الحشر والنشر ان الشرع مصدّق له. ولكنّا ننكر دعواهم دلالة مجرّد العقل عليه والاستغناء عن الشرع فيه. فلنطالبهم بالادلّة؛ ولهم فيه براهين كثيرة، بزعمهم.

الاوّل

(١٣) قولهم:

(١٤) ان العلوم العقليّة تحلّ النفس الانسانى وهى محصورة وفيها آحاد لا تنقسم. فلا بدّ وان يكون محلّه أيضا لا ينقسم. وكلّ جسم فمنقسم. فدلّ أنّ [محلّها]⁷ شىء لا ينقسم. ويمكن ايراد هذا على شرط المنطق بأشكاله، ولكن أقربه ان يقال: ان كان محلّ العلم جسما منقسما، فالعلم الحالّ فيه أيضا منقسم؛ لكنّ العلم الحالّ غير منقسم؛ فالمحلّ ليس جسما. وهذا هو قياس شرطىّ استثنى فيه نقيض التالى فينتج نقيض المقدّم بالاتفاق. فلا نظر فى صحّة شكل القياس ولا أيضا فى المقدّمتين. فان الاوّل قولنا ان كلّ حالّ فى منقسم ينقسم لا محالة بفرض القسمة فى محلّه. وهو أَوْلَى لا يمكن التشكك فيه. والثانى قولنا انّ العلم الواحد يحلّ فى الآدمى وهو لا ينقسم. لأنّه لو انقسم الى غير نهاية كان محالا، وان كان له نهاية، فيشتمل على آحاد لا محالة لا تنقسم. وعلى الجملة نحن نعلم اشياء ولا نقدر ان نفرض زوال بعضها وبقاء البعض، من حيث انّه لا بعض لها.

(١٥) والاعتراض على مقامين:

(١٦) المقام الاوّل ان يقال: بم تنكرون على من يقول محل العلم جوهر فرد متحيّز لا ينقسم؟ وقد عرف هذا من مذهب المتكلّمين. ولا

is to deem [this doctrine] unlikely—namely [to ask] "How is it that all
the cognitions would dwell in a single [indivisible] substance, all the substances surrounding [these cognitions] being deprived [of them while
yet] close by?" But deeming something unlikely [does the philosophers]
5   no good, since it [can] also be turned against their doctrine. [For one can
ask:] "How can the soul be one thing that does not occupy space, is not
referred to by pointing, is neither in the body nor outside it, is neither
connected with the body nor disconnected [from it]?" We, however, will
not favor this position [here]. For the discussion of the question of the
10   indivisible part is lengthy, and [the philosophers] have concerning it geometrical proofs that would take long to discuss. These include their
statement: "In the case of an individual atom between two atoms, would
one of its ends meet an identical thing that the other end meets, or something else? If an identical thing, this would be impossible. For from this
15   it follows necessarily that the two ends [of the atom] meet, since whatever meets that which meets another meets the former. If what [either
end] meets is another [thing], then this entails affirming multiplicity and
division."[8] This is a difficulty that will take long to resolve, and we have
no need to get involved in it; so let us, hence, turn to another position.
20   (17) The second standpoint is to say: "What you have mentioned to
the effect that everything that indwells in a body must be divisible is fal-
sified for you in terms of what the [estimative] faculty that is in the ewe
apprehends of the wolf's enmity. For it is within the domain of one thing
whose division is inconceivable, since enmity does not have a part where
25   one [could] hypothesize the apprehension of some part of it and the
ceasing to exist of another part. But, according to you, [the ewe's] apprehension [of the enmity] took place in a bodily faculty." For the soul of
beasts is imprinted in bodies, not enduring after death. This they agree
on. If, then, they are able to undertake the supposition of division in the
30   things apprehended by the five senses, the common sense, and the
faculty retentive of [material] forms, they are unable to suppose division
in these meanings that do not have as a condition their being in matter.

يبقى بعده الا استبعاد وهو انّه كيف تحلّ العلوم كلّها فى جوهر فرد،
وتكون جميع الجواهر المطيفة بها معطّلة بمجاورة؟ والاستبعاد لا خير فيه،
اذ يتوجّه على مذهبهم أيضا، انّه كيف تكون النفس شيئا واحدا لا يتحيّز،
ولا يشار اليه، ولا يكون داخل البدن ولا خارجه، ولا متّصلاً بالجسم ولا

٥ منفصلاً عنه؟ الا انّا لا نؤثر هذا المقام. فانّ القول فى مسئلة الجزء الذى لا
يتجزّى طويل، ولهم فيه أدلّة هندسية يطول الكلام عليها، ومن جملتها
قولهم جوهر فرد بين جوهرين، هل يلاقى أحد الطرفين منه عين ما يلاقيه
الآخر أو غيره؟ فان كان عينه فهو محال اذ يلزم منه تلاقى الطرفين، فان
ملاقى الملاقى ملاق؛ وان كان ما يلاقيه غيره ففيه اثبات التعدّد

١٠ والانقسام. وهذه شبهة يطول حلّها، وبنا غنية عن الخوض فيها. فلنعدل
الى مقام آخر.

(١٧) المقام الثانى ان نقول: ما ذكرتموه من انّ كلّ حالّ فى جسم
فينبغى ان ينقسم باطل عليكم بما تدركه القوّة من الشاة من عداوة
الذئب. فانّها فى حكم شىء واحد لا يتصوّر تقسيمه، اذ ليس للعداوة

١٥ بعض حتى يقدر ادراك بعضه وزوال بعضه. وقد حصل ادراكها فى
قوّة جسمانيّة عندكم. فانّ نفس البهائم منطبعة فى الاجسام لا تبقى
بعد الموت. وقد اتفقوا عليه. فان امكنهم ان يتكلّفوا تقدير الانقسام
فى المدركات بالحواس الخمس وبالحس المشترك وبالقوّة الحافظة
للصور، فلا يمكنهم تقدير الانقسام فى هذه المعانى التى ليس من

٢٠ شرطها ان تكون فى مادّة.

(18) If it is said, "The ewe does not apprehend absolute enmity, stripped from matter, but apprehends the enmity of the determinate, individuated wolf, connected with its individual [self] and frame, whereas the rational faculty apprehends truths abstracted from materials and
5   individuals," we say:

(19) The ewe has apprehended the color of the wolf, its shape, and then its enmity. If the color is imprinted in the faculty of sight, [and] similarly shape, [both] being divisible by the divisibility of the receptacle of sight, with what, then, does [the ewe] apprehend the enmity? If it is
10 apprehended by a body, then let it be divisible. But, by my word, what would be the state of that apprehension if it is divisible, and how would part of it be? Would this be apprehension of "some" of the enmity? If so, how would it have a part? Or would it be that each part is an apprehension of the whole of the enmity, whereby enmity would be known several
15 times by having its apprehension being fixed in each part of the parts of the receptacle? This, then, [remains] a difficulty in their demonstration unresolved for them. It is in dire need of a solution.

(20) [To this it may] be said:

(21) This is a contradiction [you bring] into [the things that are]
20 rationally intelligible, and intelligible things cannot be contradicted. For as long as you are unable to doubt the two premises—namely, that the one knowledge is indivisible and that whatever is indivisible does not subsist in a divisible body—you cannot doubt the conclusion.

(22) The answer is that we have written this book only to show the
25 incoherence and inconsistency in the utterances of the philosophers. This has been achieved, since one of the two things has been contradicted—either what they have said about the rational soul or what they have said about the estimative faculty. Moreover, this contradiction shows that they did not notice a place of confusion in [their] syllogism. Perhaps the
30 place of confusion lies in their statement: "Knowledge is imprinted in the body in the way color is imprinted in the colored thing, and color is divided by the division of the thing colored. Knowledge is hence divided by the division of the receptacle." The defect [here] is in the expression "being imprinted," since it is possible that the relation of knowledge to its

(١٨) فان قيل: الشاة لا تدرك العداوة المطلقة المجرّدة عن المادّة، بل تدرك عداوة الذئب المعيّن المشخّص، مقرونا بشخصه وهيكله، والقوّة العاقلة تدرك الحقائق مجرّدة عن الموادّ والاشخاص، قلنا:

(١٩) الشاة قد أدركت لون الذئب وشكله ثم عداوته. فان كان اللون ينطبع فى القوّة الباصرة، وكذى الشكل، وينقسم بانقسام محلّ البصر، فالعداوة بماذى تدركها؟ فان [ادركت]^ بجسم فلينقسم. وليت شعرى، ما حال ذلك الادراك اذا قسم؟ وكيف يكون بعضه؟ أهو ادراك لبعض العداوة؟ فكيف يكون لها بعض؟ أو كلّ قسم ادراك لكلّ العداوة، فتكون العداوة معلومة مرارا بثبوت ادراكها فى كلّ قسم من أقسام المحلّ؟ فاذن هذه شبهة مشكلة لهم فى برهانهم. فلا بد من الحلّ.

(٢٠) فان قيل:

(٢١) هذه مناقضة فى المعقولات والمعقولات لا تنقض. فانّكم مهما لم تقدروا على الشك فى المقدّمتين، وهو انّ العلم الواحد لا ينقسم وانّ ما لا ينقسم لا يقوم بجسم منقسم، لم يمكنكم الشك فى النتيجة.

(٢٢) والجواب: انّ هذا الكتاب ما صنفناه الا لبيان التهافت والتناقض فى كلام الفلاسفة؛ وقد حصل، اذ انتقض به أحد الامرين، امّا ما ذكروه فى النفس الناطقة، أو ما ذكروه فى القوّة الوهميّة. ثم نقول هذه المناقضة تبيّن انّهم غفلوا عن موضع تلبيس فى القياس. ولعلّ موضع الالتباس قولهم: انّ العلم منطبع فى الجسم انطباع اللون فى المتلوّن، وينقسم اللون بانقسام المتلوّن، فينقسم العلم بانقسام محلّه. والخلل فى لفظ الانطباع، اذ يمكن ان لا تكون نسبة العلم الى محلّه كنسبة اللون الى

receptacle is unlike the relation of color to the thing colored [where, if it were similar,] one would consequently say that it covers it, is impressed in it, and is spread over its sides, and is thus divided by its division. Perhaps the relation of knowledge to its receptacle is of a different aspect, that aspect not allowing the division [of knowledge] with the division of the receptacle. Rather, its relation may well be similar to the relation of enmity to the body. The aspects of the relation of qualities to their receptacles are not confined to one mode, nor are their details known to us in a manner in which we are [fully] confident. Hence, judging it without wholly comprehending the details of the relation would constitute an unreliable judgment.

(23) In general, one does not deny that what they have mentioned is among those things that strengthen belief, making it more likely. But what is denied is its being known with certainty, by a knowledge in which error is not allowed and which doubt does not frequent. This much [of what they say, however,] is open to doubt.

A second proof

(24) They say:

(25) If knowledge of the one intellectual object of knowledge— namely, the object of knowledge that is abstracted from material things— is imprinted in matter in the way accidents are imprinted in bodily substances, then, as previously noted, its division by virtue of the division of the body follows necessarily. If it is not imprinted in [matter] nor spread over it, and the utterance "imprinting" is found repugnant, we will exchange it for another expression, saying: "Does knowledge have or does it not have a relation to the knower?"[9] It is impossible to sever the relation. For if the relation is severed from it, then why should his being cognizant of [the object of knowledge] have preference over another [person's] being cognizant of it? If [knowledge] has a relation, then [one of] three alternatives is not excluded: either [(a)] the relation exists for each [one] of the parts of the receptacle, [or (b) it exists] for [only] some parts of the receptacle, or [(c)] no one part of the receptacle has a relation to [knowledge].

المتلوّن حتّى يقال انّه منبسط عليه ومنطبع فيه ومنتشر فى جوانبه، فينقسم بانقسامه. فلعلّ نسبة العلم الى محلّه على وجه آخر، وذلك الوجه لا يجوز فيه الانقسام عند انقسام المحلّ. بل نسبته اليه كنسبة ادراك العداوة الى الجسم. ووجوه نسبة الاوصاف الى محلّها ليست محصورة فى فنّ واحد، ولا هى معلومة التفاصيل لنا علما نثق به. فالحكم عليه دون الاحاطة بتفصيل النسبة حكم غير موثوق به.

(٢٣) وعلى الجملة، لا ينكر ان ما ذكروه ممّا يُقوّى الظنّ ويغلبه. وانما ينكر كونه معلوما يقينا علما لا يجوز الغلط فيه ولا يتطرّق اليه الشكّ. وهذا القدر مشكّك فيه.

دليل ثان

(٢٤) قالوا:

(٢٥) ان كان العلم بالمعلوم الواحد العقلىّ، وهو المعلوم المجرّد عن الموادّ، منطبعا فى المادّة انطباع الاعراض فى الجواهر الجسمانية، لزم انقسامه بالضرورة بانقسام الجسم كما سبق. وان لم يكن منطبعا [فيها]⁹ ولا منبسطا [عليها]¹⁰، واستكره لفظ الانطباع، فنعدل الى عبارة أُخرى ونقول: هل للعلم نسبة الى العالم، أم لا؟ ومحال قطع النسبة فانّه ان قطعت النسبة عنه فكونه عالما به لم صار أولى من كون غيره [عالما به]¹¹؟ وان كان له نسبة فلا يخلوا من ثلثة أقسام: امّا أن تكون النسبة لكلّ جزء من اجزاء المحلّ، او تكون لبعض اجزاء المحلّ دون البعض، أو لا يكون لواحد من الاجزاء نسبة اليه.

(26) [Now,] it is false to say that there is no relation to any one unit of the parts [of the receptacle]. For if the units have no relation, the whole would have no relation. For the compound of things separated [from an entity] is [itself] separated [from that entity]. And it is [also] false to say that the relation is [only] to some parts [of the receptacle]. For that which has no relation does not in any way [share] in the meaning ["knowledge"]. And our discussion would not pertain to it. It is, furthermore, false to say that each part which is supposed has a relation to the essence [of what is known]. For if the relation pertains to the essence of knowledge in its entirety, then what is known in each part is not restricted to a part of what is known, but to the known as [a whole]. Hence, what is known becomes known through instances that are infinite in actuality.[10] If [on the other hand] each part of [the receptacle] has a relation other than the relation which another part has to the essence of knowledge, then the essence of knowledge is divisible in meaning. But we have shown that knowledge of the one object of knowledge in all [its] aspects is not divisible in meaning. And if the relation of each [part of the receptacle] to some [part] of the essence of knowledge is other than another part's relation to it, then the division of the essence of knowledge becomes in this way even more apparent. [But] this [division] is impossible.

(27) From this it becomes clear that the sensible things imprinted in the five senses can only be representations of particular divisible forms. For apprehension means the occurrence of the representation of what is apprehended in the soul of the one who apprehends. Each part of the representation of the perceived would then have a relation to a part of the bodily organ.

(28) [Our] objection [to this] is the same as [our] previous one. For replacing the expression "imprinting" by the expression "relation" does not resolve the difficulty in the case of what is imprinted in the ewe's estimative faculty of the wolf's enmity, according to what [the philosophers] have mentioned. For this is inescapably an apprehension and has a relation to [the knower], and the things you have mentioned obtain necessarily for this relation. Enmity is not something measurable, having a measurable quantity such that its representation would be imprinted in a quantified body, its parts becoming related to its parts. The shape of the wolf being measurable is not sufficient [to resolve the difficulty]. For the ewe apprehends something other than [the wolf's] shape— namely, contrariety, opposition, and enmity. What is added to shape by

(٢٦) وباطل ان يقال: لا نسبة لواحد من الاجزاء. فانّه اذا لم يكن للآحاد نسبة، لم يكن للمجموع نسبة. فان المجتمع من المباينات مباين. وباطل أن يقال: النسبة للبعض. فانّ الذى لا نسبة له ليس هو من معناه فى شىء، وليس كلامنا فيه. وباطل ان يقال: لكلّ جزء مفروض نسبة الى الذات؛ لأنّه ان كانت النسبة الى ذات العلم باسره، فمعلوم كلّ واحد من الاجزاء ليس هو جزءًا من المعلوم، بل المعلوم كما هو. فيكون معقولا مرات لا نهاية لها بالفعل. وان كان كل جزء له نسبة أُخرى غير النسبة التى للجزء الآخر الى ذات العلم، فذات العلم اذن منقسمة فى المعنى. وقد بيّنا انّ العلم بالمعلوم الواحد من كلّ وجه لا ينقسم فى المعنى. وان كان نسبة كل واحد الى شىء من ذات العلم غير ما اليه نسبة الآخر، فانقسام ذات العلم بهذا أظهر. وهو محال.

(٢٧) ومن هذا يتبيّن انّ المحسوسات المنطبعة فى الحواسّ الخمس لا تكون الا أمثلة لصور جزئيّة منقسمة. فانّ الادراك معناه حصول مثال المدرك فى نفس المدرك ويكون لكلّ جزء من مثال المحسوس نسبة الى جزء من الآلة الجسمانية.

(٢٨) والاعتراض على هذا ما سبق. فانّ تبديل لفظ الانطباع بلفظ النسبة لا يدرأ الشبهة فيما ينطبع فى القوّة الوهميّة للشاة من عداوة الذئب، كما ذكروه. فانّه ادراك لا محالة، وله نسبة اليه، ويلزم فى تلك النسبة ما ذكرتموه. فانّ العداوة ليس امرا مقدّرا له كمّية مقدارية حتّى ينطبع مثالها فى جسم مقدّر وتنتسب اجزاؤها الى أجزائه. وكون شكل الذئب مقدّرا لا يكفى. فانّ الشاة أدركت شيئا سوى شكله، وهو المخالفة

way of enmity has no measure; but the ewe has apprehended it by means of a quantified body. This form is [also] doubtful in this demonstration, as in the case of the first.

(29) If one were then to say, "Why did you not refute these demonstrations by [arguing] that knowledge indwells in the body in a substance occupying space that is indivisible—namely, the single atom?"[11] we would say:

(30) This is because discussing the single atom is connected with geometrical matters, the discussion of whose resolution takes too long. Moreover, this does not resolve the difficulty. For it would follow that power and will would have to exist in this atom. The human has action, and this is inconceivable without power and will, and will is conceivable only with knowledge. [Now,] the power to write exists in the hand and the fingers, whereas knowledge of [writing] is not in the hand, since it does not cease with the severing of the hand. Nor is the will [to write] in the hand. For a person may will [to write] after a hand's paralysis, but it is inaccessible to him, not for lack of will, but for lack of power.

A third proof

(31) They say: "If knowledge were to be in a part of the body, then the knower would be that part, not the rest of the parts of the human. But the human is said to be a knower. The state of being a knower is an attribute belonging to him as a whole, without relating to a specific place."

(32) [We answer:] "This is madness. For one is called a seer, a hearer, and a taster, the beast also being described this way; but this does not indicate that the apprehension of sensible things is not by the body." This is a kind of metaphorical speech, in the [same] way [that] it is said that "So-and-so is in Baghdad," even though he is in part of the totality of Baghdad, not in all of it; but he is made to relate to the whole.

والمضادّة والعداوة. والزيادة على الشكل من العداوة ليس لها مقدار؛ وقد ادركته بجسم مقدّر. فهذه الصورة مشكَّكة فى هذا البرهان كما فى الاوّل.

(٢٩) فان قال قائل: هلا دفعتم هذه البراهين بانّ العلم يحلّ من الجسم فى جوهر متحيّز لا يتجزّى وهو الجزء الفرد؟ قلنا:

(٣٠) لانّ الكلام فى الجوهر الفرد يتعلق بامور هندسيّة يطول القول فى حلّها. ثم ليس فيه ما يدفع الاشكال. فانّه يلزم ان تكون القدرة والارادة أيضا فى ذلك الجزء. فانّ للانسان فعلا ولا يتصوّر ذلك الا بقدرة وارادة ولا يتصوّر الارادة الا بعلم. وقدرة الكتابة فى اليد والاصابع والعلم بها ليس فى اليد اذ لا يزول بقطع اليد؛ ولا ارادتها فى اليد. فانّه قد يريدها بعد شلل اليد وتتعذّر، لا لعدم الارادة، بل لعدم القدرة.

دليل ثالث

(٣١) قولهم: العلم لو كان فى جزء من الجسم لكان العالم ذلك الجزء دون سائر أجزاء الانسان. والانسان يقال له عالم. والعالميّة صفة له على الجملة من غير نسبة الى محلّ مخصوص.

(٣٢) وهذا هوس. فانّه يسمّى مبصرا وسامعا وذائقا، وكذى البهيمة توصف به، وذلك لا يدل على ان ادراك المحسوسات ليس بالجسم. بل هو نوع من التجوّز كما يقال فلان فى بغداد، وان كان هو فى جزء من جملة بغداد، لا فى جملتها، ولكن يضاف الى الجملة.

A fourth proof

(33) If knowledge were to reside in a part of the heart or the brain, for example, ignorance being its opposite, it ought then to be possible for it to subsist in another part of the heart or brain. Man, then, would be at one and the same time both knowing and ignorant of one thing. This being impossible, it becomes evident that the receptacle of ignorance is the receptacle of knowledge and that this receptacle is one, wherein it is impossible for the two opposites to combine. For, if it were divisible, it would not be impossible for ignorance to reside in one part [and] knowledge in another. For a thing in a place is not contradicted by its opposite in another place, just as being piebald is an attribute of the one horse and blackness and whiteness of the one eye, but in different places.

(34) This does not necessarily follow in the case of the senses. For there are no contraries to their apprehension; rather, [the sense] will either apprehend or not apprehend. There is nothing between them except the opposition of existence or nonexistence. No wonder, then, that we say, "He apprehends by some of his parts, such as the eye or the ear, but does not apprehend by the rest of his body." In this there is no contradiction.

(35) This is not dispensed with by your statement, "The state of being a knower is contrary to the state of being ignorant, the judgment being general, applying to the entire body," since it is impossible for the judgment to pertain to other than the receptacle of the cause. For the knower is the receptacle in which knowledge subsists. If the term is applied to the whole, this is only by way of metaphor, just as one would say, "He is in Baghdad," even though he is only in part of it; and just as it is said, "He has sight," when we necessarily know that the judgment of seeing is inapplicable to the foot and the hand but pertains specifically to the eye. The opposition of judgments is similar to the opposition of [their] causes. For the judgments are confined to the receptacle of the causes [of these judgments].

(36) Nor is there an escape from this in someone's saying, "The receptacle prepared for the reception of knowledge and ignorance in a human is one [and the same], and, hence, they would be in opposition in it." For,

دليل رابع

(٣٣) ان كان العلم يحلّ جزءًا من القلب أو الدماغ مثلاً، فالجهل ضدّه. فينبغى أن يجوز قيامه بجزء آخر من القلب أو الدماغ. ويكون الانسان فى حالة واحدة عالما وجاهلا بشىء واحد. فلمّا استحال ذلك، تبيّن انّ محلّ الجهل هو محلّ العلم وانّ ذلك المحل واحد يستحيل اجتماع الضدّين فيه. فانّه لو كان منقسما، لما استحال قيام الجهل ببعضه والعلم ببعضه. لانّ الشىء فى محلّ لا يضادّه ضدّه فى محلّ آخر، كما تجتمع البلقة فى الفرس الواحد، والسواد والبياض فى العين الواحدة، ولكن فى محلّين.

(٣٤) ولا يلزم هذا فى الحواس. فانّه لا ضدّ لادراكاتها؛ ولكنّه قد يدرك وقد لا يدرك. فليس بينهما الا تقابل الوجود والعدم. فلا جرم نقول: يدرك ببعض اجزائه كالعين والاذن، ولا يدرك بسائر بدنه. وليس فيه تناقض.

(٣٥) ولا يغنى عن هذا قولكم: انّ العالميّة مضادة للجاهليّة، والحكم عام لجميع البدن اذ يستحيل ان يكون الحكم فى غير محلّ العلّة. فالعالم هو المحلّ الذى قام العلم به فان أطلق الاسم على الجملة فبالمجاز، كما يقال هو فى بغداد، وان كان هو فى بعضها، وكما يقال مبصر وان كنّا بالضرورة نعلم ان حكم الابصار لا يثبت للرجل واليد، بل يختصّ بالعين. وتضادّ الاحكام كتضادّ العلل. فانّ الاحكام تقتصر على محلّ العلل.

(٣٦) ولا يخلص من هذا قول القائل: انّ المحلّ المهيّأ لقبول العلم والجهل من الانسان واحد فيتضادّان عليه. فانّ عندكم ان كلّ جسم فيه

according to you, every body that is animate is receptive of knowledge and ignorance; and you made no condition other than life [for this reception]. The remaining parts of the body, according to you, with respect to the reception of knowledge, are of one pattern.

(37) [Our] objection is that this is turned against you with respect to appetite, desire, and will. For these matters are affirmed for beasts and man, being ideas impressed in the body. It is impossible to be repelled by what one desires. For then repulsion and inclination for one thing would combine in [the individual], desire existing in one receptacle, repulsion in another receptacle. This does not prove that these two do not reside in bodies. This is because these faculties, although numerous, distributed among many organs, have one connecting link—namely, the soul. This holds for both man and beast. Once this link is unified, contradictory relations with respect to it become impossible. But this does not prove that the soul is not imprinted in the body as it is [imprinted] in the case of beasts.

A fifth proof

(38) They say:

(39) If the mind apprehends the intelligibles by a bodily organ, then it does not apprehend itself.[12] But the consequent is impossible. For [the mind] apprehends itself. The antecedent, hence, is impossible.

(40) We say:

(41) It is admitted that repeating the consequent, [but] in its contradictory form, gives as its conclusion the contradictory of the antecedent. But this is only the case if the necessary [relation] between the consequent and the antecedent is established. Rather, we say, "What renders the necessity of the consequence admissible, and what proof is there for it?"

(42) [To this they may] say:

حيوة، فهو قابل للعلم والجهل، و لم تشترطوا سوى الحيوة شريطة أُخرى. وسائر اجزاء البدن عندكم فى قبول العلم على وتيرة واحدة.

(٣٧) الاعتراض انّ هذا ينقلب عليكم فى الشهوة والشوق والارادة. فانّ هذه الامور تثبت للبهائم والانسان وهى معان تنطبع فى الجسم. ثم يستحيل ان ينفر عمّا يشتاق اليه، فيجتمع فيه النفرة والميل الى شىء واحد بوجود الشوق فى محلّ، والنفرة فى محلّ آخر. وذلك لا يدلّ على انها لا تحلّ الاجسام. وذلك لانّ هذه القوى، وان كانت كثيرة ومتوزّعة على الآت مختلفة، فلها رابطة واحدة وهى النفس، وذلك للبهيمة والانسان جميعا. واذا اتّحدت الرابطة استحالت الاضافات المتناقضة بالنسبة [اليها][١٢]. وهذا لا يدلّ على كون النفس غير [منطبعة][١٣] فى الجسم كما فى البهائم.

دليل خامس

(٣٨) قولهم:

(٣٩) ان كان العقل يدرك المعقول بآلة جسمانيّة، فهو لا يعقل نفسه. والتالى محال، فانّه يعقل نفسه. فالمقدم محال.

(٤٠) قلنا:

(٤١) مسلّم ان استثناء نقيض التالى ينتج نقيض المقدّم. ولكن اذا ثبت اللزوم بين التالى والمقدّم. بل نقول: ما يسلّم لزوم التالى وما الدليل عليه؟

(٤٢) فان قيل:

(43) The proof for it is that, since seeing is by means of a body, seeing is not connected with sight [as its object of seeing]. For seeing is not
seen and hearing is not heard, the same being the case with the rest of
the senses. If, then, mind apprehends only through a body, then it would
not apprehend itself. For just as the mind apprehends intellectually
what is other, it apprehends itself. For just as the one among us intellectually apprehends another, he apprehends himself and apprehends
intellectually that he apprehends another and that he has intellectually
apprehended himself.

(44) We say:

(45) What you have stated is false in two respects. One is that, for
us, it is possible for sight to be related to itself so that it would consist in
the seeing of another and of itself, in the same way that the one knowledge is knowledge of another and of itself. The habitual [course of
nature], however, runs contrary to this. But the disruption of the habitual courses [of nature], according to us, is possible. The second—and
this is the stronger [answer]—is for us to admit this with respect to
[some of] the senses. But why should it be the case that, if this is impossible in some of the senses, it is impossible in others? And why is it
unlikely that what governs the senses with respect to apprehension
should differ, while [the senses] yet share in being bodily? [This is] just
as sight and touch differ, in that touch does not yield apprehension
except through the contact of the tangible with the organ of touch, the
same being true of smell, whereas sight differs [from these]. For it is a
condition [of sight] that it should be separated from [the object of
sight]—so [much so] that when an individual closes his eyelids he does
not see the color of the eyelid, because it is not at a distance from him.
This difference [between sight and touch] does not necessitate a difference
in the need for a body. Hence, it is not unlikely that there would be
among the bodily senses that which is called mind, differing from the
rest in that [these] do not apprehend themselves.

(٤٣) الدليل عليه انّ الابصار، لـمّا كان بجسم، فالابصار، لا يتعلّق بالابصار. فالرؤية لا تُرَى والسمع لا يُسمع وكذى سائر الحواس. فان كان العقل ايضا لا يدرك الا بجسم، فلم يدرك نفسه. والعقل كما يعقل غيره يعقل نفسه. فانّ الواحد منّا كما يعقل غيره، يعقل نفسه، ويعقل أنّه عقل غيره، وانّه عقل نفسه.

(٤٤) قلنا:

(٤٥) ما ذكرتموه فاسد من وجهين. احدهما انّ الابصار عندنا يجوز ان يتعلّق بنفسه فيكون ابصارا لغيره ولنفسه، كما يكون العلم الواحد علما بغيره وعلما بنفسه. ولكن العادة جارية بخلاف ذلك وخرق العادات عندنا جائز. والثاني، وهو أقوى، انّا [نسلم]١٤ هذا فى الحواسّ؛ ولكن لِم اذا امتنع ذلك فى بعض الحواسّ، يمتنع فى بعض؟ وأىّ بعد فى ان يفترق حكم الحواسّ فى وجه الادراك مع اشتراكها فى انّها جسمانية؟ كما اختلف البصر واللمس فى انّ اللمس لا يفيد الادراك الا باتصال الملموس بالآلة اللامسة، وكذى الذوق، ويخالفه البصر. فانّه يشترط فيه الانفصال، حتّى [أن الواحد]١٥ لو أطبق اجفانه، لم ير لون الجفن لأنّه لم يبعد عنه. وهذا الاختلاف لا يوجب الاختلاف فى الحاجة الى الجسم. فلا يبعد ان يكون فى الحواسّ الجسمانيّة ما يسمّى عقلا ويخالف سائرها فى انّها [لا تدرك]١٦ نفسها.

A sixth proof

(46) They say:

(47) If the mind were to apprehend by a bodily organ, as with sight, it would not have apprehended its organ, as with the rest of the senses. But it apprehends the brain and the heart and what is claimed to be its organ. This proves that [the object of its apprehension][13] is for [the mind] neither an organ nor a receptacle. Otherwise, it would not have apprehended it.

(48) [Our] objection to this [argument] is similar to the objection [to the argument] that preceded it. For we say, "It is not improbable for sight to perceive its receptacle, but [this] would be a reversion away from the habitual [course of events]"; or else we can say: "Why is it impossible for the senses to differ from each other in this respect, even though, as previously mentioned, they share in being imprinted in bodies? And why do you say that what subsists in a body cannot apprehend the body which is its receptacle, when it is not necessary to make an unrestricted universal judgment based on a determinate particular?" One of the things whose falsity is agreed on and which has been stated in logic is to make a universal judgment based on a particular cause or on numerous particulars, so that [the logicians] have illustrated it by the hypothetical example of a man who states: "Every animal moves its lower jaw in chewing, because we have examined inductively all the animals, observing them to be such," [the logicians adding that he makes this error] "because of his being oblivious of the crocodile; for it moves its upper jaw." [Now,] these [philosophers] have examined inductively only the five senses, finding them to be of a known mode, and on this basis they have made a judgment on all. For the mind may well be another sense that stands in relation to the other senses, as the crocodile stands in relation to the rest of the animals. The senses, although bodily, would then be divided into those that apprehend their receptacle and those that do not, just as they divide into those, like sight, that apprehend their object without contact and those, like touch and smell, that can only apprehend through contact. Hence, if what they have also stated may bequeath opinion, it does not yield reliable certitude.

(49) [The philosophers, however, may] say:

دليل سادس

(٤٦) قالوا:

(٤٧) لو كان العقل يدرك بآلة جسمانيّة كالابصار، لما أدرك الته كسائر الحواسّ. ولكنّه يدرك الدماغ والقلب وما يدعى آلته، فدلّ انّه ليس آلة له ولا محلا. والا لما ادركه.

(٤٨) والاعتراض على هذا كالاعتراض على الذى قبله. فانّا نقول: لا يبعد ان يدرك الابصار محلّه ولكنه حوالة على العادة؛ أو نقول: لم يستحيل ان تفترق الحواسّ فى هذا المعنى، وان اشتركت فى الانطباع فى الاجسام كما سبق؟ و لم قلتم انّ ما هو قائم فى جسم، يستحيل ان يدرك الجسم الذى هو محلّه، و لم يلزم ان يحكم من جزئىّ معيّن على كلّىّ مرسل؟ ومّما عرف بالاتفاق بطلانه وذكر فى المنطق، ان يحكم بسبب جزئىّ أو جزئيات كثيرة على كلّىّ، حتّى مثّلوه بما اذا قال الانسان: انّ كل حيوان فانّه يحرّك عند المضغ فكّه الاسفل، لانّا استقرأنا الحيوانات كلّها، فرأيناها كذلك؛ فيكون ذلك لغفلته عن التمساح؛ فانّه يحرّك فكّه الاعلى. وهؤلاء لم يستقرئوا الا الحواس الخمس فوجدوها على وجه معلوم، فحكموا على الكل به. فلعلّ العقل حاسّة أخرى تجرى من سائر الحواسّ مجرى التمساح من سائر الحيوانات، فتكون اذن الحواس مع كونها جسمانيّة منقسمة الى ما يدرك محلّها، والى ما لا يدرك، كما انقسمت الى ما يدرك مدركه من غير مماسّة كالبصر، والى ما لا يدرك الا باتصال كالذوق واللمس. فما ذكروه أيضا ان أورث ظنّا، فلا يورث يقينا موثوقا به.

(٤٩) فان قيل:

(50) We do not rely solely on the inductive examination of the senses. Rather, we rely on demonstration and say:

(51) If either the heart or the brain were to constitute man's soul, then their apprehension would never escape him, such that he is never without the intellectual apprehension of both, just as he is never without apprehension of himself. For no one escapes knowing himself, but is ever affirming within himself [the existence] of his self.[14] But unless the human hears what is said about the heart and the brain, or sees them through dissection in another human, he will neither apprehend them nor believe in their existence. If mind, then, indwells in a body, it should intellectually apprehend that body permanently or not apprehend it ever. But neither of these alternatives is true. Rather, it apprehends [the body] at one time, and it does not apprehend [it] at another [time]. And this is the verification [of this]—namely, that the apprehension indwelling in the receptacle apprehends the receptacle only because of a relation it has to the receptacle. [Now,] it is inconceivable that it would have any relation to it other than that of indwelling in it. Let it, then, apprehend it always; and should this relation be insufficient, it ought not to apprehend it ever, since it can have no other relation to it. [This is] just as, in intellectually apprehending itself, it always apprehends itself, at no time being oblivious of it[self].

(52) [To this] we say:

(53) As long as man is aware of his self and is not inattentive to it, he is [merely] aware of his corpse and body. Yes, the name, form, and shape of the heart are not specifically determined for him; nonetheless, he affirms himself as a body such that he affirms himself to be in his garments and in his house, whereas the soul which [the philosophers] mention has no relation to the garment or the house.[15] His affirmation of the basis of body [in self-awareness] is constantly with him, while his unawareness of his [heart's] shape and name is akin to his unawareness of the place of smell—that it consists of two appendages at the front of the brain, similar to the nipples of the breast. For every human knows that he apprehends smell with his body; but the place of apprehension does not take shape for him and is not specified, even though he apprehends that it is closer to the

(٥٠) لسنا نعوّل على مجرّد الاستقراء للحواسّ، بل نعوّل على البرهان، ونقول:

(٥١) لو كان القلب أو الدماغ هو نفس الانسان، لكان لا يعزب عنه ادراكهما، حتّى لا يخلوا عن ان يعقلهما جميعا، كما أنّه لا يخلوا عن ادراك نفسه. فانّ احدا لا يعزب عن ذاته بل يكون مثبتا لنفسه فى نفسه أبدا. والانسان، ما لم يسمع حديث القلب والدماغ أو لم [يشاهدهما]١٧ بالتشريح من انسان آخر، لا يدركهما ولا يعتقد وجودهما. فان كان العقل حالا فى جسم، فينبغى أن يعقل ذلك الجسم أبدا أو لا يدركه أبدا. وليس واحد من الامرين بصحيح. بل يعقل حالة ولا يعقل حالة. وهذا التحقيق، وهو أن الادراك الحالّ فى محلّ انما يدرك المحلّ لنسبته له الى المحلّ، ولا يتصور ان يكون له نسبة اليه سوى الحلول فيه. فليدركه أبدا، وان [كانت]١٨ هذه النسبة لا تكفى، فينبغى أن لا يدرك ابدا، اذ لا يمكن أن يكون له نسبة اخرى اليه، كما انّه لمّا ان كان يعقل نفسه، عقل نفسه ابدا، و لم يغفل عنه بحال.

(٥٢) قلنا:

(٥٣) الانسان ما دام يشعر بنفسه ولا يغفل عنه فانّه يشعر بجسده وجسمه. نعم، لا يتعيّن له اسم القلب وصورته وشكله ولكنّه يثبت نفسه جسما حتّى يثبت نفسه فى ثيابه وفى بيته، والنفس الذى ذكروه لا يناسب البيت والثوب. فاثباته لاصل الجسم ملازم له، وغفلته عن شكله واسمه كغفلته عن محلّ الشمّ، وانّهما زائدتان فى مقدم الدماغ، شبيهتين بحلمتىّ الثدى. فانّ كل انسان يعلم انّه يدرك الرائحة بجسمه ولكن محلّ

head than to the foot and that, within the head, it is closer to the interior of the nose than it is to the interior of the ear. Similarly, man is aware of himself and knows that his haecceity through which he subsists is closer to his heart and chest than it is to his foot. For he can suppose himself to continue to exist without a foot but cannot suppose himself to survive with the nonexistence of the heart. Thus, what [the philosophers] state regarding [man's] being at one time unaware of his body and at another time aware is not the case.

A seventh proof

(54) They say:

(55) The faculties that apprehend through bodily organs undergo fatigue due to constant work through the continuing of apprehension.[16] For the continuity of motion corrupts the temperaments of bodies, fatiguing them. Similarly, strong things whose apprehension is clear weaken [these faculties] and perhaps corrupt them such that they are unable to apprehend their successively dimmer and weaker objects of apprehension—as, for example, [what] the loud sound does to hearing and great light to seeing. For they often corrupt [the faculty] or prevent the apprehension of a successive faint sound and dim objects of sight. Indeed, whoever tastes what is intensely sweet does not sense thereafter a lesser sweetness.

(56) The case is the opposite with the intellectual faculty. For its rendering continual its [act of] viewing the intelligibles does not tire it, and the apprehension of clear necessary truths renders its apprehension of hidden theoretical matters stronger, not weaker. If at times it undergoes fatigue, this is due to its utilizing the service and help of the imaginative faculty, the organ of the imaginative faculty becoming weak and hence failing to serve the intellect.

(57) [Our answer] is that this is of the same pattern as the previous one. For we say:

الادراك لا يتشكّل له ولا يتعيّن، وان كان يدرك انّه الى الرأس اقرب منه الى العقب، ومن جملة الرأس، الى داخل الانف أقرب منه الى داخل الاذن. فكذلك يشعر الانسان بنفسه ويعلم أنّ هوّيته التى بها قوامه الى قلبه وصدره أقرب منه الى رجله. فانّه يقدّر نفسه باقيا مع عدم الرجل ولا يقدّر على تقدير نفسه باقيا مع عدم القلب. فما ذكروه من أنّه يغفل عن الجسم تارة وتارة لا يغفل عنه ليس كذلك.

دليل سابع

(٥٤) قالوا:

(٥٥) القوى الدراكة بالآلات الجسمانية يعرض لها من المواظبة على العمل بادامة الادراك كلال. لانّ ادامة الحركة تفسد مزاج الاجسام، فتكلّها. وكذلك الامور القويّة الجليّة الادراك، توهنها وربما تفسدها حتّى لا تدرك عقيبها الأخفى الاضعف، كالصوت العظيم للسمع، والنور العظيم للبصر. فانّه ربّما يفسد أو يمنع عقيبه من ادراك الصوت الخفىّ والمرئيات الدقيقة. بل من ذاق الحلاوة الشديدة، لا يحسّ بعده بحلاوة دونه.

(٥٦) والامر فى القوة العقليّة بالعكس. فانّ ادامتها للنظر الى المعقولات لا يتعبها، ودرك الضروريّات الجليّة يقويها على درك النظريّات الخفيّة ولا يضعفها. وأن عرض لها كلال، فذلك لاستعمالها القوّة الخياليّة واستعانتها بها، فتضعف آلة القوّة الخياليّة فلا تخدم العقل.

(٥٧) وهذا من الطراز السابق. فانّا نقول:

(58) It is not improbable that the bodily senses should differ in these matters. For what holds for some need not necessarily hold for others. Rather, it is not improbable for bodies to differ such that some are weakened by one kind of movement while others are strengthened, not
5   weakened, by [the same] kind of movement. Should [a kind of motion] affect [the bodily sense adversely], a cause that renews its strength would [arise] so that it does not experience the effect. All this is possible, since the judgment that holds for some things need not necessarily hold for all.

An eighth proof

(59) They say:
10 (60) The powers of all parts of the body weaken at the end of growth as one reaches the age of forty or thereafter. Sight, hearing, and the rest of the faculties thus weaken, whereas the rational faculty in most cases becomes stronger after this. The inability to reflect on the intelligibles when bodily illness and senility due to old age take place is not a neces-
15 sary consequence [contradicting this]. For, as long as it is evident that [the intellect] becomes stronger as the body weakens in some instances, it becomes clear that it subsists by itself. Hence, its dysfunction when the body ceases to function does not necessitate its being subsistent in a body. For the repetition of the very consequent in a [hypothetical syllogism]
20 does not yield a valid conclusion. For we say: "If the rational faculty subsists in a body, then the weakness of the body would in every case weaken it. But the consequent is impossible; hence, the antecedent is impossible." And if we say that the consequent exists in some instances, it does not follow that the antecedent exists.
25 (61) The reason for this is that the soul has an action by itself when no obstacle impedes it and nothing distracts it. For the soul has two actions: an action in relation to the body (namely, its leading and governing it) and an action in relation to its principles and itself (namely, apprehending the intelligibles). These two are contradictory [and] irreconcilable, so that

(٥٨) لا يبعد ان تختلف الحواسّ الجسمانيّة فى هذه الامور. فليس ما يثبت منها للبعض يجب أن يثبت للآخر. بل لا يبعد ان تتفاوت الاجسام فيكون منها ما يضعفها نوع من الحركة ومنها ما يقوّيها نوع من الحركة ولا يوهنها. وان كان يؤثّر فيها فيكون ثمّ سبب يجدّد قوّتها بحيث لا تحسّ بالاثر فيها. فكلّ هذا ممكن اذ الحكم الثابت لبعض الاشياء ليس يلزم ان يثبت لكلّه.

دليل ثامن

(٥٩) قالوا:

(٦٠) أجزاء البدن كلّها تضعف قواها بعد منتهى النشو والوقوف عند الاربعين سنة فما بعدها. فيضعف البصر والسمع وسائر القوى، والقوّة العقليّة فى اكثر الامر انّما تقوى بعد ذلك. ولا يلزم على هذا تعذر النظر فى المعقولات عند حلول المرض فى البدن وعند الخرف بسبب الشيخوخة. فانّه مهما بان انّه يتقوى مع ضعف البدن فى بعض الاحوال، فقد بان ان قوامه بنفسه. فتعطّله عند تعطّل البدن لا يوجب كونه قائما بالبدن. فانّ استثناء عين التالى، لا ينتج. فانّا نقول: ان كانت القوّة العقليّة قائمة بالبدن، فيضعفها ضعف البدن بكل حال. والتالى محال، فالمقدّم محال. واذا قلنا التالى موجود فى بعض الاحوال، فلا يلزم ان يكون المقدّم موجودا.

(٦١) ثم السبب فيه أنّ النفس لها فعل بذاتها اذا لم يعق عائق ولم يشغلها شاغل. فانّ للنفس فعلين: فعل بالقياس الى البدن، وهو السياسة له وتدبيره؛ وفعل بالقياس الى مبادئه والى ذاته، وهو ادراك المعقولات.

whenever [the intellect] is occupied with one, it leaves the other, combining the two becoming not possible for it. The bodily things that preoccupy it consist of sensation, imagination, [various] appetites, anger, fear, depression, and pain. Thus, when you start to think about an intel-
5   ligible, all these things render[17] [your thought] dysfunctional. Indeed, sensation alone may well prevent the apprehension and reflection of the mind, without [this] in any way affecting the intellectual faculty or having its essence afflicted by some malady. The reason in all this is the soul's preoccupation with one act, [distracting it] from another act. For
10   this reason the mind's reflection is halted as a result of pain, sickness, and fear—for it is also a malady of the brain.

(62) How can one deem it unlikely for the two different directions of the soul's action to obstruct one another when multiplicity in the one direction may well necessitate mutual obstruction? For fright can make
15   one forget pain, appetite [can make one forget] anger, reflection on one intelligible [can make one forget] reflection on another. An indication that the illness that comes upon the body does not affect the receptacle of cognitions lies in the fact that, when [the body] returns to health, [the person] does not need to start acquiring the sciences anew. Rather, the
20   state of his soul returns as it had been, and the very same cognitions return without a [new] commencement of learning.

(63) [Our] objection [is to say]:

(64) The increase and decrease of powers has many causes that are innumerable. Thus, some powers may become stronger in early life, some
25   in middle age, and some at the end, this applying to the mind as well. The only thing remaining [for the philosophers] is a claim for probability. There is nothing unlikely about smell and sight differing in that, after forty, smell becomes stronger and sight weaker, even though they are equal in being indwellers in a body. This is just as these powers differ in degree
30   in animals, smell being stronger in some, hearing in some, and sight in some, due to differences in their bodily composition that cannot be ascertained. It is, hence, not improbable that the temperaments of organs should differ with respect to individuals and with respect to states. One of

وهما متمانعان متعاندان، فمهما اشتغل باحدهما، انصرف عن
الآخر، وتعذّر عليه الجمع بين الامرين. وشواغله من جهة البدن،
الاحساس والتخيّل والشهوات والغضب والخوف والغم والوجع. فاذا
اخذت تفكر فى معقول، تعطّل عليك كلّ هذه الاشياء الآخر. بل مجرّد
الحس قد يمنع من ادراك العقل ونظره من غير أن يصيب آلة العقل شىء
أو يصيب ذاتها آفة. والسبب فى كلّ ذلك اشتغال النفس بفعل عن
فعل. ولذلك يتعطّل نظر العقل عند الوجع والمرض والخوف، فانّه ايضا
مرض فى الدماغ.

(٦٢) وكيف يستبعد التمانع فى اختلاف جهتى فعل النفس، وتعدّد
الجهة الواحدة قد يوجب التمانع؟ فانّ الفرق يذهل عن الوجع، والشهوة
عن الغضب، والنظر فى معقول عن معقول آخر. وآية أنّ المرض الحالّ
فى البدن ليس يتعرّض لمحلّ العلوم، انّه اذا عاد صحيحا، لم يفتقر الى تعلّم
العلوم من رأس، بل تعود هيئة نفسه كما كانت، وتعود تلك العلوم
بعينها، من غير استئناف تعلّم.

(٦٣) والاعتراض أن نقول:

(٦٤) نقصان القوى وزيادتها لها أسباب كثيرة لا تنحصر. فقد
[تقوى]١٩ بعض القوى فى ابتداء العمر، وبعضها فى الوسط، وبعضها فى
الآخر. وأمر العقل أيضا كذلك. فلا يبقى الا ان يدّعى الغالب. ولا بعد
فى أن يختلف الشمّ والبصر فى أن الشمّ يقوى بعد الاربعين والبصر
يضعف، وان تساويا فى كونهما حالّين فى الجسم؛ كما تتفاوت هذه
القوى فى الحيوانات، فيقوى الشمّ من بعضها، والسمع من بعضها،
والبصر من بعضها، لاختلاف فى أمزجتها لا يمكن الوقوف على ضبطه.
فلا يبعد أن يكون مزاج الآلات أيضا يختلف فى حقّ الاشخاص وفى

the reasons for the weakening of sight before [the weakening of] mind could thus be that sight [comes] earlier [to the human]. For [the individual] sees when first created, whereas his mind is not fully developed before fifteen years or more, as is seen in the differences among people
5   in [matters like] this. Thus, it has been said that the graying in the hair [of the head] precedes [the graying in] hair of the beard because the head's hair is earlier. Hence, when one plunges into these causes and does not reduce these things to the habitual courses [of nature], one cannot build on them knowledge which is reliable. [This is] because the
10 modes of possible hypotheses regarding the increase or decrease of the faculties are innumerable. Nothing of this yields certainty.

A ninth proof

(65) They say:

(66) How could the human be [nothing but] the body with its accidents, when these [human] bodies continue to dissolve, nourishment
15 replenishing what has been dissolved? [This is] so [much the case] that when we see a [newborn] boy separate from his mother, become frequently ill, then become fat and grow, we are able to say that after the age of forty none of the parts that existed at the age of separation remain. Rather, his first existence consists of parts of the sperm; but none of the
20 parts of the sperm remain, all this having dissolved and been replaced by another. Thus, the body will be other than that [former] body. [Yet] we say that this human is that very [former] human, so that there remain with him cognitions from early boyhood, all his bodily parts having [nonetheless] been replaced. [This] proves that the self has an existence
25 other than the body and that the body is its tool.[18]

(67) [Our] objection [to this is to say]:

الاحوال. ويكون أحد الاسباب فى سبق الضعف الى البصر دون العقل ان البصر أقدم. فانّه مبصر فى أول فطرته، ولا يتمّ عقله الا بعد خمسة عشر سنة أو زيادة، على ما يشاهد اختلاف الناس فيه، حتّى قيل انّ الشيب الى شعر الرأس أسبق منه الى شعر اللحية، لانّ شعر الرأس أقدم.

٥ فهذه الاسباب ان خاض الخائض فيها و لم يردّ هذه الامور الى مجارى العادات، فلا يمكن أن يبنى عليها علم موثوق به، لانّ جهات الاحتمال فيما تزيد بها القوى أو تضعف لا تنحصر. فلا يورث شىء من ذلك يقينا.

دليل تاسع

(٦٥) قالوا:

(٦٦) اكيف يكون الانسان عبارة عن الجسم مع عوارضه، وهذه الاجسام لاتزال تنحلّ، والغذاء يسدّ مسدّ ما ينحلّ؟ حتّى اذا رأينا صبيّا ١٠ انفصل من [امه][٢٠]، [يمرض][٢١] مرارا ويذبل، ثم يسمن وينموا، فيمكننا ان نقول: لم يبق فيه بعد الاربعين شىء من الاجزاء التى كانت موجودة عند الانفصال. بل كان اوّل وجوده من اجزاء المنى فقط، و لم يبق فيه شىء من اجزاء المنى، بل انحلّ كلّ ذلك وتبدّل بغيره. فيكون هذا الجسم غير ذلك الجسم. ونقول: هذا الانسان هو ذلك الانسان بعينه [حتّى][٢٢] انّه ١٥ يبقى معه علوم من أوّل صباه ويكون قد تبدّل جميع أجسامه. فدلّ انّ للنفس وجودا سوى البدن وانّ البدن آلته.

(٦٧) الاعتراض:

(68) This is contradicted by the case of the beast and the tree when their state of old age is compared with their state of being young. For it is said that this is the very same [beast or tree] as it is said of the human, but this does not prove that [the former] have an existence other than the body. And what was mentioned regarding knowledge is refuted by the case of the retention of the forms of the imagination. For they remain from boyhood until old age, even if the rest of the parts of the brain have been replaced. Should they claim that the rest of the parts of the brain are not replaced, then the same would apply to the parts of the heart, both [heart and brain] being parts of the body. How, then, can it be imagined that all [the parts of the body] are replaced?

(69) On the contrary, we say: "Even if a human lived to be a hundred years old, for example, there would invariably remain in him parts of the [original] sperm. That these should be obliterated in him is certainly not the case.[19] For he is that [same] human by virtue of what remains [of the sperm], just as it is said that this [tree] is that tree [at its younger age] and this [horse] that horse [at its younger age]. There would remain [something of the] sperm despite the abundance of dissolution and replacement."

(70) An example of this is when a pound of water is poured in a place, another pound then poured over it so that it mixes with it, then a pound is taken and another pound poured in, this being repeated a thousand times. At the last round, we will judge that something of the original water remains and that any pound taken from it would still have some of the original water.[20] This is because it existed in the second round [of adding and pouring], in the third round to a degree close to the second, in the fourth to a degree close to the third, and so on to the end. This, in terms of [the philosophers'] principles, becomes the more necessary a consequence, since they allow the division of bodies ad infinitum. Thus, the pouring of food into the body and the dissolution of the parts of the body is similar to pouring water into this vessel and scooping [water] out from it.

(٦٨) انّ هذا ينتقض بالبهيمة والشجرة اذا قيست حالة كبرهما بحالة الصغر. فانّه يقال: انّ هذا ذاك بعينه كما يقال فى الانسان، وليس يدلّ ذلك على انّ له وجودا غير الجسم. وما ذكر فى العلم يبطل بحفظ الصور المتخيّلة. [فانّها]²³ ‹تبقى›²⁴ فى الصبى الى الكبر، وان تبدل

٥ سائر أجزاء الدماغ. فان زعموا أنّه لم يتبدّل سائر اجزاء الدماغ، فكذى سائر اجزاء القلب، وهما من البدن. فكيف يتصوّر أن يتبدّل الجميع؟

(٦٩) بل نقول: الانسان، وان عاش مائة سنة مثلاً، فلا بدّ وان يكون قد بقى فيه اجزاء من النطفة. فأمّا ان تنمحى عنه، فلا. فهو ذلك الانسان باعتبار ما بقى كما انّه يقال: هذا ذاك الشجر، وهذا ذاك الفرس. ويكون

١٠ بقاء المنى مع كثرة التحلّل والتبدّل.

(٧٠) مثاله ما اذا صبّ فى موضع رطل من الماء، ثم صبّ عليه رطل آخر حتّى اختلط به، ثم أُخذ منه رطل، ثم صبّ عليه رطل آخر، ثم أُخذ منه رطل، ثم لا يزال يفعل كذلك ألف مرّة. فنحن فى المرّة الاخيرة نحكم بانّ شيئا من الماء الاول باق، وانّه ما من رطل يؤخذ منه الا وفيه شىء من

١٥ ذلك الماء، لأنّه كان موجودا فى الكرّة الثانية، والثالثة قريبة من الثانية، والرابعة من الثالثة، وهكذى الى الآخر. وهذا على أصلهم ألزم، حيث جوّزوا انقسام الاجسام الى غير نهاية. فانصباب الغذاء فى البدن وانحلال أجزاة البدن يضاهى صبّ الماء فى هذا الاناء واغترافه عنه.

A tenth proof

(71) They say:

(72) The rational faculty apprehends the general intellectual universals which the theologians term "states." It thus apprehends the absolute human when the sense perceives a particular human individual,[21] [the former] being other than the perceived individual. For the perceived [human] is in a particular place [and] has a particular color, a particular measure, and a particular position, whereas the intellectually apprehended absolute human is stripped of these things. Rather, [absolute man] includes everything that applies to the name "human," even if [absolute man] does not have the color of the perceived [individual], [or] his measure, position, and place; indeed, [absolute man] includes that whose existence in the future is possible—nay, even if man is annihilated, the reality of man remains in the mind denuded of all these particulars. The same applies to all things which the senses perceive [as] individualized. From [the latter] there is achieved for the mind the reality of that individual as a universal stripped of materials and positions so that its descriptions are divided into what is essential for it, such as corporeality for trees and animals and animality for man, and what is accidental for it, such as whiteness and length to humans and trees. [The mind] judges its being essential and accidental [as applied] to the human genus [and the genus] of trees and to all that is [intellectually] apprehended, not to the observed individual.

(73) This proves that the universal, abstracted from sensible concomitants, is intellectually apprehended [by man] and established in his intellect. This universal, which is intellectually apprehended, is not [something] to which one points and has neither position nor measure. Hence, it is either the case that its abstraction from position and matter is [something] in relation to that from which [the universal] is grasped— which is impossible, because that from which it is grasped has position, place, and measure—or in relation to that which grasps—namely, the rational soul. It must then be the case that the soul has no position, nothing to which one points, and no measures. Otherwise, should this be affirmed [of the soul], it would then have to be affirmed of [the universal] which indwells in it.

دليل عاشر

(٧١) قالوا:

(٧٢) القوة العقليّة تدرك الكلّيّات العامّة العقليّة التى يسمّيها المتكلّمون أحوالا؛ فتدرك الانسان المطلق عند مشاهدة الحسّ لشخص انسان معيّن، وهو غير الشخص المشاهد. فان المشاهد فى مكان مخصوص ولون مخصوص ومقدار مخصوص ووضع مخصوص، والانسان المعقول المطلق مجرد عن هذه الامور. بل يدخل فيه كلّ ما ينطلق عليه اسم الانسان، وان لم يكن على لون المشاهد وقدره ووضعه ومكانه؛ بل الذى يمكن وجوده فى المستقبل يدخل فيه، بل لو عدم الانسان يبقى حقيقة الانسان فى العقل مجرّدا عن هذه الخواصّ. وهكذى كلّ شىء شاهده الحسّ مشخّصا. فيحصل منه للعقل حقيقة ذلك الشخص كلّيّا مجرّدا عن المواد والاوضاع، حتّى تنقسم أوصافه الى ما هو ذاتىّ، كالجسميّة للشجر والحيوان، والحيوانيّة للانسان، والى ما هو عرضىّ له، كالبياض والطول للانسان والشجر. ويحكم بكونه ذاتيّا وعرضيّا على جنس الانسان والشجر وكلّ ما يدرك لا على الشخص المشاهد.

(٧٣) فدلّ أن الكلّىّ المجرّد عن القرائن المحسوسة معقوله عنده وثابته فى عقله. وذلك الكلّىّ المعقول لا اشارة اليه ولا وضع له ولا مقدار. فامّا ان يكون تجرّده عن الوضع والمادّة بالاضافة الى المأخوذ منه، وهو محال، فان المأخوذ منه ذو وضع وأين ومقدار، وامّا أن يكون بالاضافة الى الآخذ، وهو النفس العاقلة. فينبغى ان لا يكون للنفس وضع ولا اليه اشارة ولا له مقدار والا لو ثبت ذلك لثبت الذى حلّ فيه.

(74) [Our] objection [is to say]:

(75) The universal meaning which you [philosophers] have posited as indwelling in the mind is not conceded. Rather, only that which inheres in the senses inheres in the mind, except that it inheres in the senses as an aggregate which the sense is unable to separate, whereas the intellect is able to separate it. Then, once separated, the thing which is separated and singled out in the mind from its associates remains, in its being particular, similar to the thing conjoined with its associates. [The thing] established in the mind, however, has one and the same relation to the thing intellectually apprehended and the things similar to it. It is thus called "universal" in this sense—namely, that there is in the mind the form of the singled-out intelligible first apprehended by the senses, the relation of that form to the individual instances of that genus being one and the same.[22] For, if [a person, for example, after seeing a human] sees another human, no new appearance will appear to him in the way [a new appearance would occur] if he sees a horse after seeing a human; for then there would occur to him two different forms.

(76) Something similar to this may happen in pure sensation. For when anyone sees water, there would occur in his imaginative faculty a form. If thereafter he sees blood, another form would then occur. If he were to see another [form of] water, another form would not come to be. Rather, the form of water [originally] imprinted in his imagination becomes a representative of each individual instance of water. It is thus thought to be a universal in this sense. Similarly, if he sees a hand, for example, there takes place in the imagination and the mind the position of its parts in relation to each other—namely, the spread of the palm, the division of the fingers in relation to it, the ending of the fingers with nails—and with this there takes place [in the imagination] its smallness, largeness, and color. If he sees another hand similar to it in all respects, no other form is renewed for him. Indeed, the second observation is not effective in producing anything new in the imagination. This is the same as when he sees consecutive instances of water in one vessel and of the same amount. He may see another hand differing in color and size [from the first], and consequently there would occur for him another color and size. A new form of the hand, however, will not occur. For the small black hand shares with the big white hand the position of the parts, but differs from

(٧٤) والاعتراض:

(٧٥) ان المعنى الكلّى الذى وضعتموه حالا فى العقل غير مسلّم. بل لا يحلّ فى العقل الا ما يحلّ فى الحسّ. ولكن يحلّ فى الحسّ مجموعا ولا يقدر الحسّ على تفصيله، والعقل يقدر على تفصيله. ثم اذا فصّل، كان المفصّل المفرد عن القرائن فى العقل فى كونه جزئيا كالمقرون بقرائنه؛ الا انّ الثابت فى العقل يناسب المعقول وامثاله مناسبة واحدة. فيقال انّه كلّى على هذا المعنى، وهو ان فى العقل صورة المعقول المفرد الذى أدركه الحس أوّلاً، ونسبة تلك الصورة الى سائر آحاد ذلك الجنس نسبة واحدة. فانّه لو رأى انسانا اخر، لم يحدث له هيئة أُخرى كما اذا رأى فرسا بعد انسان؛ فانّه يحدث فيه صورتان مختلفتان.

(٧٦) ومثل هذا قد يعرض فى مجرّد الحسّ. فانّ من رأى الماء حصل فى خياله صورة. فلو رأى الدم بعده حصلت صورة أُخرى. فلو رأى ماء اخر، لم تحدث صورة أُخرى، بل الصورة التى انطبعت فى خياله من الماء مثال لكلّ واحد من آحاد المياه. فقد يظنّ انّه كلّى بهذا المعنى؛ فكذلك اذا رأى اليد مثلا، حصل فى الخيال وفى العقل وضع اجزائه بعضها مع بعض، وهو انبساط الكفّ وانقسام الاصابع عليه وانتهاء الاصابع على الاظفار، ويحصل مع ذلك صغره وكبره ولونه؛ فان رأى يدا أُخرى تماثله فى كل شىء، لم يتجدّد له صورة أُخرى بل لا تؤثّر المشاهدة الثانية فى احداث شىء جديد فى الخيال، كما اذا رأى الماء بعد الماء فى اناء واحد على قدر واحد. وقد يرى يدا أُخرى تخالفه فى اللون والقدر فيحدث له لون اخر وقدر آخر ولا يحدث له صورة جديدة لليد. فانّ اليد <الصغيرة>٢٥ [السوداء تشارك]٢٦ اليد [الكبيرة البيضاء]٢٧ فى وضع

it in color and size. The form of what is equivalent to the first [hand] is not renewed, since that form is the very same as this form. It is the form of what is different from it that is renewed.

(77) This, then, is the meaning of the universal with respect to both the intellect and the senses. For when the mind apprehends from the animal the form of body, it does not acquire from trees a new form of corporeality, just as [it does not do this] in the imagination by apprehending the form of two [instances of water] at two [different] times, the same being the case with any two similar things. This does not allow for the affirmation of a universal that has no position at all.

(78) The mind, however, may make the judgment affirming the existence of something which is not pointed at and which has no position, as when it makes the judgment that the creator of the world exists, but only from the standpoint that this is [an existent] whose subsistence in a body is inconceivable. In this division, however, that which is utterly set apart from matter is the Intelligible in Himself, independently of[23] [a perceiving] intellect and an intellectual perceiver. But in the case of what is grasped from material things, its mode is as we have mentioned.

الاجزاء [وتخالفه]٢٨ فى اللون والقدر. فما يساوى فيه الاوّل لا تتجدّد صورته، اذ تلك الصورة هى هذه الصورة بعينها، وما يخالفه يتجدّد صورته.

(٧٧) فهذا معنى الكلّىّ فى العقل والحسّ جميعا، فانّ العقل اذا ادرك صورة الجسم من الحيوان، فلا يستفيد من الشجر صورة جديدة فى الجسميّة، كما فى الخيال بادراك صورة الماءين فى وقتين، وكذى فى كلّ متشابهين. وهذا لا يؤذن بثبوت كلّىّ لا وضع له أصلا.

(٧٨) على ان العقل قد يحكم بثبوت شىء لا اشارة اليه ولا وضع، كحكمه بوجود صانع العالم، ولكن من أين انّ ذلك لا يتصوّر قيامه بجسم. وفى هذا القسم يكون المنتزع عن المادّة هو المعقول فى نفسه دون العقل والعاقل فامّا فى المأخوذ من الموادّ فوجهه ما ذكرناه.

[Nineteenth] Discussion

On refuting their statement that it is impossible
for human souls to undergo annihilation
after [having come] to exist; that they are
everlasting, their ceasing to exist inconceivable

(1) A proof for this is hence demanded of them. They have two proofs.

[(1)]

(2) One of [these proofs] is their statement that the annihilation [of these souls] must be either [(a)] due to the death of the body, [(b)] due to the occurrence to it of a contrary, or [(c)] through the power of the one endowed with power.

(3) It is false [they argue] that [the soul] should cease to exist with the body's death. For the body is not a receptacle for it but is a tool which the soul uses through the mediation of the faculties in the body. The corruption of the tool does not necessitate the corruption of the user of the tool, unless [the latter] inheres in it and is imprinted [therein], as with bestial souls and bodily faculties. Moreover, because the soul has an act without the participation of the tool and an act that participates with it, the act it has with the participation of the tool—[consisting] of imagination, sensation, appetite, and anger—no doubt comes to corruption with the corruption of the body, ceasing as it ceases. Its act by itself [on the other hand] without the participation of the body, consists of apprehending the intelligibles abstracted from material things. In its being a perceiver of the intelligibles, it has no need of the body; on the contrary, its

مسئلة

فى ابطال قولهم انّ النفوس الانسانية يستحيل

عليها العدم بعد وجودها

وانّها سرمديّة لا يتصوّر فناؤها

(١) فيطالَبون بالدليل عليه. ولهم دليلان:

(٢) احدهما قولهم: انّ عدمها لا يخلوا امّا ان يكون بموت البدن، أو

بضدّ يطرى عليها، أو بقدرة القادر.

(٣) وباطل ان تنعدم بموت البدن. فانّ البدن ليس محلا لها، بل هو آلة

تستعملها النفس بواسطة القوى التى فى البدن. وفساد الآلة لا يوجب ٥

فساد مستعمل الالة، الا ان يكون حالا فيها، منطبعا كالنفوس البهيميّة

والقوى الجسمانيّة. ولانّ للنفس فعلا بغير مشاركة الآلة، وفعلا

بمشاركتها، فالفعل الذى لها بمشاركة الالة، التخيّل والاحساس والشهوة

والغضب، فلا جرم يفسد بفساد البدن، ويفوت بفواته. وفعلها بذاتها،

دون مشاركة البدن، ادراك المعقولات المجرّدة عن المواد. ولا حاجة فى ١٠

[كونها مدركة]¹ للمعقولات الى البدن؛ بل الاشتغال بالبدن يعوقها عن

المعقولات. ومهما كان لها فعل دون البدن ووجود دون البدن، لم تفتقر

فى قوامها الى البدن.

preoccupation with the body impedes it from [apprehending] the intelligibles. As long as it has an act independent of the body and an existence independent of the body, it does not need the body for its subsistence.

(4) It is [likewise] false to say that it ceases to exist because [of the occurrence] of a contrary, since substances have no contraries. For this reason, nothing in the world is annihilated except accidents and forms that come to exist successively over things. For the watery form is annihilated by its contrary—namely, the airy form—while matter, which is the receptacle, is never annihilated. [In the case of] every substance which is not in a receptacle, its annihilation through a contrary is inconceivable, since there is no contrary for that which is not in a receptacle. For the contraries are those [things] that succeed one another in one receptacle.

(5) It is [also] false to say that [the soul] is brought into nonexistence by power. For nonexistence is not a thing, such that its occurrence through power is conceivable. This [it should be added] is the same thing [the philosophers] have mentioned concerning the problem of the world's post-eternity, which we have discussed and settled.[1]

(6) The objection to this [is made] in a number of ways:

(7) The first is that [this proof] is built on [the theory] that the soul does not perish with the death of the body because it does not indwell in a body. This is based on [their argument] in the first discussion,[2] but we may not concede the point.

(8) The second is that even if it does not, according to them, indwell in a body, it nonetheless has a connection with the body whereby it only comes into existence when the body comes into existence. This is what Avicenna and the exacting among [the philosophers] have chosen. They disavowed Plato's statement that the soul is pre-eternal but happens to undergo preoccupation with bodies, [pursuing their refutation] through a demonstrative, ascertained method—namely [as follows]:

(9) If the souls preceding the body were one, how did they undergo division, when the division of that which has neither size nor quantity is unintelligible? If it is then claimed that [the soul] did not divide, this would be impossible, since it is known necessarily that the soul of Zayd is other than the soul of ʿAmr. If it were one, then the cognitions of Zayd would be known to ʿAmr; for knowledge is one of the essential attributes of the soul, and the essential attributes are included with the essence in every relation. If [on the other hand] the souls are multiple, then by

(٤) وباطل ان يقال انها تنعدم بالضدّ، اذ الجواهر لا ضدّ لها. ولذلك لا ينعدم فى العالم الا الاعراض والصور المتعاقبة على الاشياء، اذ تنعدم صورة المائيّة بضدها [وهي]² صورة الهوائيّة، والمادّة التى هى المحلّ، لا تنعدم قطّ. وكلّ جوهر ليس فى محلّ فلا يتصوّر عدمه بالضدّ، اذ لا ضدّ لما ليس فى محلّ. فانّ الاضداد هى المتعاقبة على محلّ واحد.

(٥) وباطل ان يقال: تفنى بالقدرة، اذ العدم ليس شيئا حتّى يتصوّر وقوعه بالقدرة. وهذا عين ما ذكروه فى مسئلة ابديّة العالم وقد قرّرناه وتكلمنا عليه.

(٦) والاعتراض عليه من وجوه:

(٧) الاول: انّه بناء على ان النفس لا [تموت]³ بموت البدن [لأنّها ليست حالّة]⁴ فى جسم. وهو بناء على المسئلة الاولى. فقد لا نسلّم ذلك.

(٨) الثانى: هو انّه مع [انّها]⁵ لا [تحلّ]⁶ البدن عندهم، [فلها]⁷ علاقة بالبدن حتى لم [تحدث]⁸ الا بحدوث البدن. هذا ما اختاره ابن سينا والمحقّقون، وانكروا على افلاطن قوله ان النفس قديمة ويعرض لها الاشتغال بالابدان، بمسلك برهانيّ محقّق، وهو:

(٩) انّ النفوس قبل الابدان، ان كانت واحدة فكيف انقسمت، وما لا عظم له ولا مقدار لا يعقل انقسامه؟ وان زعم انّه لم ينقسم، فهو محال، اذ يعلم ضرورة انّ نفس زيد غير نفس عمرو. ولو كانت واحدة لكانت معلومات زيد معلومة لعمرو، فانّ العلم من صفات ذات النفس، وصفات الذات تدخل مع الذات فى كلّ اضافة. وان كانت النفوس متكثّرة، فبماذى تكثّرت؟ و لم تتكثر بالموادّ ولا بالاماكن ولا بالازمنة ولا

what means have they been rendered multiple? They have not been
rendered multiple through materials, places, or [different] times, nor
through attributes, since they possess nothing that necessitates a difference in attribute, unlike the souls after the death of the body, which have
been rendered multiple by a difference of attributes (for those who uphold
their survival). [These] have acquired from bodies different characteristics, whereby no two souls are similar; for their characteristics result
from moral dispositions, and moral dispositions are never at all similar,
just as visible characteristics are not the same. Had they been similar,
we would confuse Zayd with ʿAmr.[3]

(10) [To proceed, then, with our objection:] In terms of this demonstration,[4] once [the soul's] creation with the creation of the sperm in the
womb and the disposition of its bodily composition to receive the governing soul is affirmed, then the specific [attachment of the soul to the body]
would only be due to a particular relation between the particular soul and
that particular body. [The sperm] receives the soul, not simply because it
is soul (for in one and the same womb two sperms may become disposed
in the same receptive state [to receive] twins, whereby two souls are
attached to them, coming into being from the First Principle, either
with or without mediation, where neither would the soul of this [twin]
manage the body of that, nor the soul of that twin manage the body of
this). This special relation can arise only from a special affinity between a
particular soul and a particular body. Otherwise, the body of one of the
two twins would have no greater claim than the other for receiving this
[particular] soul. For then two souls would have been created simultaneously and two sperms would have become disposed to jointly receive the
governing [of two souls]. What, then, is that which specifies [the attachment of one particular soul to a particular body]? If this thing that
specifies is the [very] imprinting [of the soul in the body], then it would
cease with the ceasing of the [existence] of the body. But if there is
another mode in terms of which the relation of this specific soul to this
specific body obtains, such that this relation is a condition for the soul's
creation, why should it be unlikely for it to be a condition for its durabil-
ity so that, when the relation ceases, the soul ceases [to exist], never
returning thereafter except through its being returned by God, praised
and exalted be He, by way of resurrection and revivification as conveyed
by the revealed law concerning the hereafter?

(11) [To this the philosophers may] say:

(12) Regarding the relation between soul and body, this only obtains
by way of a natural inclination and an innate desire created in it for this

بالصفات، اذ ليس فيها ما يوجب اختلاف الصفة، بخلاف النفوس بعد موت البدن، فانّها تتكثر باختلاف الصفات عند من يرى بقاءها لانّها استفادت من الابدان هيئات مختلفة، لا تتماثل نفسان منها. فانّ هيئاتها تحصل من الاخلاق والاخلاق قطّ لا تتماثل كما انّ الخلق الظاهر قطّ لا يتماثل، ولو تماثلت لاشتبه علينا زيد بعمرو.

٥

(١٠) ومهما ثبت بحكم هذا البرهان [حدوثها]⁹ عند حدوث النطفة فى الرحم، واستعداد مزاجها لقبول النفس المدبرة، ثم قبلت النفس، لا لانّها نفس فقط، اذ قد تستعد فى رحم واحد نطفتان لتوأمين فى حالة واحدة للقبول، فيتعلق بهما نفسان يحدثان من المبدأ الاول بواسطة، أو بغير واسطة، ولا يكون نفس هذا مدبّرا لجسم ذاك، ولا نفس ذاك مدبّرا لجسم هذا، فليس الاختصاص الا لعلاقة خاصّة بين النفس المخصوص، وبين ذلك البدن المخصوص، والا فلا يكون بدن احد التوأمين بقبول هذه النفس أولى من الآخر. والا فقد حدثت نفسان معا، واستعدت نطفتان لقبول التدبير معا. فما المخصّص؟ فان كان ذلك المخصّص هو الانطباع فيه، فيبطل ببطلان البدن. وان كان ثمّ وجه آخر به العلاقة بين هذه النفس على الخصوص وبين هذا البدن على الخصوص، حتّى كانت تلك العلاقة شرطا فى حدوثه، فاىّ بعد فى ان تكون شرطا فى بقائه، فاذا انقطعت العلاقة انعدمت النفس ثم لا يعود وجودها الا باعادة الله، سبحانه وتعالى، على سبيل البعث والنشور كما ورد به الشرع فى المعاد؟

١٠

١٥

٢٠

(١١) فان قيل:

(١٢) امّا العلاقة بين النفس والبدن، فليس الا بطريق نزاع طبيعى وشوق جبلّى خلق فيها الى هذا البدن خاصّة، يشغلها ذلك الشوق بها

body in particular, this desire for it distracting it from any other body and
not leaving it for one moment so that it remains, by this innate desire,
fettered to the specific body, turned away from [any] other. This does not
necessitate [the soul's] corruption with the corruption of the body, which
by its innate disposition it desires to manage. Yes, this desire may persist
after [the soul's] separation from the body if in this life its preoccupation
with the body and its turning away from overcoming the appetites and
from seeking the intelligibles had taken full control. [The soul] thus
becomes harmed by this desire, with the loss [after separation from the
body] of the instrument through which the desire attains its end.⁵

(13) As for assigning the soul of Zayd to the individual Zayd, when
first coming into existence, this is inescapably due to a cause and a relation of adaptability between the body and the soul, so that this body, for
example, is more suitable for this soul than [another] due to a greater
adaptability between them, rendering preponderant the specifying [of
this particular body for this particular soul]. It is not within human
power to apprehend the specific relations of adaptability. Our lack of
knowledge of their details, however, does not make us doubt the basic
need for something that specifies; nor does it do damage to our statement that the soul does not cease to exist with the perishing of the body.

(14) [To this] we say:

(15) As long as the relation of adaptability—it being the one that
determines specification—is hidden from us, it is not improbable that
this unknown relation is of a mode that renders the soul in need of
the body for its existence so that, if [the body] is corrupted, [the soul] is
corrupted. For with what is unknown, one cannot judge whether or not
there is a requirement of concomitance [between this relation and the
soul]. For it may well be that this relation is necessary for the existence
of the soul so that, if [the relation] ceases to exist, [the soul] ceases to
exist. Hence, one cannot rely on the proof they have mentioned.

(16) [Our] third objection is that it is not improbable to say [that]
the soul ceases to exist through the power of God, exalted be He, in the
manner we established in the discussion of [the theory] of the world's
post-eternity.⁶

(17) The fourth objection is to say: "You have stated that the three
ways concerning [the impossibility of the soul's] nonexistence [exclude
other alternatives]." This is not admitted. What proof is there that the

عن غيره من الابدان، ولا يخلّيها فى لحظة فتبقى مقيدة بذلك الشوق
الجبلىّ بالبدن المعيّن مصروفا عن غيره. وذلك لا يوجب [فسادها]^{١٠}
بفساد البدن الذى [هى]^{١١} [مشتاقه]^{١٢} بالجبلة الى تدبيره. نعم، قد يبقى
ذلك الشوق بعد مفارقة البدن ان استحكم فى الحيوة اشتغالها بالبدن
٥ وإعراضها عن كسر الشهوات وطلب المعقولات، [فتتأذى]^{١٣} بذلك
الشوق مع فوات الآلة التى [يصل بها]^{١٤} الشوق الى <مقتضاه>.^{١٥}

(١٣) وامّا تعيّن نفس زيد لشخص زيد فى أول الحدوث، فلسبب
ومناسبة بين البدن والنفس لا محالة، حتّى يكون هذا البدن مثلاً اصلح
لهذه النفس من الآخر لمزيد مناسبة بينهما، فترجّح اختصاصه. وليس فى
١٠ القوّة البشريّة ادراك خصوص تلك المناسبات. وعدم اطلاعنا على
تفصيلها^{١٦} لا يشكّكنا فى أصل الحاجة الى مخصّص، ولا يضرّنا ايضا فى
قولنا انّ النفس لا تفنى بفناء البدن.

(١٤) قلنا:

(١٥) مهما غابت المناسبة عنا، وهى المقتضية للاختصاص، فلا يبعد
١٥ ان تكون تلك المناسبة المجهولة على وجه يحوج النفس فى بقائها الى بقاء
البدن، حتّى اذا فسد فسدت. فانّ المجهول لا يمكن الحكم عليه بانّه
يقتضى التلازم أم لا. فلعلّ تلك النسبة ضروريّة فى وجود النفس. فان
انعدمت انعدمت. فلا ثقة بالدليل الذى ذكروه.

(١٦) الاعتراض الثالث هو انّه لا يبعد ان يقال تنعدم بقدرة الله تعالى
٢٠ كما قرّرناه فى مسئلة سرمديّة العالم.

(١٧) الاعتراض الرابع هو ان يقال ذكرتم انّ هذه الطرق الثلث فى
العدم تنحسم فهو [غير مسلّم]^{١٧} فما الدليل على انّ عدم الشىء لا يتصوّر

thing's nonexistence is conceivable in only one of these three ways? For if the disjunction is not [confined to] revolving between affirming and denying, it is not improbable for it to be in excess of three or four [alternatives]. It may well be that there is a fourth and a fifth way, other than the three [you mentioned], for nonexistence to come about. Restricting the ways in this to three alternatives is not known through demonstration.

[(2)]

(18) A second proof, on which they mainly depend, is that they say:

(19) For any substance that does not exist in a receptacle, nonexistence is impossible. Indeed, the simple elements are never annihilated at all. This proof establishes, to begin with, that the body's death does not necessitate the soul's nonexistence, for the reasons given [before]. After [maintaining] this, one will say that it is impossible for it to cease to exist due to [some] other cause.

(20) [This is] because whatever ceases to exist by some cause, whatever the cause, has the potentiality of corruption before [its] corruption. In other words, the possibility of annihilation precedes annihilation, in the same way that, with any event whose existence occurs, the possibility of existence precedes existence. [Now,] the possibility of existence is called the potentiality for existence, and the possibility of nonexistence the potentiality for nonexistence. And just as the possibility of existence is a relational description that must subsist in something so as to be a possibility in relation to it, the same [holds] for the possibility of nonexistence. For this reason, it is said that every temporal event needs a preceding matter wherein lies the possibility for the existence of the event and its potentiality, as has [been argued] in the discussion of the world's pre-eternity.[7] Thus, the matter which has the potentiality for existence is receptive of the occurring existence. The recipient, however, is other than the thing received. The recipient, hence, exists with the thing received when it occurs but is other than it. Similarly, the recipient of nonexistence ought to exist when nonexistence occurs, so that something in it would cease to exist in the same way as something had come to exist in it. That which ceases to exist is other than that which endures. And that which remains is the thing which possesses the potentiality for nonexistence—its reception and possibility—just as that which remains when existence occurs is other than the thing which occurs, [the former] having in it the potentiality for receiving the occurring event.

الا بطريق من هذه الطرق الثلث؟ فانّ التقسيم اذا لم يكن دائرا بين
النفى والاثبات فلا يبعد ان يزيد على الثلث والاربع. فلعلّ للعدم طريقا
رابعا وخامسا سوى ما ذكرتموه. فحصر الطرق فى هذه الثلث غير
معلوم بالبرهان.

٥ (٨١) دليل ثان، وعليه تعويلهم أن قالوا:

(١٩) كلّ جوهر ليس فى محلّ، فيستحيل عليه العدم. بل البسائط لا
تنعدم قطّ. وهذا الدليل يثبت فيه اوّلا ان موت البدن لا يوجب [انعدام
النفس][١٨] لما سبق. فبعد ذلك يقال: يستحيل ان ينعدم بسبب آخر.

(٢٠) لانّ كلّ ما ينعدم بسبب ما، أى سبب كان، ففيه قوة الفساد
١٠ قبل الفساد، اى امكان العدم سابق على الانعدام، كما ان ما يطرى
وجوده من الحوادث، فيكون امكان الوجود سابقا على الوجود.
ويسمّى امكان الوجود، قوّة الوجود، وامكان العدم قوّة الفساد. وكما
ان امكان الوجود وصف اضافىّ لا يقوم الا بشىء حتّى يكون امكانا
بالاضافة اليه، فكذلك امكان العدم. ولذلك قيل انّ كل حادث فيفتقر
١٥ الى مادة سابقة يكون فيها امكان وجود الحادث وقوته، كما سبق فى
مسئلة قدم العالم. فالمادّة التى فيها قوّة الوجود قابلة للوجود الطارى؛
والقابل غير المقبول. فيكون القابل موجودا مع المقبول عند طريانه، وهو
غيره. فكذلك قابل العدم ينبغى ان يكون موجودا عند طريان العدم حتّى
يعدم منه شىء كما وجد فيه شىء. ويكون ما عدم غير ما بقى. ويكون ما
٢٠ بقى هو الذى فيه قوّة العدم وقبوله وامكانه، كما انّ ما بقى عند طريان
الوجود يكون غير ما طرى، وقد كان ما فيه قوّة قبول الطارى.

(21) It follows necessarily that the thing to which nonexistence has occurred is composed of something that has ceased to exist and a recipient of nonexistence which continues to exist [after] the occurrence of non-existence, it having been the bearer of the potentiality of nonexistence prior to the occurrence of nonexistence. The bearer of the potentiality of [nonexistence] would be like matter, the thing that ceases to exist like form. But the soul is simple, being a form denuded of matter, having no composition. If one supposes it to have a composition of form and matter, we will transfer the explanation to matter, which is the origin and first fundament, since [the explanation] must end up with a first fundament; we will then show that nonexistence is impossible for that fundament which is called soul, just as we will show that nonexistence is impossible for the matter of bodies. For [matter] is pre-eternal and post-eternal. It is only that forms come to exist and cease to exist in it, there being in it the potentiality for the occurrence of forms and the potentiality for the forms to cease to exist. For it is equally receptive of the two contraries. From this it becomes clear that every existent, unitary in essence, cannot be annihilated.

(22) This can be explained in another way: the potentiality for a thing's existence is prior to the thing's existence and thus belongs to something other than that thing, [which,[8] when it comes into existence,] does not itself constitute the potentiality for existence. A demonstration of this is that one says of a person with sound eyesight that he is a seer in potentiality—that is, that he has the potentiality of seeing. This means that the attribute necessary for the proper [function] of seeing to take place exists. If seeing is delayed, this is due to the delay of another con-dition. Thus, for example, the potentiality to see blackness would exist in the eye before the seeing of blackness in actuality. If the seeing of black-ness takes place in actuality, the potentiality for seeing blackness does not exist with the existence of that seeing. For it is impossible to say that, so long as seeing takes place, then, in addition to its being actually existent, it exists in potentiality. Rather, the potentiality of existence never impinges on the reality of the existent that is realized in actuality. If this premise is established, then we say: "If the simple thing were to be annihilated, then the possibility of nonexistence prior to existence

(٢١) فيلزم ان يكون الشيء الذى طرى عليه العدم مركّبا من شىء انعدم ومن قابل للعدم بقى مع طريان العدم. وقد كان هو حامل قوّة العدم قبل طريان العدم؛ ويكون حامل القوّة كالمادّة والمنعدم منها كالصورة. ولكن النفس بسيطة، وهى صورة مجرّدة عن المادة، لا تركيب فيها. فان فرض فيها تركيب من صورة ومادّة، فنحن ننقل البيان الى المادّة التى هى السنخ والاصل الاول، اذ لا بدّ وان ينتهى الى أصل؛ فنحيل العدم على ذلك الاصل وهو المسمّى نفسا، كما نحيل العدم على مادّة الاجسام. فانّها أزليّة أبديّة. انّما تحدث عليها الصور وتنعدم منها الصور وفيها قوّة طريان الصور عليها وقوّة انعدام الصور منها. فانها قابلة للضدّين على السواء. وقد ظهر من هذا انّ كلّ موجود أحدىّ الذات يستحيل عليه العدم.

(٢٢) ويمكن تقهيم هذا بصيغة أُخرى، وهو انّ قوّة الوجود للشىء يكون قبل وجود الشىء، فيكون لغير ذلك الشىء، ولا يكون نفس قوّة الوجود. بيانه، انّ الصحيح البصر يقال انه بصير بالقوّة، اى فيه قوة الابصار. ومعناه انّ الصفة التى لا بدّ منها فى العين ليصحّ الابصار موجودة. فان تأخّر الابصار، فلتأخّر شرط اخر. [فتكون][١٩] قوّة الابصار للسواد مثلاً [موجودة][٢٠] للعين قبل ابصار السواد بالفعل. فان حصل ابصار السواد بالفعل لم يكن قوّة ابصار ذلك السواد موجودا عند وجود ذلك الابصار، اذ لا يمكن أن يقال: مهما حصل الابصار فهو مع كونه موجودا بالفعل، موجود بالقوّة. بل قوّة الوجود لا [تضام][٢١] حقيقة الوجود الحاصل بالفعل أبدا. واذا ثبتت هذه المقدّمة، فنقول: لو انعدم الشىء البسيط، لكان امكان العدم قبل العدم حاصلا لذلك الشىء، وهو

would have occurred to that thing, [this possibility] being what is
intended by potentiality. Thus, the possibility of existence would also
have been realized." For that whose annihilation is possible is not necessary of existence. It is thus possible of existence. We do not mean by the
potentiality of existence other than the possibility of existence. This
would thus lead to the combination in one thing of the potentiality for its
own existence and the actual realization of its existence. Its existence in
actuality would be identical with the potentiality for existence. But we
have shown that the potentiality of seeing, which is other than seeing,
exists in the eye, not in the seeing, since this would lead to [the conclu-
sion] that the thing is [simultaneously] in potentiality and in action;
these being contradictories. Rather, as long as a thing is in potentiality, it
is not in action; and, as long as it is in action, it is not in potentiality. To
affirm the potentiality of nonexistence for what is simple prior to nonexistence is to affirm the potentiality of existence in the state of existence,
which is impossible.

(23) [We answer:] This is the very thing which we have established
as [their argument] in their pursuit [to prove] the impossibility of the
temporal origination of matter and the elements and the impossibility of
their annihilation, [when we discussed] the problem of the pre-eternity
and post-eternity of the world. The source of the obfuscation is their
positing possibility as a characteristic requiring a receptacle in which to
subsist. We have said what is convincing about this, and we will not
repeat ourselves. For it is one and the same problem. There is, thus, no
difference between the thing discussed being a material substance or a
psychological substance.

المراد بالقوّة. فيكون امكان الوجود أيضا حاصلا. فان ما امكن عدمه، فليس واجب الوجود. فهو ممكن الوجود. ولا نعنى بقوّة الوجود الا امكان الوجود؛ فيؤدّى الى ان يجتمع فى الشىء الواحد قوّة وجود نفسه مع حصول وجوده بالفعل، ويكون وجوده بالفعل هو عين قوّة الوجود.

وقد بيّنا ان قوّة الابصار تكون فى العين التى هى غير الابصار، ولا تكون فى نفس الابصار، اذ يؤدّى الى ان يكون الشىء بالقوّة والفعل، وهما متناقضان. بل مهما كان الشىء بالقوّة، لم يكن بالفعل، ومهما كان بالفعل لم يكن بالقوّة. وفى اثبات قوّة العدم البسيط قبل العدم اثبات لقوّة الوجود فى [حال]٢٢ الوجود، وهو محال.

(٢٣) وهذا بعينه هو الذى قررناه لهم فى مصيرهم الى استحالة حدوث المادّة والعناصر واستحالة عدمها فى مسئلة ازليّة العالم وأبديته. ومنشأ التلبيس وضعهم الامكان وصفا مستدعيا محلا يقوم به. وقد تكلّمنا عليه بما فيه مقنع فلا نعيد. فانّ المسئلة هى المسئلة. فلا فرق بين أن يكون المتكلّم فيه جوهر مادّة أو جوهر نفس.

[Twentieth] Discussion

*On refuting their denial of bodily resurrection
and the return of spirits to bodies; of the existence
of corporeal fire; of the existence of paradise,
the wide-eyed houris, and the rest of the things people
have been promised; of their statement that all
these things are parables made for the commonality
to explain spiritual reward and punishment that
are of a higher rank than the corporeal*

(1) This is contrary to the belief of Muslims in their entirety. Let us, then, first present an explanation of their belief in matters pertaining to the other world, then object to that portion of it that is contrary to Islam.

(2) They said:

(3) The soul endures everlastingly after death either in a pleasure so great that it is beyond description or in a pain so great that it [also] is beyond description. Moreover, [either] this pain may be eternal [or] it may cease with the long passage of time. The classes of people vary in the degrees of pain and pleasure in innumerable ways, just as they vary in worldly degrees and their pleasures in innumerable ways. Everlasting pleasure belongs to perfect, pure souls, [and] everlasting pain to imperfect, tarnished souls. Pain [in the hereafter] that ceases belongs to perfect souls that have been tarnished. Thus, ultimate bliss is only attained through perfection, purity, and cleanliness. Perfection [is attained] through knowledge, [and] purity through action.

مسئلة

فى ابطال انكارهم لبعث الاجساد وردّ الارواح
الى الابدان ووجود النار الجسمانية ووجود الجنة
والحور العين وسائر ما وعد به الناس وقولهم
انّ كل ذلك أمثلة ضربت لعوام الخلق لتفهيم ثواب
وعقاب روحانيين هما أعلى رتبة من الجسمانية

(١) وهو مخالف لاعتقاد المسلمين كافّة. فلنقدم تفهيم معتقدهم فى
الامور الآخرويّة ثم لنعترض على ما يخالف الاسلام من جملته.

(٢) وقد قالوا:

(٣) انّ النفس تبقى بعد الموت بقاءً سرمديًا، امّا فى لذّة لا يحيط
الوصف بها لعظمها، وامّا فى ألم لا يحيط الوصف به لعظمه. ثم قد
يكون ذلك الالم مخلّدا، وقد ينمحى على طول الزمان. ثم تتفاوت طبقات
الناس فى درجات الالم واللذة تفاوتا غير محصور كما يتفاوتون فى
المراتب الدنيويّة ولذّاتها تفاوتا غير محصور. واللذّة السرمديّة للنفوس
الكاملة الزكيّة، والالم السرمدى للنفوس الناقصة الملطّخة، والالم المنقضى
للنفوس الكاملة الملطّخة. فلا تنال السعادة المطلقة الا بالكمال والتزكية
والطهارة والكمال بالعلم والزكاء بالعمل.

(4) The reason for the need of knowledge [lies in the fact] that the nourishment and enjoyment of the rational faculty consists in apprehending the intelligibles, just as the pleasure of the appetitive faculty consists in attaining the object of appetite, the pleasure of sight in looking at beautiful forms, and so on to the rest of the faculties. What prevents [the soul] from becoming cognizant of the intelligibles is the body and its preoccupations, its senses, and its desires. The ignorant soul in the mundane world should by right undergo pain by missing the pleasure of the soul. But preoccupation with the body makes [such a person] forget himself, distracting him from his pain in the way that one in [the grip of] fear will not feel pain and one benumbed will not feel fire. Thus, if [his soul] remains imperfect until he is unburdened of the body's preoccupation, he would be in the same state as the benumbed who, when subjected to fire, will [at first] feel no pain; but once the numbness ceases, he would then feel the great affliction that comes all at once, as an onslaught.

(5) The souls that apprehend the intelligibles may enjoy them in a faint manner, falling short of what their natures call for; this also [is] due to bodily preoccupations and the soul's being at home with its appetites. The example of this is the sick man who has a bitter [faculty of] taste. He finds the good, sweet thing distasteful and forsakes food which ought to be for him the most perfect reason for pleasure. He, however, will not enjoy it because of the illness that has afflicted him. [On the other hand, the state of those] souls perfected through knowledge that, with death, are relieved of the body's burdens and preoccupations is exemplified by the case of a person who has suffered from an impediment due to an ailment that prevents him from experiencing [taste] and who, being presented with the most enjoyable and tastiest of foods, has the impediment [suddenly] removed, experiencing [thereby] great pleasure all at once. An alternative example is the case of one whose love for a person has grown intense and who, while asleep or in a faint or a state of drunkenness, is slept with by that person, being unaware of [such a person], who suddenly awakens to experience all at once, after a long wait, the pleasure of sexual union. These pleasures, however, are base in relation to spiritual and intellectual pleasures. But one cannot explain this except through examples taken from what people experience in this life.

(٤) ووجه الحاجة الى العلم، انّ القوّة العقليّة غذاؤها ولذّتها فى درك المعقولات، كما ان القوّة الشهوانيّة لذّتها فى نيل المشتهى، والقوّة البصريّة لذّتها فى النظر الى الصور الجميلة، وكذلك سائر القوى. وانّما يمنعها من الاطلاع على المعقولات البدن وشواغله وحواسّه وشهواته.

والنفس الجاهلة فى الحيوة الدنيا حقّها ان تتألّم بفوات لذّة النفس، ولكن الاشتغال بالبدن ينسيه نفسه ويلهيه عن ألمه، كالخائف لا يحسّ بالالم، وكالخدر لا يحسّ بالنار. فاذا بقيت ناقصة حتّى انحطّ [عنها]¹ شغل البدن، كان فى صورة الخدر، اذا عرض على النار فلا يحسّ بالالم، فاذا زال الخدر شعر بالبلا العظيم دفعة واحدة هجوما.

(٥) والنفوس المدركة للمعقولات قد تلتذّ بها التذاذا خفيّا قاصرا عمّا [تقتضيه طباعها]²، وذلك أيضا لشواغل البدن وانس النفس بشهواتها. ومثاله مثال المريض الذى فيه مرارة، يستبشع الشىء الطيّب الحلو، ويستهجن الغذاء الذى هو أتمّ اسباب اللذّة فى حقّه، فلا يتلذذ به لما عرض من المرض. فالنفوس الكاملة بالعلوم اذا انحطّ عنها أعباء البدن وشواغله بالموت، كان مثاله مثال من عرض [عليه الطعم]³ الالذّ والذوق الاطيب، وكان به عارض مرض يمنعه من الادراك، فزال العارض فادرك اللذّة العظيمة دفعة. أو مثال من اشتد عشقه فى حق شخص فضاجعه ذلك الشخص وهو نائم أو مغمىّ عليه أو سكران فلا يحسّ به، فينتبه فجأة فيشعر بلذّة الوصال بعد طول الانتظار دفعة واحدة. وهذه اللذّات حقيرة بالاضافة الى اللذّات الروحانية العقلية، الا انّه لا يمكن تفهيمه الا بامثلة ممّا شاهدها الناس فى هذه الحيوة.

(6) This is just [such an instance] as when we wish to explain to the boy or to the impotent man the pleasure of sexual intercourse [and] we are unable to do so except by examples—in the case of the boy, with [the example of] play, which is the most pleasurable thing to him; and [in the case] of the impotent man, with [the example of] the pleasure of eating good food after being very hungry, so that [each] would believe the principle that there is pleasure [in this], after which [each] is apprised that what he understood by the example does not convey the reality of the pleasure of sexual intercourse and that this is only apprehended through direct experience.[1]

(7) The proof that the intellectual pleasures are nobler than bodily pleasures consists of two things:

(8) One is that the state of angels is nobler than the state of such beasts as ferocious animals and pigs, since [these angels] have no sensual pleasures by way of copulation and eating. They only have the pleasure of being aware of their own perfection and beauty that specifically belong to them through knowing the true nature of things and of being close to the Lord of the Worlds in [terms of] attributes, not space, and in rank of existence. For existents have come to be from God in an order and through intermediaries. Thus, the intermediary closer [to God] is necessarily higher [in rank].

(9) The second is that man also prefers intellectual pleasures to the sensuous. For whoever is able to defeat the enemy and gloat over him will, in achieving [this goal], abandon the pleasures of mating and food. Indeed, one may abandon food all day for the pleasure of winning in chess or backgammon, insignificant as this is, without feeling the pain of hunger. Similarly, one desirous of dignity and leadership would hesitate [when confronted with the choice] between the loss of dignity and, for example, attaining his goal with the woman he loves when another [person] would know this and [the affair] would become widely known. He would then protect his dignity, abandoning attainment of his [amorous] goal, belittling this for the sake of preserving his honor. This would thus be unquestionably more pleasurable for him. [Again,] the brave warrior may sometimes attack a host of brave warriors, belittling the danger of death, in the intense desire of what he imagines to be the pleasure of praise and honor bestowed on him after death.

(10) Hence, the intellectual otherworldly pleasures are better than the sensuous mundane pleasures. If it were not so, then God's apostle, God's prayers and peace be on him, would not have said [in conveying God's message]: "I have prepared for my righteous servants that which no eye

(٦) وهذا كما انّا لو أردنا ان نفهم الصبى أو العنين لذّة الجماع، لم نقدر عليه الا بان نمثّله فى حقّ الصبىّ باللعب الذى هو ألذّ الاشياء عنده، وفى حقّ العنين بلذّة الاكل الطيّب مع شدّة الجوع، ليصدّق باصل وجود اللذّة، ثم يعلم أنّ ما فهمه بالمثال ليس يحقّق عنده لذّة الجماع، وانّ ذلك لا يدرك الا بالذوق.

(٧) والدليل على انّ اللذات العقليّة أشرف من اللذّات الجسمانيّة امران:

(٨) أحدهما ان حال الملائكة اشرف من حال السباع والخنازير من البهائم، وليس لها اللذّات الحسيّة من الجماع والاكل. وانّما لها لذّة الشعور بكمالها وجمالها الذى [خصت به]؛ فى نفسها فى اطلاعها على حقائق الاشياء، وقربها من ربّ العالمين فى الصفات، لا فى المكان، وفى رتبة الوجود. فانّ الموجودات حصلت من الله على ترتيب وبوسائط. فالذى يقرب من الوسائط رتبته لا محالة أعلى.

(٩) والثانى انّ الانسان ايضا قد يؤثر اللذّات العقليّة على الحسيّة. فان من يتمكّن من غلبة عدوّ والشماتة به، يهجر فى تحصيله ملاذّ الانكحة والاطعمة. بل قد يهجر الاكل طول النهار فى لذّة غلبة الشطرنج والنرد، مع خسّة الامر فيه، ولا يحسّ بألم الجوع. وكذلك المتشوّف الى الحشمة والرئاسة، يتردّد بين انخرام حشمته بقضاء الوطر من عشيقته مثلا، بحيث يعرفه غيره وينتشر عنه؛ فيصون الحشمة ويترك قضاء الوطر ويستحقر ذلك محافظة على ماء الوجه. فيكون ذلك لا محالة ألذّ عنده، بل ربّما يهجم الشجاع على جمّ غفير من الشجعان، مستحقرا خطر الموت، شغفا بما يتوهمه بعد الموت، من لذّة الثناء والاطراء عليه.

(١٠) فاذن اللذّات العقليّة الآخرويّة افضل من اللذّات الحسيّة الدنيويّة. ولولا ذلك، لما قال رسول الله صلى الله عليه وسلّم، اعددت

has seen and no ear has heard and which has never occurred to the heart of mankind." And God, exalted be He, has said: "No soul knows the eye's consolation secretly kept for them" [Qurʾān 32:17].

(11) This, then, is the manner in which knowledge is needed. The beneficial parts of it are those purely intellectual sciences—namely, knowledge of God, His attributes, His angels, His books, and the way in which things come to exist through Him. Other than this, whatever is a means to [such knowledge] is beneficial. If, however, they are not a means to it—as, for example, grammar, philology, poetry, and the various kinds of sciences—these would be arts and crafts like the rest of the arts.

(12) As regards the need for works and worship, [this] is for the purpose of the soul's purification. For the soul in this body is prevented from apprehending the true nature of things, not because it is imprinted in the body, but because of its preoccupation [with it], its desire toward its appetites, and its yearning toward [the body's] requirements. This appetite and desire constitutes a disposition of the soul which becomes embedded therein, taking hold of it through the constant endeavor to pursue appetites and persistence in befriending pleasurable sensible things. If, then, it takes hold of the soul and the body dies, these attributes [remain] embedded in the soul and would be harmful in two ways. One of them is that they prevent it from the pleasures peculiar to it—namely, contact with the angels and cognizance of the beautiful divine things when the preoccupying body that would, as before death, distract [the soul] from the pain [of not being in contact with the angelic realm] is no longer with it. The second is that the care and inclination for the world [and] its meaning and pleasures remains with [the person] when the organ has been taken away from him. For the body is the instrument for the attainment of these pleasures. His state would then be the state of one who has fallen in love with a woman, become accustomed to leadership, found solace in children, attained wealth, and rejoiced in dignity; but then his beloved [woman] is killed, he is deposed from his leadership, his children and women are taken captive, his riches are taken by his enemies, and his dignity is completely destroyed. He would then suffer manifest pain. In

لعبادى الصالحين ما لا عين رأت ولا اذن سمعت ولا خطر على قلب بشر. وقال تعالى: «لا تعلم نفس ما أخفى لهم من قرّة اعين».

(١١) فهذا وجه الحاجة الى العلم. والنافع من جملته العلوم العقليّة المحضة، وهى العلم بالله وصفاته وملائكته وكتبه، وكيفيّة وجود الاشياء منه. وماوراء ذلك، ان كان وسيلة اليه فهو نافع لاجله. وان لم يكن وسيلة اليه، كالنحو واللغة والشعر وأنواع العلوم المفترقة، فهى صناعات وحرف كسائر الصناعات.

(١٢) وامّا الحاجة الى العمل والعبادة، فلزكاء النفس. فانّ النفس فى هذا البدن [مصدودة]⁵ عن درك حقائق الاشياء لا [لكونها منطبعة]⁶ فى البدن، بل [لاشتغالها ونزوعها الى شهواتها وشوقها]⁷ الى مقتضياته، وهذا النزوع والشوق هيئة للنفس تترسّخ فيها، تتمكّن منها بطول المواظبة على اتباع الشهوات والمثابرة على الانس بالمحسوسات المستلذّة. فاذا تمكّنت من النفس، [ومات]⁸ البدن، كانت هذه الصفات متمكّنة من النفس ومؤذية من وجهين: أحدهما انّها تمنعها عن لذّتها الخاصّة بها، وهو الاتصال بالملائكة والاطلاع على الامور الجميلة الالهيّة، ولا يكون [معها]⁹ البدن الشاغل [فيلهيها]¹⁰ عن التألّم، كما قبل الموت. والثانى انّه يبقى معه الحرص والميل الى الدنيا واسبابها ولذّاتها، وقد استلب منه الآلة. فانّ البدن هو الآلة للوصول الى تلك اللذّات فيكون حاله حال من عشق امرأة وألف رئاسة واستأنس باولاد واستروح الى مال وابتهج بحشمة، فقتل معشوقه، وعزل عن رئاسته، وسبى اولاده ونساؤه، واخذ امواله أعداؤه [واسقطت]¹¹ بالكلّيّة حشمته. فيقاسى من الالم ما لا يخفى.

this life, however, he would not lose all hope for the return of such things. For [the affairs of this] world come and go. But [what would be his state] when, through the loss of the body by reason of death, all hope is lost?

(13) Nothing will deliver one from wallowing in these dispositions except restraining the soul from passion, forsaking the world, and applying oneself with all seriousness to knowledge and piety, so that the soul's connection with worldly things is severed while [still] in this world and one's relations with otherworldly things are made firm. Thus, when [the person] dies he would be as one escaping from prison, arriving at all that he seeks, this being his paradise.

(14) [Now,] it is not possible to completely remove and obliterate all these attributes from the soul. For bodily necessities draw it to themselves; but it is possible to weaken this connection. For this reason the Exalted has said: "None of you but will arrive at it, this being for your Lord a decreed, determined thing" [Qurʾān 19:17]. When, however, the relation is weakened, the hurt of separation will not be severe; and the pleasure after death with knowing divine things becomes [so] great as to remove in a short time the effect of having left the mundane world. An example of this is a person who leaves his country for a great position and elevated kingship. His soul may feel sad at the time of separation from his family and homeland, and he will suffer some agony. But this is [soon] obliterated by what he encounters by way of pleasure and rejoicing in kingship and leadership.

(15) [Since] negating these [bodily] qualities is impossible, the revealed law has prescribed following the mean between every two extreme opposites. For lukewarm water is neither hot nor cold, as though remote from both qualities. Thus, [a person] must not go to extremes either in holding onto property, whereby holding fast to wealth becomes embedded in him, or in spending so as to become a spendthrift. [Again,] a person should not shrink from all things so as to be a coward, nor plunge into all things so as to be reckless. Instead, he should seek generosity,

وهو فى هذه الحيوة غير منقطع الامل عن عود امثال هذه الامور. فانّ الدنيا غاد وروائح فكيف اذا انقطع الامل بفقدان البدن بسبب الموت؟

(١٣) ولا ينجى عن التضمّخ بهذه الهيئات الا كفّ النفس عن الهوى، والاعراض عن الدنيا والاقبال بكنه الجدّ على العلم والتقوى، حتّى تنقطع علائقه عن الامور الدنيويّة وهو فى الدنيا، وتستحكم علاقته مع الامور الآخرويّة. فاذا مات كان كالمتخلص عن سجن، فالواصل الى جميع مطالبه، [فهي]١٢ جنته.

(١٤) ولا يمكن سلب جميع هذه الصفات عن النفس ومحوها بالكلّيّة. فانّ الضرورات البدنيّة جاذبة اليها؛ الا انّه يمكن تضعيف تلك العلاقة ولذلك قال تعالى: «(وان منكم الا واردها، كان على ربّك حتما مقضيًّا)»؛ الا انّه اذا ضعفت العلاقة، لم تشتدّ نكاية فراقها، وعظم الالتذاذ بما اطلع عليه عند الموت من الامور الالهيّة، فاماط اثر مفارقة الدنيا والنزوع اليها على قرب. كمن يستنهض من وطنه الى منصب عظيم وملك مرتفع. فقد ترقّ نفسه حالة الفراق على اهله ووطنه، فيتاذّى أذى ما، ولكن ينمحى بما يستأنفه من لذّة الابتهاج بالملك والرئاسة.

(١٥) [ولمّا]١٣ لم يمكن سلب هذه الصفات، ورد الشرع فى الاخلاق بالتوسط بين كل طرفين متقابلين. لانّ الماء الفاتر لا حارّ ولا بارد، فكأنه بعيد عن الصفتين. فلا ينبغى ان يبالغ فى امساك المال، فيستحكم فيه حرص المال، ولا فى الانفاق، فيكون مبذرا؛ ولا ان يكون ممتنعا عن كلّ الامور، فيكون جبانا، ولا منهمكا فى كلّ أمر فيكون متهوّرا. بل يطلب

which is the mean between stinginess and overspending; courage, which is the mean between cowardice and recklessness; and so on with all moral dispositions. Ethics is [a] lengthy [discipline], and the religious law has gone to great lengths in giving its details.[2] There is no way for cultivat-
5   ing morals[3] except through observing in works the canon of the religious law so that man would not follow his whim, such that "he makes his caprice his god" [Qurʾān 25:45; 45:22]. Rather, he must imitate the law, advancing or holding back [action], not as he chooses, [but] according to what [the law] directs, his moral dispositions becoming educated thereby.
10   Whoever is deprived of this virtue in both moral disposition and knowl-edge is the one who perishes. For this reason, God, exalted be He, said: "Whoever purifies it has achieved success, and whoever corrupts it fails" [Qurʾān 91:9–10]. Whoever combines both virtues, the epistemological and the practical, is the worshipping "knower," the absolutely blissful
15   one. Whoever has the epistemological virtue but not the practical is the knowledgeable, [believing] sinner who will be tormented for a period, which [torment] will not last because his soul had been perfected through knowledge but bodily occurrences had tarnished [it] in an accidental manner opposed to the substance of the soul. The causes renewing [these
20   accidental occurrences] are [themselves] not renewed; consequently, with lengthy time [the tarnishing accidents] are obliterated. He who has practical virtue but not the epistemological is saved and delivered but does not attain perfect bliss.

    (16) [The philosophers further] claim that whoever dies is resurrected.[4]
25   Regarding what has appeared in the religious law in terms of [sensible] representation, the intention [here] is to give analogies because of the failure [of most people] to understand these [intellectual] pleasures. They have thus been given examples in terms of what they understand, being then told that these pleasures are above what has been described to them.
30   (17) This, then, is [the philosophers'] doctrine.

    (18) We say:

    (19) Most of these things are not contrary to the religious law. For we do not deny that there are, in the hereafter, kinds of pleasures superior to the sensory. Nor do we deny the survival of the soul after separation
35   from the body. But we know this through the religious law, since it has

الجود، فانه الوسط بين البخل والتبذير، والشجاعة، فانّها الوسط بين الجبن والتهوّر، وكذلك فى جميع الاخلاق. وعلم الاخلاق طويل والشريعة بالغت فى تفصيلها، ولا سبيل فى تهذيب الاخلاق الا بمراعاة قانون الشرع فى العمل، حتّى لا يتبع الانسان هواه، فيكون قد «اتخذ الهه هواه»؛ بل يقلد الشرع، فيقدم ويحجم بمباشرته، لا باختياره، فتتهذب به اخلاقه. ومن عدم هذه الفضيلة فى الخلق والعلم جميعا فهو الهالك ولذلك قال تعالى: «قد أفلح من زكّاها وقد خاب من دسّاها». ومن جمع الفضيلتين، العلميّة والعمليّة، فهو العارف العابد، وهو السعيد المطلق. ومن له الفضيلة العلميّة دون العمليّة، فهو العالم الفاسق، ويتعذّب مدّة ولكن لا يدوم، لانّ نفسه قد [كملت]¹⁴ بالعلم ولكن العوارض البدنيّة لطخته تلطيخا عارضا، على خلاف جوهر النفس. وليس تتجدّد الاسباب المجدّدة، فينمحى على طول الزمان. ومن له الفضيلة العمليّة دون العلميّة، فيسلم وينجوا عن الالم، ولا يحظى بالسعادة الكاملة.

(١٦) وزعموا انّ من مات فقد قامت قيامته. وامّا ما ورد فى الشرع من الصور، فالقصد ضرب الامثال لقصور الافهام عن درك هذه اللذّات؛ فمثّل لهم ما يفهمون، ثم ذكر لهم ان تلك اللذّات فوق ما وصف لهم.

(١٧) فهذا مذهبهم.

(١٨) ونحن نقول:

(١٩) أكثر هذه الامور [ليست]¹⁵ على مخالفة الشرع. فانّا لا ننكر انّ فى الآخرة انواع من اللذّات اعظم من المحسوسات، ولا ننكر بقاء النفس عند مفارقة البدن، ولكنّا عرفنا ذلك بالشرع، اذ ورد بالمعاد، ولا يفهم

conveyed [that there is] resurrection. And the resurrection is only understood in terms of the soul's survival. We have previously denied only their
claim that they know this by reason alone. What is contrary to the religious law among [the things they hold] is the denial of the resurrection
of bodies, the denial of bodily pleasures in paradise and bodily torments
in the fire, and the denial of the existence of paradise and the fire as
described in the Qurʾān. What, then, is there to stand in the way of
realizing the combination of both [kinds] of happiness, the spiritual
and bodily, the same applying to misery, [in view] of His statement,⁵
"No soul knows what has been hidden from them" [Qurʾān 32:17]—that
is, it does not know all that—and [the prophet's] saying, [conveying
God's utterance,] "I have prepared for my righteous servants that which
no eye has seen . . ."? As such, the existence of these noble things does not
indicate the negation of others. Rather, combining the two represents
what is more perfect, [rendering] the thing promised the most perfect of
things. Moreover, this is possible; hence, belief in it (in accordance with
the religious law) is obligatory.

(20) [It may be] said:

(21) What has come down in [the revealed law] are parables struck
to meet the level of the understanding of created [humanity], in the same
sense that the anthropomorphic verses and reports [of the prophet] that
have come down are analogies proportionate to the understanding of
created [humanity]. The divine attributes are sanctified [high above]
what the commonality imagines.

(22) [We] answer:

(23) To make these two things equal is arbitrary. On the contrary,
they differ in two respects.

(24) One is that the anthropomorphic utterances are amenable to
interpretation in accordance with the customary practice of the Arabs in
using metaphor. But what has come down [in the law] describing paradise and the fire and the detailing of these states has attained a degree
[of explicit statement] that does not [render it] subject to metaphorical
interpretation. Nothing, then, would remain but to take [such utterances]
as obfuscation by making one imagine what is contrary to truth for the
benefit of creatures. But this is what the position of prophethood is sanctified high above.

(25) The second is that rational proofs have shown the impossibility
of [attributing] place, direction, visage, physical hand, physical eye, the
possibility of transfer, and rest to God, praise be to Him. Metaphorical

المعاد الا ببقاء النفس. وانّما انكرنا عليهم من قبل دعواهم معرفة ذلك بمجرّد العقل. ولكن المخالف للشرع منها انكار حشر الاجساد، وانكار اللذّات الجسمانيّة فى الجنة والآلام الجسمانيّة فى النار، وانكار وجود جنّة ونار، كما وصف فى القرآن. فما المانع من تحقيق الجمع بين السعادتين الروحانيّة الجسمانيّة، وكذى الشقاوة وقوله «لا تعلم نفس ما أخفى لهم»، اى لا يعلم جميع ذلك، وقوله: «اعددت لعبادى الصالحين ما لا عين رأت»؟ فكذلك وجود تلك الامور الشريفة لا يدلّ على نفى غيرها. بل الجمع بين الامرين أكمل والموعود أكمل الامور. وهو ممكن، فيجب التصديق به على وفق الشرع.

(٢٠) فان قيل:

(٢١) ما ورد فيه امثال ضربت على حدّ افهام الخلق، كما ان الوارد من آيات التشبيه واخباره، امثال على حدّ فهم الخلق. والصفات الالهيّة مقدسة عما يخيّله عامّة الناس.

(٢٢) والجواب:

(٢٣) ان التسوية بينهما تحكّم. بل هما يفترقان من وجهين:

(٢٤) احدهما انّ الالفاظ الواردة فى التشبيه تحتمل التاويل على عادة العرب فى الاستعارة. وما ورد فى وصف الجنّة والنار وتفصيل تلك الاحوال بلغ مبلغا لا يحتمل التأويل. فلا يبقى الا حمل الكلام على التلبيس بتخييل نقيض الحق لمصلحة الخلق. وذلك ممّا يتقدّس عنه منصب النبوّة.

(٢٥) والثانى ان ادلّة العقول دلّت على استحالة المكان والجهة والصورة ويد الجارحة وعين الجارحة وامكان الانتقال والاستقرار على

interpretation [here] is obligatory through rational proofs. What He has promised in the hereafter, however, is not impossible in terms of the power of God, exalted be He. Hence, one must follow the apparent [literal meaning of the revealed] speech—indeed, according to its signification, which is explicit.

(26) If it is said, "Rational proof has shown the impossibility of the resurrection of bodies, just as it has shown the impossibility of applying those [anthropomorphic] attributes to God, exalted be He," we would demand of them to bring forth [this proof]. In this they have different ways.

[(1)]

(27) The first is their statement that the supposition of the return [of souls] to bodies does not go beyond [involving] three alternatives.

(28) [The first alternative] is to say [that] the human consists of body and life, which is an accident subsisting therein, as some theologians have held; that a self-subsisting soul that manages the body has no existence; that the meaning of death is the severance of life—that is, the refraining of the Creator from creating it, whereby it ceases to exist, the body also ceasing to exist; [and] that the meaning of the resurrection is God's returning the annihilated body back to existence and the returning of the life which had been annihilated; or else, to say that the matter of the body survives as earth and that the meaning of the resurrection is that [this earth] is gathered and constructed in the form of a human, life then being created in it anew. This [then] is one alternative.

(29) [A second alternative] is to say that the soul exists and survives death but that the first body is changed back [into existence] with all its very parts. This is another alternative.

(30) [A third alternative] is to say that the soul would be returned to a body, regardless of whether [the body] is reconstituted from those [original bodily] parts or [formed] from other [parts]. The [person] resurrected would be that [identical] human inasmuch as the soul would be that [same] soul. As regards matter, no attention should be given it, since the human is not a human because of it, but by virtue of the soul.

(31) All these three alternatives [they argue] are false:

(32) In the case of the first, its falsity is clear. For once life and the body become annihilated, then the commencing of their creation would consist of bringing into existence a replica of what had been, not what is identical with what had been.[6] Indeed, what is [normally] understood by

الله سبحانه. فوجب التأويل بادلّة العقول. وما وعد من امور الآخرة ليس محالا فى قدرة الله تعالى. فيجب الجرىّ على ظاهر الكلام بل على فحواه الذى هو صريح فيه.

(٢٦) فان قيل: وقد دلّ الدليل العقلىّ على استحالة بعث الاجساد، كما دلّ على استحالة تلك الصفات على الله تعالى، فنطالبهم باظهاره. ولهم فيه مسالك.

(٢٧) المسلك الاول قولهم: تقدير العود الى الابدان لا يعدوا ثلثة اقسام. امّا أن يقال:

(٢٨) الانسان عبارة عن البدن والحيوة التى هى عرض قائم به، كما ذهب اليه بعض المتكلّمين، وانّ النفس التى هى [قائمة بنفسها ومدبّرة]¹⁶ للجسم فلا وجود[لها]¹⁷؛ ومعنى الموت انقطاع الحيوة، اى امتناع الخالق عن خلقها، فتنعدم، والبدن ايضا ينعدم؛ ومعنى المعاد اعادة الله للبدن الذى انعدم وردّه الى الوجود، واعادة الحيوة التى انعدمت، أو يقال: مادّة البدن تبقى ترابا، ومعنى المعاد أن يجمع ويركّب على شكل ادمىّ،[وتخلق]¹⁸ فيه الحيوة ابتداء. فهذا قسم.

(٢٩) وإمّا ان يقال: النفس [موجودة وتبقى]¹⁹ بعد الموت، ولكن يردّ البدن الاوّل بجمع تلك الاجزاء بعينها. وهذا قسم.

(٣٠) وإمّا ان يقال: يردّ النفس الى بدن سواء كان من تلك الاجزاء أو من غيرها، ويكون العائد ذلك الانسان من حيث انّ النفس تلك النفس. فامّا المادّة فلا التفات اليها، اذ الانسان ليس انسانا بها بل بالنفس.

(٣١) وهذه الاقسام الثلثة باطلة.

(٣٢) أمّا الاوّل، فظاهر البطلان. لانّه مهما انعدمت الحيوة والبدن فاستئناف خلقها ايجاد لمثل ما كان، لا لعين ما كان. بل العود المفهوم هو

"the return" is [that circumstance] where one supposes the endurance of
something and a renewed existence of something. [This is] just as, when
one says, "So-and-so returned to being generous," it means that the generous person continues to exist, abandoned being generous, then returned to
5   [this state]—that is, he returned to the initial [state] in terms of genus,
but [the state itself] is numerically other. It would thus be in reality a
return to what is similar, not to the same thing. [Again,] it is [also] said
that So-and-so returned to the town—that is, [after having] existed outside [it], having [previously] had an existence in the town, he then
10   returned to what is similar to this [previous state]. Thus, unless there is
something that [continues to] exist, there [also] being numerically two
things that are similar [but] separated by time, then [the meaning of]
the term "return" is not fulfilled, unless one follows the doctrine of the
Muʿtazila, where it would be said: "The nonexistent is a thing that is
15   permanent, existence being a state that occurs to it at one time, ceases
for a while, and returns at another. The meaning of 'return' would thus
be fulfilled through the consideration of the continuance of [nonexistence,
which is a pure negative, as an] entity."[7] But this would be the removal of
absolute nonexistence and an affirmation of [an] entity as being continuous
20   until existence returns to it, which is impossible.

(33) If one supporting this alternative [the philosophers continue]
resorts to a device [for resolving this difficulty] by saying, "The body's
earth does not cease to exist and thus continues to be, and life is then
returned to it," we say:

25   (34) At this point it would be correct to say that the earth has
returned to an animated state after life had been severed from it. This,
however, would not be a resurrection for the human nor a return [to life]
of that identical human being. For the human is a human not by virtue
of his matter and the earth that is in him, since all or most of [his] parts
30   are changed for him through nourishment while he remains that very
same individual. For he is what he is by virtue of his spirit or soul. If,
then, life or spirit ceases to exist, then the return of what ceases to exist
is unintelligible. What commences to exist is only that which is similar
to it. And whenever God creates human life in earth that derives from
35   the body of a tree, a horse, or a plant, this would be a creation anew of a
human. The return to existence of the nonexistent is utterly unintelligible.
That which returns is the existent; that is, it returns to a state which it
previously had—in other words, to a state similar to [the previous] state.
What, then, returns is [the capacity] of earth to [possess] the attribute of
40   life. A human is [not a human] by virtue of his body, since the body

الذى يفرض فيه بقاء شىء وتجدّد شىء، كما يقال: فلان عاد الى الانعام،
أى انّ المنعم باق وترك الانعام، ثم عاد اليه، أى عاد الى ما هو الاول
بالجنس ولكنّه غيره بالعدد. فيكون عودا بالحقيقة الى مثله، لا اليه.
ويقال: فلان عاد الى البلد، اى بقى موجودا خارجا، وقد كان له كون فى
البلد، فعاد الى مثل ذلك. فان لم يكن شىء باق، وشيئان متعدّدان ٥
متماثلان يتخلّلهما زمان، لم يتمّ اسم العود، الا ان يسلك مذهب المعتزلة
فيقال: المعدوم شىء ثابت والوجود حال يعرض له مرّة، وينقطع تارة،
ويعود اخرى؛ فيتحقّق معنى العود باعتبار بقاء الذات. ولكنّه رفع للعدم
المطلق الذى هو النفىّ المحض، وهو اثبات <لذات>٢٠ مستمرّة الثبات الى
أن يعود [اليها]٢١ الوجود، وهو محال. ١٠

(٣٣) وان احتال ناصر هذا القسم بان قال: تراب البدن لا يفنى،
فيكون باقيا، فتعاد اليه الحيوة، فنقول:

(٣٤) عند ذلك يستقيم أن يقال عاد التراب حيّا بعد ان انقطعت
الحيوة عنه [مدّة]٢٢، ولا يكون ذلك عودا للانسان، ولا رجوع ذلك
الانسان بعينه، لانّ الانسان انسان لا بمادته والتراب الذى فيه، اذ يتبدل ١٥
عليه سائر الاجزاء أو اكثرها بالغذاء، وهو ذاك الاوّل بعينه. فهو هو
باعتبار روحه أو نفسه. فاذا عدمت الحيوة او الروح، فما عدم لا يعقل
عوده؛ وانّما يستأنف مثله. ومهما خلق الله حيوة انسانيّة فى تراب
يحصل من بدن شجر أو فرس أو نبات، كان ذلك ابتداء خلق انسان،
فالمعدوم قطّ لا يعقل عوده، والعائد هو الموجود، أى عاد الى حالة كانت ٢٠
له من قبل، أى الى مثل تلك الحالة. فالعائد هو التراب الى صفة الحيوة.
وليس الانسان ببدنه، اذ قد يصير بدن الفرس غذاء الانسان فيتخلّق منه

of a horse may become the food for a human from which a sperm may be generated from which [in turn] a human may come to be. It is not said that the horse has changed into a human. Rather, a horse is a horse by virtue of its form, not its matter; [and] the form has now ceased, matter alone remaining.

(35) As regards the second alternative, which is the supposition of the survival of the soul and the returning of it to that very same body, [this,] if conceivable, would be a return—that is, a return [of the soul] to managing the body after having separated from it. But this is impossible, since the body of the dead person disintegrates into earth or is eaten by worms or birds and changes into blood, vapor, and air, mixing with the world's air, vapor, and water in a manner that renders its extraction and retrieval remote. But if this [extraction and retrieval] is supposed by trusting in God's power, then [one of two alternatives would necessarily follow]. [The first is] that only the parts of the person's body existing at the time of his death are gathered. Thus, the resurrection of the person with the severed limb, the severed nose and ear, and the defective organs would have to be [a return to the physical state such a person] had had. This is deemed bad, particularly for the people in paradise who were created imperfect at the beginning of [their] creation. To bring them back to the state of emaciation they were in when they died would constitute an extreme in punishment—this, if confined to gathering the parts existing at [the moment] of death.

(36) If, however [and this is the second alternative], all the parts of the body that existed throughout the life of [the deceased] are gathered, this would be impossible in two respects: one is that, if a human eats the flesh of another human, which is customary in some lands and becomes frequent in times of famine, the [bodily] resurrection of both together becomes impossible because one substance was the body of the individual eaten and has become, through eating, [part of] the body of the eater. And it is impossible to return two souls to the same body. The second is that one and the same part would have to be resurrected as liver, heart, and leg. For it has been proved by the medical art that some organic parts derive nourishment from the residuary nourishment of the others. Thus, the liver feeds on parts of the heart, the same being the case with the rest of the organs. Let us then suppose that individual parts had been the matter of several organs. To which organ, then, would it be returned [at the resurrection]? Indeed, there is no need to establish the impossibility of the first [alternative] by reference to cannibalism. For, if

نطفة يحصل منها انسان، فلا يقال الفرس انقلب انسانا، بل الفرس فرس بصورته، لا بمادّته، وقد انعدمت الصورة، وما بقى الا المادّة.

(٣٥) واما القسم الثانى، وهو تقدير بقاء النفس [وردّها]^{٢٣} الى ذلك البدن بعينه، فهو لو تصوّر، لكان معادا، أى عودا الى تدبير البدن بعد مفارقته، ولكنّه محال، اذ بدن الميت ينحلّ ترابا أو تأكله الديدان والطيور، ويستحيل دماً وبخارا وهواء، ويمتزج بهواء العالم وبخاره ومائه امتزاجا يبعد انتزاعه واستخلاصه. ولكن ان فرض ذلك اتكالا على قدرة الله، فلا يخلوا امّا ان [تجمع]^{٢٤} الاجزاء التى مات عليها فقط، فينبغى أن يكون معاد الاقطع ومجذوع الانف والاذن وناقص الاعضاء كما كان، وهذا مستقبح، لا سيّما فى أهل الجنة وهم الذين خلقوا ناقصين فى ابتداء الفطرة. فاعادتهم على ما كانوا عليه من الهزال عند الموت فى غاية النكال، هذا ان اقتصر على جمع الاجزاء الموجودة عند الموت.

(٣٦) وان جمع جميع اجزائه التى كانت موجودة فى جميع عمره فيه، فهو محال من وجهين. احدهما أنّ الانسان اذا تغذّى بلحم انسان، وقد جرت العادة به فى بعض البلاد، ويكثر وقوعه فى أوقات القحط، فيتعذّر حشرهما جميعا لان مادّة واحدة كانت بدنا للمأكول وصارت بالغذاء بدنا للآكل. ولا يمكن ردّ نفسين الى بدن واحد. والثانى انّه يجب ان يعاد جزء واحد كبدا وقلبا ويدا ورجلا. فانّه ثبت بالصناعة الطبية انّ الاجزاء العضويّة يغتذى بعضها بفضلة غذاء البعض، فيتغذّى الكبد باجزاء القلب، وكذلك سائر الاعضاء. فنفرض اجزاء معيّنة قد كانت مادّة لجملة من الاعضاء. فالى أىّ عضو تُعاد؟ بل لا يحتاج فى تقرير الاستحالة الاولى

you consider the surface of the inhabited earth, you would know that with the long passage of time its soil consists of corpses that have changed into soil that is seeded and planted, becoming grain and fruit that animals eat, and so becoming flesh which we eat, thus returning as bodies for us.

5 Thus, there is no matter to which one points but would have been a body for many humans, changed and transformed into soil, then to plant, then to flesh, then to animal. From this [supposition] a third impossible consequence indeed ensues. This is that the [human] souls separating from bodies are infinite, whereas bodies are finite corporeal entities. Thus,

10 the materials which had been the materials of humans would not be sufficient for the souls of all people; they would not accommodate them.[8]

(37) As regards the third alternative—namely, returning the soul to a human body composed of any matter whatsoever and whatever soil— this would be impossible in two respects: one of them is that the materials

15 receptive of generation and corruption are confined to the sphere of the moon, increment being impossible for them. They are finite, whereas the souls separating from bodies are infinite. Hence, the materials would not be sufficient for them.[9] The second is that earth, as long as it remains earth, is not receptive to being managed by the soul. Rather, the elements

20 need to be mixed in a manner similar to the composition of the sperm. Indeed, wood and iron are not receptive of this management, and it is impossible to return the human and his body [to life] from wood or iron. On the contrary, he would not be a human unless the parts of his body divide into flesh, bone, and [the four] humors. [Now,] once the body and its

25 temperament become disposed to receive a soul, they become deserving of the creation of a soul by the principles that bestow souls. But [if the third alternative is supposed], then two souls will come to the one body. It is with this [as a consequence] that the doctrine of transmigration is refuted.[10] [The view supposed in the third alternative], however, would

30 constitute the very [doctrine of] transmigration. For it reduces to the soul's preoccupation—after being delivered from one body—with directing another body [that is] other than the first body. Hence, the method adopted to refute transmigration proves the falsity of this [third] approach.

(38) [Our] objection [to all this] is to say:

الى اكل الناس الناس. فانّك اذا تأمّلت ظاهر التربة المعمورة، علمت بعد طول الزمان أنّ ترابها جثث الموتى قد تتربّت وزرع فيها وغرس [وصارت]٢٥ حبًّا وفاكهة وتناولها الدوابّ، فصارت لحما، وتناولناها فعادت بدنا لنا، فما من مادّة يشار اليها الا وقد كانت بدنا لاناس كثيرة، فاستحالت وصارت ترابا، ثم نباتا، ثم لحما ثم حيوانا. بل يلزم منه محال ثالث، وهو انّ النفوس المفارقة للابدان غير متناهية، والابدان اجسام متناهية. فلا تفى المواد التى كانت مواد الانسان بأنفس الناس كلّهم، بل تضيق عنهم.

(٣٧) وأمّا القسم الثالث، وهو ردّ النفس الى بدن انسانيّ، من ايّ مادّة كانت، وأىّ تراب اتفق، فهذا محال من وجهين. احدهما أن المواد القابلة للكون والفساد محصورة فى مقعر فلك القمر لا يمكن عليها مزيد وهى متناهية والانفس المفارقة للابدان غير متناهية فلا تفى بها. والثانى ان التراب لا يقبل تدبير النفس ما بقى ترابا، بل لا بدّ وان تمتزج العناصر امتزاجا يضاهى امتزاج النطفة؛ بل الخشب والحديد لا يقبل هذا التدبير، ولا يمكن اعادة الانسان وبدنه من خشب أو حديد، بل لا يكون انسانا الا اذا [انقسمت]٢٦ اعضاء بدنه الى اللحم والعظم والاخلاط. ومهما استعد البدن والمزاج لقبول نفس، استحق من المبادىء الواهبة للنفوس حدوث نفس. فيتوارد على البدن الواحد نفسان. وبهذا بطل مذهب التناسخ. وهذا المذهب هو عين التناسخ. فانّه رجع الى اشتغال النفس، بعد خلاصها من البدن، بتدبير بدن آخر غير البدن الاوّل. فالمسلك الذى يدلّ على بطلان التناسخ، يدلّ على بطلان هذا المسلك.

(٣٨) والاعتراض هو أن يقال:

(39) With what [argument] would you deny one who chooses the last alternative and holds the view that the soul survives death, it being a self-subsisting substance? This is not contrary to the religious law. On the contrary, the religious law indicates this in His saying: "Do not think that those who have been killed in the way of God are dead, but [they] are living with their Lord . . ." [Qurʾān 3:163] and in the saying [of the Prophet], peace be upon him, "The spirits of the righteous are in the crops of green birds that hang beneath the throne," [as well as] by what has been conveyed to us by the reports of the spirits' awareness of charitable deeds, of the questioning [in the grave] by Munkar and Nakir, of the torment in the grave and other things, all of which indicates [the soul's] survival. Yes, in addition, [this] indicates the revival and resurrection thereafter—namely, the resurrection of the body. This is possible by returning [the soul] to the body, whatever body this might be, whether [composed] of the matter of the first body [or from that] of another or from matter whose creation commences anew. For [an individual] is what he is by virtue of his soul, not his body, since the parts of the body change over for him from childhood to old age through being emaciated, becoming fat, and [undergoing] change of nourishment. His temperament changes with [all] this, while yet remaining that very same human. This lies within God's power and would be a [true] return of that soul. For [with the separation of the soul from the body] it had become not feasible for him to undergo physical pain and pleasure due to the loss of the instrument. But now an instrument similar to the first has been returned to him. This, then, becomes true resurrection.

(40) And what you [philosophers] have mentioned about the impossibility of this in that the souls would be infinite, the materials being finite, is [itself] impossible, having no basis. For it is built on [the doctrine of] the world's pre-eternity and the perpetual succession of the [celestial] circular motions. For one who does not believe in the world's eternity, the souls that separate from bodies are finite and are not greater than the existing materials. And if [for the sake of argument] one admits that [their number is] greater, God, exalted be He, is able to create and resume the creation ex nihilo.[11] To deny this is to deny God's power of temporal origination. A refutation [of such a denial] has been given previously in the discussion of the world's creation.

(٣٩) بمَ تنكرون على من يختار القسم الاخير، ويرى انّ النفس باقية بعد الموت [وهي]٢٧ جوهر قائم بنفسه؟ وانّ ذلك لا يخالف الشرع، بل دلّ عليه الشرع فى قوله، ((ولا تحسبنّ الذين قتلوا فى سبيل الله أمواتا بل احياء عند ربهم))، وبقوله عليه السلام، ((ارواح الصالحين فى حواصل طير خضر معلّقة تحت العرش))، وبما ورد من الاخبار بشعور الارواح بالصدقات والخيرات، وسؤال منكر ونكير، وعذاب القبر وغيره، وكل ذلك يدلّ على البقاء. نعم، قد دلّ مع ذلك على البعث والنشور بعده وهو بعث البدن. وذلك ممكن بردّها الى بدن، أى بدن كان، سواء كان من مادّة البدن الاوّل أو من غيره، أو من مادّة استؤنف خلقها. فانّه هو بنفسه لا ببدنه، اذ يتبدّل عليه اجزاء البدن من الصغر الى الكبر بالهزال والسمن وتبدّل الغذاء، ويختلف مزاجه مع ذلك وهو ذلك الانسان بعينه. فهذا مقدور لله ويكون ذلك عودا لذلك النفس. فانّه كان قد تعذّر عليه ان يحظى بالآلام واللذات الجسمانية بفقد الآلة، وقد أعيدت اليه آلة مثل الاولى. فكان ذلك عودا محقّقا.

(٤٠) وما ذكرتموه من استحالة هذا بكون النفوس غير متناهية وكون المواد متناهية، محال لا اصل له. فانّه بناء على قدم العالم وتعاقب الادوار على الدوام. ومن لا يعتقد قدم العالم، فالنفوس المفارقة للابدان عنده متناهية وليست اكثر من المواد الموجودة. وان سلّم انها اكثر، فالله تعالى قادر على الخلق واستئناف الاختراع. وانكاره انكار لقدرة الله على الاحداث. وقد سبق ابطاله فى مسئلة حدث العالم.

(41) As regards your second [claim of] rendering [the third alternative] impossible, in that this constitutes transmigration, there is no need to squabble about terms. What the religious law has conveyed [as true] must be believed. Let it be "transmigration." We only deny transmigration in this world. As regards the resurrection, we do not deny [it], whether or not it is called "transmigration."

(42) And your statement that every bodily composition that is prepared to receive a soul deserves the creation of a soul [for it] from the [celestial] principles is to revert to [the doctrine] of the soul's creation by nature, not voluntarily. We have refuted this in the discussion of the world's creation. How not so, when it is not unlikely in terms of the pattern of your [own] doctrine also to say that [a body] deserves the creation of a soul only if there is no soul [already] existing, so that a soul commences to be? There would remain [for the philosophers] to say: "Why is it [then] that it is [only] in this, our [present] world, that the souls attach to the bodily compositions in the wombs prepared for their reception, but not [thereafter], prior to the revival and the resurrection?"—to which it would be said:

(43) It may well be [the case] that the separated souls [in rejoining the resurrected body] require a different kind of preparation whose cause becomes complete only at that time. It is [hardly] improbable for the preparation which is a condition for the perfect separated soul [to rejoin the body] to be different from the preparation which is a condition for [the coming to be of] the soul that is initially created [and] which has not acquired perfection through managing the body for a period of time. God, exalted be He, knows best these conditions, their causes, and the times of their presence. The religious law has declared [the resurrection]. It is [in itself] possible and, hence, must be believed.

[(2)]

(44) [The philosophers'] second way is that they say:

(45) It is not within the realm of [divine] capability for iron to be transformed into a woven garment which one would wear as a turban, except through the decomposition of the particles of iron into [basic] elements by causes that control iron and decompose it into simple elements. The elements are then gathered and made to go through phases of creation until they acquire the form of cotton. Then cotton would acquire the form of yarn, yarn acquiring the known order—namely, being woven in a known shape. If it is said that changing iron into a cotton turban

(٤١) واما احالتكم الثانية بانّ هذا تناسخ، فلا مشاحة فى الاسماء. فما ورد الشرع به يجب تصديقه. فليكن تناسخا. وانّما نحن ننكر التناسخ فى هذا العالم. فامّا البعث فلا ننكره، سمّى تناسخا او لم يسمّ.

(٤٢) وقولكم انّ كلّ مزاج استعد لقبول نفس استحق حدوث نفس من المبادىء رجوع الى انّ حدوث النفس بالطبع لا بالارادة، وقد ابطل ذلك فى مسئلة حدث العالم. كيف، ولا يبعد على مساق مذهبكم أيضا ان يقال انّما يستحق حدوث نفس اذا لم يكن ثمّ نفس موجودة فتستأنف نفس؟ فيبقى ان يقال فلم لم تتعلّق بالامزجة المستعدّة فى الارحام قبل البعث والنشور، بل فى عالمنا هذا؟ فيقال:

(٤٣) لعلّ الانفس المفارقة تستدعى نوعا آخر من الاستعداد ولا يتمّ سببها الا فى ذلك الوقت. ولا بعد فى ان يفارق الاستعداد المشروط للنفس الكاملة المفارقة الاستعداد المشروط للنفس الحادثة ابتداء التى لم تستفد كمالا بتدبير البدن مدّة. والله تعالى أعرف بتلك الشروط وباسبابها واوقات حضورها. وقد ورد الشرع به وهو ممكن، فيجب التصديق به.

(٤٤) المسلك الثانى ان قالوا:

(٤٥) ليس فى المقدور ان يقلب الحديد ثوبا منسوجا بحيث يتعمّم به الا بان تحلّل اجزاء الحديد الى العناصر باسباب تستولى على الحديد فتحلّله الى بسائط العناصر؛ ثم تجمع العناصر وتدار فى اطوار فى الخلقة الى ان تكتسب صورة القطن، ثم يكتسب القطن صورة الغزل، ثم الغزل يكتسب الانتظام المعلوم الذى هو النسج على هيئة معلومة. ولو قيل انّ

is possible, without transformation through these stages according to an order, [this would be asserting what is] impossible. Yes, a human can entertain the thought that these transformations can all be realized in a short time, whose length man would not perceive, and he would think
5   that this occurred suddenly and all at once.

(46) If this is understood, then, if the body of the resurrected human were of stone, ruby, pearl, or pure earth, he would not be a human. Indeed, it is not conceivable that he would be a human unless he has a special shape formed from bones, veins, flesh, cartilages, and humors.
10   The simple parts are prior to the complex. Hence, there would be no body if there were no organs, and there would be no compound organs if there were no bones, flesh, and veins; and these single things would not be if there were no humors; and there would not be the four humors if their matters did not consist of food, and there would be no food unless
15   there were animal or plant—namely, flesh and seeds—and there would be no animals and plants if all the four elements were not mixed according to lengthy particular conditions, greater than the general treatment we have detailed. Hence, it is not possible for the body of a human to be reformed anew so that the soul would be returned to it except through
20   these things, which have many causes. Does soil, then, turn into a human by [one] saying to it, "Be," or by preparing the causes of its transformation through these phases? The causes [of its transformation] consist in placing the sperm extracted from the core of the human body into a womb so that it would derive from the blood of the menses and from
25   nourishment for a period until it is created into a lump, then a clot, then a fetus, then an infant, then a youth, then an old man. Hence, one's saying that it is said to it, "Be," is unintelligible, since earth is not addressed and its transformation into a human without undergoing these phases is impossible. And for it to undergo these stages without these causes running
30   their course is impossible. Hence, [bodily] resurrection is impossible.

(47) [Our] objection [to this is as follows]:

قلب الحديد عمامة قطنيّة ممكن من غير الاستحالة فى هذه الاطوار على سبيل الترتيب، كان محالا. نعم، يجوز ان يخطر للانسان انّ هذه الاستحالات يجوز ان تحصل كلّها فى زمان متقارب لا يحسّ الانسان بطولها، فيظنّ انّه وقع فجأة دفعة واحدة.

(٤٦) واذا عقل هذا فالانسان المبعوث المحشور لو كان بدنه من حجر أو ياقوت أو درّ او تراب محض لم يكن انسانا، بل لا يتصوّر ان يكون انسانا، الا ان يكون متشكّلا بالشكل المخصوص، مركّبا من العظام والعروق واللحوم والغضاريف والاخلاط. والاجزاء المفردة تتقدّم على المركّبة. فلا يكون البدن ما لم [تكن]²⁸ الاعضاء، ولا تكون الاعضاء المركّبة ما لم تكن العظام واللحوم والعروق، ولا تكون هذه المفردات ما لم تكن الاخلاط، ولا تكون الاخلاط الاربعة ما لم تكن موادّها من الغذاء، ولا يكون الغذاء ما لم يكن حيوان او نبات، وهو اللحم والحبوب، ولا يكون حيوان ونبات ما لم تكن العناصر الاربعة جميعا ممتزجة بشرائط مخصوصة، طويلة أكثر مما فصّلنا جملتها. فاذن لا يمكن ان يتجدّد بدن انسان لتردّ النفس اليه الا بهذه الامور، ولها أسباب كثيرة. أفينقلب التراب انسانا بان يقال له، كن، أو بان تمهّد أسباب انقلابه فى هذه الادوار؟ وأسبابه هى القاء النطفة المستخرجة من لباب بدن الانسان فى رحم حتى يستمدّ من دم الطمث ومن الغذاء مدّة، حتّى يتخلّق مضغة، ثم علقة ثم جنينا، ثم طفلا ثم شابّا ثم كهلا. فقول القائل يقال له، كن فيكون، غير معقول اذ التراب لا يخاطب وانقلابه انسانا دون التردد فى هذه الاطوار محال. وتردده فى هذه الاطوار دون جريان هذه الاسباب محال فيكون البعث محالا.

(٤٧) والاعتراض:

(48) We admit that ascending through these stages is necessary for [the earth] to become a human body, just as it is necessary for iron to become a turban. For if it remains iron, it would not become a garment. Indeed, it must [first] become spun cotton, then [be] woven. But this is possible either in a moment or a [longer] period of time. It has not been made plain to us that the resurrection takes place in the shortest possible time, since it is possible that recollecting the bones, reviving the flesh, and making them grow takes place in a long period of time. But this is not the point at issue. [The question] to be examined, however, is concerned with the progress of these stages—whether it occurs purely through [divine] power, without mediation, or through some cause or another. Both [explanations], according to us, are possible, as we have mentioned in the first question in the natural sciences when discussing [God's] making [all events] run according to a habitual course. [There we stated] that the connection of connected things in existence is not by way of necessity, but that habitual [patterns] can be disrupted, whereby these matters would come about through God's power without the existence of their causes. The second [view] consists of our saying that this is due to causes, but it is not a condition that the cause [here] would be one which we have experienced. Rather, in the treasury of things [enactable by divine] power there are unknown wondrous and strange things denied by someone who thinks that nothing exists but what he experiences, in the same way that some people deny magic, sorcery, the talismanic arts, [prophetic] miracles, and the miracles [of saints], which are affirmed, as all agree, through strange unknowable causes. Indeed, if a human had never seen a magnet and its attraction of iron and this [fact] is related to him, he would deny it, saying, "No attraction of iron is conceivable except through a string attached to it and then pulled, for this is what is observed in [things] being pulled." However, when he sees [the magnet's attraction of iron], he would be astounded by it and would realize that his knowledge falls short of encompassing the wonders of [divine] power.

(49) And it is thus with the atheists who deny the resurrection and the hereafter. When they are resurrected from the graves and see the wonders of God in [resurrecting man], they will suffer regret that will not do them any good, feeling sorry for their ingratitude—a sorrow of no benefit to them. And it will be said to them, "This is the thing which you

(٤٨) انا نسلّم ان الترقّى فى هذه الاطوار لا بدّ منه حتّى يصير بدن انسان، كما لا بدّ منه حتّى يصير الحديد عمامة. فانّه لو بقى حديدا، لما كان ثوبا. بل لا بدّ [ان]٢٩ يصير قطنا مغزولا ثم منسوجا. ولكن ذلك فى لحظة أو فى مدّة ممكن. ولم يبين لنا انّ البعث يكون فى أوحى ما يقدر، اذ يكون جمع العظام وانشاز اللحم وانباته فى زمان طويل؛ وليس المناقشة فيه. وانّما النظر فى انّ الترقّى فى هذه الاطوار يحصل بمجرّد القدرة من غير واسطة أو بسبب من الاسباب. وكلاهما ممكنان عندنا كما ذكرناه فى المسئلة الاولى من الطبيعيّات. عند الكلام على اجراء العادات، وان المقترنات فى الوجود اقترانها ليس على طريق التلازم، بل العادات يجوز خرقها فيحصل بقدرة الله تعالى هذه الامور دون وجود أسبابها. وامّا الثانى فهو ان نقول: ذلك يكون باسباب ولكن ليس من شرطه ان يكون السبب هو المعهود، بل فى خزانة المقدورات عجائب وغرائب لم يطّلع عليها، ينكرها من يظنّ انّ لا وجود الا لما شاهده، كما ينكر طائفة السحر والنارنجات والطلسمات والمعجزات والكرامات، وهى ثابتة بالاتفاق باسباب غريبة لا يطّلع عليها. بل لو لم ير انسان المغناطيس وجذبه للحديد، وحكى له ذلك، لاستنكره وقال لا يتصوّر جذب للحديد الا بخيط يشدّ عليه ويجذب؛ فانّ المشاهد فى الجذب، حتى اذا شاهده تعجّب منه وعلم ان علمه قاصر عن الاحاطة بعجائب القدرة.

(٤٩) وكذلك الملحدة المنكرة للبعث [والنشور]٣٠، اذا بعثوا ورأوا عجائب صنع الله فيه ندموا ندامة لا تنفعهم ويتحسّرون على جحودهم تحسّرا لا يغنيهم. ويقال لهم: «هذا الذى كنتم به تكذّبون»، كالذى

used to deem untrue" [Qurʾān 83:17], being like the one who deemed
false the [existence] of [hidden] properties and wondrous things. Indeed,
if a human is created rational from the very beginning and it is said to
him, "This dirty sperm, whose parts are similar, will have its similar

5   parts divide in the womb of a woman [to form] different organs, by way
of flesh, nerves, bones, veins, cartilages, and fat, from which there comes
to be the eye (with seven layers differing in constitution), the tongue, the
teeth (with the differences between them, despite their proximity, in
being soft or hard), and so on to the wonders of creation," his denial will

10   be [even] stronger than the denial of the atheists who said: "When we
were moldy bones . . ." [Qurʾān 29:11].

(50) The one who denies the resurrection does not give thought to
[the question] of how he would know the confining of the causes of existence to what he has observed. For it is not improbable that in the resur-

15   rection of bodies there is a pattern other than what he observes. In some
[of the traditional] reports it is said that at the time of the resurrection
there would cover the earth rain whose drops are akin to sperm and will
mix with the earth. What improbability is there for there being among
the divine causes something similar to this, which we do not know, that

20   results in the resurrection of bodies and their being rendered disposed
to receive the resurrected souls? Is there any basis for this denial other
than merely thinking it unlikely?

(51) [The philosophers] may [then] say:

(52) The divine act has one fixed course that does not change. For

25   this reason God, exalted be He, said: "Our command is but one, like
the flicker of the eye" [Qurʾān 54:50], and He has [also] said: "You will
not find any change in God's way" [Qurʾān 48:23]. And these causes
whose possibility you have imagined, if they exist [at all], ought also to
have sequences and would have to repeat themselves infinitely, and the

30   order of generating and being generated [continue] without end. After
acknowledging repetitions and cyclical occurrences, it is not improbable
that the pattern of things should change in a million years, for example;
but the change would also be eternal, permanent, [according to] one law.
For there is no change in God's way. This is the case because the divine

يكذّب بالخواص والاشياء الغريبة. بل لو خلق انسان عاقلا ابتداء، وقيل له ان هذه النطفة القذرة المتشابهة الاجزاء، تنقسم اجزاؤها المتشابهة فى رحم آدمية الى أعضاء مختلفة، لحمية وعصبية، وعظمية، وعرقية، وغضروفية، وشحمية، فيكون منه العين على سبع طبقات مختلفة فى المزاج، واللسان والاسنان على تفاوتهما فى الرخاوة والصلابة مع تجاورهما، وهلم جرا الى البدائع التى فى الفطرة، لكان انكاره أشد من انكار الملحدة حيث قالوا: ﴿أئذا كنا عظاما نخرة﴾. الآية.

(٥٠) فليس يتفكر المنكر للبعث انه من اين عرف انحصار اسباب الوجود فيما شاهد. و لم يبعد ان يكون فى احياء الابدان منهاج غير ما شاهده، وقد ورد فى بعض الاخبار انه يعم الارض فى وقت البعث مطر [قطراته]³¹ تشبه النطف وتختلط بالتراب. فاى بعد فى أن يكون فى الاسباب الالهية أمر يشبه ذلك ونحن لا نطلع عليه ويقتضى ذلك انبعاث الاجساد واستعدادها لقبول النفوس المحشورة؟ وهل لهذا الانكار مستند الا الاستبعاد المجرد؟

(٥١) فان قيل:

(٥٢) الفعل الالهى له مجرى واحد مضروب، لا يتغير. ولذلك قال تعالى، ﴿وما أمرنا الا واحدة كلمح بالبصر﴾، وقال ﴿ولن تجد لسنة الله تبديلا﴾. وهذه الاسباب التى أوهمتم امكانها، ان كانت، فينبغى ان تطرد أيضاً وتتكرر الى غير [نهاية]³² وان يبقى هذا النظام الموجود فى العالم من التولد والتوالد الى غير [نهاية]³³. وبعد الاعتراف بالتكرر والدور فلا يبعد أن يختلف منهاج الامور فى كل الف الف سنة مثلا، ولكن يكون ذلك التبدل أيضا دائما أبديا على سنن واحد. فان سنة الله لا تبديل فيها.

act proceeds from the divine will, and the divine will does not have a
multiple direction so as to have its order change with the change of its
directions. Thus, what proceeds from it, however [it proceeds], will have
an order that combines the first and last according to one pattern, as
5   we see it in other causes and effects.

(53) If you allow the continuous generation and procreation in the
manner now observed or the return of this pattern, even after a long
time, by way of repetition and cyclical change, you have removed the resurrection, the end of the world, and what the apparent [meanings] of the
10   religious law indicate, since it would follow that our existence would have
been preceded by this resurrection several times and will return several
times and so on, according to this order. If you said that the divine way
changes entirely to another genus, this [way] never at all returning, and
the period of possibility divides into three divisions—a division before
15   the creation of the world when God was and there was no world, a division after creation in the manner [we have now], and a part with which
there is a termination (namely, the pattern of resurrection)—then harmony and order cease and change in God's way takes place, which is
impossible. For this is only possible with a will that changes with the
20   change of circumstances. But the eternal will has one fixed course from
which it does not alter. For the [divine] act accords with the will, and the
will is of one pattern that does not change in relation to periods of time.

(54) [The philosophers further] claim that this does not contradict
our statement that God has power over all things. For [they maintain that]
25   we say that God is capable of [bringing about] the resurrection, the
afterlife, and all possible things in the sense that if He willed them He
would enact [them]. It is not a condition of the truth of this, our statement, that He wills, nor that He acts. This is just as we say that So-and-
so is capable of cutting his own throat and stabbing his [own] belly,
30   this being true in the sense that had he willed this he would have done it.
But we know that he neither wills nor does [it]. Our saying, "He neither
wills nor acts," does not contradict our statement that he is capable in
the sense that, had he willed, he would have enacted [the deed]. For the

وهذا [انما كان لأن]٣٤ الفعل الالهى يصدر عن المشيئة الالهية، والمشيئة الالهية ليست <متعددة>٣٥ الجهة حتى يختلف نظامها باختلاف جهاتها. فيكون الصادر منها، كيف ما كان، منتظما انتظاما يجمع الاول والآخر على نسق واحد، كما نراه فى سائر الاسباب والمسببات.

(٥٣) فان جوزتم استمرار التوالد والتناسل بالطريق المشاهد الآن، أو عود هذا المنهاج ولو بعد زمان طويل على سبيل التكرر والدور، فقد رفعتم القيامة والآخرة وما دل عليه ظواهر الشرع، اذ يلزم عليه ان يكون قد تقدم على وجودنا هذا البعث كرات، وسيعود كرات، وهكذى على الترتيب. وان قلتم ان السنة الالهية بالكلية تتبدل الى جنس آخر ولا تعود قط هذه السنة، وتنقسم مدة الامكان الى ثلثة أقسام، قسم قبل خلق العالم اذ كان الله ولا عالم، وقسم بعد خلقه على هذا الوجه، وقسم به الاختتام، وهو المنهاج البعثى، بطل الاتساق والانتظام وحصل التبديل لسنة الله وهو محال. فان هذا انما يمكن بمشيئة مختلفة باختلاف الاحوال. أما المشيئة الازلية فلها مجرى واحد مضروب لا تتبدل عنه، لان الفعل مضاهٍ للمشيئة، والمشيئة على سنن واحد، لا تختلف بالاضافة الى الازمان.

(٥٤) وزعموا ان هذا لا يناقض قولنا ان الله قادر على كل شىء. فانا نقول، ان الله قادر على البعث والنشور وجميع الامور الممكنة على معنى انه لو شاء لفعل. وليس من شرط صدق قولنا هذا أن يشاء ولا أن يفعل. وهذا كما أنا نقول ان فلانا قادر على ان يجز رقبة نفسه ويبعج بطن نفسه ويصدق ذلك على معنى انه لو شاء لفعل، ولكنا نعلم انه لا يشاء ولا يفعل. وقولنا لا يشاء ولا يفعل لا يناقض قولنا انه قادر بمعنى انه لو شاء

categorical statements do not contradict the hypothetical, as has been stated in logic. For our statement, "If he willed, he would have acted," is an affirmative hypothetical [statement], whereas our saying, "He did not will and he did not act," constitutes two negative categorical statements.
5 The categorical negative statement does not contradict the affirmative hypothetical [one]. Hence, the proof that shows us that His will is eternal and not varied shows us that the course of the divine decree will only be in accordance with an ordered [pattern] and [that], if it varies in individual times, its variance would also be according to order and a regular
10 pattern through [eternal] repetition and recurrence. [Anything] other than this is impossible.

(55) [Our] answer [to this is to say]:

(56) This derives from [their doctrine] of the world's eternity and [their argument] that the [divine] will is eternal so that the world is
15 eternal. We have refuted this and shown that it is not rationally improbable to posit three divisions—namely, that God exists without the world, that he then creates the world according to the order we experience, and [that he] then begins a new order which is the one promised in paradise. The whole, then, could be annihilated so that nothing would remain save
20 God. This [latter] is possible, except that the religious law has conveyed [its opposite—namely,] that reward, punishment, paradise, and the fire have no end. And this question, in whatever way it turns, is based on two questions. The first is the world's temporal origination and the possibility of the proceeding of a temporal thing from an eternal [one]; the second
25 is the disruption of the habitual [course of nature] by creating the effects without causes or creating causes on another pattern that is not customary. We have settled both these questions.

لفعل. فان الحمليات لا تناقض الشرطيات، كما ذكر فى المنطق، اذ قولنا،
لو شاء لفعل، شرطى موجب، وقولنا، ما شاء وما فعل، حمليتان سالبتان.
والسالبة الحملية لا تناقض الموجبة الشرطية. فاذن الدليل الذى دلنا على
ان مشيئته أزلية وليست متفننة، يدلنا على ان مجرى الامر الالهى لا يكون
٥   الا على انتظام، وان اختلفت فى آحاد الاوقات، فيكون اختلافها أيضاً
على انتظام واتساق بالتكرر والعود. وأما غير هذا فلا يمكن.

(٥٥) والجواب:

(٥٦) ان هذا استمداد من مسئلة قدم العالم وان المشيئة قديمة فليكن
العالم قديما. وقد أبطلنا ذلك. وبينا انه لا يبعد فى العقل وضع ثلثة أقسام
١٠   وهو، أن يكون الله موجودا ولا عالم، ثم يخلق العالم على [النظام]٣٦
المشاهد، ثم يستأنف [نظاما]٣٧ ثانيا وهو الموعود فى الجنة، ثم يعدم الكل
حتى، لا يبقى الا الله. وهو ممكن، لو لا ان الشرع قد ورد بان الثواب
والعقاب والجنة والنار لا آخر لهما. وهذه المسئلة كيف ما [دارت]٣٨،
تنبنى على مسئلتين: احديهما حدث العالم وجواز حصول حادث من
١٥   قديم، والثانية خرق العادات بخلق المسببات دون الاسباب، أو احداث
اسباب على منهج آخر غير معتاد. وقد فرغنا عن المسئلتين جميعا.

The Book's Conclusion

(1) If someone says: "You have explained the doctrines of these [philosophers]; do you then say conclusively that they are infidels and that the killing of those who uphold their beliefs is obligatory?" we say:

(2) Pronouncing them infidels is necessary in three questions. One of them is the question of the world's pre-eternity and their statement that all substances are pre-eternal. The second is their statement that God's knowledge does not encompass the temporal particulars among individual [existents]. The third is their denial of the resurrection of bodies and their assembly at the day of judgment.

(3) These three doctrines do not agree with Islam in any respect. The one who believes them believes that prophets utter falsehoods and that they said whatever they have said by way of [promoting common] utility, to give examples and explanation to the multitudes of created mankind. This is manifest infidelity which none of the Islamic sects have believed.

(4) As regards questions other than these three, such as their treatment of the divine attributes and their belief in divine unity entailed therein, their doctrine is close to that of the Muᶜtazila. Their doctrine of the necessary [connection] of natural causes [and their effects] is the one which the Muᶜtazila have explicitly expressed in [their doctrine of] generation. Similarly, all of what we have reported [of their doctrines] has been held by one or another of the Islamic sects, with the exception of these three principles. Whoever perceives the heretical innovators among the Islamic

خاتمة الكتاب

(١) فان قال قائل: قد فصلتم مذاهب هؤلاء، أفتقطعون القول بكفرهم ووجوب القتل لمن يعتقد اعتقادهم؟ قلنا:

(٢) تكفيرهم لا بد منه فى ثلث مسائل: [احداها]' مسئلة قدم العالم وقولهم ان الجواهر كلها قديمة، والثانية قولهم ان الله لا يحيط علما بالجزئيات الحادثة من الاشخاص، والثالثة فى انكارهم بعث الاجساد وحشرها.

(٣) فهذه المسائل الثلث لا تلائم الاسلام بوجه، ومعتقدها معتقد كذب الانبياء، وانهم ذكروا ما ذكروه على سبيل المصلحة، تمثيلاً لجماهير الخلق وتفهيما. وهذا هو الكفر الصراح الذى لم يعتقده احد من فرق المسلمين.

(٤) فاما ما عدا هذه المسائل الثلث من تصرفهم فى الصفات الالهية واعتقاد التوحيد فيها، فمذهبهم قريب من مذاهب المعتزلة. ومذهبهم فى تلازم الاسباب الطبيعية هو الذى صرح المعتزلة به فى التولد. وكذلك جميع ما نقلناه عنهم قد نطق به فريق من فرق

sects to be infidels will pronounce [the philosophers] also to be infidels [for the views they share]. And whoever hesitates in pronouncing [such Islamic sectarian innovators] as infidels will confine himself to pronouncing [the philosophers] infidels on these [three] questions [alone]. We, however, prefer not to plunge into [the questions] of pronouncing those who uphold heretical innovation to be infidels[1] and of which pronouncement is valid and which is not, lest the discourse should stray from the objective of this book. God, exalted be He, is the One who leads one successfully to what is correct.

◆ ◆ ◆

الاسلام، الا هذه الاصول الثلث. فمن يرى تكفير أهل البدع من فرق الاسلام، يكفرهم أيضا به. ومن يتوقف عن التكفير، يقتصر على تكفيرهم بهذه المسائل. واما نحن فلسنا نؤثر الآن الخوض فى تكفير أهل البدع، وما يصح منه وما لا يصح، كيلا يخرج الكلام عن مقصود هذا الكتاب والله تعالى الموفق للصواب.

٥

Notes to the English Text

Abbreviations

Avicenna, *Aḥwāl*
Ibn Sīnā. *Aḥwāl al-nafs.* Ed. F. Ahwānī. Cairo: Dār Ihyā al-Kutub al-ᶜArabīyah, 1952.

Avicenna, *Al-nafs*
Ibn Sīnā. *Al-shifāʾ* (Healing): *Al-ṭabīᶜiyyāt* (Physics): *Al-nafs (De Anima).* Ed. G. C. Anawati and S. Zayed. Cairo: [Wizārat al-Maᶜarif], 1975.

Avicenna, *Isagoge*
Ibn Sīnā. *Al-shifāʾ* (Healing): *Al-manṭiq* (Logic): *Al-madkhal (Isagoge).* Ed. M. Khudayri, G. C. Anawati, and A. F. Ahwānī. Cairo: [Wizārat al-Maᶜarif], 1953.

Avicenna, *Ishārāt*
Ibn Sīnā. *Kitāb al-ishārāt wa al-tanbīhāt.* Ed. J. Forget. Leiden: E. J. Brill, 1892.

Avicenna, *Metaphysics*
Ibn Sīnā. *Al-shifāʾ* (Healing): *Al-ilāhiyyāt* (Metaphysics). Ed. G. C. Anawati, S. Dunya, M. Y. Musa, and S. Zayed. 2 vols. Cairo: [Wizārat al-Maᶜarif], 1960.

Avicenna, *Najāt*
Ibn Sīnā, *Al-najāt.* Cairo: Maṭbaᶜat al-Saᶜāda, 1938.

Dunya
Al-Ghazālī. *Tahāfut al-falāsifa.* Ed. S. Dunya. Cairo: Dār al-Maᶜarif, 1957.

Iqtiṣād
Al-Ghazālī. *Al-iqtiṣād fī al-iᶜtiqād.* Ed. I. A. Çubkçu and H. Atay. Ankara: Nur Matbaasi, 1962.

Miᶜyār
Al-Ghazālī. *Miᶜyār al-ᶜilm.* Ed. S. Dunya. Cairo: Dār al-Maᶜarif, 1961.

Author's Introduction

1. The reference could be either to the group of unbelievers, to those who have deviated from true Islamic teaching, or to the Jews and Christians. The text does not make this clear.

2. This third theological group is not easy to identify. The tenth-century geographer al-Muqaddasī identifies *al-wāqiʿyya* with those who were undecided concerning the Qurʾān, presumably on the question of whether it is created or eternal. Al-Muqaddasī, *Kitab aḥsan al-taqāsīm fī maʿrifat al-aqālīm,* ed. M. J. de Goeje (Leiden: E. J. Brill, 1906), 38.

3. *Fa al-nusallim lahum jamīʿa dhālika jadalan aw iʿtiqādan:* Here appears the idea of admitting a premise to the opponent which, in this instance, could be admitted either dialectically—that is, for the sake of argument—or out of conviction, or both.

4. The title of the logical work appended to the *Tahāfut.*

5. *Min jumlatihi:* The reference seems to be to *al-nazar fī ālat al-fikr,* "examining the instruments of thought." S. Dunya suggests that this refers to the *Tahāfut*—that is, that *Miʿyār al-ʿilm* (The standard for knowledge) is part of this work. See the introduction to *Miʿyār al-ʿilm,* p. 21. This interpretation, while possible, is not certain.

Discussion 1

1. As will be seen, there are actually four proofs.

2. It is almost certain that the reference here is to the will, not to the world. But the expression is not without ambiguity.

3. See Avicenna, *Metaphysics,* 9.1 (pp. 376 ff.).

4. Literally, "if it is said . . . , we answer . . ." This is the pattern of statement and answer throughout the *Tahāfut.* But the conditional sentences usually involve lengthy discussions, and for the sake of intelligibility I resort most of the time to the pattern suggested by the translation above.

5. The terminology at this stage is that of the *kalām,* but it shifts to philosophical usage once the notion of the middle term is introduced. Knowledge by the necessity of reason *(ḍarūrat al-ʿaql)* is indubitable direct knowledge that includes self-evident truths (and this is what al-Ghazālī has in mind here) and knowledge of our own existence and of our own psychological states, as well as knowledge habitually referred to as coming to us directly through sense perception—although for the Islamic occasionalist this latter knowledge is also created in us by God. Reflection *(nazar)* is knowledge rationally inferred from the former. See al-Bāqillānī, *Kitab al-tamhīd,* ed. R. J. McCarthy (Beirut: Al-Maktabah al-Sharqiyah, 1957), 7–13; also M. E. Marmura, "Ghazāli's Attitude to the Secular Sciences and Logic," in *Essays on Islamic Philosophy and Science,* ed. G. F. Hourani (Albany: State University of New York Press, 1957), 103–5.

6. Al-Ghazālī here is voicing the doctrine of the Ashʿarite school of *kalām,* to which he belongs; it held that the divine eternal attributes are not identical with the divine essence but "additional to it."

7. Literally, "when it is not impossible for the priority and posteriority to be willed."

8. Literally, "sufficiency would take place with power."

9. *Hādhā ʿamalu tawahhumika:* Literally, "this is the work of your estimation." The reference here is to *al-wahm,* "estimation." Al-Ghazālī is using Avicennan terminology. According to Avicenna, estimation is a reasoning faculty whose

function, unlike theoretical reasoning, is to make particular judgments in terms of the particulars of sense. It is, however, incapable of abstract and universal thought. When it attempts to make judgments about nonsensible particulars, it is prone to err. Implicit in the statement above is that *wahm*, incapable of following the abstract argument that God is neither inside nor outside the world, errs when it maintains that He has spatial existence. Avicenna also attributes to animals a faculty of estimation—an internal sense which, for example, enables a ewe to apprehend the nonmaterial meaning (*ma˓nā*, or "enmity") in the wolf.

10. *Wa farḍuhu mumkin:* The underlying argument here seems to be that what is self-contradictory cannot be supposed. But since one can suppose the equality in relation to the individual's purpose, this equality is possible; hence, contrary to what the philosophers hold, it is not inconceivable.

11. *Thābita,* which can also mean "constant," as used in al-Ghazālī's reply that immediately follows. But here the term is used primarily for establishing the conclusion of the hypothetical syllogism: "If there are events in the world, there must be an [eternal] circular motion; there are events in the world; therefore, there is an eternal circular motion."

12. *Mukhtara˓atun li'llāhi ibtidā˓an:* The wording here is quite significant, as al-Ghazālī voices the Ash˓arite occasionalist doctrine that each and every event is the direct, unmediated creation of God "invented" by Him ex nihilo. The refutation of the doctrine that the celestial sphere is an animal is given in Discussion 14.

13. For the disjunctive form of this proof and an analysis of it, see M. E. Marmura, "The Logical Role of the Argument from Time in the *Tahāfut*'s Second Proof for the World's Pre-eternity," *The Muslim World* 49, no. 4 (1959): 306–14.

14. What follows is a lengthy, complex sentence. It starts with *kamā jāza*— literally, "just as it is permissible"—and is complemented five subordinate sentences later in the above translation by "similarly." For the sake of clarity, the initial *kamā* has been omitted in the translation and the complex sentence broken into shorter sentences.

15. That is, the hypothesized space between the original size of the world and the hypothesized world smaller by a cubit or two would constitute a void.

16. For a background to this argument, see Avicenna, *Metaphysics*, 4.2.7–15 (p. 182). "Every idea that exists," Avicenna writes, "either exists or does not exist in a subject. Whatever does not exist in a subject has a proper existence in terms of which it is not necessarily related. But the possible of existence is only [what] it is in relation to that of which it is possible." It is in this context that al-Ghazālī speaks of "the possibility of existence" above as "a *relative* characterization." Avicenna's "proper existence" or "special existence"—the *esse proprium*, "proper being," of his Latin translators—is distinct from *al-wujūd al-ithbātī*, "affirmative existence." The former is, in effect, a reference to the nature of a thing, regardless of whether or not it exists.

17. In other words, knowledge corresponds to the object as the object actually is. This is what makes it "knowledge." This definition is also encountered in the *kalām*.

18. *Hay³a* is a difficult term to translate. It could be translated as "form," provided that this is taken in a very general sense. Normally it means "shape" and, in astronomical contexts, "configuration."

19. The point here is that possibility can be related to what is non-material—in this case, God.

20. As pointed out in the introduction, *Qawāᶜid al-aqāᶜid* is the title of one of the books of al-Ghazāli's magnum opus, his *Iḥyā³ ᶜulūm al-dīn* (The revivification of the sciences of religion). The *Qawāᶜid* is an Ashᶜarite work but is not too detailed and does not discuss the question of the world's origin at great length. This question is quite fully treated in al-Ghazāli's *Al-iqtiṣād fī al-iᶜtiqād* (Moderation in belief), his main Ashᶜarite work, written shortly after the *Tahāfut,* in which we are told that it is concerned with the "principles of religion," although it is not referred to by its title. It is in the *Iqtiṣād* rather than the *Qawāᶜid* that al-Ghazāli fulfills the promise of "affirming" true belief. For a pertinent discussion of the dating of this work and its relation to the *Tahāfut,* see G. F. Hourani, "The Chronology of Ghazāli's Writings," *Journal of the American Oriental Society* 79, no. 4 (October–December 1959): 228; G. F. Hourani, "A Revised Chronology of Ghazāli's Writings," *Journal of the American Oriental Society* 104, no. 2 (April–June 1984): 293–94. Al-Ghazāli himself, in his *Jawāhir al-Qur³ān* (The gems of the Qur³ān), intimates that, of the two Ashᶜarite works, the *Iqtiṣād* is the deeper. Al-Ghazāli, *Jawāhir al-Qur³ān,* ed. M. R. R. al-Qabbani (Beirut: Dār Iḥyā³ al-ᶜUlūm, 1986), 39.

Discussion 2

1. *Yajūz an:* "It is permitted that." There seems to be a shift of modality here from the original argument—a shift from necessity to possibility.

2. The leading Muᶜtazilite theologian of the school of Basra (d. ca. 840).

3. That is, God would not be able to annihilate one thing without annihilating the rest of the world.

4. *Lamā tuṣuwwira fanā³uhā li hādhā al-maᶜnā:* The reference here seems to be to "endurance." In other words, the very meaning of "endurance" would exclude the meaning of "annihilation," so annihilation becomes inconceivable when, in fact, it is conceivable. It is possible, though perhaps less natural, to read *li hādhā al-maᶜnā* as referring to the accidents, where "accident" by definition is that which does not endure. Thus, the sentence could translate (somewhat elliptically) as: "For if their enduring is conceivable, then their annihilation, because of the [very] meaning [of 'accident'], would become inconceivable[—which is absurd]." But whether or not this is what is meant, the Ashᶜarite definition of "accident" as that which does not endure underlies the argument. For this definition, see al-Bāqillāni, *Al-tamhīd,* 1.4 (p. 18).

5. Although al-Ghazāli does not choose to answer the philosophers by defending any of these theological doctrines, it is this second Ashᶜarite doctrine, explaining how accidents and atoms cease to exist, to which he subscribes in *Iqtiṣād,* 37.

6. See, for example, Avicenna, *Al-nafs,* 5.4 (pp. 205–7).

Discussion 3

1. For this Avicennan argument, see, in particular, Avicenna, *Najāt,* 213–14.

2. See Avicenna, *Metaphysics,* 6.1 (p. 261) and 6.2 (p. 263). Al-Ghazālī is making the philosophers attribute to the theologians a position held by Avicenna, but with a twist. Avicenna's point is that for the building to endure there must be a sustaining cause coexisting with the effect: in this case, not the original efficient cause—the builder—but the water and dryness that acts to keep the original structure.

3. What al-Ghazālī has in mind is the example he had just given of the attribute Knowledge's being the cause of God's being a Knower. But he also seems to have in mind the relation of the divine attributes to each other. The eternal attribute Life, for example, is a necessary condition for the eternal attribute Knowledge (since without life, there can be no knowledge), but the divine attribute Knowledge is not in any real sense an act of the divine attribute Life. The divine eternal attribute Knowledge is not the enactment of the divine eternal attribute Life for the very reason that both are eternal and, hence, uncreated.

4. The reference could be to primary matter which, in the Avicennan system, is the first effect of the last of the series of intelligences emanating from God, the Active Intellect (Avicenna, *Metaphysics,* 10.1 [p. 435]), unless in this instance "first matter" refers to the matter of the outermost sphere of the world.

5. For Avicenna, each celestial intellect is in fact the only member of its species—a cardinal point for understanding his theory that God knows particulars "in a universal way."

6. In other words, it is necessary for it to apprehend the First Principle, but this necessity does not derive from the First Principle; consequently, it does not constitute any plurality in this Principle.

7. That is, if existence is a general concept that divides into the necessary and the possible.

8. *Al-wāḥid al-ḥaqq:* There is ambiguity here, as this phrase could refer either to God or to whatever is one in every respect. The argument that follows is cryptic and not entirely clear. One has to keep in mind, however, what has been stated earlier to the effect that existence is a general concept that divides into the necessary and the possible. What al-Ghazālī seems to be speaking about here is the possible in itself and the necessary in Himself. Thus, if I understand his position correctly, he is arguing (a) that, if the philosophers want to maintain that the idea of the possible in an existent that is possible in itself is not identical with its existence, then the same must apply to the necessary in itself; and (b) that, should this be the case, then the necessary in itself would not be one in every respect, which is absurd. To be one in every respect, one cannot affirm one aspect of this unity and deny another without contradiction. This is the test for true unity. The thrust of the argument is to show that the "possibility" of the first effect cannot constitute the idea of plurality.

9. *Al-ʿaql:* "Intellect," but also the *maṣdar,* or verbal noun, of *ʿaqala* (the act of intellectual apprehension) which, in the case of God, is an eternal act.

10. At first sight, what follows seems to be a continuation of the Avicennan criticism. Part of the content of the criticism—namely, that the effect would be nobler than the cause in that from the cause, God, only one thing emanates, while from His effect three things emanate—is applicable to Avicenna's theory no less than the theory he criticizes. What follows this, however, is a statement of the position of those who hold that God knows only Himself, followed by al-Ghazālī's criticism of it.

Discussion 4

1. There is an ambiguity in the argument which al-Ghazālī attributes to the philosophers: the wording suggesting that in the argument the First Principle could be the world. But the argument is a form of a reductio ad absurdum, the reasoning being something as follows:

> If an eternal world is affirmed as existing without a cause, then the principle of an existent without a cause would have been admitted. But this supposed existent without a cause—the world—entails multiplicity. Hence, it cannot be the first principle. Therefore, there must be another uncaused principle—namely, God, the First Principle—who is devoid of any multiplicity.

2. That is, within the purview of what has been supposed by the philosophers, as what follows shows.

3. In other words, it would be God. The background to this formulation is Avicenna's proof from contingency for the existence of God. The pattern of the argument is well illustrated in the version in the *Najāt* which begins:

> There is no doubt that there is existence. Every existent is either necessary or possible. If necessary, then it would be true that the necessary exists, which is the thing being sought after. If possible, we will make it evident that the existence of the possible terminates with the necessary existent. (235)

See M. E. Marmura, "Avicenna's Proof from Contingency for God's Existence in the Metaphysics of the *Shifā*ʾ," *Mediæval Studies* 42 (1980): 337–52, where different versions of the proof are discussed and translated. The version in the *Ishārāt*, 447–55 (translated on pp. 351–52 of the article), seems to be the source of al-Ghazālī's formulation.

As punctuated in Dunya's edition, al-Ghazālī's passage would translate as follows:

> The conclusive demonstration of the impossibility of infinite causes is to [ask]: In the case of each one of the individual causes, is it in itself possible or necessary? If necessary, why would it then need a cause? If possible, then the whole is characterized with possibility. Every possible needs a cause additional to itself. The whole, then, needs an extraneous cause. (143)

4. The whole series of infinite causes would be necessary (not possible in this sense), but each individual component of the series would remain possible, requiring an individual cause.

Discussion 5

1. See Avicenna, *Najāt,* 229 ff.

2. *Wa laysa Zaydun insānan li dhātihi:* The *li dhātihi* is translatable as "in himself" or "through himself." *Dhāt* also translates as "essence," sometimes simply as "entity," or even as "being." Rigid adherence to one translation sometimes misses a nuance of meaning which this expression has in one context but not another. I have adopted varying translations of the expression as dictated by context.

3. The argument is Avicennan; see, for example, Avicenna's *Metaphysics,* 8.5 (pp. 349–50). It also has a background in a logical problem which Avicenna tried to solve: that of predication. Animality as such—that is, considered simply as animality—is, he tells us, neither universal nor particular. For if it were universal—that is, if universal by its very essence (hence, by its very definition)—then there could be no such thing as a particular animal. If in its essence it were particular, then there could be only one animal: the individual animal with which animality is identified. Animality becomes a universal when universality attaches to it in the mind, rendering it predicable of many; animality becomes particular through its association with particular matter that individuates it. See Avicenna's *Isagoge,* 65; also M. E. Marmura, "Avicenna's Chapter on Universals in the *Isagoge* of His *Shifāʾ,*" in *Islam: Past Influence and Future Challenge,* ed. A. T. Welch and P. Cachia (Edinburgh: Edinburgh University Press, 1979), 34–56; and M. E. Marmura, "Quiddity and Universality in Avicenna," in *Neoplatonism and Islamic Thought,* ed. Parviz Morewedge (Albany: State University of New York Press, 1992), 77–78.

4. The reference here is to *al-ḥadd al-shāriḥ,* or lexical definition.

5. *ʿAlā ḥiyālihā:* "Individually," "independently," "in itself."

6. If this is a summary exposition of Avicenna's position, al-Ghazālī is in effect interpreting him as holding that quiddity is prior to existence—a doubtful interpretation. See note 7 below.

7. This last point represents Avicenna's position quite accurately. But whether the statement that the quiddity is "prior" to existence is an accurate interpretation of Avicenna's position is a debatable point. See, for example, Avicenna's argument denying the priority of the quiddity to existence in *Metaphysics,* 8.4 (pp. 346–47). The Avicennan distinction between essence and existence that underlies this discussion is sometimes expressed in the distinction between "affirmative existence" *(al-wujūd al-ithbātī)* and "special existence" or "proper existence," the *esse priorium* of the Latin scholastics, based on their translation of the Arabic, *al-wujūd al-khāṣṣ.* The example of the triangle's possessing this quiddity or proper existence is found in Avicenna's *Metaphysics,* 1.5 (p. 31); see also Avicenna, *Isagoge,* 34.

8. Another translation, "its meaning is known" (that is, "it does not require explanation"), is possible. The pattern of wording that follows, however, suggests that this is the less likely translation.

9. Literally, "and if not," where, in the sentence *wa illā fa laysa huwa kadhālika,* the *illā* should probably be taken as *in lā* (the translation I have adopted), the *huwa* as referring to God. The sentence is not without ambiguity.

The *illā* could be taken as "otherwise" (the meaning that first comes to mind) and the *huwa* as referring to the world, or the situation in general. Thus, a possible translation would be something as follows: "Otherwise, it is not the same," the "it" referring to the world. What immediately follows, however, suggests that the reference is to God.

Discussion 6

1. That what is intended here is a cause other than the Necessary Existent that is productive of the attributes becomes clear from al-Ghazāli's response. Implicit here is also the idea that this is a cause which not only produces the attributes but relates them to the Necessary Existent on which they depend.

2. More literally: "Hence, the regress of efficient causes of the attribute is cut with the essence, since it has no agent, just as the essence has no agent."

3. *Dhāt* (see Discussion 5, note 4, above): To translate *dhāt* in this context as "essence," while certainly possible, should perhaps be avoided, since "essence" and "quiddity" can be interchangeable in their meaning.

4. *Mawṣūfa bi al-wujūd:* For Avicenna, God has no quiddity other than existence. Hence, the divine quiddity is not something other than existence to which existence is added, so to speak.

Discussion 7

1. *Rasm:* For example, "Man is a featherless biped," as distinct from the definition, "Man is a rational animal."

2. Literally, "what is its positive."

3. More literally, "in terms of what [thing]."

4. *Biḥaythu yaqbal al-infiṣāl:* The reference is to *tarkīb*, "composition." The reasoning here seems indirect. Al-Ghazāli seems to be harking back to what he had stated earlier, to the effect that genera and differentia do not violate the unity of the essence and are, therefore, attributable to a first cause. To be a first cause does not exclude its being defined.

5. The argument can perhaps be paraphrased as follows: A difference between the supposed two necessary existents is either a necessary condition for the necessary of existence or not. If it is a necessary condition, then the two cannot be different. If the difference is not a necessary condition, then it can be dispensed with. So the difference either does not exist or it can be dispensed with, the necessity of existence being accomplished without it. The supposed difference is irrelevant to the necessity of existence. Hence, the supposed two necessary existents cannot differ and consequently cannot be two, but must be one.

6. *Al-lawniyya:* Literally, "color-ness."

Discussion 8

1. *Fatakūn al-māhiyya sababan li-al-wujūd al-ladhī huwa tābiʿun lahu,* the *lahu* being in the masculine and, hence, not referring to the *māhiyya*, which is feminine.

2. That is, if they mean by "cause" a necessary but not a sufficient condition.

3. That is, whatever is not additional to existence cannot be a quiddity. This harks back to Discussion 3, where al-Ghazālī argues against the philosophers' insistence that the necessity of existence in the divine is identical with divine existence. Here he is refuting them in terms of their own assumption that necessity and existence in the divine are identical. The argument is ad hominem.

Discussion 9

1. *Lā mūjid lahā:* Literally, "that do not have that which brings about their existence."

2. Discussion 1, First Proof, above.

Discussion 10

1. Hence, presumably, the parts must have a cause for both their existence and their combination in order to form a body.

Discussion 11

1. More literally, "As for Muslims, inasmuch as existence, according to them . . . ." One notices here that al-Ghazālī identifies Muslims with those who affirm the world's creation ex nihilo.

2. Al-Ghazālī here reaffirms his position that a pre-eternal world means the denial of the eternal will. An alternative possible translation would be: "As for you [philosophers], if you claim the world to be pre-eternal, then it is not originated through His will." This would be followed by the interrogative, "How, then, . . . ?" But if this is the intention, one would have expected the *lam yaḥduth* to read *lam yakun yaḥduth.* Moreover, one manuscript reads *lā yaḥduth,* which confirms the natural way of taking *lam yaḥduth* as a relative clause.

3. See, for example, Avicenna's *Commentary on the De Anima* in *Arisṭū ʿind al-ʿarab,* ed. A. A. Badawi (Cairo: n.p., 1947), 108.

4. This, again, is the agreed-on division of knowledge into that which is a self-evident necessary truth and that which is known to be true through "reflection" or "theory," requiring a demonstrative proof to establish it. See Discussion 1, note 5, above.

5. *Istithnāʾ naqīḍ al-muqaddam:* In the evolution of the term *istithnāʾ* in the history of Arabic logic, "adding" is one meaning, although in its final form "repeating" would be the closest to its actual meaning. Translating the term as "repeating" works ideally in the *modus ponens* argument where, in the syllogism, "If A, then B; A, therefore B," A is "repeated." To translate the above literally, however, as "repeating the contradictory of the antecedent," would be ambiguous, suggesting that the contradictory of the antecedent had already been given and is now repeated. To convey the correct meaning, one would have to give a paraphrase rather than a translation, such as "repeating the antecedent [but] in [its] contradictory [form]." For a valuable discussion of the term *istithnāʾ* in conditional syllogisms, see Kwame Gyekye, "The Term *Istithnāʾ* in

Arabic Logic," *Journal of the American Oriental Society* 92, no. 1 (January–March 1972): 88–92.

6. *Bi al-ittifāq:* Literally, "by agreement" in this context, "by coincidence" or "by chance" in other contexts. Avicenna uses it in the latter sense in his discussion of the conditional syllogism. The expression he uses is *ittafaqa ittifāqan,* which can be translated as "happening by coincidence." This is when the antecedent and the consequent both happen to be true with no immediate apparent necessary connection between them, as in the statement, "If man exists, then horse also exists." See Ibn Sīnā (Avicenna), *Al-shifāʾ* (Healing): *Al-qiyās* (Syllogism), ed. S. Zayed (Cairo: [Wizārat al-Maᶜarif], 1964), 1.1 (p. 234). For a translation and commentary, see N. Shehaby, *The Propositional Logic of Avicenna* (Dordrecht, Neth.: Reidel, 1973), 37–38.

Since both al-Ghazālī and Avicenna are using similar expressions in their discussion of the conditional syllogism, it is tempting to interpret al-Ghazālī as meaning by *bi al-ittifāq* the same as Avicenna means. This, however, does not seem to be the case.

Discussion 13

1. This means the celestial intellects as distinct from the celestial souls, the former in Avicenna's system sometimes being referred to as the cherubim and the latter as the active angels.

2. *Al-kull:* "The whole." For al-Ghazālī, this means knowledge that includes each existent in its particularity, not merely knowledge "of the whole" in a universal way.

3. Jahm, executed by the Umayyads in 749, shared with the Muᶜtazilites their doctrine of the created Qurʾān but differed from them in his being a determinist; he was classified as a Murjiᶜite by al-Ashᶜarī. He was noted for his doctrine that ultimately heaven and hell cease to exist, God alone being eternal.

4. *Lā yaṣīr fāᶜilan* can be translated as "does not become an agent," but such a translation loses the force of *fāᶜilan* in this context.

Discussion 14

1. *Qiyās al-ᶜaql:* Alternatively, "intellectual reasoning."

Discussion 16

1. *Wa al-irāda tatbaᶜ al-murād:* The will follows the thing willed in the sense that, if the thing willed is particular, the will is particular, as indicated by the train of thought that follows. See Avicenna, *Metaphysics,* 9.2 (pp. 384 ff.).

2. *Taṣawwur,* in this instance, should not be translated as "conception," which is its usual meaning.

3. *Fa inna kull irāda min ḍarūratihā taṣawwur:* Literally, "[In the case of] every will, it is necessary for it [to undergo] a *taṣawwur.*" It may not be illegitimate in this instance to translate *taṣawwur* also as "conception," since the apprehension is of a thing willed that is either a particular or a universal.

4. More literally, "If we know the more frequent and the majority of them, there would be realized for us a clear opinion of the occurrence."

5. See, for example, Avicenna, *Ishārāt*, 218.

6. This, in Avicenna's triadic emanative scheme, is the desire of the celestial soul for the celestial intellect which moves the sphere.

7. In other words, maintaining that the sphere requires particular representations for its particular motions.

8. The infinite cognitions would then coexist, "at one time," in the soul of a celestial sphere forming an actual infinite, which is impossible.

9. *Dāra:* Literally, "rotates."

10. *Ḥaqq al-nafs al-insāniyya fī jawharihā an tudrik ayḍan jamī ͨ al-ashyāʾ:* Literally, "It is the right of the human soul in its substance to apprehend also all things." *Ḥaqq* also means "truth," and *jawhar* can mean "essence"—the meaning that seems to fit the sense better. The doctrine that the soul in its natural state, unencumbered by bodily concerns, knows all things is Avicennan. See Discussion 11, note 3, above.

Part Two: Introduction

1. It is not certain whether this is a reference to Aristotle's *Historia Animalium, De Partibus Animalium,* or *De Generatione Animalium;* to all three; or simply to Avicenna's *Aristotelian Book of Animals, Kitāb al-Ḥayawān* of the *Shifāʾ.*

2. This clearly suggests that al-Ghazālī has the philosophers' theory of necessary causal connection foremost in mind. As seen in Discussion 17, he begins by subjecting this theory to a severe criticism but then discusses an alternative theory that allows natural things to cause each other, while at the same time allowing the occurrence of miracles rejected by the philosophers. The statement above supports the view that the second theory he introduces is presented simply for the sake of argument. Conclusive support for the view that this is the case is found in the *Iqtiṣād.* See M. E. Marmura, "Al-Ghazālī on Bodily Resurrection and Causality in the *Tahāfut* and the *Iqtiṣād*," *Aligarh Journal of Islamic Thought* 2 (1989): 46–75, esp. 59 ff. See also the introduction to the translation.

3. Reading *ʿalā ibṭāl,* the reading adopted by Bouyges. One manuscript reads *bi-ibṭāl,* giving the sentence a different (but possible) meaning that would translate something as follows: "They interpreted [metaphorically] the staff devouring the magic of the magicians, [thereby] negating the divine proof manifest at the hand of Moses—[this] being the doubts of those who deny." In support of this second meaning is al-Ghazālī's insistence that the miracle is created on behalf of the prophet as a proof for the authenticity of his prophethood. There is, however, a lack of clarity in the text.

4. The term used is *yatawātar,* the reference being to *tawātur,* the innumerable corroborative individual reports of a historical event or a geographical place that yield knowledge that is certain. *Tawātur* is included by the Islamic philosophers and logicians as yielding premises usable in strict demonstrative proofs.

5. See Avicenna, *Ishārāt*, 218.

6. Al-Ghazālī is summarizing Avicenna in all this—Avicenna, *Al-nafs,* 5.6 (pp. 219–20). Avicenna makes it plain that his proof is for the possibility of prophecy, not its necessity. The possibility of prophecy, however, is a premise he uses in the *Metaphysics* to prove the necessity of prophecy.

Discussion 17

1. The sentence starting from "where" in the translation is a relative clause, and so is the one that follows it. The issue here is not that two things are not identical. Avicenna, for example, is very specific in maintaining that cause and effect are two separate things. What is at stake is whether the connection between them is necessary.

2. Normally, there are relations existing between two separate things that entail each other—if A is to the left of B, then B is necessarily to the right of A, and so on. But this, according to al-Ghazālī in this passage (and elsewhere as well), is not the case with causal relations.

3. *ʿAlā al-tasāwuq:* "Side by side" or "one alongside the other," but not "one following the other" and not "in a successive order." What al-Ghazālī is talking about is concomitance, where the priority is not temporal. His critique is of the Avicennan concept of essential cause, where cause and effect are simultaneous.

4. Al-Ghazālī discusses two positions.

5. *Maʿānī:* Literally, "meanings," "ideas."

6. *Wa al-kalām maʿahum:* What al-Ghazālī means by this sentence is not entirely clear. Our understanding of the sentence would be consistent with what was stated earlier: that "there is no disagreement [with the philosophers] that the infusions of spirit . . . ; that the father does not produce his son . . ." One manuscript reads *fa lā kalām maʿahum:* "There is no dispute with them [on this issue]." This indicates that *kalām maʿahum* means "dispute with them" (though not on this issue.) Hence, an alternative translation would be "the dispute being with them."

7. *Baynahā:* It is not clear whether this contact is between the principles and observable things or between observable terrestrial bodies. If one follows al-Ghazālī's analogy of light being the cause of seeing that takes place when the eye is opened, it would seem that the contact here is between some terrestrial things and the principle, at which point an event would emanate. Alternatively, what is intended is the contact between two terrestrial bodies—for example, fire and cotton, with the enactment of burning the cotton emanating from the celestial principle. That this is what al-Ghazālī probably intends is strongly suggested by what follows.

8. *Wāhib al-ṣuwar:* Identified with the celestial principles, usually the active intellect. See Avicenna, *Metaphysics,* 9.5 (pp. 411, 413), where the giver of forms bestows forms on matter, beginning with the four elements. Avicenna's discussion in his *Metaphysics,* however, pertains to ontology, not epistemology. Though it is true that, in Avicenna's epistemology, the human rational soul receives forms from the active intellect, these are the intelligibles, not the particulars perceived by the senses. These latter are caused by the particulars of sense. If al-Ghazālī's statement above is intended as referring to an Avicennan causal

theory, this would not be accurate. If al-Ghazālī did not have Avicenna in mind, where did he get this idea? Were there philosophers advocating such a view, which would be quite close to occasionalism? Averroës does not shed much light on this question.

9. The word here, *tashnī*ᶜ, is a key term. It must be stressed that this is the *maṣdar* of the verb in its second form. This is not *shanāᶜa,* "repugnancy," but *tashnīᶜ,* "vilification." A misreading of this term as *shanāᶜa* gives an erroneous interpretation of what al-Ghazālī is saying.

10. Again, the term here is *tashnīᶜāt,* the feminine plural of *tashnīᶜ.* It is not *shanāᶜāt,* "repugnancies," but *tashnīᶜāt,* "acts of vilification."

11. *An nusallim:* "That we admit." In Avicenna's logic, the admitted premises *(al-musallamāt)* are those conceded, not necessarily because they are true, but for the sake of argument in dialectical discourse. See al-Ghazālī's Fourth Introduction and note 3, Author's Introduction, above.

12. Literally, "Our statement in this is as your statement in that."

13. That the miracle is enacted by God on behalf of the prophet is an Ashᶜarite position. See, for example, al-Juwaynī, *Al-irshād,* ed. M. Y. Musa and A. A. Abd al-Hamid (Cairo: n.p., 1950), 308–9; also al-Ghazālī's *Al-iqtiṣād,* 195–96. It is not entirely clear, however, why al-Ghazālī thinks it is also more befitting of the philosophers, unless he means that all events in this terrestrial world are caused by "the giver of forms," as he interprets the philosophers to say.

14. *Niẓām al-khayr:* The terminology is Avicennan, and al-Ghazālī follows Avicenna closely in maintaining that the prophet is needed for bringing about the good order. Avicenna, however, speaks of the "necessity" of prophethood, a term which al-Ghazālī avoids. See Avicenna's *Metaphysics,* 10.2 (pp. 441–43). In this discussion al-Ghazālī attempts as much as possible to speak in the language of the philosophers so as to show that, even in terms of some of their own principles, those miracles they reject can be upheld. In the *Iqtiṣād,* he makes his position clear: the existence of the prophet is possible, not necessary. *Iqtiṣād,* 195 ff.

15. In the *Iqtiṣād,* al-Ghazālī makes it clear that it is God, not the prophet, who renders something preponderant. *Iqtiṣād,* 194.

16. This is dictated by the sense. The text here reads simply "and."

17. The unvoweled term given is *qdra,* which is easily read as *qudra,* "power." This, however, would not make good sense, as will be seen in what follows in the argument. The most likely reading is *qidra,* "cooking pot." The normal term for this is *qidr,* without the feminine ending, but *qidra* is a variant (see Dozy). The principal Cairo edition has *kudra,* "smudge" (the reading adopted by Dunya), which would also make sense. All the other sources in Bouyges's edition, however, have it as *qdra.*

18. As al-Ghazālī explains in the *Iqtiṣād* (90 ff.), the power in us is created by God with His creation of the movement. Human power and the movement are concomitants. There is no causal efficacy between human power and the movement. Both are the simultaneous creations of the divine power. This, however, enables us to experience the distinction between the tremor and the "voluntary" movement. We experience the latter as though enacted by us, when in fact it is not. This discussion goes back to al-Ashᶜarī. Al-Ashᶜarī, *Kitāb*

al-luma^c, ed. R. J. McCarthy (Beirut: Imprimerie Catholique, 1953), 41–42. See also M. E. Marmura, "Ghazālī's Chapter on Divine Power in the *Iqtiṣād*," *Arabic Science and Philosophy* 4, no. 2 (September 1994): 279–315.

Discussion 18

1. *Wa lākin ^{c}hi:* Literally, either "there is in it," where the reference would be to the common sense, or "there is in him," where the reference would be to the individual person. In the following sentence there appears the term ^{c}*indahu,* "with him," indicating that the use of ^{c}*hi* in the previous phrase refers not to the person but to the faculty, the common sense.

2. This is the faculty which Avicenna discusses and which is not encountered in earlier Arabic philosophical writings.

3. *Qaḍāyā:* Strictly "propositions" or "judgments," as distinct from concepts. In the above, however, this is a loose way of saying things and is not intended to be taken strictly. I have translated the term as it appears in the text.

4. This statement is quite significant in understanding al-Ghazālī's attitude toward the philosophical system of the Islamic philosophers, notably that of Avicenna. What Avicenna formulates within his system based on the theory of necessitating causes and necessitated effects can be formulated in terms of what God decrees as a habitual order divested of this causal necessity. This must always be kept in mind when, in later writings, al-Ghazālī seems to be adopting Avicennan cosmological ideas; and it must be taken fully into account when interpreting him either as being inconsistent or as having changed his mind about his attitude toward the philosophers. It should also be borne in mind that the charge that the Islamic philosophers are infidels, which he levels at them in the *Tahāfut* and the *Iqtiṣād*, is repeated in works written after the *Iḥyā'*, in his *Fayṣal al-tafriqa*, and in his autobiographical *Al-munqidh min al-ḍalāl.*

5. The argument occurs in Avicenna's *Al-nafs,* 5.2 (pp. 187 ff.).

6. The term here is *istithnā',* the act of repetition, "a second time"—referring to either the antecedent, the consequent, or the negation of either. In this case, the repeated premise is the consequent, resulting in the negation of the antecedent as the conclusion. The argument is a modus tollens: if p, then q; not q, therefore not p.

7. *Bi al-ittifāq:* See Discussion 11, note 6. What may be intended here is the agreement between the negation of the consequent and the negative conclusion, which is the negation of the antecedent, rather than a reference to something on which logicians agree.

8. See Avicenna, *Al-shifā'* (Healing): *Al-ṭabī^{c}iyyāt* (Physics), ed. S. Zayed (Cairo: [Wizārat al-Ma^{c}ārif], 1983), 3.4 (pp. 188–97).

9. The point of the argument is that the material soul that is receptive of sensible things cannot be the one receptive of the abstract forms. For, even if we do not maintain that it would then be "imprinted" in the material receptacle, it would still be related to it in a manner which would render such abstract knowledge divisible, which is an impossibility. The material receptacle receives only the sensible representations, as the concluding statement of this argument asserts.

10. Like any other material thing, a material receptacle is, according to the Aristotelians, infinitely divisible in potency; but, according to the above argument, if each of its parts is related to knowledge, then, when something is known, all these parts will have knowledge, forming an infinite which is actual. But the actual infinite, for the philosophers, is impossible. Hence, on this supposition, the recipient of this knowledge cannot be material.

11. *Al-juz³ al-fard:* Literally, "the individual part."

12. Avicenna, *Al-nafs,* 5.2 (pp. 192 ff.).

13. That is, whether brain or heart.

14. This is the Avicennan view that awareness of oneself is constant and the most primary knowledge.

> The human soul is [so constituted that] it is, by its very nature, aware of existents. It is aware of some naturally; with others, it gains power to become aware of them by acquisition. That which is realized for it naturally is always actual. Thus, its awareness of itself is by nature, this being a constituent of it and, hence, belonging to it always and in actuality. Its awareness that it is aware of itself, however, is through acquisition. (Ibn Sīnā [Avicenna], *Al-taʿlīqāt,* ed. A. R. Badawi [Cairo: n.p., 1973], 30)

15. See Avicenna's *Al-nafs,* 5.7 (p. 224).

16. Ibid., 5.2 (pp. 194 ff.).

17. *Tuʿaṭṭil,* the subject being *kullu hādhihi al-ashyāʾ al-ukhar.*

18. We find in Avicenna two versions of this argument. The first is in *Al-mubāḥathāt* in *Arisṭū ʿind al-ʿarab,* ed. A. A. Badawi (Cairo: n.p., 1947), 128–29; the second is in *Risāla fī maʿrifat al-nafs al-nāṭiqa wa aḥwālihā,* in Avicenna, *Aḥwāl,* 183–84.

19. Literally, "then no."

20. The example differs from the example of Hobbes's ship of Theseus, in which all the parts are replaced and the question is then asked as to whether the ship is the same as the original ship. See Thomas Hobbes, *The English Works . . . ,* ed. W. Molesworth (London: J. Bohn, 1839–45), 1:136–38.

21. *ʿInda mushāhadat al-ḥiss li shakhṣ muʿayyan:* Literally, "at the sense's perception of a specific individual."

22. In other words, the form is the physical image separated from what is accidental and stands in a representative capacity to the individual instances of the kind. This is a reformulation of Avicenna's view in *Al-nafs,* 5.5 (pp. 209–10). For Avicenna, it is not the image but that abstract form which has this representative capacity.

23. Literally, "without."

Discussion 19

1. See Discussion 2.

2. That is, the preceding one.

3. This is Avicenna's theory, that human souls are individuated not only by the bodies with which they are created but also by their encounter with managing the body.

4. *Bi ḥukm hādha al-burhān:* "By virtue of this demonstration." This is not to be understood as al-Ghazālī's acceptance of the demonstration (which assumes the immateriality of the soul) as sound, but, rather, as granting its soundness for the sake of argument, whereby he would show that on the philosophers' own grounds the immortality of the soul does not necessarily follow.

5. See Ibn Sīnā (Avicenna), *Risalah fī ithbāt al-nubuwwāt,* ed. M. E. Marmura, 2d impression (Beirut: Dar al-Nahar, 1991), 56–58.

6. Discussion 2.

7. Discussion 1, Fourth Proof.

8. The reference is to the would-be existent when it comes into existence, as the discussion that follows shows. Linguistically, it could refer to the "bearer of potentiality" as not itself being the potentiality for existence.

Discussion 20

1. *Dhawq:* Literally, "taste," a term that acquired the meaning of "direct experience" and has also become a technical term in Islamic mystical thought.

2. One notes here that the Aristotelian doctrine of the mean is attributed to the teaching of the religious law. This is implicit in al-Fārābī and Avicenna, who hold that law is a copy, "the imitation" of philosophy. The doctrine of the mean is discussed in Avicenna, *Metaphysics,* 10.5 (pp. 454–55).

3. *Tahdhīb al-akhlāq:* The use of this expression suggests al-Ghazālī's acquaintance with Miskawayh's ethical treatise bearing this expression as its title.

4. See Avicenna, *Risalah fī ithbāt al-nubuwwāt,* 55.

5. *Wa qawluhu,* reading the *wa* as a *wāw* of circumstance; thus, literally, "when [there is] His statement . . ."

6. For this Avicennan argument, see *Metaphysics,* 1.5 (p. 36).

7. This doctrine is associated with the Muᶜtazilite al-Shaḥḥām (d. ca. 845)

8. See Avicenna, *Risāla aḍhawiyya fī amr al-maᶜād,* ed. S. Dunya (Cairo: n.p., 1949), 81; see also M. E. Marmura, "Avicenna and the Problem of the Infinite Number of Souls," *Mediæval Studies* 22 (1960): 232–39.

9. Ibid.

10. See Avicenna, *Al-nafs,* 5.4 (p. 207).

11. *Al-ikhtirāᶜ.*

Conclusion

1. Al-Ghazālī did address himself to this topic in his later work *Fayṣal al-tafriqa.*

القراءات التي اختارها بويج

مقدمة

(١) هؤلاء (٢) يوبه (٣) سوّغ (٤) العقل (٥) العقل

مسئلة ١

(١) حدث (٢) فيكون (٣) وحدوثه (٤) وحدوثه (٥) وحدوثه (٦) حدوثه (٧) أخبل (٨) يتجدد (٩) بحدث (١٠) تساوى (١١) اليه (١٢) تميز (١٣) Omitted (١٤) فرضه (١٥) وهو (١٦) Omitted (١٧) تشابه (١٨) تشابه (١٩) حادث ام قديم (٢٠) كان قديما (٢١) قلت (٢٢) سطح (٢٣) اذا (٢٤) فهذا (٢٥) تقدر (٢٦) لها (٢٧) Omitted (٢٨) منطبع (٢٩) Omitted

مسئلة ٢

(١) كان (٢) كان (٣) كان (٤) له (٥) لم (٦) لم يكن ضدا (٧) اغلى (٨) بينهم (٩) عدم

مسئلة ٣

(١) والثقل (٢) فعل (٣) الكلمات (٤) قال (٥) واذا (٦) الفعل (٧) الميشار (٨) يعرف (٩) والجواب (١٠) ومما (١١) ومعرفته

مسئلة ٤

(١) Omitted (٢) بقي (٣) وهو (٤) فيه (٥) فانه (٦) تابع (٧) المعتبرين

مسئلة ٥

(١) جعله (٢) جعل (٣) يبين (٤) تعدده (٥) Omitted (٦) Omitted (٧)
وانه (٨) غيره (٩) بحركته (١٠) نستبشع (١١) غيره

مسئلة ٦

(١) طرت (٢) قدر مقارنا (٣) طرى (٤) له (٥) لصفته (٦) اثبت (٧) الاول
(٨) يكن (٩) داخلا (١٠) كان عارضا (١١) كان (١٢) كان (١٣) وكان (١٤) يستحيل
أو (١٥) لتكثر (١٦) مذهب (١٧) وتخييله

مسئلة ٧

(١) فليس (٢) فلا (٣) أو (٤) كان (٥) بعده (٦) فليس

مسئلة ٨

(١) نفى (٢) ينفى (٣) الحقيقة (٤) بأنه

مسئلة ٩

(١) ليس (٢) نشاهد (٣) تميز

مسئلة ١١

(١) انكشف (٢) مدارك العقول (٣) يكون (٤) منه بواسطته

مسئلة ١٣

(١) ينكسف (٢) يكن (٣) فنكسفا (٤) يتجلى (٥) الكسوس (٦) حالة (٧)
فيكسف (٨) فيستتر (٩) فحالة (١٠) داخل (١١) حالة (١٢) وهذا (١٣) تشابه
(١٤) يتشابه (١٥) التسخر (١٦) التسخر (١٧) يتسخر (١٨) تسخرا

مسئلة ١٤

(١) الهوي (٢) نقرر (٣) يحدث (٤) تحكم (٥) اختص (٦) يتجزى

مسئلة ١٥

(١) مطيع (٢) بحركته (٣) فهو (٤) الرضا (٥) الرضا (٦) اطلق (٧) وانه (٨) الممكن

مسئلة ١٦

(١) فترجع (٢) سيلتقي (٣) Omitted (٤) Omitted (٥) يبقى (٦) وجه واحد (٧) وجه واحد (٨) بواسطة (٩) فبريّة

الطبيعيات

(١) وهي (٢) يموت (٣) وانه (٤) عليه (٥) كل حال (٦) وانطبع (٧) توهم (٨) له (٩) جبلته (١٠) تطيعه (١١) تطيعه غيره، فيطلع

مسئلة ١٧

(١) له (٢) ولم نقل (٣) عينه (٤) عينه (٥) عينه (٦) أو ملائكة (٧) هذه الصورة (٨) تيك (٩) يخرجه (١٠) كونه (١١) انكرت (١٢) وأضيف (١٣) يخلق (١٤) ضرورته (١٥) يخلق (١٦) فيبقى (١٧) ولا يخرجه (١٨) فيدفع (١٩) موقدة (٢٠) اليه (٢١) ظهوره (٢٢) انفتح (٢٣) فاعل (٣٤) بقدرتها

مسئلة ١٨

(١) وفيه (٢) وكان (٣) لقوى (٤) ارادة (٥) يسمى (٦) الجهات (٧) محله (٨) ادرك (٩) فيه (١٠) عليه (١١) عالما (١٢) اليه (١٣) منطبع (١٤) نسلم (١٥) Omitted (١٦) تدرك (١٧) يشاهد (١٨) كان (١٩) يقوى (٢٠) الجنين (٢١) فيمرض (٢٢) وحتى (٢٣) فانه (٢٤) يبقى (٢٥) الصغير (٢٦) الاسود يشارك (٢٧) الكبير الابيض (٢٨) ويخالفه

مسئلة ١٩

(١) كونه مدركا (٢) وهو (٣) يموت (٤) لانه ليس حالا (٥) انه (٦) انه (٧) يحل فله (٨) يحدث (٩) حدوثه (١٠) فساده (١١) هو (١٢) مشتاق (١٣) فيتأذى (١٤)

Omitted (١٥) مقتضاها (١٦) تفصيله (١٧) مسلم (١٨) انعدامه (١٩) فيكون (٢٠) موجودا (٢١) يضام (٢٢) حالة

مسئلة ٢٠

(١) عنه (٢) يقتضيه طباعه (٣) للطعم (٤) خص بها (٥) مصدود (٦) لكونه منطبعا (٧) لاشتغاله ونزوعه الى شهواته وشوقه (٨) فمات (٩) معه (١٠) فيلهيه (١١) وسقط (١٢) فهو (١٣) واذا (١٤) كمل (١٥) ليس (١٦) قائم بنفسه ومدبر (١٧) له (١٨) ويخلق (١٩) موجود ويبقى (٢٠) للذات (٢١) اليه (٢٢) مرة (٢٣) ورده (٢٤) يجمع (٢٥) وصار (٢٦) انقسم (٢٧) وهو (٢٨) يكن (٢٩) وان (٣٠) النشور (٣١) قطراتها (٣٢) غاية (٣٣) غاية (٣٤) لمكان ان (٣٥) متعينة (٣٦) النظم (٣٧) نظما (٣٨) رددت

خاتمة

(١) احديها (٢) مذاهب

Index

About the Translator

MICHAEL E. MARMURA was born in Jerusalem on November 11, 1929. He received his B.A. in 1953 from the University of Wisconsin and went on to obtain both an M.A. and a Ph.D. from the University of Michigan. He is professor emeritus at the University of Toronto, where he taught from 1959 until 1995 and where he twice chaired the Department of Middle East and Islamic Studies.

Dr. Marmura has published medieval Arabic philosophical texts and translations, as well as numerous articles on Islamic philosophy, many of them devoted to the thought of Avicenna and al-Ghazālī. His publications include an edition of Ibn Sīnā's *Fī ithbāt al-nubuwwāt* (Proof of prophecy); *Refutation by Alexander of Aphrodisias of Galen's Treatise on the Theory of Motion,* with N. Rescher; and *Islamic Theology and Philosophy: Studies in Honor of George F. Hourani,* of which he was the editor. He has also published a history of Islamic philosophy incorporated in *Der Islam II: Politische Entwicklungen und theologische Konzepte,* coauthored with W. Montgomery Watt.

A Note on the Type

The English text of this book was set in BASKERVILLE, a typeface originally designed by John Baskerville (1706–1775), a British stonecutter, letter designer, typefounder, and printer. The Baskerville type is considered to be one of the first "transitional" faces—a deliberate move away from the "old style" of the Continental humanist printer. Its rounded letterforms presented a greater differentiation of thick and thin strokes, the serifs on the lower-case letters were more nearly horizontal, and the stress was nearer the vertical—all of which would later influence the "modern" style undertaken by Bodoni and Didot in the 1790s. Because of its high readability, particularly in long texts, the type was subsequently copied by all major typefoundries. (The original punches and matrices still survive today at Cambridge University Press.) This adaptation of Baskerville, designed by the Compugraphic Corporation in the 1960s, is a notable departure from other versions in its overall typographic evenness and lightness in color. To enhance its range, supplemental diacritics and ligatures were created in 1997 for exclusive use in the Islamic Translation Series.

TYPOGRAPHY BY JONATHAN SALTZMAN

◆